THE INVENTION OF BYZANTIUM IN EARLY MODERN EUROPE

Extravagantes is a series conceived to attract exceptional books in the humanities that complement the distinctive research profile of Dumbarton Oaks. Volumes explore topics at the boundaries or intersections of disciplines and methods, or present innovative studies that call for unique formats.

THE INVENTION OF BYZANTIUM IN EARLY MODERN EUROPE

EDITED BY
NATHANAEL ASCHENBRENNER
AND JAKE RANSOHOFF

DUMBARTON OAKS RESEARCH LIBRARY AND COLLECTION
WASHINGTON, DC

Printed in the United States of America by Sheridan Books, Inc.

ISBN: 978-0-88402-484-2

Library of Congress Cataloging-in-Publication Data

NAMES: Aschenbrenner, Nathanael, 1978– editor. | Ransohoff, Jake, 1989– editor.
TITLE: The invention of Byzantium in early modern Europe / edited by Nathanael Aschenbrenner and Jake Ransohoff.
OTHER TITLES: Extravagantes (Dumbarton Oaks)
DESCRIPTION: Washington, DC : Dumbarton Oaks Research Library and Collection, [2021] | Series: Extravagantes | Chiefly papers originally presented at a conference of the same name held October 26-27, 2017 at Harvard University. | Includes bibliographical references and index. |
SUMMARY: "A gulf of centuries separates the "Byzantine Empire" from the academic field of "Byzantine studies." This book offers a new approach to the history of Byzantine scholarship, focusing on the attraction that Byzantium held for Early Modern Europeans and challenging the stereotype that they dismissed the Byzantine Empire as an object of contempt. The authors in this book focus on how and why the Byzantine past was used in Early Modern Europe: to diagnose cultural decline, to excavate the beliefs and practices of early Christians, to defend absolutism or denounce tyranny, and to write strategic ethnography against the Ottomans. By tracing Byzantium's profound impact on everything from politics to painting, this book shows that the empire and its legacy remained relevant to generations of Western writers, artists, statesmen, and intellectuals as they grappled with the most pressing issues of their day. Refuting reductive narratives of absence or progress, this book shows how "Byzantium" underwent multiple overlapping and often discordant reinventions before the institutionalization of "Byzantine studies" as an academic discipline. As this book suggests, it was precisely Byzantium's ambiguity-as both Greek and Roman, ancient and medieval, familiar and foreign-that made it such a vibrant and vital part of the Early Modern European imagination"—Provided by publisher.
IDENTIFIERS: LCCN 2021016834 | ISBN 9780884024842 (hardcover)
SUBJECTS: LCSH: Byzantine Empire—Study and teaching—Europe—History—Congresses. | Byzantine Empire—Civilization—Influence—Study and teaching—Europe—History—Congresses. | Byzantine Empire—History—Sources—Congresses. | Byzantine Empire—Historiography—Congresses.
CLASSIFICATION: LCC DF505.8.E85 I58 2021 | DDC 949.5/0207204—dc23
LC RECORD AVAILABLE AT HTTPS://lccn.loc.gov/2021016834

To the memory of
AGOSTINO PERTUSI
1918–1979

Or va, ch'un sol volere è d'ambedue:
tu duca, tu segnore e tu maestro.

—Dante, *Inferno* II.139–40

CONTENTS

FIGURES

ABBREVIATIONS

AASS *Acta sanctorum* (Paris, 1863–1940)
AB *Analecta Bollandiana*
AHR *American Historical Review*
AJNum *American Journal of Numismatics*
AOL *Archives de l'orient latin*
BalkSt *Balkan Studies*
BHG *Bibliotheca hagiographica graeca*, 3rd ed., ed. F. Halkin, SubsHag 47 (Brussels, 1957; repr. 1969)
BHL *Bibliotheca hagiographica latina antiquitae et mediae aetatis*, SubsHag 6 (Brussels, 1898–1911; new suppl., 1986)
BMGS *Byzantine and Modern Greek Studies*
BPW *Berliner philologische Wochenschrift* [and *Philologische Wochenschrift*]
BullJRylandsLib *Bulletin of the John Rylands Library*
ByzArch Byzantinisches Archiv
ByzF *Byzantinische Forschungen*
BZ *Byzantinische Zeitschrift*
CCSL Corpus christianorum, Series latina
CFHB Corpus fontium historiae byzantinae
DACL *Dictionnaire d'archéologie chrétienne et de liturgie*, ed. F. Cabrol et al., 15 vols. (Paris, 1903–53)
DBDI *Dizionario biografico degli italiani*
DOP *Dumbarton Oaks Papers*
EHR *English Historical Review*
EO *Echos d'Orient*
GRBS *Greek, Roman, and Byzantine Studies*
JMEMS *Journal of Medieval and Early Modern Studies*
JÖB *Jahrbuch der Österreichischen Byzantinistik* [note: before 1969, *JÖBG*]
JSAH *Journal of the Society of Architectural Historians*
JTS *Journal of Theological Studies*

JWarb	*Journal of the Warburg and Courtauld Institutes*
LisFil	*Listy filologické*
MarbJb	*Marburger Jahrbuch für Kunstwissenschaft*
MÉFR	*Mélanges de l'École française de Rome*
MiscByzMonac	Miscellanea byzantina monacensia
OCD	*Oxford Classical Dictionary*
ODB	*The Oxford Dictionary of Byzantium*, ed. A. Kazhdan et al. (New York, 1991)
OHBS	*The Oxford Handbook of Byzantine Studies*, ed. E. Jeffreys, J. Haldon, and R. Cormack (Oxford, 2008)
OKS	*Ostkirchliche Studien*
PG	Patrologiae cursus completus, Series graeca, ed. J.-P. Migne (Paris, 1857–66)
ProcBrAc	*Proceedings of the British Academy*
REB	*Revue des études byzantines*
REG	*Revue des études grecques*
RenQ	*Renaissance Quarterly*
RevBibl	*Revue biblique*
RHT	*Revue d'histoire des textes*
RIASA	*Rivista dell'Istituto nazionale d'archeologia e storia dell'arte*
RJ	*Rechtshistorisches Journal*
SPBS	Society for the Promotion of Byzantine Studies
SubsHag	Subsidia hagiographica
SüdostF	*Südost-Forschungen*
SVThQ	*St. Vladimir's Theological Quarterly*
Synaxarium CP	*Synaxarium ecclesiae Constantinopolitanae: Propylaeum ad Acta sanctorum Novembris*, ed. H. Delehaye (Brussels, 1902)
TAPS	*Transactions of the American Philosophical Society*
TFByzNgPhil	Texte und Forschungen zur byzantinisch-neugriechischen Philologie
TRHS	*Transactions of the Royal Historical Society*
VeröffHam	Veröffentlichung der Joachim-Jungius Gesellschaft der Wissenschaften, Hamburg
ZRVI	*Zbornik radova Vizantološkog instituta, Srpska akademija nauka*

A NOTE ON TRANSLITERATION

Classical and Byzantine names and terms are transliterated in accordance with the *Oxford Classical Dictionary* (4th ed., Oxford, 2012) and *Oxford Dictionary of Byzantium* (Oxford, 1991), respectively; in all other cases, names are rendered in their most common English-language form (e.g., Scaliger instead of Scaligerius but Grotius instead of de Groot). All quotations in Byzantine and early modern Latin and Greek retain their original orthography.

ACKNOWLEDGMENTS

This book began in unlikely circumstances one February night in 2014, when two graduate students struck up a conversation at a bar near Dumbarton Oaks. The idea took shape before the night had ended. But its successful realization—first as a conference, held at Harvard University in October 2017, and then as a book—has only come about through the labor of many hands and the wisdom of many heads.

Our first debt is to the committees, institutions, and individuals that supported the conference from which this book emerged: the Mary Jaharis Center for Byzantine Art and Culture at Hellenic College Holy Cross and its director Brandie Ratliff; Harvard University's Standing Committee on Medieval Studies and its administrative director Sean Gilsdorf, who sustained us with his unfailing energy and amiability; other Harvard-based sponsors including the Provostial Fund for Arts and Humanities, the Center for the Study of World Religions, the Department of the Classics, and the John Duffy Society; and especially the Dumbarton Oaks Research Library and Collection, whose former director Jan Ziolkowski gave this project unstinting encouragement throughout its successive phases. Dimiter Angelov and Ann Blair generously guided us through the many twists and turns of organizing and funding a major conference, while Ioli Kalavrezou and Alexander Riehle joined the aforementioned as session moderators. We also express our thanks to John Monfasani, Leonora Neville, and Leah Whittington, who enriched the conference with papers that do not appear in this volume. We owe a debt of gratitude to them all.

At Dumbarton Oaks Publications, the process of turning the conference into a book began under the experienced supervision of Joel Kalvesmaki, whose insight and discernment directed its first steps. Adopting this project with an enthusiasm for which we will remain ever grateful, Sallie Spence combined the critical acuity of an expert editor with the unflinching integrity of a true scholar—all while solving the myriad problems inevitable in a work of this nature. Measured against the countless hours she has devoted to this book, even our most effusive thanks seem small. Colin Whiting's editorial skill, support, and affability helped bring the manuscript through proofs and into print. Kathy Sparkes has managed its progress from her position as Director of Publications and overseen its design with the keen eye of an artist. In an era where rigorous academic copyediting is rapidly becoming a lost art, Alice Falk's corrections and improvements mark her as a master of her craft. Finally, Hannah Weaver of Columbia University graciously lent her expertise to reviewing the early modern French in these pages.

Among the many other people to whom we are indebted, we must thank especially Emma Dench, Stephanos Efthymiadis, James Hankins, Michael McCormick, Gregory Nagy, Charles Stang, Alice-Mary Talbot, and Nicholas Watson, all of whom gave generously of their time and wisdom. We also thank the volume's many anonymous reviewers, especially the two who read the entire manuscript and offered many helpful suggestions.

Lucky indeed are those whose personal and professional affinities intertwine, and we are exceedingly grateful to one colleague in particular whose friendship and scholarship has contributed to this book in equal measure. In addition to authoring a chapter, Shane Bobrycki of the University of Vienna was present at this idea's inception and has given us characteristically judicious advice throughout the subsequent years, improving both the conference and the book in a hundred different ways. Ὁ δὲ εὑρὼν αὐτὸν εὗρεν θησαυρόν.

In conceiving this project, the editors drew inspiration from Agostino Pertusi and his pioneering study of the subject, cited frequently in the essays that follow. It seems only fitting, then, that the book be dedicated to his memory.

INTRODUCTION

The Invention of Byzantium in Early Modern Europe

NATHANAEL ASCHENBRENNER AND JAKE RANSOHOFF

THIS BOOK IS ABOUT THE HISTORY OF BYZANTINE STUDIES IN EUROPE BETWEEN the fifteenth and mid-nineteenth centuries. Its title, *The Invention of Byzantium in Early Modern Europe*, reflects a truism: Byzantium is something that needed to be invented.[1] No polity calling itself the "Byzantine Empire" ever existed. A scholarly neologism, "Byzantium" refers to the eastern half of the Roman Empire, which survived, in one form or another, for nearly a millennium after the end of Roman imperial power in the West. The people whom present-day scholars label "Byzantines" called themselves "Romans" (*Ῥωμαῖοι*), as did their neighbors in the Islamic world, who knew their empire as the *bilād al-Rūm*: the "land of the Romans."[2] Western

1 The present work is not the first to approach Byzantium and its legacy through the frame of "invention." The conceptual premise draws on a longer history of scholarship purporting to investigate the "making" or "invention" of categories, often ones that had previously been taken as natural: see, e.g., R. Southern, *The Making of the Middle Ages* (New Haven, 1953); R. Bartlett, *The Making of Europe: Conquest, Colonization, and Cultural Change, 950–1350* (Princeton, 1993); more recently, J. Tannous, *The Making of the Medieval Middle East: Religion, Society, and Simple Believers* (Princeton, 2018). For a useful reflection on Byzantine invention, ranging from the 4th century to the 20th, and on various forms that Byzantium's invention could assume, see J. Burke, "Inventing and Re-inventing Byzantium: Nikephoros Phokas, Byzantine Studies in Greece, and 'New Rome,'" in *Wanted, Byzantium: The Desire for a Lost Empire*, ed. I. Nilsson and P. Stephenson, Studia Byzantina Upsaliensia 15 (Uppsala, 2014), 9–42.

2 For the Arabic terms *Rūm* and *bilād al-Rūm*, see N. M. El Cheikh, *Byzantium Viewed by the Arabs* (Cambridge, MA, 2004), 21–24. For the Turkish equivalent of *diyār-ı Rūm*, and later applications of the term *Rūm* in an Ottoman context, see C. Kafadar, "A Rome of One's Own: Reflections on Cultural Geography and Identity in the Lands of Rum," *Muqarnas* 24.1 (2007): 7–25, esp. 9–10.

medieval contemporaries usually referred to them as "Greeks" (*Graeci*), reflecting the contested legacy of both the Roman Empire and Roman identity in the Middle Ages. Their state acquired many names in early modern scholarship—not only "Byzantium" but also the "Empire of Constantinople," the "Empire of the Greeks," the "Eastern Empire," the "Late Empire," the "Low Empire," and occasionally even the "Roman Empire."[3] "Byzantium" and "Byzantine Empire" came to predominate to the exclusion of these alternatives in the later nineteenth century, around the same time that European scholars first began to advocate for the study of Byzantium as a cultural and political entity in its own right. But if "Byzantine" as an exclusive category and "Byzantine studies" as a field are products of the nineteenth century, then in what sense was Byzantium "invented" in early modern Europe? The present volume offers an answer to this question.

The thirteen chapters of this book assess why early modern scholars studied the texts, artifacts, and history of the period we would now consider "Byzantine." What working methods and mental processes did early modern scholars bring to their study of these materials? What were the wider social, political, and intellectual contexts in which their research occurred? In evaluating these questions and others, this book advocates a new approach to the history of Byzantine scholarship. The early history of Byzantine studies is commonly understood as a history of absence.[4] Either the Byzantine world was absent altogether from the intellectual enterprises, scientific discoveries, scholarly debates, and cultural currents that animated early modern Europe. Or it was relevant, but only to cultures, regions, and peoples outside Europe's western core. Eastern and southeastern Europe thus remained entranced by Byzantium, as Nicolae Iorga demonstrated in his classic *Byzance après Byzance*, in which he traced the persistence of Byzantine political and cultural forms in early modern Wallachia and Moldavia.[5] Others have followed Iorga's lead to explore similar influences elsewhere across eastern Europe, from the steppes of Russia to the stony reaches of Ottoman and modern Greece.[6] Yet despite acute eastern European

3 For the variety in terminology, see, e.g., Charles Du Cange, *Histoire de l'empire de Constantinople sous les empereurs françois* (Paris, 1657); Anselmo Banduri, *Imperium Orientale, sive Antiquitates Constantinopolitanae in quatuor partes distributatae*, 2 vols. (Paris, 1711); C. Le Beau, *Histoire du Bas-Empire, en commençant à Constantin le Grand*, 27 vols. (Paris, 1757–1811).

4 Significantly, Averil Cameron begins her recent meditations on the state of the field (*Byzantine Matters* [Princeton, 2014]) with a chapter titled "Absence." See further eadem, "The Absence of Byzantium," *Nea Hestia* 163 (2008): 4–59.

5 N. Iorga, *Byzance après Byzance: Continuation de l'"Histoire de la vie byzantine"* (Bucharest, 1935). It remains an active field in the study of the Byzantine tradition: see most recently A. I. Sullivan, "The Athonite Patronage of Stephen III of Moldavia, 1457–1504," *Speculum* 94.1 (2019): 1–46.

6 See, e.g., the collected essays in D. Obolensky, *The Byzantine Inheritance of Eastern Europe* (London, 1982); L. Clucas, ed., *The Byzantine Legacy in Eastern Europe* (Boulder, CO, 1988); J. J.

and Orthodox Christian sympathy for the Byzantine legacy, its absence in scholarship on the intellectual and cultural history of the early modern West only tends to reinforce the view that Byzantium remained marginal to the manifold projects of the Renaissance, Reformation, and Enlightenment.

Compounding this sense of absence is the fact that no truly comprehensive history of Byzantine studies exists. Instead, those interested in the development of Byzantine scholarship have had to rely on breezy syntheses that cover several centuries in a few dozen pages, such as the ones that preface Alexander Vasiliev's and George Ostrogorsky's respective surveys of Byzantine history or that appear in James Westfall Thompson's classic *History of Historical Writing*.[7] Such syntheses substitute chronology for argument and tend to approach the history of the discipline between ca. 1450 and 1900 as a progression through four broad stages: (1) humanist indifference, (2) Baroque enthusiasm, (3) Enlightenment contempt, and finally (4) nineteenth-century institutionalization. To be sure, neither Vasiliev nor Thompson nor Ostrogorsky explicitly divides his survey according to this scheme, nor describes the development of Byzantine scholarship in precisely these terms. Nonetheless, the guiding themes and key moments of this "four stages" template will be easily recognizable to any student of the history of Byzantine studies.[8]

Yiannias, ed., *The Byzantine Tradition after the Fall of Constantinople* (Charlottesville, VA, 1991); D. Ricks and P. Magdalino, eds., *Byzantium and the Modern Greek Identity* (Aldershot, Hampshire, 1998). See also, for Byzantium in the early modern Adriatic, F. Barišić, "Vizantijski izvori u dalmatinskoj istoriografiji XVI i XVII veka" [Byzantine Sources in Dalmatian Historiography, 16–17th centuries], *ZRVI* 7 (1961): 227–57.

7 A. A. Vasiliev, *History of the Byzantine Empire, 324–1453*, 2 vols., 2nd ed. (Madison, WI, 1952), 1:3–42, esp. 3–30; G. Ostrogorsky, *History of the Byzantine State*, trans. J. Hussey, rev. ed. (New Brunswick, NJ, 1969), 1–21; J. W. Thompson, *A History of Historical Writing*, 2 vols. (New York, 1942), 2:512–31. An exception, notable for its brilliant and pioneering exploration of this subject, is A. Pertusi, *Storiografia umanistica e mondo bizantino*, Istituto siciliano di studi bizantini e neoellenici, quaderni 5 (Palermo, 1967). On Pertusi's significance as a model for the approach adopted in this volume, see the discussion below, p. 10.

8 While Vasiliev and Ostrogorsky in particular remain perhaps the most influential representatives of the "four stages" approach, they are neither its originators nor its sole proponents. Other treatments of the history of Byzantine scholarship in western Europe that conform to this model include J. B. Bury, introduction to Edward Gibbon, *History of the Decline and Fall of the Roman Empire*, ed. Bury, vol. 1 (London, 1896), liii–lxiii; L. Bréhier, "Le développement des études d'histoire byzantine du XVIIe au XXe siècle," *Revue d'Auvergne* (1901): 1–36; G. P. Gooch, *History and Historians in the Nineteenth Century* (New York, 1913), 490–95. Most recently in this vein, see A. G. C. Savvides, "The Birth and Development of Byzantine Historical and Philological Studies in the West: A Review Essay," *Mésogeios* 9–10 (2000): 127–80; revised and expanded as *The Beginnings and Foundation of Byzantine Studies: A Survey with a Bibliographical Appendix* (Athens, 2018), particularly valuable for its rich modern Greek bibliography and its attention to the contributions of early modern Greek scholars to western European Byzantine studies. Savvides explicitly structures his account according to a progression through four stages (16th-century

For humanists of the fifteenth and sixteenth centuries, "Byzantium," in Ostrogorsky's words, "was regarded as the store-house in which the treasures of the classical world were to be found."[9] Renaissance scholars studied ancient Greek philosophy *ad fontes* at the feet of émigrés such as John Argyropoulos and Demetrios Chalkokondyles, poached exotic manuscripts from big-game sanctuaries like Mount Athos, and drew from Byzantine scholiasts for their own lectures and commentaries on classical texts.[10] Yet while the road to Parnassus and the Platonic Academy ran through Byzantium, humanist wayfarers regarded the Byzantines themselves with a lack of interest, if not outright disdain. Hieronymus Wolf (1516–1580)—often seen as the grudging "father" of Byzantine studies—emerges as the most infamous case in point.[11] Renowned for his editions and translations of such classical Greek orators as

"heralding" [59], a 17th-century "period of efflorescence" [77], 18th-century "trials and tribulations" [91], and 19th-century "recovery" [102; cf. 105]) and reproduces the biographical focus familiar from earlier surveys such as those of Vasiliev and Ostrogorsky (see further below, n. 32). By contrast, other studies of Byzantine scholarship, such as Ernst Gerland's erudite but idiosyncratic *Das Studium der byzantinischen Geschichte vom Humanismus bis zur Jetztzeit*, TFByzNgPhil 12 (Athens, 1934), present a catalog of scholars and works without a coherent structure or guiding narrative. Many recent surveys of the discipline (Savvides excepted) tend to emphasize current approaches over historical development, but their brief treatment of the field's early history continues to reflect the conventional wisdom of the "four stages" approach: e.g., E. Jeffreys, J. F. Haldon, and R. Cormack, "Byzantine Studies as an Academic Discipline," in *OHBS*, 4–20, esp. 5–8; F. K. Haarer, "Writing Histories of Byzantium: The Historiography of Byzantine History," in *A Companion to Byzantium*, ed. L. James (Malden, MA, 2010), 9–21, esp. 10–12.

9 Ostrogorsky, *History of the Byzantine State*, 2. Cf. Vasiliev, *History of the Byzantine Empire*, 1:3; Thompson, *A History of Historical Writing* 2:513 ("there was down to the seventeenth century no true interest in Byzantine history in Europe").

10 See studies in D. J. Geanakoplos, *Greek Scholars in Venice: Studies in the Dissemination of Greek Learning from Byzantium to Western Europe* (Cambridge, MA, 1962), and idem, *Byzantine East and Latin West: Two Worlds of Christendom in Middle Ages and Renaissance. Studies in Ecclesiastical and Cultural History* (New York, 1966); G. Pfeiffer, *Studien zur Frühphase des europäischen Philhellenismus (1453–1750)* (inaugural diss., Friedrich-Alexander University Erlangen-Nürnberg, 1968); D. R. Reinsch, "Edition und Rezeption byzantinischer Historiker durch deutsche Humanisten," in *Graeca recentiora in Germania: Deutsch-griechische Kulturbeziehungen vom 15. bis 19. Jahrhundert*, ed. H. Eideneier, Wolfenbütteler Forschungen 59 (Wiesbaden, 1994), 47–63; J. Harris, *Greek Emigres in the West, 1400–1520* (Camberley, 1995); E. Jeffreys, "Byzantium as Repository of Graeco-Roman Culture," in *Byzantine Culture: Papers from the Conference "Byzantine Days of Istanbul," May 21–23 2010*, ed. D. Sakel (Ankara, 2014), 17–28. Cf. H. Lamers, *Greece Reinvented: Transformations of Byzantine Hellenism in Renaissance Italy*, Brill's Studies in Intellectual History 247 (Leiden, 2015).

11 For claims for Wolf's paternity, see H.-G. Beck, *Der Vater der deutschen Byzantinistik: Das Leben des Hieronymus Wolf von ihm selbst erzählt*, MiscByzMonac 29 (Munich, 1984), and idem, "Hieronymus Wolf," *Lebensbilder aus dem bayerischen Schwaben* 9 (1966): 168–93. Cf. D. R. Reinsch, "Hieronymus Wolf as Editor and Translator of Byzantine Texts," in *The Reception of Byzantium in European Culture since 1500*, ed. P. Marciniak and D. C. Smythe (New York, 2016), 43–53; Reinsch prefers to rank Wolf among the discipline's "grandfathers and uncles" (53). See further G. Della Rocca de Candal, "*Bibliographia Historica Byzantina*: A Historical and Bibliographical Description of the Early

Isocrates and Demosthenes, Wolf found employment with the Fugger banking family of Augsburg, who tasked him with editing and translating a series of Byzantine historical works. His prefaces to the resulting *Corpus Historiae Byzantinae* (1557–62) rail against the perfidy of Byzantine politics, the parochialism of Byzantine chroniclers, and the debased idiom of Byzantine Greek, which polluted the pure spring of Attic diction. "I am surprised, not sorry," wrote Wolf of the fall of Constantinople in 1453, "that such dregs and a bilge water of an iniquitous people so long remained unmolested, and were not conquered earlier."[12] Scholars have traditionally credited Wolf with creating the terms *Byzantine* and *Byzantium*, coined to distinguish the sterile later empire from its fecund Roman forebear.[13] By this account, Byzantine studies were born under a cloud of contempt.

This cloud lifted briefly in the middle of the seventeenth century, when a prodigious circle of French scholars began to direct their erudition and energy toward the investigation of Byzantium in its own right, marking the transition from the first stage of Byzantine studies (humanist indifference) to the second (Baroque enthusiasm). As standard narratives would have it, the political concerns of the ancien régime and the encyclopedic inclinations of *érudits* generated a microclimate ideal for the cultivation of Byzantine scholarship.[14] Imperial Byzantium offered Louis XIV both a model of ceremonial grandeur and a pedigree for his imperial ambitions, and with support from the Sun King's finance minister Jean-Baptiste Colbert a new corpus of Byzantine historical works, now known as the *Corpus Parisinum* or *Byzantine du Louvre*, began steadily to emerge from the royal printing presses. At the apex of this seventeenth-century renaissance stood Charles Du Cange (1610–1688), whose staggering oeuvre spanned Byzantine numismatics, philology, linguistics, genealogy, and historiography.[15]

Editions of the Corpus Historiae Byzantinae (1556–1645)" (PhD diss., University of Oxford, 2015), esp. 21–56, for a survey of Wolf's Byzantine scholarship and the publication history of his *Corpus*.

12 Hieronymus Wolf, *Nicephori Gregorae, Romanae, hoc est Byzantinae historiae Libri XI* (Basel, 1562), *Praefatio*, n.p. [second page], cited and translated by Shane Bobrycki in Chapter 10 of this volume.

13 E.g., J. M. Ziolkowski, introduction to *Dante and the Greeks*, ed. idem (Washington, DC, 2014), 17; P. Stephenson, introduction to part 4, "The World of Byzantine Studies," in *The Byzantine World*, ed. idem (London, 2010), 429. See also A. Pertusi, "Nuova ipotesi sull'origine dei termi Bizantini," *Aevum* 28.2 (1954): 126–50. But cf. Jeffreys, Haldon, and Cormack, "Byzantine Studies as an Academic Discipline," 4, who consider the term "Byzantine" to be of 17th-century French vintage.

14 E.g., Ostrogorsky, *History of the Byzantine State*, 3; Vasiliev, *History of the Byzantine Empire*, 1:3–4; Thompson, *A History of Historical Writing*, 2:513. See also Savvides, *The Beginnings and Foundation of Byzantine Studies*, 77–90, esp. 77–79.

15 On Du Cange as a Byzantinist see J.-M. Spieser, "Du Cange and Byzantium," in *Through the Looking Glass: Byzantium through British Eyes: Papers from the Twenty-Ninth Spring Symposium*

Du Cange equipped future scholars of the Byzantine world with marvelous technical instruments for further research. "But after these promising beginnings," writes Thompson, "something worse than neglect ensued."[16] Du Cange's successors, though learned, could not match his brilliance or breadth. The stream of Louvre corpus volumes slowed to a trickle.[17] The pledge these volumes had seemed to make—that Byzantine texts and artifacts might emerge from their long neglect to claim a place in the sun beside those of ancient Greece and Rome, or even the remnants of the medieval West—went unredeemed. What is more, by the eighteenth century the currents of European taste had turned against Byzantium once again. According to Vasiliev, "the Age of Reason . . . could no longer find anything of interest in the Byzantine Empire."[18] *Philosophes* such as Montesquieu and Voltaire came to view the empire as the antithesis of Enlightenment ideals: a stagnant, monk-ridden bastion of unenlightened despotism and parochial fanaticism. Its history amounted to "nothing but a tissue of rebellions, sedition, and treachery"; its literature presented "a worthless repertory of declamations and miracles."[19] The chill of Voltaire's contempt froze the early buds of Byzantine studies. The avalanche of Edward Gibbon's eloquence buried them for a century.[20] The author of *The History of the Decline and Fall of the Roman Empire* (1776–89) famously skimmed over five hundred years of Byzantine history ("a tedious and uniform tale of weakness and misery") in a single chapter.[21] "The subjects of the Byzantine empire," he wrote, "who assume and dishonour the names of both Greeks and Romans, present a dead uniformity of abject

---

of Byzantine Studies, London, March 1995, ed. R. Cormack and E. M. Jeffreys, SPBS 7 (Aldershot, 2000), 199–210. See Teresa Shawcross in Chapter 5 of this volume.

16 Thompson, *A History of Historical Writing*, 2:513.

17 The final volume of the *Byzantine du Louvre* is generally considered Banduri's *Imperium Orientale*, published in 1711, although the series title and numbering of C. B. Hase's *Leonis Diaconi Caloensis Historia, scriptoresque alii ad res Byzantinas pertinentes . . .* (Paris, 1819) as "Corpus Byzantinae Historiae, 34" represents an abortive effort to revive the Louvre corpus in the early 19th century. On the end of the *Byzantine du Louvre*, see E. Bianco, *La Bisanzio dei Lumi: L'impero bizantino nella cultura francese e italiana da Luigi XIV alla rivoluzione* (Bern, 2015), 105–6.

18 Vasiliev, *History of the Byzantine Empire*, 1:6. Cf. Ostrogorsky, *History of the Byzantine State*, 4–5; Thompson, *A History of Historical Writing*, 2:513–14.

19 [Charles-Louis de Secondat, baron de Montesquieu], *Considérations sur les causes de la grandeur des Romains et de leur décadence* (Amsterdam, 1734), chap. 21, p. 238; Voltaire, *Le pyrrhonisme de l'histoire*, chap. 10, lines 30–32, ed. S. Davies in *Œuvres de 1768 (III)*, ed. Davies, J. Renwick, et al., Œuvres complètes de Voltaire 67 (Oxford, 2007), 296.

20 E.g., S. Runciman, "Gibbon and Byzantium," *Daedalus* 105.3 (1976): 103–10, here 109: "The splendor of his style and the majesty of his wit killed Byzantine studies for nearly a century."

21 Runciman, "Gibbon and Byzantium," 103, in reference to E. Gibbon, *The History of the Decline and Fall of the Roman Empire*, ed. D. Womersley, 6 vols. in 3 (New York, 1994), 3:23–85 (chap. 48 of Gibbon's vol. 5); quotation at 23.

vices, which are neither softened by the weakness of humanity, nor animated by the vigour of memorable crimes."[22] Gibbon's scornful verdict captured the attitudes of his age so persuasively that Byzantinists remain fixated on its refutation more than two centuries after his death.[23]

The fourth stage of the development of Byzantine studies—the field's nineteenth-century consolidation and institutionalization—began slowly. While early nineteenth-century scholarship, as the story goes, remained in Voltaire's and Gibbon's thrall, reverence for the Enlightenment's verdict did not isolate Byzantium from the general revolution in historical and philological method that had begun to emanate from Germany. As Ostrogorsky writes, "The deeper appreciation of history which developed in the nineteenth century could not fail to modify the arrogant and unhistorical attitude of the age of Enlightenment which had so discredited Byzantium."[24] The Humboldtian program of university reform—with its emphasis on collecting, editing, and categorizing documents in large-scale scholarly enterprises—encouraged Barthold Georg Niebuhr (1776–1831) to initiate a monumental new series of edited Byzantine texts. Political events also played a role in stimulating the reevaluation of Byzantium. The outburst of Romantic philhellenism that attended the War of Greek Independence (1821–32) raised questions about the continuity of Greek history and inspired scholars such as Jakob Philipp Fallmerayer (1790–1861) and George Finlay (1799–1875) to revisit Greece's Byzantine centuries, albeit with varying degrees of sympathy.[25] Still, the scholarly study of Byzantium, in the words of Thompson, continued to languish "under the double burden of dilettantism and the lack of any organ of coordination."[26] It remained for the pantheon of later nineteenth-century worthies—John Bagnell Bury (1861–1927) in Britain, Alfred Rambaud (1842–1905) and Charles Diehl (1859–1944) in France, Vasilij Vasil'evskij (1838–1899) in Russia, and above all Karl Krumbacher (1856–1909) in Germany—to finally consolidate this study into a coherent and autonomous discipline: to erect a new, professional "Byzantine studies" upon the foundation of disparate and amateur efforts. A decisive milestone came in 1892, with the inaugural issue of *Byzantinische Zeitschrift*, the first scholarly journal specifically devoted to Byzantium, in which Krumbacher, its editor, famously declared the independence

22 Gibbon, *Decline and Fall*, 3:24.

23 E.g., J. Herrin, *Byzantium: The Surprising Life of a Medieval Empire* (Princeton, 2007), 321–22; Cameron, *Byzantine Matters* (n. 4 above), 10.

24 Ostrogorsky, *History of the Byzantine State*, 6.

25 See especially R. J. H. Jenkins, *Byzantium and Byzantinism*, Lectures in Memory of Louise Taft Semple, 1st ser. (Cincinnati, 1963); C. Mango, "Byzantinism and Romantic Hellenism," *JWarb* 28 (1965): 29–43.

26 Thompson, *A History of Historical Writing*, 2:524.

of *Byzantinistik* as a field.[27] By the turn of the century Byzantine studies had finally emerged, in Thompson's description, as "an established discipline all by itself, a subject which no scholar need be ashamed of," legitimized by the trappings of disciplinary sovereignty: its own bevy of periodicals and train of auxiliary disciplines, publication series, bibliographical supplements, international conferences, and internal schisms.[28]

Such, in brief, are the four stages of the history of Byzantine studies. Their main themes, present to different degrees in different accounts, are sometimes pitched in discordant keys. Older versions, such as those elaborated by Vasiliev, Thompson, and Ostrogorsky, strike a triumphant chord, emphasizing Byzantium's successful redemption by nineteenth- and twentieth-century scholars after long centuries of neglect.[29] Newer renderings, on the other hand, often resound with strains of regret—a persistent longing for what the discipline might be now, had it benefited from the same attention that early modern scholars lavished on the ancient world. The historic disregard for Byzantium has been offered up as an explanation for everything from the subject's perceived lack of theoretical sophistication to its heavily sexualized and sensationalized renderings in popular culture.[30] Byzantine studies, by these lights, is a discipline perennially fated to lag behind adjacent fields like classics and medieval studies, whose traditional esteem among European audiences has given them an insuperable head start in the race for academic relevance.[31]

▪▪▪

The four stages model of Byzantine scholarship, canonized by historians such as Vasiliev, Thompson, and Ostrogorsky, stresses key contributors and critical moments in the development of Byzantine studies: Wolf and Du Cange, the loping advances

27 K. Krumbacher, "Vorwort," *BZ* 1 (1892): 1–12; see Anthony Kaldellis in Chapter 13 of this volume.

28 Thompson, *A History of Historical Writing*, 2:524. See further Savvides, *The Beginnings and Foundation of Byzantine Studies* (n. 8 above), 102, 105 (on Vasil'evskij), 112–15 (on the contributions of Krumbacher, Bury, and Diehl).

29 See nn. 7–8 above.

30 Cameron, *Byzantine Matters*, 13–14, 23.

31 E.g., E. Jeffreys, "We Need to Talk about Byzantium: or, Byzantium, Its Reception of the Classical World as Discussed in Current Scholarship, and Should Classicists Pay Attention?," *Classical Receptions Journal* 6.1 (2014): 158–74; Jeffreys, Haldon, and Cormack, "Byzantine Studies as an Academic Discipline" (n. 8 above), 4–10, esp. 8; Cameron, "The Absence of Byzantium" (n. 4 above), 4–59; S. Albrecht, "Byzanz in deutschen, französischen und englischen Schulbüchern," in *Pulverfass, powder keg, baril de poudre? Südosteuropa im europäischen Geschichtsschulbuch*, ed. A. Helmedach (Hanover, 2007), 11–40; and essays in P. Odorico and P. Agapitos, eds., *Pour une "nouvelle" histoire de la littérature byzantine: Problèmes, méthodes, approches, propositions. Actes du Colloque international philologique, Nicosie, Chypre, 25–28 mai 2000*, Dossiers byzantins 1 (Paris, 2002).

of the *Byzantine du Louvre*, and sharp decline under Enlightenment contempt. These narratives reproduce the learned but conservative approach of nineteenth- and twentieth-century scholars like Ulrich von Wilamowitz-Moellendorf and John Sandys, whose histories of classical scholarship focus on titanic intellects and weighty editions.[32] Such an approach has the merit of making individual scholars, their inspirations and contributions, easily apprehended. But a biographical lens can obscure as much as it magnifies, darkening developments outside the field of vision so that the great scholar with his books seems to stand alone. It has little to say about the networks of relationships in which such figures labored, prospered, and failed; about the variety of organizations—princely courts, provincial schoolhouses, scholarly societies, universities, and religious orders—that sustained or impeded their learned research; and about the national, confessional, or personal impulses that motivated their work. The historical context remains indistinct in the background.

Equally troubling is the way hegemonic narratives of decline or redemption still condition investigations into the history of Byzantine studies as a discipline. Gibbon's epitaph in particular remains etched in the minds of Byzantinists, so that even the story of the discipline's "liberation" in the nineteenth century continues to bear the marks of his scorn.[33] Such narratives are constraining in two ways. First, as Anthony Grafton demonstrates in Chapter 3, they fail to acknowledge the complexity of scholarly engagements with Byzantium produced during the late Renaissance, homogenizing what was in fact a far more diverse and ambivalent history.[34] Like many tales of disciplinary woe or triumph, reports of Byzantium's neglect in early modern Europe tend to exaggerate the coherence of past attitudes. Second, framing decline as an archetype fashioned by Gibbon overlooks the paradigm's deep roots; as Fabio Pagani shows in Chapter 1, a sense of decline emerged even among intellectuals in the last centuries of the Byzantine Empire itself, and resounded again and again in melancholy tones over the next three centuries before Gibbon.[35]

32 An approach most recently evident in Savvides, *The Beginnings and Foundation of Byzantine Studies*. See also J. Sandys, *A History of Classical Scholarship*, 3 vols. (Cambridge, 1906–08); U. von Wilamowitz-Moellendorff, *Geschichte der Philologie*, 3rd ed., rev. A. Henrichs (Stuttgart, 1998). Cf. R. Pfeiffer, *History of Classical Scholarship from the Beginnings to the End of the Hellenistic Age* (Oxford, 1968), viii, and further A. Grafton, "The Origins of Scholarship," *American Scholar* 48.2 (1979): 236–61, for a critique of "biographical" approaches to the history of scholarship.

33 See, for instance, A. Kazhdan and G. Constable, *People and Power in Byzantium: An Introduction to Modern Byzantine Studies* (Washington, DC, 1982), 10.

34 In addition to Grafton in Chapter 3, see Pertusi, *Storiografia umanistica* (n. 7 above); Bianco, *La Bisanzio dei Lumi* (n. 17 above).

35 For an early investigation of the sense of decline among late Byzantine intellectuals, see I. Ševčenko, "The Decline of Byzantium Seen through the Eyes of Its Intellectuals," *DOP* 15 (1961): 167–86.

In addition to these limitations, accounts progressing through the four stages often take for granted the normativity of the detached, institutionally housed scholarship that the discipline ultimately embraced with Krumbacher and his contemporaries. To measure the vibrancy of Byzantine studies in early modernity by citing numbers of editions, or by counting the frequency of classroom lectures on strictly "Byzantine" topics, is to risk overlooking the diverse ways scholarship was pursued before the advent of the modern research university. Agostino Pertusi articulated this insight over half a century ago. In a landmark essay on the development of Byzantine historiography, Pertusi argued that an understanding of Byzantium's place in early modern scholarship requires not a "history of erudition that led to Byzantine studies listing dates, names, and editions of texts, but rather that of researching the motivations that led the learned men of the sixteenth and seventeenth centuries to be specifically interested in Byzantine history."[36] Or, to use terms of art drawn from the history of academic disciplines, we need to integrate the existing "internalist" research with an "externalist" narrative: one which acknowledges that scholarly endeavors not only emerged from the efforts of learned figures but also were subject to structures of power, responsive to cultural tastes and imperatives, and rife with ideological significance.[37]

In recent decades, a growing number of individual studies have begun to expand upon Pertusi's insight, encouraging us to look with greater acuity at how early modern scholars lit upon Byzantium in their varied intellectual journeys. Han Lamers has illustrated the delicate game of self-representation played by Byzantine émigrés in Italy, who found that styling themselves "Hellenes" rather than "Romans" made them more attractive to prospective patrons and employers there.[38] Humanists like Philip Melanchthon (1497–1560) and his circle may have scoffed at the Byzantines' "semibarbarous" Greek. But as Asaph Ben-Tov has shown, they also made no clear

36 Pertusi, *Storiografia umanistica*, 4: "Non credo che sia nostro compito delineare una storia esterna dell'erudizione che portò allo studio della bizantinistica, elencando date, nomi, edizioni di testi, storie universali o particolari che trattano di storia bizantina, ma piuttosto quello di ricercare le motivazioni che condussero i dotti dei secoli XVI e XVII ad interessarsi in modo specifico della storia bizantina." For a recent attempt to explicitly follow Pertusi's lead, see N. Aschenbrenner, "Contesting Ceremony, Constructing Byzantium: Reading Pseudo-Kodinos in Early Modern Europe," *DOP* 72 (2018): 197–214.

37 On "internalist" and "externalist" divisions, see P. Novick, *That Noble Dream: The "Objectivity Question" and the American Historical Profession* (Cambridge, 1988), 9: "In . . . the history of academic disciplines generally, there are 'internalists' and 'externalists.' As the names suggest, those in the former camp concern themselves with what goes on inside the discipline, slighting or ignoring its relationship with the surrounding environment; the latter focus on one or another aspect of that external relationship."

38 Lamers, *Greece Reinvented* (n. 10 above).

distinction between Greek antiquity and Byzantium; the rhetoric of disdain found in their literary preferences did not prevent their looking to Byzantine texts for solutions to a range of contemporary concerns, from the reformation of Christendom to the existential threat of the Ottomans.[39] Elisa Bianco, meanwhile, has restored to Enlightenment historiography on Byzantium its discordant voices, amplifying not only the empire's vituperative critics like Louis Maimbourg (1610–1686) but also its more equable judges like Claude Fleury (1640–1723) and Charles le Beau (1701–1778).[40] Above all, she illustrates how the Byzantine past remained fundamental to Enlightenment scholarship, playing a central role in patristic studies and ecclesiastical history as well as in ambitious histories of the Roman Empire. Still others have reassessed the withering witticisms of Voltaire, Montesquieu, and Gibbon to stress the attraction Byzantium held for this "unholy trinity" of Enlightenment critics. As David Womersley points out, Gibbon's verbose expressions of disgust are themselves evidence of his considerable fascination with the Byzantines.[41]

Meanwhile, several recent volumes have sought—and found—Byzantium outside the scholar's study, directing our attention to the empire's cultural afterlife in music, theater, literature, and architecture.[42] Studies of Byzantium's reception in European culture highlight the many ways in which craftsmen, writers, and artists have looked back to the Byzantine past as a source not only of heresy and vice, but also of elegance, piety, and power. They demonstrate that "Byzantinism" constituted a Pan-European phenomenon, vital to diverse cultural and aesthetic programs. What is more, these studies catalog the variety of Byzantinism's local and national manifestations, implicitly stressing the importance of an inductive approach to the reception of the Byzantine legacy. Rather than beginning with grand, overarching themes like

39 A. Ben-Tov, *Lutheran Humanists and Greek Antiquity: Melanchthonian Scholarship between Universal History and Pedagogy* (Leiden, 2009). See also idem, "*Turco-Graecia*: German Humanists and the End of Greek Antiquity—Cultural Exchange and Misunderstanding," in *The Renaissance and the Ottoman World*, ed. A. Contadini and C. Norton (Farnham, Surrey, 2013), 181–95.

40 Bianco, *La Bisanzio dei Lumi*, 115–52, 155–69, 239–66; see also the detailed treatment of a number of these scholars in Savvides, *The Beginning and Foundation of Byzantine Studies*, 59–122.

41 A. Louth, J. Haldon, R. Webb, J. Lowden, and D. Womersley, "Taking a Leaf from Gibbon: Appraising Byzantium," *Dialogos: Hellenic Studies Review* 6 (1999): 141–55; D. Womersley, introduction to Gibbon, *Decline and Fall*, 1:xcvii–xcviii. But cf. J. G. A. Pocock, *Barbarism and Religion*, vol. 4, *Barbarians, Saracens, and Empires* (Cambridge, 2005), 334. For the term "unholy trinity," see P. Marciniak and D. C. Smythe, introduction to their *The Reception of Byzantium* (n. 11 above), p. 4.

42 See in particular articles in Marciniak and Smythe, *The Reception of Byzantium*; M.-F. Auzépy, ed., *Byzance en Europe*, Créations Européennes (Saint-Denis, 2003); F. Kolovou, ed., *Byzanzrezeption in Europa: Spurensuche über das Mittelalter und die Renaissance bis in die Gegenwart*, ByzArch 24 (Berlin, 2012); Nilsson and Stephenson, *Wanted, Byzantium* (n. 1 above).

"decline" or "absence," these works affirm that historians of Byzantium's early modern afterlife have much to gain by approaching their subject from the ground up.

Collectively, such studies suggest that the absence or disdain of Byzantium in early modern Europe is more apparent than real: it is a product of what modern research on the history of Byzantine scholarship has tended to look for—namely, evidence of contempt to explain the discipline's marginalization—rather than an indication of what exists to be found. Still, for all their value in indicating the limitations of traditional approaches, these recent works do not actively advance toward an alternate synthesis. Monographs such as those by Lamers and Ben-Tov remain disparate in thematic focus as well as in geographic and temporal range, and they do not aim to address the development of Byzantine studies as a scholarly pursuit over time. The few works—such as Elisa Bianco's—that do aim at diachronic analysis observe tight temporal, national, and linguistic constraints. Hence while Bianco has brought much-needed attention to important historians of the Byzantine world such as Maimbourg and Louis-Sébastien Le Nain de Tillemont (1637–1698), her monograph focuses on authors writing mostly in French during the seventeenth and eighteenth centuries. Work on the reception of Byzantium in European culture also resists synthesis, ranging as it does from the salon to the stage, the concert hall, and even the cinema. Moreover, reception studies skew toward the late nineteenth and twentieth centuries, although whether this reflects Byzantinism's growing cultural relevance during this period or the individual predilections of modern researchers remains unclear.

The need for a new historical synthesis of Byzantine scholarship in early modern Europe—one focused on questions of method, motivation, and context—is therefore evident. Yet progress toward this new synthesis depends on the production of more focused, specialized scholarly studies—studies that complement the pioneering work of Lamers, Bianco, and others, but that offer individual insights coordinated within a program of research and directed toward a common end. Indeed, one reason why generalizations about Byzantium's early modern "absence" or "disdain" have proven so tenacious is that we still lack the materials to construct a different account. In many areas, primary sources for early modernity's investigations of Byzantium remain inaccessible or unstudied, while competent secondary studies based on a close examination of these original authorities are often lacking. Few scholars have rooted out the relevant documents from the archives or read the dense Latin commentaries that would significantly enhance our knowledge of the history of Byzantine scholarship in its formative centuries. We have few detailed studies of even the second rank of Byzantine scholars—figures like Bonaventura Vulcanius (1538–1614), Johannes Meursius (Johannes van Meurs, 1579–1639), or Leo Allatius (Leone Allacci, 1586–1669)—to say nothing of lesser lights working away in musty studies and lecture halls.[43] The aim of this volume is therefore not only to break with the reductive "four stages" and suggest a provisional new account of the history of Byzantine scholarship, but also to add significantly to the store of raw materials with which other scholars might corroborate, refine, or dispute our synthesis. For as Anthony Grafton once remarked in reference to the history of classical scholarship, "in a subject where so few of the individual trees have ever been identified, it is hardly reasonable to continue making blurred long-distance photographs of the forest."[44]

■■■

Taking its cue from Grafton's metaphor, the present volume approaches the historiography of Byzantine studies tree by tree—with consequences for our vision of the forest. A comprehensive history of Byzantine scholarship in early modern Europe would require multiple volumes written by teams of specialists. As we have argued, the ground has hardly been prepared for a synthesis of such encyclopedic proportions. Instead, this book offers an illustrative cross-section, the product of two days of presentation and discussion at Harvard University in October 2017. As organizers, we invited a group of scholars in different fields—early modern European history, Byzantine and medieval studies, classics, art history, and comparative literature—to speak from their varied disciplinary perspectives about the motivations for, and products of, Byzantine studies across Europe between roughly 1450 and 1850. The results of this conference persuasively affirmed that early modern scholars of all stripes brought no less diversity in aims and ends, no less innovative and systematic methods, and no less urgency to their study of Byzantium than to their study of the

43 On the Byzantine endeavors of Vulcanius, see D. van Miert, "Project Procopius: Scaliger, Vulcanius, Hoeschelius, and the Pursuit of Early Byzantine History," in *Bonaventura Vulcanius, Works and Networks: Bruges 1538–Leiden 1614*, ed. H. Cazes (Leiden, 2010), 361–86; B. Croke, "Procopius, from Manuscripts to Books: 1400–1850," *Histos* Supplement 9.1 (2019): 57–67. On Meursius, see C. L. Heesakkers, "Te weinig koren of alleen te veel kaf? Leiden's eerste Noordnederlandse filoloog Joannes Meursius (1579–1639)," in *Miro Fervore: Een bundel lezingen & artikelen over de beoefening van de klassieke wetenschappen in de zeventiende & achttiende eeuw*, ed. R. J. Langelaan and M. Simons (Leiden, 1994), 13–26; K. Skovgaard-Petersen, *Historiography at the Court of Christian IV (1588–1648): Studies in the Latin Histories of Denmark by Johannes Pontanus and Johannes Meursius* (Copenhagen, 2002), 61–84, citing what little 19th-century scholarship exists. On Allacci, see T. Cerbu, "Leone Allacci (1587–1669): The Fortunes of an Early Byzantinist" (PhD diss., Harvard University, 1986), and now K. Hartnup, *"On the Beliefs of the Greeks": Leo Allatios and Popular Orthodoxy*, Medieval Mediterranean 54 (Leiden, 2004).

44 Grafton, "The Origins of Scholarship," 256, where he observes in the same vein: "Where there are no good monographs, there can hardly be good syntheses. Further progress in the history of scholarship, like progress in any field of historical research, depends on further study of the original sources."

classical past. But diversity was not the only theme to emerge from the discussion. One surprisingly consistent note that sounded across papers was the contemporary relevance of Byzantine scholarship for the early modern West. Contrary to accounts of Byzantine studies that have treated editions and translations, tables of coins, and catalogs of monuments as detached intellectual pursuits, our contributors revealed the opposite: studies of the Byzantine past were rarely just about Byzantium—or just about the past.

The present book is the product of the exchanges and collaboration that arose during this conference, enhanced by further contributions from scholars unable to attend. Its thirteen chapters and two appendixes, organized into four chronological-thematic clusters, converge on a series of interrelated questions both about the working habits and mental processes of individual scholars and about the social, intellectual, and political contexts in which their studies occurred. What role did Byzantine scholarship play in the bitter theological disputes, reforming programs, national rivalries, and confessional crises of the European Reformation? To what extent and in what ways did the political and military fortunes of the Ottoman Empire condition interest in Byzantine history? How did philological and lexicographical scholarship on Byzantine texts influence or respond to trends in classical scholarship? What place did scholars accord Byzantium's millenary civilization in early modern constructions of historical chronology and periodization? How did scholars use Byzantium's imperial history to inform defenses and critiques of empire in an age of unprecedented European expansion and conquest across the globe? While this volume does not fully answer all these questions, it aims to erect a frame in which others might fruitfully pursue them.

One of the challenges of this volume, both in whole and in its constituent parts, is to examine the formation of "Byzantine studies" before the emergence of "Byzantium" as a coherent historical category. Setting aside the fact that there remains little current consensus about what the chronological or geographical boundaries of such a category might be, we face another problem. This challenge is, in part, a terminological one, since most of the figures examined in this volume did not consciously use the term *Byzantine* to describe the objects of their study (Martin Hanke and Philippe Labbe being notable exception). As many contributors note, it is expedient but anachronistic to describe as Byzantine the texts and artifacts that derive from the historical entity we now call Byzantium. In fact, this term—which most scholars use to signify a unique fusion of Greek, Christian, and Roman elements—elides the conceptual struggle faced by early modern scholars when engaging this period and its history. Was it an imperial Roman state and society, as Johannes Cuspinian (1473–1529) and others argued? Should it be seen as part of the continuum of Greek history, as Pletho (ca. 1355–1452) and Martin Crusius

(1526–1607) suggested? Or was it an annex of the history of Christianity, as Jean Bolland (1596–1665) and his protegés imagined? Different scholars read the empire and society centered in Constantinople in different ways. The conscious use of the anachronistic "Byzantine" by the editors and contributors throughout the volume is intended to provide a common referential domain to understand how this concept gained both coherence and independence over the course of the five centuries that their essays cover. Without this anachronism, we lack the framework to collectively analyze the diverse labors of ecclesiastical historians of the late Renaissance, the lexicographers of the sixteenth century, and the dramatists of the seventeenth century. These figures themselves may not have seen their labors as contributing to the formation of "Byzantium"—focused as they often were on seeing their historical fragments as chiefly Greek, or Roman, or Christian. But in retrospect—with the aid of the modern category of Byzantium—we can see them as participants in a collaborative process that took place over several centuries.

■■■

The chapters in this volume fall into four parts, each situated in a chronological sequence and organized around a shared thematic focus. Part 1, "Reinventing Byzantium in the Fifteenth Century," explores the reassessments, by intellectuals in both East and West, of Byzantium's history and identity in this transitional century. The two chapters here show how a confluence of factors—the increased mobility of people, materials, books, and ideas; new modes of historical inquiry and writing; the growing competence in Greek among Western scholars; and, not least, the ascent of the Ottomans as a political force in the Mediterranean—led fifteenth-century thinkers to question the conventions and antipathies of the late Middle Ages and propose new frames for understanding the Byzantine past: the first of many reinventions to follow.

The two essays in this part illustrate divergent approaches to this fifteenth-century reinvention. Drawing on the work of the idiosyncratic Byzantine philosopher George Gemistos Pletho, Fabio Pagani in Chapter 1 challenges the conventional view that Western intellectuals were the first to apply the paradigm of "decline" to Byzantium. Pletho taught that the Eastern Roman Empire was only a corruption of earlier Hellenic polities like Sparta, a belief formed through his lifelong engagement with the Platonic corpus. As Pagani shows, Pletho and his students used the study of ancient Greek literature to emphasize the empire's properly Hellenic (rather than Roman) roots as a model for cultural and political revival, with important consequences for the attitudes toward the eastern empire held by Pletho's many Western admirers. While Chapter 1 reveals the reactions among some Byzantine intellectuals to the empire's decline even before its destruction, Elena Boeck in Chapter 2 takes us to Italy, where artists and antiquarians reimagined Byzantium in the wake of its collapse—with altogether different results. Early connoisseurs of material culture such as Manuel Chrysoloras and Cyriac of Ancona saw Byzantine Constantinople as a rich field in which to investigate the materiality of the past, and to conjure the erstwhile glory of the Roman Empire. Boeck reveals that the harvest of antiquities reaped from Byzantium influenced Italian visual arts in ways that scholars have largely overlooked. Focusing on Andrea Mantegna's famous *Triumphs of Caesar*, she charts how one Byzantine monument—the column of Justinian—migrated from the pages of antiquarian literature into a tableau of Roman imperial power. Together, Pagani and Boeck disclose how fifteenth-century humanists put rejection or appropriation of Byzantium's Roman valence at the heart of their philological, antiquarian, and visual programs. But the chapters also show a surprising kind of inversion. Pletho abandoned historical orthodoxy in Byzantium by arguing that his fatherland had descended not from the Roman Empire but rather from the cities and peoples of Greek antiquity. In Italy, meanwhile, Mantegna's imperial scene challenged the consensus—predominant even among humanists—that the culture of Constantinople signified as "Greek" rather than "Roman." The near-contemporary and contradictory reinventions of Byzantium examined by Pagani and Boeck illustrate two guiding themes of the remaining essays in this volume: first, how shifting political, religious, and cultural concerns informed early modern encounters with, and reassessments of, the Byzantine past; and second, how scholars grappled with the thorny question of where Byzantium fit among the familiar categories of the classical and postclassical world.

Moving forward from the fifteenth century, the volume's "long middle" (Parts 2 and 3) traces these guiding themes across the pivotal centuries between ca. 1500 and 1750. The chapters in Part 2, "Exploiting and Enacting Byzantium," focus on questions of motivation: why did early modern scholars think the Byzantine past deserved and rewarded study? Anthony Grafton begins this section in Chapter 3 with a wide-ranging investigation into the uses of Byzantine historiography among sixteenth- and seventeenth-century humanists. He spotlights how scholars from Bruni to Bentley looked to Byzantine historians to resolve—or provoke—disputes over issues as diverse as the origins of European nations, the reformation of the church, historical chronology, sacral kingship, and the best methods for vanquishing the Ottoman Empire. Grafton shows that Byzantine historiography, far from being a neglected genre at the margins of scholarship, was capable of delivering "intellectual bombshells" that shook the learned world of early modern Europe to its foundations. Picking up where Grafton leaves off—with the seminal figure of Martin Crusius—Richard Calis in Chapter 4 examines the motivations and methods of this diligent Tübingen professor, "one of the earliest early modern consumers of Byzantine materials." Calis shows that Crusius used Byzantine texts not only to interpret the classical past but also in his search for strategic information that could be employed against the Ottomans. Both of these applications, Calis argues, stemmed from Crusius's conviction that Byzantium formed part of a continuous Greek tradition that stretched back to Homer and survived in his own day under the Ottoman yoke. Yet like many of his contemporaries, Crusius also faced daunting obstacles in the interpretation of his Byzantine texts without any *instrumenta*, and Calis illustrates the scholarly practices Crusius used to make halting advances.

In Chapter 5, Teresa Shawcross takes us from Crusius to early modernity's foremost Byzantinist, much praised but little studied in modern scholarship: the great Charles du Fresne, sieur du Cange. In tribute to his titanic influence on the discipline, Shawcross examines his labors and his legacy in two separate essays. The first of these reveals that if Du Cange was a father to Byzantine studies—as even his near contemporaries regarded him—his paternity emerged from his failure to secure royal support as a historian of France. Only after abandoning his earlier, Francocentric ambitions did Du Cange bring out his groundbreaking studies on Byzantine genealogy, topography, and numismatics, as well as his crowning achievement: the glossary of medieval Greek. Shawcross details how Du Cange's Byzantine projects in the last two decades of his life—not unlike the projects of Crusius before him—received impetus from western Europe's enduring fixation on the Ottomans, alongside other Mediterranean rivalries and ambitions central to Louis XIV's political aspirations. Chapter 6 continues the focus on Du Cange with an examination of the great scholar's posthumous reputation. Shawcross traces how Du Cange's great-nephew, Jean-Charles du Fresne D'Aubigny, expended massive effort to recover the scholar's literary legacy, which had been scattered across Europe. By the mid-eighteenth century, however, when D'Aubigny set out to revive his great-uncle's reputation, the Ottoman threat that had sparked the French crown's interest in the eastern Mediterranean—and given Du Cange's Byzantine projects contemporary relevance—had receded. In reconstructing Du Cange's archive, D'Aubigny thus strategically reframed him as a historian of France, spawning a legacy that, as Shawcross argues, has contributed to Du Cange's relative neglect by historians of scholarship. Supplementing these two essays, Shawcross contributes two appendixes, found at the end of the volume, that document this "reinvention" of Byzantium's most erudite and productive early modern scholar.

Concluding Part 2 of this volume, Przemysław Marciniak in Chapter 7 guides us out of the scholar's study and onto the early modern stage, where a different audience encountered new adaptations of Byzantium. Marciniak traces the fluctuating fortunes of Byzantine characters and themes through several centuries of dramatic works, deftly revealing how playwrights of various confessional allegiances and political proclivities detached Byzantine protagonists from their historical contexts and spun them into timeless exemplars of virtue or (more frequently) vice. Above all, the Byzantine backdrop functioned as a vague but potent catalyst, capable of activating its audiences' anxieties over royal absolutism, religious heterodoxy, or Ottoman aggression. As Marciniak argues, the key feature of this dramatized Byzantium was its plastic ahistoricity—its ability to assume whatever edifying shape the playwright chose. Such remarkable flexibility emerges as a thread linking all five chapters in this section, evident in the diverse motivations that scholars brought to their study of the Byzantine past between 1500 and 1750: as keys to the recovery of classical antiquity, as ammunition in confessional disputes, as models for both praise and criticism of absolutist regimes, and as repositories of strategic intelligence for Christendom's struggle against the Ottomans.

Part 3, "Categorizing and Contextualizing Byzantium," considers the various ways that scholars between 1500 and 1750 located Byzantine history and materials within different, and often mutually exclusive, conceptual categories. The chapters in this section collectively ask: what exactly did scholars think they were studying when they studied material we would now call "Byzantine"? In Chapter 8, John Considine examines the development of Greek lexicography. Greek-language lexica expanded rapidly in western Europe over the course of the sixteenth century, swelled by new access to the dictionaries, manuscripts, and texts of the late antique and Byzantine world. But as the circulation and study of these texts increased, scholars gradually came to sense that the postclassical language was distinctive and ill-served by a universalizing ambition to collect all Greek lexemes into a single corpus. Considine charts how the ecumenical approach of Greek lexicographers in the sixteenth century thus yielded to greater specialization in the seventeenth, with the rise of a subgenre of dictionaries specifically devoted to late Greek words called *Barbarograecum*—a term whose pejorative connotations for us efface, as Considine argues, the more nuanced view held by the compilers of these dictionaries. While lexicographers debated the place of Byzantine language within the *longue durée* of Greek, others understood Byzantine literature as the continuation of a "Roman" tradition—and none more eruditely than the Silesian schoolmaster Martin Hanke (1633–1709). As William North demonstrates in Chapter 9, Hanke ought to be placed alongside Du Cange in the vanguard of late seventeenth-century Byzantine studies. In a meticulous analysis, North shows how Hanke's history of Byzantine literature surpassed its predecessors both in depth of learning and in knowledge of published and manuscript materials. By adopting a clear and consistent method, Hanke resolved thorny problems of identity and chronology that had long bedeviled research on many Byzantine authors. But as North points out, Hanke also reframed—indeed, *renamed*—Byzantine literature as the study of *res Byzantinae*. Rather than seeing it as the end of Greek literary tradition stretching back to Homer,

Hanke conceived of a Byzantine corpus that continued the literary history of the Roman Empire through the end of the Middle Ages.

Shane Bobrycki in Chapter 10 trains the spotlight on the life of another figure critical to the development of Byzantine scholarship: a pioneering—if ambivalent—Byzantinist, the Benedictine monk Bernard de Montfaucon (1655–1741). Montfaucon founded for Byzantine studies a robust and indispensable new auxiliary discipline: the systematic study of medieval Greek scripts by which manuscripts and documents could be securely dated. Yet while Montfaucon stood beside and benefited from those scholars invested in the construction of Byzantium as a historical category, Bobrycki shows that Montfaucon himself saw it as only a part of the broad sweep of Greek civilization—another province on the map of antiquity. As the volume moves from Byzantine scripts to Byzantine saints, hagiography receives illuminating treatment in Chapter 11 from Xavier Lequeux, who investigates how the Jesuit Jean Bolland transformed, in several stages, the ambitious program envisioned by Héribert Rosweyde (1569–1629) into an ecumenical compendium of the lives of Christian saints from eastern, as well as western, Christianity. He shows us how Daniel Papebroch (1628–1714) rifled archives, leveraged scholarly connections, and traveled great distances in pursuit of this desire to comprehensively edit and publish all medieval Greek saints' lives. Though Bolland, Papebroch, and their collaborators cultivated strong relationships with other scholars interested in the Byzantine world, Lequeux stresses that for these hagiographers—no less than for Montfaucon—the idea of "the Byzantine" was subordinate to a broader category: in this case, Christian sainthood. Only a desire to catalog the latter brought them into contact with the rich world of Byzantine saints' lives, miracle tales, and menologia. The ways that scholars between 1500 and 1750 made sense of the Byzantine past were thus no less protean than were the motivations that drove them to its study. Some, such as lexicographers like Johannes Meursius or philologists like Hanke, came closer to seeing "Byzantine" materials as belonging to a distinct historical epoch; others, like Monfaucon and the Bollandists, assimilated them more or less seamlessly within broader, older categories. Nevertheless, all four chapters in this section reveal how Byzantine encounters could spur scholars to revise their mental maps of the past, from drawing sharper boundaries between classical and later Greek to expanding the frontiers of Roman literature and Christian sainthood. In this respect, Byzantium's very ambiguity—at once conforming to and complicating familiar categories of Greek, Roman, or Christian—made it instrumental to the formation of new scholarly methods and sensibilities.

Advancing to Part 4, "Chronologies of Byzantium from the Enlightenment to Modernity," we see that questions of where Byzantium "fit" within various historical schemata remained active into (and after) the nineteenth century. By the age of Gibbon—let alone that of Krumbacher—scholars working on the Byzantine Middle Ages could draw on resources unimaginable in 1500: a vast array of editions and translations; technical studies of Byzantine coins and genealogy; dense lexica compiled from the study of thousands of texts; descriptions of Byzantine monuments and architecture in Greece, Constantinople, Anatolia, and beyond; the lives of innumerable holy men and women of the Christian East; and a popular culture suffused with ribald and violent tales of the Byzantine world. In spite of these profound advances in scholarship, however, the liminality and limits of the Byzantine world proved no easier to resolve. Together, the final two chapters in this volume examine the ways scholars struggled to fix the boundaries of Byzantium between ancient and modern, Greek and Roman, West and East.

In Chapter 12, Frederic Clark reveals how Byzantium's temporal and cultural indeterminacy troubled Edward Gibbon as he agonized over the endpoint for his *History of the Decline and Fall of the Roman Empire*, a dilemma that ultimately led Gibbon to extend his masterpiece down to the Ottoman conquest of Constantinople —and beyond. Clark proceeds to shows that Gibbon was not the first to struggle with Byzantium's temporal ambiguity: it challenged scholars as early as Petrarch who sought to divide "antiquity" from "modernity." Georg Horn (1620–1670), for one, attempted to resolve the difficulty by using the Byzantine Empire's demise to mark the end of "ancient history," while signaling the advent of "modern history" with the coronation of Charlemagne—a scheme in which the start of the "modern" antedated the end of the "ancient." Such "temporal flexibility," Clark reveals, eventually gave way in the late seventeenth and eighteenth centuries to a new hegemonic scheme of *ancient-medieval-modern*. But no matter the scheme, Clark elucidates how scholars never saw Byzantium as "modern"—a category reserved for polities and peoples who had survived into the contemporary age.

In Chapter 13, Anthony Kaldellis takes us from the grand historical narratives of the late seventeenth and eighteenth centuries to the political machinations of the mid-nineteenth century, introducing the final "invention" of Byzantium that gave the concept its recognizably modern form. Under the pressures of Great Power politics and the geopolitical tensions emerging from the Crimean War (1853–56), "Byzantine Empire" displaced "Greek Empire" as the favored formulation for many European scholars. Kaldellis underscores how this terminological change reflected ideological anxiety: the fear among many Europeans that the history of the "Greek empire" might legitimate the irredentist ambitions of Greek nationalists and Russian imperialists to recover Constantinople. The term *Byzantium*, Kaldellis argues, enabled scholars to avoid the slippage between an acceptable Greek nation and an intolerable Greek empire, while also walling it off from problematic associations with imperial Rome. This invention of Byzantium remained an ideological imposition, but one that granted the young discipline the independent status its Western devotees craved. Both Clark and Kaldellis show us scholars confronting similar challenges of periodizing and categorizing a liminal culture. In this way, the struggles of the eighteenth and nineteenth centuries echoed those of every era since the fifteenth. In each part of this volume we encounter scholars constantly reassessing and reinventing Byzantium's relationship to the ancient and medieval past, struggling to fit Byzantium into familiar chronologies and categories. The book concludes with a synthesis that integrates the insights derived from these thirteen chapters, in an effort both to sketch the contours for a new history of Byzantine scholarship in early modern Europe and to point the way forward for future research.

***

Taken together, the chapters in this volume make a twofold contribution to the history of Byzantine studies. First, they cumulatively step aside from the conventional "four stages" anatomized above, which narrate the history of the field as a succession of advances and setbacks toward the realization of an autonomous discipline. Rather, these essays equip us to see the study of Byzantium as a series of "inventions" and "reinventions" informed by the contemporary conditions and concerns that shaped these scholarly encounters. Second, they build on the insight that tales of Byzantium's early modern neglect—and subsequent nineteenth-century redemption—continue to hold sway because there has been no effort to provide an alternative vision of the history of Byzantine studies as a whole. Thus, this book intends not merely to critique the standard narrative of the development of Byzantine studies. Rather, it attempts to synthesize the insights of its individual studies into a provisional alternative, if only to galvanize further research and provoke fresh criticism.

However broad its coverage, the present volume can till only some fields while others—inevitably, but no less lamentably—are left fallow. While several un- or understudied scholars such as Martin Hanke and Martin Crusius benefit from close attention in the following pages, the achievements of others, hardly inferior, receive but passing mention: learned churchmen, many of whom collaborated in the *Byzantine du Louvre*, such as Denis Pétau (1583–1652), Leone Allacci, Jacques Goar (1601–1653), and François Combefis (1605–1679), to name only a few.[45] The labors of the jurists—Jacques Cujas (1522–1590), Denis and Jacques Godefroy

45 While not addressed at length in this volume, several of these figures have been studied elsewhere in varying degrees of detail. On Pétau, see M. Hofmann, *Theologie, Dogma und Dogmenentwicklung im theologischen Werk Denis Petau's: Mit einem biographischen und einembibliographischen Anhang*, Regensburger Studien zur Theologie 1 (Bern, 1976). On Goar: C. Newman, "'In vestitu deaurato circumdata varietate': Some Observations on the Commentary of Jacques Goar, O.P., on the Liturgy of St John Chrysostom," *SVThQ* 53.4 (2009): 461–76. On Combefis: R. Darricau,

(1549–1622; 1587–1652), and Charles Annibal Fabrot (1580–1659)—who sought to reconstruct Roman-Byzantine law are likewise absent.[46] Nor was the development of Byzantine scholarship purely a bookish endeavor. Intrepid travelers including Pierre Gilles (1490–1555), Hans Dernschwam (1494–1568/69), John Covel (1638–1722), and Jacob Spon (1647–1685)—to say nothing of the erudite and perceptive Mary Wortley Montagu (1689–1762)—played a critical role in recording and circulating accounts or images of monumental Byzantine architecture and inscriptions.[47] Meanwhile, collector-scholars like Nicolas-Claude Fabri de Peiresc (1580–1637) and Charles Olier de Nointel (1635–1685) slowly compiled archives of coins and seals, efforts that fostered engagement with the visual and representational culture of the Byzantine world.[48] Such projects of travel, collection, and compilation developed as European colonial empires spread across the globe, and colonialism's role in providing material and ideological stimulus for scholarship on Byzantium remains a largely neglected subject.[49]

"A Hellenist of the Grand Siècle: The Dominican François Combefis (1605–1679)," *Res publica litterarum* 1 (1978): 21–41. On Allacci, see n. 42 above.

46 For an introduction see H. E. Troje, *Graeca leguntur: Die Aneignung des byzantinischen Rechts und die Entstehung eines humanistischen Corpus iuris civilis in der Jurisprudenz des 16. Jahrhunderts* (Böhlau, 1971).

47 For early modern travelers from the West to Greece, Anatolia, and Istanbul, see in general H. Omont, ed., *Missions archéologiques françaises en Orient aux XVIIe et XVIIIe siècles*, 2 vols. (Paris, 1902); H. Pignot, *Christians under the Ottoman Turks: French and English Travellers in Greece and Anatolia, 1615–1694*, Gorgias Ottoman Travelers 2 (Piscataway, NJ, 2009); L. Pollard, *The Quest for Classical Greece: Early Modern Travel to the Greek World* (London, 2015). On Gilles, see K. Byrd, introduction to Pierre Gilles, *Pierre Gilles' Constantinople*, ed. and trans. Byrd (New York, 2008), xiii–xxvi. On Dernschwam: F. Babinger, *Hans Dernschwam's Tagebuch einer Reise nach Konstantinopel und Kleinasien*, trans. J. Reicke (Berlin, 2014), xix–xxxi, and M. D. Birnbaum, "The Fuggers, Hans Dernschwam, and the Ottoman Empire," *SüdostF* 50 (1991): 119–44. On Covel, see especially his diaries, published as *Voyages en Turquie, 1675–1677*, ed. J.-P. Grélois, with a preface by C. Mango, Réalités byzantines 6 (Paris, 1998). On Spon: R. Étienne and J.-C. Mossière, eds., *Jacob Spon: Un humaniste lyonnais du XVIIème siècle*, Bibliothèque Salomon-Reinach 4 (Paris, 1993). For Mary Wortley Montagu's interest in Byzantine antiquities during her yearlong residence in Constantinople (May 1717–July 1718), see I. Grundy, *Lady Mary Wortley Montagu: Comet of the Enlightenment* (Oxford, 2001), 152–66, esp. 163, 166.

48 On Peiresc as collector and interpreter of coins, see P. N. Miller, *Peiresc's Orient: Antiquarianism as Cultural History in the Seventeenth Century* (Farnham, 2012), 103–58; his interest in the Byzantine world is examined in A.-M. Cheny, *Une bibliothèque byzantine: Nicolas-Claude Fabri de Peiresc et la fabrique du savoir* (Ceyzérieu, 2015). The most comprehensive study of Nointel remains A. Vandal, *L'odyssée d'un ambassadeur: Les voyages du Marquis de Nointel* (Paris, 1900); see also Omont, *Missions archéologiques*, 1:175–221.

49 For an initial reflection on this topic, see N. Aschenbrenner and J. Ransohoff, "Hieronymus Wolf's Silver Tongue: Early Byzantine Scholarship at the Intersection of Slavery, Colonialism, and the Crusades," in *Is Byzantine Studies a Colonialist Discipline? Towards a Critical Historiography of Byzantine Studies*, ed. B. Anderson and M. Ivanona (State College, PA, forthcoming).

Given these and other important lacunae, the conclusions advanced by the present volume are necessarily tentative. But we will count this project successful if, despite its limitations, it stimulates scholars of the Byzantine, medieval, and early modern worlds alike to approach the history of Byzantine studies in a new way. Without minimizing the significance of the institutionalization of Byzantine scholarship in the late nineteenth century, the contributions in the present volume invite us to see that moment less as the redemption of a field that finally achieved disciplinary legitimacy than as the latest "invention" in a long series of scholarly encounters with Byzantium that stretch back to the fifteenth century and before. When we shift our focus away from enumerating editions of texts, or recording what Wolf or Gibbon thought and said (or left unsaid); when we focus instead on *how* and *why* scholars labored over the texts, artifacts, and history we would now consider to be "Byzantine"; and when we look at the *uses* of Byzantium rather than its reputation or the coherence of its identity—we find that Byzantium moves from the margins to the center of early modern European culture and erudition.

PART ONE

REINVENTING BYZANTIUM IN THE FIFTEENTH CENTURY

ONE

GREEK IDENTITY AND IDEAS OF DECLINE IN FIFTEENTH-CENTURY BYZANTIUM

Gemistos Pletho and Bessarion

FABIO PAGANI

THE INVENTION OF BYZANTINE STUDIES PRESUPPOSES BOTH THE CATEGORY OF Byzantium and the category of a scholarship specifically devoted to it. The latter, however, became possible only after the former was conceptualized and validated. This process developed over a long period of time and relied on various presuppositions that need to be clearly articulated. In general terms, Byzantium has to be different from both its Roman predecessor and its medieval contemporaries. But the task of providing a clear definition of Byzantium is by no means easy. Temporally, it is not clear where exactly to place the break (if any) between the ancient and medieval empire.[1] Spatially, since the area of influence of the Roman Empire in the East varied considerably, it is far from obvious where to set the geographical boundaries of Byzantium.[2] Semantically, even the use of the name *Byzantium* to refer to the Eastern Roman Empire is debatable. Rather than going through the history of how Byzantium emerged as a word defining a specific field of study in its own right,[3] this chapter focuses on the fifteenth century, with essentially two aims.

1 See, e.g., the recent discussion by P. Agapitos, "Contesting Conceptual Boundaries," *Interfaces* 1 (2015): 62–91, esp. 68, 73, and J. O. Rosenqvist, *Die byzantinische Literatur: Vom 6. Jahrhundert bis zum Fall Konstantinopels 1453* (Berlin, 2007), 1–3.

2 See A. Laiou and C. Morrisson, *The Byzantine Economy* (Cambridge, 2007), 8–13.

3 See Anthony Kaldellis in Chapter 13 of this volume. In this chapter I intentionally appropriate the term "Greek-speaking Roman scholars" to define the group that scholars usually refer to, using their Italian name, as *dotti bizantini*. I do so in order to avoid linking them to the label *Byzantium*, whose origin this volume is investigating.

On the one hand, I investigate the relationship between the political downfall of the empire and idealized representations of the past, in order to argue that the very same process that led to the reappropriation (or reinvention, from a contemporary perspective) of ancient Greece was also responsible for the devaluing of the post-classical history of the Eastern Roman Empire. On the other hand, I argue that this very reappropriation of ancient Greece was embedded in a set of scholarly practices that, for at least some of the protagonists of this story, we have only recently come to understand with greater precision.

By teasing out the ideological tensions beyond the creation of a discourse about ancient Greece, I intend to shed light on why some of the most respected Greek-speaking Roman (i.e., Byzantine) scholars of the fifteenth century—especially Gemistos Pletho and Cardinal Bessarion—did *not* apply the same methodologies and create a comparable discourse about the postclassical history of the Eastern Roman Empire. Therefore, instead of directly tackling the problem of when and how the concept of Byzantium was crafted, I deal with when it could *not* have been crafted as such—that is, in the fifteenth century by those talented Greek-speaking Roman scholars who were especially invested in the reappropriation of ancient Greece by means of the philological study of ancient texts. My goal is, first, to show why this group of highly educated intellectuals, who certainly possessed both the personal skills and the practical resources to produce the best scholarship, did not in fact conceptualize Byzantium and, second, to clarify which assumptions ended up having an impact on those who later on did conceptualize such a category. By doing so, I seek to illuminate the background against which other scholars in this volume will place their investigations.

Gemistos Pletho and Byzantium

In a recent book titled *Greece Reinvented: Transformations of Byzantine Hellenism in Renaissance Italy*, Han Lamers investigates the history of Greek national discourse in the fifteenth century. By analyzing a large selection of Greek-speaking eastern Roman *eruditi*, he provides an all-encompassing study of the symbolic constructions of Greek nationalism in early modernity.[4] In his study, Lamers shows how

4 Here is how Lamers sums up his conclusions: "Although this study did not aim to rewrite the history of Greek national identity or national thought, it does confirm the increasingly accepted view that symbolical constructions we now construe as specifically 'national' and therefore 'modern' have a history that pre-dates the era in which nationalist ideologists began to re-appropriate them and adapted them to their needs. As such, the reinvention of the ancient Greeks by the Byzantine intelligentsia in Italy shows the importance of studying the archaeology of national symbols and images to understand, historically, the particular symbolic force and cultural

Greek-speaking eastern Roman scholars ended up embracing a Greek identity, for a variety of reasons. For those who made their way to Italy, a Greek identity was the only way to avoid an open conflict with Italian elites, obviously unprepared to share with them the legacy of ancient Rome.[5] Admittedly, a certain degree of tension was bound to arise between Greek-speaking eastern Roman scholars and their Italian colleagues, but ultimately the émigrés were too dependent on their Western hosts to mount any kind of long-term resistance.

But, more interestingly, even some of the Greek-speaking eastern Roman scholars who spent the overwhelming majority of their career in the eastern empire had their own good reasons for disavowing their Roman identity. A famous case in point is provided by Gemistos Pletho, perhaps the most respected philosopher and scholar of the late Palaiologan era.[6] Known to modern scholars above all for his controversial treatise *Laws* (*Νόμοι*), he is studied by Lamers especially for his famous speeches to the emperor Manuel II and to the despot of the Morea Theodore II, in which he vigorously argued for the Greekness of both himself and his fellow eastern Romans.[7] Born around 1360 in Constantinople, Gemistos relocated at the beginning of the fifteenth century to Mistra, where he worked as a *kritēs* (a provincial judge) and taught some of the most noteworthy students of his time, including Markos Eugenikos, Cardinal Bessarion, and various members of the Palaiologan family.[8]

---

significance of modern nationalism" (H. Lamers, *Greece Reinvented: Transformations of Byzantine Hellenism in Renaissance Italy* [Leiden, 2015], 280–81).

5 See ibid., 62–72.

6 In referring to Gemistos as "Pletho" instead of the more common "Plethon," I follow John Monfasani's argument, expressed in a conversation with me, that this form of his name emphasizes the intended association with Plato.

7 A general analysis of these texts from the point of view of political theory is provided by N. P. Peritore, "The Political Thought of Gemistos Plethon: A Renaissance Byzantine Reformer," *Polity* 10.2 (1977): 168–91. For Pletho's reappropriation of Plato's political philosophy, see P. Garnsey, "Plethon and Platonic Political Philosophy," in *Transformations of Late Antiquity*, ed. P. Rousseau and E. Papoutsakis (Aldershot, 2009), 327–40. Intriguingly, Garnsey comes to the conclusion that Gemistos was a more accurate interpreter of Platonic political philosophy than Thomas More. On nationalism in Gemistos, see also N. Siniossoglou, "Plethon and the Philosophy of Nationalism," in *Georgios Gemistos Plethon: The Byzantine and the Latin Renaissance*, ed. J. Matula and P. R. Blum (Olomouc, 2014), 415–31.

8 See C. M. Woodhouse, *George Gemistos Plethon: The Last of the Hellenes* (Oxford, 1986), 32–47, and F. Masai, *Pléthon et le Platonisme de Mystra* (Paris, 1956). Among the most recent bibliography see at least N. Siniossoglou, *Radical Platonism in Byzantium: Illumination and Utopia in Gemistos Plethon* (Cambridge, 2011); T. Shawcross, "A New Lykourgos for a New Sparta: George Gemistos Plethon and the Despotate of Morea," in *Viewing the Morea: Land and People in the Late Medieval Peloponnese*, ed. S. E. Gerstel (Washington, DC, 2013), 419–52; Matula and Blum, *Georgios Gemistos Plethon*; V. Hladký, *The Philosophy of Gemistos Plethon: Platonism in Late Byzantium, between Hellenism and Orthodoxy* (Farnham, Surrey, 2014). On Gemistos and Scholarios, see S. Siniossoglou, "Plethon, Scholarios and the Byzantine State of Emergency," in

Highly praised by such famous students, Gemistos has long been considered one of the most learned men of his generation.

Recently, however, a series of scattered palaeographical discoveries in manuscripts connected with him have put us in a better position to assess the nature of his work as a scholar. While a full discussion of this material is not possible here, a few introductory remarks will be helpful. First, Gemistos's manuscripts fall into two general categories: Gemistos's autographs and those manuscripts containing texts by other authors whom Gemistos read or annotated. While manuscripts in the second category, containing works by classical authors, have emerged only in the past few years, those in the first category have long been known; it is precisely on the basis of a careful study of this first group of manuscripts that scholars such as François Masai and C. M. Woodhouse have put forward the image of a Gemistos interested primarily in ancient historiography, geography, and philosophy.[9] Though substantial evidence indicates that he took an interest in later authors such as Demetrios Kydones, there is as yet no evidence that he made a systematic attempt at reconstructing their original writings.

Second, far from being merely a reader of selected classical authors, Gemistos was responsible for a large series of erasures aimed at improving or at censoring portions of texts.[10] Crucially, the overarching goal of his work was to make Plato (along with some other authors) as consistent as possible with the philosophical ideas he advanced in his own treatise, the *Laws*. The aim of these emendations and erasures was to show the consistency between ancient texts and his own work, buttressing his contention that the bulk of his own philosophical ideas were part of a long tradition going back to antiquity. This project protected him from the allegations of his intellectual/ideological opponents that he was introducing new and dangerous ideas. It is hardly surprising, then, that signs of his "philological" activity have so far been identified in manuscripts containing classical authors such as Plato, Herodotus, and Euclid. Even though no general and systematic investigation has been undertaken and we cannot rule out the possibility that future discoveries might change the present picture, for the time being it seems as if Gemistos's textual work was focused on Greek authors of antiquity, not on the postclassical body of texts that we are accustomed to call Byzantine literature.[11]

The Cambridge Intellectual History of Byzantium, ed. A. Kaldellis and N. Siniossoglou (Cambridge, 2019), 633–52.

9 See Masai, *Pléthon et le Platonisme*, 102–43; Woodhouse, *George Gemistos Plethon*, 32–48.

10 See F. Pagani, "Damnata Verba: Censure di Pletone in alcuni codici platonici," *BZ* 102.1 (2009): 167–202. For Euclid, see F. Acerbi, S. Martinelli Tempesta, and B. Vitrac, "Gli interventi autografi di Giorgio Gemisto Pletone nel codice matematico Marc. Gr. Z 301," *Segno e Testo* (2016): 411–56.

11 Late antique authors, such as Synesius, were certainly of interest to Pletho. But in those cases in which their texts have been found in one of his manuscripts (for Synesius, see Biblioteca Medicea

Moreover, Gemistos's very understanding of the word *Byzantium* differs from ours. To him, Βυζάντιον was in the first instance the name of an ancient village on the Bosphorus about which he knew from ancient Greek historians (and which I will henceforth refer to as *Byzantion*, to avoid confusion). In chapter 19 of his *Adnotationes e Diodoro*, based on Diodorus Siculus's account of the expedition by Philip of Macedonia against Perinthus in 341/40 BCE, he discussed the town extensively.[12] In his eyes, however, Byzantion had something more to its credit than Perinthus, or any other city attacked by Philip. Indeed, this little town was both the "mother" of Constantinople and a Dorian colony, on account of the Peloponnesian origins of its founders. In his speech to the emperor Manuel II Palaiologos, Gemistos emphatically sketches out his plan to reform the dying empire:

> Out of all this <Greek> land, the Peloponnesos is agreed to be the place that has carried the first and most celebrated offspring of the Greeks, and it was rising from the Peloponnesos that the Greeks accomplished the greatest and most famous deeds. And for those who think rationally, this land is to be considered as the mother and a starting point of the great city on the Bosphorus, which is now the seat of your imperial power. This is because the first peoples who inhabited Byzantion were Greeks and Dorians, and the Dorians are clearly Peloponnesians.[13]

The Dorian origin of Byzantion thus enabled Gemistos to establish a direct connection between Constantinople and the Peloponnesos, and therefore to provide an alternative genealogy to the commonly held belief that Constantinople was established by the Romans.

Laurenziana, Plut. 80.19), no attempt at philologically reconstructing the text of these works in a systematic way has been detected. A group of authors that were obviously crucial for Gemistos are the Neoplatonists. But so far, no manuscript of their works has been linked to Gemistos's library.

12 As Gemistos states in chapter 19 of his *Adnotationes e Diodoro*: see *Georgii Gemisti Plethonis Adnotationes e Diodoro et Plutarco*, ed. E. Maltese (Leipzig, 1989), 38–39; for another occurrence of the word *Byzantines*, see ibid., p. 8 (para. 14).

13 Gemistos Pletho, "Εἰς Μανουὴλ Παλαιολόγον περὶ τῶν ἐν Πελοποννήσῳ πραγμάτων," in *Παλαιολόγεια καὶ Πελοποννησιακά*, ed. S. Lampros, 4 vols. (Athens, 1912–26), 3:248: Συμπάσης δὲ ταύτης τῆς χώρας αὐτὴ Πελοπόννησος ὁμολογεῖται τὰ πρῶτά τε καὶ γνωριμώτατα ἐνεγκοῦσα τῶν Ἑλλήνων γένη, καὶ ἀπὸ ταύτης ὁρμώμενοι τὰ μέγιστά τε καὶ ἐνδοξότατα Ἕλληνες ἔργα ἀπεδείξαντο· καὶ μὲν δὴ καὶ τῆς μεγάλης ταυτησὶ πόλεως τῆς πρὸς Βοσπόρῳ, ἥπερ νῦν ὑμῖν βασίλειόν ἐστι, τήνδε τὴν χώραν εἴη ἂν λογιζομένοις οἷον μητέρα τε οὖσαν καὶ ἀφορμήν τινα ἰδεῖν, τοῦτο μὲν ἐπειδὴ Βυζάντιον οἱ προενῳκηκότες Ἕλληνές τε καὶ Δωριεῖς, Δωριεῖς δὲ Πελοποννήσιοι περιφανῶς. This passage and the following one have been thoroughly discussed by Lamers, *Greece Reinvented*, 36–42.

Gemistos Pletho's attempt to "Hellenize" the conventional Roman origin of the empire was rooted in his recovery of ancient historical sources. Yet the methodology he uses when handling these sources would not necessarily win the approval of modern historians. For the origin of Constantinople from the Dorian colony of Byzantion, an interesting case in point is provided by an excerpt from Dionysius of Halicarnassus's *Roman History* (1.61, 68–69), which is found in Gemistos's personal workbook, now Marcianus Graecus Z 406, fols. 117r–119r.[14] In these chapters Dionysius provides an account of the origins of the Trojans (not the inhabitants of the ancient town of Byzantion!) as coming from Arcadia, the central and mountainous region of the Peloponnesos. When a great deluge flooded the region and the Arcadians realized that the remaining land would not be sufficient to feed them all, they divided themselves into two groups. One remained in Arcadia under the reign of King Deimas, while the other sailed toward Asia Minor via Samothrace and arrived at the region called the Troad. Here Dardanus built a city named after himself. Therefore, according to Dionysius's account, the ultimate origins of Troy are to be found in the central Peloponnesian region of Arcadia.

But because the Trojans were not the only peoples of Peloponnesian origin who came to live on the shore of the Hellespont, Gemistos had a second reason to connect Constantinople with the Peloponnesos. While Constantinople had been founded by the Romans, the Romans themselves may have had (at least some) Peloponnesian blood in their veins. In another passage of his *Roman History* (2.49) Dionysius argued that the Sabines, ancestors of the Romans, were also of Peloponnesian origin.[15]

All in all, Gemistos's familiarity with Dionysius's *Roman History* permitted him to advance two arguments indirectly linking Constantinople's foundation to peoples from the Peloponnesos. Woodhouse described Gemistos's model as a "sound enough" foundation for patriotic propaganda.[16] Yet, far more than being mere

14 On this manuscript, apart from E. Mioni, *Bibliothecae Divi Marci Venetiarum Codices Graeci Manuscripti: Thesaurus Antiquus*, 2 vols. (Rome, 1985), 2:157–59, see also the recent description by C. Giacomelli in "Commentaria in Aristotelem Graeca et Byzantina," https://cagb-db.bbaw.de/handschriften/handschrift.xql?id=69877, and F. Pontani, "L'Homère de Pléthon," *Scriptorium* 68 (2014): 25–48. There are various other hands at work in the manuscript, apart from that of Gemistos Pletho. Among them was John Dokeianos, a teacher and colleague of Gemistos at the court of Mistra. The hand that copied the Dionysian excerpt has not been identified but is certainly closely connected with the court of Mistra. For Aubrey Diller's purely hypothetical suggestion that the scribe can be identified with Johannes Kanaboutzes, see Diller, "Johannes Canabutzes," *Byzantion* 40 (1970): 271–75, esp. 274.

15 Gemistos was familiar with this passage; see "Georgius Gemistus Plethon's Denkschriften über die Angelegenheiten des Peloponnesos," in *Analekten der Mittel- und Neugriechischen Literatur*, ed. A. Ellissen, 5 vols. (1855–62; repr., Leipzig, 1976), 4:135, n. 5.

16 See Woodhouse, *Gemistos Plethon*, 108: "It was true that Byzantium had been founded by Megarians, who were Dorian by origin."

political propaganda, Gemistos's claims were rooted in his ideological reappropriation of Dionysius. This connection lends strong support to Lamers's conclusion that Gemistos "offered an ethnographical background theory to account for the Greekness of the Byzantine Romans."[17]

That conclusion, if correct, raises the questions of (1) whether such an ethnographical theory is well grounded and (2) what its implications are. This is not the place to give a systematic answer to the first question, which would lead to a discussion of whether other ethnographical models might have been possible and which ultimately pertains to the relationship between Gemistos and classical antiquity as a whole. We can simply observe that the model created by Gemistos is in reality a combination of three different ancient accounts: one about the ancient town of Byzantion, another about some Peloponnesian settlements at Troy, and a third about the Peloponnesian roots of the Romans. A modern scholar would probably draw the conclusion that some passages from Dionysius point to direct or indirect connections between various Peloponnesian peoples and settlements on the Hellespont at various times in history. (And needless to say, the literary evidence from Dionysius would be compared with the evidence, if any, coming from material culture.) But instead of acknowledging the complex interactions of ancient populations in the founding of subsequent settlements, Gemistos cuts through the complexity of this process by using Dionysius's account to project his own categories of "Peloponnesos" and "Constantinople" back in time.

By handling the pre-Roman Greek colony of Byzantion together with Troy, Gemistos creates a fictional continuum: Arcadia → Troy → Byzantion → Constantinople.[18] Then, instead of referring to Arcadia, he uses the broader geographical term *Peloponnesos,* without accounting for this shift.[19] But why does Gemistos feel the need to turn "Arcadia" into "Peloponnesos"? I maintain that it was because this terminological shift allowed him to unite two paradigms. Since he refers to the military victories achieved by the Peloponnesians, it seems that Gemistos intended to use the catchall category of Peloponnesos to include the Spartans, whose glorious deeds were

17 Lamers, *Greece Reinvented,* 40. On the problem of Greek vs. Roman, see also A. Kaldellis, *A New Herodotos: Laonikos Chalkokondyles on the Ottoman Empire, the Fall of Byzantium, and the Emergence of the West* (Washington, DC, 2014), 223–24.

18 The genetic continuity between ancient Minoans and Mycenaeans down to modern Greeks has been discussed by I. Lazaridis et al., "Genetic Origins of the Minoans and Mycenaeans," *Nature* 548 (2017): 214–18, esp. 214 (abstract): "Our results supports the idea of continuity but not isolation in the history of the populations in the Aegean, before and after the time of its earliest civilizations."

19 Lamers has rightly pointed out that Gemistos uses the word γένη to refer to the offspring of the Peloponnesos (*Greece Reinvented,* 39).

known to him from Herodotus. Ultimately, the model he had in mind was Peloponnesos (Sparta) → Troy → Byzantion → Constantinople. In this model, the colony of Byzantion is not located at the absolute beginning of the history of Constantinople, but rather is regarded as the direct antecedent (the "mother") of the imperial capital within a genealogy that goes all the way back through Troy to ancient Sparta. Vitally, however, the construction of this historiographical model relied on Gemistos's appropriation of the passages cited above from Dionysius of Halicarnassus's *Roman History*. Dionysius's connection of Peloponnesian settlements to the Bosphorus makes it impossible to rule out that some Spartans may have been among the ancestors of the inhabitants of the Eastern Roman Empire. But his account in the *Roman History* presents a much more complex situation, one that Gemistos oversimplified in his political speeches. Rather than being grounded in compelling evidence, this model instead reflected the desire of Gemistos (and possibly members of the despot's court at Mistra) to present Sparta as the political and military ideal that every citizen of the empire should strive to imitate in the current political crisis. Changing "Arcadia" to "the Peloponnesos" enabled Gemistos to fuse these two narratives.

Spartan Model and National Identity

It is now time to turn to the second question and to investigate the consequences of this selective and ideologically charged model, examining its strong connection to the contemporary political situation of the empire. The ethnographical model devised by Gemistos, in which the origins of Constantinople could be traced back to the Peloponnesos, and especially to Sparta, had important consequences. The first, and most evident, was that it allowed him to defend his political claims with ancient historical authorities whose narratives spoke to contemporary anxieties.

In his *Advisory Discourse* (*Συμβουλευτικός*) to the despot Theodore II Palaiologos, Gemistos elaborated on the current political situation of the empire.[20] From his point of view, despite multiple internal issues, the most pressing concerns arose outside it:

> This is the situation for you, but for us the political situation is turning out to be very dangerous, because we are attacked on many sides, both from land and sea. I should also add that <we are under siege> even at home, from both barbarians and from peoples of our own lineage, but we are especially threatened by these barbarians, who are currently close to us. We

20 For the tradition of political thought before these political speeches, see D. Angelov, *Imperial Ideology and Political Thought in Byzantium, 1204–1330* (Cambridge, 2007).

have been stripped by them of the greatest and dearest part of our dominion. They were called in antiquity *Parapamisadai*, and they were attacked and defeated by Alexander, son of Philip, and by the Greeks who were with him on his way to the <land of> the Indians. Now, *because we are Greeks*, they are seeking revenge against us for the things they suffered a long time ago, and in different ways. And now they possess a stronger military force than we do, and they are ever intent on our destruction.[21]

The enemies feared by Gemistos were, of course, the Ottomans, but he called them *Parapamisadai*, connecting them to a population living south of the Hindu Kush (in modern Afghanistan) who were defeated by Alexander the Great during his campaign to India.[22]

While the claim about the Peloponnesian origin of the Trojans and Sabines had at least a veneer of ancient authority in Dionysius (2.49), Gemistos's statement that the Ottomans were descendants of Alexander's ancient foes, the Parapamisadai, was controversial even in the fifteenth century. According to Theodore Gazes, who discussed this problem in his 1472 treatise *On the Origin of the Turks* (*De origine Turcarum*), the Turks originally came from the Caucasus, as Skylitzes had stated in his *Synopsis Historiarum*.[23] Since, however, Strabo and Arrian used the word *Caucasus* to refer not only to the area between the Black and Caspian Seas but also to a group of mountains in the Hindu Kush, Gemistos argued that the Turks ought to be identified with a population living in the latter region. Because the Parapamisadai had once inhabited that area, they must be the ancestors of the Ottoman Turks.

21 Gemistos Pletho, "*Συμβουλευτικὸς πρὸς τὸν δεσπότην Θεόδωρον περὶ τῆς Πελοποννήσου,*" in Lampros, *Παλαιολόγεια καὶ Πελοποννησιακά*, 4:114–15: Ἔχοντι δὲ σοὶ μὲν οὕτω, τῶν δὲ πραγμάτων ἡμῖν ἐν μεγάλῳ κινδύνῳ φερομένων ὡς ἂν πολλαχόθεν μὲν ἡμῶν ἐπιβουλευομένων καὶ ἐκ γῆς καὶ ἐκ θαλάττης· προσθείην δ' ἂν ὅτι καὶ οἴκοθεν ἐκ τῆς χώρας ὑπό τε βαρβάρων ἅμα καὶ ὁμοφύλων, μάλιστα δ' ὑπὸ τῶν πλησιοχώρων τανῦν τούτων βαρβάρων, ὑφ' ὧν καὶ τῆς ἄλλης ἐπικρατείας τὸ πλεῖστον καὶ οἰκειότατον περιῃρήμεθα, οἵ, Παραπαμισάδαι μὲν τὸ πάλαι ὄντες, ὑπὸ δὲ Ἀλεξάνδρου τοῦ Φιλίππου καὶ τῶν μετ' ἐκείνου Ἑλλήνων ἐπιβουλευθέντες τε καὶ κρατηθέντες, πάρεργον τῆς ἐς Ἰνδοὺς τότε παρόδου δίκας νῦν ἡμᾶς ταύτας διὰ μακροῦ μέν, πολλαπλασίας δὲ τῶν ὑπηργμένων εἰσπράττουσιν, Ἕλληνας ὄντας, καὶ νῦν, πολλαπλασίαν τὴν δύναμιν κεκτημένοι ἢ ἡμεῖς, τὰ ἔσχατα περὶ ἡμῶν βουλευόμενοι ἑκάστοτε διατελοῦσιν.

22 The main sources concerning the Parapamisadai are Strabo in his *Geography* and Arrian of Nicomedia in his *Anabasis of Alexander*, who refer to this population in various passages. A geographical description of the area is provided by Strabo, *Geography* 15.2.8. The identification between the land of the *Parapamisadai* with the Caucasus is discussed in Arrian, *Anabasis of Alexander* 5.3. On the origins of the Turks in the imagination of the Byzantines, see M. Meserve, *Empires of Islam in Renaissance Historical Thought* (Cambridge, MA, 2008), esp. 135–38.

23 See Theodore Gazes, *De origine Turcarum*, in PG 161, 997–1006, esp. 1000–1001; John Skylitzes, *Synopsis Historiarum*, ed. J. Thurn, CFHB, Series Berolinesis 5 (Berlin, 1973), 442–45.

For Gemistos, this was not just a matter of geography. Building on his idea of the Greekness of the empire, he extracted from his study of Strabo and Arrian the ultimate reason for the current attack on the empire. Having been defeated centuries ago by the Greek soldiers of Alexander the Great, the Parapamisadai were now eager to take their long-awaited revenge against the descendants of those Greeks—that is, the people who currently inhabited the Eastern Roman Empire. By framing contemporary events as part of an age-old battle between East and West, Asia and Greece, Gemistos intended to call for a new deployment of ancient strategies: in short, he was inviting his own people to act like the glorious Greeks of antiquity. If, however, the Turks actually came from the region between the Black and Caspian Seas, then they could not possibly have had any contact with Alexander the Great, because he had never traveled to that area—which, of course, would mean that Gemistos could not use ancient history to help his contemporaries make sense of the Turkish attack on the Eastern Roman Empire.

Since both premises—the Peloponnesian origins of Constantinople and the ethnic continuity between the Parapamisadai and the Ottomans—were, to different degrees, highly questionable, it is no wonder that the theories Gemistos built upon them can only be regarded as ideology. By basing his arguments on ancient texts, he advocated a certain normative order, one in which his compatriots inhabiting the embattled Eastern Roman Empire were enjoined to abandon their Roman identity and embrace their Greekness. This new political agenda was presented (and therefore validated) as a rediscovery of their supposedly ancient, and therefore original, national identity. Whatever we may think of such a strategy, this historical model, which was designed to explain the Ottoman pressure from the East, had interesting implications.

First, the idea of Greekness was defined within the framework of a conflict against another population from Asia, as it was in Herodotus. As in antiquity during the Persian wars, Greek identity was defined in opposition to a "barbarian" at the gates.[24] Second, according to Gemistos, Greek identity was a fact that was accepted by the barbarian *in the first place*. It was because the barbarians had *already* identified the inhabitants of the empire as their ethnic enemy that Gemistos's compatriots had to defend themselves, therefore implicitly acknowledging their Greek identity.

Defining National Identity: *Phōnē* and *Patrios Politeia*

Despite Gemistos's beliefs regarding the attack of the Parapamisadai from the East, the Greek identity of the empire required some further clarification. What elements

24 See E. Hall, *Inventing the Barbarian: Greek Self-Definition through Tragedy* (Oxford, 1989), 7.

defined the national identity of the Greeks? Gemistos tackled this issue in his discourse to the emperor Manuel II: "And we, the ones you lead and rule, are Greeks by birth, as both our language and traditional education prove."[25] So, according to Gemistos, Greek identity was defined by language and traditional education. Yet, as the word γένος clearly implies, in the fifteenth century national identity also had ancestral and kinship connotations. Those connotations, however, were assumed, since all those who spoke Greek and had been educated in the Greek way could prove (μαρτυρεῖ) *in this way* their Greekness. For Gemistos, then, Greek language and education were proof of Greek blood.

The ideological nature of this model was evident. To be sure, this model did not account for those who learned Greek and were exposed to Greek culture but did not have Greek as their first language. For instance, did Gemistos regard as Greek those Italians, like Francesco Filelfo, who became fluent in Greek after spending substantial time in Constantinople? Or those Florentines educated by Manuel Chrysoloras in Florence, such as Leonardo Bruni? Yet these questions may not have mattered for Gemistos's purposes, because in the *Advisory Discourse* he was addressing the emperor and the inhabitants of Greek-speaking regions such as Constantinople and the Peloponnesos. What he was saying is that all people sharing the same Greek language and education should rise up against the Turks, who are linguistically (and therefore culturally) different. Gemistos's discourse was ultimately a patriotic appeal to resistance against the Turks, grounded in his reading and interpretation of the ancient Greek historians.

At this point, however, the attentive reader will probably have spotted the elephant in the room. For as he sketched the distinctions between the invading Turks and the inhabitants of the Eastern Roman Empire, Gemistos remained silent about the most obvious difference of all: religion. While his compatriots saw the Turks primarily as infidels, Gemistos did not make a single reference to their lack of faith. But this silence is surprising only if we do not take into account the complex issue of his own religious outlook. As recent palaeographical discoveries have shown, Gemistos was so invested in a philosophical system which reconstructed a *prisca theologia* that he did not even hesitate to modify the text of Plato in order to make it consistent with his project. Seen from this perspective, not only Islam but also Christianity could only be understood as a corruption of this original religion.

Gemistos's definition of Greekness as based on φωνή lends itself to a comparison with a passage by Cardinal Bessarion written a few decades later, soon after the

25 Gemistos Pletho, "Εἰς Μανουὴλ Παλαιολόγον περὶ τῶν ἐν Πελοποννήσῳ πραγμάτων," 3:247: Ἐσμὲν γὰρ οὖν ὧν ἡγεῖσθέ τε καὶ βασιλεύετε Ἕλληνες τὸ γένος, ὡς ἥ τε φωνὴ καὶ ἡ πάτριος παιδεία μαρτυρεῖ.

fall of Constantinople. In one of his letters, Bessarion mentions his personal project of gathering all the Greek books that could be found,

> so that, if some Greeks are left and if in the future they fare better—many things can happen in the long run—they can have a place where their entire language, as it currently is, can be found stored all together in a safe place. And after they find <this archive>, they can add to it and not remain completely speechless, differing in no way from barbarians and slaves, because they (sc. the Greeks) have lost even these few books that are left, on top of the many and great treatises of divine ancient men that we have lost <already>.[26]

Crucially, the goal of his collection was not to provide himself with a personal library but to produce an archive for future generations of Ἕλληνες, a place where they would be able to recover their φωνή. Here the word obviously refers to books written in Greek, not to spoken language. A true student of his teacher Gemistos, Bessarion saw the Greek φωνή as the authentic sign of Greekness, a belief that rested on the implicit assumption that language was the key to defining national identity. Hence, his mission of collecting all Greek books should be seen as a cultural means toward a political end: the preservation of Greekness after the fall of the empire.

The Downfall of Postclassical Greece

There is a second consequence of Gemistos's ethnographic theory that the history of Constantinople had started in the Peloponnesos and was coming to an end with the current political emergency. While ancient Sparta was the political and cultural model to be restored in order to fight the Ottomans, the later history of the "Greeks" was less conducive to Gemistos's political claims. If the reason for the Turkish aggression was seen as revenge for the ancient defeat inflicted on their ancestors by Alexander the Great, then post-Hellenistic history—comprising the ancient and medieval Roman Empire—was merely an uneventful period between the ancient

26 *Kardinal Bessarion als Theologe, Humanist und Staatsman: Funde und Forschungen*, ed. L. Mohler, 3 vols. (Paderborn, 1923–42), 3:479: ἀλλ' ὡς ἄν, εἴ που νῦν τέ τινες λειφθεῖεν Ἕλληνες, εἴ τέ τι εἰς ἔπειτα βέλτιον πράξαιεν—πολλὰ δ' ἐν τῷ μακρῷ χρόνῳ γένοιτ' ἄν—, ἔχοιεν ὅπῃ τὴν αὐτῶν φωνὴν ἅπασαν, τήν γε νῦν οὖσαν, ἔν τινι ὁμοῦ ἀποκειμένην ἀσφαλεῖ τόπῳ εὕροιεν καὶ εὑρόντες πολλαπλασιάσαιεν καὶ μὴ πρὸς οἷς πολλοῖς τε καὶ καλοῖς τῶν θείων ἐκείνων ἀνδρῶν πάλαι ἀπολωλέκαμεν ὑπομνήμασι καὶ τὰ ὀλίγα ταῦτα νῦν ἀπολέσαντες ἄφωνοι τὸ πάμπαν μένοιεν καὶ βαρβάρων τε καὶ ἀνδραπόδων οὐδὲν διαφέροιεν. According to Mohler the letter was addressed to Michael Apostoles, but David Speranzi has recently cast serious doubts on the identity of the addressee (see Speranzi, "Scritture, libri e uomini all'ombra di Bessarione, I. Appunti sulle lettere del Marc. Gr. Z 527," *Rinascimento* 57 [2017]: 137–95, esp. 143–47, 187).

cause and the contemporary effect. More to the point, since Constantinople had been reduced to a shadow of its former power, then post-Hellenistic history was the time that led up to the current political emergency. In other words, post-Hellenistic history was the stage on which the virtue of the "Greeks" had collapsed, resulting in the present misery.

But what caused this collapse? Assuming that a modern scholar would ever accept such a notion (which I very much doubt), he or she would look for the answer by using the methodologies of historic investigation. But instead of considering such things as demography or economics, Gemistos framed his interpretation of history within the epistemological categories of his own idiosyncratic philosophical Platonism. For a Platonist, the corruption of virtue is a process that cannot be investigated merely by piecing together historical sources. Rather, it can only be seen, and therefore understood, through the lens of a priori philosophical principles. Here, a glance at the relevant Platonic passages on this subject will come in handy.

In the *Republic,* Plato had famously argued that the first principle of reality is intrinsically good.[27] Consequently, no evil can come into the world from it. In the *Timaeus* (31b–38a)—a text we now are sure, on the basis of palaeographical findings, that Gemistos knew intimately—Plato had described how the Demiurge built the universe by means of mathematical structures. Even if the Demiurge may not be identified with the Idea of the Good, there is no doubt that the world is seen as intrinsically good, because it derives from a good principle. This model hardly accounts for the existence of evil in the world, however. In the Platonic tradition, the way out of this conundrum is to see evil not as a principle opposed to the Good but as the corruption of the Good itself. This is not to say that history is just a constant decay from the archetypical perfection to future apocalypse. As Plato clarifies both in the *Timaeus* (22c–23d) and in the third book of the *Laws* (3.677a–678a), human history works in cycles—every phase starts from original perfection and then slides down into corruption until a catastrophic event ends one era and begins a new one.

If we use this philosophical assumption to make sense of Gemistos's model of Peloponnesos (Sparta) → Troy → Byzantium → Constantinople, it is clear that it sets out a historical cycle within which contemporary Constantinople represents a state of corruption of Greekness, while Sparta is the authentic archetype that the Greeks should aspire to bring back to life. By restoring vitality to ancient Sparta, the Greeks will not only defend themselves but also revive their original, uncorrupted (or, at least, less corrupted) identity. From a scholarly and philological point of view, this project necessitates studying the texts of classical antiquity, such as Plato and the

27 Plato, *Republic* 2.379a–382e, esp. 379b–c. For the comparison with the sun, see Plato, *Republic* 6.508a–509c.

ancient historians. From a political point of view, it also implies that the ideal *renaissance* of Greece would entail abandoning Constantinople to (re)establish the capital of the "Greeks" at Sparta/Mistra. Doing so would restore the greatness of the Greeks for the time being and postpone the inevitable arrival of the catastrophic event.

But what have all these weighty philosophical assumptions to do with our present investigation of "Byzantium" as a modern historical category? Quite simply, they explain why, for Gemistos, there was no Byzantium in the highly debatable sense familiar to modern scholars. There was only the small colony of Byzantion, an intermediary stage in the genealogical process of the corruption of "Greekness." While there can be no doubt that Gemistos mastered Greek literature in its entirety, I maintain that it is not by chance that his philological work, as modern palaeographical discoveries have shown, focused especially on authors such as Plato, Herodotus, Euclid, and Plutarch, who formed the core of *ancient* Greek history, philosophy, and mathematics. Of course, this does not mean that Gemistos would not have owned, read, and annotated those authors whom we are accustomed to call Byzantines. His student Bessarion played a decisive role in collecting and rescuing manuscripts of these authors—to cite but one example, Marc. Gr. Z 450, the manuscript of Photios's *Bibliotheca*.[28] But even Bessarion seems not to have engaged with these texts in the way that he did with Plato, Aristotle, and their commentators.

To be more precise, while manuscripts of medieval authors were certainly collected, read, and annotated by Gemistos and his students, they were not the object of a specific philological study aimed at reconstructing the original text. In the end, philological work relies on the assumption that the *ipsissima verba* of a certain author are important and worth understanding. By contrast, if we believe that a text and its author are uninteresting, there is little point in devoting to them the time and effort philological scholarship requires. Medieval authors, especially those bordering on contemporary times, did not matter nearly as much to Gemistos as did classical texts.

As for Bessarion, his attitude toward intellectuals of his own age was often self-deprecating. Contrary to Manuel II in his letter to Gabriel of Thessalonike, the cardinal said not merely that contemporary scholars were inferior to the ancients in their literary expression but also that they were not as knowledgeable as the ancients.[29] In a letter to Michael Apostoles written in Viterbo on 19 May 1462, Bessarion discusses the recent development of the so-called Plato–Aristotle controversy, in which Theodore Gazes has intervened: "Shall we, little men or dwarfs in comparison with those heroes, dare to call them, alas, ignorant, and mock them with

28 He refers to an ancient manuscript of Photios in a letter to Nardo Palmerio written on 24 June 1459. See Mohler, *Kardinal Bessarion*, 3:493.

29 See *The Letters of Manuel II Palaeologus*, ed. G. T. Dennis (Washington, DC, 1977), 148–51.

insults more abusive than those of comedy toward Cleon and Hyperbolus? Who are we to do so? What knowledge, what science of the things that are do we have?"[30] In this passage Bessarion belittles and dismisses the points about Plato and Aristotle raised by Gazes, one of his closest acolytes. He characterizes the scholars of his own generation as "little men" (ἀνθρωπίσκοι) vis-à-vis the great philosophers of the past.[31]

We might be tempted to play down the significance of such statements and see in them nothing more than the usual medieval refrain of "dwarves on the shoulders of giants." Yet in another important letter, written immediately after the fall of Constantinople, Bessarion makes it clear that his dismissive attitude toward his fellow Greeks extended far beyond the narrow world of scholarship: "We are the last of the Greeks, in the *entirety* of virtue as well as in time. Our destiny, alas, is that our race was defeated and no longer survives anywhere. If only we had perished before witnessing the complete defeat and death of our people."[32] With a deeply felt sense of desperation, Bessarion regarded himself and his compatriots as the "last of the Greeks," applying his negative judgment to the entire nation. Of particular importance for the present chapter, he clarified that ἔσχατοι was to be understood in the sense both of time *and* of virtue. In other words, he mourned the lack of a political future for the Greeks now that their capital had fallen. At the same time, he was painfully aware of the steady decline of their virtue from the heights of their past.

Bessarion was not the only author to have blamed the military defeats of the eastern empire on the shortcomings of its citizens. In his history of the Fourth Crusade, Niketas Choniates ironically narrated how the guards fled "as if they were unified and fused together in one cowardly soul," upon seeing the first knight who made it through the city gate.[33] In the *Povest' o Car' grade*, the account of the fall of

30 Mohler, *Kardinal Bessarion*, 3:512–13: Ἡμεῖς δὲ ἀνθρωπίσκοι ἢ πίθηκοί τινες πρὸς ἐκείνους ἥρωας ὄντες τολμήσομεν αὐτούς, φεῦ, ἀμαθεῖς λέγειν, καὶ τὰ ἐξ ἀμαξῶν σκώπτειν μᾶλλον ἢ ἡ κωμῳδία τοὺς περὶ Κλέωνά τε καὶ Ὑπέρβολον; τίνες ὄντες; ποίαν γνῶσιν, ποίαν τῶν ὄντων ἔχοντες ἐπιστήμην;

31 Bessarion's Latin secretary Niccolò Perotti twice mentions Byzantium in his *Refutatio Deliramentorum Georgii Trapezuntii Cretensis*. In both cases, the word *Byzantium* means Constantinople (see Mohler, *Kardinal Bessarion*, 3:363, 366). The word is also used with precisely this meaning by Nicholas Capranica, the bishop of Fermo, in his funeral oration for Bessarion (Mohler, *Kardinal Bessarion*, 3:406–7).

32 Mohler, *Kardinal Bessarion*, 3:480: ἔσχατοι τῶν Ἑλλήνων ἡμεῖς, ὥσπερ τῇ ὅλῃ ἀρετῇ, οὕτω δὴ καὶ τῷ χρόνῳ. ἐφ' ἡμῶν εἵμαρτο, φεῦ, τὸ φῦλον ἐκεῖνο καταστραφῆναι καὶ μηδαμοῦ ἔτι εἶναι. ὤφελον ἡμεῖς ἀπολώλειμεν πρότερον, ἢ παντελῆ καταστροφήν τε καὶ ἀπώλειαν τοῦ γένους ἰδεῖν. The word ὅλη presupposes the διαίρεσις of virtue into φρόνησις, δικαιοσύνη, ἀνδρεία, and σωφροσύνη. See, e.g., Gemistos Pletho, *Περὶ αρετῶν*, B14 (ed. B. Tambrun-Krasker, *Georges Gémiste Plethon: Traité des vertus* [Leiden, 1987], 14–15).

33 See Niketas Choniates, *Historia*, ed. J. van Dieten, CFHB, Series Berolinensis 11.1 (Berlin, 1975), 570: ὥσπερ εἰς μίαν ἐνισθέντες τε καὶ συντακέντες ἀγεννῆ ψυχήν. Choniates mocked the emperor's guards who, he writes, were unable to stand the sight of a helmet, let alone face the actual knight.

the city attributed to Nestor Iskinder, the emperor Constantine XI raised his hands to the heavens and begged the Lord to allow his city to repent its sins and return to the path of justice.[34] In his lament for the fall of the city, the Armenian poet Abraham of Ankara ascribed the disaster to the declining number of saints and the neglect of religious practice, both by the clergy and by laypeople.[35] Yet, despite their different contexts, Niketas, Nestor, and Abraham of Ankara ultimately attributed the eastern Romans' catastrophic defeats to sin, which brought about God's punishment. Bessarion's words imply instead a rather different explanation—one in which the ultimate reason for the fall of the city was not sin but the steady decline in the virtue of the Hellenes (not Rhomaioi!). The use of both the word *Hellenes* and the adjective ὅλῃ makes clear that Bessarion's understanding of the events of 1453 was much more in tune with the philosophy of his teacher Gemistos than with the lamentations of Nestor or Abraham. Nor was Bessarion the only eastern Roman scholar to explain the decline in this way. Raoul Kabakes, son of Gemistos's former student Demetrios, in one of his poems expressed the utter desperation he felt for his country:

> Whatever envious fate has snatched you, fatherland, away, put its presence in face of yours, and turned you from a gentle appearance into a wild beast? You speak out your words uncertainly and must disguise yourself in a new dress. And while you are looking for yourself deep inside, you are unrecognisable to your own son. Oh, where have your customs and ancient splendour gone?[36]

Decline (Well) before Gibbon

Within this framework, those scholars who were particularly active in the study of Greek texts, such as Gemistos Pletho and his student Bessarion, did not understand postclassical Greek literature or history as an independent field of study. Nor could they ever have done so. Precisely because Gemistos was vigorously advocating the replacement of a Roman identity with a Hellenic one, he was bound to see not the differences but rather the *continuity* between what we now define as Byzantine literature and its classical predecessor. Vital to both his scholarly work and his philosophical and political ideas was the assumption that the blood of the ancient Greeks

34 See A. Pertusi, ed., *La Caduta di Costantinopoli*, 2 vols. (Milan, 1976), 1:268 (in Pertusi's Italian translation): "A causa dei nostri peccati hai provocato tutto ciò che si è rivolto contro di noi e contro la città tua santa, con un giudizio giusto e vero, e noi non possiamo aprire la bocca per parlare in nostra difesa."

35 See ibid., 2:418.

36 Quoted in Lamers, *Greece Reinvented* (n. 4 above), 229.

was coursing through his veins. By removing the category of "Roman" and assuming an uninterrupted continuity between Homer and himself, Gemistos ended up by placing Byzantion halfway along the path leading from the Peloponnesos, and especially Sparta, to Constantinople. In a bid to define the Greekness he was so passionately advocating, he focused on language and education. As a consequence, he spent enormous time and energy in reconstructing ancient texts, for which we are gradually uncovering the palaeographical evidence. In his attempt to restore the "original" version of those ancient texts—consistent, as far as possible, with his own philosophical program—he doubtless felt that his philological program mirrored his Platonic beliefs. Indeed, removing the mistakes that had arisen over time was a way to halt the evil of corruption—whether textual, cultural, or political—and return to the immaculate purity of the original.

As for education, it has long been known that Gemistos played a fundamental role in educating humanists of the caliber of Bessarion and Kabakes, to mention just two of his many students. Yet it could still be argued that the same textual work that he did on Plato or Herodotus could also, at least in theory, have been devoted to postclassical authors. As a Platonist, however, Gemistos's philosophy of history led him to see the long continuity between antiquity and his own day not as a straight line but rather as an inclined plane. Taking for granted the perfect Goodness of the First Principle, Gemistos had a strong faith in the rational nature of the world. In such a perfect and good construction, evil could have crept in only as decline over time from the original goodness. This same dynamic also applies to the nature of human beings, whose virtue had been declining from antiquity to the present time. But history is not simply one long inclined plane starting from perfection and ending in apocalyptic destruction. Instead, history is made up of cycles: from time to time major catastrophic events close an era, reset everything, and begin the process afresh. For Gemistos, the cycle that had started in antiquity had undergone a gradual process of decline, eventually leading to the present deplorable state of the Eastern Roman Empire.

At this point, we need to turn our attention to the *Memoranda*, a couple of political pamphlets that Gemistos addressed to the emperor Manuel II and to the despot Theodore. In them, he suggests various political reforms that would help the imperial family in the (otherwise impossible) task of saving the empire. Now, it is reasonable to ask why Gemistos was putting forward the apparently optimistic reforms of the *Memoranda*, if he thought that history was doomed to decline. The answer is that he did not believe that decline was absolutely unavoidable. By modifying the current (corrupted) state of affairs and restoring the virtue of ancient Sparta, Gemistos thought he could effectively defer the end of the current historical cycle. As Teresa Shawcross has pointed out, other fourteenth-century intellectuals such as Theodore

Metochites, Nikephoros Gregoras, and Ibn Khaldūn had also advanced theories of decline, showing that they accepted the view that historical cycles governed the course of history.[37] But Gemistos went a step further: by framing this decline within a Platonic paradigm, he also suggested a way to *reverse* such a decline. By calling for a return to the archetypical virtue of antiquity, Gemistos, in his orations addressed to the Palaiologan emperor Manuel and to the despot Theodore, offered an antidote to the current intolerable state of the empire.

Consequently, from Gemistos's philosophical point of view, the body of textual material that we are accustomed to classify as Byzantine literature was less morally valuable than Plato, Herodotus, or Euclid because it was produced during a period when virtue was in decline. He certainly admired scholars such as Michael Psellos, Nikephoros Gregoras, and Theodore Metochites, and there is much to be said about his engagement with Constantine Harmenopoulos's legal compilation, the *Hexabiblion*. But as far as we know, he drew on all these authors *without* making them the object of a textual investigation or philological reconstruction. His student Bessarion, so deeply influenced by the philosophical ideas of his teacher, saw the fall of Constantinople as the result of the extreme degradation of (Hellenic) virtue, thereby appropriating Gemistos's paradigm of Hellenic continuity. He also shared his teacher's conviction that the Greek language must be preserved, and it was this belief that motivated him to gather together the greatest Greek library of his generation. But this very model of continuity made it impossible for him to conceptualize Byzantium as a field of study distinct from Greek antiquity.[38]

If all of this is true, then the idea of decline predates not only the most famous modern history of Byzantium—Edward Gibbon's *History of the Decline and Fall of the Roman Empire*—but also the establishing of Byzantium as a category worthy of independent investigation.[39] Even more interestingly, the idea of decline was not a judgment imposed on eastern Romans from the outside by the chauvinism of some Western intellectuals; instead, it was deeply rooted in the self-perception

37 See T. Shawcross, "Theories of Decline from Metochites to Ibn Khaldūn," in Kaldellis and Siniossoglou, *The Cambridge Intellectual History of Byzantium* (n. 8 above), 615–32.

38 This approach was not merely shared by the last generations of the dying Eastern Roman Empire, it was still operational well into the second part of the 16th century. As Asaph Ben-Tov has argued in his monograph *Lutheran Humanists and Greek Antiquity: Melanchthonian Scholarship between Universal History and Pedagogy* (Leiden, 2009), 216–17, Lutheran humanists, even after the publication of the *Corpus historiae Byzantinae*, saw a clear continuity between ancient and medieval Greece.

39 On the emergence of Byzantium as a distinct field of studies in the 18th century, see J. Monfasani, "Byzantium and the End of the Middle Ages," *Mediterranea: International Journal for the Transfer of Knowledge* 4 (2019): 245–53, esp. 252–53.

of some of the most gifted Greek-speaking Roman scholars.[40] In attempting to rediscover their Spartan origin as a means of invigorating the fight back against the Ottoman enemy, Gemistos Pletho and his students singled out ancient Greece as the object of their scholarship. In their burning desire to restore ancient Greekness, they effectively crafted the myth of its original superiority. This superiority, however, forced them to accept the *inferiority* of postclassical Greek-speaking culture, to which they themselves belonged. It is this deeply felt sense of their own unworthiness that was at the origin of *both* their idealization of classical Greekness and their devaluation of its postclassical continuation.

40 For an overview of various receptions of Hellenism in early modernity, see N. Constantinidou and H. Lamers, eds., *Receptions of Hellenism in Early Modern Europe: 15th–17th Centuries*, Brill's Studies in Intellectual History 303 (Leiden, 2020).

TWO

MAKING THE ROMAN PAST(S) COME ALIVE

Manuel Chrysoloras, Cyriac of Ancona, and Andrea Mantegna's Triumphs of Caesar

ELENA N. BOECK

> Andrea Mantegna, a painter of great renown, who commanded painting to aspire to its ancient beauties. . . . His paintings are filled with vases, arms, costumes and ornaments sought from the richest repositories of the ancients.[1]

ANDREA MANTEGNA'S MONUMENTAL CYCLE *TRIUMPHS OF CAESAR* (1480S–1506?) has been called "the first great masterpiece where imagination and scholarship effectively combine to recreate and reinterpret a past event."[2] Acclaimed as one of the "central icons of the Imperial Renaissance,"[3] the much-admired nine-panel cycle, now a highlight of the British Royal Collection, celebrates imperial power by visualizing in meticulous detail a Roman triumph.[4] Though their precise historical subject remains elusive, the panels are replete with careful representations of authentic, known ancient objects. At the same time, a triumphal column surmounted by a colossal bronze horseman that features prominently on one of the panels remains a historiographic mystery. I argue here that the legacy of two intellectuals steeped

1 This is the assessment of Lorenzo Pignoria (d. 1631), a renowned Paduan antiquary; quoted in R. Lightbown, *Mantegna: With a Complete Catalogue of the Paintings, Drawings and Prints* (Oxford, 1986), 153.

2 A. H. R. Martindale, *Andrea Mantegna: Historicus et Antiquarius: Inaugural Lecture Delivered before the University of East Anglia on 3 December 1974* (Norwich, 1976), n.p.

3 T. J. Dandelet, *The Renaissance of Empire in Early Modern Europe* (Cambridge, 2014), 271.

4 Dandelet called this cycle "one of the most important series of Renaissance paintings celebrating the imperial theme created in the entire period" (ibid., 37).

in knowledge of Byzantium, Manuel Chrysoloras and Cyriac of Ancona, provided the inspiration for this prominent elevated horseman. Memories of the triumphal column of Justinian, the Constantinopolitan signifier of empire, were instrumental in Mantegna's decision to populate *his* historical landscape of old Rome with a colossal monument.

The towering column surmounted by a bronze horseman has puzzled scholars of Mantegna, since there was "no obvious prototype among the surviving monuments of antiquity."[5] But this assessment is accurate only if one chooses to exclude Byzantium from antiquity. Art historians have also noted Mantegna's "success in creating a plausible and consistent image of ancient Roman power and civilization."[6] From this perspective, the horseman atop the column constitutes an apparent breach of consistency. Hypothetical sources of his inspiration have included the columns of Trajan and Marcus Aurelius in Rome,[7] as well as illustrations from Felice Feliciano's manuscript *Collectio antiquitatum*.[8] To my knowledge, no scholar has rigorously argued the proposition that Justinian's column in Constantinople served as Mantegna's main referent.[9] Drawing on the work of two important antiquarians, Mantegna inserted the column into his monumental vision of ancient Rome to elide the historical space between the Old and the New Rome, and in doing so implicitly expanded the category of monuments redolent of Rome's imperial past.

Evidence and Imagination: Learning How to Behold the Past

Before Constantinople's fall in 1453, two remarkable intellectuals directed a keen antiquarian gaze toward Byzantium's monuments. Originating with Manuel Chrysoloras (ca. 1350–1415) in 1411, this intellectual endeavor was continued by his admirer Cyriac of Ancona (1391–1452). While the former became a legend in Italian intellectual circles, the latter's work became the cornerstone of Renaissance

5 C. Hope, "Canvas VI: *Bearers of coins and plate, trophies of royal armour (The Corselet Bearers)*," in *Andrea Mantegna*, ed. Jane Martineau, Suzanne Boorsch, et al. (London, 1992), 367, no. 113.

6 C. Hope, "The Triumph of Caesar," in ibid., 350.

7 Hope, "Canvas VI: *Bearers of coins and plate, trophies of royal armour (The Corselet Bearers)*," 367, no. 113.

8 This is Princeton, MS Garrett 158. In Paola Tosetti Grandi's view, the inspiration for the monument came from the illustration of a triumphal arch on fol. 5r, where the viewer can see two equestrian "carvings" on each side of the arch—one in a frontal view, the other from the posterior. Tosetti Grandi, *I Trionfi di Cesare di Andrea Mantegna: Fonti umanistiche e cultura antiquaria alla corte dei Gonzaga* (Mantua, 2008), 127–28.

9 The connection is suggested by M. Vickers, "Mantegna and Constantinople," *Burlington Magazine* 118.883 (1976): 684.

knowledge about the eastern Mediterranean. Chrysoloras also stands at the forefront of the movement to incorporate visual evidence into the study of the past, and to begin the process of classifying that evidence. Though neither author lived to lament the fall of Constantinople, their works resonated long after 1453. The ekphrasis of Manuel Chrysoloras on Constantinople and Rome was poignantly translated into Latin in 1454, as a direct response to the Ottoman conquest.[10] Cyriac of Ancona's works continued to circulate in Italy through copies created by his friend Felice Feliciano.[11] Both figures contributed to Mantegna's emergence as an "antiquarian humanist."[12]

Chrysoloras was a Byzantine scholar and diplomat who became a Renaissance intellectual, converted to Catholicism, and entered papal service.[13] Chrysoloras was truly a special individual, and his teaching career had an enormous impact: he created an intellectual bridge between Byzantium and Italy, and yet he left very little written work.[14] He traveled to Florence in 1397 after receiving an invitation to

10 F. Niutta, ed., *Le Due Rome: Confronto tra Roma e Constantinopoli: Con la traduzione Latina di Francesco Aleardi* (Bologna, 2001). Furthermore, in 1453 Flavio Biondo dedicated the treatise *De expedition in Turchos* to Alfonso V of Aragon. Tosetti Grandi, *I Trionfi di Cesare di Andrea Mantegna*, 37.

11 On Felice Feliciano, see A. Contò and L. Quaquarelli, eds., *L'"antiquario" Felice Feliciano Veronese: Tra epigrafia antica, letteratura e arti del libro* (Padua, 1995); P. Tosetti Grandi, "Andrea Mantegna, Giovanni Marcanova e Felice Feliciano," in *Andrea Mantegna, impronta del genio*, ed. R. Signorini, V. Rebonato, and S. Tammaccaro (Florence, 2010), 273–361. For a succinct introduction to Cyriac, see P. N. Miller, "Major Trends in European Antiquarianism, Petrarch to Peiresc," in *The Oxford History of Historical Writing*, ed. D. Woolf, vol. 3, *1400–1800*, ed. J. Rabasa et al. (Oxford, 2012), 253–54.

12 For the term "antiquarian humanist," see F. Ames-Lewis, introduction to *Mantegna and 15th-Century Court Culture: Lectures Delivered in Connection with the Andrea Mantegna Exhibition at the Royal Academy of Arts, London 1992*, ed. Ames-Lewis and A. Bednarek (London, 1993), 13.

13 The epitaph on Manuel's tomb pronounced: *Ante aram situs est dominus Manuel Chrysoloras, eques Constantinopolitanus e vetusto genere romanorum qui cum Constantino imperatore migrarunt*... Quoted in G. Dagron, "Manuel Chrysoloras: Constantinople ou Rome," *ByzF* 12 (1987): 282. See L. Thorn-Wickert's *Manuel Chrysoloras (ca. 1350–1415): Eine Biographie des byzantinischen Intellektuellen vor dem Hintergrund der hellenistischen Studien in der italienischen Renaissance* (Frankfurt am Main, 2006).

14 Michael Baxandall characterized him thusly: "What is not in doubt is that Manuel left a deep impression on an astonishingly large number of the more talented Italian humanists, and if that impression may sometimes have been not much more than the elements of Greek grammar and an admiration for Manuel's Levantine urbanity it was none the less real for that. It was a main source and stimulus for the curiosity about Greek things that became the most expansive element in Quattrocento humanism" (Baxandall, *Giotto and the Orators: Humanist Observers of Painting in Italy and the Discovery of Pictorial Composition, 1350–1450* [Oxford, 1971], 79). See also J. W. Barker, "Emperors, Embassies, and Scholars: Diplomacy and the Transmission of Byzantine Humanism to Renaissance Italy," in *Church and Society in Late Byzantium*, ed. D. G. Angelov (Kalamazoo, MI, 2009), 158–79; D. J. Geanakoplos, *Constantinople and the West: Essays on the Late*

teach Greek at the University of Florence, becoming "the first Byzantine professor of Greek in the Latin West."[15] There he wrote a textbook of Greek grammar.[16] It transformed Renaissance scholarship, for Greek grammar had not been taught in western Europe for centuries. Some scholars even credit him with the revival of the art of Latin eloquence.[17] His Italian contemporaries saw him as a teacher of scholars: "even in this age, Manuel Chrysoloras, a great man and a great philosopher, educated many men."[18] In recent scholarship the impact of Chrysoloras's arrival has been characterized as a transformative civilizational event: "It is thus 1397 which has to be seen as a key date in the history of humanism and even of European culture."[19]

In 1411 Chrysoloras wrote his famous *Comparison of Old and New Rome*; though ostensibly a letter to the Byzantine emperor Manuel II, it also circulated widely in Italy.[20] This letter, his best-known work, is a unique literary exercise that was simultaneously one of the last of its kind in the Byzantine tradition and the first of its kind in the Renaissance tradition.[21] His comparison of two Romes stands as a profoundly influential work of Byzantine rhetoric, which began in the fourth century with the

---

Byzantine (Paleologan) and Italian Renaissances and the Byzantine and Roman Churches (Madison, WI, 1989), 3–37; I. Thomson, "Manuel Chrysoloras and the Early Italian Renaissance," *GRBS* 7.1 (1966): 63–82.

15 H. Lamers, *Greece Reinvented: Transformations of Byzantine Hellenism in Renaissance Italy*, Brill's Studies in Intellectual History 247 (Leiden, 2015), 6.

16 M. Reeve, "Classical Scholarship," in *The Cambridge Companion to Renaissance Humanism*, ed. J. Kraye, 9th ed. (Cambridge, 2008), 33–34.

17 C. Smith, *Architecture in the Culture of Early Humanism: Ethics, Aesthetics, and Eloquence, 1400–1470* (Oxford, 1992), 134.

18 Guarino of Verona, quoted in J. Hankins, "Humanism and the Origins of Modern Political Thought," in Kraye, *The Cambridge Companion to Renaissance Humanism*, 119.

19 N. Mann, "The Origins of Humanism," in ibid., 16–17. Smith states: "Most scholars accept that the recovery of Greek letters in the Italian Renaissance began with Manuel Chrysoloras's instruction in Florence in the last years of the fourteenth century" (*Architecture in the Culture of Early Humanism*, 133). Chrysoloras was also at the beginning of the movement to acquire (Byzantine) Greek manuscripts of the classics for the Renaissance scholars. In addition, he translated Greek works into Latin.

20 The critical edition of the text was published by C. Billò, "Manuele Crisolora, 'L'Antica e la Nuova Roma,'" *Medievo Greco: Rivista di storia e filologia bizantina* (2000): 6–26. For previous analysis, see Smith, *Architecture in the Culture of Early Humanism*, chap. 8; M. Baxandall, "Guarino, Pisanello and Manuel Chrysoloras," *JWarb* 28 (1965): 183–204; Thomson, "Manuel Chrysoloras and the Early Italian Renaissance."

21 It had a great impact on his Italian contemporaries; see Smith, *Architecture in the Culture of Early Humanism*, 136–37.

foundation of Constantinople.[22] It also became the earliest example of an "epideictic work from Renaissance Rome."[23]

The *Comparison* made the case for the inclusion of visual evidence into scholarly efforts to understand the past. Chrysoloras brought this heretofore ignored trove of evidence into the purview of antiquarian scholars by elevating it to a status equal to texts. He wrote that "[the sculptural remains] speak of Rome's victories, her general well-being, dominion, dignity, and deeds in war."[24] His was nothing less than a monumental effort to awaken the past through the direct testimony of visual evidence:

> These reliefs show how things were in past times. . . . Thus they make our knowledge of history precise or, rather, they grant us eyewitness knowledge of everything that has happened just as if it were present.[25]

For Chrysoloras the glorious past literally and repeatedly came alive in minute details when he beheld ancient, sculptural monuments:

> All these things are represented as if alive by the images, and each is identified by an inscription. Thus one can see clearly what kinds of arms the Ancients had, what kind of clothes they wore, what the devices of their rulers were, how they formed lines of battle, fought, laid siege, and built encampments.[26]

The remarkable artistic skill of a past civilization created a simulacrum of reality:

> The skill of the artists rivals and contends with reality itself, so that one seems to see a real man or horse, a city or a whole army; a breastplate,

22 Dagron characterized it as "la dernière oeuvre significative et une fort belle conclusion" ("Manuel Chrysoloras," 281). See also R. Webb, "Describing Rome in Greek: Manuel Chrysoloras' Comparison of Old and New Rome," in *Villes de toute beauté: L'ekphrasis de cités dans la littérature byzantine et byzantino-slaves*, ed. P. Odorico and Ch. Messis, Dossiers byzantins 12 (Paris, 2012), 123–33.

23 C. Stinger, "The Campidoglio as the Locus of *Renovatio Imperii* in Renaissance Rome," in *Art and Politics in Late Medieval and Early Renaissance Italy, 1250–1500*, ed. C. M. Rosenberg (Notre Dame, IN, 1990), 137.

24 Chrysoloras, ed. Billò, 8, lines 32–34, para. 8; Chrysoloras, "Comparison of Old and New Rome," trans. in Smith, *Architecture in the Culture of Early Humanism*, 201. Patricia Fortini Brown links the views of Chrysoloras with those on Cyriac: "And like Chrysoloras he saw the material object as a witness to past deeds, to be given 'more faith and notice than books themselves'" (P. Brown, *Venice and Antiquity: The Venetian Sense of the Past* [New Haven, 1996], 81).

25 Chrysoloras, ed. Billò, 9, lines 27–31, para. 10; trans. "Comparison of Old and New Rome," 202.

26 Chrysoloras, ed. Billò, 9, lines 16–20, para. 10; trans. "Comparison of Old and New Rome," 201.

> sword, or a suit of armour; and people being captured or fleeing, laughing or crying, in a state of exultation or anger.[27]

Thus ancient objects directly addressed the interested viewer without selective Christian mediation.

Chrysoloras initiated a shift from a Christian perspective on the past to a mode of engagement with ancient history on its own terms. This process is exemplified by his lament on the mistreatment of ancient monuments at the hands of Christian pilgrims: "[The pilgrims] trample them [physical remains of ancient monuments] underfoot, strike them with their fists, break off pieces, spit on them—as I said—and throwing them to the ground, smash them."[28] What had for centuries been confusing and frequently negative testimonies about the pre-Christian past that was shrouded by myth was now being made available for new taxonomies of knowledge.[29] By championing visual evidence as essential for understanding the ancient past, Chrysoloras was a full century ahead of his Renaissance peers.[30]

At the heart of the *Comparison of Old and New Rome* was an argument for shared values between Rome and Constantinople. This was not surprising for a man who strove to broker a union between the Catholic and Orthodox churches. It was also unsurprising that he deployed a familial metaphor in articulating the relationship between the two Romes: though the old Rome is like a mother to Constantinople, the latter is more beautiful.[31] He tempered familial rancor by claiming that no rivalry existed between the two.[32] And yet the relationship was still competitive, when great monuments of the past are taken into account: "Had I wished to enumerate the memorials, the tombs, the monuments and statues that are or have been in our city [Constantinople], I would not have been at a loss to do so. I might have had to

27 Chrysoloras, ed. Billò, 9, lines 32–36, para 11; trans. "Comparison of Old and New Rome," 202.

28 Chrysoloras, ed. Billò, 12, lines 7–9, para. 19; trans. "Comparison of Old and New Rome," 203.

29 According to Roberto Weiss "Modern archaeology really began when the *Mirabilia* ceased to be taken seriously" (Weiss, *The Renaissance Discovery of Classical Antiquity*, 2nd ed. [Oxford, 1988], 204).

30 Charles Hope and Elizabeth McGrath state: "It was only in the next century that the value of Chrysoloras's insight was generally recognized, as scholars came to see in archaeological remains key evidence for the study of ancient civilization" (Hope and McGrath, "Artists and Humanists," in Kraye, *The Cambridge Companion to Renaissance Humanism*, 164).

31 Chrysoloras, ed. Billò, 16, para. 33; trans. "Comparison of Old and New Rome," 207.

32 Chrysoloras, ed. Billò, 15, lines 15–19, para. 29; 15, line 32 to 16, line 2, para. 31; trans. "Comparison of Old and New Rome," 206.

acknowledge that there are fewer of them than there are here [in Rome], but some of them are much more beautiful and splendid."[33]

One of the most evocative monuments for him was the monument of Justinian in Constantinople (fig. 2.1). This was a colossal equestrian monument, which stood at the top of a triumphal column in the Augustaion, adjacent to Hagia Sophia. Erected by the emperor Justinian in ca. 543, the column likely projected even above the dome of Hagia Sophia (almost 56 m), possibly rising to a height of ca. 60 meters. For centuries it served as a landmark for travelers approaching Constantinople from the south.[34] As I demonstrate in my forthcoming book, well before the Palaiologan period this monument became a talisman of the Byzantine Empire and was celebrated internationally.[35]

Justinian's monument evoked the misty-eyed memory of other lost monuments. A relic of the past, it testified to what had been, rather than to what it was on its own merits:

> What about the commemorative monument of the law-giving emperor? And near it, to the east if I remember rightly, are other commemorative statues, many of which are supported by extraordinary columns. That there were once many other such statues in the city is shown by their bases, which are still to be seen, and by inscriptions on them. Some are scattered throughout the city, but most were in the Hippodrome.[36]

33 Chrysoloras, ed. Billò, 20, lines 25–28, para. 46; trans. in C. Mango, comp., *The Art of the Byzantine Empire, 312–1453: Sources and Documents* (Englewood Cliffs, NJ, 1972), 250.

34 Pero Tafur, who visited Constantinople in 1437–38, reports: "As we came out [of the Hagia Sophia] we saw at the door of the church a great column of stone, higher than the great chapel itself" (Tafur, *Travels and Adventures: 1435–1439*, trans. M. Letts [New York, 1926], 140–41). In a 12th-century account, Al-Herewy commented that the column was visible a day's journey before reaching Constantinople and was used by navigators to chart their course to the city; see C. Schefer, "Aboul Hassan Aly el Herewy: Indications sur les lieux de Pelerinage: Extraits," *AOL* 1:589. The 14th-century Russian pilgrim Stephen of Novgorod similarly pronounced that the column "can be seen from far away at sea" (G. Majeska, *Russian Travelers to Constantinople in the Fourteenth and Fifteenth Centuries* [Washington, DC, 1984], 28). Stephen, who would have approached by land from the north rather than from the south, was either repeating a topos or communicating a key fact about piloting in the period.

35 E. N. Boeck, *The Bronze Horseman of Justinian in Constantinople: The Cross-Cultural Biography of a Monument* (Cambridge, 2021).

36 Chrysoloras, ed. Billò, 20, line 33 to 21, line 2, paras. 46, 47; trans. Smith, "Comparison of Old and New Rome," 210.

Fig. 2.1 Job gazes upon his former city while seated on a pile of dung. Book of Job, late 12th–early 13th c. Vaticanus gr. 751, fol. 26r. Reproduced by permission of Biblioteca Apostolica Vaticana,

By referring to Justinian as a lawgiver, Chrysoloras underscored the emperor's acclaimed, shared, and foundational legacy for both Romes. In fifteenth-century Italy Justinian was classified as a Roman emperor.[37] Thus framed, his monument became a shared legacy. It also bore witness to the erasure of the past and the purported destruction of cultural heritage even within the author's living memory. It had become a symbol of past grandeur that alone persisted in the face of loss and persevered against the ravages of time and the tides of history.

Christine Smith, the first scholar to translate and comprehensively analyze the *Comparison*, suggested the influence of Constantine of Rhodes (tenth century)

37 Flavio Biondo repeatedly referred to Justinian as a Roman emperor (Lamers, *Greece Reinvented*, 65). Biondo extensively used Procopius's *Wars* in crafting his historical narrative *Decades*. According to Brian Croke, Biondo "is often said to be the first historian to formulate the notion of decline in the Roman empire from the fifth century" (Croke, "Procopius, from Manuscripts to Books: 1400–1850," *Histos* supplement 9.1 [2019]: 20).

upon the narrative structure.[38] The two narratives are very different, however. As I argue elsewhere, Constantine of Rhodes repeatedly emphasized the monument of Justinian as the foremost wonder of the city, while Chrysoloras evoked it in order to bring to life the theater of his imagination and populate other columns with lost or toppled monuments.[39] Furthermore, unlike the iconographic immediacy of Constantine of Rhodes, Chrysoloras's vagueness in narrating Constantinople's monuments was likely a result of the author's absence from the city for nearly a decade by the time the *Comparison* was composed.[40]

His Constantinople is a shadowy place, a space of past greatness and present loss. It is reminiscent of the landscape of Shelley's "Ozymandias." Pervaded with nostalgia for the lost magnificence of Constantinople, the present city emerges as a diminished witness to what it had once been.[41] Chrysoloras finds solace in the past, rather than in the present. The past has become a memory space:

> It is also said that the column on the Xêrolophos and the one facing it to the east, the one named after the bull (*tauros*), on the other hill, once supported statues of beaten silver, the former of the elder, the latter of the younger Theodosius. How big, precious and beautiful these statues must have been may be surmised from the beauty, height, splendor and magnificence of the bases. In recalling these to my mind, I also remembered that in line with the same street, to the west, there was once a gate of the city big enough to let through entire towers and fortifications (if only these could move) and cargo-ships with all their sails and masts.[42]

This is a world that bears sad witness to the lost giants of a past age (expressed by the scale of these buildings) and to the implicit and explicit insignificance of the present era. His only recourse was to bear witness to its demise with memory-tinted eyes. At

38 Smith, *Architecture in the Culture of Early Humanism*, 165.

39 Boeck, *The Bronze Horseman of Justinian*, chap. 6.

40 Smith, *Architecture in the Culture of Early Humanism*, 153.

41 Just two centuries earlier, Gerald of Wales made the opposite comparison between Constantinople and Rome in the context of narrating the Fourth Crusade. According to Paul Magdalino he compared them "after Constantine's *translatio imperii*: the space which, in Old Rome, was half covered by ruins or *inaedificatum* had been covered in the New Rome by important residences and palaces 'before the destruction and conquest of this city by the Latins of our day'" (Magdalino, *Studies on the History and Topography of Byzantine Constantinople* [Aldershot, 2007], 62). For the original, see Giraldus Cambrensis, *Speculum Ecclesiae*, ed. J. S. Brewer, in *Rerum britannicarum medii aevi scriptores* 21.4 (1873): 282.

42 Chrysoloras, ed. Billò, 21, lines 2–13, paras. 47, 48; trans. in Mango, *Art of the Byzantine Empire*, 250–51.

the same time, he provocatively proposes that art has the power to bring back to life what is lost. This goal would be realized by Mantegna.

Chrysoloras's text became a model for his Italian contemporaries.[43] *Comparison of Old and New Rome* was translated into Latin by Francesco Aleardi shortly after the fall of Constantinople to the Ottomans in 1453. Its impact and reception can be gleaned from rhetorical echoes in other texts. In 1454 Niccolò Sagundino related to Alfonso V of Aragon the fall of Constantinople and used the same mother/daughter model to describe the conqueror of Constantinople, Mehmed II, and his geopolitical intentions: "on the basis of old prophecies and omens, the conqueror of Constantinople had resolved to make himself the master of Rome and all Italy; just as he had taken possession of the daughter, Byzantium, so he would also conquer Rome, the mother."[44] Cyriac of Ancona was able to traverse the eastern Mediterranean and collect fragments of the past before the events lamented by Sagundino.

Cyriac of Ancona was an intellectual disciple of Manuel Chrysoloras, who profoundly shaped scholarship with his inquisitive explorations of the eastern Mediterranean.[45] A larger-than-life figure, he wore many hats during his restless wanderings as a "merchant, accountant, politician, traveler, antiquarian, spy, . . . father of archaeology."[46] A celebrated polymath of the early Renaissance, he studiously collected Greek and Latin inscriptions during his extensive Mediterranean travels (to Constantinople, Damascus, Cyprus, etc.) and produced numerous drawings and measurements of ancient monuments, thereby laying the foundation for the modern disciplines of epigraphy and archaeology.[47] He likewise dedicated himself to "awakening the dead."[48] His notebooks profoundly influenced his Renaissance contemporaries, particularly in Venice and Padua.[49] At the same time his corpus is virtually

43 His own model for the misty-eyed views of past greatness was likely the "Roman Oration" of Aelius Aristides, which was written in Greek in the mid-2nd century CE and would have probably been part of his Palaiologan education. Stinger, "The Campidoglio as the Locus of *Renovatio Imperii*," 137. See also Smith, *Architecture in the Culture of Early Humanism*, 139–40, 152–53, 168; Webb, "Describing Rome in Greek" (n. 22 above).

44 Sagundino is paraphrased by F. Babinger, *Mehmed the Conqueror and His Time*, trans. R. Manheim (Princeton, 1978), 494–95. See also Tosetti Grandi, *I Trionfi di Cesare di Andrea Mantegna* (n. 8 above), 37.

45 For a recent biographical summary, see F. Forner, "Pizzicolli, Ciriaco de' (Ciriaco d'Ancona)," in *DBDI* 84:61–364.

46 C. Foss, introduction to Cyriac of Ancona, *Life and Early Travels*, ed. and trans. C. Mitchell, E. W. Bodnar, and Foss (Cambridge, MA, 2015), vii.

47 See, e.g., B. Ashmole, "Cyriac of Ancona and the Temple of Hadrian at Cyzicus," *JWarb* 19.3/4 (1956): 179–91.

48 P. Brown, *Venice and Antiquity* (n. 24 above), 82.

49 According to P. Brown, "one might say that Cyriacus brought the Greek east into the drawing rooms and *studioli* of the Latin west, supplying his clients and friends in Italy not only with

inaccessible to modern scholars, except for a few surviving copies of his works.[50] His legacy perished in the fire of the Sforza Library in Pesaro in 1514.[51]

Though his original Constantinopolitan drawings do not survive, on the authority of his biographer Francesco Scalamonti we know that Cyriac admired Byzantine monuments on his first visit to the city. Justinian's horseman received his attention in word and image:

> Next, inside the city, he first inspected its great ornate churches and, especially, the huge and magnificent temple of Hagia Sophia founded by Justinian with its vast dome, its marble-faced walls, its remarkable pavement and its numerous tall, weighty porphyry and serpentine columns, and in front of it the marvelous bronze equestrian statue of Heraclius, conspicuously placed on the top of its high column (*alta columna Heracleam illam mirificam aeneam equestrem statuam, arduum quippe et conspicuum opus*).[52]

It should be noted that Scalamonti's narrative contains substantive errors and still reflects the crusader identification of the monument as Herakleios.[53] Nonetheless his summary of Constantinople's marvels effectively encapsulates the early Renaissance preoccupation with audacious architecture, variegated stones, and great sculpture. Hagia Sophia had already become an example of architectural genius admired by Renaissance thinkers.[54] A copy of Cyriac's drawing of Hagia Sophia survives to the present day.[55]

---

antiquities, but also—through his inscriptions and excerpts—first-hand eye-witness knowledge of the ancient world" (ibid., 83). She also noted, "One of [Cyriac's] most important contributions may be in his privileging the object over the literary text, a paradigm shift announced by Chrysoloras but implemented by Cyriacus" (84).

50 B. L. Brown and D. E. E. Kleiner, "Giuliano da Sangallo's Drawings after Ciriaco d'Ancona: Transformations of Greek and Roman Antiquities in Athens," *JSAH* 42.2 (1983): 321–35. See also P. Brown, *Venice and Antiquity*, 82, 306, n. 47.

51 D. Howard, "Responses to Ancient Greek Architecture in Renaissance Venice," *Annali di architettura* 6 (1994): 29.

52 Cyriac of Ancona, *Life and Early Travels*, 32, 33.

53 For a more extensive discussion of this quote, see Boeck, *The Bronze Horseman of Justinian*, chap. 12. See also the discussion by Mitchell, Bodnar, and Foss in Cyriac of Ancona, *Life and Early Travels*.

54 S. Foschi, "Santa Sofia di Constantinopoli: Immagini dall'Occidente," *Annali di architettura* 14 (2002): 7–34.

55 Its accuracy in reproducing Cyriac's original is questionable. Originally Cyriac appears to have made eight drawings. Their headings are preserved in a 15th-century manuscript (Bibliotheca Palatina, MS Parm. 1191). See Cyriac of Ancona, *Life and Early Travels*, 265–71.

Identification of the bronze horseman as Herakleios testifies to the medieval dynamism of "interrogatory spectatorship."[56] Though in this particular context the identification demonstrates Scalamonti's reliance on a lost record of an early journey by Cyriac, it also reflects a preference of medieval Latin visitors to behold in this stupendous monument the emperor who was celebrated as a protocrusader. Antiquarians were seeking to correct precisely this kind of flexibility of ascribed identity and dependence on *mirabilia* narratives by letting the monuments speak in their own voice. And correct it they did.

On a subsequent visit around 1427, Cyriac scored a victory for Renaissance scholarship by recording and publicizing a Theodosian inscription on the colossal bronze monument.[57] A greatly renowned, hallowed monument of Constantinople, which was long believed to be the monument of Justinian (or, by a few, of Constantine or Herakleios), was re-identified as Theodosius. On the body of the horse and above its mane an inscription read FON(S) GLORIAE PERENNIS THEODOSI (fig. 2.2).[58] The inscription most likely initially came to light following the fourteenth-century cleaning/"restoration" of the equestrian monument, when nearly a millennium of corrosion was removed from the rider and his horse.[59] Here we behold a triumph of the antiquarian approach—inscriptions could uncover lost truths and correct the errors of the past.[60] This inscription was meant to be appreciated by antiquarian collectors of knowledge. Its brevity conceals the depth of historical tradition that the new knowledge cut through, allowing the monument to speak for itself for the first time since late antiquity. This was a coup for the science of epigraphy. The inscription was widely circulated, and a number of manuscripts dedicated to the monuments of Constantinople were emended to reflect the new knowledge. Cyriac, in effect, had corrected the knowledge of Manuel Chrysoloras.

56 D. Kinney, "The Horse, the King, and the Cuckoo: Medieval Narrations of the Statue of Marcus Aurelius," *Word and Image* 18.1 (2002): 384.

57 Boeck, *The Bronze Horseman of Justinian*, chap. 12.

58 A famous eye-level drawing of Justinian's equestrian monument (Budapest University Library, Cod. Ital. 3, fol. 144v), shown in figure 2.2, includes the inscription and has frequently been associated with Cyriac. For another illustration, see *From Byzantion to Istanbul: 8000 Years of a Capital* (Istanbul, 2010), 452, no. 91. This drawing generated a heated exchange between Cyril Mango and Phyllis Lehmann, with the arguments and evidence summarized by Mango in the article "The Columns of Justinian and His Successors," in his *Studies on Constantinople* (Aldershot, 1993), X.

59 Boeck, *The Bronze Horseman of Justinian*, chap. 11.

60 The full inscription, possibly in Cyriac's own hand, was recorded in a manuscript that is now in Florence (Biblioteca Nazionale di Firenze, MS Conv. Sopp. I.IX.30). See C. Buondelmonti, *Liber insularum archipelagi: Transkription des Exemplars Universitäts- und Landesbibliothek Düsseldorf Ms. G 13*, ed. K. Bayer (Wiesbaden, 2007), 44; C. Barsanti, "Constantinopoli e l'Egeo nei primi decennia del XV secolo: La testimonianza di Cristoforo Buondelmonti," *RIASA* 56 (2001): 218.

Fig. 2.2.
A Renaissance drawing of the Constantinopolitan Bronze Horseman, 15th c. Budapest, University Library and Archive of Eötvös Loránd University, Cod. Ital. 3, fol. 144v. Courtesy University Library and Archives, Eötvös Loránd University.

Cyriac's discovery came at a perfect time. Fifteenth-century intellectuals, patrons, and artists were keenly interested in equestrian monuments. For antiquarians, Justinian's horseman was the kind of colossus that affirmed the veracity of Pliny's *Natural History*, the Roman encyclopedic compilation that was a revelation to Renaissance scholars. Meanwhile artists including Raphael and Leonardo da Vinci were studying, measuring, or planning to cast equestrian monuments for ambitious generals and princes.

Depicting Rome(s), Defending Caesar

Triumphs of Caesar has been called the "centerpiece of Mantegna's legacy."[61] Mantegna completed it in Mantua, where he moved in 1460 to become the court

61 K. Christiansen, *The Genius of Andrea Mantegna* (New Haven, 2009), 38.

artist to the Gonzagas.[62] Elevated in status and titled "marquis" by the Holy Roman emperor Sigismund in 1433, Gonzaga rulers were lavish patrons who cultivated an image as successors to Roman emperors.[63] The Gonzagas also assembled a legendary collection of ancient art. It included the Gemma Felix, which served as an inspiration for a triumphal column in panel III.[64]

Though Mantegna took more than two decades to complete the cycle, its theme of Roman triumphalism reflected the unwavering interest of the Gonzaga rulers in the Roman imperial past.[65] It was most likely Francesco Gonzaga (r. 1484–1519) who commissioned *Triumphs of Caesar*—originally for the great hall of his *castello,* though it was moved to the new palace of San Sebastiano by 1512.[66] The patron was very well pleased with Mantegna's paintings, referring to them as "the work of your hands and genius."[67]

Triumphs of Caesar brings to life a ceremonial entry into Rome of a victorious Roman army.[68] Heavily laden with the extensive spoils of war, the procession unswervingly moves toward the left through a classicizing landscape. Beginning with trumpeters and standard-bearers (panel I), the cycle culminates with Caesar riding in an enormous chariot, which appears against the backdrop of a triumphal arch (panel IX). The inscription "VENI VIDI VICI" appears on one of the standards above Caesar's head.[69]

62 C. Elam, "Mantegna at Mantua," in *Splendours of the Gonzaga: Catalogue,* ed. D. Chambers and J. Martineau (London, 1982), 15–25.

63 Dandelet, *The Renaissance of Empire* (n. 3 above), 36, 40.

64 Canvas III: *Trophies and bearers of coin and vases (The Trophy Bearers)* in the distant background includes a nude figure of Poseidon/Neptune with a trident standing on a column. Tosetti Grandi connected this figure with the ancient Gemma Felix, which is now in the Ashmolean Museum but was in the collection of Francesco Gonzaga. The comparison between Mantegna's figure and the ancient representation is remarkably close, even though Mantegna slightly changed some iconographic elements (Tosetti Grandi, *I Trionfi di Cesare di Andrea Mantegna,* 91–96). Mantegna repeated this figure in a drawing of sea deities.

65 In addition to *Triumphs of Caesar* Mantegna painted images of the first eight Roman emperors (1465–74), which were juxtaposed with a Gonzaga cycle in the personal apartments of Ludovico II Gonzaga (d. 1478). Dandelet, *The Renaissance of Empire,* 40.

66 Lightbown, *Mantegna* (n. 1 above), 142, 428–30. It is also worth noting that Francesco II Gonzaga maintained active diplomatic relations with the Ottoman court and showed an interest in the Ottoman court and culture. M. Bourne, "The Turban'd Turk in Renaissance Mantua: Francesco II Gonzaga's Interest in Ottoman Fashion," in *Mantova e il Rinascimento italiano: Studi in onore di David S. Chambers,* ed. P. Jackson and G. Rebecchini (Mantua, 2011), 53–64.

67 Lightbown, *Mantegna,* 144.

68 Martindale, *Andrea Mantegna: Historicus et Antiquarius* (n. 2 above). See also A. S. Halliday, "The Literary Sources of Mantegna's *Triumphs of Caesar,*" in *La corte di Mantova nell'età di Andrea Mantegna, 1450–1550,* ed. C. Mozzarelli, R. Oresko, and L. Ventura (Rome, 1997), 187–95.

69 Lightbown, *Mantegna,* 425.

Vasari called *Triumphs* Mantegna's best work, King Charles I of England acquired the set as the centerpiece of his collection, and Cromwell intervened to prevent its sale.[70] Before the panels departed for England in the second decade of the seventeenth century, *Triumphs of Caesar* was a tourist attraction in Mantua, was the subject of woodcuts, and was copied several times by different artists, including Rubens.[71]

Despite centuries of royal and scholarly accolades for Mantegna's *Triumphs,* much about the acclaimed masterpiece remains uncertain. The nine-tableaux cycle celebrates Julius Caesar, but scholars still question which of Caesar's triumphs Mantegna chose to paint.[72] The minute archaeological details of these images have intrigued scholars, since there are very few ancient sources that describe in detail Caesar's triumphs (particularly the triumph over the Gauls). Mantegna's intellectual inspiration for the cycle is also complex. In constructing the narrative progression, Mantegna used a number of ancient textual sources (Plutarch in Greek, Suetonius) and was in dialogue with contemporary publications (such as *De re militari* of Roberto Valturio and *Roma Triumphans* of Flavio Biondo).[73] It is possible that Mantegna came into contact with Biondo (who served as papal secretary) during the church council that assembled in Mantua in 1459 in order to discuss the Ottoman menace in the aftermath of the fall of Constantinople.[74] Several of the monuments that served as Mantegna's inspiration for this cycle are known. Thus, the triumphal arch of Caesar is based on the Arch of Sergii (Pula, Istria), which incidentally had also been admired by Cyriac of Ancona.[75]

Mantegna associated with many remarkable people—patrons, scholars, antiquarians, collectors, cardinals—who were keenly interested in the monuments of the past. Nonetheless, he drew on the pioneering methodological and visual approaches of Chrysoloras and Cyriac of Ancona to engage with the past in a new

70 Martindale, *Andrea Mantegna: Historicus et Antiquarius.*

71 T. Arlt, *Andrea Mantegna, Triumph Caesars: Ein Meisterwerk der Renaissance in neuem Licht* (Vienna, 2005).

72 Though Caesar had celebrated five triumphs during his reign, it is not clear whether Mantegna fused elements of all five or intended to emphasize one in particular (i.e., his Gallic or Pontic triumph). His main textual sources would have been Suetonius, Plutarch, and Appian. Lightbown, *Mantegna,* 144–45; Tosetti Grandi, *I Trionfi di Cesare di Andrea Mantegna*; Arlt, *Andrea Mantegna, Triumph Caesars.*

73 For his use of Plutarch in Greek, see Halliday, "The Literary Sources of Mantegna's *Triumphs of Caesar*," 188, 190. For the discussion of other sources, see Tosetti Grandi, *I Trionfi di Cesare di Andrea Mantegna,* 28–38.

74 Dandelet, *The Renaissance of Empire,* 37–38.

75 J. Gudelj, "The King of Naples Emulates Salvia Postuma? The Arch of Castel Nuovo in Naples and Its Antique Model," in *Dalmatia and the Mediterranean: Portable Archaeology and the Poetics of Influence,* ed. A. Payne (Leiden, 2014), 440, 431.

way. Mantegna was close to the circles that translated Chrysoloras and circulated his work in Italy.[76] He also had access to the works of Cyriac of Ancona via the copies of Felice Feliciano.[77] Mantegna appears to have known copies of the notebooks of Cyriac of Ancona; it is possible that the two men met, since both were in Ferrara in 1449.[78] We also know that Mantegna displayed his knowledge of Cyriac's collection of ancient inscriptions in a fresco he completed in 1451, where he reproduced one of the inscriptions known to have been collected by Cyriac.[79]

The image that concerns us is panel VI, *The Corselet Bearers* (or *Bearers of coins and plate, trophies of royal armor*) (fig. 2.3).[80] It is the sixth of a series of nine monumental panels that culminate with Caesar triumphant. The panel under discussion here measures 268 by 278 centimeters.[81] This means that the figures represented in the foreground are life-size. The canvases were originally intended to be seen slightly above eye level.[82] Interestingly, this is one of the panels that has attracted relatively little attention from scholars. And yet, following in the footsteps of Chrysoloras, Mantegna made antiquity come to life in these images through their meticulous details, realia (breastplates, spears, silver objects, chariots), and architecture.[83]

Our panel is composed of three registers. In the foreground, monumental victors carry precious, mostly metal, trophies either on their shoulders or above their heads. Above them the viewer beholds a monumental cityscape. The colossal

76 Marzia Faietti notes that Chrysoloras's comparison of Rome and Constantinople "became acutely topical [after 1453], [when] the Veronese scholar Francesco Aleardi decided to translate it into Latin. Paola Tosetti Grandi has convincingly argued that Mantegna was aware of the *Elogio* while still in Padua, as a result of his friendship with Nofri Strozzi, to whom Aleardi had sent two copies of the Latin version, and through the contact between Aleardi and the sons of Guarino, as well as Mantegna's own connections with Battista Guarini" (Faietti, "From Solomon's Temple to Hagia Sophia: A Metaphorical Journey for Andrea Mantegna," in Payne, *Dalmatia and the Mediterranean*, 130). She also says that Mantegna knew Lamy's miniature in *Notitia Dignitatum* (ibid.).

77 Contò and Quaquarelli, *L'"antiquario" Felice Feliciano Veronese* (n. 11 above).

78 F. Ames-Lewis, "The Agony in the Garden and Mantegna's Treatment of Narrative," in Ames-Lewis and Bednarek, *Mantegna and 15th-Century Court Culture* (n. 12 above), 41. See also P. W. Lehmann and K. Lehmann, *Samothracian Reflections: Aspects of the Revival of the Antique* (Princeton, 1973), 108.

79 This inscription is on a triumphal arch in his fresco *St. James before Herod Agrippa* (Ovetari Chapel). Ames-Lewis, introduction to *Mantegna and 15th-Century Court Culture*, 9.

80 Originally there were no individual titles for each panel. According to Lightbown, "They have no true single titles, since they are a processional sequence, not a series of independent compositions" (*Mantegna*, 143).

81 Ibid., 425. It is possible that this panel might not have been fully finished (see 148).

82 Ibid., 143.

83 Christiansen, *The Genius of Andrea Mantegna* (n. 61 above), 39–40. Mantegna drew other ancient monuments, including part of the Trajanic frieze and a seated female figure on a sarcophagus. See Martineau, Boorsch, et al., *Andrea Mantegna* (n. 5 above), 445–48, no. 145.

Fig. 2.3. Andrea Mantegna, *Triumphs of Caesar*, panel VI, *The Corselet Bearers*. Hampton Court. Courtesy Bridgeman Images.

architecture of an enormous, sloping, diagonal, arched structure (aqueduct?) looms over the scene. In the upper left corner of the composition, a triumphal column surmounted by a bronze horseman towers over everything else in the image. The direction of the rider is aligned with the direction of the procession.

We behold a rhythmic movement from right to left. Several statuesque soldiers carry trophies of conquest. They follow closely behind an elephant's rump, which is decorated with a textile evocative of the brocaded textiles produced in the Muslim world (including a pseudo-Arabic inscription along its edge).[84] Three men occupy

84 For a good discussion of Islamic objects in the European imagination, see C. Schmidt Arcangeli and G. Wolf, eds., *Islamic Artefacts in the Mediterranean World: Trade, Gift Exchange and Artistic Transfer* (Venice, 2010).

the foreground and several others are visible behind them. Their heavy treasures consist primarily of armor, metal vessels, and diadems. Most striking are two suits of "Roman" armor held aloft above their heads. From a distance these suits of armor evoke representations of military trophies on Roman imperial monuments, such as the base of Trajan's triumphal column or the column of Arcadius in Constantinople. At first glance it appears as if the archaeological precision of detail makes history come alive in a measured and steady movement of calmly triumphal participants. The attention to detail is striking—one of the breastplates is given a highly realistic scaly texture and accentuated by a decorative "relief" of a putto-like face surrounded by wings. The helmets have finely detailed crests and feathers, the blades of swords show beautiful inlays of floral design, and their handles are shaped into birds of prey. All reflect the naturalistic tendencies current in late *quattrocento* painting.

Many of the vessels display Mantegna's strong awareness of ancient shapes—from the elegantly curving handles to the narrowing necks of pouring vessels to the Bacchic-themed "reliefs" on a very large gilded vessel. Several large carved gems, pearls, and other treasures add texture to the variegated display of Roman glory. Mantegna strove to bring history to life by envisioning an ancient triumph that would flatter his own Renaissance patron. He activated the past by representing ancient monuments. In executing this panel he appears to have emulated the ancient artists celebrated by Chrysoloras for creating images with such skill that one "contends with reality itself, so that one seems to see a real man[,] . . . a breastplate, sword, or a suit of armour."

Cyriac of Ancona's legacy could even explain why Mantegna chose to highlight a triumph of Julius Caesar. In a letter written in 1436, Cyriac addressed the controversy that surrounded Julius Caesar at the time, lamenting "that in Italy divine Caesar is the subject of undeserved verbal attacks."[85] At the heart of the issue was a debate regarding the best system of government—republican vs. monarchical. Supporters of the republican model felt that Caesar had changed the Roman republican system into a monarchy. Cyriac was a dedicated monarchist who eloquently praised Caesar: "Caesar founded the very monarchy. . . . It was divinely inspired and modeled on heaven itself."[86] The debate even included the question of whether equestrian monuments could have been erected in an ancient republican context or were instead exclusively monuments of empire.[87] As part of the cycle on Caesar's triumph for a Gonzaga

85 Cyriac of Ancona, letter to Leonardo Bruni, 30 January 1436, in *Life and Early Travels* (n. 46 above), 205. For a summary of Bruni's views, see S. G. Casu, "'Veluti Caesar Triumphans': Ciriaco d'Ancona e la statuaria equestre," *Paragone: Arte* 55–56 (2004): 21–23.

86 Cyriac, letter to Bruni, 30 January 1436, in *Life and Early Travels*, 207.

87 Plutarch mentions an equestrian monument erected during a republican regime in a text that was starting to be disseminated by humanists in 1436—evidence that equestrian monuments were

patron, Mantegna's panels celebrated monarchy as a spectacular and powerful form of government.[88] The popularity of Caesar's triumph in the 1450s–60s also seems to have stemmed from a not-so-hidden dialogue with the Ottomans, since Mehmed II was rhetorically fashioned by his supporters into a new Alexander the Great.[89]

A Conspicuous Bronze Horseman on a Column

Mantegna was a sophisticated connoisseur of history who knew that neither the column of Trajan nor the column of Marcus Aurelius could have witnessed a triumph of Julius Caesar. Because no details in his images were accidental, the column presents a fascinating referent to be decoded. What did his column signify? Its towering presence testifies to Cyriac's sentiments about the honorific value of equestrian monuments.[90] It was a colossus that had recently become only a memory but still signified the greatness of the Roman imperial past.

The formidable height of the equestrian statue echoes the visual impact of Constantinople's elevated bronze horseman. While for Chrysoloras Constantinople's horseman was the springboard for recollecting other imperial monuments of Constantinople, Mantegna recalled this monument in a learned representation of old Rome. By the time Mantegna represented it, the colossal statue had been pulled down by the Ottomans and consigned to historical memory. Constantinople's bronze horseman had become part of the archaeology of knowledge. Prior to its demise shortly after the city fell in 1453, it was the only surviving imperial monument that embodied such a towering vision of imperial triumph. A cluster of iconographic features make such a source of inspiration probable. Justinian's bronze horseman had been the only equestrian monument standing atop a colossal triumphal column. We should not forget the impact that the sheer height and audacity of ancient engineering would have conveyed to medieval and Renaissance viewers.

The dynamism of the composition evokes several features of the recently dismantled Constantinopolitan colossus without necessarily striving for perfect

---

not exclusively erected in monarchies. Casu, "'Veluti Caesar Triumphans,'" 25. The question was important, since equestrian monuments were being erected in different cities in Italy.

88 For a discussion of Gonzaga and the Caesar cycle, see D. S. Chambers, "Il marchese Federico I Gonzaga (1441–1484) e Il Trionfo di Giulio Cesare di Andrea Mantegna," in Signorini, Rebonato, and Tammaccaro, *Andrea Mantegna, impronta del genio* (n. 11 above), 507–20.

89 According to Martindale, "The answer lies in the place that Caesar occupied in the general esteem of educated men. People argued violently about his political career; but everybody agreed that he was the greatest general the world had ever seen— the only real rival he had was Alexander the Great" (*Andrea Mantegna: Historicus et Antiquarius* [n. 2 above], n.p.).

90 He wrote *statua quondam ex aere vel marmore, honoris causa, donatum* (Casu, "'Veluti Caesar Triumphans,'" 11).

Fig. 2.4. Detail of figure 2.3.

faithfulness. A particularly interesting facet of the *Triumphs* is its simultaneous combination of imaginative invention and archaeological accuracy (fig. 2.4). In this case the height of the monument, the advance of the horse's right foot, the steed's turned head, the raised right hand of the rider, and the noticeable cape that appears to float in the air all represent well-known features of the Byzantine bronze horseman, which reinforce Roman typology of imperial equestrian representations. More crucially, the plinth on which Mantegna installed his equestrian monument initiates a particularly strong dialogue with the bronze horseman of Constantinople. The plinth attracted considerable attention for its sheer size, on the one hand, and for the excellent visibility of the rider that it afforded, on the other hand.[91] No other equestrian

91 See, e.g., Robert de Clari and George Pachymeres. For the text of Robert de Clari, see *La conquête de Constantinople*, chap. 86, in *Historiens et Chroniqueurs du Moyen Age: Robert de Clari, Villehardouin, Joinville, Froissart, Commynes*, ed. A. Pauphilet (Paris, 1952), 86; *The Conquest of Constantinople*, trans. E. H. McNeal (1936; repr., Toronto, 1996), 107. Pachymeres is most easily accessible in Mango, *Art of the Byzantine Empire* (n. 33 above), 111–13.

monument had such an ingenious base or such audacious elevation. Bertrandon de la Broquière, who visited Constantinople in the 1430s, was struck by the technological prowess required to achieve the monument's elevation: "I have no idea how the statue was put up there, given its size and weight."[92]

That the monument was admired by both Chrysoloras and Cyriac of Ancona must have impressed Mantegna. Chrysolaras drew attention to Justinian's equestrian statue as a lone relic from a series of grandiose, lost monuments as he made the case for a filial relationship between Constantinople and Rome. A logical extension of the analogy he advanced is the implication that if New Rome had such a monument and marvel, then Old Rome should have had one too. Mantegna's panel is nothing less than an imaginative visualization of Cyriac's equestrian statue "conspicuously placed on the top of its high column" in service of Chrysoloras's notion of values shared between Constantinople and Rome.

The alignment of an imperial past shared by the two Romes is mirrored in the directional alignment of the painted colossus and Caesar's triumph. This is where the function of gesture in Mantegna's work and in Renaissance theory becomes particularly significant. Mantegna hewed closely to the prescripts of the defining Renaissance intellectual Leon Battista Alberti,[93] who, in line with antiquarians, argued that images did not have to be subordinate to texts as primary sources of information. As Jack M. Greenstein puts it, "If the actions and reactions of depicted characters could be conveyed as well through gesture as through words, a picture no longer need function merely as an illustration; it could serve as a primary source of information, a kind of 'visible speech.'"[94]

This is ideologically and structurally significant, since in the Albertian mode the viewer was expected to experience the direction of history through body language and gesture. The direction of the procession is aligned with the directional position of the colossal monument. Mantegna very closely followed the vision of historical painting formulated by Alberti (who also served Ludovico Gonzaga).[95] Greenstein explains, "When Alberti demanded that all the depicted bodies move in definite harmony with the matter being performed, he was insisting that the subject of painting was the matter of history, that is, 'something done.' Since the viewer perceived this matter through vision, painting was *historia*, that is, a representation of things 'that

92 Bertrandon de la Broquière, *The Voyage d'Outremer*, trans. G. R. Kline (New York, 1988), 101–2.

93 D. Chambers, J. Martineau, and R. Signorini, "Mantegna and the Men of Letters," in Martineau, Boorsch, et al., *Andrea Mantegna*, 18. For Mantegna's dialogue with Alberti, see J. M. Greenstein, *Mantegna and Painting as Historical Narrative* (Chicago, 1992), chaps. 2, 3.

94 Greenstein, *Mantegna and Painting as Historical Narrative*, 38–39.

95 Ibid., 60; see also M. Murano, "Alberti e Mantegna," in *Arte, pensiero e cultura a Mantova nel primo Rinascimento in rapporto con la Toscana e con il Veneto* (Florence, 1965), 103–15.

are done and seen.'"[96] Mantegna's understanding of *historia* was complex. Though it could mean "a visually unified pictorial narrative," it also became "the act of concentrating meaning in a pictorial work through the collation of images or even through the composition of parts."[97] The juxtaposition between the column and the triumph literally and figuratively responds to an important facet of Albertian aesthetics: "The great work of the painter is not a colossus but a 'historia,' for there is far more merit in a 'historia' than in a colossus."[98] Mantegna, however, succeeded in incorporating this colossus into his "historia." In this panel it was positioned as a witness to a key turning point in history—Rome on the brink of empire. In Mantegna's lifetime the world appeared to be changing yet again, when the Ottomans took Constantinople and toppled the last surviving ancient colossus from its lofty pedestal shortly after 1453.

▪▪▪

Mantegna's antiquarian relocation of Constantinople's greatest imperial monument to Rome brought Manuel Chrysoloras's ideas full circle. Chrysoloras elevated monuments of the past as worthy evidence. Cyriac of Ancona made them worthy of admiration, demonstrating their value to antiquarian pursuits and alerting scholars to the enormous importance of visual and epigraphic evidence. After the fall of Constantinople, the lost monument was granted new life in intellectual spaces between the real and the imagined, the antiquarian and the allegorical. It took Andrea Mantegna to give this lost monument a place in history. Taking the greatest and most cross-culturally significant Byzantine sculptural monument, he projected it back into the past of Rome and into a vision of Roman and Western history cherished by antiquarians.

I would like to thank Nathanael Aschenbrenner and Jake Ransohoff for the invitation to participate in the very stimulating conference "Invention of Byzantine Studies in Early Modern Europe" and for their helpful editorial suggestions on the earlier version of this chapter. I am also grateful to the anonymous readers for their thoughtful comments.

96 Greenstein, *Mantegna and Painting as Historical Narrative*, 49.

97 Ibid., 221.

98 Alberti, *De pictura*, para. 35; trans. in L. Barkan, *Unearthing the Past: Archaeology and Aesthetics in the Making of Renaissance Culture* (New Haven, 1999), 113.

PART TWO

EXPLOITING AND ENACTING BYZANTIUM, CA. 1500–1750

THREE

WESTERN HUMANISTS AND BYZANTINE HISTORIANS

ANTHONY GRAFTON

IN THE MIDDLE OF THE SIXTEENTH CENTURY, EUROPEAN HUMANISTS SAW THE Byzantine historical texts they knew as reliable sources, not only for the history of the Byzantine Empire but for earlier periods as well. In 1560 Philip Melanchthon, Luther's right-hand man and the creator of the German classical gymnasium, obtained a handsome Wittenberg edition of the Bible. On the flyleaf, he entered a detailed description of Jesus. "Nicephorus," he explained, "a minister of the Church of Constantinople and a writer of ecclesiastical history and the greatest deeds of the Emperors of the East, describes the appearance of our Lord Jesus Christ at the end of the first book, in these words, translated accurately from the Greek text."[1] The source in question seems late, at least to serve as a source for information about Jesus. Nikephoros Kallistos Xanthopoulos lived in the early fourteenth century. But as an ecclesiastical history, his book belonged to a highly recognizable genre: the series of histories of the church in Greek that began with the work of Eusebius, completed not long after 300 CE, and that stood out for the many earlier primary documents that they preserved. Nikephoros compiled his work from the writings of predecessors

1 *Biblia* (Wittenberg, 1556), Princeton University Library (HSVR) 2018-0002F, flyleaf recto: *Nicephorus Ecclesiae Constantinopolitanae minister, Scriptor historiae ecclesiasticae & maximarum rerum, quas gesserunt Imperatores Orientis, figuram Domini nostri IESV CHristi in fine primi libri, his verbis, ex graeca narratione fideliter conversis, describit.* The passage comes from Nikephoros Kallistos Xanthopoulos, *Ecclesiastical History* 1.40, which Melanchthon read in the recently published translation by the imperial councillor Johannes Lange: Nikephoros Kallistos Xanthopoulos, *Ecclesiasticae historiae libri decem & octo* (Basel, 1553), 89.

like Eusebius and Sozomen, as well as other documents, as his surviving notes show.[2] It was only natural that Melanchthon—like many contemporary scholars—treated his work as informative and reliable, and assumed that the description of the Savior that it preserved was ancient and genuine.

A hundred and thirty-one years later, in 1691, Byzantine studies and classical scholarship celebrated their divorce. The man who came between them—and who defined the differences that made them split up—was a Byzantine historian, the sixth-century Antiochene chronicler John Malalas. Just over sixty years before, Oxford University had bought the Barocci manuscripts, a rich collection of Greek codices gathered on Crete and in Venice by the Italian scholar Francesco Barozzi and his nephew Iacopo.[3] MS 182 was Malalas's universal history. In the age of William Laud, who fostered scholarship on Christian Greek texts of all periods and hoped, at times, for reunion with the Greek Orthodox Church, a new Byzantine history attracted interest. Edmund Chilmead, a canon of Christ Church, began preparing an edition and translation. He knew the context in which to set this text: a note at the beginning of the Bodleian manuscript calls attention to a parallel passage in the "Chronicum Alexandrinum"—that is, the *Paschal Chronicle*.[4] The Civil War and Glorious Revolution intervened, but at last, in 1691, John Mill reworked the text and put it through the press. Richard Bentley, a Cambridge scholar whose reputation for brilliance was showing a little tarnish as he neared thirty with few publications, asked if he could see the proofs. Mill replied that he could, but only on condition that he would supply a commentary.[5]

This Bentley did, in a characteristically original way. He wrote a Latin *Letter to Mill* that has often been celebrated as the beginning of modern classical scholarship—and that had little to do with its ostensible Byzantine subject. Malalas's references to classical writers and events often looked foolish to a classicist's eye. At

2 Nikephoros's notes are preserved in Bodleian Library, MS Barocci 142. See N. G. Wilson, "The Autograph of Nicephorus Callistus Xanthopoulos," *JTS* 25.2 (1974): 437–42; see more generally *Ecclesiastical History and Nikephoros Kallistou Xanthopoulos: Proceedings of the International Symposium, Vienna, 15th–16th December 2011*, ed. C. Gastgeber and S. Panteghini (Vienna, 2015). For the rediscovery of Nikephoros's history, see C. Gastgeber, "Die Kirchengeschichte des Nikephoros Kallistos Xanthopoulos: Ihre Entdeckung und Verwendung in der Zeit der Reformation," *OKS* 58.2 (2009): 237–47. On the explicit citation of sources as a distinctive characteristic of ecclesiastical history, see A. D. Momigliano, "Pagan and Christian Historiography in the Fourth Century A.D.," in *The Conflict between Paganism and Christianity in the Fourth Century*, ed. Momigliano (Oxford, 1963), 79–99.

3 See *DBDI*, s.v. "Barozzi, Francesco" (G. Spiazzi).

4 Bodleian Library, MS Barocci 182, fol. 1r: *Vide fol. 106. Chronici Alexandrini, ubi haec et sequentia habentur.*

5 K. Haugen, *Richard Bentley: Poetry and Enlightenment* (Cambridge, MA, 2011), 81–83.

one point he mentioned three tragedians: Themis, whom he dated to the time of the Trojan War, Minos, and Auleas. "I know nothing of these fantastic people," said Bentley, opening up a vein of contemptuous humor that would become endemic to classical scholarship.[6] It was the work of a moment for him to replace these inappropriate names with Themis, Ion, and Aeschylus. Bentley then proceeded, in a series of short essays, to rewrite the chronology of Greek drama, which he tied to Athens and to the sixth and fifth centuries. Here and elsewhere, Malalas played the butt of Bentley's pedantic humor. When the chronicler identified Stestichorus and Bacchylides as inventors of the dance, for example, Bentley was at his most jocose: "Say what? . . . May I ask, you most lazy of men, did you never peruse the Sacred Scriptures? Is there not frequent mention of dancing long, long before Stestichorus was born? So? Did you never look at Homer?"[7] Bentley himself, as Kristine Haugen has shown, would soon abandon this sort of polyhistoric, bibliographical scholarship—and late Greek texts like that of Malalas—to concentrate on the textual and literary criticism of Latin poetry. But he provided an attractive model for others. For centuries to come, classicists would look on late Greek and Byzantine writers—as on the "cathedral builders" who were their counterparts in the Latin world—as of interest only when they copied or quoted older texts that had been lost. Bentley, it was said, treated his manuscripts as roughly as he did the fellows of his college, Trinity. He treated late Greek texts more roughly than either of them—and classical scholars followed his example until living memory. A sign of the times is the index of authors, provided for readers who—like Bentley—wanted only Malalas's quotations, not his own words.[8]

Yet the coin, as Haugen points out, had its other side.[9] The Oxford scholar Humphrey Hody composed a lengthy introduction to the text, in which he made clear its composite character and argued at length about its date. He listed all the parallels to the *Paschal Chronicle*.[10] Mill, moreover, made clear that he too thought the text had much to offer those who took an interest in the world it came from. Scholars across Europe, after all, now agreed that the world of the Eastern Roman Empire—and its historians in particular—deserved and rewarded study. In 1648—the year when Chilmead was expelled by the Parliamentarians from his post in Oxford—the Jesuit Philippe Labbe published a detailed review of the historians of Byzantium.

6 Bentley, quoted in ibid., 87.

7 Bentley, quoted in ibid., 97.

8 "Index autorum a Jo. Malala citatorum," in *Joannis Anticheni cognomento Malalae Historia chronica* (Oxford, 1691), sig. [*******8r–v].

9 Haugen, *Bentley*, 83.

10 Humphrey Hody, "Prolegomena," in ibid., sigs. *r–[*******7v].

"All scholars," he wrote with slightly exaggerated confidence, "love and cultivate Byzantine history. Its eventful history arouses wonder, its variety causes pleasure, and its duration—just short of that of Old Rome—inspires respect. Naturally, they eagerly seek out the books that contain it."[11] True, Labbe admitted that these collectors' desire outran performance. "For the most part, their empty bookshelves have waited in vain. The majority of those noble historians are still in dusty manuscripts, struggling with bookworms and moths."[12] Since 1648, however, the Louvre corpus of Byzantine histories had made much of this canon accessible. Access to texts, in turn, enabled new forms of study. Mill made clear that he knew and used these new tools of Byzantine scholarship. His edition includes a list of "words and expressions employed by Malalas that are barbarous, or used in a novel sense, which do not appear in Charles Du Cange's recently published *Glossary of Medieval and Later Greek*."[13] The 1691 Malalas was interdisciplinary, but—like all too many modern collaborations—only in the sense that distinct disciplines had been applied to the same project.

The banns for the marriage that ended in 1691 had been announced long before—longer, in fact, than is usually realized. The Latin West always had its fragments of Byzantine historical writing. In the early Middle Ages and again in the fourteenth century and after, debates about doctrine and authority in the church were fierce, and history—apparently reliable history—played a prominent role. In order to provide a continuation to Eusebius's *Church History*, which left off before the great series of late antique ecclesiastical controversies began, Cassiodorus commissioned and Epiphanius carried out a Latin translation of selected materials from an epitome of three fifth-century Byzantine church historians—Socrates, Sozomen, and Theodoret—made by Theodore the Lector. Manuscripts made clear the sources of this so-called *Historia Tripartita*, which engaged the interest of learned Latins for centuries.[14]

The traffic between late Palaiologan Byzantium and the Latin West—the human and literary traffic that brought teachers and clerics, books and methods across the Mediterranean from the late fourteenth century onward—made Byzantine histories available. By the 1440s, as we will see, Leonardo Bruni had produced a work on the Italian Wars of Justinian and Belisarius largely translated from the Greek of Procopius. Cristopher Persona soon made a full version.

11 P. Labbe, *De Byzantinae historiae scriptoribus*, 2nd ed. (Venice, 1729), sig. * iij r.

12 Ibid.

13 J. Mill, *Index vocum & dictionum quarundam barbararum aut novatae significationis, a Joanna Malala usurpatarum, quae in Caroli Dufresnii Glossario Graecitatis mediae & infimae, novissime edito, non reperiuntur*, in Malalas, *Historia* (unpaginated).

14 J. O'Donnell, *Cassiodorus* (Berkeley, 1979), chap. 6.

But the first prominent sign of change—as Agostino Pertusi pointed out in his still essential survey of the subject—was a now forgotten work by a largely forgotten scholar, Angelo Cospo. In 1517 a Venetian press brought out, posthumously, his translation of two books of Diodorus Siculus that dealt with Philip and Alexander. Casting about for supplementary materials, Cospo explained in his dedication, he had found a chronicle by one John the Monk—Zonaras—which offered the only detailed account he had ever seen of imperial history through the time of Alexios Komnenos. More remarkable still, this history was uniquely full. Ancient writers had ignored or insulted Christians and omitted the miracles, martyrdoms, heresies, and conciliar decrees that made up their history. "This monk," by contrast, "goes through all of these so clearly and seriously that we do not know what inspired him in passing, or what inspired him principally, to write: the affairs of the Roman rulers or the varied condition of the Church of Christ."[15] Cospo planned to produce a Latin rendering of the whole text. Here, for the first time, a humanist not only praised a Byzantine historian but noted his particular quality: his willingness, presumably the result of his career, to combine the genres of secular and ecclesiastical history. Unfortunately, all Cospo managed to translate was what Zonaras had to say about Alexander, which came, unbeknownst to him, from Plutarch. But something new was happening.

It was no accident that Cospo dedicated his book and described his plan to the Holy Roman emperor Maximilian: at the end of his life he left Bologna for Vienna. In the Holy Roman Empire, the history of the empire—eastern as well as western—mattered. And it was in the north that Byzantine historians began to be studied and translated in a more systematic way. From Melanchthon on, German Protestant scholars took a strong interest in the history of the Roman Empire. They tried to fit its history, eastern and western, to the prophecy of the Four Empires in the book of Daniel. They worried about the Ottoman Turks, both eschatologically—the sultan, they thought, might be the Antichrist, though a strong majority held out for the pope—and politically, especially after Süleyman besieged Vienna in 1529. And they began to use and debate Byzantine sources systematically.[16] So did Catholics. Johann Cuspinian, for example, published in 1540 a detailed history of the Roman emperors

15 Angelo Cospo, ded. to Diodorus Siculus, *Libri duo*, trans. Cospo (Venice, 1517), sig. [AA iiir]. In addition to A. Pertusi, *Storiografia umanistica e mondo bizantino*, Istituto siciliano di studi bizantini e neoellenici, quaderni 5 (Palermo, 1967), see the review of early scholarship in A. Savvides, *The Beginnings and Foundations of Byzantine Studies: A Survey with a Bibliographical Appendix* (Athens, 2018), 59–75, and the very recent and informative study by B. Croke, "Procopius, from Manuscripts to Books: 1400–1850," *Histos* supplement 9.1 (2019): 11–73, which ranges more widely than its title indicates.

16 See the full treatment in A. Ben-Tov, *Lutheran Humanists and Greek Antiquity: Melanchthonian Scholarship between Universal History and Pedagogy* (Leiden, 2009), 83–131.

from the beginnings to his own day, juxtaposing eastern and western emperors. Drawing information from Zonaras and later writers, he offered rich information about palace intrigues and much more.[17] Cuspinian had much to say about the early history of the Ottomans.[18]

Northern collections of Greek texts began to grow, not only in Vienna. The wealthy mercantile and manufacturing city of Augsburg bought 100 Greek manuscripts from Antonios Eparchos in 1544, for its own public library. Hans Dernschwam, a former employee of the Fugger, turned up in Augsburg eleven years later after a lively career managing copper mines for the Fugger in Hungary and traveling to Constantinople with a diplomatic party sent by the future emperor Ferdinand I. He brought with him three bulky Greek manuscripts, now in Munich, which contained the histories of Zonaras and Choniates. Texts mattered: two published catalogs would make clear how rich Augsburg became in Greek manuscripts.

But people mattered more. In 1551, Hieronymus Wolf, an expert on classical Greek oratory who had studied with Melanchthon himself, became Johann Jakob Fugger's Latin secretary and librarian.[19] Once the codices of Zonaras arrived, Wolf found himself assigned the task of making a translation. Soon he formalized the marriage that Bentley would dissolve. He did not serve willingly. Wolf was unusually self-obsessed, even for a scholar.[20] His autobiography gives a sense of his character:

> I go to see no one except when I am called for or forced to do so: no one comes to see me, except if someone needs my help.... Hence I learn too late what everyone in town has known for long. Children are born to many, they fall ill and die, some marry.... But since they tell me nothing, I know what happens to them no better than what happens beyond the pillars of Hercules. And so, in this swarming city in the midst of its hustle and bustle,

17 Johannes Cuspinian, *De caesaribus atque imperatoribus Romanis opus insigne* (Basel, 1561).

18 M. Meserve, *Empires of Islam in Renaissance Historical Thought* (Cambridge, MA, 2008), 241.

19 See in general F. Husner, "Die Editio Princeps des 'Corpus Historiae Byzantinae': Johannes Oporin, Hieronymus Wolf und die Fugger," in *Festschrift Karl Schwarber; Beiträge zur schweizerischen Bibliotheks-, Buch- und Gelehrtengeschichte: Zum 60. Geburtstag am 22. November 1949 dargebracht* (Basel, 1949), 143–62.

20 See the marvelous study by G. Algazi, "Food for Thought: Hieronymus Wolf Grapples with the Scholarly Habitus," in *Egodocuments in History: Autobiographical Writing in Its Social Context since the Middle Ages*, ed. R. Dekker (Hilversum, 2002), 21–44, as well as V. Jung, "Die Leiden des Hieronymus Wolf: Krankengeschichten eines Gelehrten im 16. Jahrhundert," *Historische Anthropologie* 9.3 (2001): 333–57, and, for the wider context, A. D. Nuttall, *Dead from the Waist Down: Scholars and Scholarship in Literature and the Popular Imagination* (New Haven, 2011).

> I lead the life of an anchorite. . . . I don't visit the sick since there is nothing I can do to help them.[21]

Wolf found plenty of reasons not to welcome his commission. As a student of the classics, he had to adapt to Zonaras's "monastic style" and his Greek wordiness, which required many omissions to produce a reasonable Latin version.[22] He also found it hard to decipher the manuscripts "because of their script, which though very elegant was also very hard to read, because of those far-fetched abbreviations and the effort to write prettily, which is the source of many errors. For it is easy to switch letters, which, though in other respects they are not dissimilar, have a totally different force."[23] And when he finished it—characteristically, he compared himself to a more successful Sisyphus, who had rolled his stone to the top of the hill—his reward was to be assigned to render Niketas Choniates and then Nikephoros Gregoras into Latin as well. As he recalled, "[In 1558] I finished the Nikephoros Gregoras, not because I wanted the money—it was 100 guilders—but because I did not wish to offend my patron."[24] It probably came as a relief when he found that

21 Wolf's autobiography, *Commentariolus, coeptus quidem scribi anno 1564 sed aliquot annis post demum absolutus, de vitae suae ratione, ac potius fortuna*, magnificently edited and translated into German by Helmut Zäh (2013), is available, along with Wolf's letters, in an online edition (http://mateo.uni-mannheim.de/cera/autoren/wolf_cera.html). For this passage, see 37–38.

22 Hieronymus Wolf, in Zonaras, *Historia imperatorum Romanorum a Constantino Magno, qui primus imperii sedem et dignitatem ex urbe Roma ac Italia in Orientem atque Constantinopolim transtulit, usque ad Constantinum postremum & Constantinopolim a Turcis occupatam, continua serie rerum ac temporum exposita a quatuor Scriptoribus Graecis, latinitate ab Hieronymo Vvolfio donatis*... (Frankfurt, 1578), sig. a3v: *Nunc etiam de stylo autoris nonnihil est dicendum, qui cum non unius sit generis & formae, sed pro varietate autorum, e quibus haec petita sunt, & ipse variet, in ultimo Tomo praesertim, qua aetate Graeca pariter & Romana lingua degeneravit: eruditi homines in eo nonnihil desiderabunt. Desideravi & ipse nonnihil, parsimoniam inprimis Demosthenicae orationis, quae meo palato longe fuit gratior, & ad convertendum non tantum iucundior, sed etiam facilior: utut alijs difficilis videatur, & mea tenuitate superior. Nam in hoc autore multae sunt, aut mihi certe esse videntur, περισσολογίαι, quae ut Graecum sermonem suo quodam genio saepe non infeliciter lascivientem deceant: Latinis auribus multo severioribus, nisi multum ego fallor, permolestae futurae erant. eaque de causa, ubi citra sententiae detrimentum fieri potuit, a me alicubi praetermissae sunt. idque cum non tam mea sponte, quam monitu doctissimorum virorum IOACHIMI CAMERARII ET LVDOVICI CARINI fecerim, me facile viris doctis probaturum confido.* The *Historia imperatorum* was Wolf's second edition of Zonaras. The work was first published in his Basel 1557 edition, under the title *Compendium historiarum*.

23 Wolf in Zonaras, *Historia imperatorum*, sigs. a3v–[a4r]: *Nam ut de conversionis ipsius aerumnis taceam, quantum difficultatis in ipsa lectione fuit? ob characteres elegantissimos illos quidem, sed lectu difficillimos, propter affectata illa scribendi compendia, &c. τῆς καλλιγραφίας studium, unde infinita errata oriuntur, ex facili notarum mutatione: quae cum alicubi non dissimiles sint, vim diversissimam habent. Vnde factum, ut quemadmodum Plutarchus se Latina verba ex cognitione rerum assequutum profitetur: ita ego saepe de veritate lectionis ex sensu & constructione divinare sim coactus, ratione plane praepostera. Nam & verba rerum, & literae verborum notae ut essent, sunt inventae.*

24 Wolf, *Commentariolus*, ed. Zäh, 77.

instead of translating Chalkokondyles himself, he could polish an earlier Latin version by Conrad Clauser.

What Wolf began, complaining all the way, would be continued in many of the centers of the Republic of Letters—especially, though not only, in the empire. In Augsburg itself Wolf's pupil David Hoeschel put out a series of important editions from the press *Ad insigne pinus* funded by his patron, Markus Welser: the *Bibliotheca* of Photios, the *Excerpta de legationibus* of Constantine Porphyrogennetos, and the *Alexiad* of Anna Komnene.[25] In Leiden, Joseph Scaliger, who dominated not only the thrusting and innovative university where he held his chair but much of the north European world of learning, encouraged his colleague Bonaventura Vulcanius, who edited Agathias. When Vulcanius went off the boil, Scaliger helped and encouraged Hoeschel.[26] Rising interest in the history of the Goths spurred Hugo Grotius and others to work on Byzantine sources.[27] Soon Jesuits, Benedictines, jurists, and others began to collaborate, first in Munich and then, with help from laymen as well, on the great series of editions printed at the Louvre Press between 1648 and 1711, the first really comprehensive corpus of Byzantine historians.

At what point in these developments—it seems reasonable to ask—did scholars begin to regard Byzantine historiography, and Byzantine studies more generally, as separate from the study of Greek texts? Clearly Wolf saw the Byzantine scholarship he carried out for pay as different from the classical scholarship he did for love. Yet his first efforts to define his enterprise seem fairly laudatory. After completing his translation of Zonaras, he wrote to his patron in 1556 that the Byzantine historian had set out to create what he called a "discipline" of history, by gathering "members and parts" scattered in many volumes "into a sort of single body" (*in unum quoddam corpus*).[28] In 1557, writing the dedication to his translation of Niketas Choniates,

25 See J. Bellot, "*Ad insigne pinus*: Kulturgeschichte der Reichsstadt Augsburg im Spiegel einer Verlages an der Wende des 16./17. Jahrhunderts," *Buchhandelsgeschichte* 14 (1978): B 697–B 709, and M. Völkel, "Von Augsburg nach Paris, von Oporin zu Cramoisy: Die reichsstädtische Byzantinistik und die europäische Respublica litteraria in der Frühen Neuzeit," in *Humanismus und Renaissance in Augsburg: Kulturgeschichte einer Stadt Zwischen Spätmittelalter und Dreissigjährigem Krieg*, ed. G. M. Müller, Frühe Neuzeit 144 (Berlin, 2010), 293–308.

26 D. van Miert, "Project Procopius: Scaliger, Vulcanius, Hoeschelius and the Pursuit of Early Byzantine History," in *Bonaventura Vulcanius, Works and Networks: Brugge 1538–Leiden 1614*, ed. H. Cazes (Leiden, 2010), 361–86; Croke, "Procopius," 57–74.

27 Croke, "Procopius," 94–104.

28 Wolf, ep. ded. to Zonaras, in *Historia Imperatorum*, sig. a3r: *Cuius rei Zonaras noster exempla pene innumera, in postremo Tomo praesertim (absque quo si esset, posteriorum imperatorum res gestas magna ex parte ignoraremus) compendio proponit: in quo etsi alij alia desiderare possunt (quis enim satisfaciat omnibus?) tamen conatus eius egregius atque institutum praeclarum fuit, certam quandam historiae quasi disciplinam constituendi, & dispersa in plurimis voluminibus membra & partes eius, in unum quoddam corpus redigendi: ea moderatione adhibita, ut instar lauti magis quam copiosi*

Wolf remarked that Choniates, "a man not only of high distinction in his own time, but also outstanding in intellect and erudition, and, in my view, dedicated to true history, follows Zonaras, in an order that is both very fitting and most useful to readers. This order, since it adds and connects the events that follow to those that preceded it, creates a sort of corpus of history."[29] A complete and perfect corpus of Byzantine history: Wolf seems to have liked this phrase, which reappeared on the title page of his collected translations. And it certainly had an impact. Gradually, Wolf's chosen term "Byzantine" replaced "East Roman" and other terms as the accepted title for the history and literature of the eastern empire.

Yet as Wolf almost certainly knew, he was not the first to argue that a comprehensive history or set of histories—one that covered a long time span and brought together events across the earth—was especially instructive. The Rostock professor David Chytraeus, a fellow student of Melanchthon, gave lectures on how to study history, which eventually transformed themselves into manuals. "The marvelous goodness of God," he reflected, "brought it about, that at almost the very moment where the prophetic history [of the Old Testament] runs out, Herodotus of Halicarnassus begins his history."[30] Thucydides, he noted, "follows directly on the trail of Herodotus"; and where Herodotus explored monarchies, Thucydides analyzed cities. Xenophon in turn followed Thucydides, and so on.[31] He made clear that God, who had provided a complete history, expected humans to read it in order: "God wishes us to read the principal writers, who have traced the records of the greatest events and the continuous history of the world from the Creation down to our

---

continuatoris, optima potius quam plurima apponeret, nec convivas cum fastidio dimitteret, sed ita affectos, ut Timotheum de Platone dixisse ferunt, coenas eius etiam postridie delectare. [Printed marginal note: *Zonaras Synopsin sive corpus quoddam historiarum edere voluit.*] *Delegit enim sibi non omnium, sed praecipuarum gentium historias: neque eas omnes, sed vel praecipuas duntaxat, vel eas quae ad Ecclesiae seriem perspiciendam facere videbantur, consilio iudicioque suo. quod sive probarit, sive non probarit omnibus: hoc illi cum multis, illud cum paucissimis scriptoribus, ne dicam nullis, commune erit.* Note that in 1557 Wolf titled Zonaras's work *Compendium historiarum* (see n. 22 above).

29 Wolf, ep. ded. to Choniates, in *Historia imperatorum*, sig. A2r: *Zonaram tuum, Vir amplissime, CHONIATES sequitur, homo sua aetate non tantum magnis dignitatibus ornatus, sed etiam ingenio & multiplici doctrina praestans, & veritatis historiae (ut mihi videtur) ubique studiosus, ordine aptissimo & lectoribus utilissimo: qui ordo cum sequentia ijs quae antecessere adiungat atque annectat, historiae quoddam quasi corpus absolvit, & in suo genere homines eruditos reddit.* On the title page of the 1557 edition Wolf notes that Choniates' work starts from the year *in quo Zonaras desinit.*

30 David Chytraeus, *De lectione historiarum recte instituenda*, in *Artis historicae penus*, ed. Johannes Wolf, 2 vols. (Basel, 1579), 2:471–72: *Miranda autem & ingenti bonitate Dei factum est, ut fere in eo ipso momento, ubi prophetica historia desinit, Herodotus Halicarnassaeus . . . suam historiam ordiatur.*

31 Ibid., 472–73.

times."[32] Here as elsewhere, Chytraeus followed Melanchthon. As he started to read his way through the Basel 1549 edition of the Greek historian Polybius, Melanchthon reflected, following Polybius himself, "that historical knowledge yields its greatest fruits if we mentally grasp the body (*corpus*) of events, so to speak, and contemplate their full order."[33] In describing the Byzantine historians in the same terms, Wolf was claiming, in effect, that they offered as complete and instructive a picture of East Rome and its world as the Greek and Latin historians did of Greece and Rome.

Wolf and his colleagues, moreover, made the same arguments in their prefaces that they might have advanced in prefaces to classical texts. Conrad Clauser, the country schoolmaster outside Zurich who first translated Laonikos Chalkokondyles into Latin, argued in 1544 that the author "places graphically before our eyes" what happened when the "eastern church fought with the western, and religious concord could not be established between them: the Turk attacked the disputants, and conquered the head or metropolis of the eastern empire and added it to his own."[34] Modern Christians, he insisted, must restore the ancient military discipline that had given them power during the Crusades. Reading Chalkokondyles and other historians who described the Crusades and the Turkish way of war would provide "excellent counsels and examples" for the leader of an expedition against them.[35] The blurb for a late edition of Hieronymus Wolf's translations of Zonaras, Gregoras, and others made a similar point, though more generally: "This work includes remarkable changes in the empire and various struggles in the church that are quite like our

32 David Chytraeus, *Chronologia historiae Herodoti & Thucydidis* (Strasbourg, 1563), sig. Bv: *Vult Deus legi a nobis praecipuos scriptores, qui maximarum rerum memoriam & continuam Mundi historiam a prima conditione ad nostra usque tempora deduxerunt.*

33 Melanchthon, note in his copy of Polybius, *Historiarum libri priores quinque* (Basel, 1549), Princeton University Library (EX) 2018-0009Q, 2: *Maximus fructus ex historiae cognitione percipitur si rerum gestarum quasi corpus animo complectamur et totam* οἰκονομίαν *aspiciamus.* Melanchthon was ruminating on Polybius 1.4.7–9: Polybius uses the metaphor of the body in 1.4.7.

34 Laonikos Chalkokondyles, *De origine et rebus gestis Turcorum libri decem*, trans. Conrad Clauser (Basel, 1556), 21: *Haec omnia graphice ob oculos nobis ponit Nicolaus Calchocondiles. Nam (ut ipse perhibet) cum orientalis ecclesia cum occidentali contenderet, & nulla inter utranque posset constitui concordia in religionis causa, dissidentibus supervenit Turcus, & caput sive metropolim orientalis imperij expugnat & suo imperio adiungit. Idem quoque author demonstrabit, quomodo ante captam Constantinopolim Graecorum regum & principum discordia Turcum in Europam exciverit: necnon patefaciet, quid porro in Europa molitus sit. Ex eodem autore patebit corrupta disciplina militaris Graecorum multis exemplis.*

35 Ibid., 15: *Hic* [Germany's chosen war leader] *praeter alias historias, quae stratagematum & consiliorum subitorum magnam praebent copiam, legerit Robertum Monachum, Gulielmum Tyrium, Nicolaum Calchocondilem, & alios scriptores, qui res Turcicas persequuti sunt. Hinc poterit se informare egregijs consilijs & exemplis, dum videt quid maioribus nostris in diversis & varijs Turcicis expeditionibus vel profuerit, vel obfuerit. Quicquid casus obtulerit, semper habebit exemplum aut consilium, quo se referat, ne aliquem errorem in re militari commitat: ubi non facile est invenire errori remedium.*

present ones, and therefore are as necessary as they are pleasant to read now."[36] Like their ancient counterparts, in other words, Byzantine historians were presented as writers of exemplar history: so far as the scholars who edited and translated them were concerned, they offered examples and counsels from the past that could be applied directly to the present.

By the middle of the sixteenth century, a fair number of Byzantine historians had become available, whether in the Greek manuscripts to which the luckiest and most skillful scholars gained access or in translations into Latin and the vernacular.[37] Critical discussion began to take place. In 1566 the French jurist Jean Bodin brought out his *Method for the Easy Comprehension of History*. This was a comprehensive guide to historical literature, eastern and western, African and American. Like many sixteenth-century students of the Roman law, Bodin had ceased to see the *Corpus iuris civilis* as an eternally valid body of legal argument and decrees. It was a Byzantine product, appropriate only to the Eastern Roman Empire. Each nation, he argued, should draw on laws and histories from around the world to develop a legal code of its own, which fit its origins and the qualities that climate and countryside had imposed on it. Bodin set few limits on the literature that he saw as relevant to this enterprise: for example, he studied the Talmud, the Jewish law code, which Catholic authorities had burned in public in 1553 and after. And he insisted that the jurist must master history, as well as formal laws, in order to understand why the latter were made and whether they functioned well. His *Method for the Easy Comprehension of History* guided the reader to materials from the ancient Near East and modern Africa as well as ancient Greece and Rome and modern Europe.[38]

As a Roman lawyer, Bodin was well acquainted with Justinian and his world. Yet he did not try to impose a special identity on Byzantine texts from Justinian's time and after. In the rich universal bibliography of historians that concluded Bodin's book, Greek history began with Herodotus—more precisely, with Dares and Dictys—and ended with Niketas Choniates. Bodin argued at length that Procopius—though prone to error and given to silly extremes of flattery toward

36 Zonaras, *Historia Imperatorum*, title page: *Opus complectens et insignes in imperio mutationes, et varia Ecclesiae certamina praesentibus haud dissimilia, ideoque hoc tempore non minus lectu necessarium, quam iucundum, Dum quibus de causis florentissimum Orientis Imperium conciderit quibusque dissidiis Ecclesia distracta lacerataque sit, ostendit, animos eorum, qui cum ad Reip. gubernacula sedent, tum vero Ecclesijs praesunt, utilissimo exemplo ab intestinis aemulationibus atque dissidiis ad mutuae coniunctionis & amicitiae studium revocat. In gratiam & utilitatem omnium veritatis amantium nunc denuo editum.*

37 For a case in point, see the impressive list in Croke, "Procopius," 144–57.

38 See, e.g., J. Franklin, *Jean Bodin and the Sixteenth-Century Revolution in the Methodology of Law and History* (New York, 1963); A. Grafton, *What Was History? The Art of History in Renaissance Europe* (2007; repr., Cambridge, 2012).

Belisarius—was an excellent historian, much more reliable than his Renaissance successor Pietro Bembo. His argument moved on more than one line of attack. The first was already traditional. When Leonardo Bruni translated Procopius's *Wars* 5–8 into Latin, he made clear that he saw Procopius not as a colleague but only as an eyewitness to events: "I have taken only my knowledge of events from Procopius . . . and departed from him in every other respect. He has only one good quality: he was present during this war. The rest of his work is despicable."[39] Bodin agreed that Procopius, though no stylist, was a useful eyewitness source: "He was the constant companion of Belisarius in his enterprises, and took part in all public deliberations."[40]

But Bodin found another, quite different, reason to trust Procopius. Byzantine readers had already noted that his histories quoted a good many letters, as well as speeches. Some marked these in the margins of their texts, while others made collections of documentary extracts.[41] In 1492, the most brilliant forger of the Renaissance, Giovanni Nanni or Annius of Viterbo, had argued that modern readers should give their trust not to Greek historians like Herodotus and Thucydides, who wrote whatever they wanted to and regularly lied, but to Near Eastern historians like Berosus and Manetho. Though fragmentarily preserved, their works showed that they had worked as official "notaries" of their kingdoms, drawing on official chronicles and archival records.[42] Bodin believed that Procopius deserved credence because he too had preserved original documents: "Since he copies individual letters, decrees, treaties and speeches in a range of genres and styles, he provides strong proof that he is a very truthful historian."[43] Yet he also noted that Procopius committed a range of errors, from praising Belisarius to excess and trying to excuse his crimes to claiming that ash from the eruption of Vesuvius in 472 CE had reached Byzantium, frightening its inhabitants so much that they began to pray for safety from the volcano every

39 Leonardo Bruni, *Epistolarum libri VIII*, ed. L. Mehus, 2 vols. (Florence, 1741), 2:157: *eodem item modo ipse noticiam tantum rerum gestarum de illo sumens, in ceteris omnibus ab eo recessi, utpote qui hoc unum habeat boni, quod bello interfuit. Cetera illius sunt spernenda.* See Croke, "Procopius," 13–27, esp. 19, and G. Ianziti, "Bruni on Writing History," *RenQ* 51.2 (1998): 367–91.

40 Jean Bodin, *Methodus ad facilem historiarum cognitionem*, ed. and trans. Sara Miglietti (Pisa, 2013), 206: *At Bembi omnino dissimilis est Procopius, qui ornamenta historiarum et Graeci sermonis puritatem aut nescisse, aut neglexisse videtur: sed quae ad historiarum pertinent singula commemorat, ac res quoque levissimas magno studio consectatur, et quoniam in rebus gerendis perpetuus Belisarii comes, ac totius publici consilii particeps fuit, saepius etiam pro Republica legationes obiit; denique mediocriter est a doctrina informatus, non dubitem illum inter selectos recensere.*

41 Croke, "Procopius," 11.

42 See most recently A. Grafton, "Matthew Parker: The Book as Archive," *History of Humanities* 2.1 (2017): 45.

43 Bodin, *Methodus*, 206: *cum vero singulas epistolas, decreta, foedera, conciones vario dicendi genere ac stilo describit, magnum verissimi scriptoris praebet argumentum.*

year.[44] Accounts of prodigies like this one, Bodin commented, "give off the scent of Greek vanity, and have often cost not only profane historians but ecclesiastical ones their credibility."[45]

At this point, Bodin had in mind a current scholarly debate about the credibility of ecclesiastical historians. In 1553 Johannes Lange published a Latin translation of the *Ecclesiastical History* of Nikephoros Kallistos Xanthopoulos—the very book from which Melanchthon plucked the description of the appearance of Jesus that he entered in his Bible. Lange presented the text enthusiastically, as a well-organized and accurate epitome of the older ecclesiastical histories by Eusebius and his successors.[46] The Protestant church historian Flacius Illyricus, eagerly gathering materials for his own project to create a massive, source-based history of the church, came across this newly published text. Perhaps Caspar von Nidbruck, also an imperial councillor and one of Flacius's most diligent suppliers of material, called his attention to it.[47] One passage in particular caught Flacius's eye: book 12, chapter 34, where Nikephoros argued, giving many examples, that the early Christians had followed a wide variety of customs, rather than a single law, in their rituals and liturgies, "and that did no harm to true piety."[48] Flacius enthusiastically cited this passage in his *Catalogus testium veritatis,* noting that it seemed to refute "the pope and his spirituals, who reject and demolish the commands of God with their little human traditions."[49]

Not everyone was so enthusiastic. Whether the *casus belli* was Nikephoros's account of custom, his account of the face of Jesus, or something else, I do not know, but a scholar known for his learning soon dismissed both Josephus and Nikephoros, claiming that the latter offered "oxcarts full of nonsense and blasphemy."[50] François

44 Ibid.: *nisi quod suum Belisarium saepius quam decuit, et ineptis plerunque laudibus oneravit: ineptius quoque caedem Constantiani, qui apud Iustinianum stabuli magistrum egit, Belisarii iussu perpetratam ita excusavit, ut in fatis esse diceret Constantianum sic mori debuisse: ridicule quoque xxx. porcorum et statuae Theodorici coniecturas eximo: quodque Thulen decies Britannia maiorem facit, quae tamen altero tanto minor est. Sed illud fidem omnium superat: cineres Vesuvii montis, qui citra Neapolim situs est; Bizantium usque delatas, ac populum ita exterritum, ut annuis supplicationibus Deum placaret.*

45 Ibid., 206–8: *quae prodigia sapiunt Graecam vanitatem, et historicis non modo prophanis, verumetiam ecclesiasticis fidem saepe derogarunt.*

46 Lange, ep. ded. to Nikephoros Kallistos Xanthopoulos, *Ecclesiasticae historiae libri decem & octo* (n. 1 above), ed. Lange, 5–6.

47 Gastgeber, "Die Kirchengeschichte" (n. 2 above), 245–46.

48 Nikephoros Kallistos Xanthopoulos, *Ecclesiasticae historiae libri decem & octo*, ed. Lange, 631–34, quotation at 631: *Neque id verae pietati detrimento fuit.*

49 Matthias Flacius Illyricus, *Catalogus testium veritatis* (Basel, 1556), 930bis–931bis.

50 François Baudouin, *De Institutione historiae universae et eius cum iurisprudentia coniunctione προλεγομένων libri ii* (Paris, 1561), 45: *audio nuper hominem alioqui eruditum publice scripsisse,*

Baudouin, a lawyer like Bodin, disagreed: he argued sharply in 1561 that "there is nothing to criticize in Nikephoros that is not also to be criticized in Eusebius."[51] But Bodin agreed with the critic: "Nicephorus Callistus is full of fables of this kind, and Zonaras, in other respects a solid historian, and Nikephoros Gregoras often take pleasure in them: and sometimes Eusebius of Caesarea does the same."[52] As an example, he cited a miracle reported by Eusebius in his *Ecclesiastical History* (7.18.2). Here—as in his bibliography—Bodin treated Byzantine sources not as a separate, late branch of the Greek tradition of historical writing but as an integral part of it. Late Byzantine writers could shed light backward on Eusebius. All of them, for Bodin, belonged to the same historical tradition—one in which genre borders were sometimes crossed and individual writers could not be assessed simply as credible or worthless.

Byzantine history, moreover, was meant to be studied in the same way as any other form of history: by commonplacing. In 1564 Wolf brought out with Oporinus in Basel what he called *Suidae historica*—"The Histories of Suidas"—a Latin translation of the tenth-century *Suda* lexicon.[53] As always, the enterprise proved harder than expected. Wolf had to give the printer his drafts, which made it impossible to check the proofs properly. The title page promised an alphabetical index. But as Wolf explained in a note inscribed in a copy he gave to a friend, Johannes Maior,

> The index wasn't made, and the work itself was so badly printed in many passages that I couldn't understand my translation unless I could check the Greek. The reason was the plague, which was then raging in Oporinus's house, and which meant that the best workers were not available. The same plague, creeping around the area and even in my house, worried me, but with God's help I was saved.[54]

Iosephum esse referendum inter scriptores deliros & fabulosos: Nicephorique historiam Ecclesiasticam nihil aliud quam plaustra ineptiarum & blasphemiarum.

51 Ibid.: *Et quid tandem reprehendere in Nicephoro possunt, quod non possint in ipso Eusebio?*

52 Bodin, *Methodus*, 208: *Plenus est eiusmodi fabulis Nicephorus Callistus, quibus etiam Zonaras, alioqui probatus historicus, et Nicephorus Gregoras saepe delectantur: ac interdum Eusebius Caesariensis: cuiusmodi est illud quod se vidisse omni asseveratione confirmat: Plantam in basi qua nitebatur aenea Christi statua (quam ante annos CCC. foemina sanguinis profluvio curata SERVATORI dicarat) sponte natam, quae cumprimum extremam statuae vestem attigisset, omnia morborum genera curabat.*

53 *Suidae historica, caeteraque omnia quae ulla ex parte ad cognitionem rerum spectant*, ed. and trans. Hieronymus Wolf (Basel, 1564; 2nd ed., Basel, 1581).

54 *Suidae historica* (1564), Augsburg Staats- und Stadtbibliothek 2 LG 341, manuscript note on title page: *Non est factum* [sc. Index]*: & ipsum opus ita mendose excusum: ut multis in locis conversionem meam (inquit W+) (nisi pa[ginae] Graecae ad manum essent) non intelligerem. In causa fuit grassans tunc in aedibus Oporini pestilentia, optimis quibusque operarijs e medio sublatis. Eadem lues in vicinia atque adeo in aedibus meis serpens, solicitum me habuit,* ἀλλ' ἐσώθημεν σὺν θεῷ.

But the hardships had all been worthwhile. Wolf praised the text to the skies for its organization: it arranged a vast amount of material in alphabetical order, making it easy to memorize. True, all this well-organized information served as a reproach to Wolf himself:

> I wish that this advice had been given to me when I was young, and that we had had as many books as we do now. What a treasury I would now have, of things that, as my mind was distracted by various studies, I have largely forgotten, and can't be sought out without trouble and wasted time, and sometimes not at all. To confess the weakness of my own mind: sometimes, I not only don't remember what I have read and heard, but even doubt if I have ever read or heard them, and where. Though my books, with their margins full of annotations, refute these doubts. Hence if I had not relied too much on my memory in my youth, but rather had had regard for the long term, I could now come up with much more material, and more rapidly. This was written as a warning to the young.[55]

For students, though, it was a splendid example. As Ann Blair and others have shown, the sixteenth century was the golden age of commonplacing. Erasmus and the many other pedagogues gave detailed instructions on how to slice and dice a text into excerpts and store them under the proper headings.[56] Bodin himself did the same.[57] The *Suda* was not a Byzantine *Kunst- und Wunderkammer* but a classical model in its own right for scholarly learning.

Yet the *Suda* was also something more: a storehouse of lost texts. The editor of the first edition of the Greek text, Demetrios Chalkokondyles, had already noted that "the lexicon contains not only the most accurate interpretation of poetic and rhetorical terms and of those used by the most eloquent authors, but also many fine histories

55 *Suidae historica* (1581), 4–5: *Atque utinam & hoc qualecunque consilium adolescenti mihi datum, & ea copia optimorum librorum, quae nunc est, etiam tum fuisset. Quantam enim variae lectionis gazam nunc in promptu haberem, quae animo, varietate studiorum & occupationum distracto, bona ex parte exciderunt: nec sine molestia iacturaque temporis, cum opus est, inquirendae sunt, nec tamen semper repe- riuntur. Fit enim (ut imbecillitatem ingenij mei fatear) aliquando, ut non modo quod legi & audivi, non satis meminerim: sed illud etiam dubitem, an & ubi legerim atque audiverim? Quanquam hanc haesitationem meam, libri mei marginum annotationibus plerunque refellunt. Quod si adolescens memoria non nimis fretus fuissem, sed in longitudinem potius consuluissem: nunc multo essem promptior atque uberior, & minus occupatus. Et haec admonendae adolescentiae causa scripta sint.*

56 A. Blair, *Too Much to Know: Managing Scholarly Information before the Modern Age* (New Haven, 2010); H. Zedelmaier, *Werkstätten des Wissens zwischen Renaissance und Aufklärung* (Tübingen, 2015).

57 See Bodin, *Methodus*, 116, 118–40.

that it would not be easy to find elsewhere, since many of the books from which they were taken, that is Greek and Roman and Hebrew, have perished."[58] Wolf, who translated Chalkokondyles' preface into Latin, agreed. And he knew that it was by no means the only Byzantine text produced by rewriting older ones: he himself noted that Zonaras had produced the early sections of his history in much the same way.[59] Isaac Casaubon, similarly, noted on the title page of his working copy of Polybius that many uncollected fragments remained in the *Suda*.[60] Studying Byzantine texts, in other words, could yield dividends to classical scholars—just as Bentley still believed.

When Wolf—who became rector of the St. Anna Gymnasium in Augsburg—used the *Suda* in his teaching, he treated it not only as a model for compiling copybooks but also as an object of research. Presumably working with advanced students, he handed out the material for four late letters in the alphabet—Τ, Υ, Φ, and Χ—to them to translate. He not only named these research assistants—a practice rarely followed by humanists—but also described them, with obvious pride, as "pupils of Wolf" (*Vuolfij auditores*).[61] In doing so, as he knew, he was bringing them into contact with a rich and puzzling mass of material, much of it taken without naming names from ancient and late antique sources—and thus rich territory for anyone interested in enlarging the corpus of, for example, ancient historiography. Byzantine history, in other words, became for Wolf a kind of advanced class, in which he supervised students as they translated texts from a wide variety of sources and periods. That

58 See Chalkokondyles' preface to his edition of the *Suda*, *Suida* (Milan, 1499), translated into Latin by Wolf, *Suidae historica* (1564), 5: *Nec enim verba tantum historicorum & oratorum, & quorumvis eloquentium autorum interpretatur (quam rem liber praecipue profitetur) sed & multas variasque historias, quae non temere alibi reperiuntur, eo quod libri & Graeci & Romani & Hebraei, unde haec sumpta sunt, periere, complectitur.* [Chalkokondyles: οὐ γὰρ μόνον λέξεων ποιητικῶν τε καὶ ῥητορικῶν καὶ τῶν ὁπωσοῦν ἐν λόγοις εὐδοκιμησάντων ἀκριβεστάτην ἑρμηνείαν περιέχει, ἀλλὰ καὶ ἱστορίας πολλὰς καὶ ποικίλας καὶ ἃς οὐκ ἄν τις ἀλλαχοῦ ῥάδίως εὕροι, διὰ τὸ πολλὰ τῶν βιβλίων ἀφ᾽ὧν αὑταὶ περελήφθησαν, ἀπολωλέναι. Ἑλληνικάς φημι καὶ Ῥωμαικὰς καὶ Ἑβραικάς.]

59 Wolf, in Zonaras, *Historia Imperatorum* (n. 22 above), sig. a3r: *Non inficior, posse videri Zonaram alias prolixiorem, ut in Iudaica historia: alias breviorem, ut in exterarum gentium rebus gestis. In quo si culpa commissa est, excusationem habere videtur hanc, quod ipse non ex suo ingenio deprompsit ea quae scripsit, sed ex varijs autoribus collecta, in certum ordinem redegit, qui autores inter se dissimillimi sunt.*

60 Bodleian Library, MS Casaubon 19, title page of Basel 1549 edition of Polybius's Greek text: Ση[αι] *Ad editionem Polybii possunt colligi multa egregia fragmenta ex Suida quae quod non haberent nomen Polybii adiectum, praetermissa sunt a Fulvio Vrsino. Versato in historia Polybii facile erit dignoscere. Nunc in nostro libro pleraque omnia notata habemus.* Casaubon's copy of the *Suda* (Basel, 1544), Leiden University Library 759 B 16, has many notes in his hand identifying the fragments of Polybius.

61 *Suidae historica* (1564), 944: *Litera T Christophoro Macellario Augustano, Vuolfii auditore interprete*; 978: *Hactenus Christophorus Macellarius, reliqua huius literae Vuolfius*; 996: *Litera Y. Georgio Mylio Augustano, Vuolfii auditore, interprete*; 1015: *Principium literae Φ, id est, Ph vel F, Ioanne Scheurlino, Vuolfii auditore, interprete; Principium literae X Rodolpho Briuio Memmingensi, Vuolfij auditore, interprete.*

helps to explain why—for all Wolf's complaints about the miseries of Byzantine scholarship—it became the chosen field of his favorite gymnasium pupil, David Hoeschel. He too probably began to learn his craft as a philologist by working as an apprentice for his erudite master.

Byzantine historians were more than a source of general advice, however. For one thing, the learned agreed, they offered concrete information about the Turks, their military discipline, their order of battle, and their tactics—as well as about the larger, longer-term history of Islam. Sometimes this was literally true: Laonikos Chalkokondyles provided a vast amount of information, much of it firsthand, about the Turks.[62] But humanists believed that the qualities of nations and religions were durable. Accordingly, the fact that other sources were very old did not prevent them from being of practical utility. Perhaps the most exciting feature of Cuspinian's book on the Roman emperors was the detailed digression on the origins of Islam that appeared after his account of the emperor Herakleios. One reader noted: "On Muhammad and the beginning of the sect and the kingdom of Muhammad, which began during the reign of Herakleios, see Philip [Melanchthon] in his Chronicle and in other historians."[63] The title page of Wolf's corpus of Byzantine historians in Latin blatantly advertised its importance for anyone involved in the struggle with the Ottomans. Even well-traveled scholars like Hugo Blotius, librarian for the imperial collection in Vienna, saw Byzantine texts as crucial sources of what he called "Turcica."[64] The corpus of Byzantine history, in other words, was unified by its promise of precise, practical information about the Ottoman world—even if it was only the scholars who believed that.

The scholars, moreover, were not wholly wrong. Though Byzantine historians might not offer the best tips for dealing with contemporary Turks, they did portray a rich and exotic past. Byzantine history, as presented in the *Suda*, included a description of ancient techniques for making the spirits of the dead speak, Xenophanes' views on the transmigration of souls, a sharp distinction between the worldly wisdom of the statesman and the proper qualities of a priest, and a textual correction of

62 A. Kaldellis, *A New Herodotos: Laonikos Chalkokondyles on the Ottoman Empire, the Fall of Byzantium, and the Emergence of the West* (Washington, DC, 2014); for the larger context see idem, *Ethnography after Antiquity: Foreign Lands and Peoples in Byzantine Literature* (Philadelphia, 2013).

63 Wolfgang Hunger, note in Johannes Cuspinian, *De caesaribus atque imperatoribus Romanis opus insigne* (Basel, 1561), Princeton University Library (EX) 2958.279q, 532, at the heading *De Mahomete Saracenorum phylarcho et pseudopropheta*: *De Mahomete et de initijs sectae et regni Mahumetici. Quod sub Heraclij gubernatione cepit. Lege Philip: in suo Carione et in Alijs Hystoricis.*

64 P. Molino, "World Bibliographies: Libraries and the Organization of Knowledge in Late Renaissance Europe," in *Canonical Texts and Scholarly Practices: A Global Comparative Approach*, ed. A. Grafton and G. W. Most (Cambridge, 2016), 299–322; see esp. 303.

John 1:28. These and other exciting passages actually found their way onto the *Index of Forbidden Books*. As late as 1620, a Catholic censor working in Lucca crossed out each of them, and others.[65] No wonder that the *Bibliotheca* of Photios—the man blamed by the Catholic Church for the Great Schism—seemed even more frightening to the censors.

Beginning early in the fifteenth century, Byzantine historians opened up new possibilities for studying and debating periods and peoples not recorded by Latin authors—or at least by standard ones.[66] Flavio Biondo—a rival of Leonardo Bruni's who shared his belief that the fall of Rome, for all the destruction it had brought with it, had done some good—identified the sole source that Bruni had used for his history of the Italian wars as Procopius. He savaged the Greek historian for his ignorance about Italy: how, he asked, could a writer who thought Ravenna was divided by the Po have anything useful to say? Comparing Procopius to other historians and even to surviving mosaics, Biondo did his best to convict him—and Bruni, who had relied on him—of gross unreliability.[67]

Over time, more and more writers came to share Bruni's and Biondo's interest in the period that would now be referred to as late antiquity. The northern humanists Konrad Peutinger and Beatus Rhenanus scoured extant texts in Latin for information, for example, about the barbarian peoples who had entered and, they believed, destroyed the Roman Empire—and the others that had remained outside it and were, in some cases, the ancestors of modern nations.[68] Gradually it became clear that Byzantine writers offered a wealth of information about worlds that Latin sources did not describe in such detail. Procopius described the buildings of Constantinople and the customs of the Goths. When Bonaventura Vulcanius edited and translated Agathias, who drew on and continued Procopius, he emphasized the cosmopolitan richness of the text: "First, Agathias describes many great wars waged against very populous and powerful nations—the Franks, the Goths, the Vandals, the Huns and the Persians. Second, he also records many things very much worth knowing about their customs and laws, and especially about the genealogy and government of the Persian kings, which cannot be found anywhere in other writers."[69]

65 *Suidae historica* (1581), Princeton University Library Rare Books Offsite Storage 2773.2581q, censored in Lucca on 22 August 1620, col. 1035 on ψυχαγωγεῖ; col. 638 on ξενοφάνης; col. 770 on πολιτικὴν ἀρετὴν . . .; col. 180 on Bethania.

66 See the still valuable account of S. Mazzarino, *The End of the Ancient World*, trans. George Holmes (New York, 1966), 77–87.

67 Ianziti, "Bruni on Writing History" (n. 38 above), 385–88.

68 Mazzarino, *End of the Ancient World*, 87–88.

69 Bonaventura Vulcanius, in Agathias, *De imperio et rebus gestis Iustiniani imperatoris libri quinque*, ed. and trans. Vulcanius (Leiden, 1594), sig. *3r: *Quam enim varia gravissimaque bella adversus*

Vulcanius, as Dirk van Miert has shown, situated this new text in an appropriately rich context, by publishing Jordanes' Latin history of the Goths and his own treatment of the Gothic language and alphabet.[70] Late Byzantine history flowed into Turkish history, and the humanists argued that that gave it relevance. But early Byzantine history flowed into the history of barbarous peoples, which attracted increasing interest in the late sixteenth-century Gothic Revival, as the Dutch, the English, the French, the Spanish, and others began to re-create—or invent—pasts independent of Rome. As the definition of historical knowledge expanded—a phenomenon observed earlier when Jean Bodin was discussed—so did the special value of Byzantine history.

Another special feature of Byzantine histories, of course, was their language—or rather the variety of forms of Greek in which they wrote. Wolf was ambivalent, as usual. The style of Zonaras, he argued, "is not of one kind and form, but varies with the variety of authors on whom he drew—especially in the last volume, in which period both the Greek and the Latin language changed for the worse. Learned men will find that it lacks something. I too found that it lacks the economy of the language of Demosthenes."[71] The language of Choniates was more puzzling. Coming across both a manuscript of the original text and a later verse paraphrase, Wolf took the latter for the original. Since he found it largely unintelligible, however, he based his edition on the genuine text. And though he appreciated Choniates' copiousness—for example, he liked the long passage on Anna Komnene—he treated Choniates' prose as affected and hyperbolic: an example of the degeneration of the Greek language caused by commerce with foreign nations and writers with too much time on their hands.[72]

---

populosissimas potentissimasque nationes, Francos scilicet, Gotthos, Vandalos, Hunnos, & Persas gesta, describat: tum vero de eorum moribus atque institutis, ac praecipue de Persicorum regum genealogia ac politia, multa commemorat scitu dignissima, quae apud alios scriptores nusquam reperiantur.

70 Van Miert, "Project Procopius" (n. 26 above).

71 Wolf, in Zonaras, *Historia Imperatorum*, sig. a3v: *Nunc etiam de stylo autoris nonnihil est dicendum, qui cum non unius sit generis & formae, sed pro varietate autorum, e quibus haec petita sunt, & ipse variet, in ultimo Tomo praesertim, qua aetate Graeca pariter & Romana lingua degeneravit: eruditi homines in eo nonnihil desiderabunt. Desideravi & ipse nonnihil, parsimoniam inprimis Demosthenicae orationis, quae meo palato longe fuit gratior, & ad convertendum non tantum iucundior, sed etiam facilior: utut alijs difficilis videatur, & mea tenuitate superior.*

72 Ibid., vol. 2, sig. A3v: *Nunc de hoc opere dicendum est, quod etsi labore non multo minore, longe tamen maiori cum voluptate converti, propter historias mihi ante hac fere incognitas, & planius ac fusius orationis genus. In quo tamen immodicam nescio cuius insolentis eloquentiae affectionem, non semper sequendam mihi duxi: quod quicquid eius generis est, non ipsius auctoris scriptum, sed paraphrastae & aemuli alicuius assumentum esse videtur. Contuli enim hic quoque duos codices, cum eo quem Amplitudo tua Constantinopoli ab Alexandro Chartophylace comparavit: atque operam dedi, ut ex ea collatione opus hoc quam integerrimum ederetur: & Graeca itidem, ut in Zonara nostro factum est, cum*

Yet Wolf also learned a good deal of Byzantine Greek, and used his knowledge to emend the text. The study of Byzantine history and Byzantine Greek remained tightly connected. By 1610 Wolf's pupil Hoeschel was complaining about Anna Komnene's partiality to her fatherland and father, which led to her "womanish" habit of hurling insults at the Latins and the pope.[73] But he did not complain about Anna's Greek usage. In some cases—as when Anna referred to the "purple room" where she was born—he simply explained that it referred not to a color *sed locus Palatij*.[74] In others he resorted to higher authority. Johannes Meursius had devoted himself to Byzantine antiquities: he had drawn up studies of the imperial palace, the church, the military, and the treasury. "I watched the language grow corrupt as the Empire fell," he wrote, "and become as different from the ancient language as Italian is from Latin."[75] Meursius collected any of these deviations from classical usage in a "Greek-barbarian lexicon," to which Hoeschel simply referred his readers for particularly "barbarous" words. Seventy years later, Charles Du Cange published his massive *Historia Byzantina*, an 800-page guide to the families of Byzantium and its neighbors and to the buildings of Constantinople. He then packed up the thousands of *fiches* he had compiled on the meaning of particular terms and sent them off to the publisher Anisson in Lyon.[76] Horrified by the ease with which slips of paper could be lost or misfiled, Anisson demanded that Du Cange put some sort of manuscript together. Never disinclined to work, Du Cange created the *Glossarium mediae et infimae Graecitatis* (1688): one of the few reference books to stay in everyday use for more than 300 years. The readers of Byzantine histories never argued that the Greek they found there was simply different from, not worse than, that of the classics. But they made mastering it part of their craft. The study of Byzantine history was deeply philological, almost from the start. As Meursius's title suggests, it was at first an ambivalent philology: a study of a language that scholars saw as changing steadily for the worse. But eventually the evaluative note dropped away. Du Cange, for example,

---

Latinis coniungerentur. Quamvis enim Graeci sermonis puritas & proprietas, cum exterarum nationum commercijs, tum ociosorum hominum ineptijs corrupta est: nec fieri nequit, in hoc scriptorum genere, ut interpretis non indocti nec indiserti oratio, ipsi auctori praeferatur: tamen nec eum ego me interpretem profiteri ausim: & Graeca lingua, qualiscunque adhuc, nescio quem genium retinet ac ubertatem, Latinis inimitabilem.

73 David Hoeschel, in Anna Komnene, *Alexiados libri viii*, ed. Hoeschel (Augsburg, 1610), sig. [A IIv]: *Hic est foedissimorum convitiorum fons, quibus Anna interdum muliebriter in Latinos, Pontificem, aliosque Principes indulget.*

74 Ibid., *Notae*, 177.

75 Johannes Meursius, *Glossarium Graeco-Barbarum*, 2nd ed. (Leiden, 1614), sig. * iij r.

76 H. Omont, "Le glossaire grec de Du Cange: Lettres d'Anisson à Du Cange relatives à l'impression du *Glossaire* (1682–1688)," *REG* 5.18 (1892): 212–49, at 214–17. For Du Cange's use of fiches, see also J.-F. Bert, *Une histoire de la fiche érudite* (Villeurbaine, 2017), 36.

like Martin Crusius before him, seems to have set no borders on what he saw as genuine Greek.

The study of Byzantine historians was a cautious, technical domain, sometimes inhabited by men, like Wolf and Meursius, of legendary shyness. But it was also the site of intellectual explosions, a place where discoveries were made that shook the intellectual world. Johannes Löwenklau, or Leunclavius (1541–1594), learned Greek at Wittenberg and taught it at Heidelberg. He became an expert Byzantinist: a master student, in fact, of Byzantine law, who edited, translated, and sometimes drastically reconfigured Byzantine legal texts.[77] But he also spent much of his life in contact with equivocal figures: liberal scholars from the imperial court, such as Hugo Blotius and Carolus Clusius; the erudite and tolerant Catholic captain Lazarus von Schwendi; and the brilliant adventurer Jacob Heraclides, the well-educated soldier of fortune who ruled for two years in Moldovia as the first Protestant monarch of an east European land and founded a humanist school before the boyars overthrew and killed him. Leunclavius seems to have shared the aspirations of men like Jacob to bring about a religious peace under Protestant auspices. In 1584–85 he accompanied a Habsburg embassy to Constantinople. There he met Hungarians, as well as Ottomans of Hungarian origin, and observed, and had sketches made, of Ottoman subjects. With the help of his informants he produced a series of studies of Ottoman history that gave a new and favorable picture of Ottoman life, based on Ottoman sources. The richest of them was actually written in Latin by Murad Bey, an Ottoman interpreter of Hungarian origin, who collected and translated Ottoman works.[78]

But Leunclavius brought out his most radical publication in 1576, when he was in his mid-thirties. It was a Latin translation of the *New History* of Zosimus, an imperial official who lived around 500 CE. Scholars had known that the work existed before Leunclavius found his manuscript. The sixth-century Syrian scholar Evagrius devoted two chapters of his *Ecclesiastical History* to denouncing Zosimus, whom he addressed as a demon:

77 B. Stolte, "Joannes Leunclavius (1541–1594), Civilian and Byzantinist?," in *Reassessing Legal Humanism and Its Claims: Petere Fontes?*, ed. P. du Plessis and J. Cairns (Edinburgh, 2016), 194–210. On Leunclavius's studies of Ottoman history, see A. Höfert, "Hans Löwenklau," in *Christian-Muslim Relations 1500–1900*, ed. D. Thomas (2015), http://dx.doi.org.ezproxy.princeton.edu/10.1163/2451-9537_cmrii_COM_27730.

78 P. Ács, "*Pro Turcis and contra Turcos*. Curiosity, Scholarship and Spiritualism in Turkish Histories by Johannes Löwenklau," *Acta Comeniana* 25 (2011): 25–46. On his career see also M.-P. Burtin, "Un apôtre de la tolerance: L'humaniste allemand Johannes Löwenklaw, dit Leunclavius," *Bibliothèque d'Humanisme et Renaissance* 52.3 (1990): 561–70.

> ZOSIMUS, a follower of the accursed and foul religion of the Greeks, in his anger against Constantine, because he was the first emperor that had adopted Christianity, abandoning the abominable superstition of the Greeks, says, that he was the person who devised the tax called Chrysargyrum, and enacted that it should be levied every five years. He has on many other grounds also reviled that pious and magnificent monarch; for he affirms that he contrived many other intolerable proceedings against every class of persons; that he miserably destroyed his son Crispus, and made away with his wife Fausta by inclosing her in an overheated bath; and that, after having in vain endeavoured to procure purification from murders so detestable at the hands of the priests of his own religion (for they plainly declared its impossibility), he met with an Egyptian who had come from Iberia; and, having been assured by him that the faith of the Christians had the power of blotting out every sin, he embraced what the Egyptian had imparted to him, and thenceforward abandoning the faith of his fathers, he made the commencement of his impiety. The falsehood of these assertions I will forthwith shew, and in the first place treat of the matter of the Chrysargyrum.[79] (3.40; see also 3.41)

One manuscript of Zosimus's work, now Vaticanus gr. 156, survived the centuries in Byzantium, accumulating denunciatory marginal comments from scholar after scholar.[80] Zosimus offered a richly detailed account of the *Ludi saeculares*, a festival splendidly staged by Augustus and Aterius Capito and designed to be held at the ends of *saecula* of 110 years.[81] The late fifteenth-century Florentine philologist Angelo Poliziano, who saw the manuscript of Zosimus's history in the Vatican and later managed to borrow it, incorporated this material into his own discussion of the *Ludi*, which formed one chapter of his *Miscellaneorum centuria prima* (1489).[82] Poliziano dodged the question of Zosimus's own views about Roman history and Christianity.[83] So, half a century later, did Pierre Gilles, to the extent that he could manage it. As he worked up his magnificently detailed survey of the ruins—and parts of the modern city—of Constantinople, he made regular use of Zosimus's work, to

79 Evagrius Scholasticus, *Ecclesiastical History: A History of the Church in Six Books, from* A.D. *431 to* A.D. *594*, trans. and ed. E. Walford (London, 1846), 176–77.

80 See Paolo Megna's exemplary study, *Poliziano e la storiografia bizantina: Il cap. LVIII dei primi "Miscellanea"* (Messina, 2012), 45–60.

81 *OCD*, s.v. "Secular Games" (S. B. Dunning).

82 Megna, *Poliziano e la storiografia bizantina*, 61–130 (Megna provides a critical text of and commentary on Poliziano's chapter, as well as a full analysis of its creation).

83 Ibid., 70–71.

which he accorded considerable authority, especially on questions of topography.[84] *Zosimus antiquus historicus* was, after all, older than many of the other sources Gilles used, as he repeatedly pointed out.[85]

But the ground Zosimus covered was mined, and in the sixteenth century the mines had sensitive fuses. Through the course of the Reformation and Counter-Reformation, evaluating the career and impact of Constantine became—as it still is—a delicate and controversial business.[86] Luther and other magisterial reformers saw Constantine as an exemplary Christian prince, who had taken responsibility both for making Rome Christian and for imposing order on the church at Nicaea. In 1549 Wolfgang Musculus produced the first Latin translation of Eusebius's *Life of Constantine*, which had been published in Greek five years before. He dedicated it to Edward VI, in the hope that the young prince would find it a model.[87] A decade and a half later, John Foxe dedicated his *Acts and Monuments*—a Protestant martyrology modeled on the *Ecclesiastical History* of Eusebius—to his new queen, Elizabeth. The first word in his text was "Constantine."[88] Foxe's printer began the emperor's name with an immense initial C, in which Queen Elizabeth was depicted, riding the letter like a swing: clear evidence of the hopes nourished by Foxe and others that she would be a new Constantine. Catholic scholars agreed about Constantine's greatness. But they were likely to describe the immense basilicas he and his family had built in Rome, not to mention his supposed donation of the western empire to the papacy, where Protestants were likely to see the former as evidence of the corruption of the church and the latter as a fable.

What to do, then, with Zosimus, who accused Constantine both of crimes, such as the murder of his son Crispus, and mistakes, such as the *chrysargyron* tax, which had crippled the empire? Every detail called for careful treatment. The Byzantine church historians had refused to believe that Constantine had murdered Crispus,

84 Pierre Gilles, *De topographia Constantinopoleos atque de illius antiquitatibus libri quatuor* (Lyon, 1561), 16–17, 83, 90, 105–6, 112, 126, 135–36, 182, 193–95; trans. by Kimberly Byrd as *Pierre Gilles' Constantinople* (New York, 2008), 6–7, 67, 75, 89, 95, 107, 131, 177, 185–87.

85 Gilles, *Topographia*, 182, 16, 83, 90, 193–95; Byrd, *Gilles' Constantinople*, 177, 6, 67, 75, 185–87.

86 For some sense of the problems involved, see *The Cambridge Companion to the Age of Constantine*, ed. N. Lenski (Cambridge, 2007).

87 Wolfgang Musculus, ep. ded. to Edward VI, in *Ecclesiasticae historiae autores*, trans. and ed. Musculus (Basel, 1549), ep. ded. sigs. *2r–*3v.

88 The English preface of the 1563 edition of Foxe's work begins: "COnstantine the greate and mightie Emperour, the sonne of Helene an Englyshe woman of this youre Realme and countrie (moste Christian and renowmed Pryncesse Queene Elizabeth) after he had pacified and established the churche of Christ, being long before vnder persecution, frō the tyme of our sauiour Christ almost 400 yeres[.]" John Foxe, *The Acts and Monuments Online* (Sheffield, 2011), https://www.dhi.ac.uk/foxe/index.php?realm=text&gototype=&edition=1563&pageid=5.

since Eusebius, his contemporary, did not mention the event. Gilles, by contrast, repeated the story in detail, while insisting that Zosimus was a hostile witness, and therefore not credible:

> So says Zosimus, a follower of Julian the Apostate and hostile to Constantine on account of his religion. I shrink from his views, and do not agree about impious crimes he falsely ascribed assigned to this Constantine. I would try to show in detail that all of these things were completely distant to the thought of Constantine, an immensely pious and humane man, but so great a digression would not fit within the limits of the present task, and Sozomen and Evagrius have already refuted and contradicted him well enough.[89]

Still, he could not deny that he found Zosimus's description of the city useful: it was, after all, the work of a genuinely old author.[90]

Zosimus's text, while full of useful information, also bristled with difficulties. One of the most prominent Roman scholars of the mid-sixteenth century, Onofrio Panvinio, laid bare some of these problems. He knew perfectly well that Zosimus was in bad odor with Latin scholars, as he had been with Greek ones. In an antiquarian work on the Ludi saeculares, which appeared in 1558, he not only followed Poliziano in relying on Zosimus but had the relevant passage translated into Latin and included it in his text.[91] Unlike Poliziano, however, Panvinio worked for patrons committed to the ongoing defense and reform of the Catholic Church, and at their behest he devoted himself in his later years to the study of ecclesiastical history.[92] In 1558 he also published a massive historical commentary on the Roman *Fasti consulares*, the list of the city's consuls. When he arrived at the early fourth century CE, he included a long, fervent discussion of Constantine's decision, impelled by a vision, to take the

89 Gilles, *Topographia*, 20–21: *Haec quidem Zosimus Iuliani studiosus Constantino ob religionem infensus, a cuius sensibus, ut penitus abhorreo, ut ei non assentio de sceleribus impiis, quae falso impingit Constantino, quae alienissima a mente Constantini maxime pii humanissimique copiose monstrare conarer, nisi hoc praesens institutum tantam digressionem non pateretur, nisi etiam satis Sozomenus & Evagrius ea redarguissent & confutassent*; translation from Byrd, *Gilles' Constantinople*, 9 (revised).

90 Gilles, *Topographia*, 21; Byrd, *Gilles' Constantinople*, 9–10.

91 Onofrio Panvinio, *De ludis saecularibus liber* (Venice, 1558), 23; Panvinio, *De ludis saecularibus*, in *Libri tres. I. De ludis saecularibus. II. De Sibyllis et carminibus sibyllinis. III. De antiquis Romanorum nominibus* ([Heidelberg], 1588), 19: *Caeterum quo omnia quae dixi magis confirmari possint, antequam ad huius disputationis finem veniam, ipsius Zosimi verba ad amussim translata ex initio secundi historiarum suarum libri, qui acephalus est, suggerere volui.*

92 See S. Bauer, *The Invention of Papal History: Onofrio Panvinio between Renaissance and Catholic Reform* (Oxford, 2020).

Christian God as his divine patron and the labarum as his symbol.[93] Panvinio was a pious as well as an erudite—and, sometimes, over-imaginative—scholar.[94] Zosimus claimed that Constantine had deprived Rome of the favor of the true gods by canceling the Ludi saeculares and other pious festivals. Panvinio, accordingly, could not cite Zosimus's richly detailed description of the Ludi without further comment. He noted that Zosimus "strives to persuade" his readers that the Christians who ceased to practice these "superstitions" also "caused the decline of the city and the empire."[95] And he took care to point out that Augustine, in the *City of God*, and other Christian writers had refuted such views so completely "that I think it unlawful to discuss those matters further."[96] Zosimus, in other words, was exactly the sort of pagan observer of events against whom Augustine had warned Christian readers. After such knowledge, what forgiveness? By 1572 the French scholar Marc-Antoine Muret, who lived and worked in Rome, wrote to his friend Claude Dupuy that "I wouldn't dare to touch Zosimus." True, Zosimus was in the Vatican Library. But Cardinal Sirleto, the prefect, had "seen to it some time ago that he was hidden away in the deepest recesses of the library." Muret eventually managed to provide Dupuy with a partial version of the text, but he could not arrange for a more prominent friend, the jurist and historian Jacques-Auguste de Thou, to consult the manuscript at Florence.[97]

Like Panvinio, Leunclavius came to Zosimus with formidable preparation. But he used both his erudition and his critical skills to find a new path to the *New History*. As the translator of Gregory of Nyssa and the editor of an early Byzantine collection of ecclesiastical legislation, the *Collectio Tripartita*, he had experience in textual criticism and deep knowledge of his author's period and empire.[98] He

93 Onofrio Panvinio, *Fastorum libri V a Romulo rege usque ad Imp. Caesarem Carolum V. Austrium Augustum* (Venice, 1558; repr., Heidelberg, 1588), 277–79.

94 For Panvinio's inventions see R. Bizzocchi, *Genealogie fantastiche: Scritti di storia nell'Europa moderna* (Bologna, 2009), and Bauer, *Invention of Papal History*.

95 Panvinio, *De ludis saecularibus* (1558), 23; (1588), 19: *Post Honorium autem imperatorem omnino fieri desierunt, siquidem tempus centum & decem annorum, in Christianorum tempora devenit, qui his superstitionibus adversi, eos agere desierunt. Quare etiam imperii urbisque declinationem factam fuisse nititur Zosimum persuadere, quum inquit: Quarto vero Constantini & Licinii consulatu, tempus statum ludis saecularibus celebrandis centum videlicet & decem annorum exactum est, in quo ex antiquorum consuetudine sacra ipsa agere necesse erat, eisque non factis, in eas molestias, in quibus nunc res sunt devenire oportuit. Siquidem tanta urbs tamque praeclara barbarorum mancipium effecta est, &c.*

96 Ibid. (1558), 23; (1588), 19: *Quibus omnibus & similibus calumniis, quum divus pater Augustinus in libris de Civitate dei, & plerique alii veteres Christiani scriptores accuratissime satisfecerint, nefas esse arbitror de iisdem rebus amplius disserere.*

97 The story is told in detail by Megna, *Poliziano e la storiografia bizantina*, 49, n. 1.

98 Mazzarino, *End of the Ancient World* (n. 66 above), 93; B. H. Stolte, "The Lion's Paws: Observations on Johannes Leunclavius (1541–1594) at Work," *RJ* 13 (1994): 219–33. Stolte examines Leunclavius's work as an editor of legal texts in detail.

also knew the new techniques of the antiquarians, as he showed when he had the chance to examine the Ottoman coins available in Constantinople.[99] Above all, he had mastered cutting-edge philological techniques. In 1572, when Leunclavius translated the chronicle of the twelfth-century polymath Michael Glykas, he explained in his dedicatory letter that Glykas provided many valuable fragments.[100] A list of the "unpublished authors and books, from which Glykas gathered his material," confirmed this assessment.[101] Leuclavius's defense of Zosimus showed a similar command of critical techniques. It included an attack on the ecclesiastical authors who had refuted Zosimus, and whom Leunclavius dismissed as uncritical, especially of their patrons: "But what if this testimony be not good? For I must tell you, this kind of Historians, Prelates I mean, Priests and Monks have but a scurvy reputation for their fidelity this way; for those Princes who preferr'd them, they do not onely praise immoderately, but studiously endeavour not onely to free from the guild, but from the very suspicion too of those Villanies."[102] Pretending to relent from his assault on the "eminent" Eusebius, Leunclavius then returned to it, noting that the historian could not have mentioned the murder of Crispus without risking his own life. As for the *chrysargyron*, he argued that Zosimus had shown "out of the writers of those times" that Constantine introduced it—and even if he did not, Zosimus provided good evidence that Constantine had needed to raise taxes in order to pay for his own extravagance.[103] Those who denied Constantine's sins and errors had forgotten "the duty of Historians, and seem rather to write Panegyrics and Declamations

99 J. R. Jones, "Leunclavius' Notes on European and Ottoman Coins," *BalkSt* 2 (1970): 190–96.

100 Johannes Leunclavius, ep. ded. to Michael Glykas, *Annales Michaelis Glycae Siculi, qui lectori praeter alia cognitu iucunda & utilia, Byzantinam historiam universam exhibent*, trans. Leunclavius (Basel, 1572), sigs. α4v–α5r: *Secundam temporum seriem ab initio mundi usque ad Christum ex Ecclesiae doctrina praecipue tradit, & eius caussa, cui librum elaboravit (appellat autem hunc filium), plurima de sacris intertexit. Quippe primorum imperiorum tam initia, quam progressus ex ijs, tanquam certis testibus, petere maluit: quum de Nabuchodonosore, de liberis eius, totoque Assyriorum imperio (ut omittam antiquiora) perpauca, vel nulla potius memoratu digna in extrariorum, quod gentiles dicimus, scriptorum monumentis reperiantur. Sic autem haec tractat, ut obiter de quaestionibus minime vulgaribus disserat, citatis auctorum gravissimorum testimonijs: quorum quum non pauca nobis plane sint incogniti, pretium nos operae facturos existimabamus, si antiquitatis studiosorum in gratiam, illorum nomina statim huic prooemio subijceremus.*

101 Ibid., sig. [α8r–v]: *AVCTORES ET LIBRI NON editi, de quibus Glycas sua collegit. Nam editos omittere libuit, quorum tamen fragmenta quaedam habet, in editis non exstantia.*

102 Leunclavius, "Apology," in *The New History of Count Zosimus* (London, 1684), [a7r]; "Apologia pro Zosimo," in Zosimus, *Historiae novae libri sex* (Basel, 1576), β 2v: *Quid si testem hunc non admisero? nam male genus hoc historicorum, antistites inquam & monachi, solent audire: quod liberales in se principes et laudent prolixius, et studiosius a facinorum non modo culpa, sed etiam suspicione liberent.*

103 Leunclavius, "Apology," sig. a2v; "Apologia pro Zosimo," sig. β 2v.

than History."[104] Evagrius and Nikephoros insisted that Zosimus was inconsistent, since he credited Constantine with some good deeds. Leunclavius retorted that a historian could praise Christian princes "without approving all that they did."[105] Even more sharply, he pointed out that Julian and some other pagan emperors "for their abstinence, gentleness and moderation in Government have been a reproach to some who profes'd a better Religion."[106]

Leunclavius not only read and translated Zosimus, in short: he used his work as a lens, through which he saw the history of the late empire and the characters of Christian and pagan emperors in a new, differentiated way. From 1576 on, no one interested in the fall of Rome or the rise of Christianity could tell either story in the traditional, simple terms. And anyone who read Zosimus and Leunclavius carefully began to see that rulers were not the cardboard figures of exemplar history, all of a piece, but complex humans, capable of both good and evil, wisdom and folly.[107] Some, like Isaac Casaubon, took Zosimus as a credible historian and used his work without question to help explain Rome's collapse.[108] Others, like Caesar Baronius, denounced him for his bias.[109] Gibbon, at his most Gibbonian, played down the special importance of Zosimus: "Eusebius and Zosimus form indeed the two extremes of flattery and invective."[110] But Zosimus sketched Gibbon's problem for the first time. No one could ignore his way of thinking about history in more complex terms—or his emphasis on economic and financial questions, as well as on rituals and murders. The rediscovery and legitimation of one mediocre Byzantine historian transformed historiography.

Thirty years later, another dramatic figure—Joseph Scaliger—made a second Byzantine discovery. Scaliger had won fame as a textual critic of Latin poetry and a chronologer: an expert on the dates of events and the nature of calendars, ancient and modern, eastern and western. In 1593 he came to the University of Leiden, which offered him special treatment. Though he offered no lectures, he did provide a form

104 Leunclavius, "Apology," sig. a3r; "Apologia pro Zosimo," sig. β v.

105 Leunclavius, "Apology," sig. [a5r]; "Apologia pro Zosimo," sig. β 2r.

106 Ibid.

107 See the excellent discussion of Leunclavius's views in Mazzarino, *End of the Ancient World*, 92–99.

108 Isaac Casaubon, "Imperii Romani eversio, ac primum καθόλου de causis eversionis," Bibliothèque Nationale de France, MS lat. 4855, fol. 82r: *Vide omnino librum doctis quibusdam decantissimi Lazii de migratione gentium. Itaque sub Honorio et Arcadio juvenibus Theodosii fil. fuit Resp. R. corruptissima ab omni parte, quod et Zosimus et alii declarant*[.]

109 Caesar Baronius, *Annales ecclesiastici*, vol. 3 (Mainz, 1601), col. 130 (sec. 313.15): *cum nullam prorsus aliam scribendae historiae inierit rationem, quam ut doceret, culpa Christianorum Romanum Imperium esse collapsum.*

110 Edward Gibbon, *The History of the Decline and Fall of the Roman Empire*, ed. D. Womersley, 3 vols. (New York, 1994), chap. 18, n. 1 (1:643).

of advanced teaching, for everyone from the eleven-year-old Leiden student Hugo Grotius, whom he taught to edit texts, to adult friends like Hoeschel and Janus Gruter, whose scholarly projects he directed from a distance. Under attack from the Jesuits, he was also irritated by the success of the great Catholic church history of Caesar Baronius. Scaliger set out on a massive project. Though Baronius criticized Eusebius for his Arian views, he accepted his authority as a historian. Eusebius's *Chronicle*—a massive timeline that began with Abraham and came down to Constantine—was one of Baronius's major sources. But he—and everyone else—knew the text only in the Latin adaptation by Jerome. Scaliger set out to reconstruct the original Greek text of the *Chronicle*—which, he thought, would prove that Eusebius's work was derivative and inaccurate.[111]

Eventually, Scaliger's friend Isaac Casaubon turned up, in the French Royal Library, the massive Greek chronicle of George Synkellos, composed around 800. As Scaliger had suspected, it seemed to contain masses of material from Eusebius. After long and annoying negotiations, Casaubon managed to send the codex from Paris to Leiden. Scaliger used it, in part, exactly as he had planned. He reconstructed the Greek text of Eusebius's timeline and put it at the heart of a great synthetic work on chronology, the *Thesaurus temporum*, which appeared in 1606. Here he argued, at great length, that Eusebius had based his work on the lost earlier chronology of Julius Africanus, and that where he differed from Africanus and other sources, he was usually wrong. His commentary—which Casaubon worked his way through, column by column—offered material for endless debate with Baronius's defenders, who materialized in force.[112]

But one aspect of the materials discovered by Scaliger startled even him. Reading Synkellos, he found that the original *Chronicle* of Eusebius consisted of two books, not one. He realized that he could reconstruct the first book as well as the second—even though he had no Latin translation by Jerome to use as model. But the nature of the first book, and the materials it had contained, took him by surprise. The early sections of Eusebius's *Chronicle* traced the history of the earliest kingdoms, Assyria and Egypt. They were oddly suggestive: though Egyptian history began after the Flood, it began with the sixteenth dynasty of kings. Had Egypt perhaps existed before the Flood? Adventurous chronologers like Gerardus Mercator had suspected

111 See in general A. Grafton, *Joseph Scaliger: A Study in the History of Classical Scholarship*, vol. 2, *Historical Chronology* (Oxford, 1993).

112 Casaubon's copy of the *Thesaurus temporum* (Leiden, 1606) is Cambridge University Library Adv.a.3.4.

as much, connecting the lost early dynasties with the account of Egyptian antiquity given by Plato in the *Timaeus*.

Reading the remains of Eusebius's first book, Scaliger discovered that they included strange chronological tables: a canon of Near Eastern kings, beginning with Nabonassar of Babylon, and a full list of thirty Egyptian dynasties, compiled in Greek by an Egyptian priest, Manetho of Sebbenytos, in the third century BCE. He copied them out in a notebook. The total duration of Manetho's king list, he discovered, was some 5,000 years—which meant that they had begun not only before the Flood but before the creation of the world. Scaliger, a good if independent Calvinist, was anything but eager to relinquish his belief in the authority and accuracy of biblical history. Worries about the minor discrepancies between the Gospels kept him up at night, as he confided to the students who lodged with him. When he copied out the Canon of Kings, he noted beside it in his manuscript that it was a typical pagan fabrication. He thought the same about Manetho.

But Scaliger was the greatest historical and textual critic of his time. Like his friend Casaubon, he had a gift for detecting forgeries. It was second nature to him to notice the inconsistencies that revealed that the Sibylline Oracles were not the inspired prophecies of a female pagan seer, and to accept Casaubon's argument that the dialogues of Hermes Trismegistus were not genuine Egyptian antiquities. Even rarer, however, was Scaliger's gift for detecting texts that looked like forgeries but were genuine. He decided that no forger he could imagine would have been capable of creating the strange lists of names that Manetho had drawn up. Scaliger crossed out his original remark. He accepted the dynasty list, impossible though it was, as a genuine piece of Egyptian lore, passed on by native priests. Scaliger was right. In the nineteenth century, when the Turin papyrus was deciphered, it proved to offer the same list that Manetho had translated into Greek. Scaliger had no way of proving, or even knowing, this, however. He had to posit a period of proleptic time, which ran before the Creation, simply in order to provide a grid of years long enough to accommodate all these kings. Scaliger was re-creating a world history that directly contradicted the Bible—a deeply uncomfortable position for a leading Calvinist professor.

Scaliger's discovery set off a long war among chronologers. But it did much more. It provided ammunition—ammunition of weight and power—for scholars who were already inclined to challenge the authority of the Bible. It inspired speculative historians like Athanasius Kircher to trace not only the kingdom of the Egyptians but also its traditions of learning to a period long before the Flood—and to suggest that Egyptian wisdom was in fact the source from which not only Greeks like Plato but the Jews themselves had drawn their theology and their rituals. For two centuries to come, as Dimitri Levitin and others have shown, the libraries of colleges and the studies of learned clerics across Europe buzzed with debates that Scaliger had provoked by what he found in Synkellos.[113] Byzantine historiography, in this erudite age, produced intellectual bombshells.

Twenty years after Scaliger—and at the other end of the Christian world—another very erudite man supposedly found, but more precisely created, the most subversive Byzantine historical text of all. The *Suda* mentioned a work by Procopius titled Ἀνέκδοτα. This was, of course, the work in which the warmly supportive historian of Justinian's wars turned into a savage critic of the emperor's stupidity and cowardice—as well as of the domination exercised over him by his undeserving wife, the onetime dancer Theodora. As early as 1506 the erudite Volterran humanist Raffaele Maffei noted that Procopius "wrote another book, which he entitled Ἀνέκδοτα, that is, 'Do Not Publish' or 'Unpublished.' In it he sets out a denunciation of Justinian and his wife Theodora, in the form of a comedy. So much from Suidas. We saw this author, who as of now has not been translated for the Latins, in the Vatican Library."[114] Maffei exaggerated what he read in the short entry on Procopius in the *Suda*. That describes the *Secret History* as "the one called unpublished" (τὰ καλούμενα Ἀνέκδοτα). Although the lexicon noted that the text "contains abuse and mockery of the emperor Justinian and his wife Theodora, and indeed of Belisarius himself as well, and his wife," it did not call for or record any effort at suppression of a text that it cited elsewhere as well.[115] Thanks to Maffei's embroidery, an air of scandal surrounded the text. Beatus Rhenanus, who published the first edition of the *Buildings*, thought the *Secret History* had probably been suppressed for good reason.[116] Still, copies circulated. Half a century after Maffei, Gilles quoted the text in both his

113 D. Levitin, *Ancient Wisdom in the Age of the New Science: Histories of Philosophy in England, c. 1640–1700* (Cambridge, 2015). See also D. Stolzenberg, *Egyptian Oedipus: Athanasius Kircher and the Secrets of Antiquity* (Chicago, 2013). P. Rossi, *The Dark Abyss of Time: The History of the Earth and the History of Nations from Hooke to Vico*, trans. L. Cochrane (Chicago, 1984), and C. Kidd, *The World of Mr Casaubon: Britain's Wars of Mythography, 1700–1870* (Cambridge, 2016), also follow the explosions touched off by Scaliger's work, but are less precise than Levitin about the impact of his work on Manetho.

114 Raffaele Maffei, *Commentariorum urbanorum . . . octo et triginta libri* (Basel, 1559), 426: *Composuit item alterum librum, quem inscripsit Ἀνέκδοτα, id est, non edenda sive non edita: ubi comoedia quadam Iustiniani & eius uxoris Theodorae vituperationem describit. ex Suida. Hunc hodie autorem non adhuc redditum Latinis cernimus in bibliotheca Vaticana*. See Croke, "Procopius" (n. 14 above), 18–19, 31, 39, for this and other early references.

115 *Suda*, s.v. "Προκόπιος Ἰλλούστριος"; translation from *Suda On Line*, https://www.stoa.org/sol-entries/pi/2479 (accessed 28 May 2020).

116 Croke, "Procopius," 39.

book on the Thracian Bosporus and his book on Constantinople.[117] By the end of the sixteenth century, the great collector Gian Vincenzo Pinelli, the erudite jurists Guido Panciroli and Pierre Pithou, and a number of other scholars had manuscript copies of the book.[118]

But Niccolò Alemanni (1583–1626) turned this well-known if unpublished text into a printed bombshell. The scion of a family from Chios and a star student in the Greek College at Rome, he taught even more brilliant future stars like Leone Allacci. Swarming nimbly up the greasy pole, he served as secretary to two cardinals before becoming the primary custodian of the Vatican Library and archive—two separate institutions—in 1614. A skilled antiquary, he surveyed and described the Lateran Basilica. When Urban VIII prepared to excavate the space needed for the new altar of Saint Peter's, Alemanni was called in to consult about the doubts and objects raised against the violation of the sacred space (sadly, his report does not survive).[119]

Early in the 1620s, Alemanni came across two Vatican manuscripts of the *Secret History* of Procopius. Using these he established a Greek text, translated it into Latin, and provided it with a detailed, learned, and imaginative commentary.[120] He drew on all the resources of contemporary scholarship. Alemanni's mastery of patristic and later Greek enabled him to solve complicated problems presented by the text. His knowledge of Roman law allowed him to find evidence that confirmed that Theodora had started life as a dancer. Even his antiquarian expertise came into play, when he used reproductions of the Justinian and Theodora mosaics from San Vitale in Ravenna to confirm Procopius's physical descriptions of the emperor and empress.[121]

Alemanni shirked no effort to prove that Procopius's portrait of the imperial house was as truthful as it was savage. Procopius noted that Justinian's predecessor, Justin, was illiterate; indeed, he could not even sign his name to imperial documents but could only trace four letters, using a wooden template. Alemanni had heard that the monastery at Monte Cassino had documents signed by Justin, which he sent for, in the hope of verifying Procopius's account. When he received a report that they bore Justin's full name, he rejected them as forgeries—thus anticipating the paleographical intuition with which his pupil Leone Allacci would reject the Etruscan

117 Ibid., 44, for the book on the Thracian Bosporus; for Gilles's use of the text in his book on Constantinople, see K. Byrd, introduction to *Gilles' Constantinople*, xxiii.

118 Croke, "Procopius," 61–67.

119 See *DBDI*, s.v. "Alemanni, Nicolò (1960)" (S. G. Mercati).

120 Procopius, *ANEKΔOTA: Arcana historia, qui est liber nonus historiarum*, ed. Nicolò Alemanni (Lyon, 1623).

121 Ibid., *Notae*, 28, 47.

forgeries of Tommaso Inghirami.[122] Some aspects of Procopius's text were so brutal that Alemanni could not bring himself to print them, far less to translate them into Latin—especially the descriptions of Theodora. But he did explain to his reader that he had to omit certain passages. Alemanni's scholarship would not have allowed him to make such changes without noting them.

But the most important decision that Alemanni made had to do with the Latin title he devised for Procopius's little book. Alemanni decided that the proper translation for Ἀνέκδοτα was *Historia arcana*—"secret history." In the past, the term *arcanum*, in humanist political writing, had borne the sense given it by Tacitus when he described how the Roman armies discovered the *arcanum imperii* (secret of empire)—that is, that an emperor could be made outside Rome (*Histories* 1.4)—and went on to discuss other arcana in the *Annales*. The fashion for Tacitus was taken up by political journalists like Arnold Clapmarius, who popularized the term and expanded its purview in a book that first appeared in 1605.[123] Clapmarius carefully distinguished between the legitimate arcana of monarchical rule and the *flagitia dominationis* committed by a good many Roman emperors inside and outside their households—as when they entered into incestuous marriages or insisted on arbitrary divorces, "both to enhance power and to gain pleasure."[124] But the effect of his influential book was to sweep up many forms of secret imperial behavior, from the prudent to the scandalous, and associate all of them with the term *arcanum*. Clapmarius and his ilk offered Alemanni a perfect category term for his text, and he followed their direction when he decided that the secrets of empire also included the discreditable family secrets that could, if known, destroy popular respect for a ruler.[125]

When Alemanni's edition appeared, in 1623, it made a stir: but it also aroused fierce opposition. Sir Thomas Ryves, an English lawyer, issued a counterblast just three years later. In it he insisted that Procopius's book was a blow not just to Justinian but to all royal authority. Justinian, he argued, could not have been so inconsistent as Procopius made him. Like Evagrius criticizing Zosimus, Ryves used the principle

122 Ibid., 19. On Allacci and Inghirami, see I. Rowland, *The Scarith of Scornello: A Tale of Renaissance Forgery* (Chicago, 2004).

123 See M. Stolleis, *Arcana imperii und Ratio status: Bemerkungen zur politischen Theorie des frühen 17. Jahrhunderts*, VeröffHam 39 (Göttingen, 1980); P. Donaldson, *Machiavelli and Mystery of State* (Cambridge, 1992), 113; H. Dreitzel, "Reason of State and the Crisis of Political Aristotelianism: An Essay on the Development of 17th Century Political Philosophy," *History of European Ideas* 28 (2002): 163–87.

124 Arnold Clapmarius, *De arcanis rerum publicarum* (Amsterdam, 1644). For the *flagitia dominationis*, see book 5 (221–69), esp. 5.3. The passage quoted in the text is from 226: *Sed primum videamus de flagitiis regiis. Qualia sunt eorum qui incestas nuptias contrahunt, vel divortia pro lubitu faciunt, cum dominationis augendae, tum libidinis exercendae causa.*

125 For the full story of Alemanni's editorial work and its reception, see Croke, "Procopius," 74–89.

of decorum to work out how a past emperor would or could have acted, arguing that Procopius's Justinian was too indecorous to have lived. He also insisted that Alemanni had mistranslated the title of the book.[126]

Ryves and other critics notwithstanding, Alemanni's title stuck. In 1674, when the first English translation of Procopius's book appeared, it was titled *The Secret History of the Court of the Emperor Justinian*. In England and elsewhere, in the last decades of the seventeenth century, Procopius's work became the source and model for a rich new vein of writing: exposés of life at the top that claimed to be historical but often used the methods of fiction to make themselves credible.[127] Secret histories fell from the presses like autumn leaves in Vallombrosa—eighty of them in England alone between 1674 and 1724. There were secret histories of the Stuarts and secret histories of the House of Orange, secret histories of favorites and secret histories of great noblemen, even a secret history of the East India Company.[128] Books like these, as Brendan Dooley and Jacob Soll have argued, had powerful effects on political as well as cultural life.[129] They stripped monarchy of something of its sacred character and provided new and effective ways to criticize authoritarian old regimes, whether in the court of Louis XIV or the republic of Venice. Once again, a Byzantine text proved capable of shaking the pillars of authority: in this case, not only intellectual but political authority as well.

One of Leunclavius's colleagues and friends, Martin Crusius of Tübingen, was Latin Europe's greatest expert, in the late sixteenth century, on Byzantine and modern Greek. He entertained dozens of Greek informants in his house and interviewed them about contemporary Greek. He also collected letters from learned friends both Western and Greek who managed to visit Turkey and, when possible, amassed images of the Grand Patriarch and the complex he occupied in Constantinople—images that Crusius discussed with his Greek informants.[130]

When Leunclavius visited Constantinople in 1584–85, he went more than twenty times to the house of one of Crusius's Greek correspondents, the protonotary Theodosios Zygomalas. There, he had absorbing conversations with his host. He

126 Thomas Ryves, *Imperatoris Iustiniani Defensio contra Alemannum* (London, 1626), esp. 9–10.

127 P. Burke, *Secret History and Historical Consciousness from the Renaissance to Romanticism* (Brighton, 2016).

128 M. Brownley, "The Secret History and Seventeenth-Century Historiography," in *The Secret History in Literature, 1660–1820*, ed. R. Bullard and R. Carnell (Cambridge, 2017), 33–45.

129 B. Dooley, *The Social History of Skepticism: Experience and Doubt in Early Modern Culture* (Baltimore, 1999); J. Soll, *Publishing "The Prince": History, Reading and the Birth of Political Criticism* (Ann Arbor, 2005).

130 R. Calis, "Reconstructing the Ottoman Greek World: Early Modern Ethnography in the Household of Martin Crusius," *RenQ* 72.1 (2019): 148–93.

also saw, on the walls of Zygomalas's "own room in his house," portraits of Crusius himself and of "the great men of Tübingen": the exact counterpart of what a Greek would have seen in Crusius's house.[131] I wonder if Leunclavius was able to see the world outside Europe in his characteristic open way—to see Greeks as subjects, as well as objects—because he had begun his scholarly career thinking about Zosimus and the way in which he taught readers to go beyond the traditions of rhetoric and decorum. If that conjecture is correct, then the study of Byzantine history and historians was at the core of later Renaissance humanism and its cosmopolitan culture of inquiry.

My thanks to Alexander Bevilacqua, Richard Calis, and Christian Flow for discussion, to Paola Megna for providing me with a copy of her book on Poliziano and Zosimus, and to the referees for their very helpful corrections and suggestions.

131 Leunclavius to Crusius, 20 July 1586, published in B. A. Mystikades, "Notes sur Martin Crusius: Ses livres, ses ouvrages et ses manuscrits," *REG* 11.43 (1898): 294; also discussed in C. Pitsakis, "Leunclavius Neo-Graecus," *RJ* 13 (1994): 243.

FOUR

MARTIN CRUSIUS'S LOST BYZANTINE LEGACY

RICHARD CALIS

ONE OF THE EARLIEST EARLY MODERN CONSUMERS OF BYZANTINE MATERIALS was a professor of Latin and Greek at the University of Tübingen. Over the years, Martin Crusius (1526–1607) acquired dozens of Byzantine texts of all genres and from all periods, in print and in manuscript, and, importantly, both in Greek and in Latin. Diligently he would mark his way through the massive Homer commentaries of Eustathios of Thessalonike and the *Epitome of History* of John Zonaras; through Manuel Moschopoulos's seminal Greek grammar as well as the massive *Etymologicum Magnum* and the equally voluminous *Suda* lexicon. He made manuscript copies of Symeon Metaphrastes' *Menologion*—a collection of saints' lives organized according to the church calendar—and even owned such a colorful work as the *Lexicon on the Properties of Foods*, that classic on dietetics published by the medieval physician Symeon Seth. Through contacts in Venice and Istanbul, Augsburg and Basel, Crusius managed to collect no fewer than fifty different books and manuscripts from the Byzantine period and often enriched them with thick layers of critical commentary.

Crusius is no stranger in the field of Byzantine and modern Greek studies. Byzantinists interested in the history of their field have often grouped him together with better-known pioneers of Byzantine studies such as Hieronymus Wolf and his student David Hoeschel.[1] Yet reasons for Crusius's inclusion in this story have often

1 H.-G. Beck, "Die byzantinischen Studien in Deutschland vor Karl Krumbacher," in *ΧΑΛΙΚΕΣ: Festgabe für die Teilnehmer am XI. internationalen Byzantinistenkongreß, München 15.–20. September*

been based on his seminal publication on the Ottoman Greek world, the *Turcograecia* of 1584. This chapter posits that to gauge Crusius's exact position in the field of Byzantine studies and the full richness of his engagement with Byzantine materials, it is more productive to examine the books and manuscripts that he so thoroughly annotated. This vast mass of materials, which has survived in the Tübingen University Library, lets us gain a rich sense of how Crusius envisioned Byzantine texts and histories and also enables us to read his *Turcograecia* in a different way, since it sheds so much light on the terminology and framing used there.

My analysis of these documents demonstrates that in the hands of an early modern reader such as Crusius, Byzantine materials formed an incredibly fertile field of learning—and one that he harvested with multiple objectives in mind. Crusius read Byzantine commentaries and lexica to clarify and add depth to his understanding of ancient authors such as Homer. He mined these and other works for evidence of the postclassical development of the Greek language. The Byzantine historical tradition offered Crusius a means to confront one vitally important contemporary issue: the existential threat that he and others believed the Ottoman Turks posed to the Christian world. Byzantium was nevertheless also relatively unfamiliar ground; in Byzantine historical works Crusius encountered a seemingly endless string of historical actors who required careful contextualization and historical explanation. And so did the authors who narrated their histories: in the second half of the sixteenth century Byzantine historians still lacked a coherent chronology. To find his way through these uncharted terrains, Crusius resorted, as his marginal annotations reveal and this chapter reconstructs, to the scholarly principles of biobibliography, historical chronology, and genealogy.

Tracing the technicalities of these forms of readerly interaction also affords insight into the conceptual framework by which Crusius arranged his texts. He did not yet conceive of Byzantium as a period in Greek history in its own right. He did not treat the Byzantine texts that he had acquired as a fixed canon. Instead, he sought to

---

1958 (Freising, 1958), 67–119, at 82–83 (repr. in idem, *Ideen und Realitäten in Byzanz: Gesammelte Aufsätze*, Variorum Reprints [London, 1972], I); D. R. Reinsch, "Hieronymus Wolf as Editor and Translator of Byzantine Texts," in *The Reception of Byzantium in European Culture since 1500*, ed. P. Marciniak and D. C. Smythe (New York, 2016), 43–53; F. Tinnefeld, "Die Erinnerung an Vergessenes in der Byzantinistik seit ihren Anfängen im 15./16. Jahrhundert," in *Erinnerungskultur in Südosteuropa: Bericht über die Konferenzen der Kommission für Interdisziplinäre Südosteuropa-Forschung im Januar 2004, Februar 2005 und März 2006 in Göttingen*, ed. R. Lauer (Berlin, 2011), 83–104, at 87. See also K.-H. Suchland, "Das Byzanzbild des Tübinger Philhellenen Martin Crusius (1526–1607)" (PhD diss., Universität Würzburg, 2001), 5, and the many references to Crusius in Karl Krumbacher's foundational *Geschichte der byzantinischen Litteratur: Von Justinian bis zum Ende des oströmischen Reiches (527–1453)* (Munich, 1891). For a more in-depth assessment, see A. Ben-Tov, *Lutheran Humanists and Greek Antiquity: Melanchthonian Scholarship between Universal History and Pedagogy* (Leiden, 2009), 83–131.

trace how the story of the Greeks had continued into his own time, as is borne out not only by his marginalia but also by his editorial work. In the *Turcograecia*, Crusius inserted two historical chronicles that presented his readers with a "Byzantium" slightly different from the constructions of his scholarly forebears. For Crusius, who approached Byzantine and Ottoman history as a continuum, Byzantium was not a political and cultural entity of the past; it was the living present. To understand how he came to see these periods as part of one continuous Greek history, it is necessary to move beyond questions of terminology. Crusius used *Greek* and *Byzantine* interchangeably when referring to the period in Greek history that we now call Byzantine. It is telling that on the first page of his diary, which he initially kept to collect evidence about the Ottoman Greek world, *Byzantium* was the term he used when talking about sixteenth-century Ottoman Greek affairs. His terminology, in other words, elides what others were turning into historical distinctions in the field of Greek history and literature, so that Byzantine and post-Byzantine materials came to exist in the same matrix. It is more fruitful in this context, as this chapter sets out to show, to examine how Crusius classified the Greek language: one could say that for Crusius "Byzantium"—even when called something else—was born as the ancient Greek language, which he studied so zealously in his Tübingen home, started to become corrupt.

Biobibliography and the Uses of Byzantine Scholarship

Byzantine materials were central to Crusius's professional life. In 1559, after a short stint as rector of a Latin school in Memmingen, he accepted a position to teach at the University of Tübingen, where he would stay until his death in 1607. Throughout his long career, he explicated many ancient texts, including Cicero's orations as well as the historical work of Thucydides. The epics of Homer, which he taught year after year, particularly interested him and brought him great renown: at one point the university decided to break down one of the lecture room's walls to accommodate all the students who wished to attend his lectures.[2] Homer was also one of two ancient authors to whom Crusius ever dedicated a commentary (the other was Heliodoros).[3] This work, as well as Crusius's lectures—as can be gleaned from his

2 The anecdote is told in Martin Crusius, *Germanograeciae libri sex* (Basel, 1585), 39. See also N. Hofmann, *Die Artistenfakultät an der Universität Tübingen 1534–1601* (Tübingen, 1982), 148.

3 Martin Crusius, *Commentationes in I. lib. Iliad. Homeri grammaticae, rhetoricae, poëticae, historicae, philosophicae* (Heidelberg, 1612). Only his notes to the first book of the *Iliad* were published. The rest of the commentary is lost; see R. Stahlecker, "Martinus Crusius der erste deutsche Verfasser eines Kommentars zum gesamten Homer," *BPW* 59 (1939): 1196–207. The work was a commercial disaster: Crusius initially struggled to find a printer for it, and eventually about two-thirds of the print run remained unsold. See I. Maclean, *Scholarship, Commerce, Religion: The Learned Book in*

working copy of Homer, which has survived—demonstrates that he approached the poet as a storehouse of knowledge, ready to be plundered for intellectual gain, as many contemporaries did.[4]

Studying Homer as a fountain of learning was an approach with deep roots in Greek tradition. Crusius himself readily admitted that many of his own observations were based on ancient and Byzantine commentators on Homer who had read the poet in precisely that way. Chief among these was that apex of Byzantine learning Eustathios of Thessalonike, whose monumental *parekbolai* were held in high regard by early modern scholars. Crusius read this work in the formidable Rome edition of 1549–50.[5] He had acquired the three thick volumes in 1560 and started reading them in the fall of 1563 in preparation for his lecture course (which began in January of the next year).[6] But the scale of this learned tome demanded prolonged attention: Crusius came back to Eustathios for many years to come, finishing the third and final volume only on 14 March 1581, nearly twenty years after he marked his way through the first pages of the *parekbolai*.[7] Throughout the work, he discovered numerous explications that helped him peel back the many layers of Homer's epics. On the frontispiece of his copy, in a single, comical note, Crusius testified to the reverence that Eustathios's learnedness had instilled in him: "[*parekbolai*] are marginal annotations . . . which are thrown, that is, placed next to or close to the text, as when a mole throws soil over and next to himself in a garden."[8]

---

the Age of Confessions, 1560–1630 (Cambridge, 2012), 94–96. For his commentary on Heliodoros, see Martin Crusius, *Aethiopicae Heliodori Historiae Epitome. Cum observationis eiusdem . . . Eiusdem de parentibus suis narratio. Cum indice copioso* (Frankfurt, 1584).

4 For general assessments of the early modern legacy of Homer, see J. Wolfe, *Homer and the Question of Strife from Erasmus to Hobbes* (Toronto, 2015); T. Demetriou, "The Homeric Question in the Sixteenth Century: Early Modern Scholarship and the Text of Homer," *RenQ* 68.2 (2015): 496–557. For two concise analyses of Crusius's Homer, which has survived in the Princeton University Library, see A. Grafton, "Martin Crusius Reads His Homer," *Princeton University Library Chronicle* 64.1 (2002): 63–86, and Ben-Tov, *Lutheran Humanists and Greek Antiquity*, 174–79.

5 Eustathios, *Παρεκβολαὶ εἰς τὴν Ὁμήρου Ἰλιάδα καὶ Ὀδύσσειαν*, 3 vols. (Rome, 1549–50). Crusius's copy is Universitätsbibliothek Tübingen (hereafter UBT) Cd 2936.

6 Eustathios, *Παρεκβολαί*, UBT Cd 2936, vol. 1, title page: *M. Martini Crusii 1560 28 Iunii à Micaëlo Toxite poeta. Constant omnes 3 tomi 11 fl. minus 10 kr. Tybingae. 1: 1563 25 Novemb: incepi ego M. Crusius.* In his working copy of Homer, Crusius noted that he began teaching Homer on 24 January 1564; see Jacob Micyllus and Joachim Camerarius, *Opus utrumque Homeri Iliados et Odysseae* (Basel, 1541), Princeton University Library PA4018.A31 M52 1541q, 1: *Incepi 24 Ianu: 1564 Tybginae publice explicare.*

7 Eustathios, *Παρεκβολαί*, UBT Cd 2936, vol. 3, 1970: *Absolvi ego M. Martinus Crusius, Graecolatinus Tybing. Academiae professor, die 14 Mart. 1581 die martis, media 3 hora pomeridiana. Laus Deo.*

8 Ibid., vol. 1, title page: "÷ *marginales annotationes (sic mihi M. Crusio videtur) quae extra et prope textum iactae ÷ positae sunt*: als wann ein maulwurff (talpa) in einem Garten das Aertrich übersich naebenzu würfft. 1 Sept. 1567 παρὰ *iuxtra* ἐκ *extra*, βάλλω *iacio*."

The lumps of learned clay, which Eustathios had hurled at Homer's epics, became incredibly fertile soil in Crusius's hands. Eustathios, Crusius realized, was instrumental for the correct explication and teaching of classical authors like Homer. The passage, for instance, where the Byzantine commentator analyzed the prudence and eloquence of Nestor, king of Pylos—who had tried to mediate between Agamemnon and Achilles—attracted Crusius's attention because as a teacher he focused on explicating the epic's many speeches and highlighting their rhetorical potential.[9] Elsewhere Crusius took an interest in how Eustathios explicated the plot by way of allegory. One such comment discussed the role of Hephaestus in reconciling his parents, Zeus and Hera, at the beginning of the *Iliad*. Eustathios had drawn from earlier allegorical discussions of this passage when he had interpreted Hephaestus as Heat (τὸ θερμὸν), Zeus as Ether (αἰθήρ), and Hera as Air (ἀήρ), showing that because both ether and air have warm qualities, it was Hephaestus who was bound to reunite his parents. Crusius underlined key sentences of this physical allegory, which runs to three pages, and also summarized its content in the margins.[10] The section then formed the basis of Crusius's own commentary on this passage, where he succinctly paraphrased Eustathios's allegorical explanation.[11] Eustathios, in other words, served Crusius as a source for what he regarded as plausible learned interpretations of Homer, some of which he accepted with no sense of irony or distance.

Approaching Byzantine texts as repositories of ancient learning was not idiosyncratic. It was, in fact, a common way to read Byzantine scholarship throughout the early modern period. Early modern luminaries as diverse as Angelo Poliziano and Meric Casaubon, Guillaume Budé, and Madame Dacier knew the rewards (and pitfalls) to be found in Byzantine scholarship.[12] In preparing his commanding *Thesaurus Temporum*, Joseph Scaliger (1540–1609) zealously looked for a manuscript copy of George Synkellos's selection from the Greek chronographers to learn more about the chronicle of Eusebius. The great Hellenist Isaac Casaubon (1559–1614) read the seventh-century *Chronicon Paschale* for what it revealed about the ancient Greek Olympiads.[13] In late seventeenth-century Cambridge, the notable and

9 Grafton, "Martin Crusius," 82–84.

10 Eustathios, *Παρεκβολαί*, UBT Cd 2936, vol. 1, 150–51. In the margin of p. 150 Crusius noted: *Vulcani allegoria, aetherem et aerem componentis.*

11 Crusius, *Commentationes in I. lib. Iliad*, 186.

12 A. Grafton, *Commerce with the Classics: Ancient Books and Renaissance Readers* (Ann Arbor, 1997), 168; F. Pontani, "'Captain of Homer's Guard': The Reception of Eustathius in Modern Europe," in *Reading Eustathios of Thessalonike*, ed. F. Pontani, V. Katsaros, and V. Sarris (Berlin, 2017), 199–226.

13 A. Grafton, *Joseph Scaliger: A Study in the History of Classical Scholarship*, vol. 2, *Historical Chronology* (Oxford, 1993), 538 (on Casaubon), 540–48 (on Scaliger).

notorious English philologist Richard Bentley (1662–1742) turned his critical acumen to the work of John Malalas of Antioch to reconstruct the numerous fragments of ancient Greek poetry that the author had misquoted to disastrous effect.[14]

Yet Crusius read Eustathios not just to learn more about an ancient author. Eustathios's work was more than just a vast commentary or a proverbial treasure trove. Crusius also sought to position the Byzantine scholar himself in his direct historical and linguistic context by applying the principles of biobibliography. Biobibliography was a way to fix an author in time and place by bringing the account of an author's life to bear on their work. It was a method that could help scholars discern the so-called *scopus*, or goal, of a given text.[15] From Niketas Choniates' *Histories*, for instance—which Crusius read in Hieronymus Wolf's 1557 *editio princeps*—he learned about the courageous behavior of Eustathios as archbishop of Thessalonike: the emperor Manuel I Komnenos (r. 1143–1180) had once suggested that an anathema against Islam be abolished in order to prevent future converts from Islam from having to blaspheme against their former God. Of all the ecclesiastics present at the synod that the emperor had convened, it was Eustathios who denounced the abolition at length. Elsewhere Choniates narrated how Eustathios, when the Sicilians besieged and entered Thessalonike, interceded on behalf of the city's inhabitants and thereby managed to alleviate some of their suffering. Both passages in Crusius's copy of Choniates contain traces of readerly interaction, indicating that he examined them with serious attention.[16] This is also borne out by the frontispiece, where Crusius referenced both passages and stressed the archbishop's "praiseworthy freedom of speech" (*laudabilem* ... παρρησίαν).[17] Indeed, Eustathios, his actions, and his commentaries were apparently so commendable that Crusius even acknowledged them in his university oration on the *Odyssey*, given on 19 November 1572.[18] For Crusius, then, Eustathios was not just an explicator of Homer but also a historical actor

14 A. Grafton, *Defenders of the Text: The Traditions of Scholarship in an Age of Science, 1450–1800* (Cambridge, MA, 1991), 13. For the broader context, see K. Haugen, *Richard Bentley: Poetry and Enlightenment* (Cambridge, MA, 2011).

15 K. Eden, *Hermeneutics and the Rhetorical Tradition: Chapters in the Ancient Legacy and Its Humanist Reception* (New Haven, 1997).

16 Hieronymus Wolf, *Nicetae Acominati Choniatae ... LXXXVI annorum historia: Uidelicet ab anno restitutae Salutis circiter MCXVII, in quo Zonaras desinit, usque ad annum MCCIII, libris XIX descripta* (Basel, 1557), UBT Cd 4980, 109, 153. In the margins of the first passage Crusius also copied out part of Eustathios's preface to his commentary on Dionysius Periegetes from Robert Estienne's 1547 edition of this work.

17 Eustathios, *Παρεκβολαί*, UBT Cd 2936, vol. 1, title page: *Laudabilem Eustathii contra Manuelem Comnenum παῤῥησίαν, vide Nicetae Choniatae pag. 109. et pro civibus, Thessalonica à siculis capta, intercessionem. 153.*

18 Crusius, *Germanograecia* (n. 2 above), 38–39.

himself, and in some ways an exemplary one, on whom other near-contemporary testimonies could shed an important light.

This was far from the only moment when Crusius mined one Byzantine author for biographical details about another. The title pages and flyleaves of his Byzantine books are often decorated with similar notes on authors and their writings. On the title page of Niketas Choniates' history, Crusius brought together all the bio-bibliographical details that he could find to contextualize this work. Crusius took Choniates to be a historian with poetic phrasing, an imitator of Homer who was pleasant to read "because of his profuseness of language and bombastic words. He was pious, learned, and prudent. Not unlike Ammianus Marcelinus."[19] Elsewhere on the page, he referred to Eustathios's commentary on the *Iliad*, when he noted that the historian's first name, Νικήτας, was a Doric version of the common noun νικήτης, meaning "victor." So just as Crusius had read Choniates to understand Eustathios better, so he also read the latter to make sense of the former. Similarly, in the back of John Chrysostom's *On the Priesthood*, Crusius copied out a lengthy excerpt from the *Suda* lexicon's entry on the Greek church father.[20] Likewise, when Crusius read Eusebius of Caesarea's *Ecclesiastical History* he again copied details from the *Suda* lexicon for further contextualization.[21] Crusius's own copy of the *Suda*—Aldus's 1514 edition—evinces a similar approach. Not only did he read and mark up the entries of important ancient writers, such as those on Epicurus and Euripides, he also sought to anchor the lexicon in time and place. Following an earlier tradition, Crusius still believed that this work had been written by a man called Suidas: on the frontispiece he remarked that one could gather from the entry on Adam that "Suidas" had lived in

19 Wolf, *Nicetae Acominati Choniatae . . . LXXXVI annorum historia*, UBT Cd 4980, title page: νικήτας *doricè, pro* νικήτης *Iliad. 18. Eustats. 1166* and *Est historicus* φράσει *poeticus, et Homeri imitator. Est suavis propter copiam, et ampullosa verba. . . . Fuit pius, doctus, prudens. Talis est Ammianus Marcell.*

20 John Chrysostom, *Qvod multae quidem dignitatis, sed difficile sit episcopum agere: Dialogi sex* (Tübingen, 1548), UBT Gb 98, blank flyleaf in the back: *Vitam Ioan. Chrysost. Suidas habet. Ioan. Antiochenus, ὁ ἐπικληθεὶς Χρυσόστομος, primo presbyter Antiochiae: Eusebii vero Emeseni philosophi, et Diodori,* ἀκόλουθος. *Is multa scripsit:* ἀφ> ὧν οἱ περὶ ἱερωσύνης ὑπερβάλλουσι λόγοι, τῷ τε ὕψει καὶ τῇ φράσει, καὶ τῇ λειότητι, καὶ τῷ κάλλει τῶν ὀνομάτων. *Scripsit in omnes Iudaeorum et Chistianorum libros.* οὐδεὶς τῶν ἀπ' αἰῶνος τοσαύτην λόγων ηὐπόρησεν εὔροιαν, ἣν μόνος αὐτὸς ἐπλούτησε: καὶ μόνος ἀκιβδήλως τὸ χρυσοῦν τε καὶ θεῖον ἐκληρονόμησεν ὄνομα. τῶν δὲ συγγραμμάτων αὐτοῦ καταλέγειν τὸν ἀριθμὸν, οὐκ ἀνθρώπου: θεοῦ δὲ μᾶλλον, τοῦ τὰ πάντα γινώσκοντος. *Erat* πολυάγρυπνος, καὶ φιλήσυχος λίαν, καὶ διὰ ζῆλον σωφροσύνης εὐπαρρησίαστος, καὶ ἀκρόχολος: θυμῷ γὰρ μᾶλλον ἢ αἰδοῖ ἐχαρίζετο: καὶ ἐλευθεροστομίᾳ πρὸς τοὺς ἐντυγχάνοντας ἀμέτρως ἐκέχρητο. *Epsicopus factus,* μείζονι ὀφρύϊ κατὰ τῶν ὑπηκόων ἐκέχρητο: πρὸς διόρθωσιν ἑκάστου, καὶ σωτηρίαν, καὶ τοὺς τρόπους, καὶ τοὺς λόγους, μεταλλάττων.

21 Eusebius, *Ecclesiasticae historiae libri X* (Paris, 1544), UBT Gb 407, **iii: *Suidas addit προσκείμενος τῇ ἀρειανῇ αἱρέσει idem de eo sentitur in synodi Nicaenae ii actione 6 in disputatione Epiphanii diaconi contra Gregor. Neocaesariensem.*

the reign of the emperor John I Tzimiskes (r. 969–976). On that same page Crusius also referenced the *Magdeburg Centuries*, a polemical Gnesio-Lutheran ecclesiastical history that he used repeatedly to understand Byzantine history. This work mentioned that the English statesman, bishop, and philosopher Robert Grosseteste (ca. 1175–1253) had translated the *Suda* from Greek into Latin.[22] On the final page of the lexicon, Crusius copied out, in full, Demetrios Chalkokondyles' preface to the 1499 Milan edition of the *Suda*—a passage in which the editor had called attention to the lexicon's utility for scholars with diverse interests.[23] Crusius thus turned his copy of the *Suda* into a site of biobibliographical research, full of easily retrievable information on the author of this foundational lexicon.

Dry, succinct, and technical as they may sometimes be, these notes nevertheless yield important clues about how Crusius used one Byzantine text to understand another. Early modern readers, as specialists in different fields have shown, often referenced what other materials they had read in the margins of texts they were reading.[24] But in this case Crusius's reliance on biobibliography demonstrates a hugely important point: texts from the Byzantine period required a form of universal bibliography in the tradition of Conrad Gessner (1516–1565). The Swiss physician's 1545 *Bibliotheca universalis* purported to catalog, in shorter or longer alphabetically organized entries, all known books and authors printed in Latin, Greek, or Hebrew. Although Gessner's work is not listed as one of the more than 700 hundred books that have survived from Crusius's private library, it is evident that he shared with his Swiss colleague a vision about the potential of universal bibliography: in situating texts in their biobibliographical context, Crusius created an inventory that helped him escape the "labyrinth"—to borrow Gessner's metaphor—of Byzantine texts and authors, not unlike the summaries offered by Gessner in the *Bibliotheca universalis*.[25] But Crusius's notes also demonstrate that the tradition of

22 *Suida* (Venice, 1514), UBT Cd 4643, title page: *Robertus Grossetest... in Anglia Lincolniensis Episcopus, Suidam e Greco latine convertit. Obiit 1253. Illyric. Eccles. Histor. Centur. 13. Cap. 10.* and *Suidas videtur, in dict. ἀδὰμ, vixisse tempore Ioannis Tzemiscae.*

23 Ibid., final page: *Idem hoc opus antea anno domini 1499 die 15 novemb. excusum fuit Mediolani, impensa et dexteritate D. Demetrii Chalcocondylae, Ioannis Bissoli, Benedicti Mangii, Carpensium.*

24 The literature is vast. For some works relevant to the story here, see Grafton, *Commerce with the Classics*, 34; L. Jardine and A. Grafton, "'Studied for Action': How Gabriel Harvey Read His Livy," *Past and Present* 129 (1990): 30–78; W. H. Sherman, *Used Books: Marking Readers in Renaissance England* (Philadelphia, 2008).

25 On Crusius's library, see T. Wilhelmi, *Die griechischen Handschriften der Universitätsbibliothek Tübingen: Sonderband Martin Crusius: Handschriftenverzeichnis und Bibliographie* (Wiesbaden, 2002). On Gessner and bibliography, see H. Zedelmaier, *Bibliotheca Universalis und Bibliotheca Selecta: Das Problem der Ordnung des gelehrten Wissens in der frühen Neuzeit* (Cologne, 1992); P. Nelles, "Reading and Memory in the Universal Library: Conrad Gessner and the Renaissance Book," in *Ars Reminiscendi: Mind and Memory in Renaissance Culture*, ed. D. Beecher and G. Williams

universal bibliography started by Gessner was as continuous as the publishing of books: the discovery and publication of (new) texts required Crusius and other heirs of Gessner's bibliographical tradition to continue the compilatory research of their illustrious predecessor. This is not to say that Crusius saw Byzantine texts, or Byzantium, as a self-contained, internally coherent field (a point to which I will return); it demonstrates rather that he sought to integrate the world of Byzantine scholarship into the wider world of learning.

Chronology, Genealogy, and the Byzantine Historiographical Tradition

To wring knowledge out of texts from the Byzantine period was evidently not easy: Crusius had to actively make his Byzantine books serve his scholarly needs and put them in conversation with other scholarship. This holds true to an even greater extent for the Byzantine historians that passed through his hands. By the second half of the sixteenth century there was not a single historian who narrated the whole sweep of Byzantine history. Instead, those wishing to familiarize themselves with the postclassical fate of the Greeks needed to read widely and comparatively. This realization—together, admittedly, with the availability of manuscripts and funds—had already dictated the decision of the Basel printer and publisher Oporinus to publish four authors—Zonaras, Choniates, Gregoras, and Chalkokondyles—and arrange them into a single narrative. "In comparing these four writers," the learned world would have "an integral corpus of Byzantine history from Constantine the Great to Constantine the last [emperor], and the capture of Constantinople by the Turks." In other words, this bilingual edition, which had been edited by Hieronymus Wolf, bracketed off Byzantium as the period between the glory days of Constantine the Great and the rise of the Ottomans at the expense of the Greeks.[26]

(Toronto, 2009), 147–69; F. Sabba, *La 'Bibliotheca Universalis' di Conrad Gesner: Monumento della cultura europea* (Rome, 2012).

26 Hieronymus Wolf, *Nicephori Gregorae, Romanae, hoc est Byzantiae historae libri XI* (Basel, 1562), title page: *Ita quatuor his scriptoribus, Zonara, Choniate, Gregora, Chalcondyla coniunctis, integrum Byzantinae historiae corpus a Constantino magno ad Constantinum postremum, & Constantinopolim a Turcis occupatam & possessam, habituri sunt studiosi, utraque lingua expositum, ut & de fide interpretum constaret: & tam rudibus Graecarum litterarum, quam doctis, maiore commoditate quam sumptu consuleretur.* For Wolf's editorial practices, see D. R. Reinsch, "The History of Editing Byzantine Historiographical Texts," in *The Byzantine World*, ed. P. Stephenson (London, 2010), 438–39, and idem, "Hieronymus Wolf as Editor and Translator." On the creation of this "corpus," see the excellent discussion in F. Husner, "Die Editio Princeps des 'Corpus Historiae Byzantinae': Johannes Oporin, Hieronymus Wolf und die Fugger," in *Festschrift Karl Schwarber: Beiträge zur schweizerischen Bibliotheks-, Buch- und Gelehrtengeschichte* (Basel, 1949), 143–62. For the suggestion that Oporinus and not Wolf coined the term *Corpus historiae byzantinae*, see Ben-Tov, *Lutheran Humanists and Greek Antiquity* (n. 1 above), 106–9.

Yet the historians in the "corpus" were but four authors out of a much larger pool of Byzantine historical writing. Crusius, for one, owned and read many other Byzantine historians as well: Anna Komnene, John Skylitzes, George Pachymeres, George Kedrenos, Pseudo-Kodinos, Michael Glykas, Constantine Manasses, and late antique historical works such as Eusebius's *Church History* also stocked his library. These historians needed to be synchronized with the timeline offered by Oporinus's corpus and placed on the timeline of world history as well. Some of these texts, after all, narrated events in early Byzantine history in much more detail than, say, the universal history of Zonaras, whose eighteen books spanned the time from Creation to the death of Alexios I Komnenos in 1118. So one of the first tasks that Crusius set himself echoed the editorial principle of the corpus, but at the same time went far beyond it: connecting all the various Byzantine texts that he owned so that they lined up chronologically.

Crusius did so in the first instance by cross-referencing his way through these works, and by mining them for chronological clues. One of the Byzantine books that he owned was a copy of Joachim Camerarius's 1566 Latin translation of Patriarch Nikephoros's *Chronographikon*. In this work, which lists all the various rulers from the creation of the world to the ninth century CE, Crusius cross-referenced passages that enabled him to reconstruct and date the life of the author, who, he (erroneously) believed, had been patriarch of Constantinople until 845—evidence in itself that his biobibliographical and chronological approach were two sides of the same coin.[27] In other cases, Crusius worked comparatively: in Wilhelm Xylander's 1566 bilingual edition of George Kedrenos, Crusius turned to the final page, which narrated the abdication of Michael VI Stratiotikos (r. 1056–1057), and noted that this heralded the beginning of Isaac I Komnenos's reign, as told by the historian Zonaras.[28] Here Crusius relied on Johann Funck, a Lutheran historian and theologian whose 1554 *Chronologia* was highly influential in the period, to understand Byzantine imperial succession.[29] (A set of chronological tables, which Xylander had appended to his edition and which placed the rulers of the world from Adam to Charles V neatly side by side, may have helped Crusius here as well.) On the front flyleaf and frontispiece of his copy of Zonaras, Crusius made a list of Greek

27 Joachim Camerarius, *Chronologia secundum Graecorum rationem temporibus expositis, autore Nicephoro archiepiscopo Constantinopolis* (Basel, 1561), UBT Cd 3860.2, title page: *qui dixit usque ad annum Christi 845 pag. 96.*

28 Wilhelm Xylander, *Georgii Cedreni Annales, sive historiae ab exordio mundi ad Isaacium Commenum usque Compendium* (Basel, 1566), UBT Cd 2440.2, 662: *Iam imperium Isaacii Comneni incipit anno Christi 1059. Funccio, apud Ioan. Zonaras.*

29 Wolf, *Nicetae Acominati Choniatae . . . LXXXVI annorum historia*, UBT Cd 4980, title page: *Chr. 1117 Secundum Ioan. Funccium.*

authors that had chronicled the history of Byzantium. It was complemented by another one on the front pastedown.[30] These may not have been chronological, but in bringing them together Crusius, at the very least, created a neat list of authorities on the subject he was studying.[31] Moreover, at the very end of the historian's work, where Zonaras narrated the life of Alexios I Komnenos (r. 1081–1118), Crusius noted that the emperor's own daughter, "the most learned Anna Komnene," had also described her father's life. Zonaras, Crusius argued, had in fact borrowed from her work.[32] Turning to the front flyleaf of Crusius's manuscript copy of the *Alexiad*, we find a similar note about Zonaras's reliance on Anna Komnene—information that Crusius had taken from the Benedictine theologian Gilbert Génébrard's 1585 *Chronographia*.[33] Similarly, in the margin of Hieronymus Wolf's preface to his edition of Niketas Choniates, Crusius noted that he had seen the *Alexiad* in a mutilated manuscript version from the imperial library in Augsburg.[34] Crusius also remarked—on the frontispiece, as usual—that John Skylitzes had written a history from the death of the emperor Nikephoros I (r. 802–811) to the reign of

30 Zonaras, *Compendium Historiarum, in tres Tomos distinctum ... Opus praeclarum ... labore Hieronymi Vvolfii, Graece ac Latine ... in lucem editum*, UBT Cd 4980, front pastedown: *Historici graeci de imperio orientis. Gregorius monachus. Theophanes. Psellus Philosophus. Theodorus. Nicetas Paphlagon. Iosephus. Genesius et Manuel Byzantii. Nicephorus Diaconus Phocorum. Leo Asianus. Theodorus Proedrus. Sidis. Demetrius Cyzicenus. Ioan, Monachus Lydius. Scylax. Ioan. Curopalates Cilix. Zonaras monachus. Acropolites. Ephren carmine iambico* and title page: *Scriptores Graeci Byzantinae Historiae. Gregorius monachus et syncellus. Ioan. Zonaras. Niceta Acuminatus Choniata. Georg. Cedrenus. Anna Comnena Caesarissa. Niceph. Gregoras. Laonic. Chalcondyles. Ioan. Curopalates, Scylax. Michaël Glyces. Constantinus Manastes. Theodorus Spanduginus Byzantius.* This edition was printed in March 1557, several months prior to Wolf's 1557 edition of Niketas Choniates (see n. 16 above); thereafter, the two texts were often bound together. See G. Della Rocca de Candal, "*Bibliographia Historica Byzantina*: A Historical and Bibliographical Description of the Early Editions of the Corpus Historiae Byzantinae (1556–1645)" (PhD diss., University of Oxford, 2015), 43.

31 On these and other types of lists as devices to locate information, see A. Blair, *Too Much to Know: Managing Scholarly Information before the Modern Age* (New Haven, 2010), 132–44, and, more philosophically, U. Eco, *The Infinity of Lists: From Homer to Joyce*, trans. A. McEwen (New York, 2009).

32 Zonaras, *Compendium Historiarum*, UBT Cd 4980, book 3, 234: *Vita huius Alexii filia ipsius Anna descripsit: cuius libros 8 (reliquae deest) mutilatos, perlegi ego M. Crusius Graecos Tybingae, manuscriptos, ex Bibliothec. Augustana, anno 1575. ex quibus Zonaras multa sumpsit* and 242: *Anna Comnena doctissima.*

33 Anna Komnene, *Alexiad*, UBT Mb 11, fol. b-I: *Gilb. Genebrardus, in Chronographia 1585. Parisiis excusa, Lib. 4. Anna Alexias Libris 20. de rebus ab Alexio patre gestis, Zonarae narrationem persequitur.*

34 Wolf, *Nicetae Acominati Choniatae ... LXXXVI annorum historia*, UBT Cd 4980, unpaginated preface: *Anna Comnena. Eius libros legi Christi 1575, quorum tum 8 mutili extant in Bibliotheca Augustana.*

Isaac I Komnenos (r. 1057–1059) and that Michael Glykas in his world history had narrated the events up to the death of Alexios I Komnenos.[35]

Comparison, in other words, enabled Crusius to read the Byzantine historians within a common chronological frame. It taught him which of these authors narrated the same events, how they supplemented one another, and who had borrowed from whom; and it enabled him to construe an extraordinarily rich, fine-grained timeline of Byzantine events. Yet in a way, that was only the beginning: early modern readers of Byzantine materials must have quickly realized that different historians had construed different histories and that, despite their overlap, disagreement between them was no exception. Worse still, the Byzantine historiographical tradition had its own unique way of reckoning time. Byzantine historians used the Greek calendar based on the World Era: that is, they computed the years from the starting point of the creation of the world, whose date was hotly debated.[36] The date that Niketas Choniates, for instance, gave for the sack of Constantinople by the crusaders was not 1204 CE but "on the twelfth day of the month of April of the seventh indiction in the year 6712."[37] This meant that reading Byzantine historians in early modern Europe always involved an exercise in synchronization.

Crusius's marginalia demonstrate just how complex any comparison between this Greek way of dating the world and chronologies offered in Latin treatises would be. On the very top of the frontispiece of his Zonaras copy, for instance, Crusius confidently asserted that "Christ [is the] main point of chronology," only to list the different dates for Christ's birth given by four different authorities (Johann Funck, Bibliander, George Kedrenos, and Patriarch Nikephoros).[38] Crusius made the same comparison between these four authors on the frontispiece of his copy of Kedrenos, where he echoed the tagline about the importance of Christ in historical chronology.[39] In his copy of Patriarch Nikephoros's *Chronographikon*, Crusius

35 Ibid., title page: *huc usque, describendo annales suos mundi, Michael Glycas Siculus pervenit.* and *Ioan. Curopalates historiam scripsit à morte Nicephori Imp. usque ad Isaacum Comnenum.*

36 V. Grumel, "L'année du monde dans l'ère byzantine," *EO* 34 (1935): 327–31.

37 I. Bekker, ed., *Nicetae Choniatae Historia* (Bonn, 1835), 752: ἡ ἐνάτη τοῦ Ἀπριλλίου μηνὸς τῆς ἑβδόμης ἰνδικιτῶνος τοῦ ἑξακισχιλιοστοῦ ἑπτακοσιοστοῦ δωδεκάτου ἔτους.

38 Zonaras, *Compendium Historiarum*, UBT Cd 4980, title page: *Christus,* κεφάλαιον *Chronologiae* and *Christus est natus anno mundi {5506} autore {Georgio Cedreno, pag. 143 5500 Nicephoro Archiepiscopo Constantinop. p. 36 in conversio Camerarii Ioan. Funccius 3963} natum scribit. Bibliander 3979.* For an overview of the importance of Jesus Christ's life in early modern historical chronology, see C. P. E. Nothaft, *Dating the Passion: The Life of Jesus and the Emergence of Scientific Chronology (200–1600)* (Leiden, 2012).

39 Xylander, *Georgii Cedreni Annales*, UBT Cd 2440, title page: *Christus,* κεφάλαιον *Χρονολογίας* and "*Christus est natus anno mundi {Georgio Cedreno 5506. Nicephoro Archiepiscopo Constantinop. 5500 Funccio 3963 Bibliandro 3979.*

flagged part of the appendix where Joachim Camerarius—the translator and commentator of the work—compared how Greek and Hebrew writers had dated Creation.[40] Elsewhere Crusius again turned to Funck to understand in precisely what year the reign of Alexios I Komnenos ended.[41]

Again and again Crusius brought to bear on these chronological issues every bit of learning that he could find in his study. Even such an unlikely voice in the early modern debate on historical chronology as Nikolaus Selnecker (1530–1592)—known primarily as a hymnographer and theologian—made an appearance. Selnecker had published not only collections of psalms but also more than a few biblical commentaries. One of the theologian's earliest scholarly works, which Crusius owned and read, was a collection of proposition and questions on Aristotle's *Physics*. At the very end of the work Crusius learned from Selnecker that Greek and Latin writers had voiced markedly different opinions on the age of the world. This detail was apparently so important that Crusius replicated it on the title page of his personal copy of Nikephoros's history.[42] It also tells us with what kind of sources Crusius tackled his Byzantine books.

But Crusius confronted and compared Byzantine chronologies not just to synchronize them with his own way of dividing time. He also sought to understand how human history had unfolded since biblical times. Crusius dated page after page after page in Zonaras's *Epitome of History*—a book that in a general sense lacked precise dating—by inserting single-sentence summaries that identified scenes from the Old Testament, such as the creation of Adam and Eve, the Exodus from Egypt, the reign of King David, and Judith beheading Holofernes, as well as chapters in the life of Jesus.[43] Elsewhere Crusius flagged and dated *capita selecta* from ancient Roman history, such as the founding of the city, the end of the Second Punic War, the life of Caesar, and the reign of Constantine the Great, as well as moments when biblical and Roman history intersected, such as the siege of Jerusalem by the future emperor Titus.[44] Throughout Zonaras's historical work Crusius meticulously dated biblical

40 Camerarius, *Chronologia*, UBT Cd 3860.2, 51.

41 Wolf, *Nicetae Acominati Choniatae . . . LXXXVI annorum historia*, UBT Cd 4980, title page: *Chr. 1117 Secundum Ioan. Funccium.*

42 Camerarius, *Chronologia*, UBT Cd 3860.2, title page: *Graecorum et latinorum errorem in annis mundi numerandis, vide sub finem Nicol: Selnecceri Physices 148.*

43 Zonaras, *Compendium Historiarum*, UBT Cd 4980, book 1, 7 (*Adamus et Eva, creati*), 21 (*Israelitarum exitus de Aegypto. Ante Chr. 1509*), 48 (*Davidis regnum. Incepit regnare ante Chr. 1072.*), 98 (*historia Iudithae, et Holofernis, Ante Chr. circit. 630*), 191 (*Iesu Christi adventus in natura humana. Anno Mundi 3963*).

44 Zonaras, *Compendium Historiarum*, UBT Cd 4980, book 1, 209 (*Hierosolyma obsessa, Chr. 72. die April 14. direpta et incense Septemb. 8*); book 2, 5 (*Roma conditur, ante Chr. 750*), 97 (*Finis secondi belli*

events, as well as the history of the Roman Empire, seemingly in an attempt to put human interaction on a timeline that connected biblical and secular history.

To some extent ancient and biblical histories could be considered episodes in the history of mankind that were well-known to early modern scholars. However, determining the details of what happened in the Eastern Roman Empire after these events required more work. Making individual histories line up chronologically was one thing; sorting out the extensive list of kings and queens, emperors and empresses—and ultimately sultans and sultanas—that Byzantine historians wrote about was quite another. In order to connect these protagonists with those from other histories Crusius turned to genealogy, historical chronology's twin sister in the pursuit of knowledge. In an early modern political climate dominated by noble families and hereditary monarchies, genealogy constituted a vital branch of scholarly research, as scholars of this discipline have shown. Early modern rulers often commissioned elaborate and complex genealogies that were used to substantiate dynastic claims or confirm royal status, testifying to their ever-present concerns with lineage.[45] But genealogy was also a key way of understanding historical writings. Reiner Reineccius, a German professor of history and a contemporary of Crusius, would go as far as claiming that genealogy illuminated "all the other parts of history, and without it they bear basically no fruit at all."[46] Indeed, early modern readers of historical works often structured the past by studying its protagonists. Genealogical tables and diagrams helped a given reader resolve chronological inconsistencies, as happened, for instance, in the case of the conflicting accounts of Christ's parentage found in the Bible.[47] More generally, genealogy helped readers of history find links between past and present: while history offered precedent, genealogy uncovered pedigree.

In Crusius's case this period interest in genealogical data morphed into a method to tackle the intricacies of Byzantine historical writing. He relied on genealogy to identify vital links of kinship. He used chronology, and a whole range of Latin erudite scholarship, to position these ties and events within the larger history of the world. On the second page of his copy of Choniates, for instance, he listed the first

---

punici, ante Chr. 198), 125 (*Ante Chr. 45 factus monarcha [est Iulius Caesar]*); book 3, 3 (*[Imperium Constantini magni] Anno Christi 310.*).

45 V. Bauer, *Wurzel, Stamm, Krone: Fürstliche Genealogie in frühneuzeitlichen Druckwerken* (Wiesbaden, 2013); M. Friedrich, "Genealogy as Archive-Driven Research Enterprise in Early Modern Europe," *Osiris* 32.1 (2017): 65–84.

46 Reineccius, quoted in A. Grafton, *What Was History? The Art of History in Early Modern Europe* (2007; repr., Cambridge, 2012), 147.

47 K. Macfarlane, "The Biblical Genealogies of the King James Bible (1611): Their Purpose, Sources and Significance," *The Library* 19.2 (2018): 131–48.

five emperors from the Komnenian dynasty as well as the offspring of the emperor Alexios I Komnenos and his wife Irene, referencing a similar passage in the history of Zonaras.[48] Elsewhere, relying on information he had taken from Wolfgang Lazius's seminal work on late antique migrations (*De aliquot gentium migrationibus*), Crusius listed the children of Berengar II of Sulzbach (ca. 1083–1125), count of Sulzbach, and his wife Adelheid von Dießen-Wolfratshausen (d. 1126). Their daughter Bertha, Crusius discovered, had been the first wife and empress of the Byzantine emperor Manuel I Komnenos (r. 1143–1180), and as such embodied the intertwined history of Byzantine and Western affairs.[49] Lazius's work, itself the product of systematic genealogical research, thus enabled Crusius to insert Byzantine history into the fabric of history writ large. This was an exercise that Crusius routinely performed while reading Byzantine texts. In other words, he practiced in the margins of his books what advocates of genealogy as a critical method preached on a much larger scale in their printed works and lecture courses.

More than anything, it seems that Crusius's interests in the details of Byzantine genealogy reflect an effort to synchronize Byzantine with Ottoman history. Such a contextualization was not unusual in Crusius's world: the rapid fifteenth- and sixteenth-century advances of the Ottomans into Hungary and Austria had provoked a strong sense of anxiety throughout Western Christendom, but especially in Italy and in the Germanic lands of the Holy Roman Empire. In sermons, broadsheets, single-leaf pamphlets, and numerous other treatises concerning the "Turkish menace" (*Türkengefahr*), authors voiced their fears that the Ottomans might root out the Christian religion and their way of life and began to perceive the Turks as a natural enemy to the Christian world.[50] In scholarly circles, the arrival of the Ottomans and the havoc that they had caused propelled scholars to establish the origins of

48 Wolf, *Nicetae Acominati Choniatae . . . LXXXVI annorum historia*, UBT Cd 4980, 2: *Comneni. 1. Isaacius. 2. Alexius 1. 3. Caloioannes, Isaacius, Andronicus. 4. Manuel. 5. Alexius 2.* and: *Alexii Comn. Liberi, ex Irena: {filii 3.}1. Ioannes, Imp. -Manuel Imp. 2. Andronicus 3. Isaacius -Andronicos Tyrannus. filiae 4. {1. Anna, Nicephoro Bryennio nupta 2. Maria 3. Theodora 4. Eudocia. Sup. 3. Tomo Zonar. 237.*

49 Ibid., 20: *Berengarius, Comes Sulzbach (qui obiit 1126) et Adelhaida, comitissa de Wolfratzhausen, eius exor. Horum liberi {Berengarius. 100. Gerardus. Gertrudis, nupta Conrado 3 Imp. Qui obiit 1138. Bertha, Emanueli Imp. Graeco nupta, dicta Irene. Adelhaidis, nupta Graeco principi de Kvolą Abbatissa quaedam Wolfgang Lazius de migrationibus gentium.*

50 J. W. Bohnstedt, "The Infidel Scourge of God: The *Turkish Menace* as Seen by German Pamphleteers of the Reformation Era," *TAPS* 56.9 (1968): 1–58; W. Schulze, *Reich und Türkengefahr im späten 16. Jahrhundert: Studien zu den politischen und gesellschaftlichen Auswirkungen einer äußeren Bedrohung* (Munich, 1978); A. Höfert, *Den Feind beschreiben: "Türkengefahr" und europäisches Wissen über das Osmanischen Reich, 1450–1600* (Frankfurt, 2003); T. Kaufmann, "Aspekte der Wahrnehmung der 'türkischen Religion' bei christlichen Autoren des 15. und 16. Jahrhunderts," in *Wahrnehmung des Islam zwischen Reformation und Aufklärung*, ed. D. Klein and B. Platow (Munich, 2008), 9–26; F. Konrad, "From the 'Turkish Menace' to Exoticism and Orientalism: Islam as Antithesis of

this people by drawing on ancient and in particular medieval sources, as Margaret Meserve has shown in an excellent study.[51] In a similar move, Crusius—and many of his colleagues—turned to Byzantine texts for answers, assuming that reading through the whole of Greek and Byzantine history would reveal more about the unsettling incursions of the Ottoman Turks into Christian territories: to understand the Ottoman Turks and their rapid rise at the expense of the Greeks was to delve into the Byzantine historians who chronicled this phenomenon and its prehistory.[52]

In that sense Crusius turned his Byzantine books not only into sites of chronological research but also into repositories of knowledge about the advances of the Ottoman Turks. This is borne out most clearly by his perusal of two texts that he had bound together in a single volume: an excerpt from Anna Komnene's *Alexiad* and Laonikos Chalkokondyles' *Histories*, the latter being the single most detailed Greek account of the arrival of the Ottomans. Crusius dedicated a full page in front of the *Alexiad* to organizing all the rulers of Constantinople from 1056 until 1261—a list he had compiled from Funck and had compared to Gerardus Mercator's chronological work.[53] He continued this reconstruction of imperial succession in his copy of Chalkokondyles' histories. On the recto of the title page, he first listed "the rulers of Osman, a Turkish tribe, in the following genealogy, on which [there is material] in this work."[54] This record of Ottoman sultans was followed by a similar list of the Palaiologan dynasty since Michael VIII Palaiologos (r. 1259–1282) recovered the city from Baldwin II, the last Latin emperor, in 1261 (figs. 4.1 and 4.2). Individually these genealogies can be read as condensed but tidy and easily navigable records of the last Byzantine and first Ottoman rulers of Constantinople since 1056. Together their full potential comes into play: they afforded Crusius a rare insight into how Byzantine and Ottoman cultures came to exist side by side, and how Ottoman sovereignty had come to replace Byzantine authority in the political sphere.

Europe (1453–1914)?," *European History Online* (2011), http://ieg-ego.eu/en/threads/models-and-stereotypes/from-the-turkish-menace-to-orientalism.

51 M. Meserve, *Empires of Islam in Renaissance Historical Thought* (Cambridge, MA, 2008).

52 For the importance of the Byzantine historical tradition for understanding the Ottomans, see Anthony Grafton in Chapter 3 of this volume and D. R. Reinsch, "Edition und Rezeption byzantinischer Historiker durch deutsche Humanisten," in *Graeca recentiora in Germania: Deutsch-griechische Kulturbeziehungen vom 15. bis 19. Jahrhundert*, ed. H. Eideneier, Wolfenbütteler Forschungen 59 (Wiesbaden, 1994), 47–63, at 49.

53 UBT Mb 11, fol. B-III: *Ex Chronologia Ioannis Funccii, anni imperatorum. Sed rectius ex Ger. Merc. Imperarunt Constantinopoli, anno Christi*. For a short analysis of this manuscript and Crusius's annotations, see D. R. Reinsch, "Die Editio Princeps eines Auszugs aus der Alexias Anna Komnenes aus dem Jahr 1562; ein unabhängiger Überlieferungsträger," *BZ* 84/85 (1991–92): 12–16.

54 UBT, Mb 11, fol. C-III: *Oguziorum (Turcicae tribus) duces, sequenti genealogia, de quibus in hoc opera.*

This was never an easy exercise, though. In most cases, Crusius had to rely on the expertise of more than a single author. It is worth examining this point in more depth, because whether Crusius worked his way through John Zonaras or Niketas Choniates, Anna Komnene or Laonikos Chalkokondyles, George Pachymeres or George Kedrenos, and whether he read these authors in Greek or in a Latin translation, he always relied on a broad range of other books for further contextualization. Crusius's method of marking up his manuscript copy of Chalkokondyles is particularly revealing of this process. He referenced learned and weighty scholarly tomes in his usual way. These included Paulus Aemilius's *De rebus gestis Francorum*, Johannes Leunclavius's studies of the Ottomans, and even such a rare and obscure work of history as *De origine et rebus gestis Polonorum* by the Polish historian and diplomat Marcin Kromer (1512–1589).[55] Such references often elucidated specific passages or problems from Chalkokondyles' work. Aeneas Sylvius Piccolomini's *Cosmographia*, for instance, told Crusius that the Ottomans were Scythians rather than Trojans—a hotly debated issue at the time.[56] The world chronicle of Johannes Nauclerus, a local humanist and historian who became the first rector of the University of Tübingen after its foundation in 1477, contextualized the passage where Chalkokondyles mentioned the city of Prague.[57] Paolo Giovio offered Crusius further particulars about the history of Samarkand, mentioned by Chalkokondyles in the beginning of book 2.[58]

But Crusius also pondered other textual genres, such as travelogues, in the hope of finding valuable information to enrich Byzantine history. The journals of Leonhard Rauwolf and Johann Schiltberger, for example, provided Crusius with direct empirical testimonies. Rauwolf, a learned botanist, had set out for the Levant in 1573 to search for medicinal herbs, which he hoped to sell through his brother-in-law's Augsburg firm.[59] From the account that Rauwolf published of his journey in 1582—under the title *Aigentliche Beschreibung der Raiß inn die Morgenländerin*—Crusius took a passage concerning Turkish marriage customs and copied it next to a passage where Chalkokondyles discussed a similar topic, seemingly to

55 Chalkokondyles, *Historiae*, UBT Mb 11, fol. 74, 94.

56 Ibid., fol. 5. For the debate, see Meserve, *Empires of Islam*, passim.

57 Chalkokondyles, *Historiae*, UBT Mb 11, fol. 94.

58 Ibid., fol. 44.

59 K. H. Dannenfeldt, *Leonhard Rauwolf: Sixteenth-Century Physician, Botanist, and Traveler* (Cambridge, 1968); F. Babinger, "Leonhard Rauwolf, ein Augsburger Botaniker und Ostenreisender des sechzehnten Jahrhunderts," *Archiv für die Geschichte der Naturwissenschaften und der Technik* 4 (1913): 148–61.

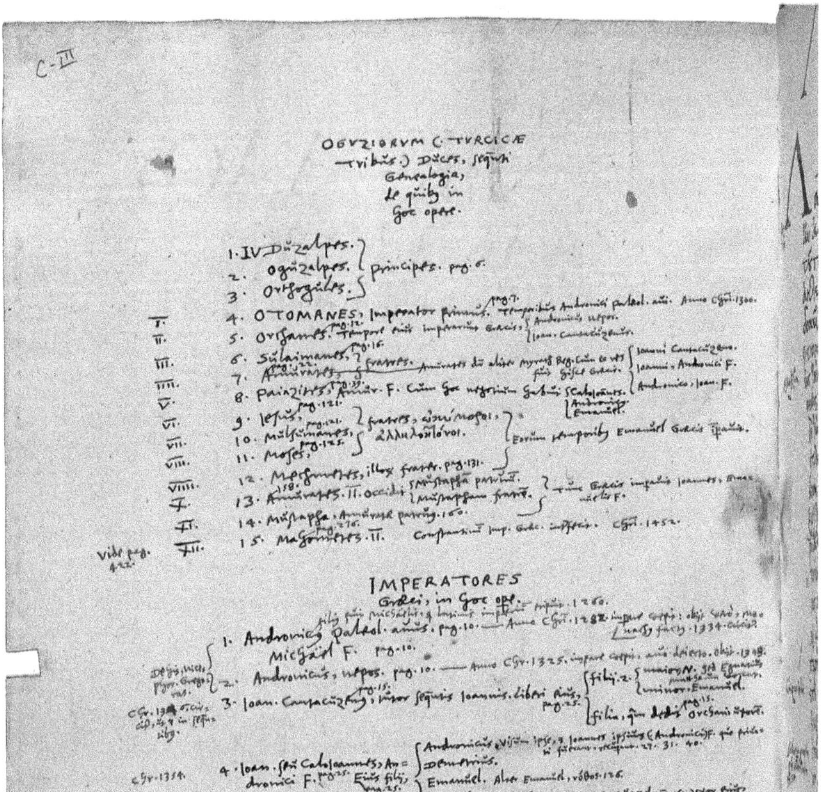

Fig. 4.1. Crusius's genealogy of the House of Osman. Chalkokondyles, *Historiae*. Universitätsbibliothek Tübingen Mb 11, fol. C-III. Courtesy Universitätsbibliothek, Universität Tübingen.

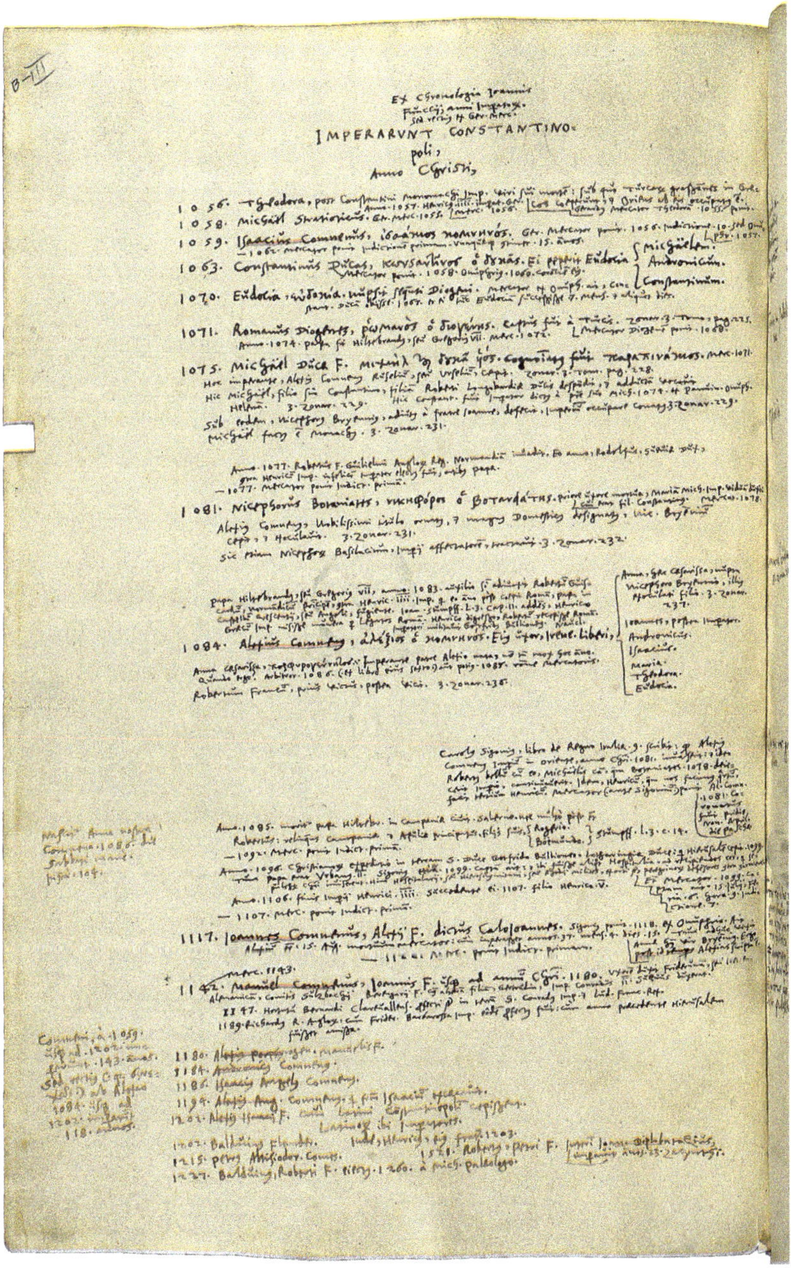

Fig. 4.2. Crusius's genealogy of the Palaiologan dynasty. Chalkokondyles, *Historiae*. Universitätsbibliothek Tübingen Mb 11, fol. B-III. Courtesy Universitätsbibliothek, Universität Tübingen.

corroborate evidence given by the historian.[60] Crusius valued Schiltberger, on the other hand, for the deeply personal testimony on the Battle of Nikopolis (1396) that the author provided. In the second book of his *Histories*, Chalkokondyles narrated the events building up to this dramatic confrontation in which an allied crusader army under Holy Roman Emperor Sigismund (1368–1437) suffered a crushing defeat by the Ottoman forces of Sultan Bayezid I (1360–1403). Amid other learned works Schiltberger stood out for the colorful brushstrokes that his life could add to Chalkokondyles' narrative depiction of these events: as a teenager Schiltberger had been taken captive in the Battle of Nicopolis. He subsequently entered the services of a host of Turkish and Mongol overlords, with whom he traveled to many corners of the world, from Siberia and Mongolia to the Balkans. Thirty years later he escaped and returned to Bavaria, where he became a chamberlain of Duke Albert III. In other words, his travelogue afforded readers like Crusius a testimony of survival from troubled times.[61]

History and travel writing, then, added some unusual color to Chalkokondyles' narrative. Contemporary pamphlets and other ephemera helped Crusius further visualize the movements of the Ottoman sultans and their armies as described in the *Histories*. On 10 November 1444 another military campaign that European monarchs had mounted against the rapidly advancing Ottomans came to nothing when the army of Sultan Murad II ambushed the Christian troops in the Battle of Varna. Book 7 narrated this event and, apparently, Chalkokondyles' technical description of how Murat had positioned his forces caught Crusius's attention: on the bottom of the page he added a drawing of the battle (fig. 4.3).[62] Not without a sense of proportion, he sketched the fortified city, the Christian troops with their Jerusalem cross, and the various contingents of the Ottoman army at whose center, surrounded by Janissaries, was the Ottoman leader. He even labeled individual parts of the drawing and explained them in a legend—almost exactly as Chalkokondyles had described it.

60 Chalkokondyles, *Historiae*, UBT Mb 11, fol. 74: *Leonhard. Rhauwolf. peregrinat. suae lib. 1 cap. 7 scribit: si quis Turca uxorem ter repudiatam, etiam quarto recipiat: eum haberi pro viro nihili et turpi.*

61 Ibid., fol. 51: *Schiltberger, ex patria sua Monaco Bavariae, anno 1394 cum suo domino, Leonhardo Reichertingero, profectus in barbarorum regionem (in die Haidenschafft) fuit: et inde rediit 1427. Interfuit praelio huic, apud Nicopolin (Schiltaw) commisso: in quo dominus eius periit, et Werner Bentzenawer, Ulrich Kugler, und ein kleiner steiner, und alle Baierischen haerren. Germanice suas peregrinationes descripsit, qui liber editus est. Ait, se post praelium fuisse ductum (quia captus fuerat) ut cum caeteris captivis occideretur: sed quod tunc vix 16 annorum esset, deprecatione filii Turc. imperatoris conservatum fuisse. Inde Adrianopolin ductus fuit, et Callipolin: ubi vidit Sigism. regem praetervehementem domum versus, et à Turcis derisum. Als nun Weiesit von Taemerlin gefangen ward: una etiam Schiltberger captus fuit. Postea ad filium eius Scharochum venit, etc. Tandem delatus Byzantium, imperatoris et patriarchae favore in patriam rediit.*

62 Ibid., fol. 239.

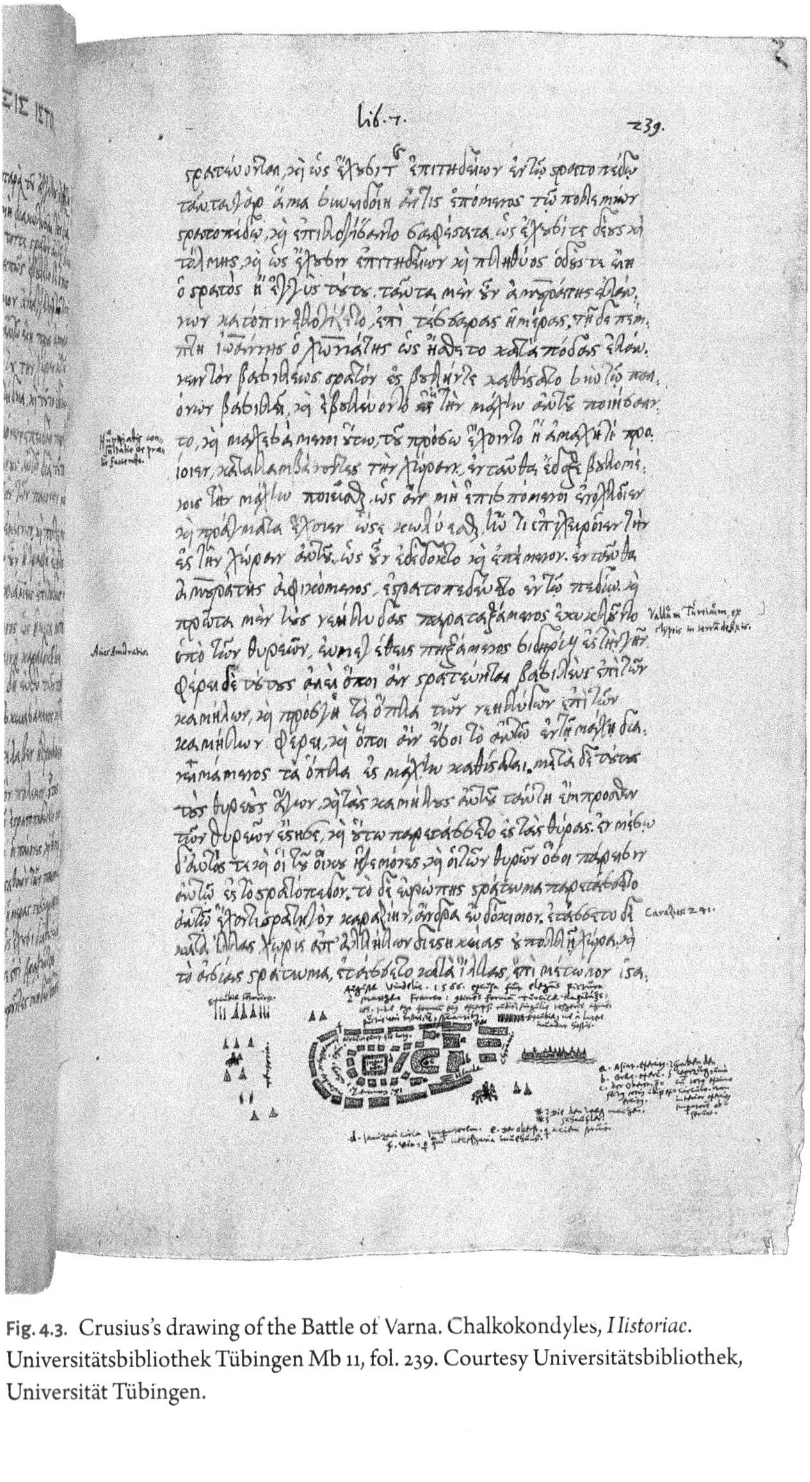

Fig. 4.3. Crusius's drawing of the Battle of Varna. Chalkokondyles, *Historiae.* Universitätsbibliothek Tübingen Mb 11, fol. 239. Courtesy Universitätsbibliothek, Universität Tübingen.

But it was not just Chalkokondyles' text that inspired the drawing. The shape of the Turkish ranks, Crusius revealed in a marginal note, was taken from a pamphlet that Matthaeus Franck had printed in Augsburg in 1566.[63] Intriguingly, this pamphlet detailed not the fifteenth-century Battle of Varna but the famous 1566 Siege of Szigetvár in Hungary, during which thousands of Habsburg and Ottoman soldiers had clashed and lost their lives. That confrontation had resulted in nothing but a pyrrhic victory for the Ottomans: although they had managed to take control over the Habsburg stronghold, Sultan Süleyman the Magnificent was one of the casualties. Yet in the pamphlet it was not the outcome of the campaign but the Siege of Szigetvár, which was surrounded by water on all sides, that took center stage: on the right thundering cannons had bombarded a part of the city that had completely burned down. On top, troops marched in formation and prepared for battle. Below, cavalry charged at full gallop. Ottoman tents, recognizable by their emblematic star and crescent, had been erected everywhere. Bodies lay all over the place. It was an ominous sight (fig. 4.4).[64] Crusius, rather than carefully evaluating the pamphlet as a source in its own right, transformed this suggestive image into a generic one. The pamphlet may have depicted an altogether different siege, but it evidently helped Crusius conjure up an image of the Battle of Varna. The illustration thus became an icon.

In the practice of reading, then, distance and time could dissolve. This is also borne out by what was perhaps the most valuable description that Crusius found in Chalkokondyles: the account of the 1453 fall of Constantinople in book 8 of the *Histories*. Crusius enveloped this particular passage in an even greater number of marginalia than was usual for him. Two notes of a particular kind stand out among the numerous other references. The first is the testimony of Stephan Gerlach, a student from Tübingen who had joined the imperial ambassador David Ungnad as chaplain on an embassy to Constantinople in 1573.[65] In a letter sent back to Tübingen in 1576, Gerlach told Crusius that the last Byzantine emperor, Constantine XI Palaiologos (r. 1449–1453), had died by the "Roman Gate."[66] In the second note Crusius recalled

63 Ibid.: *Augusta Vindelic. 1566 excusa fuit elegans pictura à Mattheo Franco: continens formam Turcicae* παρατάξεως *inde ego formam eius excerpsi ruditer: singulis tesseris agmen, punctis verò hastas, etc. seccantibus.*

64 *Warhafftige Contrafactur und verzeychnuß, des gewaltigen Schloß Zigeth, mit allen seinen Festungen: Sampt der belegerung des Erbfeinds Christlichs Namens, des Türcken* (Augsburg, 1566), UBT Ke XVIII 4 a.2-20FF.

65 M. Kriebel, "Stephan Gerlach: Deutscher evangelischer Botschaftsprediger in Konstantinopel 1573–1578: Diasporafürsorge in der Türkei und die ersten Beziehungen zur Griechisch-orthodoxen Kirche im 16. Jahrhundert," *Die evangelische Diaspora* 29 (1958): 71–96.

66 Chalkokondyles, *Historiae*, UBT Mb 11, fol. 290: *M. Stephanus Gerlachius, 18 Iunii 1576 mihi Crusio Tybingam e Constantinopoli scripsit: Constantium ultimum in porta romani perisse.*

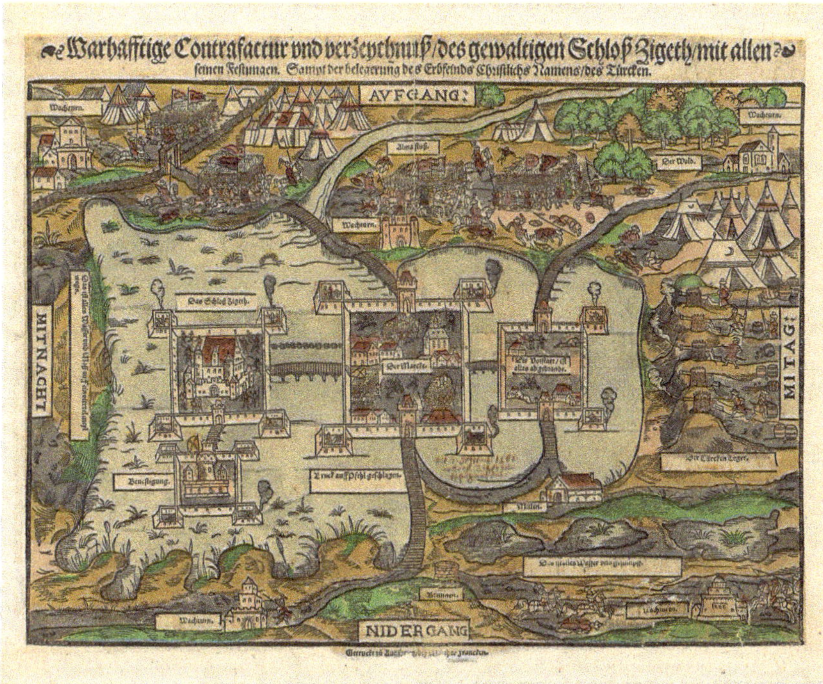

Fig. 4.4. Matthaeus Franck's 1566 pamphlet of the Siege of Szigetvár. Universitätsbibliothek Tübingen Ke XVIII 4 a.2-20FF. Courtesy Universitätsbibliothek, Universität Tübingen.

a news report he had read and received in February 1575, in which the death of Sultan Selim II was reported. Crusius then drew a comparison between the remuneration that the Janissaries received after Mehmed conquered the Byzantine capital and the money that the corps was given when subsequent sultans started their reign.[67] In the margins, Crusius thus set up conversations between this Byzantine history and the other texts in his library. He also repeatedly brought the past to bear on the present and the present to bear on the past in such a way that the continuous story of Greece came into sharper focus.

67 Ibid., fol. 291: *1575 die 23 Februar. ego M. Crusius hic Tybingae legi Nova, ex Constantinopoli die 9 Ianuar. hoc anno scripta. Die 9 Decemb. 74 Selimo II mortuo, successisse filium Amuratem III die 22 Decemb. qui proceres suos muneraverit: Ianizaris autem singulis (numero 15700 circiter) donaverit 3000 asperle: cum tamen 6000 expectassent singuli. Nam Mahometen, expugnata Constantinopoli, donasse singulis Ianizaris 1000 Asperle: propter hanc urbem, et imperium Graeciae, capta: et ordinasse, ut quisque successor 1000 Asperle addat. Debuissent ergo esse 6000 quod 6 imperatores sunt: scil. Mahometes, Baiazites, Selinus I, Solimannus, Selinus II et Amurates III. qui fratres suos (puerulos) strangulavit. 1 Asperle (ὀβολὸς) facit 2 kr. 1000 Asperle sunt 20 Ducati.*

Fig. 4.5. Crusius's annotated map of Constantinople, pasted in his copy of Choniates' *Histories*. Universitätsbibliothek Tübingen Cd4980, rear pastedown. Courtesy Universitätsbibliothek, Universität Tübingen.

One final bit of evidence illustrates this point in strikingly visual form. On the rear pastedown of his copy of Choniates' *Histories*, Crusius pasted a map of Istanbul taken from Pierre Gilles's account of his travels to the Ottoman capital (fig. 4.5). This map by a sixteenth-century French antiquarian, which Crusius enriched by layers of interpretive annotation, offered insight into Choniates' historical work—and perhaps in particular the latter's graphic description of the occupation of Constantinople in 1204—not unlike how Stephan Gerlach's firsthand observations had helped him understand Chalkokondyles' history better. Here as elsewhere Crusius envisioned Byzantine and Ottoman affairs as part of one continuous history.

Past and Present

Crusius's desire to read past and present through a single lens emerges also from some of the other books in his study. Histories of the Ottomans and their movements, for instance, such as the one by Francesco Sansovino, yielded vital clues about the survival of the Greeks into Ottoman times and about the lineage of the Ottoman sultans. Crusius read the travelogues of Pierre Belon, Ogier Ghiselin de Busbecq, George Dousa, and others for their detailed descriptions of what and whom they encountered on their journeys through the Ottoman Empire.[68] Even popular chronologies and summaries of world history could be made to serve his interest in the intertwined history of Byzantine and Ottoman affairs. In the 1551 German translation of Martin Luther's *Supputatio annorum mundi*—an eschatological reckoning of the world's expected six-thousand-year history—Crusius filled up the individual columns and margins with references to key passages in late Byzantine and Ottoman history: the 1204 sack of Constantinople, the 1261 reconquest of the city by Michael VIII Palaiologos, and the bloody military conflicts with the Ottomans that ultimately culminated in the loss of Byzantine political power and the establishment of Ottoman rule. Tellingly, Crusius inserted the names and dates of the reigns and deeds of successive Byzantine emperors and Ottoman sultans, starting in 1261 and continuing to the death of Süleyman the Magnificent in 1566 and the accession of his son Selim II.[69] Crusius thus envisioned the rise of the Ottomans and the fall of the Greeks as key points on the timeline of salvation. In the end such chronologies, travelogues, and works of history functioned not unlike the two genealogies that Crusius compiled of Byzantine and Ottoman rulers and the many notes that he left in the margins of his Chalkokondyles: they demonstrate how Crusius approached Byzantine and Ottoman history as a continuum.

To see this continuum in living color, Crusius supplemented his readings with inquiries of a different kind. For years he also sought to understand the Ottoman advance into Christian territories by collecting news reports. He kept close tabs on battles lost and won, the deaths of famous sultans, and the births of their Christian adversaries. Sometimes he could even corroborate the historical events described in some of his books with more accurate evidence brought to Tübingen through the postal network.[70] For instance, in Wolfgang Dreschler's 1550 account of the origins and history of the Ottomans—which he had bound together with Conrad

68 Pierre Belon, *Les observations de plusieurs singularitez et choses memorables, trouvées en Grèce, Asie, Indée, Egypte, Arabie, et autres pays estranges* (Antwerp, 1555), UBT Fc 33.4; Ogier Ghislain de Busbecq, *Itinera Constantinopolitanum et Amasianum* (Antwerp, 1582), UBT Fo XI 4c; Georgius Dousa, *De itinere suo Constantinopolitano epistola* (Leiden, 1544), Fo XI 25; Pierre Gilles, *De Bosporo Thracico libri III* (Lyon, 1561) and *De topographia Constantinopoleos et de illius antiquitatibus libri 4* (Lyon, 1562), UBT Fo XI 5.4; Francesco Sansovino, *Historia universale dell'origine et imperio de' Turchi* (Venice, 1573), UBT, Fo XI 2.4.

69 Martin Luther, *Cronica . . . Deudsch* (Wittenberg, 1551), UBT Ce 1094. For Luther's method of reckoning the years, see J. Barr, "Luther and Biblical Chronology," *BullJRylandsLib* 72.1 (1990): 51–68.

70 For the various news networks that Crusius subscribed to, see T. Gloning, "'Nova Wellingiana'—Nachrichten-Exzerpte in den Tagebüchern von Martin Crusius (1526–1607): Ein Beitrag zur Frühgeschichte der Presse und der Zeitungssprache," in *Bausteine zur Tübinger Universitätsgeschichte*, vol. 5, ed. V. Schäfer (Tübingen, 1991), 13–52.

Clauser's Latin translation of Chalkokondyles—Crusius read that Sultan Süleyman the Magnificent may have died in 1550: "In the beginning of this year," Dreschler revealed, "Süleyman, who for thirty years had tormented the people of God, was rumored to have died."[71] But when Crusius read this entry in 1566, he knew these rumors were "evidently false"—"if only he had died then!" he exclaimed in the margin, adding with relief:

> The death of this [sultan] was announced in Tubingen, yesterday 28 October 1566. [It was said] that he died in the month of September of this year in the fortress of Sziget, which he had recently besieged. If it is true, Crusius prays that he may rest in pitch (*quiescat in pice*): just as there today was a lunar eclipse after the third hour in the afternoon.[72]

This last note is not only reflective of the anxiety that Crusius, like his contemporaries, experienced about the Ottomans. It also illustrates how for Crusius the record of Byzantine and Ottoman affairs had to be maintained with great diligence. In his world every tiny bit of information mattered.

Crusius's reasons for compiling so much data can be traced back to a specific chapter in his life. Between 1573 and 1581 he was the driving force behind the lengthy correspondence that Lutheran theologians from Tübingen maintained with the Greek Orthodox patriarch Jeremias II (ca. 1536–1595). The Lutherans, convinced as they were that their evangelical principles were in agreement with the teachings of the Greek Orthodox Church, had written the patriarch to pass his judgment on the evangelical movement. They were soon proven wrong, however, and eventually the patriarch simply asked them "to write no longer about dogma, but only for friendship's sake."[73] This unsuccessful exchange of letters instilled in Crusius a deep sense

71 Wolfgang Drechsler, *De Saracenis et Turcis Chronicon: Item de origine et progressu et fine Machometi* (Strasbourg, 1550), UBT Gi 128, 235: *Ineunte hoc anno Solimano mors rumoribus nunciata est, qui triginta annos populum dei afflixit.* For some scant bibliographical details on Drechsler, see C. G. Jöcher, *Allgemeines Gelehrten-Lexicon*, 4 vols. (Leipzig 1750–51), 2:213. Clauser's Latin translation was the one printed by Oporinus: Conrad Clauser, *Laonici Chalcondylae Atheniensis, de origine et rebus gestis Turcorum Libri Decem* (Basel, 1556).

72 UBT Gi 128, 235: *prorsus falsis* and *Utinam tunc mortuus fuisset* and *Eiusdem mors hodie rursus .28. Octob. 1566. Tybingae nuntiatur. scilicet nuper mortuum esse in arce Zigetha, quam nuper expugnaverat, mense scilicet septembri. si verum est: precatur ei Crusius, ut quiescat in pice: sicut et hodie eclipsis lunae post tertiam pomeridianam fuit.*

73 *Acta et scripta theologorum Wirtembergensium, et patriarchae Constantinopolitani D. Hieremiae: quae utrique ab anno 1576 usque ad annum 1581 de Augustana Confessione inter se miserunt: Graece & Latine ab ijsdem theologis edita* (Wittenberg, 1584), 370: *Quamobrem quantum ad vos attinet, liberastis nos curis. Vestram ergo viam euntes, ne amplius de Dogmatibus, sed amicitiae tantum causa, si volueritis, scribete.* For a detailed analysis of this exchange, see D. Wendebourg, *Reformation und*

of disappointment about the religion of the Greeks. In his Lutheran eyes, they had erred and fallen into superstitious ways, which is why he believed that Greece's "misfortune should be lamented."[74]

This disappointment, however, did stimulate Crusius to find out as much as he could about how the Greeks and their church had survived in Ottoman times. In addition to the books that he read and the news reports that he collected, Crusius also managed to acquire two Greek texts unknown to earlier scholars of Byzantine materials. Stephan Gerlach, upon his return to Tübingen in 1578, had brought Crusius these manuscripts from the Ottoman capital. The first consisted of a political history of Constantinople from 1391 to 1578, written for Crusius by Theodosios Zygomalas, the *protonotarios* of the Greek Orthodox patriarchate in Constantinople.[75] The second manuscript, copied by the Greek scribe Manuel Malaxos, contained an account of the Greek Orthodox patriarchate between 1454 and 1578.[76] In 1584 Crusius published both texts in his *Turcograeciae libri octo*, the book he is best known for today. In this wide-ranging work, Crusius meticulously edited several sets of Greek texts, translated them into Latin, and explicated them in lengthy sets of notes, creating a vast repository of evidence that illuminated the social, cultural, religious, and political nature of the Ottoman Greek world.

In itself, the decision to include these two histories in the *Turcograecia* underscores that for Crusius Ottoman and Byzantine affairs were deeply intertwined: the "political history of Constantinople from 1391 to 1571" chronicled a transitional phase in the history of the city—namely, the period of its transformation, when the Ottoman Empire succeeded the Byzantine one and Constantinople became a Muslim capital.[77] The patriarchal history, similarly, narrated how the Greek Orthodox patriarchate—an age-old institute that dated back to at least the fourth century—had survived into Ottoman times, sometimes even with support of the sultan.[78] The annotations that Crusius appended to these texts offer another hint in this direction: he began his commentary on the political history by bringing together on a single page some chronological material (including Funck and

---

Orthodoxie: Der ökumenische Briefwechsel zwischen der Leitung der Württembergischen Kirche und Patriarch Jeremias II. von Konstantinopel in den Jahren 1573–1581 (Göttingen, 1986).

74 Martin Crusius, *Turcograeciae libri octo* (Basel, 1584), *2^{v}: ἑλλας *ibi* ἐκτουρκωθεῖσα *est: Graecia servituti Turcicae subiecta: insuperque multis in Religione erroribus & superstitionibus (quod initio nos latebat) obnoxia: ideoque merito infelicitas eius deploranda.*

75 Bibliothèque Nationale de France, Supplément Grec 1152, 1: *Accepi ego Mart. Crusius 10 Ianuar. 1579 à D. Theodosio Zygomala patriarchico Byzantii Protonotario, per D. Steph. Gerlach Tybingae.*

76 UBT Mb 18.

77 Crusius, *Turcograecia*, 1–68.

78 Ibid., 107–212.

Patriarch Nikephoros) in order to explicate how the Greeks counted the years.[79] What followed was a genealogy, taken from Gregoras and Chalkokondyles, of the Palaiologan dynasty "from the moment when the city was taken from the Latins until the Turkish siege."[80] This list was complemented by a reproduction of the genealogy of the Ottoman sultans that Crusius had compiled in his copy of Chalkokondyles, updated by himself so that all Turkish rulers until Murad III (r. 1574–1595) were neatly listed.[81] In such notes, and more generally in editing these two Greek histories, Crusius showed himself to be the successor of Chalkokondyles and the whole Byzantine historiographical tradition. Note, moreover, how Crusius did not start his work after the fall of Constantinople in 1453, but homed in on the much longer process of transformation and transition that began in the thirteenth century and continued into his own times.

Crusius thus contributed to a chronology of Byzantine affairs that is slightly different from the timelines that other pioneers in the field of Byzantine studies devised: the "corpus" of Byzantine history had presented Chalkokondyles as the culmination of a Byzantine historical tradition. Crusius shared with Oporinus and Wolf the notion that Greek history began properly from the creation of the world. But unlike them Crusius did not believe that Byzantine history had ended in 1453. For Wolf Byzantine history was a closed story, told in a circumscribed corpus, written in a style that he held in thinly disguised contempt, as shown below. Crusius did not look reflectively at Byzantium. He saw Byzantium as a precursor of the Ottoman state: Ottoman Greek history was a continuation of late Byzantine history and part of universal history since Creation. Ultimately, then, Crusius's project of reading—and eventually editing—Byzantine materials was aimed at weaving the rapid Ottoman advances of the past century into the larger fabric of Christian history told by such Byzantine luminaries as Zonaras and Choniates, Komnene and Chalkokondyles. For him every Greek period, including Ottoman times, formed part of a single, coherent, though not exactly uniform tradition.

This is perhaps also why Crusius had no single definition of *Byzantium* and *Byzantine*. In his copy of Zonaras, for instance, Crusius used "Greek" and "Byzantine" interchangeably when listing historians of what we would call the Byzantine period.[82]

79 Ibid., 44: *Graeci solent tempora ab annis Mundi conditi annotare: multoque plures annos numerant, quam nos. certe annum Mundi 5353. Ioannis Fuccii, in quam annus Christi 1391 cadit, annis 1547 excedunt. causa quaeratur a doctis: cum Eusebius tantum 1236 annos habeat superfluos, qui 72 interpretes sequitur.*

80 Ibid., 45: *Stirps Paleologinae familiae, ab erepta Latinis urbe, usque ad eiusdem per Turcas expugnationem, ex Gregora & Chalcondyle.*

81 Ibid., 47.

82 Zonaras, *Compendium Historiarum* (n. 30 above), UBT Cd 4980, front pastedown: *Historici graeci de imperio orientis* and title page: *Scriptores Graeci Byzantinae Historiae.* Once he even used both

Elsewhere he used the term "Greek empire" for the period in Greek history before the arrival of the Ottomans and "Byzantium" when talking about sixteenth-century Ottoman Greek affairs.[83] In my estimation, this does not reflect any slippage on Crusius's part or any blurring of categories. On the contrary: Crusius's terminology indicates that the notion of "Byzantium" was still very much in flux in this period and its contours not yet fully determined. Crusius's perusal of his Byzantine books and manuscripts offers a keyhole through which we can see how Byzantium crystalized into a historical entity. This is not to suggest, though, that Crusius saw the history of the Greeks—whether it was called Byzantine or not—as one dense and indistinguishable cluster of events and people. His attempts at creating chronological order when reading Choniates, Zonaras, and other historians should be evidence enough that he was not blind to change over time. My suggestion is rather that Crusius made no serious attempt to divide Greek history into distinct periods, as others including Wolf and Oporinus did. Indeed: the closest Crusius ever came to something like a division of Greek history manifested itself not in his views on history but, as we will see in the final section, in how he conceptualized the development of the Greek language.

The Language of Byzantium

Reading and making sense of Byzantine texts also meant examining the stylistic register, as well as the language, in which these materials were written. Certainly in the sixteenth century this was still a daunting task and one relevant for many of the authors that Crusius read. The subscript that Hieronymus Wolf had appended to his 1557 edition of Choniates is revealing in this respect. In this "admonition," Wolf admitted to having included in his index vernacular Greek words (*barbarica vocabula*), marked with an asterisk, whose meaning had remained unknown to him. He then called on "those who have expert knowledge of the corrupt language to compile a vernacular Greek lexicon from recent writers in which vernacular words appear often, placing vernacular expressions first and [then] adding the [ancient] Greek ones, so that those who only know the ancient language will not be deterred

in a single sentence; see Crusius, *Germanograecia* (n. 2 above), 5: *Denique adhuc hodie apud cives Byzantinos & in totius Graeciae urbibus, Graeci sermonis, licet corrupti, usus est.*

83 UBT Mb 13, first pagination, fol. 520: *Menda autographi de industria relinui: ut Graeciae ruditas, etiam stante imperio adhuc Greco, conspiciatur*; and UBT Mh 466, vol. 1, fol. 1: *Historica quaedam a me M. Martino Crusio, utriusque linguae professore in inclyta Academia Tybingensi, comportata, de nostris temporibus, praesertim Graecorum Byzantii rebus*, respectively.

from reading them."[84] Throughout the work Crusius rose to the occasion: he duly annotated the passage ("Barbarograeca"), underlined the words marked as uncertain in the index, and identified the "vernacular" Greek words in the main text, the index, and the notes that Wolf had printed in the back of the book.

He even systematically compared Wolf's edition with a vernacular Greek manuscript version of the text that he had borrowed from the imperial library in Augsburg. For nearly three hundred pages, Crusius diligently reproduced from this manuscript copy what he called variant readings of the print edition, but what in actuality are often radically different versions of substantial passages (fig. 4.6).[85] The manuscript that Crusius read in conjunction with the printed text was a later translation (*metaphrasis*) into a lower linguistic register. In 1544 the Greek manuscript dealer Antonios Eparchos had sold this text, together with dozens of other Greek manuscripts, to the city of Augsburg.[86] It was also one of three manuscripts of Choniates' text that Wolf had known. Intriguingly, though, Wolf had not recognized it as a later adaptation but instead believed it to be the original text that Choniates had written. For this reason, Wolf considered Choniates a *semibarbarus* and decided to jettison what he deemed was the original version in favor of text in a more elevated register. The two other manuscripts that Wolf *did* use—brought to the Fugger family in 1553 by Hans Dernschwam, one of their retired employees, from his journey to the Ottoman Empire—offered him exactly such a version: one that deftly complied with the type of rhetorical register he expected and sought in Byzantine writers.[87] Wolf, in other words, made the evidence fulfill the expectations he held about Choniates.

Nowhere in his copy does Crusius explicitly express his disagreement with Wolf on this matter. In fact, it is somewhat unclear which version Crusius thought

84 Wolf, *Nicetae Acominati Choniatae . . . LXXXVI annorum historia* (n. 16 above), unpaginated *annotationes: Admonitio de indice. Barbarica vocabula ex vetusto codice annotata, in hoc opera non reperiuntur: sed Graeca duntaxat, quibus illa explicantur. Quibus ubi nulla interpretatione adiicitur, aut * apponitur, sciat lector significationem eius nobis vel ignotam esse, vel dubiam. Rogo autem eos qui corruptae linguae periti sunt, ut propter scriptores, in quibus subinde barbara vocabula occurrunt barbaricum lexicon conficiant, vocibus barbaris praepositis & Graecis subjunctis, ne veteris duntaxat linguae periti ab eorum lectione deterreantur.*

85 Wolf, *Nicetae Acominati Choniatae . . . LXXXVI annorum historia*, UBT Cd 4980, 13: + *hoc loco incipit (quod principio caret) Barbarograecum Nicetae Acom. Choniatae manuscriptum exemplar quod ego Martinus Crusius 25 April. 1580 accepi.*

86 For Eparchos as a manuscript dealer, see E. Benz, *Wittenberg und Byzanz* (Marburg, 1949), 4–33, and H. Zäh, "Wolfgang Musculus und der Verkauf griechischer Handschriften für die Augsburger Stadtbibliothek 1543/44," in *Wolfgang Musculus (1497–1563) und die oberdeutsche Reformation*, ed. R. Dellsperger, R. Freudenberger, and W. Weber (Berlin, 1997), 226–45.

87 On Dernschwam and his journey, see F. Babinger, *Hans Dernschwam's Tagebuch einer Reise nach Konstantinopel und Kleinasien*, trans. J. Reickel (Berlin, 2014), and M. D. Birnbaum, "The Fuggers, Hans Dernschwam, and the Ottoman Empire," *SüdostF* 50 (1991): 119–44.

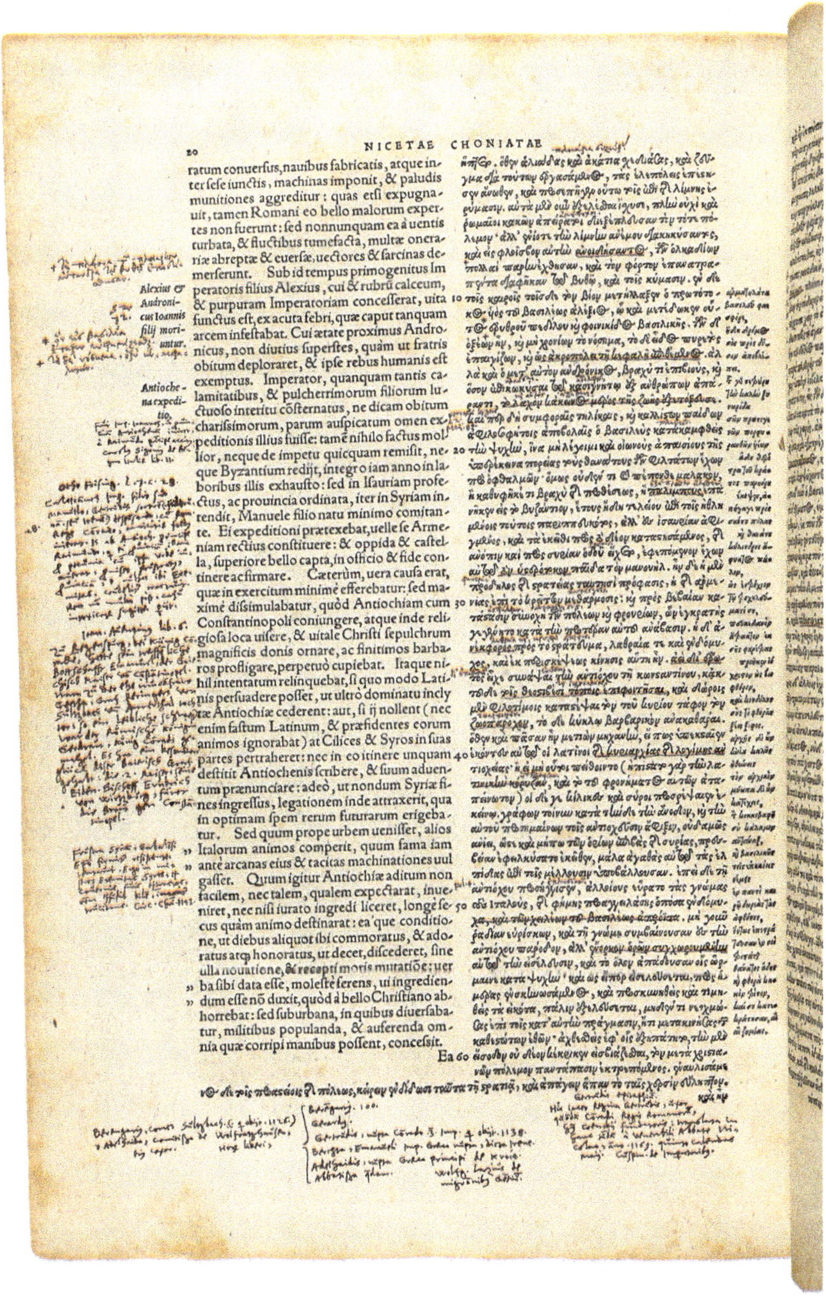

Fig. 4.6. Crusius's record in his copy of Choniates' *Histories* of what he thought were variant readings, found in a manuscript version of this text. Universitätsbibliothek Tübingen Cd 4980, 20. Courtesy Universitätsbibliothek, Universität Tübingen.

had been Choniates' original. But it is clear beyond doubt that a comparison of all versions, whether in a lower or higher stylistic register, seemed to serve Crusius's scholarly needs, and his interests in language in particular. More than any of his contemporaries, Crusius was attuned to the full linguistic and dialectical diversity of the Greek world. Whereas Wolf had outright dismissed the vernacular metaphrasis of Choniates' copy, even though he considered it the original, Crusius searched this work and other Byzantine works for evidence of the postclassical development of the Greek language and the type of spoken Greek that was current in the time of a given Byzantine author. Indeed, there is hardly a Byzantine text in his collection whose flyleaves or pastedowns he did not use for compiling lists of colloquial Greek words.

Crusius's perusal of a manuscript copy of Symeon Metaphrastes' *Menologion* offers some clues as to why he so diligently mined such texts for colloquialisms. Saints' lives like these, which are often included in office books in Greek Orthodox Christianity, sparked Crusius's interest first of all for the rich details they afforded about the celebration of feast and saint days in the Eastern Church. (He intimated that he enjoyed reading the *vita* of John Chrysostom more than any of the others.[88]) But he had also turned to these religious texts to better understand what type of vernacular language had developed out of ancient Greek: "I have now finished this old manuscript codex of martyrs and saints," he wrote, "in order to become better acquainted with ecclesiastical affairs and the Greek language."[89] Indeed, on some spare pages in front of the third and final section of the manuscript Crusius listed all the "barbarian words" that he had encountered while reading, which could signal the process of "barbarization" that Greek had undergone "for many centuries."[90] His use of the plural ("centuries") is relevant here: this development had in Crusius's estimation started not with the arrival of the Ottomans but, as he revealed here and elsewhere, "while the Greek empire was still standing."[91]

Orthography also attested to these developments. Crusius's engagement with Byzantine manuscripts meant confronting the many vowel shifts that had occurred in nonclassical Greek:

88 Symeon Metaphrastes, *Menologion*, UBT Mb 12, second pagination, fol. 242: *Chrysostomi vita, plus caeteris me delectavit: et Theoctistae legenda,* διὰ τὸ ἐμπαθὲς γλυκυτάτη.

89 Ibid.: *Absolvi hunc etiam, Martyrum et Sanctorum, codicem antiquum manuscriptum: propter ecclesiastica et linguam graecam melius cognoscenda.*"

90 Ibid., unpaginated page: *vocabula Barbara, aut obscura.* In the margin Crusius added: *Ergo lingua Graeca fuit ante multa secula* βαρβαρωθεῖσα.

91 UBT Mb 13, fol. 520: *Menda autographi de industria retinui: ut Graeciae ruditas, etiam stante imperio adhuc Graeco, conspiciatur.*

> The writing of this book was faulty and its orthography neglected. . . . But in all that I have thus far excerpted, I have retained the mistakes. Frequently, the *iota* in the autograph was written not below but next to the letter, as in τῶι θεῶι for τῷ θεῷ. It also appears that already before Greece was captured by the Turks the vowels and the diphthongs were pronounced like today in the vernacular, as in τὰ ἀπεῶνος τετιρειμένα ἄρρητα ἀγαθὰ τοῖς ἀγαθοῖς.[92]

Crusius often retained these mistakes because they indicated the "ignorance and the negligence of those that transcribed" these manuscripts.[93] After all, differences in orthography could tell Crusius a great deal about how the Greek language had developed. Here he followed a basic philological principle established by Lorenzo Valla and Poliziano in the fifteenth century and adopted by the best students of Greek glossaries: errors could reveal indispensable things about a language's developments and needed to be preserved and studied, whether one is working on manuscript transmission or on spelling.[94]

Language, then, and its manifestation in written form, was the yardstick that Crusius used to contextualize a given Greek text. His consuming interest in the intricacies of the Greek language also extended to forms of spoken Greek. I have shown elsewhere how Crusius studied the Greek vernacular not just by collecting books but also by talking to numerous Greek Orthodox Christians in his Tübingen home. These men and women, who came from different social strata, had traveled through Europe in search for alms to ransom family members whom the Ottoman Turks had taken captive. In Crusius they found a sympathetic ear: not only did he give these beggars some money, he also interviewed them and made systematic lists of the *barbarograeca vocabula* that they explained to him. Crusius also corresponded with members of the Greek Orthodox patriarchate, often sending requests to the Ottoman capital for translations of specific vernacular words that he had

92 UBT Mb 37, fol. 141v: *Absolvi ego M. Mart. Crusius 27 Augusti 1580 die sabbati, domi meae, Tybingae. Liber fuit valde mendosè scriptus, neglecta orthographia. . . . Ego autem quicquid huc excerpsi, emendatè descripsi. Frequenter autem iota in Autographo non subscriptum est, sed ad latus scriptum: ut,* τῶι θεῶι*: per,* τῷ θεῷ*. Apparet etiam, olim, quoque (ante Graeciam a Turcis captam) vocales et Diphthongos fuisse in praenuntiatas, ut hodie, vulgo: ut* τὰ ἀπεῶνος τετιρειμένα ἄρρητα ἀγαθὰ τοῖς ἀγαθοῖς.

93 UBT Mb 10, fol. 1: *Menda in plerisque studio retinui ut describentium ruditas negligentiave (non autem una manus fuit) conspiciatur.* See also UBT Mc 62, fol. 382: *Ita mendose haec (ut alia multa) sunt in Autogr. scripta. Unde ruditas etiam nunc graecorum apparet.*

94 For Valla and Poliziano, see A. Grafton, "On the Scholarship of Politian and Its Context," *JWarb* 40 (1977): 150–88; L. D. Reynolds and N. G. Wilson, *Scribes and Scholars: A Guide to the Transmission of Greek and Latin Literature*, 3rd rev. ed. (Oxford, 1991), 140–46: S. Timpanaro, *La genesi del metodo del Lachmann* (Turin, 2010), 15–21. For the broader context, see A. C. Dionisotti, "From Stephanus to Du Cange: Glossary Stories," *RHT* 14–15 (1984–85): 303–36.

encountered in his Greek books.[95] Whether it was spoken or written down, Crusius sought to collect every bit of information available.

In Crusius's eyes all forms of Greek were connected. He more or less classified the Greek language into three categories: "classical," "vernacular," and "ecclesiastical" —with "vernacular," the *barbarograeca vocabula,* covering both spoken Greek and the deviations from the classical norm that he found in his Byzantine books. Leaving aside the thorny question of how exactly these three versions differed from one another—Crusius is again not always consistent on this point—it is worth emphasizing just how much this classification implied a story of decline: although Crusius was passionate about learning the Greek vernacular, and at one point even proudly asserted that he was the first to teach it at a German university, the vernacular was essentially a corrupted version of a pure ancient form. And in an age in which language and culture were thought to be deeply intertwined, such an assessment could easily be applied to the history of Greece as a whole: in an oration on why the Greek language needed to be preserved, Crusius exclaimed: "How many corruptions in all the arts have poured out of the ignorance of this [Greek] language, how much darkness in philosophy, and how big a perversion of the Christian religion." Only the recent and fortunate "rebirth of Greek letters" in Germany and Italy had "dispelled this darkness."[96]

Many contemporaries of Crusius approached languages in similar ways. Frederic Clark has shown how throughout the early modern period, in their attempts to divide time, scholars had to grapple with the diversity of the past and come to terms with the period in between antiquity and the present. The threefold scheme of ancient–medieval–modern that they devised and that eventually crystallized in the course of the late seventeenth and early eighteenth centuries was strongly influenced by ideas about the postclassical development of an ancient Latinity.[97] Interpretations of the ways in which Latin texts and their authors had to be classified and temporally organized varied. But the ambivalences that some scholars expressed toward later Latin, which they studied with great zeal even as they decried its decadence, closely

95 R. Calis, "Reconstructing the Ottoman Greek World: Early Modern Ethnography in the Household of Martin Crusius," *RenQ* 72.1 (2019): 148–93. For Crusius's interests in the Greek vernacular, see P. Toufexis, *Das "Alphabetum vulgaris linguae graecae" des deutschen Humanisten Martin Crusius (1526–1607): Ein Beitrag zur Erforschung der gesprochenen griechischen Sprache im 16. Jh.* (Cologne, 2005).

96 Crusius, *Germanograecia,* 7: *Ex quali ignoratione linguarum, quantae corruptelae in omnes artes, quantae tenebrae in Philosophiam, quanta perversio in Religionem Christianam, redundaverint.... Has tenebras, renascens graeca literatura, ut clarissimus Sol, dispulit.*

97 F. Clark, "Dividing Time: The Making of Historical Periodization in Early Modern Europe" (PhD diss., Princeton University, 2014).

resembled Crusius's attitude toward Greek: in all cases the language in which a given text was written offered valuable clues about its position in history and its relationship to developments in the world at large—be they corruptions or rebirths.

But Crusius's deep consciousness of decline was not calibrated as Western visions of development and decline normally were. It is, somewhat frustratingly, not immediately apparent what exactly Crusius considered the high period of Greek cultural and scholarly life from which decline ensued. Nor did he—in his published works or in his manuscripts—lay out the specific moment when that decline set in. On the contrary: in the aforementioned oration, to illustrate the antiquity of the Greek language, Crusius drew up a seemingly indiscriminate list of Greek writers that started with Hermes Trismegistus, Orpheus, Musaeus, and Homer; included the "Byzantine" historians discussed in this chapter (e.g., Choniates, Zonaras, and Chalkokondyles); and ended with a letter by Antonios Eparchos to Melanchthon and with Alexios Rarturos's collection of vernacular sermons (which, paradoxically, he mentions were written in a mixed form).[98] His pessimism about the decline of the Greek world thus implied a timeless period of purity and florescence somewhere in the ancient Greek past—a vision that projected Homer and Hesiod, Herodotus and Thucydides, Pindar and Plato, and Aeschylus and Aeschines onto the same canvas, but a vision that had no clear contours. Crusius's ideal Greece, that center of culture, had become an insignificant point on the map of letters and learning when knowledge of ancient Greek was either disappearing or at a low point. It was at some point in that process that Byzantium was born. Nowhere in his writings did Crusius explicitly equate Byzantium or the writers who chronicled its history with that decline, but the Byzantine books and manuscripts on his desk belonged and testified to that narrative. This admittedly somewhat nebulous conceptual framework is ultimately also the one through which Crusius came to see the history of Greek in the Byzantine period and, consequently, Byzantine history as a whole.

Though Crusius shared the prejudices of other humanists who worked on Byzantine texts and agreed that Greece was now something of a sad relic, he ultimately told a different story from that of Wolf and others—one that began, like theirs, with Creation, since some of the Byzantine histories started there, but that set the history of later Greece into a world-historical context in which Byzantium did not disappear but, as he wrote in the *Turcograecia*, slowly became "Turkified."[99] One could point out that Crusius's vision of history had developed in a deeply Lutheran context: he shared the Lutheran interest in chronology, which always set out to correlate the histories of Greeks and Latins with those of others, and his engagement

98 Crusius, *Germanograecia*, 4–5.

99 Crusius, ded. ep., *Turcograecia* (n. 74 above), 2v: ἑλλας *ibi* ἐκτουρκωθεῖσα *est*.

with the tabular world histories of, for instance, Funck can thus help explain why he saw the past rather differently from Wolf, the editor of particular texts. But Crusius's vision of history was ultimately also mediated by his deep engagement with all episodes in the history of the Greek language and the vast but neglected world of later Greek. That too is a lesson that Crusius's annotated books and manuscripts tell us.

■■■

The individual observations and notes discussed here yield important clues to why and how Crusius perused his Byzantine books and manuscripts. Crusius mined materials from the Byzantine world mainly to inform himself about other periods in Greek history: Eustathios could shed a new light on Homer. The Byzantine historiographical tradition offered a framework for understanding the rapid advancements of the Ottomans. Thus, whether Crusius marked his way through the hefty tomes of Byzantine scholarship or sought to synchronize the Byzantine historical tradition, Byzantium was never the only or even the primary subject of scrutiny. Byzantium enabled early modern readers such as Crusius to deepen their understanding of periods of history that went beyond what we now consider Byzantine.

To be sure, perusing Byzantine books and manuscripts was never straightforward or easy in Crusius's world. The challenges that he and presumably many other sixteenth-century scholars faced as they attempted to make sense of Byzantine materials were considerable. It bears emphasizing that there was no reliable canon of commentaries or reference works in place to guide Crusius and his colleagues through the unfamiliar names, places, and references that they found in their Byzantine texts. In fact, it is telling that the Byzantine reference works and commentaries that he *did* read informed him about earlier periods of Greek (literary) history. At first glance, then, these works provided little guidance for understanding the context in which they originated. It was only by bringing methods developed in other fields of scholarship to bear on these and other materials that Crusius began to reap their fruits. Biobibliography, historical chronology, and genealogy offered him valuable tools for unlocking Byzantium's many mysteries.

It is clear that Crusius went to the trouble of trying to figure out Byzantine texts because he believed they were also applicable to a wide array of pressing contemporary issues. More than anything else, it was the arrival of the Ottoman Turks in the eastern Mediterranean that made Byzantium a matter of poignant urgency. In the decades following the Reformation, it was becoming increasingly probable that the Ottoman presence could be a permanent one. Not a small number of Crusius's contemporaries equated the Ottoman Turks with the Antichrist. Others tried to determine the apocalyptic significance of the capture of Constantinople. Still others worried how far into Christian territories the Ottomans would eventually advance. All contemplated the significance of the Ottomans for Christian life. In the Byzantine historical tradition, scholars like Crusius found perhaps not any clear-cut answers, but at least a template for framing their questions and concerns.

Over time, while enriching his Byzantine materials with layers of annotation, Crusius generated a sort of working database of Byzantine knowledge that developed cumulatively author by author, expanding constantly and shifting as new texts passed through his hands. This database shows us something of the possibilities of the burgeoning discipline of Byzantine studies in early modern Europe. It illuminates the discipline's dynamic response to contemporary politics and religion and its appropriation of methodologies from adjacent disciplines. It shows us how Crusius saw Byzantine and Ottoman history as a continuum and how for this early modern reader "Byzantium" was still a rather malleable concept whose contours were yet to be determined. His scholarly engagement with materials from the Byzantine world thus serves as a powerful reminder that if we come to Crusius—and any other early modern reader, for that matter—with our own axiomatic understanding of what Byzantium is or is supposed to be, we risk missing what makes Crusius distinct as a reader. It is therefore all the more unfortunate that much of Crusius's diligent work has withered on the vine: the methodological innovations that he developed as he faced a welter of unfamiliar vocabulary, names, places, and references left no mark on later readers of Byzantine materials. For centuries, this material lay dormant in Crusius's marginal notes and scrawls, until historians of reading made them speak to us again by pointing out their importance for understanding intellectual and scholarly practices.

That is not to say that Crusius had no influence at all. The scaffolding that he erected in his book and manuscripts may have been primarily intended to meet the needs of those specific texts, but ultimately it did end up serving to support the works of others. It is perhaps one of history's many ironies that Crusius's *Nachlass* in seventeenth- and eighteenth-century scholarly circles consisted solely of his published works, and of the *Turcograecia* in particular. Not his practice but the results it yielded left their trace. In the footnotes to Edward Gibbon's masterly account of the decline and fall of Rome, for instance, Crusius's *Turcograecia* rubbed elbows with the works of better-known early modern Byzantinists such as Charles du Fresne, sieur Du Cange (1610–1688), and, tellingly, Hieronymus Wolf. Crusius's seminal work also appears frequently in the dictionaries of Byzantine and other vernacular versions of Greek that different lexicographers compiled in the early modern period. Although these scholars' engagement with Byzantine materials was prompted by altogether different concerns than Crusius's, they nevertheless found something in the *Turcograecia* that spoke to their particular interests. Yet to understand Crusius's legacy without looking at his annotated books and manuscripts would be to miss a crucial point: to some extent this now largely forgotten reader of Byzantine texts also laid the foundations for what would ultimately become Byzantine (and modern Greek) studies, but without having anything like that as his aim, and in unexpected ways. Crusius had found himself a path through the uncharted terrain of the Byzantine world that—although less often trodden by later generations of scholars—would still branch off into numerous other directions.

FIVE

EDITING, LEXICOGRAPHY, AND HISTORY UNDER LOUIS XIV

Charles Du Cange and La byzantine du Louvre

TERESA SHAWCROSS

> Learned men have experienced a great loss in the person of Sir Charles du Fresne, Lord Du Cange, Treasurer of France at Amiens, who died on the twenty-third of last month at seventy-eight years of age. He had acquired a knowledge of the innermost secrets of Antiquity that was so profound and detailed that no one else had outdone him in this science. He left us the marks of his learning in his Works on the History of France and of Constantinople. His two Glossaries on the Greek Language and the Latin Language explain an infinity of terms, both specific and ancient, which were unknown until our day. It is difficult to conceive of the number of Manuscripts and printed Books he read.[1]

SUCH WAS THE OBITUARY OF THE *MERCURE GALANT* FOR CHARLES DU CANGE, WHO had been born in Amiens in 1610 and died in Paris in 1688. At his death, Du Cange (fig. 5.1) had seen eight of his books published, and a ninth in press. Among them

1 *Mercure galant* (Paris, 30 November 1688), 235–36. Other obituaries include *La Gazette* 29 (30 October 1688), 570; and Étienne Baluse, "Epistola Stephani Baluzii Tutelensis ad virum clarissimum Eusebium Renaudotum de vita et morte Caroli Dufresnii Cangii," in Du Cange, *Πασχάλιον seu Chronicon paschale a mundo condito ad Heraclii Imperatoris annum vicesimum. Opus Hactenus Fastorum Siculorum nomine laudatum, deinde Chronicæ temporum Epitomes, ac denique Chronici Alexandrini lemmate vulgatum: Nunc tandem auctius et emendatius prodit, cum nova Latina versione & Notis Chronicis ac Historicis* (Paris, 1688), xlix–lii. Unless otherwise indicated, all translations in this chapter are mine.

Fig. 5.1. Unknown artist, *Charles du Fresne, Sieur du Cange*. Engraving, France, 17th century. Inv.-Nr. 12/143. Courtesy Universitätsbibliothek Leipzig Porträtstichsammlung.

was a work of scholarship so important and daunting that—it was said—"Scaliger had desired it, Meursius promised it, and Spellman and Vossius undertaken it," but real progress could not be made until Du Cange had appeared on the scene, since he alone possessed the "immense erudition and indefatigable toil" required.[2] Indeed, the learned man's reputation for an absolute dedication to study was so great that the tale circulated while he was alive—and was repeated posthumously—that even on his wedding day he had chosen to set aside "six or seven hours" to spend with his books.[3] The surviving portion of the compendium Du Cange kept of his reading, which gives short references to printed and manuscript works organized in columns under "things, cities, names, [etc.]," is over a thousand pages long and contains tens of thousands of entries.[4] Indeed, in his survey of the seventeenth-century French authors, Voltaire would remark regarding Du Cange that one could only be terror-struck when confronted by the extent of his knowledge and the number of his works.[5]

Even though many of the publications he produced continue to be used, little has been written recently about their author.[6] Examining Du Cange's printed writings

2 The work in question was the Latin *Glossarium*. Lesage de Samine [pseud. of J.-L. Baron], *Éloge de Charles Dufresne, seigneur du Cange, avec une notice de ses ouvrages: Discours qui a remporté le Prix de l'Académie en 1764* (Amiens, 1764), 13.

3 Ibid., 4; L. Feugère, *Étude sur la vie et les ouvrages de Du Cange* (Paris, 1852), 8; this anecdote about Du Cange echoes a similar story about Guillaume Budé that can be traced as far back as Pierre Bayle, *Dictionnaire historique et critique*, 2 vols. (Amsterdam, 1697), 1:690; J. Considine, *Dictionaries in Early Modern Europe: Lexicography and the Making of Heritage* (Cambridge, 2008), 34, 262.

4 N. Edelman, *Attitudes of Seventeenth-Century France toward the Middle Ages* (New York, 1946), 80.

5 Feugère, *Étude sur la vie et les ouvrages de Du Cange*, 42; [François Marie Arouet de] Voltaire, "Du Cange (Charles du Fresne)," in *Catalogue de la plupart des écrivains français qui ont paru dans le siècle de Louis XIV, pour servir à l'histoire littéraire de ce temps*, in *Siècle de Louis XIV (II): Listes et "Catalogue des écrivains,"* ed. D. Venturino, Œuvres complètes de Voltaire 12 (Oxford, 2017), 47–206, at 74. Voltaire's praise of Du Cange was absent from the original *Catalogue des écrivains* that appeared in the Berlin edition of 1751; its inclusion in 1768 can be attributed specifically to activism on the part of the writer Nicolas-Claude Thiriot and perhaps more generally to the growth of interest in Du Cange's work from such scholars as Baron and D'Aubigny in the 1750s and 1760s. See the notes on Du Cange in Voltaire's *Catalogue des écrivains*, 306, for more details.

6 Historical treatments of Du Cange include [Jean-Charles Du Fresne D'Aubigny], *Mémoire sur les manuscrits de M. Du Cange* (n.p., 1752), and idem, *Mémoire historique pour servir à l'éloge de Charles Du Fresne Sieur Du Cange, et à l'intelligence du plan général de ses études sur l'histoire de France* (Paris, 1766); H. Hardouin, *Essai sur la vie et sur les ouvrages de Charles Dufresne Du Cange* (Amiens, 1849); Feugère, *Étude sur la vie et les ouvrages de Du Cange*; C. Samaran, *Du Cange à Paris, rue des Écouffes: D'après son testament et son inventaire après décès* (Nogent-le-Routrou, France, 1922); J.-M. Spieser, "Du Cange and Byzantium," in *Through the Looking Glass: Byzantium through British Eyes. Papers from the Twenty-Ninth Spring Symposium of Byzantine Studies, London, March 1995*, ed. R. Cormack and E. Jeffreys, SPBS 7 (Aldershot, 2000), 199–210; and Considine, *Dictionaries in Early Modern Europe*, 250–87.

and unpublished papers,[7] I seek to shed light on the man and his intellectual trajectory, situating his work in the seventeenth-century context in which he operated as a scholar. I argue that Du Cange was a disciple of the new historical school that had emerged in Paris a generation earlier. Informed by the approaches of older contemporaries, he prepared himself to succeed them as the foremost historian of France and the Latin West; but circumstances made him instead a Byzantinist. Ultimately, however, the career he traced was that of a versatile polymath, who threw himself into complex editorial, lexicographic, and historical projects at different points in his life, and who became so devoted to Byzantine history—and so proud of the series on the subject directed by him under the patronage of Louis XIV—that on his death bed it was impossible to prise him away from his proofs. Considered today to be the founding father of Byzantine studies, Du Cange had a trajectory shaped by geopolitical shifts—especially the Bourbons' temporary alliance with the Habsburgs and engagement in hostilities against the Ottomans, culminating with French participation in the War of Crete—that sparked an interest on the part of the French crown in the past of the eastern Mediterranean world.

The Amiens Years

After legal studies in Paris as a young man until 1631, Du Cange had returned to his hometown of Amiens, where he integrated himself into the ranks of the regional officials of the crown by purchasing the post of local magistrate and marrying the daughter of the city's treasurer general; he would later serve as the councillor-treasurer of the region of Picardy, from 1645 to 1668.[8] Although his library—with its statues interspersed among weighty tomes in the bookcases and inscriptions adorning the walls above—suggested a concern with the classical past,[9] it was not in this guise that he established himself initially as a scholar in the 1640s, but rather through a series of editions of texts and studies relating to French involvement in the Crusades. His native Picardy and neighboring Champagne had been among the foremost recruiting grounds for the movement. In 1657 he produced the *History of the Empire of Constantinople* (*Histoire de l'empire de Constantinople*), a new edition and translation of Geoffroi de Villehardouin's account of the sack of Constantinople in 1204.

7 For a list of the works published by Du Cange during his lifetime or in press at his death, see Appendix I; for unpublished works, see Appendix II.

8 Hardouin, *Essai sur la vie et sur les ouvrages de Du Cange*, 12; Feugère, *Étude sur la vie et les ouvrages de Du Cange*, 8–9.

9 L. Delisle, *Le Cabinet des manuscrits de la Bibliothèque impériale*, vol. 1 (Paris, 1868), 425; Samaran, *Du Cange à Paris*, 1–2; P. Rickard, "From Villehardouin to Du Cange via Vigenère," *Zeitschrift für Französische Sprache und Literatur* 103 (1993): 113–43.

Du Cange accompanied Villehardouin's work with a narrative and institutional history of the Crusader states founded in the former territories of the Byzantine Empire.[10] According to him, the work was concerned not with "foreign lands" and "new worlds," but rather with places formerly conquered by Frenchmen to which their descendants continued to retain "authentic titles" and "well-founded claims."[11] While he defined the events in question as being "part" of the history "of France," he also acknowledged that "there was no doubt" it was also "Byzantine."[12]

In 1665 Du Cange followed this publication with the *Historical Treatise on the Head of John the Baptist* (*Traité historiqve du chef de S. Iean Baptiste*), the relic behind the foundation of Amiens Cathedral. This book examined one of the main phenomena that followed in the wake of the Fourth Crusade: the influx of relics from Byzantium to western Europe, especially France.[13] Then, in 1668, he brought out the *History of Saint Louis, IXth King of France of That Name* (*Histoire de S. Lovys IX. dv nom Roy de France*), a new edition of Jean de Joinville's historical biography of Saint Louis accompanied by an account of the later Crusades (fig. 5.2).[14]

10 Du Cange, *Histoire de l'empire de Constantinople sovs les emperevrs françois, divisée en deux Parties, dont la premiere contient l'Histoire de la conquête de la ville de Constantinople par les François & les Venitiens, écrite par Geoffroy de Ville-Hardovin Maréchal de Champagne & de Romanie: Reueuë & corrigée en cette Edition sur le Manuscrit de la Bibliotheque du Roy, & illustrée d'Obseruations Historiques, & d'vn glossaire, pour les termes de l'Auteur, à present hors d'vsage. Avec la Suitte de cette Histoire, iusques en l'an MCCXL. tirée de l'Histoire de France MS. de Philippes Movskes Chanoine & depuis Euesque de Tournay. La seconde contient vne Histoire Generale de ce que les François & les Latins ont fait de plus memorable dans l'empire de Constantinople, depuis qu'ils s'en rendirent maistres, iusques à ce que les Turcs s'en sont emparez: Iustifiée par les ecriuains du temps, & par plusieurs Chroniques, Chartes, & autres Pieces non encore publiées* (Paris, 1657). In his "Preface svr l'histoire de Geoffroy de Ville-Hardovin," Du Cange mentions two earlier printings consulted by him: Blaise de Vigenère, *Histoire de Geoffroy de Villehardovin, svr la Conqveste de Constantinople, en 1204* (Paris, 1585), and Guillaume Rouillé, *L'Histoire ov Chroniqve dv Seignevr Geoffroy de Ville-Hardvin, Mareschal de Champaigne & de Romanie. Representee de mot à mot en ancienne langue Françoise, d'un vieil exemplaire escrit à la main, qui se trouue dans les anciens archives de la Serenissime Republique de Venise: Contenant la Conqveste de l'Empire de Constantinople faicte par des Barons François, confederez & vnis auec les Seigneurs Venitiens, l'an 1204. Ensemble la description de la prinse de Constantinople, extraicte de la fin des Annales de Nicete Coniates, historien Grec, & Chancelier des Empereurs Constantinopolitains. De nouueau mise en François* (Lyons, 1601).

11 Du Cange, "Au Roy," dedication to *Histoire de l'empire de Constantinople sovs les emperevrs françois*, [i–ii].

12 Du Cange, "Preface svr l'histoire de Geoffroy de Ville-Hardovin," [i].

13 Du Cange, *Traité historiqve dv chef de S. Iean Baptiste, contenant vne discussion exacte de ce que les auteurs anciens & modernes en ont écrit, & particulierement de ses trois Inuentions. Il y est aussi parlé par occasion des autres Reliques du mesme Saint. Et à la fin sont inserez quelques Traitez Grecs, tirez de la Bibliotheque du Roy, & de celle de M. le Cardinal Mazarin, auec leurs versions latines seruans de fondement & de preuue à toute cette dissertation* (Paris, 1665).

14 Du Cange, "Au Roy," dedication to *Histoire de S. Lovys IX. dv nom Roy de France, ecrite par Iean Sire de Ioinville Senéchal de Champagne: Enrichie de nouuelles observations & Dissertations*

Fig. 5.2. Unknown artist, *Saint Louis, IXth King of France of That Name*. From Du Cange, *Histoire de Saint Lovys IX. du nom Roy de France* (Paris, 1668), frontispiece. Courtesy Bibliothèque nationale de France.

The *History of Saint Louis* was one of several works across his career that Du Cange would offer to his monarch, Louis XIV. Its epistolary dedication explicitly compared the long-dead saint and his youthful namesake, expressing the confident assertion that the "same genius that inspired Saint Louis" was now also guiding Louis XIV, ensuring that the latter ruler would not merely grow into a fitting heir for the former but surpass him in both judgment and deeds.[15] The conceit was one calculated to appeal to the Sun King. While Louis XIV exploited classical figures from myth or history (such as Apollo, Alexander, or Augustus) as allegories of his kingship throughout his long reign, the monarch would also be celebrated extensively with religious imagery as the "Most Christian King."[16] As his father Louis XIII had done before him, Louis XIV encouraged his association with his eponym, Saint Louis, the patron saint of the Bourbon dynasty and France's ultimate symbol of holy kingship.[17] This was perhaps to be expected in one who, as a child, had been given a stack of cards to play with that held up Saint Louis as "Pious, fair-handed, chaste, prudent, valiant, a true model of good Kings" (fig. 5.3).[18] Louis XIV dedicated his chapel at Versailles to the saint, whose feast day he celebrated, together with his court, with increasing pomp. The process would culminate in 1693 with the foundation of the military Order of Saint Louis and in 1702 with the decoration of the

---

Historiques. Avec les Établissemens de S. Lovys, le Conseil de Pierre de Fontaines, & plusieurs autres Pieces concernant ce regne, tirées des Manuscrits (Paris, 1668). Excerpts from contemporary reviews of Du Cange's book are reprinted in J. Le Long, *Bibliothèque historique de la France; contenant le catalogue de tous les ouvrages, tant imprimez que manuscrits, qui traitent de l'histoire de ce roïaume, ou qui y ont rapport: Avec des Notes critiques & historiques* (Paris, 1719), 358–59. Du Cange did not have access to what is today the oldest surviving manuscript edition of Joinville's work, which was rediscovered in Brussels only in 1746: Jean de Joinville, *Vie de saint Louis* (ca. 1340–50), Bibliothèque nationale de France (hereafter BnF), MS fr. 13568. Du Cange wrote in his "Preface svr l'histoire de Saint Lovys contenant tovte l'œconomie de ce volume," in the *Histoire de S. Lovys IX. dv nom Roy de France*, [i–iii], that his edition of Joinville was based on two printed editions: Antoine Pierre de Rieux, *L'histoire & Chroniqve dv treschrestien Roy S. Loys, IX. du Nom, & XLIIII. Roy de France. Escripte par feu messire Iehan Sire, seigneur de Ionuille, & Seneschal de Champaigne, amy & contemporain dudict Roy S. Loys* (Poitiers, 1547), and Claude Ménard, *Histoire de S. Loys IX. dv nom, Roy de France. Par Messire Iean Sire de Ionuille, Seneschal de Champagne. Novvellement mise en lumiere, suiuant l'original ancien de l'Autheur. Avec diverses pieces dv mesme temps non encor imprimees, & quelques Obseruations Historiques* (Paris, 1617).

15 Du Cange, "Au Roy," dedication to *Histoire de S. Lovys IX. dv nom Roy de France* (1668).

16 J.-M. Apostolidès, *Le roi-machine: Spectacle et politique au temps de Louis XIV* (Paris, 1981); L. Norman, *The Shock of the Ancient: Literature and History in Early Modern France* (Chicago, 2011), 95–106; M. M. S. Edmunds, *Piety and Politics: Imagining Divine Kingship in Louis XIV's Chapel at Versailles* (Newark, DE, 2002), 36.

17 P. Burke, *The Fabrication of Louis XIV* (New Haven, 1992), 28, 96, 185; S. Heath, *Sacral Kingship in Bourbon France: The Cult of Saint Louis, 1589–1830* (London, 2021). 5.

18 See H. G. Hall, *Richelieu's Desmarets and the Century of Louis XIV* (Oxford, 1990), 230–36.

Fig. 5.3. Jean Desmarets de Saint-Sorlin (author, 1595–1676) and Stefano Della Bella (artist, 1610–1664), "Saint Louis IX." *Cartes des Rois de France* (Paris, 1644), card 44. Courtesy Bibliothèque nationale de France. The text reads: "Pious, fair-handed, chaste, prudent, valiant, a true model of good Kings. He pacified his Kingdom, passed good laws, then went two times to the Holy Land, where he first took Damietta [in Egypt], but in the end he met misfortune there, and died there on his second voyage."

Invalides, a complex built for war veterans, with portraits and scenes from the life of Saint Louis.[19]

But the 1650s and 1660s already saw the production of a wealth of texts and artistic works that celebrated ongoing military campaigns against the Ottomans as a continuation of the medieval Crusades. Sculptors and painters produced numerous images of Saint Louis guiding or interceding for Louis XIV (e.g., Charles Le Brun's *Louis XIV Adoring the Risen Christ* of 1674), or of Saint Louis with the features of Louis XIV (e.g., *Louis Performing a Miracle* at the Jesuit College of Poitiers, dating from 1655–60).[20] Writers such as Jean Desmarets de Saint-Sorlin in his *Clovis, or Christian France* (*Clovis, ov la France chrestienne*, 1657), Antoine Godeau in his *Historical Encomia of Emperors* (*Éloges historiques des Empereurs*, 1667), and Charles de La Rue and Pierre Corneille in *The Victories of the King* (*Regi Epinicion*, or *Les Victoires du Roi*, 1667) repeatedly presented Louis XIV as following "in the footsteps of Saint Louis, who was the true model of a most Christian prince," by leading a spiritual and military crusade.[21] The promise was made that someday the church "would see among the number of the saints a Louis XIV as it already counts a Louis IX."[22] That these tendencies percolated well beyond the court and capital is demonstrated by the erection in 1675 of a statue of Louis XIV as Saint Louis in the village of Guimiliau in Finistère, at the westernmost extremity of Brittany.[23] The culmination would be the chapels at Versailles (1682–1710) and in the Invalides (1676–1702): the ceiling of the latter has an image from 1692 by Charles de La Fosse of Louis XIV depicted as Louis IX, wearing a royal mantel and presenting arms to Christ.[24]

19 Burke, *Fabrication of Louis XIV*, 115; Edmunds, *Piety and Politics*, 209–11; F. Polleroß, *Das sakrale Identifikationsporträt: Ein höfischer Bildtypus vom 13. bis zum 20. Jahrhundert*, 2 vols. (Worms, 1988), 1:258; 2:fig. 583.

20 Edmunds, *Piety and Politics*, 211 and fig. 155; Polleroß, *Das sakrale Identifikationsporträt*, 2:fig. 257. The city of Poitiers also displayed a statue of Louis XIV as Louis IX, sculpted by Jean Girouard, on the saint's feast day (25 August 1687): Burke, *Fabrication of Louis XIV*, 96.

21 Jean Desmarets de Saint-Sorlin, *Clovis; ov La France chrestienne. Poëme heroïqve* (Leiden, 1657); Antoine Godeau, *Éloges historiqves des Emperevrs, des Roys, des Princes, des Imperatrices, des Reynes, et des Princesses, Qui dans tous les Siécles ont excellé en piété* (Paris, 1667); and Charles de La Rue, *Regi Epinicion*, trans. Pierre Corneille as *Poème sur les victoires du Roy* (Paris, 1667). The quotation is from Bossuet, letter of 1679 to Innocent XI, cited and translated in Edmunds, *Piety and Politics*, 210; see Hall, *Richelieu's Desmarets*.

22 Godeau, "Au Roy," dedication to the *Éloges historiqves des Emperevrs*, [vi–vii]; Edmunds, *Piety and Politics*, 210.

23 Burke, *Fabrication of Louis XIV*, 158; Polleroß, *Das sakrale Identifikationsporträt*, 1:258; 2:fig. 555.

24 Edmunds, *Piety and Politics*, fig. 163.

Establishment in Paris

Du Cange's growing relationship while in Amiens with the Royal Printing Press of the Louvre (Imprimerie royale du Louvre) anticipated his move in 1668 back to Paris, where he set about cultivating the particular patronage of Louis XIV and his minister of finance, Jean-Baptiste Colbert, who acted as a Maecenas to many learned men and institutions (fig. 5.4).[25] In 1665 Colbert had purchased the Hôtel Bautru de Serrant on the rue Vivienne in Paris for his own library, the Colbertine, and a few months later he had moved the Royal Library (Bibliothèque royale) next door. From then on the Royal Library was reformed along the lines of the Colbertine and became to some extent integrated with it: the two collections would to all intents and purposes function as a single operational unit during Colbert's life, with holdings being regularly transferred from one to the other and curatorial appointments in both being in the minister's gift.[26]

Recent decades had seen a gradual revolution in the way in which French scholars treated the classical and especially the medieval past. Ambitious projects had been developed for great histories numbering multiple volumes and thousands of pages, whose emphasis was less on narrative than on a more composite presentation based on the meticulous edition of textual sources together with the reproduction of material artifacts, accompanied with extensive analysis and commentary.[27] Historical culture—as a form of antiquarianism—bolstered royal claims and legitimated the authority of the state. In a world of the competing rights of secular and religious authorities, governments recruited individuals and encouraged the establishment of networks whose scholarship could reconstitute the past as confirmation of legitimacy. This was a propaganda war fought by ransacking libraries and archives for their treasures—and by countering source with source in heated debates.[28] Symptomatic of these changes was Colbert's relocation, reorganization, and expansion in 1666 of the collection of printed books and manuscripts of the Royal Library, as well as his assemblage of a vast bank of documents, coins, medals, and seals—and his employment of groups of experts to conserve, catalog, and study all this material

25 Burke, *Fabrication of Louis XIV*, 49.

26 For the history of the Colbertine and Royal Libraries, see S. Saunders, "Public Administration and the Library of Jean-Baptiste Colbert," *Libraries & Culture* 26 (1991): 283–300; J. Soll, *The Information Master: Jean-Baptiste Colbert's Secret State Intelligence System* (Ann Arbor, 2009), 7.

27 B. Barret-Kriegel, *Les historiens et la monarchie*, 4 vols. (Paris, 1988), 1:78–79; L. Doucette, *Emery Bigot: Seventeenth-Century French Humanist* (Toronto, 1970), 162; A. Momigliano, "Ancient History and the Antiquarian," *JWarb* 13.3 (1950): 285–315.

28 Soll, *Information Master*, 26–29, 94–105. On the antiquarian inclusion of material objects as evidence in historical debates, see Momigliano, "Ancient History and the Antiquarian," 294–97.

Fig. 5.4. Henri Testelin Huygens (1616–1695), *Colbert Presenting the Members of the Royal Academy of the Sciences to Louis XIV*. Painting, 17th c. Photo by Gérard Blot, Chateaux de Versailles et de Trianon, Versailles, France, via RMN-Grand Palais / Art Resource, NY.

so that it could be used by the state. In his *History of the Capitularies of the French Kings* (*Histoire des capitulaires des rois français*), the legal scholar Étienne Baluze, who was the head librarian of Colbert's personal library, outlined a new archival method: it would allow for the managing of the resources provided by diplomatic documents and the creation of the most efficient repository of knowledge dealing with the history of titles and rights—and the establishment of legal precedents—that was available for administrative purposes to any European monarchy.[29]

In this enterprise, in addition to those he employed directly in his libraries, Colbert relied increasingly on the services of Jean Mabillon, a learned Benedictine who, at his abbey of Saint-Germain-des-Prés just across the river from the Louvre, gathered together a group of monastics with similar interests and twice a week presided over scholarly meetings that secular men could also attend.[30] Du Cange was among those invited to these meetings. He and Mabillon became well acquainted over time, each declaring a profound respect for the other's knowledge. Contemporaries recalled a story about a provincial scholar who came to Paris in order to consult Du Cange, only to be told to go instead and find "Father Mabillon, for it is he who is informed of these

29 Soll, *Information Master*, 94; Barret-Kriegel, *Les historiens et la monarchie*, 4:97–100.

30 Barret-Kriegel, *Les historiens et la monarchie*, 1:51–58, 3:108–111; Doucette, *Emery Bigot*, 83–84, 93; Considine, *Dictionaries in Early Modern Europe* (n. 3 above), 264.

matters and can satisfy you"; but then, upon addressing himself to Mabillon, he found himself sent straight back to "Monsieur Du Cange, who will know how to answer your request."[31] Du Cange and Mabillon joined Baluze as contributors to Colbert's development of the Colbertine and reform of the Royal Library.[32] While Mabillon oversaw Latin manuscripts, Du Cange had charge of Greek manuscripts together with Jean-Baptiste Cotelier, a Hellenist with expertise in ancient texts.[33] Like the Latinists, the Hellenists advocated less for the acquisition of theological or fictional works (there is no evidence, for example, that they engaged in Counter-Reformation biblical scholarship, or in literary analyses of ancient Latin or Greek prosody) than for the acquisition of technical works of utility to the state: "You must not let escape any historical book, or any book on civil or ecclesiastical law, that is to say: the canons." Instructed to triage material, they systematized the assessment of the evidence available by composing a formulary to be used specifically for Greek texts.[34] Other specialists who were made responsible for the Hebrew, Syriac, Arabic, Armenian, Persian, and Turkish collections to some extent also pursued similar objectives.[35]

31 Edelman, *Attitudes of Seventeenth-Century France toward the Middle Ages* (n. 4 above), 83.

32 Baluze would go on to write Du Cange's eulogy in the introduction to his colleague's last work of scholarship, published posthumously. See the "Epistola Stephani Baluzii Tutelensis" (n. 1 above), xlix–lii.

33 While some 18th-century accounts state that Du Cange had hired Cotelier as his assistant, Cotelier's heavy presence in the library archives calls into question the relationship between the two scholars. Cotelier's earliest memorandum from the Royal Library has a possible date of 1667, while Du Cange must have started work there after his move to Paris in 1668. One cannot help wondering exactly what Du Cange's linguistic competence was when he first arrived in Paris to undertake editorial work, and how much his mastery of medieval Greek owed to his collaborative study with Cotelier of the collection they curated together. It is noteworthy that the editions Du Cange produced of Greek material were not of new texts but were revised editions of texts that had already been edited and studied. However, this does not prove lack of sureness in the language, for the same was also true of his editions of Latin texts. It seems that Du Cange was interested less in making undiscovered or obscure works accessible than in providing through detailed commentaries a better understanding of works whose importance had already been acknowledged. His edition of the text of Villehardouin, for example, which stretched to some 200 folio pages, was accompanied by another 600 pages of supplementary materials—including notes, commentary, glossary, and index; a similar distribution can be seen in his edition of Zonaras. See Soll, *Information Master*, 105–6 and notes, for further documentation on Cotelier. On Cotelier as Du Cange's assistant, see Delisle, "Jean-Baptiste Cotelier," in J.-J. Expilly, *Dictionnaire géographique, historique et politique des Gaules et de la France*, vol. 5 (Amsterdam, 1768), 190–91. On Du Cange as an editor, see Considine, *Dictionaries in Early Modern Europe*, 263–65.

34 Soll, *Information Master*, 105–6. The quotation by Jean-Baptiste Cotelier can be found in [Cotelier,] "Remarques sur les manuscrits grecs" (ca. 1667), in H. Omont, *Missions archéologiques en Orient aux XVIIe et XVIIIe siècles* (Paris, 1902), 30–32.

35 D'Aubigny, *Mémoire sur les manuscrits de M. Du Cange* (n. 6 above), 25; Barret-Kriegel, *Les historiens et la monarchie*, 4:100. François Banier, for instance, was engaged in collecting information

In Paris, Du Cange initially continued to elucidate the crusaders' eastern theater of action. He provided editions and analyses of Greek narrative sources relating to the Byzantine Empire at the time of the Crusades: his *History in Six Books of John Kinnamos* (*Ἰωάννου Κιννάμου βασιλικοῦ γραμματικοῦ ἱστοριῶν λόγοι ϛ΄*), with extensive observations on Nikephoros Bryennios and Anna Komnene, was published in 1670;[36] his *Chronicle of John Zonaras* (*Ἰωάννου τοῦ ἀσκητοῦ τοῦ Ζωναρᾶ γεγονότος τοῦ μεγάλου δρουγγαρίου τῆς βίγλας καὶ πρωτοασηκρήτις χρονικόν*) was completed in 1687.[37] He also had plans to edit and translate the "political verses in vulgar Greek" of the *Chronicle of Morea* (*Τὸ χρονικὸν τοῦ Μορέως*), which recounted the story of the crusader settlers in the century after their occupation of the Byzantine provinces. He described the *Chronicle* as being about the "deeds of the French in the Morea, or Peloponnese," beginning with the "sack of Constantinople" and continuing with "our war in the Morea."[38] While these editions may have been spurred on by a keen interest in the inception and development of the crusading movement, the research required for them also led to an exploration of the interactions of western Europeans with the Byzantine Empire, from their first contact with the Komnenian dynasty during the campaign launched in 1095 to fight the Turks and retake Jerusalem to the seizure of the empire from the Angelid dynasty by French and Venetian forces in 1204.

on the Mughal Empire that could be used for diplomatic purposes. See Soll, *The Information Master*, 105.

36 Du Cange, *Ἰωάννου Κιννάμου βασιλικοῦ γραμματικοῦ ἱστοριῶν λόγοι ϛ΄. Joannis Cinnami imperatorii grammatici historiarum libri sex, sev de rebvs gestis a Joanne et Manuele Comnenis impp. CP. Accedunt Caroli dv Fresne, D. dv Cange, Regi a Consiliis, & Franciæ apud Ambianos Quaestoris, in Nicephori Bryennii cæsaris, Annæ Commenæ cæsarissæ & ejusdem Joannis Cinnami Historiam Comnenicam Notæ Historicæ & Philologicæ. His adivngitvr Pauli Silentiarii descriptio sanctæ Sophiæ, quæ nunc primum prodit Græce & Latine, cum vberiori Commentario* (Paris, 1670).

37 Du Cange, *Ἰωάννου τοῦ ἀσκητοῦ τοῦ Ζωναρᾶ γεγονότος τοῦ μεγάλου δρουγγαρίου τῆς βίγλας καὶ πρωτοασηκρήτις χρονικόν. Joannis Zonaræ monachi magni antea vigilum præfecti et primi a secretis annales. Carolus du Fresne, Dom. Du Cange, Regi a Consiliis, & Franciae apud Ambianos Quæstor, Wolfianam Editionem cum scriptis Codicibus contulit: Latinam Versionem recensuit, Annales Notis illustravit*, 2 vols. (Paris, 1686–87).

38 J. A. Buchon, *Chronique de la conquête de Constantinople et de l'établissement des français en Morée, écrite en vers politiques par un auteur anonyme dans les premières années du XIVe siècle et traduite pour la première fois d'après le manuscrit grec inédit* (Paris, 1825), xx–xxi; Du Cange, "De bellis Francorum in Morea," *Index auctorum graecorum ineditorum ac editorum, qui in hocce Glossario laudantur & illustrantur*, 23–70, in the second appendix to Du Cange, *Glossarium ad scriptores mediæ & infimæ Græcitatis, in quo Græca vocabula novatæ significationis, aut usus rarioris, Barbara, Exotica, Ecclesiastica, Liturgica, Tactica, Nomica, Jatrica, Botanica, Chymica explicantur, eorum Notiones & Originationes reteguntur: Complures ævi medii Ritus & Mores; Dignitates Ecclesiasticæ, Monasticæ, Palatinæ, Politicæ, & quamplurima alia observatione digna, & ad Historiam Byzantinam præsertim spectantia, recensentur ac enucleantur. E libris editis, ineditis, veteribusque monumentis. Accedit Appendix ad Glossarium mediæ & infimæ Latinitatis, unà cùm brevi Etymologico Linguæ Gallicæ ex utroque Glossario*, 2 vols. (Lyons, 1688), vol. 2, col. 34.

Out of these concerns, therefore, grew a deeper engagement with Byzantium. In 1680 Du Cange published his *Byzantine History* (*Historia Byzantina*), a lengthy introduction to the empire's prosopographical, topographical, and institutional past, accompanied by an innovative program of illustrations.[39] The volume opens with a frontispiece depicting the allegorical figure of Constantinople as a crowned woman in imperial robes reclining in front of her city—whose identity is immediately recognizable from the representation of its most famous monument, the Justinianic Church of the Holy Wisdom (Hagia Sophia) (fig. 5.5); a detailed bird's-eye view of the city and its most eminent features is subsequently provided (fig. 5.6). In addition, many pages throughout the work contain highly detailed reproductions of the images and inscriptions found on Byzantine coins, medals, icons, reliquaries, frescoes, and monuments.[40] Du Cange's compositional method was one that sought to support all statements advanced, so that a concise exposition was accompanied by citations that were often as long as, if not longer than, the main text.[41]

Already in 1648, the French crown had established under Colbert's direction the series *Of the Writers of Byzantine History under the Most Happy Louis XIV* (*De Byzantinae historiae scriptoribus sub Felicissimis Ludovici XIV*), also known as the *Corpus of Byzantine History* (*Corpus Byzantinae historiae*), as the *Corpus of Writers of Byzantine History* (*Corpus scriptorum historiae Byzantinae*), and—more familiarly—as the *Byzantine Series of the Louvre* (*La byzantine du Louvre*).[42] In the programmatic preface he wrote for the first volume in the series, its founding editor, Philippe Labbe—a Jesuit theologian who was learned in both Latin and Greek—had defined the project as being concerned with "Byzantine history" of the type that was not only "admirable because of its events, both agreeable in their variety and remarkable in their duration," but also so closely related to that of "ancient Rome"

39 Du Cange, *Historia Byzantina duplici commentario illustrata. Prior familias ac stemmata imperatorum Constantinopolitanorum, cum eorundem Augustorum Nomismatibus, & aliquot Iconibus: Prætererea Familias Dalmaticas & Turcicas complectitur: Alter descriptionem urbis Constantinopolitanæ, qualis extitit sub Imperatoribus Christianis*, 2 vols. (Paris, 1680).

40 Ibid. See the "Index tabellarum, quae ad huius operis, atque adeò totius Historiae Byzantinae illustrationem, in eo passim inseruntur," 1:9–10, and the "Syllabus, seu index descriptionis urbis Constantinopolitanae" at the beginning of 2:n.p., for more engravings throughout the work.

41 D'Aubigny, *Mémoire historique pour servir à l'éloge de Charles Du Cange* (n. 6 above), 17; Feugère, *Étude sur la vie et les ouvrages de Du Cange* (n. 6 above), 28–33.

42 H. Omont, "La collection byzantine de Labbe et le projet de J.-M. Suarès," *REG* 17 (1904): 18–32; L. Bréhier, "Le développement des études d'histoire byzantine du XVIIe au XXe siècle," *Revue d'Auvergne* 18 (1901): 1–36; A. Pertusi, *Storiografia umanistica e mondo bizantino*, Istituto siciliano di studi bizantini e neoellenici, quaderni 5 (Palermo, 1967), 82–93; M.-F. Auzépy and J.-P. Grélois, eds., *Byzance retrouvée: Érudits et voyageurs français (XVIe–XVIIIe siècles)* (Paris, 2001), 70–80.

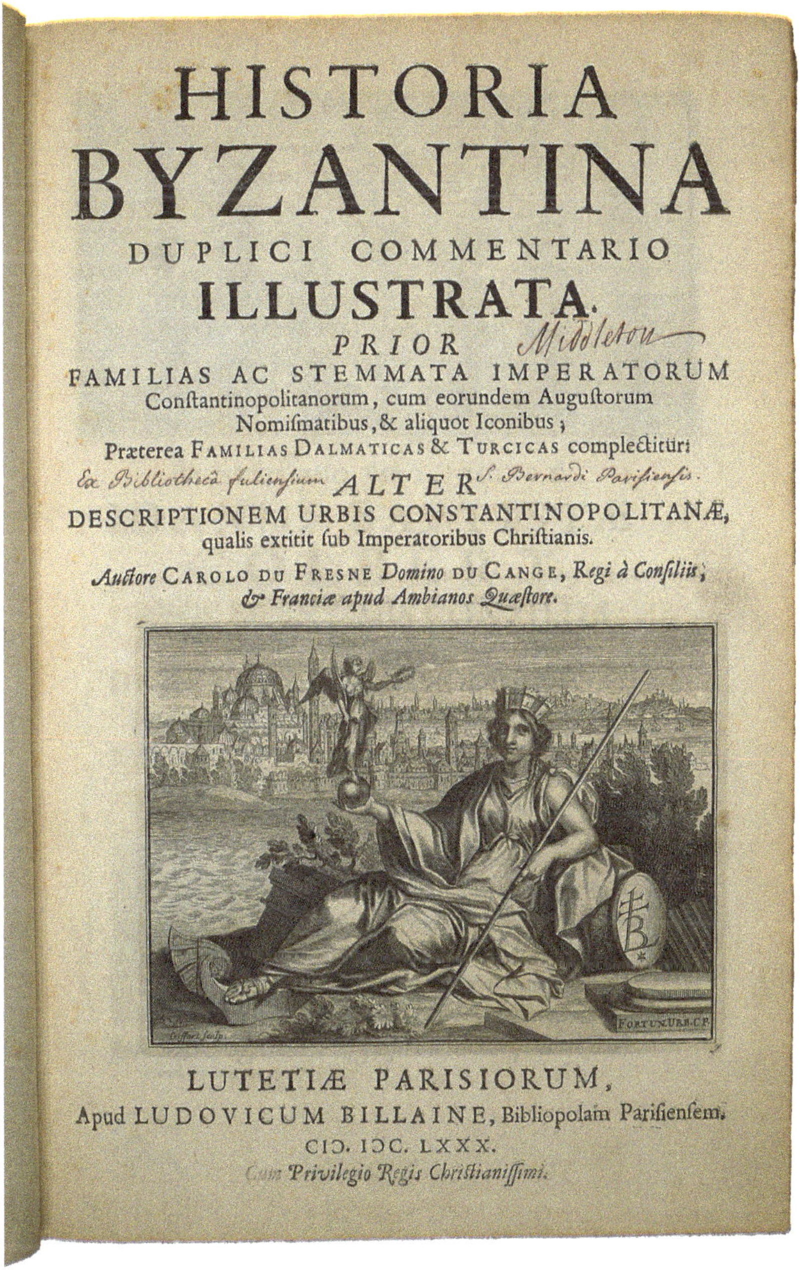

HISTORIA
BYZANTINA
DUPLICI COMMENTARIO
ILLUSTRATA.
PRIOR
FAMILIAS AC STEMMATA IMPERATORUM
Constantinopolitanorum, cum eorundem Augustorum
Nomismatibus, & aliquot Iconibus;
Præterea FAMILIAS DALMATICAS & TURCICAS complectitur:
ALTER
DESCRIPTIONEM URBIS CONSTANTINOPOLITANÆ,
qualis extitit sub Imperatoribus Christianis.
Auctore CAROLO DU FRESNE *Domino* DU CANGE, *Regi à Consiliis;*
& Franciæ apud Ambianos Quæstore.

LUTETIÆ PARISIORUM,
Apud LUDOVICUM BILLAINE, Bibliopolam Parisiensem.
CIϽ. IϽC. LXXX.
Cum Privilegio Regis Christianissimi.

Fig. 5.5. Pierre Giffart (engraver, 1643–1723), personification of the city of Constantinople. From Du Cange, *Historia Byzantina duplici commentario illustrata,* vol. 1 (Paris, 1680), title page. Courtesy Rare Book Division, Special Collections, Princeton University Library.

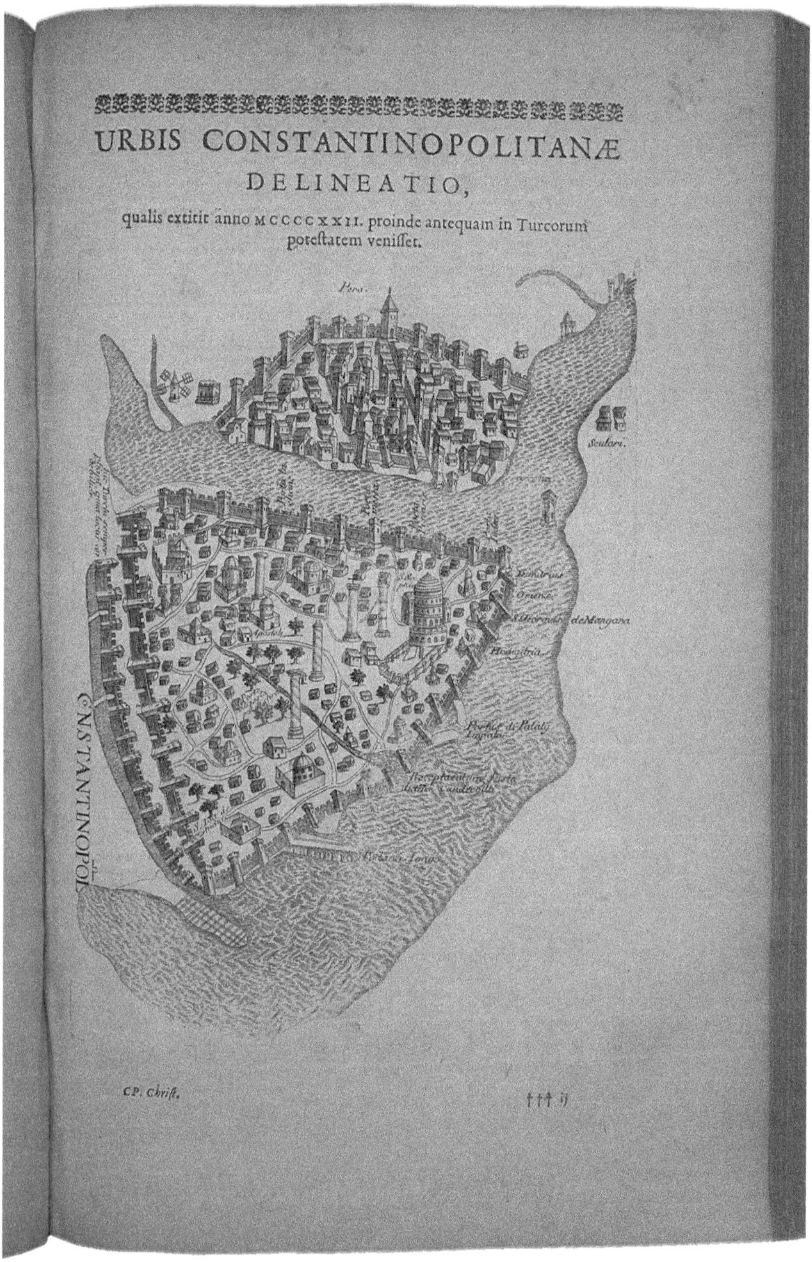

Fig. 5.6. Unknown engraver after Christoforo Buondelmonti (1386–ca. 1430), *A Sketch of the City of Constantinople as It Stood in the Year 1422, Thus Before the Turks Came to Power*. From Du Cange, *Historia Byzantina duplici commentario illustrata*, vol. 2 (Paris, 1680), n.p. [xvii]. Courtesy Rare Book Division, Special Collections, Princeton University Library.

that all scholars "love and cultivate it," and "all books containing it are sought after."[43] The series was dedicated to the printing of original sources—mainly in medieval Greek, but occasionally in Latin and even French—that elucidated aspects of the history of the Byzantium and of Constantinople; the editions were accompanied by translations, commentaries, and other apparatuses. Although Labbe had originally outlined the content of thirty-two volumes, the twenty-seven he actually produced ended up being composed of somewhat different material.[44] Du Cange, who had already been a contributing editor, took care to cast himself as a fitting overseer of the revival of the project, which had been struggling since Labbe's death in 1667. Not only did he offer his offices to revise the manuscript Labbe had been working on at his death and see it through the press, but he decided to dedicate his own monograph on Byzantine history to Colbert. In 1679 he arranged for the *abbé* Jean Gallois, a tutor attached to Colbert's household, to show him a draft of the introductory letter in which he expressed a "great desire that the King have the *Byzantine History* continued." This solicitation was apparently well received, because Du Cange was instructed shortly thereafter to send "a project of what you would like to do together with a succinct catalog of the principal authors" whose works "had not yet been printed" and were to be found in "the library of the King."[45] Six volumes from the series would later be attributed to him.[46]

Because of his work as a curatorial librarian, Du Cange was eminently qualified to draw up a proposal for a series on Byzantine history. Together with Jean-Baptiste Cotelier, he had cataloged both the Royal Library's legacy holdings in Greek and its new acquisitions. He used several hundred of these manuscripts—as well as additional manuscripts, some already in Paris and others sent to him from afar, and also existing word lists by Cotelier, Labbe, Emery Bigot, Étienne Baluze, and others—as the basis for the production of his great *Glossary to Middle and Low Greek Authors* (*Glossarium ad scriptores mediæ et infimæ Græcitatis*).[47] His method of composition

43 Philippe Labbe, preface to *De Byzantinæ historiæ scriptoribvs, svb felicissimis Lvdovici XIV. Francorum ac Navarræorvm Regis Christianissimi Avspiciis[.] Publicam in lucem e Lvparæa Typographia emittendis: Ad omnes per orbe ervditos προτρεπτικόν* (Paris, 1648), [i]. See also Bréhier, "Le développement des études d'histoire byzantine," 6; Auzépy and Grélois, *Byzance retrouvée*, 71.

44 D. R. Reinsch, "The History of Editing Byzantine Historiographical Texts," in *The Byzantine World*, ed. P. Stephenson (London, 2010), 440. Auzépy and Grélois, *Byzance retrouvée*, 70–80, includes a catalog that compares Labbe's provisional 32-volume series with the ultimate output of an informally defined 57-volume series that continued until 1819.

45 Gallois to Du Cange, 11 October 1679, in H. Omont, "Du Cange et la Collection Byzantine du Louvre," *REG* 17 (1904): 33–34. See also Considine, *Dictionaries in Early Modern Europe*, 266.

46 Auzépy and Grélois, *Byzance retrouvée*, 71–72, 76–77 (nos. 28–33); the inclusion of two of these works in the series appears to have been an 18th-century convention.

47 Du Cange, *Glossarium ad scriptores mediæ & infimæ Græcitatis.*

led to individual entries that frequently grew into short essays covering an encyclopedic range of topics.[48] In order to bring out the Greek *Glossary*, moreover, Du Cange had to go to great lengths to identify a printer who could adequately handle its linguistic complexity. Although he initially hoped to work with Louis Billaine, who printed and closely collaborated with him on the Latin *Glossary*, Billaine's death before the project could be undertaken meant that an alternative had to be found. After several false starts in Paris, Du Cange therefore began negotiations in July 1682 with an ambitious Lyonnais printer, Jean Anisson, who promised to spare neither money nor effort.[49]

The preserved correspondence of Anisson to Du Cange (fragments of fifty-eight letters written over five and a half years) reveals that the process of setting and printing the work did not go smoothly. Du Cange had worked by creating *fiches* in octavo format for individual entries, employing a rapid, firm, but often difficult-to-read hand and making numerous emendations—adding more material in the margins as well as attaching bits of paper with corrections, revisions, and additions. When initially submitted to the printer, the work appears to have been not "in a very good state to be printed far from the author's eyes."[50] It was internally badly ordered and contained a number of duplicates for words that the author had forgotten he had already done. The printer, after repeatedly complaining of the poor state of his copy and asking for guidance, and having spent several days trying to order the letter "A," was so discouraged that he felt he had no recourse other than to return the manuscript to its author and demand that it be properly copied out, ordered, and numbered.[51] Even so, problems with legibility remained: for example, the author's handwriting made little distinction between the letters "ν" (nu) and "υ" (upsilon). And the manuscript had been prepared prior to Anisson's innovative decision to include accents and breathings above capital letters—not only unprecedented for a Greek dictionary, but also a rare accomplishment in the printing of any sort of Greek text—and therefore had not been suitably marked up.[52]

48 H. Omont, "Le glossaire grec de Du Cange: Lettres d'Anisson à Du Cange relatives à l'impression du *Glossaire* (1682–1688)," *REG* 5.18 (1892): 212–49, esp. 216.

49 Ibid., 214–16.

50 Ibid., 320.

51 Ibid., 223, 226, 227, 229.

52 Ibid., 221, 231, 235. As no correspondence with Du Cange's other printers survives, we cannot determine with certainty how unusual the tensions in his relationship with Anisson were. But an examination of Du Cange's manuscript of the projected revised second edition of *The History of the Empire of Constantinople* (*Histoire de l'empire de Constantinople*)—based on the existing first edition, another book supervised from afar since it was produced in Paris while the author was still in Amiens—shows that in this instance at least the author felt that his insistence on detail during production had already resulted in a printed work he considered to be satisfyingly

The physical distance also meant impractical delays with proofs. To avoid this, Anisson had recruited a local Hellenist, Jacob Spon, to assist with the task at the press. But Du Cange, used to making his own corrections, did not approve of the arrangement; alleging that Spon was sloppy, he insisted on reviewing everything himself as well. And so packets of galleys traveled back and forth every few days or weeks across the breadth of France. Pages were reset again and again at considerable cost, a process only aggravated by Du Cange's continued consultation of new texts previously unknown to him and addition of further examples to entries. Attempts to obtain a royal privilege for Anisson that would relocate him to the capital to be near his most important author dragged on. Finally, out of frustration with the lack of progress, Du Cange turned to his old printer, Sébastien Cramoisy, who had published his very first works in Paris, to print the final portions of the work.[53]

To avoid such extreme measures, Anisson had proposed that the author come to Lyons and, while the book was in press, take up residence in the printer's own home, but Du Cange had turned down that solution—despite being offered a valet and carriage of his own. The reason for Du Cange's refusal must have been that he was by then already too ill to travel, although, circumspect about his personal life, he chose not to share the news of his deteriorating health with his printer. Certainly, his decision in early 1686 to compose his last will and testament appears to have been motivated by his belief already at that date that he was not long for this world. Anisson was initially irritated but then, when he discovered the truth of the situation, became more sympathetic. "I had not known, Sir, about your indisposition," he wrote, "and I despair to see you exposed to pain. You ought never to have to suffer."[54] In any case, the work's birth pangs appear to have been forgotten once the finished product—for whose letters a very beautiful set of type had been specially commissioned and whose illustrations were engraved by "masters"—finally appeared in 1688 in two large volumes and Anisson was able at long last to send Du Cange thirty leather-bound copies of the work, with his compliments.[55] The *Journal des sçavans*, in its positive review of the Greek *Glossary*, praised Du Cange's scholarship but also

error-free as far as typographical matters were concerned. The manuscript reveals that in the course of his work on the second edition, Du Cange saw the need to make no corrections to the numerous Greek quotations included in the first edition and very few corrections to the passages in other languages. His primary concern was rather to insert information not previously known to him and to nuance his earlier interpretation of several decades earlier. BnF, MS fr. 9473 and 9474.

53 Omont, "Le glossaire grec de Du Cange," 219, 223, 230, 241.

54 Ibid., 240; also 212–14, 233, 236–37, 244, 248; "Testament de Charles Du Fresne, sieur du Cange, et de sa femme, Catherine Du Bos," 22 February 1686, from Samaran, *Du Cange à Paris*, 9–11.

55 Omont, "Le glossaire grec de Du Cange," 216, 219, 244, 249; Feugère, *Étude sur la vie et les ouvrages de Du Cange*, 99.

commended his printer; indeed, the typographical layout of the work was so greatly admired that Anisson would be rewarded with promotion to director of the Royal Printing Press.[56]

In the months before his death, Du Cange remained extremely active as a scholar working in Greek. He busied himself with the final touches of an edition of a seventh-century chronicle, the *Paschal Chronicle* (*Πασχάλιον seu Chronicon paschale*), for the *Writers of Byzantine History*, while at the same time beginning preparations for an edition and commentary for the same series on the fourteenth-century narrative history of Nikephoros Gregoras—editions that, when added to those he had already produced, effectively provided readers with coverage of the entire period of existence of the Byzantine Empire.[57] He had become a fixture at the royal court. Not only Colbert but others close to the person of the king, such as Chancellor Boucherat, entrusted him with delicate tasks, such as the revision of a series of "historical and chronological tables" that Louis XIV had previously rejected on religious grounds. Drawing an annual pension himself, and through his work securing a further gift of money from the king for his family, he was acknowledged as a scholar of the Middle Ages especially well versed in the history of the Crusades and, latterly, of Byzantium.[58]

The Bid to Become the King's Historian

Yet an episode some years before he became editor in chief of the series of Byzantine historians suggests that Du Cange had other interests, and that he had for a time conceived of his work on the Crusades not as a prelude to the development of expertise in Byzantium but as preparation for a career as a historian of France.

In 1676 Du Cange had already composed a memorandum for Colbert that prefigured his later proposal for the *Writers of Byzantine History*. This older memorandum was for a similarly ambitious editorial project, but with different intended subject matter. It outlined a plan for another multivolume series: the *Collection of French Historians* (*Recueil des historiens françois*, or *Historiae Francorum Scriptores*).[59]

56 *Journal des sçavans* 16 (Amsterdam, June–Dec. 1688): 374–84, esp. 378–79 for the passage on Anisson; Omont, "Le glossaire grec de Du Cange," 212.

57 Du Cange, *Πασχάλιον seu Chronicon paschale* (n. 1 above); Doucette, *Emery Bigot* (n. 27 above), 110–11. Jean Boivin later published Du Cange's notes on the Gregoras as "Notæ postumæ Caroli Du Fresne D. Du Cange," in *Νικηφόρου τοῦ Γρηγορᾶ ῥωμαϊκὴ ἱστορία: Nicephori Gregoræ Byzantina historia*, ed. Boivin and H. Wolf, 2 vols. (Paris, 1702), 2:720–48. See D'Aubigny, *Mémoire historique pour servir à l'éloge de Charles Du Cange*, 24.

58 Feugère, *Étude sur la vie et les ouvrages de Du Cange*, 53.

59 D'Aubigny, *Mémoire historique pour servir à l'éloge de Charles Du Cange*, 23–24; Feugère, *Étude sur la vie et les ouvrages de Du Cange*, 87; Baron, *Éloge de Charles Du Cange* (n. 2 above), 25.

Such a plan was not Du Cange's invention, since, as early as 1633, André Du Chesne had begun a *Series of All the Authors Who Wrote . . . the History of France* (*Series auctorum omnium qui de Francorum historia . . . scripserunt*), drawing up a list of twelve and then twenty volumes to be published by the Royal Printing Press.[60] According to Du Cange, Du Chesne had wished to divide the collection into two parts: the one devoted to "the general history of France . . . [and] of each king," and the other to "the particular histories of the provinces, and of the cities, dukes, counts, churches and monasteries within those provinces."[61] Moreover, the range of excerpts from the sources that had been collected and published so far was interpreted by Du Cange as evincing a capacious understanding on the founder's part of the purview of the series devoted to French history. Specifically, Du Cange argued that "the history of the Holy Wars undertaken at various times by our Frenchmen belongs too closely to our history not to find its place in such a vast and glorious enterprise." And he added that, since these wars had taken place with "the Greeks and Saracens," material should also be gleaned from the Byzantine and Islamic sources.[62]

Du Cange's memorandum responded to Colbert's recent acquisition of André Du Chesne's papers relating to the series *Historians of France* and his request for advice about how best to restart the project.[63] Mindful that André Du Chesne had received, in recompense for his series of editions of French historical sources, not only substantial financial remuneration but also the position of "King's Historian"—which identified its holder as one of the foremost historians in France—Du Cange

60 André Du Chesne, *Series auctorum omnium qui de Francorum historia et rebus Francicis, cum ecclesiasticis, tum secularibus, scripserunt. Ab exordio Regniæ ad nostra usque tempora* (Paris, 1633). Jacques Le Long provides information on Du Chesne's work and the full publication history of its subsequent editions under both André du Chesne and his son François in his *Bibliothèque historique de la France* (n. 14 above), 311, 953–54.

61 Le Long, introduction to "André du Chesne," a section of "Mémoires historiques sur quelques historiens modernes de France," in *Bibliothèque historique de la France*, 952–55, esp. 953–54. See also "Remarques de M. l'Abbé Gallois sur le Projet de l'Histoire de France, dressé par M. Du Cange" and "Plan général du Recueil des Historiens de France dressé par M. Du Cange," in Le Long, *Bibliothèque historique de la France*, 958–60.

62 "Mémoire sur le Projet d'un nouveau Recueil des Historiens de France, qui sert de Preface au Plan de Charles Du Fresne du Cange," in Le Long, *Bibliothèque historique de la France*, 955–59, esp. 957.

63 Others involved in discussions about the Du Chesne papers included the priest Charles Le Cointe, Antoine Wion d'Herouval, Adrien De Valois, the *abbé* Gallois, and Étienne Baluze. Later scholars thought that Du Cange may have been appointed as a member of an official committee charged to deal with the 1676 acquisition of André Du Chesne's papers from his son François; however, this supposition may instead reflect the mechanism for the revival of the project in the 18th century. Le Long, "André Du Chesne," in *Bibliothèque historique de la France*, 954; D'Aubigny, *Mémoire sur les manuscrits de M. Du Cange*, 9.

would have considered it well worth expending every possible effort in order to advance his candidature.[64]

It was in this context that he advertised, in 1676, and then published two years later, in 1678, his *Glossary to Middle and Low Latin Authors* (*Glossarium ad scriptores mediæ et infimæ Latinitatis*).[65] Drawing on some 6,000 authors and covering 140,000 words, the *Glossary*, which was a far more substantial undertaking than the later Greek equivalent, showcased Du Cange's staggeringly extensive familiarity with medieval Latin vocabulary and scripts, and therefore would have been counted on as an especially effective way to draw attention to his qualifications as prospective editor in chief of the most prestigious publishing project of the age.[66]

He also engaged in composing a series of studies of the history of France, assuming this task in a way that sought to improve upon the ideas of the previous generation of historians regarding the proper scope and methodological approaches to be adopted. Publications by the cohort over which Du Chesne presided—compilations of the "authors" and "antiquities . . . of the towns, castles, and most remarkable places of all France"; "descriptions entire" of "the celebrated kingdom of France"; local histories of Burgundy, Normandy and other regions; and genealogies of noble houses of the Montmorency, Laval, La Rochefoucauld, Vergy, Coucy, and so on—had transformed the writing of history when Du Cange was growing up and had continued to be admired during the period when he himself was beginning to contribute to the discipline; they provided models with which the contents and structure of his projected works engaged.[67] Du Cange sought to apply the practice of

64 See C. Grell, "Les Historiographes en France, XVIe–XVIIIe siècles," in *Les historiographes en Europe de la fin du Moyen Âge à la Révolution*, ed. eadem (Paris, 2006), 127–56, on the origins and development of the *Historiographe du roi*.

65 Du Cange, *Glossarium ad Scriptores mediæ & infimæ Latinitatis, in quo Latina vocabula novatæ significationis, aut usus rarioris, barbara & exotica explicantur, eorum Notiones & Originationes reteguntur: Complures ævi medii Ritus & Mores, Legum, Consuetudinum municipalium, & Iurisprudentiæ recentioris Formulæ, & obsoletæ voces: Vtriusque Ordinis, Ecclesiastici & Laici, Dignitates & Officia, & quamplurima alia observatione digna recensetur, enucleantur, illustrantur. E libris editis, ineditis, aliisque monumentis cùm publicis, tum privatis* (Paris, 1678).

66 Baron, *Éloge de Charles Du Cange*, 13; D. Bloch, "Charles Du Cange (1610–1688): Exposition organisée à l'occasion du tricentenaire du *Glossarium mediae et infimae latinitatis* par la Bibliothèque Nationale," in *La lexicographie du latin médiéval*, ed. Y. Lefevre (Paris, 1981), 509–47.

67 See, e.g., André Du Chesne, *Les antiquités et recherches des villes, châteaux et places plus remarquables de toute la France* (Paris, 1609), and *Bibliothèque des autheurs, qui ont escript l'histoire et topographie de la France, divisée en deux parties, selon l'ordre des temps, & des matières* (Paris, 1618), for compilations. The most famous of Du Chesne's almost a dozen genealogical volumes was his *Histoire généalogique de la maison de Montmorency et de Laval. Ivstifiee par chartes, tiltres, arrests, & autres bonnes & certaines preuues. Enrichie de plusievrs Figvres, & divisée en XII. livre* (Paris, 1624). His *Historiæ Normannorum scriptores antiqvi, res ab illis per Galliam, Angliam, Apvliam, Capuæ principatvm, Siciliam, & Orientem gestas explicantes, ab anno christi DCCCXXXVIII ad annum*

close study and the heavy referencing of narrative sources and documents, but also of material culture, to a "native" history of the French that gave particular weight to the Middle Ages. He embarked upon three main historiographic endeavors: first, a regional political and cultural history dealing with his own homeland, Amiens, and the province of Picardy; second, a historical geography of what he called "Gallia"—that is to say, France, conceived not as its current territory, but rather at its greatest extent; and, finally, a comparative genealogy explaining the formation of the main secular noble houses and religious institutions of France that would provide full lineages and uninterrupted lists for these.[68]

With François Du Chesne, the son of the late founder of the series *Historians of France*, positioning himself to succeed to his father's editorial work, Du Cange countered by advising that the project could not simply be resumed but needed to be rethought radically.[69] He emphasized the importance of revising the list of projected publications so that it would include items that reflected a level of multilingualism and a set of technical skills peculiar to himself. When his proposal was rejected,[70] he had to cast around for something else with which to apply once more to Colbert; the series *Writers of Byzantine History* was his fallback.

That, despite Du Cange's disappointment, later generations would still come to remember him as a historian primarily of France was due to the determination of his great-nephew Jean-Charles du Fresne D'Aubigny. In the 1730s and 1740s, D'Aubigny

MCCXX... (Paris, 1619) and *Histoire des Roys, Dvcs, et comtes de Bovrgogne, et d'Arles. Extraicte de diverses Chartes & Chroniques anciennes, & divisée en IIII. Liures* (Paris, 1619) advocate for a wide-ranging interpretation of "French" history. And, of course, there was the *Dessein de la description entière et accomplie du très-florissant et très-célèbre royaume de France* (Paris, 1614), as well as the ensuing *Historians of France* series begun by André Du Chesne, *Historiae Francorum scriptores coaetanei: ab ipsius gentis origine, ad pipinum vsque regem...*, 5 vols. (Paris, 1636–49). Edelman discusses further precedents in *Attitudes of Seventeenth-Century France toward the Middle Ages* (n. 4 above), 64–65.

68 Acquisitions des manuscrits (26) 1667–1758, BnF, Archives Ancien Régime 65, fols. 366r–368. For a different division of these projects, see D'Aubigny, *Mémoire historique pour servir à l'éloge de Charles Du Cange*, 3–21.

69 Feugère, *Étude sur la vie et les ouvrages de Du Cange*, 87.

70 Le Long, writing in 1719, stated that Du Cange's strident advocacy for a new series for the *Historians of France* led Colbert to strip him of his royal pension for several years; see Le Long, "André Du Chesne," in *Bibliothèque historique de la France*, 954. It is worth noting that Le Long published this account of Du Cange's plan as a way to advocate for a continuation of the *Historians of France* series in 1717 (see ibid.). Du Cange's kinsman D'Aubigny denied the story's veracity and countered that Du Cange had submitted a similar proposal to Colbert's successor Louvois; subsequent scholarship on Du Cange has been similarly skeptical of Le Long's claims. See D'Aubigny, *Mémoire sur les manuscrits de M. Du Cange*, 8–9; D'Aubigny, *Mémoire historique pour servir à l'éloge de Du Cange*, 23–24; Baron, *Éloge de Charles Du Cange*, 25; Feugère, *Étude sur la vie et les ouvrages de Du Cange*, 87; Hardouin, *Essai sur la vie et les ouvrages de Du Cange* (n. 6 above), 19–20.

devoted himself to reassembling the writings that Du Cange had left unfinished or unpublished at his death, and that had been dispersed. He managed to locate many papers, especially in the collections of the francophone Prince Eugene of Savoy that were then housed in Vienna. He negotiated their acquisition either by gift or by purchase, secured the diplomatic and pecuniary assistance of the French crown, prepared the material for entry into the Royal Library, and composed the first inventory of the collection.[71]

These activities resulted in the survival of a highly selective portion of Du Cange's papers. There are indications that from the start, D'Aubigny may not have been concerned with attempting to replicate the true range of Du Cange's interests, but instead sought out traces of a supposed historian of France above all else. At the very least, the assembly of autographs—to the exclusion of related material such as professional correspondence or notes written in other hands, or indeed annotated printed books from the study library—preserves almost no record of intellectual influence and collaborative exchange, making Du Cange seem to have worked in far greater isolation than had actually been the case.[72] Moreover, the emphasis on material that had not yet been published drew attention not to the projects on Byzantium,

71 N. Le Prince, *Essai historique sur la Bibliothèque du Roi, et sur chacun des dépôts qui la composent, avec la description des bâtimens, & des objets les plus curieux à voir dans ces différens dépôts* (Paris, 1782), 208–13; Samaran, *Du Cange à Paris* (n. 6 above). On Eugene of Savoy and the afterlife of Du Cange's manuscripts, see D'Aubigny, *Mémoire sur les manuscrits de M. Du Cange*, 2–8; H. Hardouin, "Sort des manuscrits de Du Cange," in *Essai sur la vie et les ouvrages de Du Cange*, 24–26; Feugère, *Étude sur la vie et les ouvrages de Du Cange*, 64–65; and J. W. Thompson, "The Age of Mabillon and Montfaucon," *AHR* 47, no. 2 (1942): 225–44, at 244.

72 Such letters as survive are for the most part eulogistic pieces contributing to the myth of Du Cange as the font of all knowledge, rather than workaday exchanges on the practical matters of scholarship; the notable exceptions are the letters from the printer Anisson, which were appended to the main collection in a separate box. Only two books that once belonged to Du Cange's working library have so far been identified: a copy of Hephaestion now in the Bodleian Library in Oxford, and a Terence that was in Vienna in the 18th century but whose whereabouts is now not certain. In a single instance in D'Aubigny's inventory of Du Cange's "manuscripts," a box containing historical sources or notes does not have its contents designated as being "all in the hand of Du Cange"; rather, the contents in question are described as "three different manuscript works of the sixteenth century, of which the last is in a very bad hand." See *Copie des titres originaux que j'ai (du Fresne d'Aubigny, arrière-neveu de Du Cange) pu recueillir sur la maison de Relly, dont étoit la mère de M. Du Cange: il en avoit vu et il en cite beaucoup que je n'ai point trouvé, et il a laissé aussi beaucoup à travailler sur la teste de cette famille, dont il paroît qu'il étoit embarrassé de trouver la descendance*, 2 vols., BnF: Bibliothèque de l'Arsenal, MSS 4922–23; Acquisitions de Manuscrits (26) 1667–1758, BnF, Archives Ancien Régime 65, fols. 372r–v; D'Aubigny, *Mémoire sur les manuscrits de M. Du Cange*, 4–5, 25; Feugère, *Étude sur la vie et les ouvrages de Du Cange*, 93; Considine, *Dictionaries in Early Modern Europe* (n. 3 above), 267. Some of the culling, particularly of the letters, most probably antedated d'Aubigny's interventions and was the work of other family members.

where Du Cange's publication rate had been good, but to those on France, where it had been poor. The writings on the geography, history, and culture of the Byzantine Empire are a notably faint presence in the archive as it is currently constituted.[73]

The Scholar at Work

Even so, when taken alongside the printed works, the manuscripts and papers do allow a glimpse into Du Cange's working method. They suggest that the scholar himself never definitively saw his expertise as being in either the Byzantine Empire or France; rather, he identified himself as a polymath who could be different things at different points of his career depending not just on the opportunities available to him or the exigencies of his intended patrons, but also on the directions in which he was pulled by his training. Developing into a researcher with a methodological virtuosity and an extraordinary breadth of knowledge, he was interested in the study of the past less because he sought entertaining or instructive examples of universal truths than because a scientific understanding of artifacts allowed the achievements of earlier civilizations to be revived and capitalized upon in the present.[74] His method emphasized the value of being able to evaluate and interpret medieval sources in their authentic form. In this, he followed in the footsteps of an earlier lexicographer of medieval Greek, Johannes Meursius, for whom the reading of narratives on the history of Byzantium represented an engagement with "the external appearance of the empire, and account of things done at diverse times" that needed to be extended through familiarity with the language—since this familiarity allowed one to "inquire more deeply" into a culture and acquire access to its "interior workings."[75] Du Cange did not take this position regarding linguistic knowledge to shame others, for he never underscored his authority by introducing original quotations with flourishes that drew attention to them. On the contrary, he tried to make concessions by adding translations for those of his contemporary readers—in practice, almost all his readers—who could be expected to be well-educated in Latin but not to have Greek as good as his own. He was thus concerned with making material in Greek accessible, even if he sometimes struggled to achieve this goal. Scribbling away day in, day out in his study on the top floor of his home in the Marais, he had noble intentions with

73 See Teresa Shawcross in Chapter 6 of this volume.

74 Anthony Grafton, *What Was History? The Art of History in Early Modern Europe* (Cambridge, 2007), 189–254.

75 Johannes Meursius, *Glossarium Graeco-Barbarum, in qvo Præter Vocabvla amplius ter mille sexcenta, Officia atque; Dignitates Imperii Constantinop. tam in Palatio, quàm Ecclesia aut Militia explicantur, & illustrantur* (Leiden, 1610), 2v–3r; see also Considine, *Dictionaries in Early Modern Europe*, 253–56.

regard to the assistance to be provided to his public, but he could also forget that that public was not as erudite as himself.

When conducting his initial exploratory research, Du Cange often behaved as if he considered materials in Greek to be one of the many types of sources that were at his disposal. Instead of discriminating between different languages, he treated Greek, Latin, and Old French as if they were comparable. Thus, the master catalog he kept of everything he read listed "keywords relating to the principal matters contained within the most learned Greek and Latin Authors, and especially the historians, and in some of the old French romances, poets, and historians."[76] His notes for a specific work in progress, perhaps the early stages of a "Universal Dictionary," had "a mixture of names and things taken from different Greek, French, Latin, etc. authors on the sciences; arts; languages; religion; the law; philosophy; tales; poetry; ancient, modern, sacred, profane, civil, political etc. history; antiquities etc. These names or things having below them the references or citations of authors written indiscriminately as they came up."[77] Even the marginalia in the books from his library, such as his copy of the printed edition of Adrien de la Morlière's *Antiquities of Amiens* (*Antiquitez d'Amiens*), contained "notes, citations, corrections, additions, insertions in Greek, in Latin and in French."[78]

As he shaped his notes into finished studies, such as the *Byzantine History*, Du Cange sought to render his quotations in Greek more comprehensible by providing a short summary by way of introduction (e.g., *Paulus Silentiarius in ejus Descriptione . . . Addit . . . eam esse aedis pulchritudinem, ut qui semel hanc ingrediuntur, pedem inde referre renuant, dum huc illuc oculos circuserunt, & tot eximiis quibus ubique decoratur ornamentis detinentur.* Εἰ δέ τις ἐν τεμένεασι Θεουδέσιν ἴχνος ερείσει, / Οὐκ ἐθελει παλίνορσον ἄγειν πόδα· θελγομένοις δε / Ομμασιν ἔνθα καὶ ἔνθα πολύστροφον ἀυχένα πάλλει / Πας΄ κόρος εὐπήληκος ἐλήλατο ἔκτοθεν οἴκου [*sic*]) or including a full translation afterward (e.g., *Theophanes:* Τῷ ἀυτῷ ἔτει ἐπληρώθη και ὁ χαλκοῦς κίων ὁ μεγας πλησίον τοῦ Παλατίου, ὁ λεγόμενος Αὐγουστεὺς, καὶ ἀνηνέχθη ἡ στήλη τοῦ Βασιλέως Ιουστινιανοῦ ἔφιππου. *Hoc ipso anno ingens illa aenea columna ad Palatium posita, qua dicitur Augusteus, absoluta est, & equistris imperatoris Iustiniani statua in eam sublata* [*sic*]).[79] Concern for accessibility can be associated even more strongly with

76 Acquisitions de Manuscrits (26) 1667–1758, BnF, Archives Ancien Régime 65, fol. 374r; see also Augustin Belley, *Notice des ouvrages manuscrits de Monsieur Du Cange* (Paris, 1750), 23, and BnF, MS fr. 9489.

77 BnF, MSS fr. 9594–95; Acquisitions de Manuscrits (26) 1667–1758, BnF, Archives Ancien Régime 65, fol. 374r. For more information, see Shawcross, Chapter 6 of this volume.

78 Adrien de Morlière, *Antiquitez de la Ville d'Amiens* (Paris, 1627); BnF, MS fr. 9475; Acquisitions de Manuscrits (26) 1667–1758, BnF, Archives Ancien Régime 65, fol. 379v.

79 Du Cange, *Historia Byzantina duplici commentario illustrata* (n. 39 above), vol. 2, book 3, pp. 5, 23. See also vol. 1, book 1, pp. 31, 34, 35, 39, 42, 74, 77. Unless another scholar had produced a rendition

Du Cange's projects to create free-standing tools to facilitate the navigation of the Greek sources. Yet a focus less on educational intent than on the satisfaction of listing Greek authorities and assembling Greek quotations for their own sake remains evident in the working draft of the Greek *Glossary*. A single manuscript fiche of that draft has been handed down to us: the entry for the word "μονόζωνοι" (fig. 5.7). It offers only the briefest of explanations in Latin (*Milites Expediti, Praedatores*); this appears to have been characteristic, the author having to be pressed repeatedly to "insert as many Latin explanations as you can" in order to assist "the reader who wishes to instruct himself and is not yet learned."[80]

As for the series *Writers of Byzantine History*, Du Cange's avowed aim was the creation of a canon of Greek texts, and to this end he duly printed revised editions of important works that had already been discovered by others. However, these editions were dwarfed by supplements and appendixes containing additional texts—and other extensive paratextual material.[81] In the case of his printed *Kinnamos*, for example, he provided editions not only of the twelfth-century chronicle by John Kinnamos of the deeds of the Byzantine emperors John II and Manuel I Komnenos, but also of Paul the Silentiary's sixth-century description of the Church of the Holy Wisdom

with literary pretensions, Du Cange rarely used an existing translation, preferring instead to provide his own version. When citing Manasses, Du Cange used not the edition produced by the Royal Press in Paris in 1655 (Leone Allacci and Charles-Annibal Fabrot, *Κωνσταντίνου τοῦ Μανασσῆ σύνοψις ἱστορική. Const. Manassis breviarvm historicvm. Ex interpretatione Ioannis Levnclavii, cum eiusdem, & Ioannis Mevrsii Notis* [Paris, 1655]), but the earlier 1616 Leiden edition (Johannes Meursius, *Constantini Manassis annales, Græcè ac Latinè* [Leiden, 1616]); he did not reproduce either of the Latin translations these editions offered, nor that published in Basel in 1573 without the Greek original (Johannes Leunclavius, *Annales Constantini Manassis: Nvnc primùm in lucem prolati, & de Græcis Latini facti* [Basel, 1573]). Indeed, even when a translation had been published and could be consulted, he sometimes not only chose to avoid using it but gave no translation at all. In such cases, often involving religious prose or formulaic inscriptions, he apparently hoped that the Greek vocabulary was sufficiently familiar and the syntax sufficiently simple not to pose problems.

80 When he was not forthcoming despite being told that entries without explanations or with inadequate explanations gave the impression that he had not been able to discover the meaning of the word, his publishers felt they had to intervene directly. For example, for the entry on cured fish roe, "Αὐγὸ τάρηχο," his copyeditor and proofreader added the explanation "Italis *Botarga*," which was then submitted for approval; similarly, for "le mot BANTA [*sic*]," he amended "pars navis" to "Pars navis lateralis, *Banda* Italis." Some of the emendations may reflect a knowledge of contemporary language possessed by Spon, a traveler in the Mediterranean, but not by Du Cange, who never left northern France; in any case, these would constitute a tiny handful of corrections in a dictionary covering thousands of words. See Omont, "Le glossaire grec de Du Cange," 213, 220, 225–28, 232 (quotations), 235; compare with the *Glossarium ad scriptores mediæ & infimæ Græcitatis* (n. 38 above), 950–51. The only other extant part of the manuscript of the *Glossary* is one of the appendixes: BnF, MS fr. 9467.

81 Du Cange, *Ἰωάννου τοῦ ἀσκητοῦ τοῦ Ζωναρᾶ γεγονότος τοῦ μεγάλου δρουγγαρίου τῆς βίγλας καὶ πρωτοασηκρήτις χρονικόν. Joannis Zonaræ monachi magni antea vigilum præfecti, et primi a secretis annales* (n. 37 above); Du Cange, *Πασχάλιον seu Chronicon paschale* (n. 1 above).

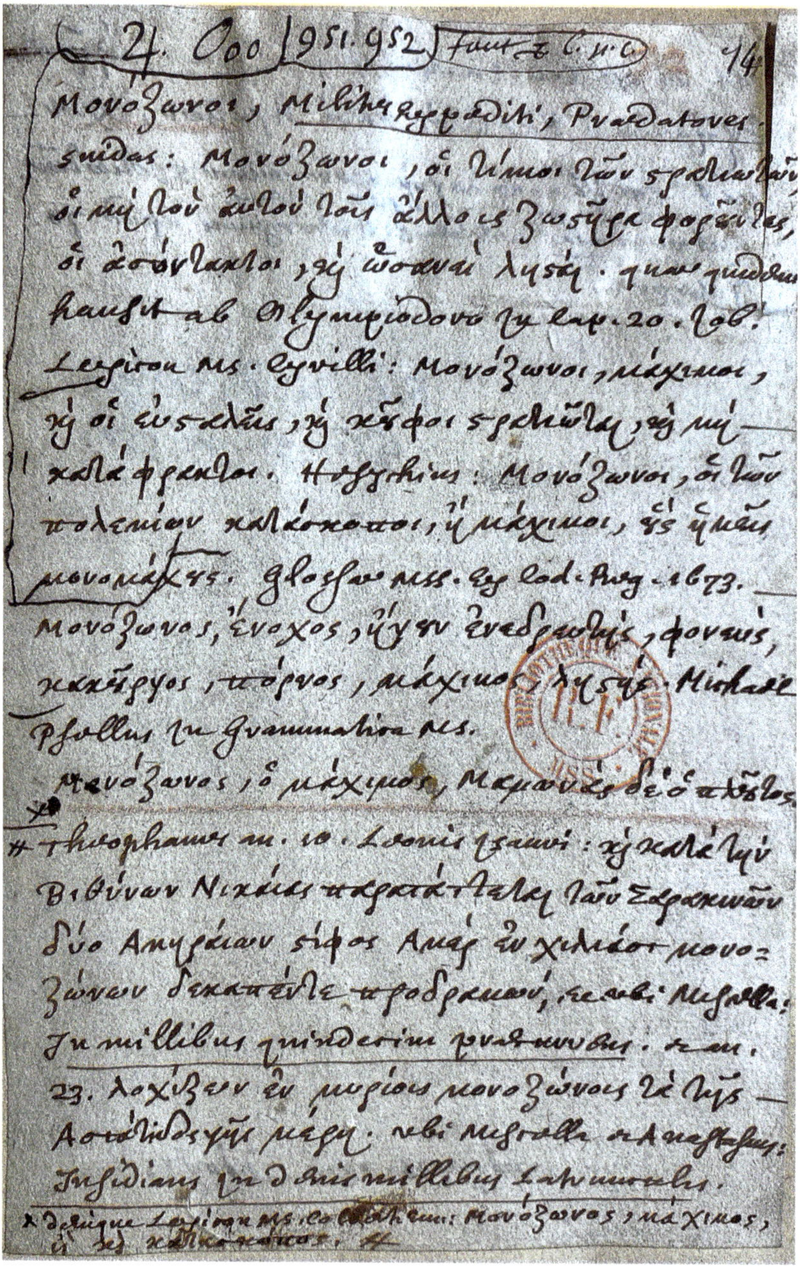

Fig. 5.7. Du Cange, a preparatory version of fiche in-8º for the *Glossarium ad scriptores mediæ & infimæ Græcitatis*. Paris, ca. 1682–88. From "Papiers divers recueillis par Emmanuel Miller (1886) sur différents sujets d'histoire et de littérature," NAF 5057, fol. 14. Courtesy Bibliothèque nationale de France.

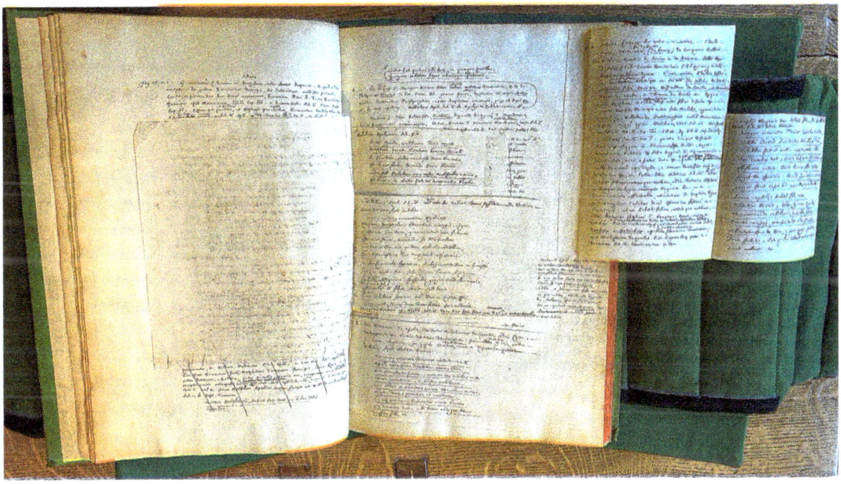

Fig. 5.8. Du Cange, opening from the draft of "Notes on Anna Komnene's *Alexiad*" with pasted *feuilles volantes*. Paris, 17th c. From "Caroli Du-Fresnii in Annae Comnenae Alexiadem notae," Bibliothèque de l'Arsenal MS–1000, fols. 4v–5r. Courtesy Bibliothèque nationale de France.

(Hagia Sophia). The method of composition Du Cange followed for the accompanying commentary, as can be seen from the surviving manuscript of a draft section for the *Kinnamos*, was first to write detailed analytical notes giving the relevant Greek comparative material—in this instance, Anna Komnene's *Alexiad* (Ἀλεξιάς), her biography of her father, Alexios I Komnenos, but also Bryennios, Tzetzes, Choniates, and so on—together with some initial Latin material. Subsequently, when revising, he inserted longer quotations from Latin.[82] Indicative are the insertions delineating a discovery he had made after having completed his initial research: that of the existence of parallels between the *Alexiad* and William of Apulia's *Deeds of Robert Guisard* (*Gesta Roberti Wiscardi*). These parallels suggested to him the hypothesis that the Byzantine historian had known of the Latin text and drawn from it.[83]

The endless crossings out, rewritings, and additions made in the *Kinnamos* to the exposition both in the margins of the pages and on separate leaves inserted and glued onto the pages—together with the highly detailed "proofs" or references that

82 Du Cange, *Ἰωάννου Κιννάμου βασιλικοῦ γραμματικοῦ ἱστοριῶν λόγοι ϛ΄. Joannis Cinnami imperatorii grammatici historiarum libri sex* (n. 36 above); BnF: Bibliothèque de l'Arsenal, MS fr. 1000.

83 The significance of Du Cange's discovery concerning the *Alexiad*'s possible Latin source has not been fully appreciated until recently. See J. Howard-Johnston, "Bilingual Reading, the *Alexiad* and the *Gesta Roberti Wiscardi*," in *Reading in the Byzantine Empire and Beyond*, ed. T. Shawcross and I. Toth (Cambridge, 2018), 467–98.

accompany each point—indicate a command of an extremely wide range of sources as well as a significant investment in making sense of them (see fig. 5.8).[84] One gets the impression here and elsewhere in Du Cange's papers of a scholarly obsessiveness that bordered on perfectionism. Indeed, if Du Cange considered his writings as being, in some sense, offspring, he came to see the labor expended on his last edition for the series *Writers of Byzantine History*, the *Paschal Chronicle*, as producing not merely an adopted child but rather the closest thing he had to a true child. Such was his devotion to this edition that he was chided for refusing to let anything get in the way of his "proofs for the Louvre."[85]

Commitment to the Study of Byzantium

If the texts of the Byzantine Empire were of great significance to Du Cange, his was an insatiable curiosity directed not just at them but also at the material objects and even the living descendants of the people themselves. Two such items are of particular interest. The first of these, dating to the Amiens years, is a sequence of drawings of the layout and appearance of the enamel plaques found on a reliquary of the True Cross at Amiens Cathedral. Even though the drawings are known only by a copy made from Du Cange's original in the eighteenth century, we can still see that the scholar, having identified the geographical provenance of the plaques, had undertaken to decipher the inscriptions, as well as to represent the images accurately enough for them to be recognizable. He even recorded minutiae such as the holes for the nails by which the plaques were fixed (compare Du Cange's drawing of the lost plaques, fig. 5.9, with an extant example of similar type, fig. 5.10).

The other item, this time dating to shortly before Du Cange's death in Paris, is a group of letters accompanied by a large-scale genealogy—provided by the Savoyard historiographer Samuel Guichenon—of a branch of the Byzantine imperial dynasty of the Komnenoi (fig. 5.11).[86] Preserved in the original, though lacunose and misfiled across several dossiers, the letters provide traces of an exchange between Du Cange and a certain "Jean-Constantin Comnène." Comnène wanted to prove his descent from the former imperial house of Byzantium, but his ancestors had fled westward as refugees in the face of Turkish encroachment and there was little documentation he could provide. Even though genealogical research was normally highly paid and his

84 Feugère compares Du Cange's system of textual accumulation to the methods that Pascal used to compile his *Pensées*. Feugère, *Étude sur la vie et les ouvrages de Du Cange*, 93.

85 Omont, "Le glossaire grec de Du Cange," 33–34.

86 "Comnène (Arbre généalogique des), original envoyé à Du Cange par l'entremise de Guichenon," BnF: Bibliothèque de l'Arsenal, MS 5047, "Recueil formé des papiers de Du Cange et de sa famille," division 20°, fol. 329.

interlocutor, a hanger-on at the fringes of the household of Prince Eugene of Savoy, had limited resources, Du Cange undertook to aid him, and was generous with both his expertise and his time.[87]

These items from the archive point to Du Cange as someone who was not merely plodding away but cared deeply about what he did: a scholar who did not see investigation into a faraway and distant past as a gratuitous pursuit, but instead felt keenly the continuing relevance of both the time and the place of his studies to his own homeland and lifetime. Du Cange was putting the finishing touches to his very first publication of an edition of a Byzantine text just as Candia, the capital of Crete, fell to the Ottomans after an unremitting siege that lasted from 1646 to 1669.[88] Across the previous decades, France had repeatedly—in 1646, 1660, 1667, and again in 1669—contributed troops to the defense of Venetian Crete, the last Greek-speaking former Byzantine province and Crusader lordship that had remained outside Muslim control.[89] Thousands of Frenchmen had fought as part of a large expeditionary force sent by Louis XIV under the flagship *La Thérèse* during the last weeks. Their eyewitness accounts circulated in popular pamphlets, illustrated with dramatic engravings (fig. 5.12).[90] From the 1640s to the 1670s, the Bourbons thus abandoned their alliance with the Ottomans and, by supporting Venice, found themselves instead on the same side as their customary rivals, the Habsburgs. Indeed, they established an entente with the latter that lasted several decades (until 1688), during which the two states combined forces in the struggle against Islam. The shift had been instigated by Louis' minister, the Italian Cardinal Mazarin, whose own early career had been spent at the French court as the legate of Urban VIII—the pope who had announced the beginning of his reign with "Peace be in thy Strength," a crusader prayer that wished for the preservation of Jerusalem in Christian hands. Mazarin's personal ambitions regarding the papal miter had led him to pursue policies that won him credit for

87 D'Aubigny, *Mémoire sur les manuscrits de M. Du Cange*, 52.

88 Ö. Bardaçı and F. Pugnière, *La dernière croisade: Les français et la guerre de Candie, 1669* (Rennes, 2008). The text in question is the *Joannis Cinnami imperatorii grammatici historiarum libri sex* (1670).

89 Bardaçı and Pugnière, *La dernière croisade*, 61–77.

90 See, e.g., *Journal de l'expédition de M. de La Feuillade pour le secours de Candie. Par un volontaire* (Lyons, 1669); L. P. Nicole, *Au Roy sur l'embarquement de ses troupes pour le secours de Candie* (Paris, 1669); Louis de La Solaye, *Mémoires ou relation militaire contenant ce qui s'est passé de plus considérable dans les attaques et dans la deffense de la ville de Candie*... (Paris, 1670); François Savinien D'Alquié, *Les mémoires du voyage de Monsieur le Marquis de Ville au Levant, ou l'histoire curieuse du siège de Candie* (Amsterdam, 1671); Des Roches, *Journal véritable de ce qui s'est passé en Candie sous le commandement de M. le duc de La Feuillade* (Paris, 1671); Des Réaux de La Richardière, *Le voyage de Candie fait par l'armée de France en l'année 1669* (Paris, 1671); Pierre Domenisse, *Mémoire des choses les plus remarquables qui se sont faites au voyage de Candie* (n.p., n.d.). These and other sources are discussed in Bardaçı and Pugnière, *La dernière croisade*, 79–167. Once Crete fell, only the Ionian Islands remained under Venetian control.

Fig. 5.9. Unknown hand, sketch of five of the enamel medallions from the True Cross of Amiens. After Du Cange, filed at Passy in 1754. From "Copie des Recueils manuscrits de Du Cange, cotés A, B, C, D, E. Recueils d'extraits," Bibliothèque de l'Arsenal Ms–5259, division 53°, fol. 211. Courtesy Bibliothèque nationale de France.

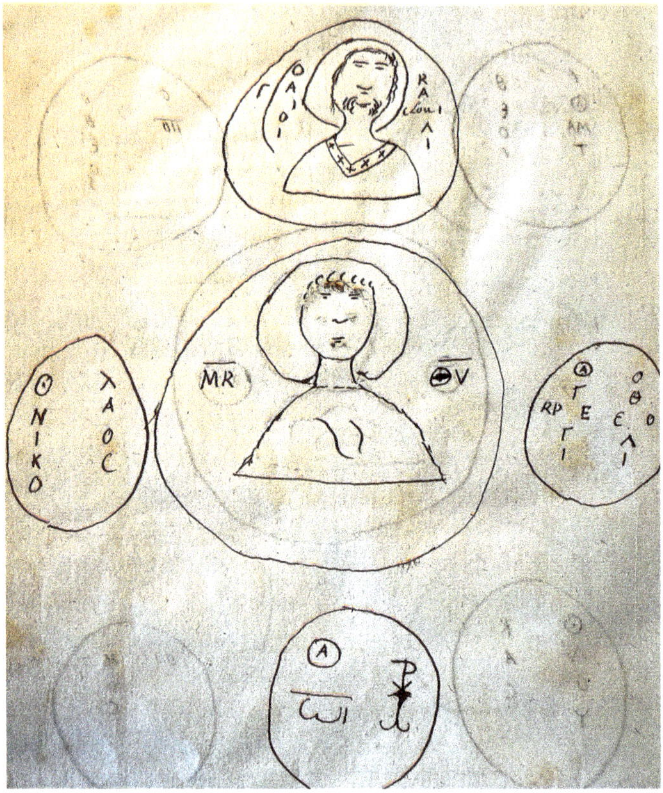

invigorating the traditions of the crusading movement in which the French, as loyal sons of the Mother Church, had played such a prominent role in the Middle Ages.[91]

In 1648, at the beginning of these developments, Joseph-Marie Suarès, who was at that time bishop of Vaison, recalled to the French chancellor Séguier a project he had first envisaged while serving as the librarian of Cardinal Barberini in Rome during the papacy of Urban VIII. Suarès alleged that, even before 1633, he had wanted to undertake to publish, through a compilation of Byzantine historians, a "history from creation to the fall of Constantinople to the Turks." Though circumstances had not allowed him to carry out this project at the Curia, he expressed the belief that it ought to be revived under Louis XIV. He noted that Louis could lay claim to the legacy of both the Western and Eastern Roman Empires, a privilege no other ruler had

91 Bardaçı and Pugnière, *La dernière croisade*, 63–65; R. Darricau, "Mazarin et l'Empire ottoman: L'expédition de Candie (1660)," *Revue d'histoire diplomatique* 74 (1960): 339–40; M. K. Averett, "The Annual Medals of Pope Urban VIII Barberini," *AJNum* 25 (2013): 303–4.

Fig. 5.10. Unknown artist, enamel medallion with Saint John the Baptist. Constantinople, ca. 1100. Gold, silver, and enamel worked in cloisonné, 8.3 cm. Object number 17.190.677, The Metropolitan Museum of Art via Art Resource, NY.

had since Constantine the Great. The king was the legitimate heir to the "Byzantine Empire" in addition to the Carolingian Empire. This was so not only because he had recently incorporated into his realm the County of Flanders—the native land of the crusading dynasty that had conquered and ruled Byzantium in the thirteenth century—but also because the French monarchs, by intermarriage with that dynasty, had inherited the imperial title of "Emperor of Constantinople."[92] These statements by Suarès constituted a two-pronged attack on behalf of the Bourbons, advocating for their new but still rather uncertain policy of imperial rivalry against the Ottomans

92 Omont, "La Collection byzantine de Labbe" (n. 42 above), 21, 31–32.

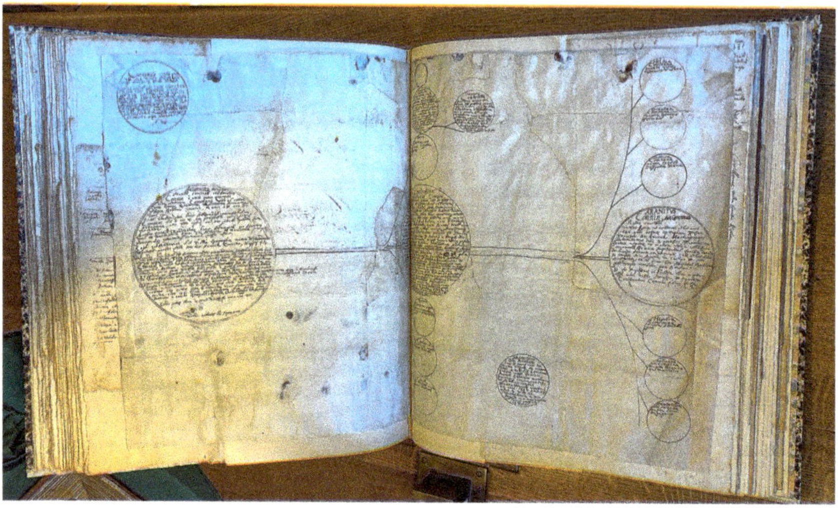

Fig. 5.11. Genealogy of the Komnenoi. Original sent to Du Cange via Samuel Guichenon (1607–1664), country and date unknown. From "Recueil formé des papiers de Du Cange et de sa famille," Bibliothèque de l'Arsenal, MS-5047, division 20°, fol. 329. Courtesy Bibliothèque nationale de France.

without completely abandoning the enmity they had maintained until recently against the Habsburgs.[93]

Du Cange deployed and revised tropes similar to those found in Suarès regarding the Bourbons' pretensions to an imperial heritage. In the late 1630s, when Du Cange had drawn up a genealogical tree of the Bourbons, ornamented with a rosette (fig. 5.13) illustrating the various thrones to which they could lay claim in addition to that of France, he had depicted, in a privileged position at the very top left, the coat of arms of the "Empire of the West" and, next to it at the top right, that of the "Empire of the East."[94] By the 1650s and 1660s, however, he preferred—since the Habsburgs had become established as French allies—to frame in his published writings the French crown's claims as being directed mainly against the Ottomans. At the beginning of his *History of the Empire of Constantinople*, for example, he offered his work

93 For the rival claims to the imperial past made by the Bourbons and the Habsburgs, see Pertusi, *Storiografia umanistica* (n. 42 above), 24–40, 82–93.

94 See D'Aubigny, *Mémoire sur les manuscrits de M. Du Cange*, 26–30, followed by a fold-out engraving incompletely reproducing Du Cange's genealogical chart, n.p.; Auzépy and Grélois, *Byzance retrouvée* (n. 42 above), 37–38 and fig. 10. The genealogical tree appears to have been separated from Du Cange's papers before or when they entered the Royal Library in 1756; see Shawcross, Chapter 6 in this volume.

Fig. 5.12. Allain Manesson Mallet (cartographer, 1630–1706) and Johann David Zunner (engraver, d. 1704), *The City of Candia* depicted under siege (1669), cartographic detail. Frankfurt-am-Main, 1685. HMC01.6660. Courtesy Historic Maps Collections, Special Collections, Princeton University Library.

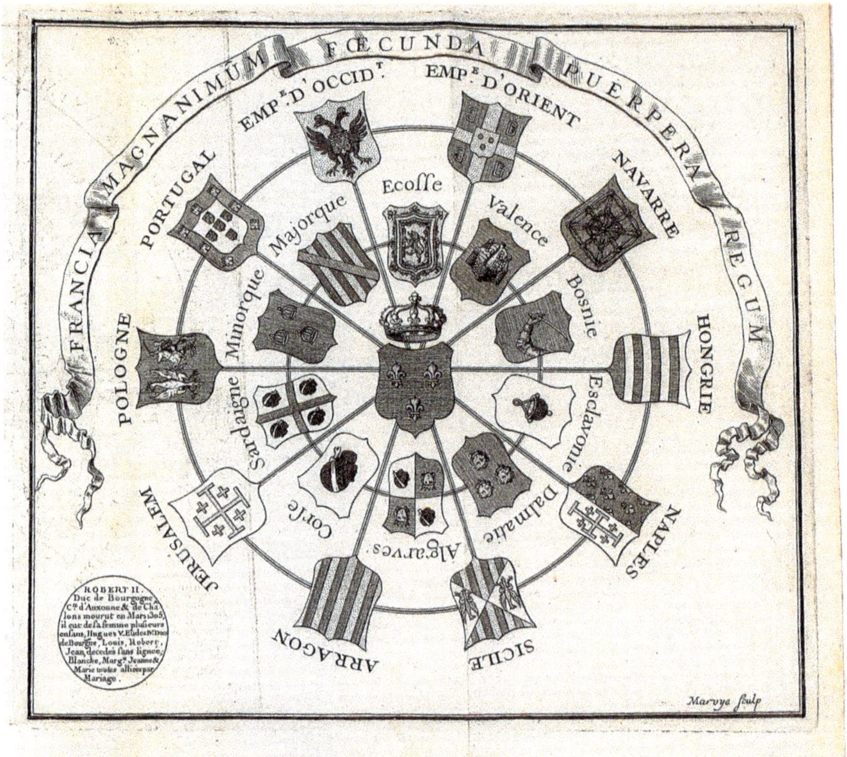

Fig. 5.13. Martin Marvie (engraver, 1713–1813), *France, Fertile Mother of Great-Hearted Kings.* A detail in the form of a rosette after Du Cange, "Genealogical Chart of the Kings of France" (Amiens (?), 1630s). Folded sheet from [Jean-Charles Du Fresne D'Aubigny], *Mémoire sur les manuscrits de M. Du Cange* (n.p., 1752), inside back cover. Public domain; courtesy Getty Research Institute and HathiTrust. The title, *Francia magnanimûm fœcunda puerpera regum,* is taken from "Lilium," or "Fleur-de-lys" (1608?), a poem on the history of France by the humanist Jacques-Auguste de Thou.

to Louis XIV, claiming that the "Throne" of the Byzantine Empire "was one upon which valor and virtue had raised Your Ancestors." He added that French rights to the city of Constantinople, the "proud mistress of the world . . . the New Rome," which Louis had inherited as king of France, were currently being trampled upon by "usurpers" and "tyrants" of the most primitive kind—an allusion to Ottoman rule.[95] When dedicating his *Byzantine History* to Colbert, he was even more explicit. He

95 Du Cange, "Au Roy," dedication to the *Histoire de l'empire de Constantinople sovs les emperevrs françois* (n. 10 above), n.p. [i, v, x].

conjured up an image of the glories of Constantinople when it had been in Christian hands, lamented its desecration by Islam, and identified in Louis the sovereign who would liberate it from Turkish tyranny. It would appear that he was so transported by his own rhetoric advocating the launch of crusades against the Ottomans that he was led in a manuscript draft of the text to continue with further statements Colbert found overblown, asking for their expurgation before publication.[96]

The allusions to the Ottoman threat in Du Cange's dedicatory epistles and prefaces suggest that while he was far from the battlements of Candia, he saw himself, as he saw the French soldiers who defended Crete against the Ottoman Grand Vizier Köprülü Fazıl Ahmed Pasha, to be engaged in a race to save the remnants of civilization from Turkish barbarism.[97] Overseeing and contributing editions to the series *Writers of Byzantine History*, founded by Colbert, may not have been his earliest or indeed main passion, but rather the consolation prize of his old age. Yet the field of study was one he had grown to know and love dearly. He thought research on the Byzantine Empire mattered not only from the perspective of scholarship but also from that of current affairs. This viewpoint was one his contemporaries shared. It is perhaps no coincidence that a prince raised in Louis XIV's court, Eugene of Savoy—the same prince whose retainer of Byzantine descent Du Cange had once helped with his genealogical tree—would buy for his personal library not only copies of all thirty-three printed volumes of *Writers of Byzantine History*, the series for which Du Cange acted as editor in chief, but also as many of Du Cange's manuscript papers as could be obtained.[98] The Prince of Savoy, after all, not only was the great-nephew of Cardinal Mazarin, having inherited the family ardor for resisting Islam, but built his own reputation as one of the most skilled generals of his age through a series of spectacular campaigns against the Ottomans, the most famous of which culminated with his victory at Zenta in 1697.[99] Of course, it was precisely these victories that, by ending the Turkish advance across Europe, ultimately rendered obsolete the geopolitical

96 Du Cange, dedication to the *Historia Byzantina duplici commentario illustrata* (n. 39 above); Omont, "Du Cange et la Collection Byzantine du Louvre" (n. 45 above), 33–34; Considine, *Dictionaries in Early Modern Europe* (n. 3 above), 286–87; Spieser, "Du Cange and Byzantium" (n. 6 above), 200.

97 Considine, *Dictionaries in Early Modern Europe*, 286–87; Spieser, "Du Cange and Byzantium," 200.

98 See the discussion of Eugene of Savoy earlier in this chapter, and also M. Braubach, *Prinz Eugen von Savoyen: Eine Biographie*, 5 vols. (Munich, 1963–65), 1:93–111; and K. Smentek, *Mariette and the Science of the Connoisseur in Eighteenth-Century Europe* (Burlington, VT, 2014), 42–44. We are unlikely ever to know for certain whether Du Cange and Eugene of Savoy came into contact with each other when the latter was a young boy in Paris.

99 Bardaçı and Pugnière, *La dernière croisade*, 63; Braubach, *Prinz Eugen von Savoyen*, 1:258–59. See also Shawcross, Chapter 6 of this volume.

concerns that underpinned Du Cange's research on the history of the Crusades and the Byzantine Empire. His later readers—starting with his great-nephew Jean-Charles Du Cange D'Aubigny—were thus obliged to reinvent the scholar as having been preoccupied with forging the kind of nationalist history that, focused on events within continental France, was beginning to find favor in the eighteenth century.

This chapter originated as a paper given at the conference "Invention of Byzantine Studies in Early Modern Europe," held at Harvard University on 26–27 October 2017. I am grateful to the audience for their comments, as well as to Matthew McDonald for his assistance with the final revisions to the piece.

SIX

THE EIGHTEENTH-CENTURY REINVENTION OF DU CANGE AS THE FRENCH NATION'S HISTORIAN

TERESA SHAWCROSS

When Charles du Fresne, sieur Du Cange, moved from Amiens to Paris in 1668, he must have been sorry to leave his study behind. It was, by all accounts, a "most agreeable" room, which he had taken some trouble to decorate. Less well appointed than his family's provincial home, the house in the capital in which he established himself and his dependents was one of the smaller dwellings on the rue des Écouffes, an old medieval street on the margins of the aristocratic part of the Marais. As the place was rented, there was little incentive for him to make the kinds of changes that would have allowed replication of the elegant comfort of his earlier workspace.[1] Instead, he simply claimed two rooms on the top floor in which to sleep and work: a bedchamber containing a bed and a few chairs, as well as his clothes, and, next door, his study—equipped with a table and chair of plain wood, a folding stool, and a large chest. On the walls of the rooms were three prints in gilt frames and, hanging by a pair of red batons, a youthful work that had shown his promise as a scholar: a gigantic parchment roll, measuring 11 feet (*pieds*) by almost 8 feet, with an elaborately drawn genealogy of the kings of France. There were also a few pieces of fine porcelain and a small display cabinet containing twenty-one gold and silver medals, while six flowerpots dotted about contributed a more homely touch.[2]

1 C. Samaran, *Du Cange à Paris, rue des Écouffes: D'après son testament et son inventaire après décès* (Nogent-le-Routrou, 1922), 1–2.

2 Ibid., 5–6, 16; [Jean-Charles Du Fresne D'Aubigny], *Mémoire sur les manuscrits de M. Du Cange* (n.p., 1752), 4–5.

With nothing above him except the attic, Du Cange must have had as much peace and quiet as his home could offer. Of course, that his suite was on the same floor as a number of other rooms, mainly bedrooms, would have meant there was some unavoidable commotion. Still, the setup appears to have been congenial enough for him to read and write successfully there on a daily basis—and entertain colleagues—for two decades, from his late fifties to his late seventies.[3] The single element most important to this routine was ready access to the tools of his chosen profession: books. Du Cange's working library numbered just under 1,500 printed volumes. Eight hundred and forty books were located in his study in five bookcases of varying size whose uppermost shelves could be accessed only by a set of stairs. The remaining 650 spilled over into his chamber.[4] It is not known how he organized his papers so as to distinguish between current, dormant, and completed projects. Observers were left with the impression of considerable disarray: an anecdote has him inviting some printers to his study and showing them an old chest in the corner containing a pile of tattered scraps of paper that seemed not to have any value, but proved upon close examination to be the *fiches* of the draft of one of his dictionaries.[5] The absence of a rigid filing system made it difficult after his death for others to appreciate exactly what it was that he had been busy producing, or to use what he left behind.

Upon Du Cange's demise, his library and his autograph manuscripts and working papers were dispersed and entered the private collections of other notable scholars or collectors, not only in Paris but also in Vienna and London. Drafts and notes that were bound together as multivolume sets or otherwise formed constitutive parts of a single work in progress were broken up. Material—it is impossible to gauge how much, but it must have been substantial—was destroyed.

3 Du Cange perished not from a stroke or some other sudden attack while at work but from a lengthy, painful illness, passing away on 23 October 1688 in the grandest reception room on the floor below, which had been converted into a sick room. He died from the retention of urine, thought to have been caused by sitting at his desk for overly long spells. The medical problem was one known to affect the scholars of his era (most notably Casaubon, who purportedly had a grossly swollen and diseased bladder because he refused to allow himself toilet breaks). See "Epistola Stephani Baluzii Tutelensis ad virum clarissimum Eusebium Renaudotum de vita et morte Caroli Dufresnii Cangii," in Du Cange, *Πασχάλιον seu Chronicon paschale a mundo condito ad Heraclii Imperatoris annum vicesimum. Opus Hactenus Fastorum Siculorum nomine laudatum, deinde Chronicæ temporum Epitomes, ac denique Chronici Alexandrini lemmate vulgatum: Nunc tandem auctius et emendatius prodit, cum nova Latina versione & Notis Chronicis ac Historicis* (Paris, 1688), xlix–lii; M. Pattison, *Isaac Casaubon, 1559–1614* (London, 1875), 469.

4 C. Samaran, "Inventaire après décès de Du Cange," in *Du Cange à Paris*, 16.

5 The story is told in G.-T. Raynal, *Anecdotes littéraires, ou Histoire de ce qui est arrivé de plus singulier & de plus intéressant aux ecrivains françois depuis le renouvellement des lettres sous François I jusqu'à nos jours*, new ed., 3 vols. (La Haye, 1756), 2:53–54; Samaran, *Du Cange à Paris*, 6.

Eventually, however, a great-nephew, Jean-Charles Du Fresne D'Aubigny, would make it his life's work to reassemble as many unpublished writings as he could locate and arrange them into a coherent collection that was deposited in the Royal Library. The dossier on the collection, begun with its deposition, contains extensive and detailed information on the state of the writings.[6] Its primary document is the inventory of acquisitions dating to 1756. Published for the first time here (see Appendix II), this document constitutes particularly precious evidence, since the papers had not been inventoried during Du Cange's lifetime or upon the execution of his will.

The ideological preoccupations of the periods during which the papers were first dispersed, then reassembled affected the preservation of material. The content of the inventory reveals that emphasis was put on Du Cange's research on France to the exclusion of his other work. The way in which the scholar's memory was constructed as a result of this process meant that he came to be lionized in the eighteenth and nineteenth centuries less for the successes he saw during his lifetime in publishing on Byzantium than for his projects on France that remained incomplete. As shown most powerfully by the disquisitions on the subject penned by D'Aubigny, Du Cange's would-be intellectual heirs interpreted the scholar's career and output in such a way as to enable him to be given a place as one of the founding fathers of the rising genre of national history. He was identified as a remarkably prescient scholar who had not been allowed by circumstances to publish his most innovative projects while he was still alive—leaving it to later generations to grant him the recognition he deserved.

Dispersal of the Papers

After Du Cange's death, his books as well as his autograph manuscripts and other papers passed to his children (fig. 6.1). A few years previously, in 1686, when his illness had first begun to trouble him, Du Cange had had a will drawn up together with his wife Catherine (née Du Bos). The couple bestowed upon each of their surviving children an equitable portion of their immovable and movable property, as required by the inheritance laws of Paris, but they also ensured that particular children received particular bequests in accordance with their order of seniority, and with their individual needs and interests. They declared that their eldest son Philippe and younger son François, together with their younger daughter Jeanne, were each to inherit equal portions of property valued at 30,000 livres; their eldest daughter,

6 Acquisitions de Manuscrits (26) 1667–1758, Bibliothèque nationale de France (hereafter BnF), Archives Ancien Régime 65, fols. 362r–381v.

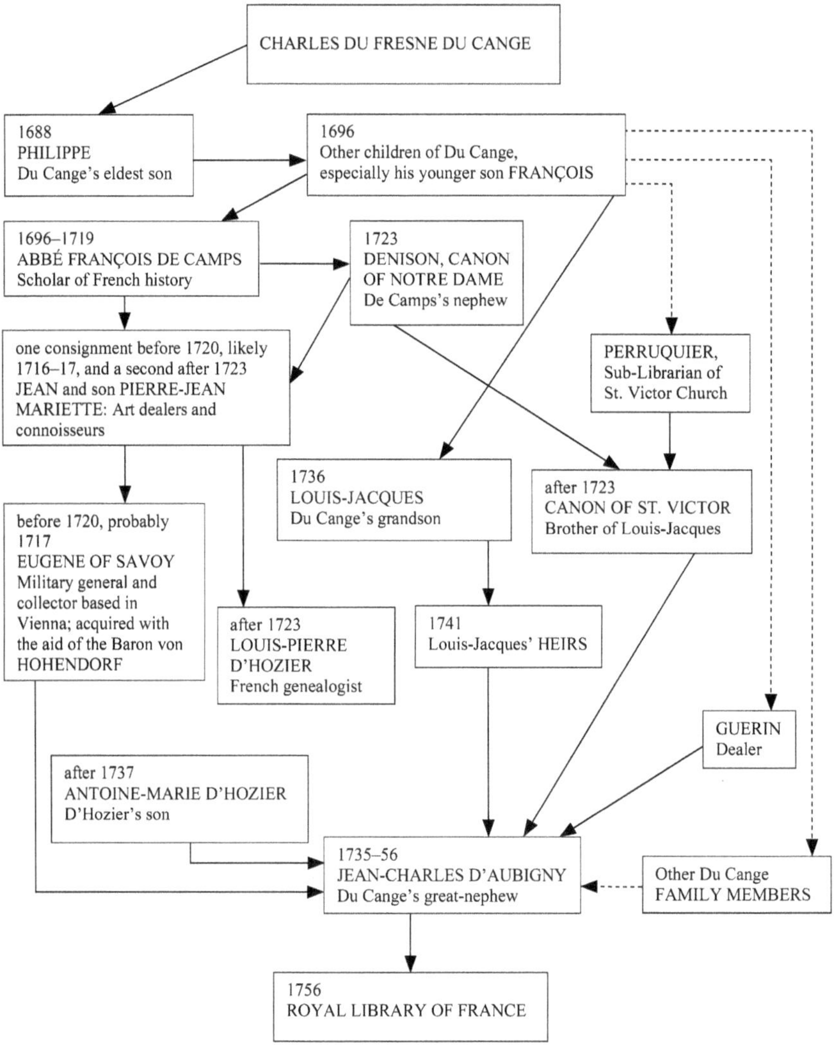

Fig. 6.1. The transmission of the papers of Charles du Fresne Du Cange. Prepared by Teresa Shawcross with the assistance of Matthew McDonald.

Catherine, had already been given her portion as a dowry upon her marriage and so was not entitled to receive anything. Philippe, who was to act as executor, was to come into the family estate, "the fiefs and lands of Cange," so that these would be handed down the male line; he was also given the option to keep, against 3,500 livres of his inheritance, his father's "manuscripts and memoranda," the coins and medals together with their display cabinet, and also the equipment of the bureau: the candelabra, the ink stand engraved with family crest, and the other writing materials of silver.[7]

The only one of the children with any intellectual ambitions, Philippe did claim his father's unpublished writings as part of his share and may well have had the notion of doing something with them when his other duties as a landowner and public servant permitted it. But, if so, he never acted on his intentions, for he followed his father to the grave in 1696. As he was a bachelor with no legitimate issue, his part of the parental inheritance was redistributed among his siblings. Du Cange's library was sold, with the exception of a few stray volumes. Although many manuscript works and papers were also put up for sale at this time, a still larger number were retained by the remaining son, François, while other relatives also held on to some odds and ends.[8]

François kept in his possession a selection of items from Du Cange's correspondence: documents concerning Du Cange's family history; manuscripts and notes relating to the history of the Du Cange's home town, Amiens, and home region, Picardy; and also most of Du Cange's genealogical and heraldic writings. He likewise kept the manuscript compendium that served as the general repository of and key to Du Cange's research, containing as it did lists of references to both the printed books in his library and his notes; given that in his initial drafts Du Cange was in the habit of including only shorthand citations to the sources he intended to give in fuller form in the printed version of the text, access to this volume was of paramount importance for any reader of the unfinished works. Finally, he hung on to the manuscript of a projected second edition of the Du Cange's breakthrough work, the *History of the Empire of Constantinople under the French Emperors* (*Histoire de l'empire de Constantinople sovs les empereurs françois*); its first edition had been printed in 1657 by the Royal Printing Press of the Louvre (Imprimerie royale du Louvre) and had established the scholar's reputation outside his native Picardy.[9] This last decision, however, may reflect accident more

7 "Testament de Charles Du Fresne, sieur du Cange, et de sa femme, Catherine Du Bos," 22 February 1686, from Samaran, *Du Cange à Paris*, 9–11; [Jean-Charles Du Fresne D'Aubigny, in] *Le grand dictionnaire historique, ou Le mélange curieux de l'histoire sacrée et profane*, ed. L. Moréri, new ed., 10 vols. (Paris, 1759), 3:130.

8 Jean-Charles Du Fresne D'Aubigny, *Mémoire historique pour servir à l'éloge de Charles Du Fresne Sieur Du Cange, et à l'intelligence du plan général de ses études sur l'histoire de France* (Paris, 1766), 2–3; Moréri, *Le grand dictionnaire historique*, 3:130.

9 Du Cange, *Histoire de l'empire de Constantinople sovs les emperevrs françois, divisée en deux Parties, dont la premiere contient l'Histoire de la conquéte de la ville de Constantinople par les François & les Venitiens, écrite par Geoffroy de Ville-Hardovin Maréchal de Champagne & de Romanie: reueuë & corrigée en cette Edition sur le Manuscrit de la Bibliotheque du Roy, & illustrée d'Obseruations Historiques, & d'vn glossaire, pour les termes de l'Auteur, à present hors d'vsage. Avec la Suitte de cette Histoire, iusques en l'an MCCXL. tirée de l'Histoire de France MS. de Philippes Movskes Chanoine*

than design, since there is nothing to suggest François was aware that the copious notes in the author's own copy of the printed first edition constituted revisions intended for a second edition.[10]

When François died in 1736, his son and heir Louis-Jacques gave or sold some of his holdings to other family members and also contemplated sales to outside buyers. Louis-Jacques retained other items, including the revised *History of the Empire of Constantinople*, until his own death in 1741.[11]

The material initially sold by the Du Cange family went to the *abbé* François de Camps, a fellow scholar and compatriot from Amiens with whom Du Cange himself—and perhaps also his family—must have been acquainted. De Camps collected rare medieval manuscripts, especially those pertaining to the history of France. The subject, along with numismatics, was his abiding passion. It seems that it was in order to gather material on French history that he had sought to acquire Du Cange's papers.[12] He showed his holdings to a colleague, Jacques Le Long, who was encouraged to use the information they contained to promote the reestablishment of an edited series by André Du Chesne and his son François under royal patronage known as the *Collection of French Historians* (*Recueil des Historiens François*, or *Historiae Francorum Scriptores*)—formerly also a concern of Du Cange's.[13] Indeed, to

& depuis Euesque de Tournay. La seconde contient vne Histoire Generale de ce que les François & les Latins ont fait de plus memorable dans l'empire de Constantinople, depuis qu'ils s'en rendirent maistres, iusques à ce que les Turcs s'en sont emparez: Iustifiée par les ecriuains du temps, & par plusieurs Chroniques, Chartes, & autres Pieces non encore publiées (Paris, 1657).

10 D'Aubigny, *Mémoire sur les manuscrits de M. Du Cange*, 2–5; Augustin Belley, *Notice des ouvrages manuscrits de Monsieur Du Cange* (Paris, 1750), 23; BnF, MSS fr. 9473–74, 9489.

11 D'Aubigny, *Mémoire sur les manuscrits de M. Du Cange*, 5.

12 T. Sarmant, *Le Cabinet des médailles de la Bibliothèque nationale, 1661–1848* (Paris, 1994), 84; Pierre Bayle, *Dictionnaire Historique et Critique*, 5th ed., 4 vols. (Amsterdam, The Hague, Leiden and Utrecht, 1740), 4:196. François de Camps' numismatic catalog, the *Selectiora Numismata in ære maximi moduli e Museo illustrissimi* (Paris, 1693), formed the basis for the French Royal Library's own holdings in the 18th century.

13 The first edition of the original series was published by André Du Chesne, *Series auctorum omnium qui de Francorum historia et rebus Francicis, cum ecclesiasticis, tum secularibus, scripserunt. Ab exordio Regniæ ad nostra usque tempora* (Paris, 1633). D'Aubigny, in his *Mémoire sur les manuscrits de M. Du Cange*, 3, notes that he had found a reference to Du Cange's manuscript *Histoire des principautés et des Royaumes de Hierusalem, de Cypre et d'Armenie, et des familles qui les ont possedées*, in J. Le Long, *Bibliothèque historique de la France; contenant le catalogue de tous les ouvrages, tant imprimez que manuscrits, qui traitent de l'histoire de ce roïaume, ou qui y ont rapport: Avec des notes critiques & historiques* (Paris, 1719), 836, no. 16236. Le Long sourced this and scores of other manuscripts from the collection of De Camps: see Le Long, *Bibliothèque historique de la France*, 175, no. 3605; 196, no. 4144; 197, no. 4167; 206, no. 4419; 240, no. 5221; 248, no. 5350; 323, no. 6645; 352, no. 7056; 374, no. 7383; 591, no. 11469; 593, no. 11521; 624, no. 12133; 625, no. 12168; 636, no. 12412; 637, no. 12416; 641, no. 12588; 692, no. 13576; 720, no. 14082; 733, no. 14394; 751, no. 14674; 780, no. 15165; 810, no. 15365; 828, no. 16073; 837, no. 16260; 846, no. 16449.

bolster his own argument in favor of the series, Le Long duly cited a memorandum on the subject by Du Cange as an authoritative precedent.[14]

De Camps offloaded a number of Du Cange's papers with a dealer, Jean Mariette, and his son, Pierre-Jean.[15] Perhaps as early as 1713, and certainly in 1716–17, the Mariettes, who specialized in rare engravings and prints but also dealt in paintings, books, and manuscripts, were working for Baron Georg Wilhelm von Hohendorf. Hohendorf was himself a prominent agent of Prince Eugene of Savoy in Paris who, over the years, had sourced thousands of works of art and other objects for his patron.[16] Among the items with which Hohendorf arranged to have the Mariettes supply Eugene were eleven manuscripts (later divided into fifteen) by Du Cange: one volume titled *Collection of Histories and Coats of Arms* (*Recueil d'histoires et de Blazons*), constituting the first of a two-volume set mainly containing genealogies and lists of coats of arms; seven volumes and boxes of drafts and notes for the *Geography of France* (*Geographie de la France*), later divided into ten volumes and boxes, namely one volume of references and one box of introductory material, followed by eight boxes devoted to the various provinces; one volume labeled *Collections* (*Recueils*) and underneath "A. B.," containing originally parts 1 and 2 of a five-part set containing various types of genealogical material mainly excerpted from cartularies and rolls and relating to Picardy, especially Amiens; and two volumes that were labeled *Greek Authors* (*Authores Graeci*) and *Investigation and Interpretation of Civil Law* (*Juris Civilis Cognitio et Interpretatio*), but that seem to have been repurposed to collect material, perhaps for a "Universal Dictionary," from "the letter A to the letter V."[17] Also possibly

14 See Teresa Shawcross, Chapter 5 of this volume, pp. 162–65, for details on Du Cange's project to revive the *Collection of the French Historians*. Le Long, *Bibliothèque historique de la France*, 954–60.

15 K. Smentek, *Mariette and the Science of the Connoisseur in Eighteenth-Century Europe* (Burlington, VT, 2014), 40–55.

16 On Hohendorf, see M. Braubach, "Hohendorff, Georg Wilhelm von," in *Neue Deutsche Biographie*, 26 vols. (1953–2016), 9:478, and idem, *Prinz Eugen von Savoyen: Eine Biographie*, 5 vols. (Munich, 1963–65), 1:93, 97.

17 The eleven volumes from Vienna are described in [Jean-Charles du Fresne D'Aubigny], "Notice des ouvrages Manuscrits de M. du Cange," *Le Journal des Sçavans* (December 1749): 1:2316–43, 2:2487–520, with the Viennese material in 1:2321–43; see also D'Aubigny, *Mémoire sur les manuscrits de M. Du Cange*, 10–16, 25; and D'Aubigny in Moréri, *Le grand dictionnaire historique*, 3:131–32 (inv. nos. 3, 6, 25). The volume of genealogical material and coats of arms is included in the 1756 inventory (Acquisitions de Manuscrits [26] 1667–1758, BnF, Archives Ancien Régime 65, fol. 371v, and in this volume, p. 396); it is found today as BnF, MS fr. 9477, while its companion volume is BnF, MS fr. 9491. The seven volumes owned by Eugene of Savoy on Gaul were divided into ten when they entered the Royal Library (Acquisitions de Manuscrits [26] 1667–1758, BnF, Archives Ancien Régime 65, fols. 376v–377v, and in this volume, pp. 412–16), but are found today in five as MSS fr. 9492, 9504–8. The double collection labeled A and B on Picardy remained as one volume when it entered the Royal Library (Acquisitions de Manuscrits [26] 1667–1758, BnF, Archives Ancien Régime 65, fols. 377v–378r, and in this volume, pp. 416–18); it can be found today

acquired were printed books from Du Cange's library.[18] It may be that Mariette's son Pierre-Jean took this material with him when he traveled in 1717 to Vienna, where he spent over a year until the end of 1718 as part of Eugene's household, engaged in organizing the material that he and his father had supplied to the prince.[19]

Eugene of Savoy's library collections were wide-ranging, described by visitors as containing "the most beautiful, rare and select books written in the Latin, Italian, French, Spanish, and German languages—of which the like could not easily be found in a single place."[20] There is no way of knowing for sure what motivated the acquisition of the material originating with Du Cange. Part of the appeal may have been knowledge of Du Cange's repeated insistence in his published works that he aimed, by memorializing the struggles of the crusaders and Byzantines against Islam and holding these up as examples to be imitated, to contribute through his scholarship to the war effort against the Ottomans—his pen acting as a counterpart to the soldier's sword.[21] It may be noted that Eugene of Savoy was both the great-nephew of Louis XIV's chief minister, the Cardinal Mazarin—who had advocated for French participation in the revival of the crusading movement—and a military general who in 1691 had made his youthful reputation as the hero of the Battle of Zenta against the Ottomans.[22] For his part, Hohendorf was a career diplomat and spy who during the same period had been dispatched on a mission to Constantinople, developing first-hand expertise of Ottoman affairs by working for the Venetian ambassador there. Eugene of Savoy and Georg Wilhelm von Hohendorf were thus two men for whom the struggle against Ottoman expansion in the seventeenth century had been a matter of great concern during their own careers.[23]

---

as MS fr. 9496. The two alphabetical volumes, perhaps intended for a dictionary, are included in the 1756 inventory (Acquisitions de Manuscrits [26] 1667–1758, BnF, Archives Ancien Régime 65, fol. 373v, and in this volume, pp. 402–4) and are found today as MSS fr. 9494–95.

18 Since at least one printed book known to have originally belonged in Du Cange's library, an edition of Terence, is recorded as having entered the royal library in Vienna by 1752, it is also possible that he acquired printed books from the Mariettes, which suggests that the latter dealt also in Du Cange's library—perhaps initially for the Du Cange family in 1696, or around 1716 for de Camps, if he had previously acquired the volume.

19 See Smentek, *Mariette*, 42–45; Braubach, *Prinz Eugen von Savoyen*, 5:94–96.

20 Braubach, *Prinz Eugen von Savoyen*, 5:92.

21 J.-M. Spieser, "Du Cange and Byzantium," 199–210, in *Through the Looking Glass: Byzantium through British Eyes. Papers from the Twenty-Ninth Spring Symposium of Byzantine Studies, London, March 1995*, ed. R. Cormack and E. Jeffreys, SPBS 7 (Aldershot, 2000), 200–201.

22 Ö. Bardaçı and F. Pugnière, *La dernière croisade: Les français et la guerre de Candie, 1669* (Rennes, 2008), 63.

23 Braubach, *Prinz Eugen von Savoyen*, 1:258–59; 5:93, 97; see also Shawcross, Chapter 5 of this volume.

But it is also possible that Eugene, who had grown up at the royal court in Paris but in 1683 transferred his allegiance to the Bourbon's enemies, the Habsburgs, wished to counter the arguments of the pro-Bourbon material produced by the curators of the French Royal Library. The rulers of the Duchy of Savoy in the transalpine region—Charles Emmanuel II, his wife and regent Marie-Jeanne-Baptiste de Savoie-Nemours, and her son Victor Amadeus II, Eugene's second cousin—had a turbulent relationship with Louis XIV, with whom they allied themselves by marriage but by whom they were also constantly threatened with annexation.[24] The escalation into armed conflict from 1690 onward, which included a French attempt to besiege Turin in 1706, led Eugene to come to the aid of his cousins in Savoy with a Habsburg army and seek to break the Bourbon hold over northern Italy.[25] These developments appear to have intensified Savoy's desire to create a state collection of manuscripts and documents that emulated the scholarly administrative tradition of a centralized repository created by Jean-Baptiste Colbert for Louis XIV, and that could be used to generate defensive propaganda. By 1720 Victor Amadeus II had attached to the palace a building housing both the state archive and the royal library. He announced that it was intended to guard "treasure," in the form of "papers, bulls, briefs, diplomas, investitures, treaties, marriage contracts," which was to be managed by state scholars. Perhaps witnessing these efforts in Savoy to appropriate and counter the French state's apparatus of information gathering and archiving was what encouraged Eugene to devote serious resources to create similar collections for his own political use.[26]

Eugene's collecting took off in earnest only in 1715, when he took advantage of an uneasy entente between the Bourbons and the Habsburgs, begun in 1713, and sent his representative to the rival power's heart, Paris, to see what could be obtained. It would have been a coup for him to secure works of Du Cange, who had been one of the most prominent scholars employed by Colbert to work on the royal collections. The items acquired may have been of special interest to Eugene because they defined France as including much of the European continent, and thus offered information useful to Habsburg attempts to assert influence on territories that were claimed by the Bourbons but not central to them. In particular, the manuscripts

24 Eugene of Savoy was a member of the related House of Savoy-Carignan. Braubach, *Prinz Eugen von Savoyen*, 1:28.

25 Braubach, *Prinz Eugen von Savoyen*, 4:151–167.

26 J. Soll, *The Information Master: Jean-Baptiste Colbert's Secret State Intelligence System* (Ann Arbor, 2009), 162–63. Victor Amadeus II's statement (ibid., 241) is from M. Carassi and I. M. Ricci, "Gli archivi del principe: L'organizzazione della memoria per il governo dello Stato," in *Il Tesoro del principe: Titoli, carte, memorie per il governo dello Stato*, ed. Carassi, A. Griseri, Ricci, and E. Mongiano (Turin, 1989), 21.

contained material that focused on one such territory, Eugene's ancestral homeland of "Savoy" and "the Alps."[27] It is notable that Eugene was scrupulous in defining himself as something more than French—signing his name in a combination of Italian, German, and French as "Eugenio von Savoie" to emphasize his polyglot nature and multiethnic affiliations.[28]

At de Camps' death in 1723, his nephew and heir, the *abbé* Denison, canon of Notre-Dame in Paris, found a number of Du Cange's unpublished works and notes still among his uncle's effects. Denison returned at least two of these manuscripts to the Du Cange family in the person of one of its youngest members—Du Cange's grandson, the canon of Saint Victor in Paris; the Victorine may have personally kept some material and given the remainder to his monastery's noted library. However, Denison placed the majority of de Camps' collection for sale with the Mariettes, who had dealt in the earlier portion. These included various items which had acquired multiple titles that could suggest a historical content or a more narrowly genealogical one: for example, bound manuscripts such as a work known as *History of the Principalities and Kingdoms of Jerusalem, Cyprus, and Armenia, and the Families That Possessed Them* or on the spine as *Families of the Crusader States* (*Histoire des principautés et des Royaumes de Hierusalem, de Cypre et d'Armenie, et des familles qui les ont possedées*, or *Familles d'Outremer*); unbound portfolios containing notes for a projected *Peerage of France* (*Nobilier de France*); and also miscellaneous detached sheets of paper.[29] The Mariettes sold the works to another former acquaintance of Du Cange's, Louis-Pierre d'Hozier, who held the appointment from the king of Judge of the Coats of Arms of France and who, together with his son, Antoine-Marie d'Hozier, was responsible from 1696 onward for composing the gigantic *General Armorial of France* (*Armorial général de la France*). Louis-Pierre d'Hozier reorganized the papers as best suited his needs, using them actively for his own work; although they did not include all Du Cange's genealogical and heraldic writings, they did contain much research—enough to fill several boxes—on the subject. After his father's death, Antoine-Marie appears to have continued to consider these papers to be of value: when pressed in 1735 to give them up and return them to the Du Cange family, he displayed considerable reluctance to do so.[30]

27 See Acquisitions de Manuscrits (26) 1667–1758, BnF, Archives Ancien Régime 65, fols. 379v, 377v, as well as the inventory in this volume, Appendix II.

28 T. Blanning, *The Culture of Power and the Power of Culture: Old Regime Europe, 1660–1789* (Oxford, 2002), 235.

29 See Acquisitions de Manuscrits (26) 1667–1758, BnF, Archives Ancien Régime 65, fol. 369r, and the inventory in this volume, Appendix II; also BnF, MSS fr. 9469–72, 9493.

30 BnF, MSS fr. 9469–72; D'Aubigny, *Mémoire sur les manuscrits de M. Du Cange*, 4–5, 22; *L'Armorial général de 1696: Une source méconnue de l'histoire sociale et institutionnelle de la France d'Ancien Régime*, special 2-volume issue of *Révue française d'héraldique et de sigillographie* 67–68 (1997–98).

At some point before 1752, the book dealer Guérin came into possession of an isolated manuscript book formerly belonging to Du Cange: a sixteenth-century handwritten copy of three treatises titled *On Heraldry* (*Sur le Blason*), into which the scholar had copied and inserted further extensive material.[31] When conducting his research, Du Cange rarely defaced the unpublished manuscript sources that he consulted by covering their margins with his annotations—and almost never inserted into these sources interleaved scraps of paper with his own handwritten drafts.[32] Given this, it is unlikely that anyone handling volumes from his library would have looked at the copy of the treatises in sufficient detail to realize it had been transformed into what was effectively a new work in progress. It makes sense that this item should have been treated as something that could be separated from Du Cange's own works, since it was valued less for its association with the scholar than for its age. There are hints that Guérin purchased the manuscript from Louis-Jacques Du Cange or from his heirs. Certainly, before his death in 1741 Louis-Jacques was advertising material for sale, spreading the rumor that some foreigners—referred to as "the Englishmen"—had got wind of what he possessed and had expressed interest in acquiring it; if these "Englishmen" had ever truly existed and were not fabrications intended to drive up domestic prices, they seem to have concentrated primarily on buying not Du Cange's papers but rather other items that had formerly belonged to him. Evidence of this interest is provided by a medieval manuscript and an incunable that had been in the scholar's library and respectively ended up in London and Oxford.[33]

During this process of the dispersal of Du Cange's papers, draft works and notes that should have been kept together were separated and sent to different locations, perhaps because they were misidentified. For example, one of the works that in Eugene of Savoy's library in Vienna corresponded to two volumes (A and B) of a multivolume set, rebound in one volume; the remaining three volumes (C, D, and E) were in the possession of de Camps and then passed on to d'Hozier. This set formed Du Cange's research notes on Amiens and Picardy, containing all his excerpts and notes from the sources he had read and analyzed; it thus ought to have been kept together with the manuscript drafts of the *Portfolio Containing the Charters for the History of Picardy* (*Porte-feuille contenant les Titres pour l'Histoire de Picardie*) and the *Manuscript of the Counts of Amiens, with the Portfolio of Titles* (*Manuscrit des Comtes*

31 BnF, MS fr. 9491; D'Aubigny, *Mémoire sur les manuscrits de Du Cange*, 5, 22.

32 Du Cange generally confined himself to adding descriptions of the manuscripts' contents; see, e.g., the slip pasted into BnF, Ancien fonds grec 2898, fol. 1r.

33 D'Aubigny, *Mémoire sur les manuscrits de M. Du Cange*, 5–6; British Library, Additional 3811, and Bodleian Library, Auct. S. 2. 35.

d'Amiens, avec le Porte-feuille des Titres), which were retained by the Du Cange family.[34] Another work sent to Vienna contained notes that may have appeared at first sight to be diverse and haphazard but that in fact recorded sources on genealogy and heraldry. It properly belonged with the drafts of the *Treaty on Armorial Bearings, Considering Their Origin and Use* (*Traité du Droit des Armes, de leur Origine et Usage*), which the Du Cange family had kept for themselves, and also with the notes for the *Peerage*, at least a portion of which d'Hozier had acquired.[35]

Reassembly of the Papers

We owe the preservation of Du Cange's papers as a coherent collection primarily to the activities of one man: his great-nephew, Jean-Charles du Fresne D'Aubigny. In an obituary published shortly after his death in 1766, D'Aubigny was described as "having devoted himself for a long time to the cares of reassembling those manuscripts that had been dispersed; collecting them, putting them in order, and, by means of notices he published . . . , making them known to the public." In two published treatises, the 1752 description of the manuscripts, *Memoir on the Manuscripts of M. Du Cange* (*Mémoire sur les manuscrits de M. Du Cange*), and 1766 biography of their author, *Historical Memorandum Serving for the Eulogy of Charles Du Cange, and for the Comprehension of the General Plan of His Studies on the History of France* (*Mémoire historique pour servir à l'éloge de Charles Du Fresne Sieur Du Cange, et à l'intelligence du plan général de ses études sur l'histoire de France*), as well as in an unpublished memorandum dating to around 1756, D'Aubigny reviewed his endeavor after it had been substantially completed, insisting that he had been motivated above all by patriotism. He was persuaded, he wrote, that he had discovered "the universal plan of all M. Du Cange's studies." According to him, the driving force behind the immensity of Du Cange's "readings and literary labors" was that, from his earliest years, the scholar had always had "as his objective the History of France in all its parts and all its ages." In his program of study, Du Cange allegedly "never lost from sight the History of France: all his compositions, whether printed or manuscript, are united under this project." It could be demonstrated, furthermore, that everything he had

34 D'Aubigny, *Mémoire sur les manuscrits de M. Du Cange*, 4–5; Acquisitions de Manuscrits (26) 1667–1758, BnF, Archives Ancien Régime 65, fols. 377v–378v; BnF, MSS fr. 9496–500. For a different interpretation of these volumes, see J. Considine, *Dictionaries in Early Modern Europe: Lexicography and the Making of Heritage* (Cambridge, 2008), 272.

35 BnF, MSS fr. 9466, 9469–72; D'Aubigny, *Mémoire sur les manuscrits de M. Du Cange*, 4; Acquisitions de Manuscrits (26) 1667–1758, BnF, Archives Ancien Régime 65, fol. 370v; see also the inventory in this volume, Appendix II.

written, "both printed and manuscript, had a very intimate and marked relationship with Our History."[36]

D'Aubigny claimed that Du Cange had already shown signs of his future trajectory in his very first work, produced when merely twenty years old: a "genealogical chart of the kings and house of France, eleven feet high and seven or eight feet wide" that was "a masterpiece." And his papers contained numerous books on France that were to all intents and purposes finished and needed only to be sent to press.[37] D'Aubigny further asserted that because of the vagaries of publication, the scholar had been subjected by his immediate posterity to an undeserved "oblivion" from which his loftiness of vision—and the degree to which his work anticipated the nationalist preoccupations of current generations—required that he be rescued. There was an urgent need to concentrate on locating unpublished manuscripts in Du Cange's own hand.[38]

D'Aubigny stated that his interest in the material had first been sparked when he came across isolated references in his readings of Le Long and other authors to Du Cange's unpublished manuscripts and documents, such as the *History of the Principalities and Kingdoms of Jerusalem, Cyprus and Armenia, and the Families That Possessed Them* and the *Genealogical Chart of the Kings of France* (*Carte Généalogique des Rois de France*). In 1735, claiming to represent the Du Cange family in the matter, he launched negotiations for the return from Denison and Antoine-Marie d'Hozier of material that had been owned by Louis-Pierre d'Hozier. A year or two later, in 1736 or 1737, he started adding to this material by consolidating papers previously held by other family members, obtaining a substantial number from Louis-Jacques Du Cange—together with still others from further relatives. He occupied himself "solely with the finding, examination, and subsequent fate of these manuscripts, having renounced for this objective all other future employment and projects."[39] Additional items were surrendered by the Library of Saint Victor and by the book dealer Guérin. The outstanding material from Vienna was secured only decades later, following a publicity campaign in the press. The acquisition occurred during

36 D'Aubigny, *Mémoire sur les manuscrits de M. Du Cange*, 7–9; idem, *Mémoire historique pour servir à l'éloge de Du Cange* (n. 8 above).

37 Belley, *Notice des ouvrages manuscrits de Monsieur Du Cange* (n. 10 above), 18. While the article appeared under Belley's name, D'Aubigny had provided the greater portion of the "clarifications and observations" contained in it (ibid., 5).

38 Acquisitions de Manuscrits (26) 1667–1758, BnF, Archives Ancien Régime 65, fol. 367v.; D'Aubigny, *Mémoire sur les manuscrits de M. Du Cange*, 6–7, esp. 3; "Mémoire historique pour servir à l'éloge de Charles Dufresne sieur du Cange," *Journal des Sçavans*, August 1767, 585–86.

39 Acquisitions de Manuscrits (26) 1667–1758, BnF, Archives Ancien Régime 65, fols. 368r–v; see also D'Aubigny, *Mémoire sur les manuscrits de M. Du Cange*, 3–6, 18.

the lull in Habsburg–Bourbon hostilities that occurred with the end of the War of the Austrian Succession in 1748: an imperial order was issued around the year 1751 by the Court of Vienna that "the manuscripts of the renowned Du Cange" were to be sent back "immediately."[40]

In his task D'Aubigny was assisted by his patron, Chancellor Henri-François d'Aguesseau, who in 1735 intervened on his behalf with Antoine-Marie d'Hozier and then in 1743 commenced a similar intervention regarding the material in Vienna.[41] D'Aguesseau's willingness to assist may initially have been nothing more than a show of personal interest in scholarly matters as was befitting an honorary member of the French Academy of the Sciences. But his enthusiasm was apparently strengthened by practical considerations following the burning on 27 October 1737 of the Chamber of Accounts (Chambre des Comptes) in Paris and the destruction of the archives it contained. Since Du Cange had made unique copies of a number of documents, his papers could be used to reconstruct lost records vital for administering fiscal and other state affairs in France.[42] That royal clerks had already found other aspects of Du Cange's scholarship useful in executing their professional duties was emphasized in one early eighteenth-century account: "The gentlemen of the Chamber of Accounts always have M. Du Cange's Latin glossary on their desk so that they can turn to it when ancient deeds present difficulties."[43]

In 1756 the collection of manuscripts and papers assembled by D'Aubigny entered the French Royal Library. The event was accompanied by a petition by D'Aubigny, who declared he had received no remuneration so far and put forward his case for meriting a pension from the king, both in recognition of what he had already achieved and to support his further work on the collection. He explained he had already begun to make a detailed index organized by proper names and by topics, and he argued that a program of publication of the material should be instituted.[44] He also explained that his task was not yet complete and that further manuscripts and papers awaited discovery—a claim with some truth, since additional manuscripts seem to have entered the library later. One possible example of a delayed acquisition is Du Cange's handwritten working copy of his analysis of Anna Komnene's *Alexiad*, a life of the Byzantine

40 D'Aubigny, *Mémoire sur les manuscrits de M. Du Cange*, 7.

41 Acquisitions de Manuscrits (26) 1667–1758, BnF, Archives Ancien Régime 65, fol. 368r.

42 P. Bondois, "Le procureur général Joly de Fleury et les papiers de Du Cange," *Bibliothèque de l'école des chartes* 89 (1928): 83–84; D'Aubigny, *Mémoire sur les manuscrits de M. Du Cange*, 6–7; Acquisitions de Manuscrits (26) 1667–1758, BnF, Archives Ancien Régime 65, fols. 366v–367v.

43 Lesage de Samine [pseud. J.-L. Baron], *Éloge de Charles Dufresne, seigneur du Cange, avec une notice de ses ouvrages: Discours qui a remporté le Prix de l'Académie en 1764* (Amiens, 1764), 50; see also Considine, *Dictionaries in Early Modern Europe*, 278.

44 Acquisitions de Manuscrits (26) 1667–1758, BnF, Archives Ancien Régime 65, fols. 368r–v.

emperor Alexios I Komnenos. As this work had already been published in 1670 as part of the edition of the *History in Six Books of John Kinnamos* (*Ἰωάννου Κιννάμου βασιλικοῦ γραμματικοῦ ἱστοριῶν λόγοι ς´*), it may not have been considered to have been of significance when the collection was initially established.[45]

For the remainder of his life, D'Aubigny continued to promote the fame of his great-uncle Charles Du Cange, sharing material about him with others who were working on projects concerning the seventeenth century—such as the continuation of the massive biographical encyclopedia *The Great Historical Dictionary, or the Curious Anthology of Sacred and Secular History* (*Le Grand Dictionaire historique, ou le mélange curieux de l'histoire sacrée et profane*), commenced by Louis Moréri in 1674 and subsequently revised and reprinted many times until 1759—and penning a number of publications himself.[46] The final eulogy he wrote to the life of his forebear, the *Historical Memorandum Serving for the Eulogy of Charles Du Cange, and for the Comprehension of the General Plan of His Studies on the History of France*, came out in 1766, just weeks before D'Aubigny himself died.[47] His success in revising people's opinion of Du Cange can be seen from a comparison of the 1751 and 1768 editions of Voltaire's catalog of French writers that accompanied the *Century of Louis XIV* ("Catalogue de la plupart des écrivains français qui ont paru dans le siècle de Louis XIV, pour servir à l'histoire littéraire de ce temps"), for in the later edition the entry regarding Du Cange is much expanded.[48]

Following its entry into the Royal Library, the Du Cange collection experienced losses that may have been connected with the upheavals of the French Revolution. These losses—which included items such as Du Cange's early notes relating to antiquities in the area surrounding Amiens—were mitigated only in part by the existence

45 D'Aubigny, *Mémoire sur les manuscrits de M. Du Cange*, 6; BnF, MS fr. 1000; Charles Du Cange, *Ἰωάννου Κιννάμου βασιλικοῦ γραμματικοῦ ἱστοριῶν λόγοι ς´. Joannis Cinnami imperatorii grammatici historiarum libri sex, sev de rebvs gestis a Joanne et Manuele Comnenis impp. CP. Accedunt Caroli dv Fresne, D. dv Cange, Regi a Consiliis, & Franciæ apud Ambianos Quaestoris, in Nicephori Bryennii cæsaris, Annæ Commenæ cæsarissæ & ejusdem Joannis Cinnami Historiam Comnenicam Notæ Historicæ & Philologicæ. His adivngitvr Pauli Silentiarii descriptio sanctæ Sophiæ, quæ nunc primum prodit Græce & Latine, cum vberiori Commentario* (Paris, 1670).

46 D'Aubigny, in Moréri, *Le grand dictionnaire historique* (n. 7 above), 3:130–32.

47 D'Aubigny, *Mémoire historique pour servir à l'éloge de Charles Du Cange.*

48 [François Marie Arouet de] Voltaire, "Du Cange (Charles du Fresne)," in *Catalogue de la plupart des écrivains français qui ont paru dans le siècle de Louis XIV, pour servir à l'histoire littéraire de ce temps*, in *Le Siècle de Louis XIV (II): Listes et "Catalogue des écrivains,"* ed. D. Venturino, Œuvres complètes de Voltaire 12 (Oxford, 2017), 47–206, at 74. See the notes in the *Siècle de Louis XIV*, 306, for information on the expanded entry for Du Cange in the 1768 edition; see also Shawcross, Chapter 5 of this volume, p. 145, with n. 5.

already of copies of some of the material.[49] Since then, the entire collection has been repeatedly inventoried and cataloged, eventually being assigned new reference codes as part of a larger project of recataloging the library's holdings. Specific manuscripts and papers have been reorganized, trimmed, rebound, and conserved. The collection is divided today between two sites of the National Library of France (Bibliothèque nationale de France), the Richelieu and the Arsénal; some items are also accessible in microfilm or digital format.

The Inventory of 1756

An examination of the volume known as *Royal Library: Manuscript Acquisitions, 1667–1758* (*Bibliothèque royale: Acquisitions des manuscrits, 1667–1758*)[50] is instructive, providing us with a snapshot of the content and organization of Du Cange's manuscripts and other papers when the collection first entered the library. Rather than being a ledger filled out over time, this volume consists of a series of documents, on paper of varying format and size, that concerned acquisitions and were later bound together in roughly chronological order. Nestled in the middle of 1756 is a dossier relating to Du Cange. One of the documents it contains serves as an introduction of sorts to the circumstances under which the collection was acquired. This unsigned first-person memorandum (fig. 6.2), "Manuscripts of Monsieur Du Cange" ("Manuscrits de M^{r} Du Cange"), was penned by D'Aubigny himself; in it he briefly outlined his forebear's research agenda, gave an account of the process by which he himself had reassembled the collection of manuscripts and papers, and, finally, petitioned for a pension (366r–368v). The most important document of the dossier (fig. 6.3), however, is the one that follows immediately afterward (369r–381v), dated 2 May 1756 and titled "Inventory of the Manuscripts

49 In the inventory of the Du Cange papers postdating 1767 (Acquisitions de Manuscrits [26] 1667–1758, BnF, Archives Ancien Régime 65, fols. 363r–365v), for instance, it is noted of one manuscript that "there remained only a few pages." Although the library's holdings relating to royal and aristocratic titles, coats of arms, and genealogical trees were attacked by revolutionary forces, it appears that orders were given to target specific collections of an immediate practical application; research collections are not mentioned and, in any case, the losses observable in the Du Cange collection concern unrelated material. The possible exception is the *Genealogical Chart of the Kings of France* (*Carte Généalogique des Rois de France*), which seems to have been detached from Du Cange's other papers, but this may have happened in the 19th century. For the effect of the French Revolution on the Royal Library, see L. H. Thien, "La Bibliothèque Nationale sous la Révolution," *Dix-Huitième Siècle* 14 (1982): 75–88. Eighteenth-century copies of Du Cange's autograph writings include BnF, MS fr. 5259.

50 Acquisitions de Manuscrits [26] 1667–1758, BnF, Archives Ancien Régime 65, fols. 362r–381v.

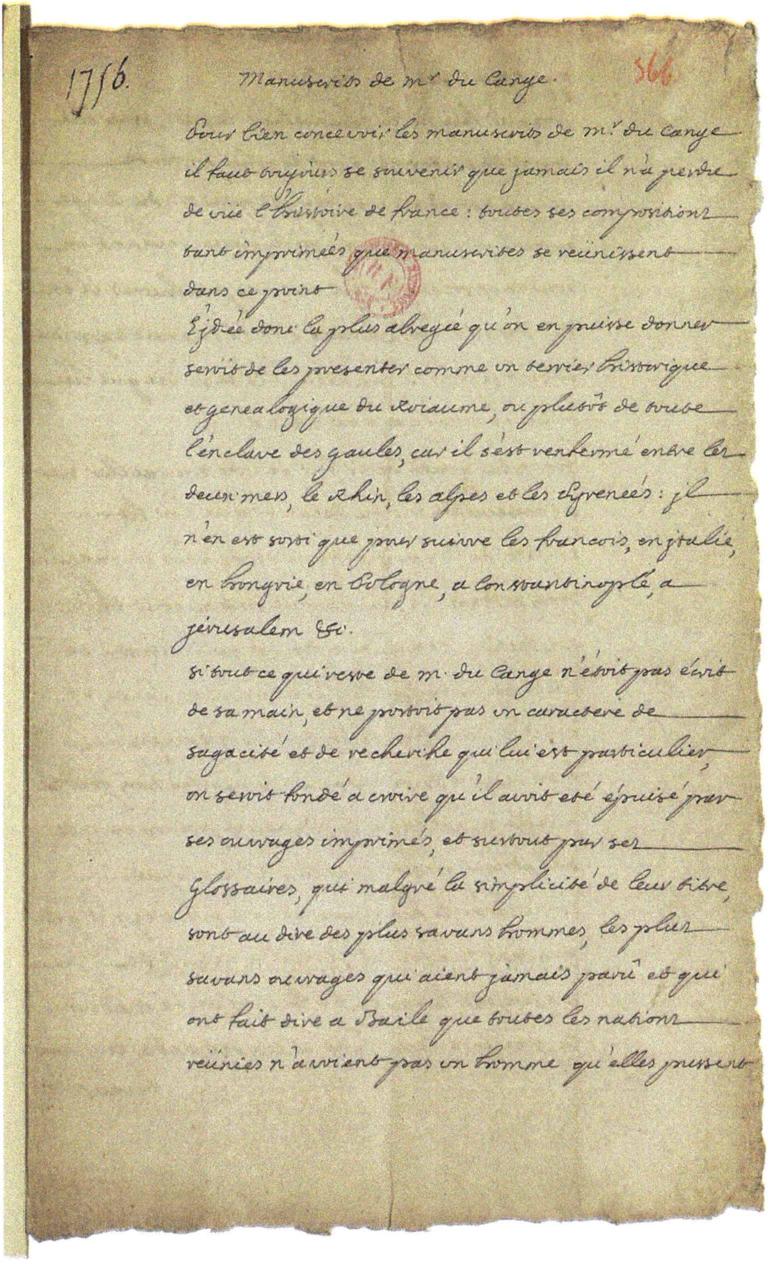

1756. Manuscrits de mr du Cange. 366

Pour bien concevoir les manuscrits de mr du cange il faut toujours se souvenir que jamais il n'a perdu de vue l'histoire de france : toutes ses compositions tant imprimées que manuscrites se reünissent dans ce point

L'idée donc la plus abregée qu'on en puisse donner seroit de les presenter comme un terrier historique et genealogique du royaume, ou plutôt de toute l'enclave des gaules, car il s'est renfermé entre les deux mers, le Rhin, les alpes et les pyrenées : il n'en est sorti que pour suivre les francois, en italie, en hongrie, en pologne, a constantinople, a jerusalem &c.

si tout ce qui reste de m. du Cange n'étoit pas écrit de sa main, et ne portoit pas un caractere de sagacité et de recherche qui lui est particulier, on seroit fondé a croire qu'il avoit été épuisé par ses ouvrages imprimés, et surtout par ses Glossaires, qui malgré la simplicité de leur titre, sont au dire des plus savans hommes, les plus savans ouvrages qui aient jamais paru et qui ont fait dire a Bayle que toutes les nations reünies n'avoient pas un homme qu'elles pussent

Fig. 6.2. Jean-Charles du Fresne D'Aubigny, "Manuscripts of Mr du Cange." Paris, 1756. Département des manuscrits, Acquisitions de manuscrits (26) 1667–1758, Bibliothèque nationale de France, Archives Ancien Régime 65, fol. 366r. Courtesy Bibliothèque nationale de France.

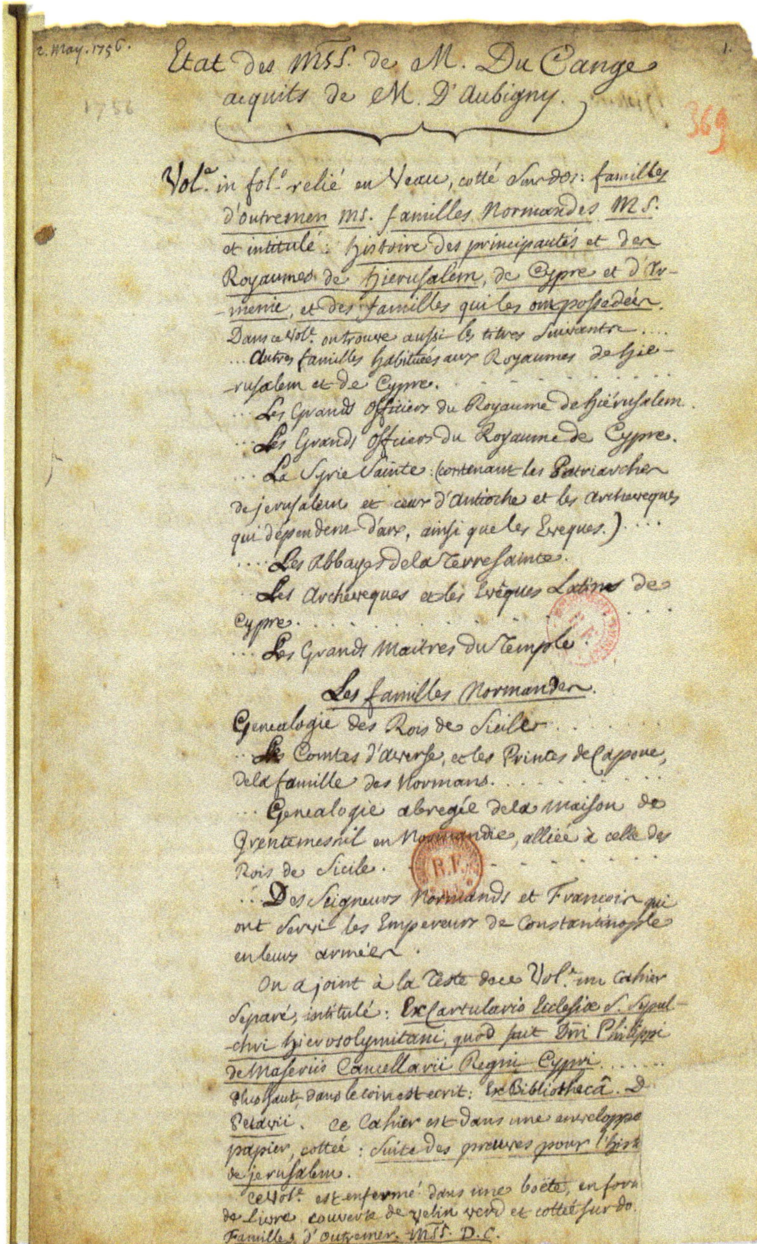
2. May. 1756.

Etat des MSS. de M. Du Cange acquits de M. D'Aubigny.

369

Vol. in fol. relié en veau, cotté sur dos: familles d'outremer MS. familles Normandes MS. et intitulé: histoire des principautés et des Royaumes de Hierusalem, de Cypre et d'Armenie, et des familles qui les ont possedées.

Dans ce Vol. on trouve aussi les titres suivants....

...Autres familles habituées aux Royaumes de Hierusalem et de Cypre.

...Les Grands Officiers du Royaume de Hierusalem.

...Les Grands Officiers du Royaume de Cypre.

...La Syrie Sainte (contenant les Patriarches de Jerusalem et ceux d'Antioche et les Archeveques qui dependent d'eux, ainsi que les Eveques.)...

...Les Abbayes de la terre sainte.

...Les Archeveques et les Evêques Latins de Cypre.

...Les Grands Maitres du temple.

Les familles Normandes.

Genealogie des Rois de Sicile.

...Les Comtes d'Averse, et les Princes de Capoue, de la famille des Normans.

...Genealogie abregée de la maison de Grentemesnil en Normandie, alliée à celle des Rois de Sicile.

...Des Seigneurs Normands et François qui ont servi les Empereurs de Constantinople en leurs armées.

On a joint à la teste de ce Vol. un cahier separé, intitulé: Ex Cartulario Ecclesiae S. Sepulchri Hierosolymitani, quod fuit Dni Philippi de Maseriis Cancellarii Regni Cypri.....

Plus haut, dans le coin est ecrit: Ex Bibliothecâ D. [illegible]. Ce Cahier est dans une enveloppe papier, cottée: Suite des preuves pour l'hist de Jerusalem.

Ce Vol. est enfermé dans une boëte, en forme de Livre couverte de velin verd et cottée sur do. Familles d'outremer MSS. D.C.

Fig. 6.3. "Inventory of the Manuscripts of M. Du Cange acquired from M. D'Aubigny." Paris, 2 May 1756. Département des manuscrits, Acquisitions des manuscrits (26) 1667–1758, Bibliothèque nationale de France, Archives Ancien Régime 65, fol. 369r. Courtesy Bibliothèque nationale de France.

of M. Du Cange Acquired from M. D'Aubigny" ("Etat des manuscrits de M. Du Cange acquits de M. D'Aubigny").[51]

This inventory lists forty-six items—bound manuscript volumes, boxes, and portfolios of unbound papers—divided into some thirteen separate research and writing projects. The writer—whose identity is not known but who was most likely a librarian or other permanent member of the library's staff, given that the same neat and vigorous hand is found in another inventory from the same year—uses indentations and other forms of spacing, the size of the lettering, and also bolding and underlining to distinguish between different levels of information regarding the items listed.

The inventory's detailed descriptions focus on external appearance and contents. Their structure closely resembles that of descriptions found in other inventories from the library (e.g., 356r–359v) and must therefore reflect standard institutional practice. They specify the fabric, size, and color of any container such as a box or folder used to protect the material (e.g., "box covered in green vellum," "red quarto folder"), as well the fabric and color of any binding or cover present (e.g., "bound in parchment," "covered in marbled paper"); if the material is unbound, they note whether sheets are sewn together into a quire, are held together with some sort of clip or pin, or are simply loose (e.g., "separate sheets held together with a pin"). They also transcribe the labeling, both that given on the outside, such as on the spine (e.g., "labeled on the spine"), and on the inside, such as on the endpapers or the opening pages of the text proper (e.g., "titled *On Oracles* inside"), noting any differences

51 The remaining two documents from the dossier in Acquisitions de Manuscrits (26) 1667–1758, BnF, Archives Ancien Régime 65, must postdate 1767, as the second includes a reference to publications from that year; they may well be 19th-century. The first document is a small scrap of paper with a short note regarding the existence of a journal in five volumes kept by Charles du Cange during the years 1651–57 about "what happened in Paris and in some other locations within the Kingdom," with entries being "enriched by a great number of portraits" (fol. 362r). There follow three larger sheets of paper, which had been folded lengthwise in half and have a crease down the middle (363r–365v) and are written in minuscule script on both front and back. The first page contains two columns in ink: a bibliography of sources about Du Cange and a list of Du Cange's published works. Subsequent pages have only the right-hand column in ink; it gives information on Du Cange's unpublished writings, summarizing and preserving the structure of publications on the subject from the 1750s and 1760s that are cited. The left-hand column has check marks in pencil and brief comments about the color of bindings or the format of the volume, and it notes the loss of material etc., suggesting that the list was used in conjunction with an examination of the library's actual holdings. The aim appears to have been to provide some sort of check on the status of the collection, exposing losses and other deterioration. Whoever composed this document appears not to have been aware of the existence of the 1756 inventory, which, with its more accurate and detailed description of the manuscripts than was available in the published material, would have suited his purposes better—indicating that the existence of the earlier inventory had most likely been forgotten.

between versions of the title and verifying this labeling against the actual contents (e.g., "these two titles are repeated"). They discuss the dimensions, such as folio or quarto (e.g., "a small folio volume"), of the paper used. More strikingly, they emphasize over and over the fact that the material is autograph by Du Cange (e.g., "All in the hand of Du Cange"); in those few cases in which Du Cange did not himself write the text, they meticulously comment that it is by another hand or printed, and evaluate the extent to which it is accompanied by Du Cange's own annotations (e.g., "with notes, citations, corrections, additions, insertions . . . written in the margins"). Also noted are changes made by Du Cange or by others after his death, such as the reordering of material, the excision or insertion of pages, the construction of tables of contents, and generally any signs of use (e.g., "has been removed from this volume in order to be bound separately," "a sheet of paper in different handwriting which has as its title: Table of Articles returned by M. d'Hozier"). Throughout, there appears to have been an effort to identify the traces of the author's research method and to speculate about his intentions regarding the finished product (e.g., "notes of memoranda to be used to make up a complete work," "apparently intended to supplement").

The inventory does not seem to be organized either by the date when works were produced or by their most recent provenance. The early research by Du Cange on the history of Picardy comes toward the end of the list, and a volume that had been in Vienna is recorded next to one that never left the possession of the Du Cange family. However, there is some attempt at thematic ordering internally. Items on the same broad topic (e.g., the history of the Crusader states) are listed one after another, and multiple volumes or boxes that belong to the same project (e.g., the notes on a peerage of France) are correctly grouped together. Miscellaneous small items, such as notebooks that were in large part blank, were included at the end of the list (380v–381v).

The Nation's Historian

D'Aubigny taught his contemporaries to see Du Cange as a "gentle hero" who brought glory to France by scholarship, just as more "strident heroes" did by fighting for their country or engaging in politics.[52] A comparison of the inventory—and of the manuscripts and other papers themselves—with D'Aubigny's claims in his published and unpublished writings on the subject reveals that Du Cange's descendant, eager to secure "recompense for the costs and labors" he had expended, as well as angling for an appointment to oversee the publication of "all these

52 Baron, *Éloge de Charles Du Cange*, 4; also Considine, *Dictionaries in Early Modern Europe*, 13.

manuscripts,"[53] deliberately exaggerated what he had found and assembled during his decades-long manuscript hunt. With one exception, what he unearthed were not finished or even largely complete books, but rather fragmentary drafts, chapter outlines, and, above all, simple compilations of sources and other research notes. As indeed Du Cange himself had specified in a note on the first leaf of a particular series of sheaves of unbound papers, these were "undigested records for the writing" of works that had not yet been advanced.[54] Thus, if Du Cange had ever desired to become a historian of France, those aspirations had resulted not in a complete and polished body of work, but rather in an undertaking that had been arrested in the form of notebooks devoted to the gathering of material and the initial formulation of ideas. In any case, these drafts envisioned history less as a rhetorical art whose arguments were framed through narrative than as an erudite method of inquiry into customs, institutions, laws, arts, and crafts—and other products of the human intellect.[55]

Though D'Aubigny's imagining of his great-uncle as one of the most important forerunners in the composition of the types of narrative histories of the nation that were beginning to emerge in eighteenth-century France does not bear detailed scrutiny, it fitted well with contemporary geopolitical concerns. Louis XIV's anti-Turkish policies from 1640 to 1670 were only a temporary aberration in a Franco-Ottoman "fraternal alliance" directed against the Habsburgs that lasted for centuries, from the time of King Francis I to the Revolution.[56] By the time Du Cange's manuscripts and other papers entered the Royal Library, the French crown was far less focused on the Ottoman threat in the Mediterranean than it had been under Louis XIV. It therefore had little interest in identifying the precedents of the Fourth Crusade and the Latin Empire as the means by which to assert that it—rather than the Turkish polity—was the true successor to the glories of the Eastern Roman, or Byzantine, Empire.

Instead, there appears to have been a tendency to argue for the continuing existence since earliest historical times of an indigenous Gallic people and culture in northwestern Europe that, already infused with Roman values during the late republic and early principate, could lay claim to a Western Roman imperial heritage. In the face of Hanoverian—and especially Habsburg—rivalries with the Bourbons, the advancement of arguments about ethnogenesis served to legitimate claims

53 Acquisitions de Manuscrits (26) 1667–1758, BnF, Archives Ancien Régime 65, fol. 368r.

54 Ibid., 370r.

55 Anthony Grafton, *What Was History? The Art of History in Early Modern Europe* (Cambridge, 2007), 189–254.

56 Bardaçı and Pugnière, *La dernière croisade* (n. 22 above), 61.

regarding the territorial integrity of France.[57] It was no coincidence that D'Aubigny was proud of having supposedly wrested manuscripts from the marauding hands of Austrian and English collectors.

The inventory of Du Cange's unpublished works duly acknowledged that the revisions for the new edition of the *History of the Empire of Constantinople under the French Emperors* sought to offer a "general history of the most memorable deeds of the Franks and Latins in the Empire of Constantinople," while the material for his *Research on the History of France* (*Recherches sur l'Histoire de France*) included a volume, labeled on the spine with the single word *Outremer*, whose subject was the families of the Crusader states.[58] But it did not dwell on these particular volumes. Instead, it emphasized that Du Cange's *Geography of France* had two aims. First, it would offer an explanation of

> the ancient names of the Gauls; the origins of the Gauls, etc.; the itineraries and division of the Gauls by Julius Caesar and under Augustus, etc.; that by archbishops, bishops, etc.; the governors of the provinces and cities of the Gauls under the Romans; the prefects of the Praetorium; the history of the Gauls under the Roman Emperors; the name of France; the origins of the French; the dukes and counts; (palatine inspectors) the form of government in the provinces and towns of the Gauls under the French, etc.; the state of France under the third race of our kings, etc. etc. etc.

And, second, it would provide an exposition of the topographical characteristics of all the different territories that could notionally be part of mainland France, from Belgium to Normandy and from Gascony to Switzerland. Moreover, the inventory drew attention to the scholar's notes for his *Peerage of France* on the subject of the "Kingdoms, Duchies, Principalities, Sovereignties, Marquisates, Counties, Viscounties, Vidames, and other great lordships situated within the confines of the Gauls—that is to say, as much in the Kingdom of France as in the other provinces located between the Atlantic and the Mediterranean Seas, the Alps, the Pyrenees, and the Rhine."[59] Thus, the Bourbon administration—in listening to D'Aubigny's proposal, and in facilitating his endeavors and accepting their fruit—sponsored a reinvention of Du Cange that mirrored contemporary royal ambitions in continental Europe. It is, of course, a testimony to the rich and multifaceted nature of the

57 For an overview of Habsburg–Bourbon relations in this period, see J. Duindam, *Vienna and Versailles: The Courts of Europe's Dynastic Rivals, 1550–1780* (Cambridge, 2003), 14–17.

58 Acquisitions de Manuscrits (26) 1667–1758, BnF, Archives Ancien Régime 65, fols. 369v, 375v.

59 Ibid., fols. 370v, 376v–377v.

seventeenth-century scholar's output as an original researcher and thinker that such an interpretation of his legacy was possible.

During archival research in Paris in 2017, I had the good fortune to discover the documents relating to the acquisition and organization by the Royal Library of France in the eighteenth century of Du Cange's papers (Acquisitions de Manuscrits [26] 1667–1758, BnF, Archives Ancien Régime 65, fols. 362r–381v). Thanks are due to the staff of the Bibliothèque nationale de France, and especially the librarians at the Arsénal, for making archival and manuscript material pertaining to Du Cange available and for facilitating the publication of the original inventory of the collection; to Nathanael Aschenbrenner and Jake Ransohoff, for inviting this contribution; and to Matthew McDonald, for his assistance with the piece. My edition and translation of the inventory, together with an attempt to correlate the contents listed with the material extant today, are published as Appendix II of this volume.

SEVEN

PERFORMING BYZANTIUM IN EARLY MODERN THEATER

PRZEMYSŁAW MARCINIAK

IN 1778 THE PENULTIMATE PLAY WRITTEN BY THE EIGHTY-FIVE-YEAR-OLD VOLTAIRE, *Irène,* was performed. The plot of the play, described by Henri Lion as a "tragédie d'amour,"[1] is loosely based on the history of the Komnenian coup d'état of 1081. There is some irony in the fact that someone so often accused of disdain, if not hatred, toward Byzantium spent his last days writing a play that draws on the history of the eastern empire.[2] While it is not entirely clear whether Voltaire intended to write a simple love story, a satire directed against absolutism,[3] or a play inspired by his readings in Oriental ethnography,[4] the choice of theme does not seem to be

1 H. Lion, *Les Tragédies et les théories dramatiques de Voltaire* (Paris, 1895), 399.

2 On Voltaire and Byzantium see T. Palágyi, "'Une suite ininterrompue de meurtres, de parjures et de déclamations': Voltaire et les Byzantins," in *Cultivateur de son jardin, Mélanges offerts à Monsieur le Professeur Imre Vörös,* special issue of the *Revues d'études françaises* (Budapest, 2006), 149–71.

3 O. Delouis, "Byzance dans la scène littéraire française (1870–1920)," in *Byzance en Europe,* ed. M.-F. Auzépy, Créations européennes (Saint-Denis, 2003), 105.

4 M. Hua, "Irène, une autre tragédie de Voltaire qui s'inspire de la Chine," in *Le bonheur de la littérature: Variations critiques pour Béatrice Didier,* ed. C. Montalbetti and J. Neefs (Paris, 2005), 107–14, at 107, argues that *Irène* took inspiration from the story of a young Chinese Christian called Maria: "Supposons l'analyse du caractère d'Idamé connue, je voudrais attirer l'attention sur une chose curieuse et paradoxale: si Voltaire a créé en 1755 une héroïne dite chinoise, mais effectivement peu chinoise, il en fera une typiquement confucéenne vingt-deux ans plus tard. Il s'agit là d'Irène, héroïne de sa dernière tragédie représentée." This suggestion is hardly convincing, however. It is doubtful that the audience of the play would be able to read into it the Chinese context hidden behind Byzantine history. Moreover, the eastern empire was exotic enough on its own.

incidental.[5] Eleventh-century Byzantium was not unknown to the French elite, and seventeenth-century France had already evinced considerable interest in Byzantine history, long before Voltaire penned his tragedy.[6]

Voltaire's *Irène*, which marks the end of Byzantine inspirations in early modern European theater, failed, along with other important omissions, to make it onto Agostino Pertusi's list of early modern plays that draw on Byzantine motifs, even though Pertusi, ironically enough, ends his paper by quoting Montesquieu's and Voltaire's derogatory opinions of Byzantium.[7]

Voltaire's choice was somewhat unusual though not an isolated exception, since other playwrights before him drew on Byzantium; as this chapter will demonstrate, Byzantine history was and still remains neither an obvious nor a very common choice for playwrights.[8] What unites most, if not all, plays discussed here is their use of Byzantium as a floating signifier, whose meaning and referent are contextually relative and depend on the needs of a given author. This chapter shows how different cultural, political, and literary variables gave meaning to this floating signifier. It argues that in most cases, historical Byzantium (as construed by post-Byzantine historians, scholars, and writers) was in fact unimportant or irrelevant for playwrights, and the empire became instead a polysemic sign used to express different and sometimes even contradictory historical, social, and political views. This chapter begins in the sixteenth centrury, with a focus on Jesuits, and examines the role of "school plays" in disseminating Byzantium as a setting, and Byzantine figures as exemplary characters, on the European stage. It then moves on to consider how Protestant authors both adopted and adapted these Jesuit themes for their own ends. Finally, it examines Byzantium on the Restoration English stage, before reflecting on the afterlife of early modern Byzantine plays in the wake of Gibbon and the gradual crystallization of Byzantine studies as an academic discipline.

5 According to Lion (*Les Tragédies et les theories*, 397), the play was inspired by the book *Histoire de l'impératrice Irène*. But this volume by Vincent Mignot (1662) tells the story of the empress Irene, wife to Leo IV and mother to Constantine VI; it could perhaps serve as inspiration for Voltaire but not the source of the plot for a play based on a completely different story.

6 J.-M. Spieser, "Du Cange and Byzantium," in *Through the Looking-Glass: Byzantium through British Eyes. Papers from the Twenty-Ninth Spring Symposium of Byzantine Studies, London, March 1995*, ed. R. S. Cormack and E. Jeffreys, SPBS 7 (London, 2000), 199–210. See also Teresa Shawcross in Chapter 5 of this volume.

7 A. Pertusi, "Τα δράματα μὲ βυζαντινὴ καὶ τουρκική ὑποθέση στὸ εὐρωπαϊκό καὶ βενετικὸ θέατρο ἀπὸ τοῦ 16ου ως τὶς αρχὲς τοῦ 18ου αἰώνα," *Hellenikά* 22 (1969): 341–69, at 357.

8 Similarly understudied is the issue of the presence of Byzantine motifs in early modern opera. At the moment Gwendolyn Döring (University of Mainz) is preparing a PhD thesis on this neglected yet surprisingly rich topic.

Prologue: The Jesuit World of Byzantium

While it is easy to pinpoint the last, it is virtually impossible to identify the first piece of early modern theater to dramatize a Byzantine story. Pertusi's proposition to treat *Abraham sacrifiant* by Theodore Beza (1550) as Byzantium's debut on the European stage seems a stretch, since this work was a revision of the biblical story of Abraham and has almost nothing to do with Byzantium. Similarly, while plays such as *La Theodora* by Flaminius Malaguzzi (1572) and *Irene* by Vincenzo Giusti (1579) featured Greek characters or occur in Greek settings, such works bear no substantive connection to figures or events from Byzantine history.[9] The beginnings of "Byzantine plays," by which I understand works drawing on Byzantine historical events (330–1453), are, however, inextricably connected with "school theater"—that is, theater written and performed in Jesuit colleges as a means of rhetorical and moral instruction. The first school plays to dramatize both the events and the characters of the eastern empire were penned by Jesuits,[10] and later such plays were composed by members of other orders that ran their own schools; they also became part of the school practices of Protestants.[11] Jesuits' interest in Byzantine topics—fully realized by the end of the sixteenth century—derived from their sense that Byzantium represented "an ideal union between Church and state."[12] Thus Byzantine history became mostly a source of rulers both exemplary (e.g., Constantine the Great, r. 306–337) and errant (e.g., the Iconoclast Leo V the Armenian, r. 813–820), whose lives illustrated the ideal relationship between a Christian monarchy and the church.

Two Byzantine figures proved particularly attractive to the authors of school theater (and indeed, to other authors as well): Belisarius and the emperor Maurice (r. 582–602). Several dozen plays exist in which these two characters act as protagonists.[13] Of course, the fates of both Maurice and Belisarius offered excellent

9 A. Pertusi, "I drammi di soggetto bizantino e turco nel teatro europeo dalla fine del sec. XVI all'inizio del sec. XVIII," in *Bisanzio e i Turchi nella cultura del Rinascimento e del Barocco*, ed. C. M. Mazzucchi, Bibliotheca erudita studi e documenti di storia e filologia 25 (Milan, 2004), 93, no. 258.

10 The scholarly bibliography on the school theater of Jesuits is rich. For a good introduction, see W. H. McCabe, *An Introduction to the Jesuit Theatre: A Posthumous Work*, ed. L. J. Oldani (St. Louis, 1983).

11 See, e.g., P. Marciniak, "The Silesian Tragedy 'Avaritia crudelis et punita' in Mauritio Imperatore as a Political Commentary on Its Times," *LisFil* 124.3–4 (2001): 274–79. For school plays in a Protestant context, see J. Budzyński, *Dramat i teatr szkolny na Śląsku (XVI–XVIII wiek)* [School drama and theater in Silesia, 16th–18th c.] (Katowice, 1996), 7.

12 J. A. Parente, "Tyranny and Revolution on the Baroque Stage: The Dramas of Joseph Simons," *Humanistica Lovaniensia* 32 (1983): 317.

13 See *Tragoediae Mauritius et Belisarius*, ed. Z. Piszczek (Wrocław, 1971), 208–15.

examples of *fortuna mutabilis*, the "changing fate" or wheel of fortune—a metaphor of particular potency throughout the Middle Ages and well into the seventeenth century.[14] The emblematic utility of these two Byzantine personages must have been one of the reasons for their popularity among early modern playwrights. Yet while dramatizations of Maurice's career were mostly limited to school theater, the invented story of Belisarius's fall became a powerful symbol and inspiration among writers and artists in the centuries to come.[15] Moreover, school theater, and the Jesuit interest in Byzantium more broadly, came to influence plays written for the professional stage by renowned authors. Pierre Corneille, schooled by the Jesuits, penned the play *Héraclius, Empereur d'Orient* (1647), which is actually a variation on a popular story about the emperor Maurice and his fall caused by his avarice. In his introduction to the play, Corneille notes the changes he made to the original story, saying that he mostly retained the order of the emperors but changed everything else—for instance, making Herakleios into the son of Maurice (in reality these two were not even related, and Herakleios was not in Constantinople when Maurice was dethroned and killed by Phokas). It is interesting that Corneille felt compelled to excuse himself. We might safely assume that since the story he decided to alter was so well known, Corneille believed it necessary to explain to readers and reviewers the intentions behind his changing of the facts.

In his preface to *Héraclius*, Corneille refers to Baronius, a historian, as one of the main sources of his knowledge about the eastern empire.[16] This was Caesar Baronius, whose hugely successful *Annales Ecclesiastici* (1588–1607) helped disseminate knowledge of Byzantine history. Baronius's laboriously researched work, which narrated the history of the church up until 1198 and was meant to be one of the Counter-Reformation tools in the debate with the Protestants, became a principal

14 While the history of the fall of Maurice was rooted in history, the story of Belisarius—who supposedly died as a blind beggar after falling out of favor with Justinian—is purely anecdotal.

15 See, e.g., K. Weschenfelder, "Belisar und sein Begleiter: Die Karriere eines Blinden in der Kunst vom 17. bis zum 19. Jahrhundert," *MarbJb* 30 (2003): 245–68; N. Lebermann, *Belisar in der Literatur der romanischen und germanischen Nationen*, inaugural diss., Heidelberg (Nürnberg, 1899), 64–109; A. S. Barrovecchio, "Histoire de Bélisaire dans la literature française (sous la direction de J. Dagen, Université Paris IV–Sorbonne)," *Revue Voltaire* 6 (2006): 339–47. There is no convincing answer to the question of why the fictional story of Belisarius, but not that of Maurice, became popular outside of school walls. We can only speculate that in the case of Belisarius, the immensely popular novel *Bélisaire* (1767), by Jean-François Marmontel, helped transfer the story of the general from the educational realm to popular literature. A similar mechanism, in my opinion, boosted the literary career of Empress Theodora, which was launched after Victorien Sardou's play *Theodora* (1884), discussed below.

16 "Baronius, parlant de la mort de l'empereur Maurice et de celle de ses fils . . . "; P. Corneille, *Œuvres completes*, textes établis, présentés et annotés par G. Couton, 3 vols. (Paris, 1980–87), 2:355.

source for playwrights in search of Byzantine source material.[17] Although a handy tool, Baronius's *Annales* was not perfect—his Greek was not very good and he often relied on (not always correct) translations.[18] It nonetheless offered authors of Byzantine dramas a tentative outline of personalities and events that could be adjusted as needed. Still, Byzantium would probably have remained just one possible—and relatively marginal—source of inspiration for Jesuit writers,[19] were it not for Joseph Simons (1593?–1671): his Byzantine plays not only became quite famous but also sparked literary responses in various parts of Europe that pushed Byzantine drama beyond the horizons of school theater.

Joseph Simons (also Simeon/Simon), born Emmanuel Lobb in Portsmouth in 1593, first entered the English College of St. Omers in Artois, and then, in 1616, the English College of Rome.[20] He returned to St. Omers to teach classics, and there he wrote and produced his five tragedies.[21] Three of these five drew on Byzantine historical events: *Leo Armenus seu Impietas Punita* (first performed between 1624 and 1629), *Theoctistus sive Constans in Aula Virtus* (first performed in 1624), and *Zeno sive Ambitio Infelix* (first performed in 1631).[22] William McCabe notes that Simons was one of the first authors to write plays inspired by Byzantine history.[23] This is not entirely true; there were other tragedies set in Byzantium, some of them much earlier.[24] Some of these plays enjoyed considerable popularity and were staged in different Jesuit colleges in various countries.[25] None of them, however, was as influential or as popular as Simons's plays, which captivated audiences with their novel takes on Byzantine themes.

The "argument" of *Leo Armenus* reveals Simons's source for his Byzantine plays—which was, quite unsurprisingly, Baronius's *Annales*:

17 On Baronius and his work, see C. K. Pullapilly, *Caesar Baronius. Counter Reformation Historian* (Notre Dame, IN, 1975).

18 Ibid., 156.

19 McCabe, *An Introduction to the Jesuit Theatre*, 23.

20 On Simons's life, see G. P. Sandham, "An English Jesuit Dramatist: Fr. Joseph Simeon 1593–1671," *The Month* 210 (1960): 308–13.

21 McCabe, *An Introduction to the Jesuit Theatre*, 135.

22 I am using the editions and translations of the plays available at the University of Birmingham's online Philological Museum, at http://www.philological.bham.ac.uk/library.html.

23 McCabe, *An Introduction to the Jesuit Theatre*, 139: "His Byzantine plays represent, to the best of my knowledge, one of the first calls made by a tragic playwright on this rich treasury of plot."

24 See, e.g., *Heraclius. Exaltatio s. Crucis* (Turnai, 1596), a tragedy on Maurice by J. Keller (*Mauritius*, 1603); *Mauritius* (anonymous, Poznań, written between 1604 and 1611).

25 Z. Piszczek, "Die Geschichte vom Kaiser Mauritius auf der Bühne der Kollegien Societatis Jesu in Polen," *Humanistica Lovaniensia* 18 (1969): 127.

> Leo the Armenian, Emperor of the East, was a very bitter foe of holy images, and after making great and protracted trouble for the Catholic cause, in the end, he paid the penalties for his impiety. For Michael Balbus, the most preeminent of his nobility, condemned to death by burning after his conspiracy had been revealed, broke free of his bonds when Leo was assassinated by his friends on Christmas Eve itself, was created emperor, and banished Leo's family. Baronius, vol. 9.[26]

In the case of *Zeno*, Simons states that the subject matter was taken "Ex Hist. Niceph., Procop., Evag., Zonar."; but since these are exactly the same historians mentioned by Baronius in his treatment of the emperor Zeno (r. 474–475, 476–491), Simons likely cribbed the citation directly from Baronius's *Annales* without consulting the Byzantine texts themselves. Simons's approach to Byzantium thus foreshadows perhaps one of the most common, and problematic, features of the reception of Byzantine material in Jesuit theater and also in later plays. What these texts often have in common is their expression of a mediated opinion. Simons, like his predecessors, relied on secondhand accounts rather than primary sources. There is no evidence that the Jesuit knew anything beyond what he could read in the *Annales*, itself a highly polemical account.

Simons did not care about the eastern empire per se; for him, Byzantium was a medieval, Christian version of the exotic Mediterranean places portrayed by Elizabethan drama.[27] On a more symbolic level, it could represent Protestants (as Christians who deviated from the true faith). Simons thus fills the annalistic narrative of Baronius with gory, exotic, and supernatural details, which both were enticing for his audience and, at the same time, embedded and reinforced the decadent image of the eastern empire in the minds of viewers.[28] Simons's Emperor Leo (*Leo Armenus*), for instance, is a suspicious tyrant interested above all in drinking, while

26 Trans. D. W. Sutton (5 November 2013; see n. 22 above): *Leo Armenus, orientis imperator, sacrarum imaginum hostis acerrimus, cum diu multumque rem Catholicam vexasset, tandem impietatis poenas persolvit. Nam Michael Balbus, procerum princeps, detecta coniuratione, ad flammas damnatus, ipsa nascentis Christi nocte, caeso per amicos Leone, vincula perfringit et imperator efficitur, totamque Leonis familiam evertit.* Baronius tomo 9.

27 Parente, "Tyranny and Revolution on the Baroque Stage," 317. On the imagery of the Mediterranean, see *Remapping the Mediterranean World in Early Modern English Writings*, ed. G. Stanivukovic (New York, 2007).

28 See, e.g., McCabe, *An Introduction to the Jesuit Theatre*, 134: "Here, in a luxury, which our imagination can scarcely reconstruct, amid marbles, mosaics and gold, costly tapestries, purples, and precious stones, governed by a daily program at once petty in its precision and marvelous in its display, the *basileus* was the center of the gorgeous ceremonial of the Byzantine Court." This passage also reveals how McCabe himself perceived the eastern empire.

the young emperor Michael III (featured in the play *Theoctistus*) is surrounded by his gay lovers. Drinking, homosexuality, and luxury: these clichés were not invented by Simons. He builds on ideas that had already circulated in the chronicles of medieval authors. The Polish chronicler Jan Długosz (1415–1480), while commenting on the fall of Constantinople, remarked that the city contained brothels with young boys.[29] Given the popularity of his plays, however, it is possible that Simons helped disseminate these lurid associations with the eastern empire.[30] At the same time, Simons aimed not merely to entertain his audience with gory and sensational stories. He also saw in Byzantine history the potential to convey a political message. Unlike the works of his predecessors, Simons's plays were not only didactic or religious pieces but also political manifestos. Whether he retrojected his stories into the remote past to avoid giving offense to his contemporaries, as Dana Sutton suggested, remains debatable.[31] As James Parente argues, English students must have been able to read the Byzantine state in Simons's plays as a medieval version of the absolutist Stuart monarchy.[32] Therefore, in dramatizing two (successful) attempts at removing emperors (Zeno and Leo Armenus) who renounced orthodox Christianity, Simons seemed to support the idea that one day, Protestant rulers would be similarly ousted from power for their apostasy.[33] Byzantium was effectively reduced to the role of avatar: a disguise for the author's political manifesto.

Act I: Andreas Gryphius

Simons emerges as a major figure in Byzantium's reception on the early modern stage, not only because his plays were performed, read, and copied throughout Europe but also because his works were imitated. One such imitator might have been Andreas Gryphius (1616–1664), a prominent Protestant poet and playwright of the German Baroque who penned his own version of the story of Leo V the Armenian, titled *Leo Armenius oder Fürsten-Mord* (1650).[34] There is no undisputable proof that Gryphius was inspired by Simons's tragedy, but he visited Rome in 1646 and might

29 Jan Długosz, *Roczniki czyli Kroniki sławnego Królestwa Polskiego* [Annals of the famous Kingdom of Poland], vol. 5, ed. D. Turkowska and M. Kowalczyk, trans. J. Mrukówna (Warsaw, 1974), 145.

30 Parente, "Tyranny and Revolution on the Baroque Stage," 310.

31 D. F. Sutton, introduction to Joseph Simons, *Theoctistus* (1654), 6 September 2013, http://www.philological.bham.ac.uk/theo/intro.html.

32 Parente, "Tyranny and Revolution on the Baroque Stage," 317.

33 Ibid., 318.

34 The title of the 1650 version was slightly different: *Ein Fürften-Mörderifches Trawer-Spiel/genant. Leo Armenius.* I have consulted a digitalized version of the first edition, available at http://www.deutschestextarchiv.de/book/view/gryphius_leoarmenius_1650?p=1.

have seen a performance of *Leo Armenus* while there. Moreover, his play bears some resemblance to the work of the English Jesuit.[35] But their use of the sources sets these two texts apart. While Simons's drama was based mostly on Baronius's *Annales*, Gryphius turns to the Byzantine historians John Zonaras and George Kedrenos, whose works were available in the editions of Hieronymous Wolf and Wilhelm Holtzmann (Xylander), respectively. Therefore, Gryphius's declaration that he based his play on the accounts of these two medieval historians is not purely an embellishment.[36] Janifer Gerl Stackhouse has shown in detail how Gryphius appropriated and adapted his historical materials.[37] His tragic *Leo Armenius* is not a "history play" in the strict sense, for it is does not attempt an accurate reconstruction of the events that led to the murder of Leo. As Karl-Heinz Habersetzer puts it, in commenting on Gryphius's other tragedy *Papianus*, here history is not limited to the facts but transcends itself "because of a statement contained in it."[38] The events described in the play are "stripped of concrete reality and frozen into a picture that is related to the universal truth."[39] In other words, like Simons's goal in his Byzantine plays, Gryphius's main purpose was not to dramatize the history of the eastern empire but rather to tell a story with contemporary relevance, be it political or moral, using Byzantium to disguise it.

35 Willi Harring presented a very detailed analysis supporting this claim. However, not all of his arguments are equally compelling. He argues for instance that the Greek word παπίας (janitor/keeper of the Palace) was transferred into a proper name in the works of both Simons and Gryphius (Harring, *Andreas Gryphius und das Drama der Jesuiten* [Halle, 1907], 67–74). However, Baronius's *Annales* might be the common source of the confusion. Contrary to what McCabe suggests (*An Introduction to the Jesuit Theatre*, 140, n. 27), Paul Stachel also acknowledges Simons's input (even if he doesn't mention him by name); see Stachel, *Seneca und das deutsche Renaissancedrama: Studien zur Literatur- und Stilgeschichte des 16. und 17. Jahrhunderts* (Berlin, 1907), 218.

36 H. Palm and F.-W. Wentzlaff-Eggebert, eds., *Andreas Gryphius: Werke in drei Bänden mit Ergänzungsband*, 4 vols. (Darmstadt, 1961), 2:16: "Die historie erzehlen weitläufftiger Cedrenus und Zonaras in ihrem Leone und Michael Balbo." Moreover, Gryphius used the material from Kedrenos to write an epigram for the wife of Maurice, comparing her to Hecuba and Niobe: "Der Kaiserin Constantinae, Mauritij Ehegemahlin Grabschrift. Aus dem Grichischen Cedreni." But we should note that, as mentioned earlier, the history of Maurice was quite well known at that time.

37 J. G. Stackhouse, *The Constructive Art of Gryphius' Historical Tragedies* (Bern, 1986), 19–23.

38 K.-H. Habersetzer, *Politische Typologie und dramatisches Exemplum: Studien zum historisch-ästhetischen Horizont des barocken Trauerspiels, am Beispiel von Andreas Gryphius' "Carolus Stuardus" und "Papinianus"* (Stuttgart, 1985), 60. See also A. Menhennet, *The Historical Experience in German Drama from Gryphius to Brecht* (Rochester, NY, 2003), 13.

39 J. H. Tisch, *Andreas Gryphius: Leo Armenius: An Inaugural Lecture Delivered before the University of Tasmania on Monday, 27th February 1967* (Hobart, 1968), 16.

At first glance, the contemporary message that Gryphius wanted to convey appears different from that of Simons. The subtitle of the Jesuit's play reads *seu Impietas Punita* (*or Impiety Punished*), while the German play has *oder Fürsten-Mord* (*or the Regicide*). These are two different messages, which emphasize two different interpretations of the same story. In the German version the Iconoclastic struggle between Leo and his opponents is downplayed. As suggested by the drama's title, the fall of Leo V—murdered by his confidant Michael Balbus (Michael "the Stammerer")—warns against the crime of regicide as a breach of human and divine justice, to give just one possible interpretation of Gryphius's complex text.[40] On the other hand, Simons's play is not a simple praise of regicide and encouragement of revolution: although Leo deserved punishment for his actions against the church, it does not follow that Michael Balbus's deeds are praiseworthy.[41]

To a certain extent, Gryphius's play might thus be read as a Protestant answer to the Catholic version of the story of Leo V.[42] But it also shows that following seventeenth-century literary norms, the same historical material—Leo V's reign and deposition—could accommodate various contradictory interpretations. This plasticity of Byzantine history, along with its largely negative valence, was to become one of the most important features of the empire's reception in early modern theater. Gryphius, much like Simons, repeats negative clichés concerning Byzantium. He explicitly states in the introduction to the play: "Nevertheless, I only have to remind you that since our Leo was a Greek Emperor he will exhibit much to his reader that is partially not praised and partially not tolerated for princes who now rule."[43]

In particular, Gryphius reiterates stereotypes about the inferiority of the Byzantines already found in medieval crusader chronicles, and such statements paved the way for later negative imagery of the Byzantine Empire. For the German playwright no less than his Jesuit counterpart, however, Byzantium itself was of little importance; it was the message the empire could convey, transcending its historical context, that counted. This message might have a moral dimension, but it could also be political. Interestingly, Andreas's son Christopher Gryphius, a pedagogue and classical philologist from Breslau, wrote a school play, *Graecorum imperium a*

40 Ibid., 5.

41 Parente, "Tyranny and Revolution on the Baroque Stage," 319.

42 As Parente notes: "Thus, *Leo Armenius* was written to counter Joseph Simons' historical tragedy, *Leo Armenus*." See J. A. Parente, *Religious Drama and the Humanist Tradition: Christian Theater in Germany and in the Netherlands, 1500–1680* (Leiden, 1987), 168.

43 Palm and Wentzlaff-Eggebert, *Andreas Gryphius: Werke in drei Bänden*, 2:13: "Gleichwol muss ich nur erinnern dass, wie unser Leo ein griechischer kaiser, also auch viel seinem leser auffweisen wird, was bey regierenden fürsten theils nicht gelobet, theils nicht gestattet wird." Translated in Stackhouse, *The Constructive Art*, 17.

Muhamede secundo eversum, or *The Greek Empire Destroyed by Mohammed the Second*. This play, performed in 1682, details the history of the fall of Constantinople.[44] The onset of the Great Turkish War, and the imminent Ottoman siege of Vienna (1683), provided the impetus for such a drama in Breslau, then under Austrian rule. In this context, contemporary events offered yet another dynamic that activated the political code of Byzantine history—namely, a Turkish attack on a Christian empire.

Act II: Sir William Killigrew et al.

In 1669 a play titled *The Imperial Tragedy Taken out of a Latin Play, and Very Much Altered* was published anonymously in England. Today, it is accepted that this play was written by Sir William Killigrew (ca. 1606–1695).[45] The author himself reveals the source of his inspiration in the prologue:

> Methinks I hear some travl'd gallant say,
> When he was last at Rome, he saw this play,
> That *Zeno* there was acted, we confess,
> And hope that here he'll have as good success.
> ....
> That model which in Italy was fram'd
> He has new moulded for our English stage,
> Hoping 'twill fit the temper of the age,
> And the learn'd Latin author not offend,
> For alt'ring what he dares not think to mend.[46]

The "learn'd Latin Author" in question is none other than Joseph Simons, and *The Imperial Tragedy* is based on Simons's successful *Zeno sive Ambitio Infelix*, which was staged throughout Europe.[47] In her article on *The Imperial Tragedy*, Alison Shell observes, regarding the Byzantine-inspired plays in Restoration drama, that

44 K. Gajek, ed., *Das Breslauer Schultheater: Das Breslauer Schultheater im 17. und 18. Jahrhundert. Einladungsschriften zu den Schulactus und Szenare zu den Aufführungen förmlicher Comödien an den protestantischen Gymnasien* (Tübingen, 1994), 93–96.

45 W. H. McCabe, "The Imperial Tragedy," *Philological Quarterly* 15.3 (1936): 311–14.

46 *The Imperial Tragedy*, http://www.philological.bham.ac.uk/killigrew/act1.html, 25 January 2014.

47 The Greek version of the play, written by an unknown author, was performed at Zakynthos in 1682 or 1683; see B. Merry, *Encyclopedia of Modern Greek Literature* (Westport, CT, 2004), 419, and more importantly W. Puchner, "Paralipomena allo Zenone," *Ausgewählte Studien zur Theaterwissenschaft Griechenlands und Südosteuropas* (Vienna, 2018), 459–63. There was also a German version of the play, "Wol-Bewärte Tugend Pelagij," performed in Lucerne in 1642. In addition, two Italian operas thematized the fate of Zeno: see W. Puchner, "Ο Ζήνων και το

"Killigrew's imaginative interest in the Byzantine period is unusual—despite the fact that it abounds in stories of courtly plotting, often with a lavish dose of the supernatural, which might have been very appealing to audiences of Tudor and Stuart professional drama."[48] Shell's characterization of Killigrew's interest in Byzantium as "unusual" is overstated, as is her example of Byzantine eccentricities—a history of Justinian and Theodora drawn from Procopius's *Anecdota*.[49] While Byzantium occupied an admittedly marginal place in the history of Restoration drama, especially in comparison to other topics, it nonetheless remained a presence.[50]

In 1642 Thomas Fuller published a very successful collection of character sketches, *The Holy State and the Profane State*. It featured a short biography of the emperor Andronikos I Komnenos (r. 1183–1185), which was later expanded as *The Life of Andronicus, or the Unfortunate Politician* (1646).[51] Fuller's source for these works was the Byzantine historian Niketas Choniates, whose account he followed quite faithfully.[52] Fuller's fascination with the Byzantine emperor was understandable: he saw Andronikos I as the medieval version of the contemporary English dictator Oliver Cromwell (1599–1658), for both men seized power through acts of regicide. Thomas Fuller also wrote a play in 1643 that dramatized the fate of this Byzantine emperor, *Andronicus: A Tragedy*, which remained unpublished until the Restoration.

Fuller's hugely popular *Life of Andronicus* sparked an interest in the life of the emperor and consequently, during the Restoration, several so-called usurper plays

πρότυπό του," *Ελληνική Θεατρολογία* (Athens, 1988), 215–97, esp. 233–42, 244. I am grateful to one of the anonymous readers for this information.

48 A. Shell, "Byzantine Tragedy in Restoration England: Joseph Simons's *Zeno* and Sir William Killigrew's *The Imperial Tragedy*," *Renaissance Studies* 30.4 (2016): 624.

49 Interestingly enough, the play titled *El ejemplo mayor de la desdicha*, penned by Antonio Mira de Amescua (1625) and detailing the story of Belisarius, was inspired by Procopius's *Anecdota*.

50 Some Byzantine plays were lost: for instance, *Phocas* by Samuel Bernard, performed in Oxford in Magdalene College, or *Andronicus*, another play by the same author. The content of the latter is unknown and the assumption that it dealt with Andronikos is only conjectural; both plays are listed in *Annals of English Drama, 975–1700*, ed. A. Harbage, rev. S. Schoenbaum and S. S. Wagonheim, 3rd ed. (Padstow, 1989), 110, 112.

51 W. L. Wesel, "Thomas Fuller: Historian" (MA thesis, University of Montana, 1966), 36. The expanded sketch, which appeared in 1646, was later incorporated into *The Holy State*. Andronikos is also mentioned in *The Holy Warre* of 1639. On the life of Andronikos, who was commonly regarded as a murderous tyrant, see H. Magoulias, "Andronikos I Komnenos: A Greek Tragedy," *Byzantina Symmeikta* 21 (2011): 101–36.

52 For *The Holy Warre* Fuller used the edition of Choniates' *History* published in Geneva in 1593, which included the translation by Hieronymus Wolf. The Bodleian Library has still the copy used by Fuller; see also J. O. Wood, "Thomas Fuller's Oxford Interlude," *Huntington Library Quarterly* 17.3 (1954): 192–93, 196.

were written:[53] John Wilson's *Andronicus Comnenius* (1664)[54] and two anonymous plays, *Andronicus Impiety's Long Success, or Heaven's Late Revenge* (1661) and *The Unfortunate Usurper* (1663). These plays, however, were based not on the account of Choniates but rather on Fuller's work. Once again, similarities with contemporary politics sparked interest in Byzantium; Byzantine history was performed because it seemed to foreshadow the current political situation. In *The Unfortunate Usurper*, the demon conjured by a character named Seth, by the end of his very long speech, is clearly speaking of England and not Byzantium:

> Shall with his Tail
> Have tossed up and down the Kingdom's ship,
> Great Charles shall by his prudence safely
> Steer it[.]
>
> (*THE UNFORTUNATE USURPER*, ACT 5, SCENE 3)[55]

If there is anything unusual in this interest in Byzantium, it is that Fuller based his *Life of Andronicus* directly on Choniates' account. As mentioned above, one of the characteristic features of the reception of Byzantium is that Byzantine motifs and inspirations were taken not from Byzantine sources, but instead from some intermediary, usually pejorative, accounts. This was clearly the case with Neville Payne's 1675 play, *The Siege of Constantinople*, which was based almost entirely on a famous, and very popular, book by Richard Knolles, *Generall Historie of the Turkes* (1603).[56] Knolles had dedicated his book to the newly crowned James I (r. 1603–1625), and he promised that this account of the "glorious Empire of the Turkes . . . the present terror of the world" might instruct James "concerning the state and good of the English commonwealth."[57] To strengthen his warning, Knolles lists the Christian kingdoms conquered by the Turks, starting with the "utter ruin and subversion of the empire of the East." Payne freely adapted his source material to write a critique of the

53 A. Harbage, *Cavalier Drama: An Historical and Critical Supplement to the Study of the Elizabethan and Restoration Stage* (New York, 1936), 187.

54 On Wilson's play see A. Hammond, "John Wilson and the Andronicus Plays: A Re-consideration," *The Yearbook of English Studies* 4 (1974): 112–19.

55 Quoted in Harbage, *Cavalier Drama*, 187.

56 In his works Knolles used texts of late Byzantine historians such as Chalkokondyles; see the extensive list of sources in V. J. Parry, *Richard Knolles' History on the Turks* (Istanbul, 2003), 32–45.

57 Richard Knolles, *The Turkish History from the Original of that Nation, to the Growth of the Ottoman Empire: With the Lives and Conquests of their Princes and Emperours*, 6th ed., 2 vols. (London, 1687–1700), 1:1. See also S. J. Owen, "Restoration Drama and Politics: An Overview," in *A Companion to Restoration Drama*, ed. idem (Oxford, 2008), 128–39.

contemporary political scene.[58] The plot of his play is rather fantastic, although there are historical elements to it. Payne describes a fictitious story of Irene, fiancée of Thomazo, the Emperor's brother, and her kidnapping by the Sultan's soldiers. Prince Thomazo manages to recapture her and, in the process, is given the kingdom of Morea by the Sultan. But Payne's drama is much more than just a love story set in the past. According to an anonymous author from 1680, Payne "composes a tragedy of a certain Emperor of Constantinople, whom he never knew; but in whose person he vilifies a certain Prince, whom he very well knows."[59] Matthew Birchwood claims that this statement is "a fairly comprehensive misreading of the play."[60] What is important for our purposes, however, is the direct acknowledgment that Byzantium was understood as a cipher used to conceal contemporary matters. The conflict between Byzantium and the Ottomans is portrayed in the play as the clash between two religions. At the beginning, the Emperor states:

> The grand concern this Council has debated
> Affects no less than all the Christian world:
> It is indeed, chuse Christ or Mahomet,
> Whose law shall have the universal sway.
>
> (*THE SIEGE OF CONSTANTINOPLE*, ACT 1)[61]

Payne's choice of the fall of Constantinople was not incidental. It is a story of a Christian state betrayed by other Christians because of theological—and consequently political—quarrels. As has been noted, it is difficult not to notice the parallel between this medieval Orthodox/Muslim rivalry and contemporary tensions between Catholics and Protestants, but *The Siege* is a multilayered work, which also mirrors the concerns and problems of post–Civil War England.[62] Ultimately, Payne's Constantinople is not substantively "Byzantine"; he is not interested in Byzantine

58 P. Monod, "A Voyage out of Staffordshire; or, Samuel Johnson's Jacobite Journey," in *Samuel Johnson in Historical Context*, ed. J. C. D. Clark and H. Erskine-Hill (New York, 2002), 19.

59 Quoted in W. Thorp, "Henry Nevil Payne, Dramatist and Jacobite Conspirator," in *Essays in Dramatic Literature: The Parrott Presentation Volume*, ed. H. Craig (Princeton, 1935), 9.

60 M. Birchwood, "Plotting the Succession: Exclusion, Oates and the News from Vienna," in his *Staging Islam in England: Drama and Culture, 1640–1685* (Cambridge, 2007), 159.

61 H. N. Payne, *The Siege of Constantinople* (London, 1675), Act 1, p. 2, https://quod.lib.umich.edu/e/eebo2/A70911.0001.001, accessed 12 October 2020.

62 A more extensive discussion on this topic, including the relation of the play to the contemporary debates on politics and language, can be found in G. D. Parker, "History as Nightmare in Nevil Payne's *The Siege of Constantinople* and Nathaniel Lee's *Lucius Junius Brutus*," *Papers on Language and Literature* 21 (1985): 3–18.

history. Byzantium is rather an oriental place par excellence, reminding potential readers of "the enigma of the Turkish Empire."[63]

Byzantium could also be appropriated by English playwrights through the translation and adaptation of preexisting plays. One such example is the tragedy *Heraclius, Emperor of the East* (1664), translated from Corneille's *Héraclius* by Lodowick Carlell (1601/2–1675). Samuel Pepys (1633–1703) mentions in his diary that he saw a performance of the play, making the interesting comment that "[t]he garments like Romans very well."[64] This is a good reminder that in the seventeenth century, Byzantium was not an entity in itself but remained legible to audiences simply as a transformed version of the Roman Empire.[65]

This brings us back to 1669, and the publication of Killigrew's *The Imperial Tragedy*. It is clear that Killigrew's interest in Byzantine themes was hardly "unusual." Sutton, for his part, claims that Killigrew's tragedy is a simplified version of Simons's Latin original.[66] As Jean-Pierre Vander Motten has pointed out, however, *The Imperial Tragedy* also represented a new kind of tragedy, one that performed its didactic function by presenting the audience with an execrable rather than an admirable example.[67] Be that as it may, Killigrew's interest in the Byzantine material is differently motivated yet again than that of Simons and Gryphius. Killigrew had no profound political or historico-philosophical agenda. He intended to build on the popularity of a well-known play that happened to be both "Byzantine" and interesting enough to be used for the author's own purposes.

Epilogue

As mentioned earlier, Voltaire's *Irène* marks, purely chronologically, the end of the use of Byzantium in early modern European drama. Samuel Johnson penned a play with the same title, *Irene* (performed in 1749), whose plot was taken from Knolles's history. Although it featured Greek (Byzantine) characters, it was not really about

63 Birchwood, "Plotting the Succession," 169.

64 *The Diary of Samuel Pepys, M.A., F.R.S.*, ed. H. B. Wheatley, vol. 4 (London, 1894), 69.

65 For a similar statement regarding 17th-century France, see Spieser, "Du Cange and Byzantium" (n. 6 above), 207. Of course, such codes and descriptions could be changed if needed—sometimes the Greek aspect of Byzantium was emphasized by referring to "Greek emperors." Often this language was used when a negative message was to be conveyed.

66 D. F. Sutton, introduction to Joseph Simons, *Zeno* (1645), 10 January 2014, http://www.philological.bham.ac.uk/zeno/intro.html.

67 J.-P. Vander Motten, "Sir Willian Killigrew's *The Imperial Tragedy* as a Transitional Play," *Studia Germanica Gandensia* 15 (1974): 202.

Byzantium.[68] It tells the story of Irene, who converts to Islam to become the queen at the court of Mehmed the Conqueror. Ultimately, she is killed when Mehmed becomes convinced that she is plotting against him. Despite its tenuous connection to Byzantine history, the play nonetheless reiterated what became the established imagery of the eastern empire. At the beginning of the text a Greek nobleman, Demetrius, comments in the following way on the fall of Constantinople:

> Demetrius.
> A thousand horrid prodigies foretold it:
> A feeble government, eluded laws,
> A factious populace, luxurious nobles,
> And all the maladies of sinking states.
> When publick villany, too strong for justice,
> Shows his bold front, the harbinger of ruin.
>
> (*Irene*, Act I)[69]

The next Byzantine play, chronologically speaking, was Joanna Baillie's *Constantine Paleologus or the Last of the Caesars*, published in 1804. Baillie's work not only reinterprets but also, to some extent, rejects Edward Gibbon's influential *History of the Decline and Fall of the Roman Empire* (1776–89) by understanding Christianity as the crucial, rather than destructive, element in the empire's history. In doing so, it opened up new vistas for the next generation of writers. Baillie, much like earlier authors, uses the fall of Constantinople to discuss contemporary social and political issues, including how to define the relationship between the state and the people in the wake of the Napoleonic wars, and how to deal with the atrocities of the French Revolution.[70]

Gibbon's *Decline and Fall of the Roman Empire* became for nineteenth-century century writers what Baronius's history was for early modern playwrights. A plethora of early nineteenth-century dramas on the fall of Constantinople were written

68 See D. N. Smith, *Samuel Johnson's "Irene"* (Oxford, 1929); B. Moran, "The Irene Story and Dr. Johnson's Sources," *Modern Language Notes* 7.2 (1956): 87–91. Johnson considered this play to be his greatest failure. Extant contemporary texts also discuss *Irene* in a fairly critical way; see *Samuel Johnson: The Critical Heritage*, ed. J. T. Boulton (1971; repr., London, 2002), 51–62.

69 S. Johnson, *Irene*, in *The British Drama Comprehending the Best Plays in the English Language* (London, 1804), 609. Interestingly enough, the same passage became the epigraph to Chapter 1 of the first modern novel whose plot was set in Byzantium—*Count Robert of Paris* (1832) by Sir Walter Scott.

70 See, e.g., B. H. Friedmann-Romell, "Staging the State: Joanna Baillie's *Constantine Paleologus*," in *Women and Playwriting in Nineteenth-Century Britain*, ed. T. C. Davis and E. Donkin (Cambridge, 1999), 151–73.

in England, Greece, Germany, and Denmark by authors who drew inspiration from Gibbon's work. These authors became interested in the fall during the War of Greek Independence (1821–32).[71] As I argued earlier, Byzantium's latent potential as a political code was activated by a contemporary situation. Although both the historical circumstances and the main source of inspiration for this activation changed, its mechanism remained the same, and playwrights continued to demonstrate a lack of interest in Byzantium as such. This situation changed only in the last decades of the nineteenth century, when Byzantine studies were consolidated into an independent discipline and Byzantium entered the popular imagination on a much larger scale than before.[72] Victorien Sardou's *Theodora* (1884), an immensely popular play based on the life of the sixth-century empress, embodies this new trend. In displaying an interest in Byzantium as such, this play stands in sharp contrast to the earlier works. Sardou's Byzantine Empire is no longer simply a metaphor for contemporary concerns; rather, it is a historically grounded entity worthy of interest its own right.

Byzantium in early modern theater was by no means a marginal topic. While its function could range from the didactic—a repository of some good and many bad examples—to the political, each individual manifestation of its use was different, and its reception was shaped by local, political, and social conditions. As Constantinos Patrides notes, Catholic surveys of history cited the Ottoman conquest of "proud Bizantium" as the capital proof of God's vengeance against schismatics.[73] This, in turn, implied that Protestants might meet a similar fate one day. Moreover, Renaissance authors and audiences (not unlike medieval ones) perceived the world as full of divine scourges—which "ranged," in the words of S. R. Arjana, "from Timur, particularly under his Marlovian guise as Tamburlaine, to the less probable instance of lawyers. But the most consistent invocation of the traditional theory was made in connection with the Ottoman Empire."[74] The Turkish danger, in both the sixteenth and seventeenth centuries, made Byzantium interesting, because it could provide the Europeans with insights regarding the Ottoman Empire.[75]

71 On the plays on this topic, see W. Puchner, "Der Fall Konstantinopels in der europäischen und griechischen Dramatik," in his *Ausgewählte Studien zur Theaterwissenschaft Griechenlands und Südosteuropas* (Vienna, 2018), 105–15.

72 See L. Leveque, "La Vision de Byzance chez les historiens du XIXe siècle, en France, en Angleterre et en Allemagne" (PhD diss., Toulouse, 1999).

73 C. A. Patrides, *Premises and Motifs in Renaissance Thoughts and Literature* (Princeton, 1982), 142.

74 S. R. Arjana, *Muslims in the Western Imagination* (Oxford, 2015), 45.

75 As John Haldon put it, "it was to Byzantine authors and texts that Renaissance scholars and leaders turned when they wanted to find out about the Ottomans and how to deal with them" (A. Louth, J. Haldon, R. Webb, J. Loweden, and D. Womersley, "Taking a Leaf from Gibbon: Appraising Byzantium," *Dialogos: Hellenic Studies Review* 6 [2000]: 143).

The salient feature of Byzantium's use in early modern theater was its *ahistoricity*.[76] This was partly a consequence of how playwrights such as Gryphius understood history and its uses. Transforming Byzantine history into a series of emblematic events whose significance transcended their immediate contemporary (i.e., Byzantine) context was crucial to the project of using Byzantium for various, often contradictory, purposes. In this way, Byzantium could be appropriated by Catholics and Protestants alike. Byzantium, the Empire of the East or the Oriental Empire, was not interesting per se. To paraphrase Stendhal, it was interesting inasmuch as it could provide a mirror for each author's own agenda. The authors of Byzantine plays often relied on intermediaries—be they secondary (that is, not Byzantine) historians such as Baronius, or texts that stood between the real and imaginary, such as political pamphlets or even other plays. Today almost all of these "Byzantine plays" have fallen into oblivion; in their own times, however, at least some of them were very popular. We know little about the audiences for such plays, but it seems safe to assume that these plays (as well as operas) reached a much wider audience than the rarified works of historians. Therefore, it could be argued that by disseminating negative associations with Byzantium, works such as Simons's *Leo Armenus* or Fuller's *Andronicus* played a crucial if underappreciated role in the slow but steady process (already under way in the Middle Ages)[77] of imprinting adverse stereotypes about the eastern empire in the common imagination.

76 This was clearly the case in Jean Gambert de Campistron's drama *Andronic* (1685), in which the author is so uninterested in historical accuracy that one of the protagonists is called simply Paleologos I and the Byzantine characters are in fact Prince Don Carlos and his father, Philip II of Spain, in disguise.

77 See, e.g., S. Runciman, *The Emperor Romanus Lecapenus and His Reign: A Study of Tenth-Century Byzantium* (Cambridge, 1988), 27: "Ever since our rough crusading forefathers first saw Constantinople and met, to their contemptuous disgust, a society where everyone read and wrote, ate food with forks and preferred diplomacy to war, it has been fashionable to pass the Byzantines by with scorn and to use their name as synonymous with decadence." For a more detailed analysis see M. Carrier, "L'image du Grec selon les chroniquers des croisades: Perceptions et reaction face au cérémoniel byzantine 1096 à 1204" (PhD diss., Sherbrooke, 2000).

PART THREE

CATEGORIZING AND CONTEXTUALIZING BYZANTIUM, CA. 1500–1750

EIGHT

THE LEXICOGRAPHY OF BYZANTINE GREEK FROM ANNA NOTARAS TO JOHANNES MEURSIUS

JOHN CONSIDINE

THE FUNDAMENTAL CHALLENGE OF THE LEXICOGRAPHY OF GREEK IN EARLY modern Europe was the challenge that is always present in the lexicography of a well-documented language with multiple overlapping varieties: how—and whether—to differentiate one variety from another. In the case of Greek, as the great length of its written tradition became apparent to scholars in Latinate Europe, so too did the possibility of chronological differentiation—in other words, of periodization. The theory and practice of the engagement with later Greek by early modern makers and readers of dictionaries developed slowly, from a first encounter with the dictionaries produced in the Byzantine world, in which they were seen simply as guides to ancient Greek, to the eventual emergence of a sense that Byzantine authors used a distinctive vocabulary that might call for treatment in separate, periodized dictionaries.

The story of that development will be told here in five chronologically overlapping sections. The first will show how the early printed editions of the great Byzantine dictionaries, which appeared from 1499 onward, were initially received as guides to ancient Greek, and then, gradually, as works that had their own place in the history of the Greek language, and that might therefore include words which were comparatively recent. The second and third sections will present the envisioning of very different dictionaries of later Greek by two scholars in the mid-sixteenth century: Hieronymus Wolf, who worked on pre-contemporary written texts, and Martin Crusius, who worked on the contemporary Greek language, as spoken by informants and printed in popular texts. The subject of the fourth section is the use of dictionaries from the Byzantine world, and the inclusion and exclusion of the Greek of Byzantine authors, by Henri Estienne in his *Thesaurus graecae linguae,* published in 1572. The fifth gives an account of the compilation of the first printed dictionaries of Byzantine Greek by Nicolas Rigault and Johannes Meursius, published in 1601 and 1610 respectively, with a second edition of the latter in 1614.[1] From the work of Meursius, a further step might of course be taken to the wonderful *Glossarium ad scriptores mediae et infimae graecitatis* of Charles Du Cange, published in 1688. But it might be said that the subject treated by Du Cange had already been defined by Meursius: that is why, for instance, Meursius's work was placed first in Karl Krumbacher's chronological account of the dictionaries useful for the reader of *byzantinische Literatur.*[2]

A prehistory of a social construct—a nation, a language, a discipline—is always embarrassed by a sort of double vision: what we see with our own eyes is never the same as what we try to see through the eyes of the actors. To take an example from the lexicography that is the subject of this chapter, Meursius's sources for his dictionary ranged from Hesychius of Alexandria to sixteenth-century Venetian imprints in contemporary Greek. That is intelligible to a modern reader with a concept of Byzantine studies. But "Byzantine studies" was surely not a fully developed concept for Meursius, let alone for most sixteenth-century readers of a source of Meursius's such as the *Novels of Justinian I,* and it would have been quite alien to any fifteenth-century reader of the first edition of the *Etymologicum magnum.* Likewise, "the inclusion and exclusion of the Greek of Byzantine authors" was not, as such, a conscious concern of Henri Estienne's. So, although I think that it makes sense to apply "Byzantine" retrospectively both to the Greek texts of the period from late antiquity to the fifteenth century and to the Greek language as used in those texts, and to see how early modern lexicographers understood those texts and their language, I note that I am not working with a category available to the actors when I do so.

The First Editions of the Byzantine Dictionaries

The *Lexicon* of Hesychius, the *Suda,* and the *Etymologicum magnum* were all read in manuscript in early modern Latinate Europe before they were made available in

1 I have discussed the 16th-century lexicography of modern Greek and the early 17th-century lexicography of Byzantine Greek from other perspectives in my *Small Dictionaries and Curiosity: Lexicography and Fieldwork in Post-medieval Europe* (Oxford, 2017), 79–82, and *Dictionaries in Early Modern Europe: Lexicography and the Making of Heritage* (Cambridge, 2008), 250–56, respectively; a few paragraphs of this chapter rework material from those discussions.

2 K. Krumbacher, *Geschichte der byzantinischen Litteratur* (Munich, 1891), 395.

printed editions.[3] For our purposes, we may call even the earliest of these works a Byzantine dictionary, as Robert Browning did in the *Oxford Dictionary of Byzantium*, and as Stefano Valente does in the *Cambridge World History of Lexicography*.[4] The *Ethnica* of Stephen of Byzantium was also read in manuscript in fifteenth-century Italy, but whether we see this as a highly specialized dictionary or as an encyclopedia, it is rather different from the other texts to be discussed in this chapter, and will not be noticed further below.[5] Nor will extended attention be given to bilingual word lists such as the late antique Latin–Greek dictionary sometimes known as *Ps. Philoxenus*, and to the Greek–Latin dictionary sometimes, and confusingly, known as *Ps. Cyril* (it has nothing to do with the monolingual Greek lexicon ascribed to St. Cyril in some manuscripts); these, although they have their wellspring in the Byzantine world, are at some distance from the main currents of Byzantine lexicography.[6]

The first Greek–Latin dictionaries of the fifteenth century, which were in the business of providing simple Latin glosses for Greek words, did not borrow extensively from Byzantine lexicography, although some had sporadic additions from the Greek–Latin *Ps. Cyril*.[7] The slender boughs of their lexicographical structure would have been overburdened if older wood heavily laden with the fruits of Byzantine scholarship had been grafted onto them. The *Lexicon* prepared for the press by Giovanni Crastone or Crastoni, first published before 28 March 1478, stood at the head of a long tradition of printed Greek–Latin dictionaries, enlarged from edition to edition, a number of which were given the title *Lexicon graecolatinum*, which may stand as a name for the tradition as a whole. As we will see, though their foundation was not Byzantine, they had material added to them from the printed Byzantine dictionaries.

From 1499 onward, major Byzantine dictionaries began to be made available in printed editions. The first was the *Etymologicum magnum*, published at Venice by Zacharias Kallierges, in a tall folio of 224 leaves.[8] A prefatory text by Marcus Musurus pointed out that the publication had been undertaken entirely by Greeks,

3 P. Botley, *Learning Greek in Western Europe, 1396–1529: Grammars, Lexica, and Classroom Texts* (Philadelphia, 2010), 55–61.

4 *ODB*, s.v. "Hesychios of Alexandria" and "Lexika" (R. Browning); S. Valente, "Byzantine Greek," in *The Cambridge World History of Lexicography*, ed. J. Considine (Cambridge, 2019), 247–66.

5 Botley, *Learning Greek in Western Europe*, 60–61.

6 For these bilingual word lists, see A. C. Dionisotti, "Greek Grammars and Dictionaries in Carolingian Europe," in *The Sacred Nectar of the Greeks: The Study of Greek in the West in the Early Middle Ages*, ed. M. W. Herren with S. A. Brown (London, 1988), 1–56, at 6–13.

7 Botley, *Learning Greek in Western Europe*, 65.

8 The copy sold at Christie's, New York, 9–10 April 2013, was 416 × 276 mm.

and indeed Anna Notaras, one of its financial backers, was a child of the Byzantine Empire itself rather than the Byzantine diaspora; she was born in Constantinople before 1453, the daughter of the *megas doux* Loukas Notaras.[9] This book is dated 8 July 1499; the *Suda* appeared in an edition of 800 copies on 15 November of the same year, edited by Demetrios Chalkokondyles and printed in Milan. By 1503 Aldus Manutius—who had already published Guarino Favorino's *Thesaurus cornu copiae,* a rearrangement of material from Byzantine grammatical texts and commentaries (notably Eustathios), in 1496—seems to have acquired the unsold copies of both editions.[10] In February 1514 he published a new edition of the *Suda,* which was based on a better manuscript than that used for the *princeps,* and which was joined in August of the same year by the *princeps* of Hesychius, edited by Musurus. Thereafter, Hesychius went through two more editions in rapid succession, published by the house of Giunti in Florence in 1520 and by Thomas Anshelm in Hagenau in the following year; the latter was reissued, perhaps in Basel, around 1530. Although it was not in itself a Byzantine dictionary, the *Magnum et perutile dictionarium* of Favorino, published in 1523, was very much a compilation from Byzantine sources, many of them unpublished.[11]

But then there was a sudden deceleration: six complete editions of major Byzantine dictionaries, plus the dictionary of Favorino, were printed in the 25 years beginning in 1499 and ending in 1523, and only nine more, plus a second edition of Favorino, in the next 145 years. A second edition of the *Etymologicum magnum* did not appear until 1549, and a third in 1594. A third edition of the *Suda* was published in 1544 (Hieronymus Wolf also extracted material of historical significance from the *Suda,* published with a facing Latin translation as *Suidae historica* in editions of 1564 and 1581), and a Graeco-Latin edition appeared in 1619, reissued in 1630. After that, there was no new edition of the *Etymologicum magnum* or of the *Suda* until the eighteenth century. Hesychius appeared in a Geneva edition of 1607, the rarity of which suggests that only a few copies were printed; it was not until 1668 that a new edition became widely available to succeed the three of 1514–21.

An explanation for the decline in the production of editions of Byzantine dictionaries after 1521 is that in that year, the addition of material from the *Suda* and Hesychius to dictionaries in the *Lexicon graecolatinum* tradition started to be widely acknowledged. One of these, edited by Valentino Curio and published in Basel in

9 On Anna Notaras, see D. M. Nicol, *The Byzantine Lady: Ten Portraits, 1250–1500* (Cambridge, 1994), 96–109, esp. 106.

10 They are in his catalog of that year: see A. A. Renouard, *Annales de l'imprimerie des Alde,* 3rd ed. (Paris, 1834), 334.

11 See A. Guida, "Il Dictionarium di Favorino e il Lexicon Vindobonense," *Prometheus* 8 (1982): 264–86, esp. 273, n. 23.

1519, already cited Hesychius occasionally, for instance as an authority for the sense *unigenitus* (only begotten) of ἀγαπητός, and its successor, published in Paris in 1521, remarked explicitly that most of the additions to the 1519 dictionary had come from Hesychius and the *Suda*.[12] Curio countered in the next edition of his dictionary, published in the following year, that it included words which were not even to be found in these sources, implying perhaps, and if so falsely, that his dictionary had absorbed all their material.[13] The early editions of the Byzantine dictionaries had been presented, and received, as contributions to the study of ancient Greek in general. Once dictionaries in the *Lexicon graecolatinum* tradition could claim to have absorbed those contributions, they could drive the Byzantine dictionaries out of the market.

Even the sixteenth-century editors of the Byzantine dictionaries showed little interest in their age, the particular kind of Greek that they documented, or their textual integrity. So it was that Aldus Manutius's brother-in-law Federico Torresani stated on the title page of the 1549 *Etymologicum magnum* that he had improved it by adding numerous new entries, which he marked with maniculi, and the learned Friedrich Sylburg retained the added entries in his edition of 1594, changing the maniculi to asterisks.[14]

But this early editorial willingness to interpolate was followed at no great interval by its converse: an awareness that a text like the one transmitted in the single extant manuscript of the *Lexicon* of Hesychius might be the product of the lexicography of different periods, or in other words that it might be seen as an ancient base text with later interpolations. So, by the end of the sixteenth century Isaac Casaubon argued that Hesychius was a Christian, remarking that there were persons who disagreed with this judgment: those who disagreed were surely aware of the Christian material in the *Lexicon*, but they regarded the dictionary as the work of a late pagan compiler, to which the Christian material had been added.[15] Readers who accepted that the Christian elements in the *Lexicon* were not ipso facto interpolations might still argue, as did Caspar Barth in the mid-seventeenth century, that it included much

12 *Dictionarium graecum* (1521), quoted in Botley, *Learning Greek in Western Europe*, 68–69: *omnia, praesertim quae recens adiecta erant, reposuisse ex Hesychii, Suidae, aliorum lectione.*

13 Valentino Curio, *Lexicon graecum iam secundum* (Basel, 1522), sig. a1v: *dictionum ingentem numerum . . . quorum bona pars non modo in uulgatis dictionarijs, sed in Suida etiam, atq[ue] Hesychio, non proderentur.*

14 Federico Torresani, *Magnum etymologicum Graecae linguae* (Venice, 1549), title page: *innumerabilibus pene dictionibus locupletatum. Quas ut facilius cognoscere Lector possit, singulis manus index est apposita*; Friedrich Sylburg, *Etymologicon magnum* ([Heidelberg], 1594).

15 Isaac Casaubon, *Animadversionum in Athenaei Dipnosophistas libri XV* (Lyon, 1600), 19: *doctissimum illum grammaticum scimus fuisse Christianu[m], contra quam sit quibusdam visum.*

material which should be ejected from the text as belonging to a later age.[16] This led to considerable doubt as to the date of the original compilation of the *Lexicon*: at the end of the seventeenth century, the orientalist Thomas Hyde did not know whether Julius Pollux or Hesychius came first; and well into the eighteenth century, Johannes Alberti thought Hyde's uncertainty worth citing, and admitted that his own belief that Hesychius might belong to the fifth century depended on an assessment of the degree of interpolation in the extant text.[17] The whole concept of the *Lexicon* as an ancient text with later interpolations depended on a sense that a line could be drawn between works that were "ancient" (including some early Christian texts, at least for those who saw Hesychius as a Christian author) and works that were "later." This line might, at least by the seventeenth century, be defined in terms of language. In 1660 Tannegui Le Fèvre thus warned readers of the *Lexicon* that "in that most precious treasury of Greek, we find rubbishy scraps from the *graecum vulgare* which is now called Romaic":[18] to his eyes, some later Greek lexical items in the text of Hesychius as he knew it stood out in sharp contrast to the classical language. As we will see, he was writing at a time when—quite apart from other advances in the understanding of the development of the Greek language from antiquity onward—a good dictionary of Byzantine and post-Byzantine Greek was available to support the kind of distinction that he was making.

Before leaving the topic of the first printed editions of Byzantine dictionaries, we should add that those which remained in manuscript throughout the early modern period might nevertheless circulate in that form. As Paul Botley has shown, for instance, the *codex Galeanus* of the *Lexicon* of Photios was read by Scaliger in Leiden, by Casaubon in Paris, and by others, thanks to the generosity of its then owner, Richard Thomson.[19] Manuscripts and printed books might coexist: Henri Estienne owned and, as we will see, used a manuscript of the *Etymologicum magnum*, which he made available to Sylburg for use in his edition.[20] But it was through the

16 Caspar Barth, *Adversariorum commentariorum libri LX* (Frankfurt am Main, 1648), col. 1918, suspects that a given word *ut glossema posterioris aevi ejicienda sit, ut plurimae insunt luculento operi, quas nullo negotio per paginas singulas deprehendas.*

17 Thomas Hyde, *De ludis orientalibus*, 2 vols. (Oxford, 1694), 2:156: *Hunc [Pollucem] fortassis (vel vice versa, ut solent Lexicographi ex se invicem exscribere,) secutus est Hesychius*; J. Alberti, in Hesychius, *Lexicon*, vol. 1 (Leiden, 1746), sig. ††1r.

18 Tannegui Le Fèvre, in *Anacreontis et Sapphonis Carmina*, ed. Le Fèvre (Saumur, 1660), 117: *Addam et hoc monitum, reperiri in illo pretiosissimo Hellenismi thesauro carbones ex Graeco vulgari, quod hodie Ρωμαϊκὸν vocant.*

19 P. Botley, *Richard "Dutch" Thomson, c. 1569–1613: The Life and Letters of a Renaissance Scholar* (Leiden, 2016), 86–89.

20 Henri Estienne cites this manuscript as *Lexicon meum vetus*: e.g., in *Thesaurus Graecae linguae*, 5 vols. ([Geneva], 1572), 5 [index]:col. 307, where he reports its statement that αἰθερίως means

medium of printed books that knowledge of the Byzantine lexicographical tradition circulated most freely.

Hieronymus Wolf

An early attempt to assign a date to the *Suda* was made, as one might expect, by Hieronymus Wolf, who wrote in the preface to the *Suidae historica* of 1564 that he supposed the compiler to have lived "not much after the emperors Honorius and Arcadius,"[21] who ruled jointly between 393 and 408. His thoughts on the subject then developed, and in his marked-up copy of the first edition of the *Suidae historica,* he corrected the reference to Honorius and Arcadius to read "diu post Justinianum," thus moving the date from the early fifth century into the sixth or later.[22] By the time of the second edition, published in 1581, he had considered the internal evidence for the dating of the *Suda* further, and altered his preface accordingly: "since [the compiler] cites Metochites the Logothete, who lived under the Palaeologi, it appears that he compiled this lexicon scarcely three hundred years ago" (in other words, in the later thirteenth century).[23] A century later, Richard Bentley was able to draw on a richer and more precise understanding of the chronology of the Byzantine world to correct Wolf's revised date: "*Logotheta* indeed is quoted, but not the *Logotheta,* that Wolfius understood, *Theodorus Metochita Logotheta,* that died 1332, but *Symeon Metaphrastes Logotheta,* that flourished in the beginning of the 10th Century."[24] What concerns us here is not that Wolf got the date of the *Suda* wrong, but that he sought to ascertain the date at all—and thereby to see the *Suda* as a Byzantine document, the product of a particular time and hence a particular cultural world, and not simply as a timeless aid to the understanding of the ancient world.

By the time that Wolf first tried to ascertain the date of the *Suda,* he had been using material from it for nearly thirty years. The first Greek dictionary he ever owned had been a work in the *Lexicon graecolatinum* tradition, edited by Gisbert

---

the same as καθαρῶς. Sylburg refers to it in *Etymologicon magnum,* iii–iv (in the issue with preliminary matter numbered iii–viii).

21 *Suidae historica,* ed. and trans. Hieronymus Wolf (Basel, 1564), 5: *non multo post Honorium et Arcadiu[m] Impp. uixisse conijcio.*

22 The annotation is reported from Augsburg, Staats- und Stadtbibliothek, 2 LG 341, in G. C. Mezger, *Memoria Hieronymi Wolfii* (Augsburg, 1862), 71; page images of this copy are available online at digitale-sammlungen.de.

23 *Suidae historica,* ed. and trans. Hieronymus Wolf, 2nd ed. (Basel, 1581), 4: *cum Metochiten Logothetam citet, qui sub Pal[a]eologis uixit: apparet, eum uix annis ab hinc CCC Lexicon hoc composuisse.*

24 Richard Bentley, *A Dissertation upon the Epistles of Phalaris,* 2nd ed. (London, 1699), 23; the quotations in the *Suda* are from the Metaphrastian *Menologion.*

Longeuil, which he had bought in 1533, the year of its publication, when he had just turned seventeen, and a prefatory epistle to this work boasted the addition of "gleanings from the *Suda*, Pollux, and Hesychius," all of which were indeed cited from time to time in its text.[25]

In 1564 Wolf had, however, been studying Byzantine texts intensely only for less than a decade, beginning with the edition of the chronicle of Zonaras that he published in March 1557. The making of this edition had been undertaken at the urging of his employer Johann Jakob Fugger, after three manuscripts of Zonaras had entered the Fugger family library. One of these manuscripts included a text of the *History* of Niketas Choniates, which Wolf was invited to edit once he had finished Zonaras.[26] Another manuscript of Choniates was also in the Fugger library, and a third was in the Augsburg Stadtbibliothek, where Wolf was about to take up the position of librarian as he worked on his edition; Wolf consulted all three. The Stadtbibliothek manuscript was in fact a copy of the metaphrase of the *History* of Choniates, a transposition of the original text into a simplified, declassicized linguistic register, and Wolf found it very difficult to read.[27] He regarded it as the original text of the work, not, I think, on account of a "general prejudice that the Byzantines could only write a barbarised version of Greek"[28]—the editor of Zonaras knew that not all Byzantine Greek has a very strong vernacular flavor—but because he expected rewriting to make a difficult text easier, not the other way around, and therefore concluded that the version of Choniates which he, as a reader trained in classical Greek, found more difficult must precede the one which he found less difficult. So it was that he called Choniates *semibarbarus* in his *Commentariolum de vita sua*, remarking there that the dialect he used "has so many *verba et phrases barbaras*, not understood by me, that I could not have translated it had not someone else (Alexander Chartophylax of Byzantium, I believe) written the paraphrase which is available in print."[29] Cataloging the Augsburg manuscript of the metaphrase, he likewise saw its

25 *Lexicon Graecolatinum*, ed. Gisbert Longeuil (Köln, 1533), sig. π4v: *racemationem ex Suida, Polluce, Hesychio*. For Wolf's purchase of this dictionary, see his *Commentariolum de vita sua* in J. J. Reiske, *Oratores Graeci*, 12 vols. (Leipzig, 1770–75), 8:772–876, at 796.

26 For Wolf, Zonaras, and Choniates, see D. R. Reinsch, "Hieronymus Wolf as Editor and Translator of Byzantine Texts," in *The Reception of Byzantium in European Culture since 1500*, ed. P. Marciniak and D. C. Smythe (New York, 2016), 43–53, at 46–49; quotation at 48.

27 For a discussion of the metaphrase, see J. Davis, "Anna Komnene and Niketas Choniates 'Translated': The Fourteenth-Century Byzantine Metaphrases," in *History as Literature in Byzantium: Papers from the Fortieth Spring Symposium of Byzantine Studies, University of Birmingham, March 2007*, ed. R. Macrides (Farnham, Surrey, 2010), 55–70.

28 Reinsch, "Hieronymus Wolf as Editor and Translator," 48.

29 Wolf, *Commentariolum de vita sua*, 859: *exstat enim in Augustana bibliotheca Choniates, vsitata tum dialecto, quae plurima verba et phrases barbaras, mihi non intellectas, habet, nec a me conuerti*

language as *graecobarbarus*, and likewise added that the text had been written out "in Greek" by Alexander Chartophylax.[30]

Wolf's use of *barbarus* and its derivatives *graecobarbarus* and *semibarbarus* is early: such forms became common in discussions of Byzantine Greek from the later sixteenth century to the eighteenth, but I have not noticed them used before 1557 (Conrad Gessner remarked two years earlier that modern Greek differed from the ancient language owing to the admixture of *vocabula barbara*, but he simply called the modern language *lingua graeca hodie uulgaris*).[31] In classical Latin, *barbarus* is used of language that falls short of the highest standards: Quintilian remarked that it might be applied to words which had been borrowed into Latin from less prestigious languages such as Gaulish, and Aulus Gellius said that *barbarum* was used of language in his day in the sense in which *rusticum* had been used previously.[32] Wolf's vision of the quality of the Greek of Choniates was harsher than that: "The purity and essential character of the Greek language has been corrupted both by intercourse with foreign nations and by the incompetence of idle persons."[33] The English word *barbarous* has even more strongly negative connotations, and I will therefore leave *barbarus* and its derivatives untranslated in this chapter; as I will argue toward the end of the chapter, I am not sure that early modern writers after Wolf intended these words in a sense as pejorative as his own, let alone in one approximating the range of senses in which the English word is generally used.

Wolf's belief that the *semibarbarus* or *graecobarbarus* vocabulary of Choniates had been transposed into Greek by Alexander led him to introduce the index of his edition with words that were to ring in the ears of later Byzantinists:

> The *barbarica uocabula* noted from the ancient manuscript will not be found in this edition, but only the Greek words by which they are

---

potuisset, nisi alius quispiam (Alexander Chartophylax Byzantinus, vt opinor) paraphrasin eam, quae edita est, conscripsisset.

30 *Catalogus graecorum librorum manuscriptorum Augustanae bibliothecae* (Augsburg, 1575), sig. A4v (item 65): *Nicetae Acominati historiae Byzantinae libri aliquot graecobarbari. (Hos Alexander Chartophylax Byzantinus graece descripsi . . .).*

31 Conrad Gessner, *Mithridates* (Zurich, 1555), fol. 46v: *Lingua Graeca hodie uulgaris . . . a uetere Graeca recessit tum uocabulis barbaris admixtis [etc.]*. Marc D. Lauxtermann, in stating that Gessner says that Greek "has become a barbaric language" ("Of Frogs and Hangmen: The Production and Reception of the *Corona preciosa*," *BMGS* 35.2 [2011]: 170–84, at 174), goes a little further than Gessner's actual words.

32 Quintilian, *Institutiones oratoriae* 1.5.8; Aulus Gellius, *Noctes Atticae* 13.6.2.

33 Hieronymus Wolf, in Niketas Choniates, *LXXXVI annorum historia*, ed. and trans. Wolf (Basel, 1557), sig. α4r: *Graeci sermonis puritas et proprietas, cum exterarum nationu[m] commercijs, tum ociosorum hominum ineptijs corrupta est.*

> explained. Where no translation is given of these, or they are marked with a *, the reader should understand that their sense is unknown or in doubt. Therefore I request those who are expert in the *lingua corrupta* that, since there are more recent writers in which *barbara uocabula* occur, they should compile a *Barbaricum Lexicon*, in which the *uoces barbarae* would be placed first and the Greek [equivalents] subjoined, lest those who are expert only in the ancient language should be deterred from the reading of these writers.[34]

This passage was copied out on an endpaper of the historian Matthias Bernegger's copy of the second edition of the *Glossarium graecobarbarum* of Meursius in the early seventeenth century; it was reprinted at the beginning of Charles du Cange's *Glossarium* in 1688; and it was quoted again at the close of the foreword to one of the Greek dictionaries of Skarlatos Vyzantios in 1857.[35]

Wolf was calling for a dictionary in which later written Greek would be glossed with classical Greek and not with Latin, which was to be undertaken therefore by a person well acquainted with both varieties of the language: perhaps a Greek? The written Greek that he saw as in need of glossing was not so much the classicizing literary Greek of Byzantine high culture as the declassicized Greek of the metaphrasis of Choniates. So, although Wolf's appeal was quoted with evident approval by Du Cange, Du Cange's dictionary was not exactly what was being called for. But Wolf appears to have been the first person to see that a separate dictionary would be useful for the reading of Byzantine texts, and Du Cange was right to honor him on that account.

Martin Crusius

Like Hieronymus Wolf, Martin Crusius first became aware of Byzantine dictionaries toward the end of his schooldays: in a note on Lucas and Anna Notaras, he

34 Wolf, in ibid., sig. F1v: *Barbarica uocabula ex uetusto codice annotata, in hoc Opere non reperiuntur: sed Graeca duntaxat, quibus illa explicantur. Quibus ubi nulla interpretatio adijcitur, aut * apponitur, sciat lector significatione[m] eius nobis uel ignotam esse, uel dubiam. Rogo autem eos qui corruptae linguae periti sunt, ut propter recentiores scriptores in quibus subinde barbara uocabula occurrunt, Barbaricum Lexicon conficiant, uocibus barbaris praepositis, et graecis subiunctis, ne ueteris duntaxat linguae periti, ab eorum lectione deterreantur.*

35 The annotation to Bernegger's Meursius is reproduced in U. Moennig, "Matthias Berneggers Handexemplar des *Glossarium graecobarbarum* des Ioannes Meursius mit Korrekturen des Metrophanes Kritopulos," in *Graeca recentiora in Germania: Deutsch-griechische Kulturbeziehungen vom 15. bis 19. Jahrhundert*, ed. H. Eideneier, Wolfenbütteler Forschungen 59 (Wiesbaden, 1994), 161–98, at 190; Du Cange, *Glossarium ad scriptores mediae et infimae graecitatis* (Lyon, 1688), sig. π2v; S. Vyzantios, Λεξικον της καθ'ημας ελληνικη διαλεκτου (Athens, 1857), p. ζ'.

recollects that he often saw a copy of the 1499 edition of the *Etymologicum magnum* in the possession of his teacher Gregor Leonhardt of Ulm.[36] In 1557, the year of Wolf's editions of Zonaras and Choniates, Crusius had had the opportunity to speak for an hour to a Greek traveler and thus to get a sense of the contemporary Greek language; in 1562, he had obtained an incomplete manuscript of the fourteenth-century poem *Libistros and Rhodamne*, which is written in vernacular Greek (he called its language *Barbarograecum*); in 1564, friends had sent him some Greek books from Venice, including the *Didachai* of Alexios Rartouros, printed in 1560, a collection of sermons in somewhat archaizing ecclesiastical prose.[37] This last textual encounter fired his interest in vernacular Greek. It is to the point that Crusius mentions it together with his reading of *Libistros and Rhodamne*: just as a fourteenth-century declassicizing text had made Wolf wish for a dictionary, so a fourteenth-century vernacular text was part of the story of Crusius's linguistic curiosity.

In his *Turcograecia* of 1584, Crusius distinguished three kinds of Greek: the *antiqua et pura*, which is still an object of study but is not in active use; the *ecclesiastica*, used by priests and learned persons, which has *admixta barbara*; and the *vulgaris*, used by the common people.[38] A learned and thoughtful account of Crusius's study of the *vulgaris lingua graeca* has argued that his subject is better discussed as *frühneugriechisch* than as the *postbyzantinische Volkssprache*.[39] From our point of view, that may certainly be so. But Crusius himself saw the *vulgaris lingua* as having already existed centuries before the end of the Byzantine Empire. It was, he remarked, corrupt; and the corruption was long-standing. So it is, he pointed out, that in the *Suda*, ἠπήτριον is glossed τὸ σουβλίον, a word that evidently comes from Latin *subula* (awl): here, it is interesting to see Crusius treating the metalanguage of the *Suda*

36 Martin Crusius, *Turcograeciae libri octo* (Basel, 1584), 55: born in 1526, Crusius was Leonhardt's student between 1540 and 1545, and *Intra eos annos hunc libru[m] saepe apud eum uideram.*

37 For the encounter of 1557 and the books received in 1564, see U. Moennig, "On Martinus Crusius's Collection of Greek Vernacular and Religious Books," *BMGS* 21 (1997): 40–78, at 44–48; for the readings of the 1560s, see Crusius, *Turcograecia*, 489: *Vulgaris linguae graecae cupido magis me incessit 1564. quo anno amici mei . . . Iliadem Homeri[,] διδαχὰς Rarturi, Alexandrum M[agnum] et alios id genus minores libellos, e Veneta urbe mihi miserunt. . . . Antea uero 1562. fragmentum manusc[riptum] Barbarograecu[m], de amore Lybistri et Rhodamnae, inspiciendum, e Nyrtingae oppido acceperam.* The assessment of the language of the *Didachai* is from P. Toufexis, *Das "Alphabetum vulgaris linguae graecae" des deutschen Humanisten Martin Crusius (1526–1607): Ein Beitrag zur Erforschung der mündlichen griechischen Sprache im 16. Jh.* (Cologne, 2005), 68.

38 Crusius, *Turcograecia*, 273: *Lingua graeca, ut intelligimus, hodie triplex est. 1. Vulgaris, qua ulugus [sc. uulgus] Graecorum utitur, corrupta. . . . 2. Antiqua et pura . . . quam Graecorum docti hodie didicerunt. . . . 3. Ecclesiastica, quae puris admixta barbara habet, qua Sacerdotes, aut Docti, in scribendo utuntur.*

39 Toufexis, *Alphabetum*, 16: "hier von einer 'frühneugriechischen' und keiner 'postbyzantinischen volkssprachlichen' Sprache und Literatur die Rede sein wird."

explicitly as that of an old text.[40] Likewise, he remarks, the eighth-century emperor Constantine V was known as Kopronymos and καβαλῖνος, the latter from καβαλίνη (horse dung): Crusius does not make the point explicitly, but he must be drawing attention to καβαλῖνος and καβαλίνη because they are obviously derivatives of Latin *caballus* (horse).[41] Elsewhere, he quotes Zonaras as saying that the common people used a word τοῦφος for a kind of crown, perhaps from Greek τύφος (pride)—"from which it appears that the *corrupta lingua graeca* is very old."[42] In this case, we note that the postclassical word is part of the *corrupta lingua* even though it is formed from a Greek word. And elsewhere again, he reports that the Greeks say that the *barbarograeca lingua* is very old, and that nobody knows when it began to be used.[43]

The *vulgaris lingua* overlapped, in Crusius's view, with the spoken language of the present day. He compiled a manuscript word list of no fewer than 17,500 entries under the title "Alphabetum vulgaris linguae graecae," writing it in the margins of a printed copy of the *Thesaurus cornu copiae* of 1496 and using the alphabetization of that work as a guide to the alphabetization of his own material.[44] His "Alphabetum" included material obtained by oral elicitation (some of which also appeared in print in the *Turcograecia*), word lists sent to him from the Greek-speaking world, and material from written or printed vernacular Greek texts that he had worked out with the help of native speakers.[45] So his total picture of the *vulgaris lingua graeca* started in the Byzantine Empire, no later than the eighth century, and continued to the spoken Greek of his own day; it included the Greek of vernacular texts from the fourteenth century onward, and even Latin loanwords used unselfconsciously by the compiler of the *Suda*. To make sense of this linguistic range, we may consider Crusius's interest in the possibility of translating the Bible into Greek for contemporary readers to whom the language of the Septuagint and the original language of the New Testament was not accessible.[46] He had a sense of a widely acceptable written vernacular which had been in use well before 1453 and which was still in use,

40 Crusius, *Turcograecia*, 273 (quoting *Suda*, η 432): *Vulgaris . . . corrupta: quae corruptio, uetus est. Vt apud Suida[m], ἠπήτριον, τὸ σουβλίον (subula).*

41 Crusius, *Turcograecia*, 273: *Constantinus qui anno 750. imperauit, Copronimus, dictus fuit καβαλῖνος: quia καβαλίνη, ἡ ἵππεια κόπρος.*

42 Ibid., 514: *Vnde, ualde antiquam esse corruptam linguam Graecam, apparet.*

43 Ibid., 489: *Barbarograecam linguam . . . antiquissimam esse dicunt Graeci: quando uero coepit, ignorant.*

44 Toufexis, *Alphabetum*, 105–23.

45 Material from oral elicitation is at Crusius, *Turcograecia*, 64, 188, 208, 210, 255–56; the target language is usually Latin, occasionally supplemented with German: e.g., at 255, "στεφάγνα, *circulus*, raiff," where the Latin does not specify precisely enough that the hoop of a barrel is meant.

46 See Toufexis, *Alphabetum*, 87.

and which might be for ordinary readers of Greek more or less what the language of Luther's Bible was for readers of German.

Crusius's "Alphabetum vulgaris linguae graecae" was compiled for want of a dictionary of the sort of Greek that he was trying to master. In the decade before the appearance of the *Turcograecia* in 1584, he had hoped that such a dictionary might be in circulation in Constantinople. His inquiries after one reached Theodosios Zygomalas, *protonotarios* of the patriarchate of Constantinople, who assured him that none was extant.[47] He likewise asked Stephan Gerlach, a Tübingen theologian attached to the diplomatic mission of the Holy Roman Empire to the Sublime Porte, "whether there be a lexicon of the modern *Barbarograeca lingua*" and received the same answer.[48] Crusius sent Zygomalas lists of difficult words for explication: a ten-page "explanation of the *Barbarograeci* words, which I sent to Master Theodosius," now lost, was in his possession in 1579, and he received another in 1581.[49] But still he lamented the absence of a full dictionary, announcing how grateful he would be to have anything of the sort, and describing how he had to get hold of the explanations of difficult words from whatever source he could, in Greek or in Latin.[50] This was an early hint at the desirability of a dictionary in which late Greek words might be explained in Latin rather than in classical Greek, and Du Cange quoted it at the beginning of his *Glossarium* alongside Wolf's call for a *Barbaricum Lexicon*.[51]

Crusius did in fact have a dictionary of recent Greek, but it did not suit his purposes. This was the Italian–modern Greek–Latin–ancient Greek *Corona preciosa* of Stefano Nicolini da Sabbio; a small octavo of 128 pages and 1,526 entries, it was published in Venice in a series of editions from 1527 onward, and fairly widely circulated, besides being registered in Conrad Gessner's *Pandects*.[52] The request for a

47 Theodosios Zygomalas, letter dated 15 November 1575, in Crusius, *Turcograecia*, 428–35, at 431: περὶ βι[β]λίων ἁπλῶν τοὺ δημώδους φωνῆς, ἢ λεξικοῦ, ἴσθι. οὐδὲν ἐν τοιοῦτον τινὶ πεπόνηται, translated by Crusius (431) as *Quod ad libros vulgaris linguae attinet, aut Lexicu[m]: scito, nihil tale extare.*

48 Martin Crusius, letter of 20 March 1575 to Stephan Gerlach, in Moennig, "On Martinus Crusius's Collection," 47; for Gerlach's reply of 27 November 1575, see Toufexis, *Alphabetum*, 80, n. 136. And for Gerlach in Constantinople, see A. Ben-Tov, "*Turco-Graecia*: German Humanists and the End of Greek Antiquity—Cultural Exchange and Misunderstanding," in *The Renaissance and the Ottoman World*, ed. A. Contadini and C. Norton (Farnham, Surrey, 2013), 181–95, at 191–92.

49 Toufexis, *Alphabetum*, 98, n. 6: *Explicatio Vocabulorum BarbaroGraecorum, quae Domino Theodosio miseram*; Crusius, *Turcograecia*, 99. See also Moennig, "On Martinus Crusius's Collection," 50.

50 Crusius, *Turcograecia*, 311: *Si alium, qui ante me quicunq[ue] tale tentasset, haberem: magnas ei gratias egissem*; 524: *Doleo, nullum tale Lexicon extare. Vnde mihi necesse est, vndecunque possim, corrogare Dictionum me latentiu[m] interpretationes: quae aut puris vocabulis Graecis, aut Latinis, reddantur.*

51 Du Cange, *Glossarium ad scriptores mediae et infimae graecitatis*, sig. π2v.

52 For the *Corona preciosa*, see Lauxtermann, "Of Frogs and Hangmen" (n. 31 above); Lauxtermann (174, 179) discusses the statement of authorship in Conrad Gessner, *Pandectarum libri XXI* (Zürich, 1548), fol. 35v.

lexicon that he sent to Stephan Gerlach was followed by a parenthesis: "I only have a little book printed at Venice called *Corona preciosa*."[53] He may have received his first copy among the Greek books sent to him from Venice in 1564; he was subsequently to receive, and to give away, another.[54] The *Corona preciosa* was certainly not a sufficient support for all of Crusius's reading of later Greek texts, but as Marc Lauxtermann remarks, it is odd that he should never have quoted it in his lexicographical collections:[55] perhaps his initial disappointment in it led him to discount it as having nothing to offer him.

Henri Estienne

When we turn from the work of Wolf and of Crusius to the *Thesaurus graecae linguae* of their contemporary Henri Estienne, the preeminent early modern lexicographer of Greek, we see an interestingly selective use of Byzantine sources in the preliminary catalog of authors.[56] The historians edited by Wolf are not listed; nor, for instance, does the name of Michael Psellos appear. Those absences may at once make us feel uncertain about the argument "that the philological activity of the day did not make a clear distinction between Byzantine and ancient Greek texts."[57] We might feel more confident about the argument that sixteenth-century philology did not make a *consistent* distinction. For among the legal authors in Estienne's catalog is the fourteenth-century jurist Constantine Harmenopoulos, whose *Hexabiblos* had been available in print since 1540. The *grammatici, scholiastae, et lexicographi* in the catalog naturally include Hesychius, the *Suda*, and other Byzantine texts, notably Eustathios. Theodore Gazes is among them, but little or no use is made of sixteenth-century Greek texts; Estienne knew the *Corona preciosa* but did not think well of it, and was not interested in the very late texts for whose study it might have been relevant.[58] Christian texts were also presented in the catalog of authors, and many of these were ancient—the Septuagint, the New Testament, St. Clement of Alexandria—or at least belonged to late antiquity, such as the works of the Cappadocian fathers and St. John Chrysostom. But St. John of Damascus brings the chronological boundary of the list forward to the mid-eighth century, and the *Expositiones ab Oecumenio et*

53 Crusius, letter of 20 March 1575 to Gerlach, in Moennig, "On Martinus Crusius's Collection," 47: *tantum ego libellum, Venetiis excusum, habeo, titulo, Corona preciosa*.

54 Moennig, "On Martinus Crusius's Collection," 47, 70–72.

55 Lauxtermann, "Of Frogs and Hangmen," 176.

56 Estienne, *Thesaurus graecae linguae* (n. 20 above), 1.7–8.

57 This expression is in Ben-Tov, "*Turco-Graecia*: German Humanists and the End of Greek Antiquity," 182 (where it is not altogether endorsed).

58 For Estienne and the *Corona preciosa*, see Lauxtermann, "Of Frogs and Hangmen," 175.

Aretha collectae, which Estienne owned in the *princeps* of 1532, brings it forward as far as the tenth.[59] This suggests that Byzantine theology was more appealing to Estienne than much Byzantine secular learning, an exception being made for Harmenopoulos and of course for the writers on language.

When the latter are mentioned in Estienne's preface to the *Thesaurus*, it is often to point out instances where compilers of dictionaries in the *Lexicon graecolatinum* tradition have misunderstood them. On one occasion, he remarks mildly that the compiler of the *Suda* should, in a passage that has been misunderstood by sixteenth-century lexicographers, "have used language which a cobbler of dictionaries would understand, and which would furnish him no occasion for error"; on another, he wonders whether a copyist's error in the text of Hesychius "may have furnished occasion for such errors" to compilers in the *Lexicon graecolatinum* tradition—"but only to those who labor under dense ignorance."[60] When his predecessors in the study of the Greek language, including presumably the Byzantines, are unhelpful (indeed, "dumber than fishes"),[61] Estienne does not suggest that this is a matter of the period at which they wrote.

When we look at thirteen arbitrarily selected columns of text distributed across the *Thesaurus* (every 500th in each sequence of column numbering), we see very frequent references to Hesychius, Eustathios, and the *Suda*: they are being used as works of reference, nearly as heavily and systematically as the *Commentarii linguae graecae* of Guillaume Budé. The *Etymologicum magnum* is cited four times in the sample, three times from a printed edition as *Etymol.* or *Etymologus* and once from Estienne's own manuscript as "Lexicon meum vetus"; a handful of patristic authors appear, but only early in the alphabet; the only reference to the usage of a Byzantine text later than the sixth century is to the *Expositiones ab Oecumenio et Aretha collectae.* A working hypothesis must be that Estienne was prepared to draw on a few post-patristic Byzantine authors, but so few, and so seldom, as to suggest that he generally preferred not to do so. The eighteenth-century English theological writer Daniel Scott stated that one of his policies in his two-volume supplement to the *Thesaurus graecae linguae* was that where appropriate, "I have sought examples from what are called more 'classical' Greek authors. So, when the learned author has only taken his evidence from the Fathers and Councils of the Christian Church, or from Greek

59 For Estienne's reading of the *Expositiones*, see Considine, *Dictionaries in Early Modern Europe* (n. 1 above), 81–82.

60 Estienne, *Thesaurus graecae linguae*, 1:18: *debuit scribere quae λεξικοῤῥάφος intelligeret, et quae nullam errandi occasionem illi praeberent*; 1:19: *Praebere tamen potuit et Hesychii mendosum exemplar talium errorum occasionem: sed illis duntaxat qui crassa ignorantia laborarent.*

61 Estienne, *Thesaurus graecae linguae*, 1:11: *magis muti quam pisces*, translating the Greek ἀφωνότερος τῶν ἰχθύων, as in Lucian, *Gallus* 1.

scholiasts and lexicographers, I have not hesitated to make substitutions from writers of the best reputation for purity and elegance."[62] This policy was, I think, largely sympathetic to Estienne's own intentions.

In the year after the publication of the *Thesaurus*, Estienne produced a volume of lexicographical material, including Greek, under the title *Glossaria duo*; the two longest texts were the Latin–Greek *Ps. Philoxenus* and the Greek–Latin *Ps. Cyril*, which were mentioned earlier in this chapter.[63] Joseph Scaliger appreciated it: "Estienne's *Glossaria* are the best of all," he remarked in his table talk, adding that "someone would do well to make a glossary to the authors of the postclassical age."[64] Interest in these word lists continued, and Du Cange, who printed Scaliger's words at the beginning of his *Glossarium* in 1688, had seen a seventeenth-century rearrangement of their material through the press a few years previously.[65]

Nicolas Rigault and Johannes Meursius

By the end of the sixteenth century, quite a lot of work on the lexicography of Byzantine Greek had been done in Latinate Europe, in one way and another. Major Byzantine lexicographical texts had been printed in multiple editions, and had been drawn on in dictionaries of Greek. Their dates were beginning to be ascertained, and their usage was beginning to be studied in its own right. Lexicographers were starting to draw a boundary between Byzantine and earlier usage. The language of declassicizing and vernacular texts from the fourteenth century onward was becoming an object of inquiry. But the need for a dictionary that would help readers of difficult texts from the Byzantine Empire had not yet been answered.

In the preface to his 1604 translation of the *Chronicon maius*, which he attributed to George Sphrantzes, Jacobus Pontanus remarked that the language of this text was fantastically *depravatus* and *corruptus*, and expressed a wish that we have encountered before: "Would that someone could be found who would compile a *Lexicon ἑλληνικοβάρβαρον*: it would certainly be a great help for readers and translators of

62 D. Scott, *Appendix ad Thesaurum graecae linguae ab Henr[ico] Stephano constructum, et ad lexica Constantini et Scapulae*, vol. 1 (London, 1745), sig. a1v: *Exempla … e Graecis Auctoribus magis (ut aiunt) Classicis desumpta, conquisivi. Ubi enim Cl[arissimus] Auctor Testimonia e solis Ecclesiae Christianae Patribus et Conciliis, vel e Scholiastis et Lexicographis Graecis, deprompsit, alia e Scriptoribus puritatis et elegantiae Fama quam clarissimis, huic Operi inserere non dubitavi.*

63 A. C. Dionisotti, "From Stephanus to Du Cange: Glossary Stories," *RHT* 14.15 (1984–85): 303–36, at 313–18.

64 *Scaligeriana, sive excerpta ex ore Josephi Scaligeri* (The Hague, 1666), 144: *Glossaria Stephani omnium optima. Qui feroit un glossaire des Auteurs infimi saeculi feroit bien.*

65 Dionisotti, "From Stephanus to Du Cange," 330–36.

more recent writers among the Greeks, in whose works you will not only find many new words, but also the sense and meaning of old words changed and distorted."[66] He made a helpful start with a non-alphabetized explanation of the names of Byzantine and Turkish ranks, from *protovestiarius* (*protovestiarites*, Sphrantzes' own rank) to *beglerbegus*.[67] Du Cange prefaced the words in which Pontanus called for a dictionary to his *Glossarium*, as he had done with the similar words of Wolf, Crusius, and Scaliger.[68]

Perhaps Pontanus was a little behind the times. In the last month of the sixteenth century, Bonaventura Vulcanius had published an emended and expanded edition of Estienne's *Glossaria duo*, declaring at the end of the table of contents that "some *Glossae ἑλληνικοβάρβαροι* conducive to the understanding of Zonaras and of other historians of the later period" would have been printed at the end of the volume, had Vulcanius not heard from Nicolas Rigault that his own word list of such material was forthcoming; under this announcement, he printed a text of Rigault's letter of September 1600 heralding his "Glossarium ἑλληνικοβάρβαρον."[69]

Rigault's word list, the first printed dictionary of the written Greek of the Byzantine Empire, appeared in 1601, in or around early March, as a quarto of 220 numbered pages, registering about 250 words in alphabetical order. As the ratio of pages to entries suggests, the latter tended to be discursive, and they were generously and attractively laid out. The work, titled *Glossarium τακτικὸν μιξοβάρβαρον*, claimed to cover no more than the vocabulary of certain documents written after the age of Justinian that were concerned with the art of war, especially the tenth-century *Taktika of Leo VI* and the seventh-century (or earlier?) *Strategikon of Maurice*. It thus was a successor to Rigault's *editio princeps* of a text of the first century CE, the *Strategicus* of Onasander, on which the *Taktika of Leo VI* draws extensively. In the notes to this edition, printed in 1598 and issued with the date of 1599 on the title page, Rigault had quoted the Byzantine successors of Onasander and had told the reader that he had compiled a *Glossarium Barbarograecum*, capable of being published in

66 Jacobus Pontanus, in "Georgius Phrantzes" [really Makarios Melissenos's expansion of a text by George Sphrantzes], *Chronicon*, separately paginated section of Theophylaktos Simokattes, *Historiae*, trans. Pontanus (Ingolstadt, 1604), 5–6: *Vtinam inueniretur, qui Lexicon ἑλληνικοβάρβαρον conficeret: magnum vtique scriptores Graecorum recentiores legentibus et interpreta[n]tibus lumen praeferret, apud quos non solum vocabula multa noua, sed antiquorum etiam notiones, et significata alienata, et detorta videas.*

67 Ibid., 8–15.

68 Du Cange, *Glossarium ad scriptores mediae et infimae graecitatis*, sig. π2v.

69 *Thesaurus utriusque linguae*, ed. Bonaventura Vulcanius (Leiden, 1600), sig. *4v: *Accessissent Colophonis loco Glossae aliquot ἑλληνικοβάρβαροι, ad Zonarae aliorumque posterioris aevi Historicorum intelligentiam conducibiles; nisi Cl[arissimum] V[irum] Nicolaum Rigaltium hoc agere ex doctissimis amicissimisque ipsius ad me literis intellexissem.*

the near future, in which their vocabulary was expounded.[70] This was the *Glossarium* that saw the light in 1601, the prefatory epistle to which began by pointing out that Rigault was keeping the promise made in the edition of Onasander.[71] So whereas Crusius had been interested in a kind of Greek that he saw as beginning in the eighth century, and as looking forward to the present day, Rigault was interested in a kind of Greek that he saw as present in texts of the tenth century and earlier, and as looking backward to antiquity.

Rigault's sources were, for such a short word list, numerous—he lists fifteen manuscripts, and his index of other authors has seventy-three entries—and they included much Byzantine material. The sources that he cited five times or more, apart from Vegetius, Isidore, and Paul the Deacon, were all Byzantine: a "Glossarium vetus," and, from the sixth century, the *Novels of Justinian I*; from the tenth century, Constantine Porphyrogennetos and the *Suda*; from the eleventh, John Skylitzes (as "Curopalates"); from the twelfth, Theodore Balsamon and George Kedrenos; from the thirteenth, Niketas Choniates. Nor are very late Greek sources excluded. The sixteenth-century *Historia patriarchica* of Manuel Malaxos is cited from the *Turcograecia*; the Ποίημα *νέον* of Leonardos Phortios, published in Venice in 1531 (quite a rare book, which evaded Crusius's search for modern Greek imprints), is cited twice; and there are four references to the *Corona preciosa*.[72]

Rigault was still in his early twenties when he achieved this pioneering work, and he did not settle down to a lifetime as a lexicographer thereafter. What he showed to his contemporaries in his one separately published word list was that by using material from the *Suda* and other Byzantine dictionaries, together with material from sixteenth-century Greek texts and dictionaries, it was possible to bring together the threads of the lexicography of Byzantine Greek of sixteenth-century Latinate Europe to explicate the language of Byzantine texts written in literary prose of a high register. Perhaps Pontanus had not come across the *Glossarium τακτικὸν μιξοβάρβαρον* when he called for the compilation of a *Lexicon ἑλληνικοβάρβαρον* in 1604, or perhaps he regarded the scope of Rigault's work as too narrow for his purposes. But in the year in which Pontanus made his appeal, a more ample dictionary of Byzantine Greek was already well under way.

70 Nicolas Rigault, *Ad Onosandri Strategicum notae* [issued, with separate pagination, with Onasander, *Strategicus*, ed. Rigault (Paris, 1599)], sig. ã4r: *vocabula . . . exposui in Glossario Barbarograeco, quod breui, si ita tibi videbitur, manumissum tui iuris faciam.*

71 Nicolas Rigault, *Glossarium τακτικὸν μιξοβάρβαρον* (Paris, 1601), sig. ã4v: *Quod in Onosandri editionem pollicitus eram, Lector, soluo ecce nunc libens.*

72 The citation at ibid., 201, to *Turcograec. II* is to *Turcograecia*, 161; Lauxtermann, "Of Frogs and Hangmen," 176, identifies Meursius as the first lexicographer to use the *Corona preciosa.*

This was the work of Johannes Meursius, who had shown precocious talent as a student at Leiden (where he was taught by Vulcanius), and was by 1604 resident at The Hague as tutor to two of the sons of the statesman Johan van Oldenbarnevelt.[73] At the beginning of February 1604, Hugo Grotius wrote from The Hague to Daniel Heinsius in Leiden on Meursius's behalf—"for he is preparing a *Lexicon Barbarograecum*, of the sort which Rigault published. As you know, it is work which calls for no brains and little exertion: he reads a number of authors and makes excerpts, and he is pleased to call this a Lexicon. Zonaras and Kedrenos are still to be read," but Meursius does not have access to their works; does Heinsius have copies which he could lend?[74] These words should not be taken to include Grotius's considered judgment of all lexicography: he and Heinsius found Meursius amusing.[75] But they are of interest because they suggest that Meursius's response to Rigault's work was to see its potential, and to set out at once to broaden its scope by means of something like a systematic program of reading.

The first edition of Meursius's *Glossarium graecobarbarum* was eventually published in 1610, after a period in which the compiler's responsibilities as a traveling tutor delayed his completion of the work. It appears to have been the first printed book to use the word *graecobarbarus* in its title. It ran to 808 numbered pages, and boasted more than 3,600 entries—ten times as many as Rigault's work—with particular attention to the subject that we have already seen interesting Pontanus, namely Byzantine ranks and dignities.[76] Meursius's liminary material does not name Rigault, but it hints at his work by referring to "vocabula μιξοβάρβαρα," using a word that had been part of the title of the earlier dictionary.[77] Rigault is, however, acknowledged generously enough the first time that he is mentioned in the main text of the dictionary: at βίγλα, "watches" (from Latin *vigiliae*), after citing Niketas Choniates, pseudo-Kodinos, and the *Etymologicum magnum*, Meursius adds that "the most learned Nicolas Rigault" has more in his glossary, before turning to a different sense

73 For Vulcanius as an influence on Meursius's Byzantine studies, see H. Cazes, "The Many Lives of Bonaventura Vulcanius 1614–2010," in *Bonaventura Vulcanius, Works and Networks: Bruges 1538–Leiden 1614*, ed. Cazes (Leiden, 2010), 4–43, at 9–10.

74 Hugo Grotius, letter of 5 February 1604 to Daniel Heinsius, in Grotius, *Briefwisseling*, vol. 1, ed. P. C. Molhuysen (The Hague, 1928), 41: *Apparat igitur Lexicon Barbarograecum, quale Rigaltius vulgavit. nosti laborem in quo ingenii nihil, industriae non multum requiritur. Legit auctores plerosque et exscripsit. hoc illi placuit Lexicon vocare. Restant legendi Zonaras et Cedrenus*[.]

75 See H. J. M. Nellen, *Hugo Grotius: A Lifelong Struggle for Peace in Church and State, 1588–1645*, trans. J. C. Grayson (Leiden, 2015), 63.

76 Johannes Meursius, *Glossarium graecobarbarum* (Leiden, 1610), title page: *Praeter Vocabula amplius ter mille sexcenta, Officia atq[ue] Dignitates Imperij Constantinop[olitani] tum in Palatio quam Ecclesia aut Militia explicantur, et illustrantur.*

77 Ibid., sig.)(3r.

of βίγλα, "cross guard of a sword," which Meursius himself has found in a group of orally elicited words in the *Turcograecia*.[78]

The chronological range of the *Glossarium* is broad: on the one hand, a liminary poem by Vulcanius suggests that Meursius has done for later Greek what Hesychius did for the Greek of the ancient world, implying rightly that his coverage goes all the way back to the time of Hesychius; on the other hand, Meursius quotes the *Turcograecia*.[79] The Greek authors and texts whose entries in Meursius's index run to more than five complete lines of type are as follows, in chronological order (together with three that are hard to date—an edition of the *Euchologion*, a much-cited manuscript of "Glossa graecobarbara," and a commentary on Oppian): from late antiquity, the *Lexicon* of Hesychius, and Palladios (not to mention *Ps. Philoxenus* and the Greek–Latin *Ps. Cyril*); from the sixth century, the *Novels of Justinian I*; from the seventh century or earlier, the *Strategikon of Maurice*; from the ninth century, the *Basilika* (there is also a long entry for the "Glossa Basilicorum"); from the tenth, Constantine Porphyrogennetos, the *Suda*, and the *Taktika of Leo VI*; from the eleventh or earlier, "Achmes" (the *Oneirokritikon* of Achmet ben Sirin, published in Paris in 1603); from the eleventh, John Skylitzes; from the eleventh or twelfth, the *Etymologicum magnum*; from the twelfth, Theodore Balsamon, George Kedrenos, John Tzetzes, and John Zonaras; from the thirteenth, Niketas Choniates, John of Kitros, Nicholas Myrepsos, and Demetrios Pepagmenos from the thirteenth–fourteenth, Manuel Moschopoulos; from the fourteenth, Nikephoros Gregoras, Constantine Harmenopoulos, John Kantakouzenos, Pseudo-Kodinos, and the vernacular Greek *Chronicle of the Morea* (cited by Meursius as *De bello sacro*); from the sixteenth, the *Corona preciosa* (very frequently cited), Manuel Malaxos, Leonardos Phortios, and the *Chronicon maius* attributed to George Sphrantzes. When the second edition of the *Glossarium graecobarbarum* appeared in 1614, boasting some 1,300 new entries, it made quite extensive use of other very late texts: the late fifteenth-century Greek translation of Boccaccio's *Theseid*, printed at Venice in 1529, and an anonymous *De vulpe et lupo*, which must be the Γαδάρου Λύκου Κιαλουποῦς, διήγησις ὡραῖα printed at Venice in 1539.[80]

This is all most impressive, particularly considering that Meursius prepared his dictionary in no more than nine years, and that he did not always have ready access even to texts which were fairly readily available in print, such as the

78 Ibid., 104: *Plura in Glossario suo uir eruditissimus, Nicolaus Rigaltius*; the reference is to *Turcograecia*, 188 (Mersius gives no page cite).

79 Vulcanius's poem is in Meursius, *Glossarium graecobarbarum* (1610), sig.)()(1v; it ends Οὔ ἄτερ ἱστορικῶν νεαρῶν νόος οὐ καταληπτὸς, / Οὐδ᾽ ἄτερ Ἡσυχίου τῶν παλαιῶν πέλεται.

80 For the Γαδάρου Λύκου Κιαλουποῦς, διήγησις ὡραῖα of 1539, see É. Legrand, *Bibliographie hellénique des XVe et XVIe siècles*, vol. 1 (Paris, 1885), 234–35.

editions of Zonaras and Kedrenos. He read a number of the major sources mentioned above in manuscript—in all, the list of texts consulted in manuscript in his first edition runs to eighty-four items, with eleven more added in the second edition. A short introductory address to the reader expressed his hopes of publishing some of these, namely Constantine VII Porphyrogennetos's *De administrando imperio*, the *Taktika of Leo VI*, Palladios, the chronicles of George Akropolites and of Constantine Manasses, and the *De velitatione bellica*, which he ascribed to Nikephoros II Phokas.[81] Some of these hopes were indeed realized, and his edition of *De administrando imperio* appeared in 1611, followed by the *Taktika* in 1612 and by both Palladios and Constantine Manasses in 1616. On the other hand, Theodore Dousa, who owned the manuscript of George Akropolites from which Meursius had hoped to work, decided to edit it himself, publishing the result in 1614 (though as late as 1613, Meursius was still promising his own edition), and the edition of *De velitatione bellica* fell by the wayside.[82]

The breadth of Meursius's editorial ambitions set up part of a fivefold challenge for any lexicographer who might follow him: he would need to be familiar with the Byzantine lexicographers; conversant with sixteenth-century Greek; very widely read in the printed texts in Byzantine Greek; capable of finding, reading, and even editing new Byzantine texts—and capable of working at a high level on the lexicography of postclassical Latin. (Of course, Du Cange had all five of these distinctions.) Writing the full and appreciative third-person entry about himself in his anonymous collection, published in 1613, of biographies and portraits of the most eminent professors of the University of Leiden, Meursius followed a reference to the forthcoming new edition of the *Glossarium graecobarbarum* with the information that "he turned with equal zeal to the Latin language, and also constructed a *Glossarium latinobarbarum*, to be a counterpart to that earlier work, which is very soon to be published as well. And with this bipartite work, he will shed more than a little light on the *barbaries* of either empire, eastern and western alike."[83]

In these words, Meursius was conceiving of the lexicography of Byzantine Greek not simply as part of the deep story of the Greek language, its literature, and its speakers, but as part of a broad story of the cultures that succeeded the ancient

81 Meursius, *Glossarium graecobarbarum* (1610), sigs.)(4v–)( )(1r.

82 Theodore Dousa in George Akropolites, *Chronicon Constantinopolitanum* (Leiden, 1614), sig.)(1v; Meursius's edition is promised in [Johannes Meursius], *Illustris Academia Lugd-Batava: id est virorum clarissimorum icones, elogia ac vitae, qui eam scriptis suis illustrarunt* (Leiden, 1613), sig. O4r.

83 [Meursius], *Illustris Academia Lugd-Batava*, sigs. O3r–v: *Pari studio ad Latinam linguam se transtulit; et, quod priori illi responderet, Latinobarbarum quoque concinnauit, propediem itidem publica[n]dum. Et gemino illo opere vtriusque Imperij, Orientalis pariter atque Occidentalis, barbariem non parum illustrabit.*

Roman Empire. The texts that he handled in the *Glossarium graecobarbarum* went back, as we have seen, to late antiquity, so it and the "Glossarium latinobarbarum" would have had the same starting point; but whereas the *barbaries* of the West was surely that of the successor states to the western empire from late antiquity onward, insofar as their inhabitants used Latin, the *barbaries* of the East was that of the Byzantine Empire from late antiquity to the post-Byzantine period. Meursius was, to use a concept that was both new and exciting in 1613, seeing the lexicography of Byzantine Greek as part of the lexicography of the Middle Ages.[84] As it happens, the first word list to be printed under the title "Glossarium latinobarbarum" was published in 1613, the work of Johannes Lydius, preacher at Oudewater near Utrecht, who presented it as an annex to his edition of the late medieval church reformer Nicolas de Clamanges.[85] Whether Lydius borrowed the word *latinobarbarus* from Meursius or came up with it independently, its appearance in the writings of both men in the same year suggests its timeliness.

Meursius's "Glossarium latinobarbarum" was never published, though we know a little about its contents: there would have been entries for such forms as *butina* (vessel to contain liquid), *guerra* (war), *novigeldus* (ninefold penalty) and *werigeldus* (wergild), *sceurum* (granary), *scinca* (ham), and *tornamenta* (tournament).[86] This list suggests that the work would have surveyed some of the Latinity of law, conflict, and everyday life of the early and high Middle Ages; and what this in turn suggests is that the word *latinobarbarus* is by no means to be taken as having exclusively negative connotations.

Nor should the word *graecobarbarus*. Meursius's dedicatory epistle to the second edition of the *Glossarium graecobarbarum*, in which he gave his considered opinion of what the dictionary had achieved, stated that "in this book, I have sought to portray the public affairs of the Empire," with particular attention to civil, ecclesiastical, and military matters.[87] This does not sound like an uncivilized subject. The language of the eastern empire, he added, had changed like the empire itself: it was as far removed from that of antiquity as Italian is from Latin.[88] The analogy is suggestive:

84 For *medium aevum* and similar expressions in the first two decades of the 17th century, see Considine, *Dictionaries in Early Modern Europe* (n. 1 above), 259–61.

85 For Lydius's "Glossarium," see ibid., 258.

86 Johannes Meursius, *Glossarium Graeco-Barbarum*, 2nd ed. (Leiden, 1614), 94, 574, 102, 505, 507, 569.

87 Ibid., sigs. *2v–*3r: *hoc libro statum Imperij repraesentare conatus fui; quo pacto administratum Palatium, aut Ecclesia; denique quid Militia gestum.*

88 Ibid., sig. *3r: *adeo quidem ab antiqua illa diuersa, ut Italica a Latina non possit magis.*

the *lingua graecobarbara* had degenerated from classical Greek as Italian had from classical Latin, but Italian was not to be despised.

Overview

The story told in this chapter is not that of a single intellectual movement toward the clarification of "Byzantine" as a lexicographical concept. Rather, it is that of the slow clarification by a number of lexicographers of different boundaries between what we now see as Byzantine Greek and what we now see as earlier or later Greek, and of a simultaneous intensification of interest in the varieties of Greek that fall within those boundaries.

The boundary with earlier Greek was seldom viewed as a boundary between pagan and Christian usage: Hesychius was a Christian, who could be seen by Vulcanius as looking back on the usage of a classical period, and the Cappadocian fathers were included by Henri Estienne in his *Thesaurus graecae linguae*. Estienne drew on the *Expositiones ab Oecumenio et Aretha collectae*, but this text was a late outlier among his Christian texts; Meursius drew on Palladios in his *Glossarium graecobarbarum*, but this text was an early outlier among his. Only with the publication of the *Thesaurus ecclesiasticus* of J. C. Suicerus in 1682 would the lexicography of patristic Greek become a field of significant activity in its own right. As for secular texts, those handled by Meursius began in late antiquity and became numerous from the ninth century onward; those handled by Estienne were seldom later than late antiquity (Constantine Harmenopoulos being an outlier), with the exception of texts that he was using as secondary sources, such as Eustathios on Homer.

The boundary with later Greek was not seen by the lexicographers as a boundary between the ages of empire and diaspora: the use of the *Corona preciosa* by Meursius is revealing, as is his interest in sixteenth-century Greek texts, which are strongly represented in the first edition of the *Glossarium graecobarbarum*, and perhaps even more strongly in the second. (As for late *spoken* Greek, Crusius's interest was exceptional.) But although 1453 was not a chronological boundary for Meursius, his conceptualization of a parallel between *graecobarbarus* and *latinobarbarus* usage meant that the lexicographical field which he was defining had medieval, and not contemporary, Greece at its center.

The parallel between the Greek and Latin Middle Ages set up by the twin terms *graecobarbarus* and *latinobarbarus* ensured that both terms were ambivalent. On the one hand, medieval Greek could be seen as having declined from ancient Greek because it was mixed with a *barbaries* that was simply to be condemned. On the other hand, medieval Greek could be seen as the same sort of entity as medieval Latin—*barbarus* in a sense that might see decline from the classical to what was starting to be seen as the medieval, but that did not simply condemn the latter.[89] The wide-ranging and fine-grained study of texts, institutions, and ways of life demanded by the work of the lexicographer of medieval Greek (or Latin) could only lead him to see a picture of a complex, well-ordered, Christian society emerging from the mass of lexical detail with which he engaged. The vision expressed by Wolf of a catastrophic decline from purity to corruption and the newer vision, which I see emerging at least by the time of Meursius, of the complexity and even the virtues of postclassical societies could both be expressed with the word *graecobarbarus*: it sums up the ambivalence of the vision of Byzantine Greek in the lexicography of early modern Europe.

I am grateful for the advice and corrections of the two anonymous reviewers of this chapter.

89 See the reception of a specimen of Sir Henry Spelman's dictionary of postclassical Latin by Rigault and others in 1619: two responses quoted by Dionisotti, "From Stephanus to du Cange" (n. 63 above), 335–36, use the word *barbaries* but come to different conclusions about the work, which was generally admired, as shown by the quotations in Considine, *Dictionaries in Early Modern Europe*, 182–83.

NINE

ERUDITION, DOCUMENTATION, AND ORGANIZATION IN THE MAKING OF EARLY MODERN BYZANTINE STUDIES

The Case of Martin Hanke's De Byzantinarum rerum scriptoribus Graecis liber *(1677)*

WILLIAM NORTH

IN THE NOW CLASSIC TREATMENTS OF THE HISTORY OF THE BYZANTINE EMPIRE BY A. A. Vasiliev and George Ostrogorsky,[1] both authors began with brief accounts of the history of Byzantine studies. For each of these two great Byzantinists, the genealogy of Byzantine studies *proprio dictu* found its homeland in France and its founding fathers in the French Jesuit Philippe Labbe (1607–1667) and the polymath linguist, historian, and antiquarian Charles du Fresne, sieur Du Cange (1611–1688). These men had been intimately connected with the organization and promotion of a massive, sustained, organized, and royally sponsored effort to edit the historical sources for the Byzantine Empire, and those volumes eventually formed the series known as the Paris Corpus (1648–1711).[2] This collection, in turn, would provide the model and the textual basis for the *Corpus Scriptorum Historiae Byzantinae* or Bonn Corpus, which the philologist Barthold Niebuhr launched in the early nineteenth

1 I would like to express my thanks to the conference organizers and volume editors, Jake Ransohoff and Nathanael Aschenbrenner, for their initiative, enthusiasm, support, and patience and to the anonymous reviewers for their attentive reading and insightful suggestions. I also acknowledge the invaluable research assistance provided by Carleton College student Jonathan Dahlsten that facilitated identification of many of the early modern editions used by Hanke. A. A. Vasiliev, *History of the Byzantine Empire, 324–1453*, 2 vols., 2nd ed. (Madison, WI, 1952), 1:3–42, esp. 3–6; G. Ostrogorsky, *A History of the Byzantine State*, trans. J. Hussey, rev. ed. (New Brunswick, NJ, 1969), 1–21, at 1–4.

2 Philippe Labbe, *De Byzantinae historiae scriptoribus* (Paris, 1648). On this project and a contemporary discussion of a collection of Byzantine historians, see H. Omont, "La collection byzantine de Labbe et le projet de J.-M. Suarès," *REG* 74 (1904): 18–32.

century, intending to improve and extend the Paris Corpus.[3] Although, to be sure, the efforts of earlier scholars to edit and translate Byzantine historical sources have sometimes been acknowledged,[4] the brevity of their treatment (often limited to names, texts, and date of publication) and the lack of any clear sense of intellectual consequences create for modern readers a sense of randomness and idiosyncrasy rather than elements of a disciplinary genesis or signs of momentum. Coherence, method, and, implicitly, progress in the study of Byzantine history thus had to await the initiatives in Paris.

Published in 1677, the *De Byzantinarum rerum scriptoribus Graecis liber* by the Silesian librarian, schoolmaster, antiquarian, poet, and historian Martin Hanke (1633–1709), or Martinus Hankius, suggests a different story for the rise of Byzantine historical studies.[5] His comprehensive biobibliographical guide to the Greek witnesses to Byzantine history from the time of Constantine until the fall of Constantinople to the Ottoman Turks in 1453 signals instead that the mid-seventeenth century witnessed not the birth of Byzantine historical studies but rather their coming of age. In this period, editions, commentaries, and other critical tools—accumulated over more than a century—reached a critical mass that, once ordered and discussed, enabled scholars both to achieve a synoptic view of Byzantine historical writing and to better manage the accelerating rate of publication in Byzantine studies, of which the Paris Corpus was a part.

Yet Hanke is a figure largely unknown in accounts of Byzantine studies. He is absent from both Vasiliev's and Ostrogorsky's accounts and finds no mention in Ernst Gerland's 1934 overview of the history of Byzantine historical studies.[6] Although he does appear briefly in Hans-Georg Beck's discussion of Byzantine studies in Germany before the time of Karl Krumbacher, he does so more as curiosity, an *unicum*, than as a contributor. For Beck assumed that Hanke was, at heart, a dedicated teacher and a committed historian of Silesia; his extended guides to both Roman history and Byzantine history stemmed therefore not from serious scholarly engagement in the field but from "pedagogical and didactic motives" that bore witness either to the wide scope and rigor of gymnasium education in the

3 On the Bonn Corpus, see J. Irmscher, "Das Bonner Corpus und die Berliner Akademie," *Kretika Chronika* 7 (1953): 360–83.

4 Vasiliev, *History of the Byzantine Empire*, 1:3; Ostrogorsky, *History of the Byzantine State*, 2–3; and most recently, D. R. Reinsch, "The History of Editing Byzantine Historical Texts," in *The Byzantine World*, ed. P. Stephenson (London, 2010), 435–44.

5 Martin Hanke, *Martini Hankii De Byzantinarum rerum scriptoribus Graecis liber*... (Leipzig, 1677). This work has been digitized and can be found online.

6 E. Gerland, *Das Studium der byzantinischen Geschichte vom Humanismus bis zur Jetztzeit*, TFByzNgPhil 12 (Athens, 1934).

mid-seventeenth century or to Hanke's inflated hopes for his students' humanistic interests.[7] This casual, even dismissive, treatment echoed Karl Krumbacher's own brief assessment of Hanke's work in his *Geschichte der byzantinischen Litteratur von Justinian bis zum Ende des Oströmischen Reiches*: "Professor Hanke of Bresslau made a quite superficial literary-historical compilation"—an assessment challenged not only by the length and detail of Hanke's work but also by Krumbacher's own references to its extended discussions.[8]

Such consistent neglect or undervaluation is as regrettable as it is puzzling, for as Agostino Pertusi observed more than fifty years ago, "Hanke's work [*De Byzantinarum rerum scriptoribus Graecis*] can effectively be considered the first history of Byzantine historiography. . . . For the precision of its information it is a work that one can consult even today with profit."[9] Moreover, Pertusi saw that Hanke's scholarship bore critical witness to his own alternative chronology of Byzantine studies in Europe:

> The movement of scholarly studies on the history and civilization of Byzantium that began in Venice, then continued in Germany, and concluded in France during the reigns of Louis XIII and Louis XIV, a movement that aimed for erudite completeness in all branches of what was historically knowable, had amassed an imposing quantity of materials—blocks of stone already squared, bricks big and small, beams and poles—ready to be employed in a monumental construction: a history of Byzantium's thousand-year civilization. The rationalist and skeptical enlightenment transformed this into a history of Byzantium's thousand-year decline. It will

7 H.-G. Beck, "Die byzantinischen Studien in Deutschland vor Karl Krumbacher," in *ΧΑΛΙΚΕΣ: Festgabe für die Teilnehmer am XI. Internationalen Byzantinistenkongress, München 15.–20. September 1958* (Freising, 1958), 67–119, at 89–90 (repr. in Beck, *Ideen und Realitäten in Byzanz: Gesammelte Aufsätze*, Variorum Reprints [London, 1972], I). Hanke's 2-volume work on Roman historians was published over a five-year period (1669–74). Beck's direct engagement with Hanke's historical works seems minimal; the volumes' level of detail, documentation, and scholarly rigor all suggest that Hanke's works, though they may have had their origins in the classroom, were reworked and published for the wider Republic of Letters. Unless otherwise indicated, all translations are my own.

8 K. Krumbacher, *Geschichte der byzantinischen Litteratur: Von Justinian bis zum Ende des Oströmischen Reiches (524–1453)*, 2nd ed. (Munich, 1897), 225. Krumbacher cited extended passages from Hanke five times in his discussion of Byzantine historical writers. On Krumbacher, see now the essays in *Karl Krumbacher: Leben und Werke*, ed. P. Schreiner and E. Vogt, Bayerische Akademie der Wissenschaften, phil.-hist. Klasse, Sitzungsberichte 2011, Hft. 4 (Munich, 2011), and P. Agapitos, "Karl Krumbacher and the History of Byzantine Literature," *BZ* 108 (2015): 1–52.

9 A. Pertusi, *Storiografia umanistica e mondo bizantino*, Istituto siciliano di studi bizantini e neoellenici, quaderni 5 (Palermo, 1967), 104.

> be necessary to wait until the nineteenth century when, amid a renewed sentiment of historical evolution and in opposition to the presumptions of the Enlightenment, the erudite research of the seventeenth century would be rendered fruitful and, through them, the Byzantine world reevaluated without prejudice.[10]

Far from being an idiosyncratic historical handbook for German gymnasium students or a "superficial compilation," Hanke's work, for Pertusi, represented an important element in what had been a critical phase of synthesis, organization, and reconciliation in the Republic of Letters' treatment of the Byzantine world. The aim of the present chapter is to begin a process of scholarly reconsideration of Hanke and the nature and implications of his work for Byzantine historical writers. After reviewing Hanke's life and career, it will examine his scholarly priorities and approach as they were developed and expressed in his earlier study of Roman historical writers, before turning to the aims, method, and reception of his guide to Byzantine historical writers.

A Teaching Life

Martin Hanke was born in the village of Borna in the district of Neumarkt near Breslau (modern Wrocław), the son of Johannes Hanke, a Protestant pastor, and Agnes Pittich, daughter of another Protestant pastor. Initially educated at the Elisabeth-gymnasium in Wrocław, Hanke went on to study philosophy and history at Frankfurt and then Jena, receiving his master of art's degree in 1656 at the age of twenty-three.[11] Around the same time and thanks to the patronage of the family

10 Ibid., 116. Pertusi's view of Hanke has resonated most in Italian Byzantine studies, where he receives at least a passing mention in histories of Byzantine studies though without significant investigation. See S. Ronchey, *L'Impero Bizantino* (Milan, 2002), part 3.1, and, more recently, R. M. Parrinello, "Byzantinistica," in *Dizionario di sapere storico-religioso del Novecento*, ed. A. Melloni (Bologna, 2010), 156–86, at 157.

11 For Hanke's biography, see J. Flood, *Poets Laureate in the Holy Roman Empire: A Biobibliographical Handbook*, 4 vols. (Berlin, 2006), 2:766–69; K. Garber, *Das Alte Breslau: Kulturgeschichte einer geistigen Metropole* (Cologne, 2014), 344–47. For Flood's account, Gottlob Krantz's biographical epitaph provides essential detail: see G. Hankius, *Martini Hankii Monumenta* (Breslau, 1718), 359–64. For additional contemporary biographical detail, see "Elogium Martini Hankii," in *Acta Eruditorum anno MDCCIX publicata* (Leipzig, 1709), 332–34. See also the biographical essay in H. Markgraf, *Kleine Schriften zur Geschichte Schlesiens und Breslaus* (Breslau, 1915), 30–52, which traces Hanke's career in particular detail. Markgraf refers to diaries and other materials that formed part of a manuscript *Nachlass* but without traceable citation. The survival of Hanke's papers warrant further research. J.-P. Niceron's entry on Hanke contains additional information as well as a bibliography of his works: *Mémoires pour servir à l'histoire des hommes illustres dans la*

friend and fellow Silesian Georg Frantzke, chancellor to the Duke of Saxe-Gotha, he received the poet's *laurea* and eventually a teaching position in Gotha in 1659. Although his literary talents in poetry and rhetoric now seem modest, Hanke's output was prolific, and his orations on festive or solemn occasions and his funerary epitaphs, as well as a continuous stream of poetry, represent an important part of his published work.

He returned to Breslau in 1661 to teach at the Elisabeth-gymnasium, becoming its rector in 1688, a position that entailed his oversight of education in the city as a whole and that he held until his death in 1709. From 1670 until 1688, he also occupied the position of librarian at the Rehdiger Library, the extensive book collection donated to the city of Breslau by the sixteenth-century polymath and bibliophile Thomas Rehdiger (1540–1576) and housed at the Elisabeth-gymnasium.[12]

Methodological Laboratory: Hanke's *De Romanarum rerum scriptoribus liber*

In 1669, eight years after his return to Breslau, Hanke published the first volume of what was to be a two-volume biobibliographical survey of historians of the Roman Republic and Empire. His first major publication and one that he chose to dedicate to the city fathers of Breslau in gratitude for the city's long-standing support of his life in letters, this work was the fruit of over ten years of research that had been sparked by a request from his former student in Gotha, the young nobleman Gideon von Wangenheim. Gideon had asked Hanke for a "list (*index*) of good authors from which it would suitable to drink up the histories of all peoples, as though from wellsprings." Hanke, in turn, began to conceive of a "library of historical writers that was to be put together on a new model for benefits of various kinds."[13] Although progress on the grand project was at first slowed by limited access to books, he eventually gained access to public and private libraries: the favor of his former mentor and patron Georg Frantzke's widow opened his library to Hanke, while Duke Ernest of Saxony commissioned him to produce a *quoddam compendium historiarum* for use in

république des lettres, avec un catalogue raisonné de leurs ouvrages, 43 vols. (Paris, 1729–45), 38:202–6; it also attests to Hanke's status as a member of the European Republic of Letters.

12 On the Rehdiger Library, see now A. Lipińska, "Brothers in Collecting: Thomas and Jacob Rehdiger—Two Sixteenth-Century Silesian Art Collectors and Bibliophiles," in *Early Modern Merchants as Collectors*, ed. C. M. Anderson (New York, 2016), 169–83 with further literature.

13 *Martini Hankii De Romanarum rerum scriptoribus liber*, 1: . . . *de quadam Historicorum Scriptorum Bibliotheca, novo exemplo, in varii generis utilitates componenda cogitationem suscepi*. Further references to this work will be given parenthetically in the text with the abbreviation *R*.

law and gave him access to a library "equipped with many kinds of codices"[14] (*R* 2). Hanke recalled that he had begun his more focused work on the writers of Roman history seven years before, working on it within the narrow confines imposed by place and circumstance. Initially developing the work as lectures to his students, he continued to refine, expand, and improve the entries until a book emerged that was "now as different from its [original form] as the body of an animal is from a freshly laid egg"[15] (*R* 2).

Although it was his first foray into the field, Hanke clearly informed his readers about what they should and should not expect. They should not expect to find every possible author treated exhaustively. He had made a selection of what he considered to be the one hundred most important writers on Roman history from antiquity to the early sixteenth century, thus implicitly guiding his reader through both the complex terrain of the ancient witnesses and the increasingly dense thicket of late medieval and early modern scholarship. Readers should also not expect to find discussed ancient authors whose works had not survived to be consulted; for information about those authors, Hanke counseled consultation of the surveys of Conrad Gessner and Gerhard Vossius.[16] Finally, they should not expect to find historians who dealt primarily or exclusively with the empire of East Rome or the affairs of Constantinople, a limit that perhaps signals Hanke's early plans for a volume on Byzantine historians. What they could expect were thorough, systematic discussions of one hundred authors whose works—regardless of original genre—addressed Rome's history. These would be arranged not in alphabetical order but in chronological order so that the reader might better understand the authors in their proper historical context; a supplementary alphabetical index would enable readers seeking a given author to locate the relevant section; authors that could not be securely dated would be kept in a separate section and arranged arbitrarily. Within Hanke's treatment of each author, the reader would always find three subsections—*vita, scripta,* and *judicia*; and in these sections information as well as a selection of relevant scholarly debates would be provided (*R* 3–4, 8–9).

Most importantly, readers would find rigorous documentation of the evidence. This was a topic on which Hanke expressed strong views. He affirmed that he had

14 *[I]ta suam quoque Bibliothecam multiplici codicum genere instructam, desideriis meis patere jubebat.*

15 *Haec postea subcisivis horis et frequens augmentum et cum eo meliorem forman receipt, donec in hunc librum abiit, iam in tantum sibi dissimilis, in quantum ovo recentissimo visceribus inhaerenti exclusum animalis corpus.*

16 Gerhard Johannes Vossius, *De historicis Græcis libri quatuor* (Leiden, 1624), and Conrad Gessner, *Bibliotheca Vniuersalis, siue Catalogus omnium scriptorum locupletissimus, in tribus linguis, Latina, Græca, & Hebraica: extantium & non extantiu[m], ueterum & recentiorum in hunc usq[ue] diem, doctorum & indoctorum, publicatorum & in Bibliothecis latentium* (Zürich, 1545).

personally read all of the books that he would cite, noting that although he knew a range of others, he excluded them because he had read them before he conceived of this project and therefore his notes were inadequate (*R* 8). He promised that he would include no views that lacked evidence and indeed would often quote the evidence directly, so that his readers—who were perhaps without access to the materials cited—might nonetheless have direct access to the relevant proofs. In this approach, he explicitly challenged what he saw as scholarly culture of disquietingly variable quality.

> Indeed, in this kind of scholarship, we commend nothing less than the practice of some who provide either no evidence or unsuitable evidence for the most ancient affairs that they recount. Regarding the former problem [providing no evidence], for those endowed with the necessary books, a more inflated arrogance governed some, while a greater inclination to sloppiness ruled others. Regarding the latter problem [offering inappropriate sources], in part, it is those who work without the best books, and in part those who do not fully understand how to judge between and use books, that usually do this. Both groups simultaneously write for both the few and the many. They write for the few, that is, for those most learned in such matters for whom the things that are set forth are already known from their very foundations. They also write for the many, that is, the crowd of the *eruditi* for whom anyone writing about earlier times is satisfactory. Both drink from any spring, from any stream, since they are convinced that it does not matter: the authority of the writer alone counts as reason and evidence, since they suppose that these famous men, who at first excelled in their solid scholarship and whose genius and memory they trust too much, never fall asleep and never dream.[17] (*R* 5)

In his work, by contrast, the authority of any claim would be rooted in suitable witnesses and historical demonstrations presented to the reader. Furthermore, he

17 *Nihil enim minus in hoc studiorum genere, quam eorum morem approbamus, qui antiquissimis rebus, quas tradunt, aut nullos aut minus idoneos testes addunt. Quorum illud, necessaria quidem Bibliotheca praeditis, aliis ventosior arrogantia, pronior aliis negligentia, saepius imperavit; hoc, partim meliorum inopia codicum laborantes, partim genuinum discrimen usumque librorum non satis intelligentes, facere solent. Utrique simul et paucis et multis scribunt: paucis, id est, rerum peritissimis quibus ea quae proferuntur iam ex suis fundamentis sunt cognita: multis, id est, vulgo eruditorum, quibus aut superiorum annorum quilibet scriptor satisfacit, utrum aquas ex fonte ipso, an ex quocunque rivo bibant, nihil interesse persuasis: aut etiam sola scribentis autoritas pro ratione, pro testimonio est; celebres, inprimis solida scientia praecellentes viros, quorum ingenio nimium, nimium memoriae confidunt, nunquam domitare, nunquam somniare cogitantibus.*

promised that all writers—ancient and modern—on whose works he drew would be named and receive full credit (*R* 14–15).

Attentive to the rigor of his historical argumentation, Hanke was also sensitive to his readers' need for ease, access, and flexibility. He therefore noted that he would include translations into Latin of all quoted materials (with their bibliographical references) to give all his readers access to the arguments, "for it would have been annoying and useless to supply Greek words without a translation to those who don't understand them"[18] (*R* 11). He also included five indexes designed to assist readers with all manner of interests in finding the relevant materials quickly: (1) an alphabetical list by author; (2) a chronological list of authors with reference to the period in which they wrote; (3) a list of authors in the order treated, with the start and end dates of the period covered by their works; (4) a chronology of all the works treated in the first section, arranged by the historical periods covered; and (5) a topical index in which authors are grouped under the topics addressed by their works (*R* 308–84). In both their organizing concepts and their page layouts, these finding aids show that Hanke not only thought about the different ways in which his readers might approach their historical questions but also recognized the powerful ways in which vision could be used to enhance comprehension of textual materials and thereby historical understanding.[19]

As he concluded his methodological preface, Hanke noted that the volume, like all human creations, was incomplete; topics and authors worthy of treatment, noted throughout the published book, would await a supplemental volume (which he published six years later, in 1675). Yet Hanke also revealed to his readers that his work on Roman historical writers was just the tip of a very large historiographical project that he had conceived and hoped to execute over the remainder of his life.

> Although they may be content with this Cato for now, the many books of similar material that some of our friends are pressuring us to prepare may perhaps satisfy those who await later times. For, if I may state simply what the project is: I have gathered together in my handwritten notes—intended for individual volumes—writers not only about the Byzantines or Constantinopolitans, the Turks, the Germanic peoples, the Poles, the Bohemians, and other peoples, so that we may have their memorable deeds

18 *Nam sine interpretatione verba Graeca proferre, non intelligentibus et molestum nec utile fuisset.*

19 For extensive discussion of the ways in which early modern authors experimented with visual design, especially in presenting materials with a chronological dimension, see A. Grafton and D. Rosenberg, *Cartographies of Time: A History of the Timeline* (Princeton, 2010), esp. 26–49.

> described individually, but also about the interconnections between these peoples and especially about ecclesiastical affairs.[20] (*R* 16)

Hanke's volume on the writers of Roman history was, therefore, merely a first installment in what he imagined and hoped would be a comprehensive set of guides to the histories of the peoples of the world, each of which would provide its users with the same meticulous and abundantly documented guidance through key historical writers and works as they encountered in this volume. Of course, he warned his readers that many things could slow or even halt progress: "the completion of all books requires enduring powers of mind and body, generous leisure, and well-supplied libraries," none of which he could guarantee (*R* 16).[21] Within his larger scholarly prospectus, however, it seems clear that he had already begun to plan a volume on the writers of Byzantine history even as he worked through the 1660s and early 1670s on the Roman writers.

What was the response to Hanke's effort? Although further investigation is needed on the larger place of Hanke within the intellectual world of his time, Christian Daumius, polymath philologist and rector of the Academy of Zwickau in Saxony, offers one example of a very positive, articulate response to Hanke's effort, as well as intimations of potential contemporary critique. In a letter of 26 September 1670, Daumius remarked to his friend Johannes Gebhardt, who was also Hanke's senior colleague at the Elisabeth-gymnasium:

> I have now seen and purchased the excellently prepared book of your colleague Martin Hanke—please greet him for me with utmost duty and honor—on Roman writers. I really like it, and I wish that more would be published by him. For he has seen and carefully read the books themselves—even quite rare ones—and he is more careful and more circumspect than

20 *Hoc Catone in praesens contentis, pluros simileis materiae codices, ad quos elaborandos ab Amicis nonnullis impellimur, exspectantibus advenientia tempora forte satisfacient. Nam, ut simpliciter quod res est, dicam: equidem non tantum de Byzantinis sive Constantinopolitanis, Turcicis, Germanicis, Polonicis, Bohemicis, aliorumque populorum, quatenus eorum memorabilia seorsim habemus descripta, sed etiam de plurium gentium inter se connexis, maxime autem de Ecclesiasticis rebus Scriptores (solitariis libris destinatos) in MStis adversariis meis collectos habeo.* In this ambition to provide comprehensive guidance to vast scholarly landscapes, Hanke shared in the sensibilities of other polyhistors of his age; see A. Grafton, "The World of the Polyhistors: Humanism and Encyclopedism," *Central European History* 18 (1985): 31–47 (repr. in A. Grafton, *Bring Out Your Dead: The Past as Revelation* [Cambridge, MA, 2001], 166–80).

21 *Sed cum multa consiliis exsequendis se opponere soleant, non modo queant, et quos indicavimus, librorum omnium perfectio durabiliores animi corporisque vires, liberalius otium, Bibliothecas instructiores sibi deposcat, quam ut mihi vel possim, vel debeam polliceri, de futura publication in spes firmas neminem vocare audeo.*

Vossius in many respects. For Vossius wrote about authors not badly but in a confusing way. Hanke, in contrast, with outstanding skill, writes everything clearly: life, writings, judgments. He has set forth the lives with such hard work and accuracy that he arranges the testimonies of the ancients only in chronological order after adding the years of the Olympiads, the City [of Rome], the world, and Christ, and he has taken special care over the last years that someone lived.[22]

Daumius also remarked favorably on Hanke's inclusion of fifty writers not in Vossius's work as well as the extremely useful indexes. The book, he said, literally made him—and others better than him—hunger for more.[23] Several days later, he reiterated his enthusiasm for Hanke's approach when he noted that he had learned that Hanke was preparing another volume on "Greek writers" following the same format; when it was published he planned to buy a copy.[24]

When Hanke did publish the supplementary volume on Roman writers, Daumius was quick to acknowledge his achievement, noting that Hanke had discussed these new authors *pulcherrime*. He then expanded on his earlier comparison with the biobibliographical work of Gerhard Vossius, sharpening the sense of Hanke's superiority: "His thorough investigations surpass those of Vossius in this genre inasmuch as they are much more carefully laid out, more fully developed, and extend until our own times." Furthermore, his appreciation of Hanke's excellent scholarship, he claimed, was shared not only by those in Leipzig but also the *summi viri* in other places.[25] Once again, his reading of volume 2 of Hanke's *De scriptoribus*

22 Christianus Daumius, *Epistola* 19 to Johannes Gebhardus, in *Christiani Daumii Philologi et polyhistoris celeberrimi Epistolae Philologo-criticae ad clarissimos viros Jo. And. Bosium, Jo. Gebhardum, et Martinum Hankium* (Chemnitz, 1709), 88–89, at 88: *Clarissimi Viri, Collegae Tui, officiossime et honorificentissime a me Salutandi Martini Hankii Librum de Romanis Scriptoribus optime concinnatum vidi emique. Perplacet sane et vellem plura ab eo edi. Vidit enim et intellexit ipsos Libros, eosque aliquando rarissimos: Vossio in multis, at quanto Viro diligentior et circumspectior. Nam hic, etsi non male, tamen confuse, quicquid de Autoribus scripsit. Ille vero artificio egregio omnia distincte, Vitam, scripta, Judicia; mire laboriosus et accuratus ita Vitas disposuit, ut nonnisi secundum ordinem Temporum collocet Testimonia veterum, additis annis, et Olympiadum, et urbis, et mundi, et Christi; ubique de ultimis maxime annis, quo quisque vitam perduxerit sollicitus.*

23 Ibid., 89: *Ideo mihi et aliis me majoribus salivam movet ad plura hujus exasciati viri scripta quibus specimen adeo bonum praemisit degustanda.*

24 Daumius, *Epistola* 21 to Johannes Gebhardus, in *Philologi et polyhistoris celeberrimi Epistolae*, 91–92.

25 Daumius, *Epistola* 36 to Johannes Gebhardus, in ibid., 119–20, at 120. The letter is dated 28 December 1674. The publication is usually placed in 1675, suggesting that Daumius was among the first to receive a copy. He acknowledged Joachim Gensenius's role in sending him the work directly from Leipzig.

Romanis left him even more eager for Hanke's work on Greek writers, a project that he clearly knew about and eagerly awaited.[26]

De Byzantinarum rerum scriptoribus Graecis liber: Continuity and Focus

This extended discussion of the method and aims of Hanke's initial work has had several aims. First, it has made clear that Hanke's approach was not at all one of simply assembling a "superficial compilation" of sources: it was far more ambitious, rigorous, and methodologically articulated. Contemporaries noted this distinctive approach and acknowledged its scholarly rigor and utility: Hanke actually practiced the principles of historical research and documentation that he claimed to follow in his preface *ad lectorem*. Furthermore, it has shown that Hanke was not a "Silesian" historian dabbling in other histories outside his ken. He was a classically trained scholar of encyclopedic historical interests and broad temporal and geographical range who had been working for more than a decade, seeking out books and manuscripts and systematically reading authors ancient and modern, amassing notes, and formulating his assessments on a specific set of critical questions. Yet, importantly, as he worked he was gathering materials not only for the volume of the moment but for all the volumes in a very ambitious global historiographical project. His work on the writers of Byzantine history, in other words, represented the fruit of almost two decades of broad but meticulous reading. Hanke was, indeed, a serious student of Byzantium—but of a Byzantium that formed part of larger temporal and geographical continuities.

This extended discussion of his methods and approach in his volumes on Roman writers is highly relevant, because Hanke himself believed he was continuing this very approach in his *De Byzantinarum rerum scriptoribus Graecis*, published in 1677. As he noted in his letter to the reader in the Byzantine volume:

> The more serious and perspicacious judge of our work shall easily be able to know on his own why we set forth the reasons for the other important aspects pertaining to the whole [work] and to the individual parts. But if he should wish them to be explained, he can gain them from the Letters to the Reader with which we prefaced the first and second book about Roman writers, for this book has been developed along the same lines.[27]

26 Ibid.

27 Hanke, *De Byzantinarum rerum scriptoribus Graecis liber* (n. 5 above), C4: *Momentorum caeterorum, ad huius libri tum universitatem tum membra singula pertinentium, rationes cur asseramus, quas diligentior circumspectiorque nostri laboris Aestimator ex facili per se cogniturus sit; quod si vero,*

The formal similarities would have been immediately apparent to his readers. As in his earlier work, Hanke sought in this volume to present a select group of the most important historical writers, in this case on Byzantium; to array them in chronological order (when possible) or grouped in relative order (when precise dates or identities were unknown); to develop for each rigorously documented discussions of their lives (*vita*), their works (*scripta*), and judgments (*judicia*) about them; and to highlight and, if possible, resolve disputed aspects of their careers and works. To enhance the work's usefulness, his treatment of Byzantine writers would again conclude with a set of carefully designed indexes: (1) an alphabetical guide to authors; (2) an index organized chronologically by the latest period that the author's work discusses; (3) an alphabetically organized author guide with short summaries of the people, places, and events discussed in their works; (4) a tripartite index that ordered authors chronologically, topically, and by peoples discussed; and (5) an alphabetical index to all authors mentioned in the volume, if only in a reference. For this volume, however, he had added one more finding aid—an alphabetical guide to historical people and things (such as offices, technical terms, religious factions)—suggesting that he was continuing to consider the ways in which different readers would use his work (*B* Ad Lectorem, quires A–H).

As in his earlier volume, Hanke did not hesitate to restrict the scope of his work to serve specific scholarly aims, and those aims had become more focused with time (and perhaps with a growing sense of the limits on his own time and attention) on the Roman Empire and its heirs, the Greeks and the Germans.

> Today, although [the Roman Empire] has lost much of its size and strength, the example of this most indulgent and benign Mother shines forth in so many kingdoms that flourish in their wealth and power; and although it may seem undone by the great weight of its old age, it nonetheless imitates the nature of iron, which remains durable even in the most delicate of forms. Thus to possess with understanding the origins, the provinces, the changes, and especially the history of this empire when it was so extensive through so many ages and from the very beginning: what else is this but to render familiar the most important histories of, if not all, then the most noble peoples.[28] (*B* Ad Lectorem, c1r–v)

quantum satis, expositas velit, ex Epistolis ad Lectorem, quas de Romanis Scriptoribus primo secundoque libro praemissimus (ad quorum similitudinem hic elaboratus est) haurire possit? This work is hereafter cited parenthetically in the text, with the abbreviation *B*.

28 *Hodieque, licet amplitudinis roborisque multum amiserit, tamen in tot Regnis opulentia potentiaque florentissimis, instar indulgentissimae benignissimaeque Matris eminet; licet maxima senii gravitate videtur confectum, tamen Ferri naturam, sub formis etiam tenuioribus durabilem, imitatur. Huius*

Because of its own historical reach and rule but also because of its ongoing imprint on other polities, the history of Rome could serve, Hanke argued, as the historical skeleton key that would enable the diligent scholar to unlock many other histories. But the pathway to this key of historical understanding was difficult and full of dangers because of the need for fitting and credible guides: that is to say, reliable historical sources. Hanke sought to provide such guidance in a world where the rarity and cost of books might preclude awareness of critical materials even among the most studious, while among the less trained, trust might come to be misplaced in a writer with little or no historical care (*B* Ad Lectorem, c1v).[29]

Rome had "ennobled" three peoples in particular: the Latins, the Greeks, and the Germans (*B* Ad Lectorem, c1v).[30] Hanke's first volumes had guided readers through sources on the initial phase of Roman history. In the present volume, he stated that he would focus specifically on the development of the Roman Empire in the Greek world. He further narrowed his scope to authors writing in Greek and to those whose works, though they might discuss other regions of the empire, focused primarily on the secular and ecclesiastical affairs unfolding in Constantinople between the time of Constantine I (306–337) and Constantine XI Palaiologos (1449–1453). The consequences of this methodological choice were significant: it meant that Hanke's *De Byzantinarum rerum scriptoribus* would not map directly onto the evolving contours of the Paris Corpus of Byzantine writers, a publishing endeavor for which he had the greatest appreciation and some of whose volumes he would use.[31] In particular, he would omit Anastasius Bibliothecarius, Leone Allacci, and Philippe Labbe on the grounds that they wrote in Latin; George Synkellos, George Kedrenos, Michael Glykas, Constantine Manasses, and Joel the Chronicler would be set aside because their works focused primarily, if not exclusively, on the world prior to Constantine; and Laonikos Chalkokondyles would be excluded because he framed his work around the history of the Ottoman Turks, even though, Hanke acknowledged, "he devoted a great part to their deeds against the empire of Constantinople" (*B* Ad

imperii latissime patentis origines, provincias, mutationes, inprimis res tam multis saeculorum aetatibus gestas, a principiis suis habere cognitas, quid aliud est quam potissimas, si non omnium, certe nobilissimarum Gentium historias sibi reddidisse familiares?

29 *Quales cum solerter inquirendi, prudenter aestimandi veniant, sed alii, quos minime vulgaris usus ingeniis, curas historicas vel prorsus negligentibus, vel remissius exercentibus, relinquit obscuros, in eruditis plerosque fugiant; alii, quos insolentior seu raritas, seu caritas bibliothecis maxime privatis denegat, ne summis quidem viris, etsi reconditae scientiae librariae studiossimis, omnibus innotescant*[.]

30 *Imperium Romanum, ut Barbaros silentio premam, tres imprimis populos, quos habuit possessores, Latinos, Graecos, Germanos eminentia sua nobilitavit.*

31 See *B* Ad Lectorem, c3, where Hanke noted that the corpus had been "published for thirty years with the greatest expense and efforts and with the most refined papers and fonts, and was notable already for 25 volumes and was not yet finished."

Lectorem, c3). He also excluded earlier authors such as Eunapius, Olympiodorus, and several others because he had already dealt with them in the Roman volumes. At the same time, he noted that his treatment of Byzantine historical writers would include authors that had not yet appeared in the Paris Corpus, such as Eusebius, Ignatios the Deacon, Niketas David Paphlagon, John Kameniates, Nikephoros Gregoras, and George Sphrantzes (*B* Ad Lectorem, c3). He was, in other words, writing not an annotated handlist for the Paris Corpus but a guide constructed according to independent criteria of historical scope and significance, and he was drawing on the entire pool of available editions and translations of Byzantine works.

Although he had specific historical criteria that determined which authors would receive separate treatment in his volume, Hanke made clear that when an author was included for discussion, a full reckoning of their published corpus of writings would be offered, whether those writings related to Byzantine affairs or not (*B* Ad Lectorem, c3v).[32] In this regard, he both sought to offer his readers comprehensive guidance to his catalog of authors and implicitly claimed that to understand these writers as historians, readers needed to know about the full range of their literary production across genres. As in his Roman volumes, Hanke also manifested concern for his reader's access to the fullness of documentation and argument by either providing translations of Greek passages or simply including relevant textual materials in Latin translation—always with the translations clearly cited, so that readers could find the originals. In this way, he implicitly acknowledged and accepted the highly variable quality of Greek learning that interested readers in the Republic of Letters might bring to their study of Byzantine history, while recognizing the importance of their access to the full weight of historical evidence and arguments, even those involving finer points of philology.

From available witnesses, the response to Hanke's treatment of Byzantine historians seems to have been strongly positive, yet not unmixed. Here again Christian Daumius, Hanke's admirer and now friend, offers insight into the work's European reception. To Hanke's colleague Johannes Gebhard, Daumius enthusiastically reported in the winter of 1678 that he had heard from Nicholas Heinsius the Elder not only that Nicholas liked the work very much but also that it was already being very well received in England and Belgium, where copies had arrived in the previous year.[33] In a letter from May 1678 to Hanke himself, Daumius shared news of the

32 Although Hanke drew on manuscript evidence in his comments, was sensitive to it in his evaluation of editions, and was certainly aware of the importance of textual witnesses still in manuscript, he consciously avoided focusing primary attention on materials that were not more broadly accessible through publication (rare or expensive though such works might be).

33 Christian Daumius, *Epistola* 46 to Johannes Gebhardus, in *Philologi et polyhistoris celeberrimi Epistolae*, 136: *Id in Belgio et Anglia quo superiore anno iam pervenit, pro merito aestimari, honorifice*

work's warm reception not only among erudite Germans but also among English, French, and Italian scholars. He noted in particular Nicholas Heinsius's appreciation, as well as that of the Italian polymath and bibliophile Antonio Magliabechi (1633–1714), who spoke of Hanke as a standout among the *vulgus eruditorum* and as someone others should appreciate.[34] Having conveyed to Hanke the good news, Daumius alerted him to the fact that his work did have at least one detractor, a "hater and despiser of such scholarship" and an "incredibly ignorant" man whose own works Daumius found a "confused chaos" written in an "unsuitable style" and with "gratuitous and affected eloquence" offering nothing special to the reader save a disordered collection of remarks derived from others yet set forth as his own. Indeed, Jakobus Thomasius, the philosopher and historian of philosophy, had demonstrated that he was a plagiarist. "This fellow," Daumius concluded supportively and with a dose of academic crudity, "should shut up lest he irritate the censors [judges of critical merit] by publicizing his own ignorance that they shall greet with their middle fingers. He shits crap of this kind only to his own ruin and only dishonors himself when he spurns those who deserve honor because of scholarship that is beyond their own ken."[35] Hanke, in other words, need not worry.

nobilissimus Heinsius index mihi fuit, cui placet admodum; et vel uni placuisse satius est quam multis aliis minoris commatis.

34 Christian Daumius, *Epistola* 5 to Martin Hankius, in ibid., 154–57, at 155. Daumius notes that Magliabechi's testimony about Hanke's reputation in Italy relied on a printed estimation of Hanke's work on Roman historical writers published in the *Ephemerides italicae* (Rome, 1677) and gives the page numbers of the reference. I have not been able to consult this work. That Nicholas Heinsius knew of Hanke's work on Byzantine historians, and likely had a copy, is shown by Benedict Carpzovius's letter to Heinsius from 1678 in which he praises the clarity and rigor of Hanke's style in a quiet comparison with Vossius's work; *Epistola* 254, in *Sylloges Epistolarum a viris illustribus scriptarum*, ed. P. Burman, vol. 5, *Quo Nicolai Heinsii et Virorum Eruditorum in Succia, Germania, Belgio, Italia, et Gallia Epistolae*... (Leiden, 1727), 294–97, at 295: *Unus tamen Martinus Hankius novi operis tibi nunciandi nobis copiam dedit, emisso de Byzantinarum rerum scriptoribus graecis Commentario, in quo vitas et scripta auctorum quinquaginta, qui de Constantinopolitanis aliisque Graecis antiquitatibus monumenta nobis reliquerunt, distinctiorem in modum recensentur, judicia etiam de eorum scriptis feruntur: quem in modum jam superioribus annis idem Clarissimus autor de Rerum Romanarum scriptoribus geminos ediderat libros: de quibus aeque ac nunc publici juris facto Commentario sententiam non dico, quam amor erga virum optimum, qui mihi etiam librum, ut typographum et editorem ei conciliarem, Uratislavia miserat, cohibet. Id tamen profiteor, ut colligendi et varios Autores evolvendi laboris laude se commendant, ita ingenii gloria se minus mihi probare hujusmodi Collectanea, magis placere ab ipsorum autorum ingenio profecta opera, de quibus rectius etiam sive in bonam, sive in alteram partem ferre judicium licet.*

35 Daumius, *Epistola* 5 to Hankius, 155–56, with the final quotation: *Taceat igitur ille, ne suam prodendo inscitiam irritet censores, eam medio digito excepturos. Eiusmodi turdus certe sibi ipsi exitium cacat, et seipsum turpiter prostituit dum honorem merentes ex studiis spernit quae supra sunt ipsius captum.* I have not yet been able to identify the person referenced here.

Earlier in the year, however, Daumius had been much less confident. He had heard about a detractor of Hanke's work who did not so much attack it openly as praise it *satis frigide* and strongly imply that Hanke had merely plagiarized Gerhard Vossius's *De historicis Graecis libri IV*.[36] Initially uncertain of the truth of this charge, Daumius undertook a comparison of the two works *maiore cura*, which immediately set his mind at ease: the charge of plagiarism was entirely groundless. As a sample of his findings he offered Gebhardus the authors' treatments of two authors: Eusebius and Photios.

> What does Vossius say about these fellows? About the former, he offers one page; concerning the latter, not even half a page. In contrast, Hankius has prepared an outstanding *commentarium* about Eusebius and Photios to which he devoted more than thirty full *quaternia*. There you may find more than one hundred times more than in Vossius. Is this what it means "to owe much to Vossius"? In addition, he has no small number of authors about whom Vossius offers scarcely a word, authors of whom Vossius was completely unaware because, although available in manuscripts, they had not yet been edited.[37]

Hanke had, of course, drawn on Vossius's work as one of the sources of contemporary opinion on Greek historians, and cited him explicitly twenty-eight times.[38] But Daumius's point-by-point comparison revealed the contrast in depth and complexity that Hanke brought to his discussions of the Byzantine authors; in each case, his assessment that Hanke provided "more than a hundred times more material"

36 Daumius, *Epistola* 46 to Gebhardus, 137. Published in 1627, Vossius's work had been reprinted in Leiden in 1651. Vossius divided his work into four books, with book 3 dedicated to historians of uncertain date and book 4 to historians before the Peloponnesian War. Books 1 and 2 were dedicated to a wide-ranging sets of comments, some of which were biobibliographical, some of which were polemics on chronological matters, and others of which were notes on particular historical treatments. The alphabetical index of names at the end of the work is the only way to easily find discussions of particular writers. On Vossius's life and scholarly career, see the classic biography by C. S. M. Rademaker, *Life and Work of Gerardus Joannes Vossius (1577–1649)*, trans. H. P. Doezema (Assen, 1981). On Vossius's ideas about history and historical method, see now N. Wickenden, *G. J. Vossius and the Humanist Concept of History* (Assen, 1993).

37 Daumius, *Epistola* 46 to Gebhardus, 137: *Exemplo sint Eusebius et Photius. De his quid Vossius? de priore quidem unius folii paginam; de posteriore autem ne paginame quidem dimidiam. At quam insignem de Eusebio et Photio confecit Hankius commentarium: cui plusquam XXX integros quaterniones impendit; Ubi plusquam centies plura quam in Vossio reperias. Hocne est multa debere Vossio? Ad haec scriptores non adeo paucos habet de quibus vi ullum verbum Vossius, quos, etsi Gracecos, nondum tamen editos in MStis obvios penitus ignoravit.*

38 See *B* Index V, s.v. Vossius.

than Vossius proved true.[39] Rather than feeling the gratitude and admiration appropriately owed to such a scholarly accomplishment, Hanke's critic had succumbed to envy and the willful blindness and ignorance that it engendered.[40] Perhaps concerned to defend Vossius's work, the critic had not noticed that Hanke had entirely different objectives and that his work, as a consequence, assumed a much different form with a much different function.

Hanke at Work

As Hanke had observed early on, his wish was to set the study of Byzantine history upon a firm foundation of textual witnesses whose lives, times, works, and potential problems the reader could assess readily through reading. To that end, Hanke sought consciously to assemble and set forth for evaluation all available witnesses both in the primary sources themselves and in later commentators. Whether it concerned an author's name, birthplace, office, or other moments in their curriculum vitae, Hanke offered his reader selections from the author's own works or those of others that would help demonstrate an interpretation or explain why a question could not be decided. These selections reveal that Hanke must have been an extremely careful, focused reader of the sources, harvesting comments big and small that shed light on an author's situation. At the same time, Hanke constantly attended to the observations of these texts' editors and commentators and did not just select but displayed the *status quaestionis* on debated points. In this way, he constantly juxtaposed source and criticism, allowing the reader to see which interpretations flowed from the sources and which did not have such support. Likewise, his work offered the reader who had limited access to the full range of scholarship—a problem that afflicted many and that Hanke recalled experiencing personally—a wider and more populated toolbox of sources and scholarly opinion with which they could pursue their own historical projects.

This cumulative and synthetic work that placed, in effect, the condensed results of scholarship on Byzantine history in the reader's hand was complemented by Hanke's more critical interventions on disputed points and his explicit scholarly deconstruction of erroneous views. Matters of identification and names, offices, chronology, and larger questions of source bias preoccupied him, particularly

39 For example, Vossius devoted nine lines amid a much larger section to his discussion of Anna Komnene (*De historicis Graecis libri IV* [n. 16 above], 231); Hanke dedicated a full section (chapter 29) of six pages to Anna, its brevity prompted mainly because her life and narrative did not seem at the time to pose complex problems (*B* 507–13).

40 Daumius, *Epistola* 46 to Gebhardus, 137.

because such questions condition so much about a source's relevance and reliability. In addition, Hanke showed particular and sustained interest in several of the religious conflicts as both central to an author's lifetime and complicating the historian's reading of the sources.

Names stood at the core of authorial identity, and Hanke correspondingly was willing to spend significant time and space sorting through knotty naming problems. His patient approach was exemplified in his treatment of Eusebius, his first Byzantine historian. Hanke begins where he meant to end: "Our Eusebius took his cognomen from the martyr and priest Pamphilus of Caesarea in Palestine" (*B* 1). But he then goes on to complicate this seemingly straightforward name with a thoroughgoing analysis of Eusebius's treatment by Latin and Greek writers from antiquity to the recent past, initiated by the simple phrase: "This cognomen, which Eusebius owes to Pamphilus, is usually formed in different ways" (*B* 1)[41]. These variants are not idle curiosities, however, but signal deeper differences in the understanding of Eusebius the person. More recent medieval and early modern Latin writers used the nominative form *Pamphilus,* while ancient and more recent Greek writers never did, instead employing the genitive. When he examined the ancient Latin writers, Hanke found that they also used the genitive. Yet he noted that it was not clear to all why Eusebius had the cognomen *Pamphili.* Some thought that this meant that Eusebius was the son of Pamphilus, as some scholars insightfully (*luculenter*) invoked the Greek practice of *ellipsin* to explain the absence of the word *son.* Unfortunately, it did not always indicate "son of"; sometimes it could mean "brother," at other times "servant," and at still others "friend"—three very different relationships that Eusebius might have with Pamphilus. Drawing on the witnesses of Jerome and Photios, Hanke concludes that the meaning of the genitive form of "Pamphili" is "Eusebius, friend of Pamphilus," though he observed that this usage still was not found in available translations (*B* 1–5).

Similar questions swirled around the relationship of Caesarea to Eusebius, an issue of importance because the multiplicity of people named Eusebius led to Caesareus/Caesariensis being used as a cognomen as well. Accumulating a corpus of examples from Greek and Latin writers, Hanke observed that this geographical cognomen often seems to be used as if it designated Eusebius's birthplace. But other writers claim that it referred to Eusebius's episcopal see: "Eusebius, bishop of Caesarea." Yet "our Eusebius," Hanke noted, also was referred to as "Palestinus." Did this mean that his homeland was Palestine? Hanke warned against making this assumption, because, here again, Eusebius might have been called *Palestinus* because

41 *Eusebius noster a Caesariensium in Palestina Presbytero Pamphilo Martyre cognomen accepit.... Istud cognomen, quod Eusebius Pamphilo debet, diversis modis formari solet.*

he was bishop of Caesarea in Palestine. Nor did evidence from Eusebius himself necessarily clarify the force of the cognomen: it could mean that he ruled a bishopric in Palestine or that he had been born or raised there and therefore could be numbered among the "Palestini" (*B* 5–7). These options may not have been mutually exclusive, however, for at that time, Hanke observed—invoking his sense of difference between early Christian and later ecclesiastical custom—foreigners rarely pursued episcopal positions; he found this suspicion to be confirmed by Theodore Metochites, who noted that Eusebius remarks on being from Palestine, though Hanke added that it is not known to whom Eusebius recounted his life (*B* 7).

One final piece of Eusebius's nomenclature puzzled him, however: the use of the term *necessarius* to describe the relationship between Eusebius and Pamphilus. He admitted that such a term could be used of people unrelated by blood who were simply very close friends. Yet for someone more accustomed to the practices of Latin funeral inscriptions, the more common usage would be that "relatives by blood or by marriage were called 'necessary'" (*B* 8). Pamphilus and Eusebius were therefore not only friends but kinsmen.

Hanke's extended and richly documented probe into Eusebius's name may have struck some of his readers as much ado about very little. Yet, as his presentation showed, students interested in Eusebius were continuously exposed not only to different primary accounts that said different things but also to different translations that rendered the original Greek in different ways based on different assumptions about language and history. They therefore had to be vigilant. He also clearly rejected the idea of simply telling his reader the "answer" *ex auctoritate,* though he did begin the entry with a basic position that he maintained. Instead, he took his reader step-by-step through the process of reasoning with sources, highlighting areas of interpretive ambiguity as well as the role that an understanding of historical change can bring to the interpretation of a set of textual details—in this case, helping to reconcile them.

Occasionally, naming issues arose from the confusion of two persons closely associated in time. Such, Hanke argued, was the case with Nikephoros Bryennios the Caesar. Conrad Gessner in his *Bibliotheca universalis* (1549) and the Carmelite bibliophile Louis Jacob in his *Bibliotheca illustrium foeminarum* (1650) had both confounded the husband of Anna Komnene with his contemporary Nikephoros Melissenos through an "easy mistake, because both men were caesars."[42] Hanke presented

42 On Gessner, see now U. Leu, *Conrad Gessner (1516–1565): Universalgelehrter und Naturforscher der Renaissance* (Zurich, 2016), and the essays assembled in *Conrad Gessner: Die Renaissance der Wissenschaften / The Renaissance of Learning,* ed. U. Leu and P. Opitz (Berlin, 2019). On Louis Jacob de Saint-Charles, see I. Maclean, "Louis Jacob de Saint-Charles (1608–1670) and

excerpts from the relevant witnesses—John Zonaras and Anna Komnene—and quickly moved on (*B* 494–95).

Along with questions of identity and naming, Hanke viewed chronology as a central concern of his project: to determine, within the limits of the evidence, the lifetimes of his authors. These issues came together in Hanke's treatments of two writers named Theophanes: Theophanes Confessor and Theophanes Byzantius. In these cases, he isolated Gerhard Vossius a principal sower of confusion and misinformation.

In his treatment of Theophanes Confessor, Vossius had noted that "[e]qual to [George Synkellos] was George Theophanes Confessor: as it is known from part III of Michael Glykas's annals."[43] "As they usually do," Hanke observed, three recent writers had taken up Vossius's view in their works on Roman historical writers without question: the Trevisan Balthasar Bonifacius (1585–1659), Aubert Miraeus (1573–1640), and Martin Zeiller (1589–1660). In doing so, they followed a leader who, "if not wrong, nevertheless was rightly suspected of error." Hanke knew of no ancient source that called Theophanes George, but he surmised that the error had arisen from Vossius's consultation of the Latin translation (rather than the Greek edition) of Michael Glykas, where he misread "Post Georgium [Syncellum] Theophanes Confessor" as "Georgius Theophanes Confessor" (*B* 200). Quietly, Hanke alerted readers to Vossius's occasional sloppiness and to his failure to go back to the original language sources.

Vossius disseminated another error regarding Theophanes Confessor's death and identity when he noted—again without explanation or evidence—that "clearly this [Theophanes] seems to me to be one and the same as that Theophanes the priest and prior whose speech on the exile of S. Nicephorus, bishop of Constantinople, and the translation of his relics is available in tome II, XIII March of [Laurentius] Surius's work."[44] But this identification was a chronological impossibility, because Theophanes Confessor was known with documented certainty (as Hanke had just shown) to have died before 821 and Theophanes Presbyter could not have delivered his oration prior to 845 (*B* 217–18).

Vossius again proved a flawed guide in his treatment of "Theophanes Byzantius," an author whom Hanke placed in his section of authors with uncertain dates.

---

the Development of Specialist Bibliography," in his *Learning and the Market Place: Essays in the History of the Early Modern Book* (Leiden, 2009), 404–60 with references to earlier literature.

43 *De historicis Graecis Libri IV*, 285: *Aequalis ei fuit Georgius Theophanes Confessor, ut constat ex Michaelis Glycae Annalium parte III B 200.*

44 *Vossius, De historicis Graecis Libri IV, 285: Plane autem, inquiens, mihi hic idem videtur ac Theophanes ille presbyter et praepositus cuius oratio de exsilio S. Nicephori episcopi Constantinopolitani, deque translatione reliquiarum eius Surium exstat, tomo II, XIII Martii.*

Theophanes Byzantius was alive at the same time as Justin II, whom Justinian I chose as his successor in 565, if Gerhard Vossius does not wander from the truth (*De historicis Graecis* 2.23). "Theophanes Byzantius, who published 10 books of histories lived under Justin II, who succeeded Justinian in 565." Among those who subscribe to Vossius's view is Jacob Goar in the notes to Theophanes' chronographia.... We are not able to go against Vossius's opinion, which he confirms with no testimony and no argument, although we fear lest, led by a foolish conjecture, he judged that Theophanes lived at the time of this same emperor because he finished his ten books of histories amid the deeds of Justin II. For clearly one can find many writers who lived much later than the person amid whose deeds they ended their books.[45] (*B* 674)

Vossius, Hanke feared, had fallen into the trap of thinking that the point at which an author concluded his history could be used to date the author's own terminus ad quem. He quickly observed that this assumption was simply untrue (and, indeed, a bit naïve) but then added critical information about the uncertain state of the history, using Photios's account of Theophanes' work (a work, significantly, that Hanke explicitly showed was known to Vossius). There the ninth-century polymath made clear that the ten surviving books of Theophanes were not the total of his historical work but that he had written many more books. Could Theophanes not have written about events under later emperors? asked Hanke rhetorically before concluding: "Since it is not clear when he finished his last books, it is all the more doubtful when he lived" (*B* 675).[46]

Hanke then noted, with irritation and perhaps some amusement, that Vossius contradicted himself when raising the question of whether Theophanes Byzantius, whom he placed in the late sixth century, and Theophanes Confessor, whom he placed in the late eighth or early ninth century, were one person or two people and "leaves it to the learned to puzzle it out." For these two Theophanes to be the same

45 *Theophanes Byzantius imperatore Justino II, quem Justinianus primus A.C.565 successorem accepit, in vivis exstitit, si non a vero aberrat Gerardus Vossius lib.II, de Historicis Graecis, cap. XXII, Sub Justino Secundo, inquiens, qui Justiniano successit anno IϽ LXV vixit Theophanes Byzantius, qui inclaruit decem historiarum libris. Inter quos qui Vossio subscribunt, Jacobus Goarus in notis ad Theophanis chronographiam: ... Nos in Vossi sententiam quam nullo testimonio, argumento nullo firmat, discedere non sustinemus, verentes, ne propterea Theophanem, quoniam in Imperatoris Justini II rebus libros deem historiarum terminavit, eiusdem Imperatoris temporibus vixisse judicaverit, imbecilli conjectura ductus. Sane scriptores plurimos invenire licet, quos multo recentius habuit superstites, quam in cuius gestis codices suos finierunt.*

46 *Itaque cum minime clarum sit, ubi ultimos suos codices terminaverit, tanto magis dubium est, quando vixerit.*

person, Hanke explained, "we must assert that he was a 200-year-old man," which clearly was impossible. He personally did not see a problem with a chronology in which Theophanes Byzantius and Theophanes Confessor could be the same person, since the date of Theophanes Byzantius was uncertain. But he also stated that "we do not have anything with which we might demonstrate that those two Theophanes, one named Byzantius, the other Confessor, are not two different people" (*B* 675). Unlike Vossius, who perhaps believed it necessary to have a decided view on each question even if expressing it would lead his readers into confusion or absurdity, Hanke was prepared to remain explicitly uncertain and to state clearly the limits of the evidence. In this way, his readers would know exactly the firmness of the historical ground on which they stood. For attentive readers, his explicit critique of Vossius's handling of these Theophanes—Vossius's carelessness, his use of Latin translations rather than original texts, his flawed assumptions about authorship, his failure to reason historically, and, most importantly, his failure to provide full evidence and argument—might serve to vaccinate them against excessive and unquestioning reliance on such an authority. Yet it also identified the way in which uncritical reliance on authorities by other scholars disseminated and strengthened such errors by spreading them to wider audiences and by turning a single voice into what appeared to be consensus among different scholars.

Hanke tackled another knotty set of chronological problems in his treatments of Symeon Metaphrastes and Michael Psellos, two authors bound together because of Psellos's encomium for Symeon. He noted, "The time at which Simeon lived is very controversial," and then proceeded to detail dates proposed by various early modern scholars: prior to the third century, during the fourth century, during the seventh century, and before the year 859 (*B* 420–22). Chief among the proponents of this ninth-century date was the ecclesiastical historian and Counter-Reformation polemicist Caesar Baronius.[47] Basing his dating on an assumption that Michael Psellos was the teacher of Leo the Philosopher and on the idea that Psellos must have composed his encomium of Symeon soon after the man's death, because Psellos in his encomium says that he heard about Symeon's death from those who were present, Baronius had given Symeon a date just before 859. He, in turn, had been followed by Robert Bellarmine (*De scriptoribus ecclesiasticis liber unus*, 1613), Johannes Gerhard (*Patrologia*, 1668), and André Du Saussay (*De mysticis Galliae scriptoribus*, 1639). Yet, "because these men did not know the true era of the Psellus

47 On Baronius and his historical work (though without discussions of engagement with Byzantine history), see *Baronio storico e la Controriforma: Atti del Convegno internazionale di studi, Sora, 6–10 ottobre 1979*, ed. R. de Maio, L. Gulia, and A. Mazzacane (Sora, 1982); S. Zen, *Baronio storico: Controriforma e crisi del metodo umanistico* (Naples, 1994); and, most recently, *Baronio e le sue fonti: Atti del Convegno Internazionale di Studi, Sora, 10–13 Ottobre 2007*, ed. L. Gulia (Sora, 2009).

who wrote the posthumous encomium for our Simeon, they erred. For Psellus lived in the eleventh century after Christ, not, as Bellarmine and Baronius judge, in the ninth, as we will show in chap. 26"[48] (*B* 422). Indeed, error was rife regarding the era of Symeon's life: "Just as some deduce Simeon's lifetime from some of the lives of saints, so they bring it about that Simeon is assigned to the most various times because they wrongly judge him to be the author of many lives from the titles which bear the name of our Symeon: thus he becomes a man of many ages"[49] (*B* 422). Having identified the existing scholarly error and confusion, Hanke turned to his own positive project: "But why would we devote our energy to destroying these false opinions one by one when Symeon's authentic age, which we will soon clearly demonstrate, will easily take on the color of truth—which is beautiful to all" (*B* 423).

Later, in his treatment of Michael Psellos, Hanke continued to highlight the virus-like damage that Baronius's interpretation had caused: "Baronius deceived his followers when he offered them an utterly weak basis for his opinion, or rather, no basis at all"[50] (*B* 478). But Baronius also revealed a lack of imagination about the historical process. He had assumed that for Psellos to claim knowledge from eyewitnesses, he had to be their exact contemporary. To the contrary, Hanke observed, there were many different means of access: Psellos could have heard the stories as a young man from older men who were eyewitnesses; he could have heard oral tales about Symeon and written them down in later life; he could also have read texts by those who were present at Symeon's death but described the contents as if they had said them (*B* 478–79). The scholar thinking seriously about historical writers thus possessed no easy equations and algorithms; one had to enter imaginatively into the human processes of memory, documentation, and history making. Yet, for the final blow against this pernicious dating of Psellos, Hanke turned to the rigors of chronology, noting pointedly: "Chronology destroys Baronius's opinion"[51] (*B* 479).

48 *Sed hi, quoniam aetatem Pselli veram, qui nostro Simeoni posthumum elogium scripsit, ignoraverunt, errant. Hic enim Psellus, non, ut Baronius et Bellarminus arbitrantur, nono, sed undecimo post Christum natum saeculo vixit, quemadmodum cap. xxvi demonstrabimus.*

49 *Sicut autem Simeonis aevum ex aliis Sanctorum vitis, alii colligunt, sic efficiunt, ut Simeon, quem plurimarum vitarum autorem ex titulis nomen Simeonis nostri praeferentibus male quidam judicant, diversissimis temporibus adscribatur, adeoque multorum saeculorum homo fiat.* It is worth mentioning here that Hanke also noted scholars who had confused Symeon Metaphrastes with Symeon the New Theologian, and therefore placed Symeon Metaphrastes' life in the early 12th century, around 1200, and even around 1300, a view so egregiously incorrect that he indicted those who held it for sinning against truth: *Adhuc enormius in veritatem peccant quibus Simeon Metaphrastes anno Christi circa 1300 claruisse creditur. In quibus reperitur Raphael Volterannus (Raffaele Maffei) commentariorum libro XIX* (*B* 433).

50 *Sed asseclas suos Baronius fallit, qui sententiae suae fundamentum prorsus infirmum, imo nullum dedit.*

51 *Accedit quod Baronii sententiam chronologia destruat.*

Questions of name, title, office, and chronology occupy a central place in Hanke's treatment of each of his authors. At the same time, he spent significant time and energy on a range of debated aspects of these biographies. Two examples bring out key qualities of his approach. When discussing Procopius of Caesarea's qualities as an author, he noted that "[w]hether [Procopius] was a pagan or a Christian is not beyond debate," accumulating quotations from Procopius's works as well as modern commentaries that might suggest a pagan or agnostic position. Yet Hanke urged a more circumspect reading: "But there are reasons why we may interpret more tolerantly those things which Procopius seems to have written as a pagan. For in some passages, he shows quite clearly that he is not only a Christian but an orthodox Christian (unless he was perhaps a very perverse and shameless pretender of Christian religion)"[52] (*B* 147)—a claim that he supported, characteristically, by quoting four of the relevant proof texts.

In his extended treatment of Photios—one of the longest in the work—he took time to quash what he portrayed as a vicious rumor that was infiltrating the discussion of this prolific, complex, and controversial figure: that Photios was a eunuch. Once again, Baronius is the key vector for this idea. He derived his view (which he repeated, as Hanke observed, multiple times) from a single letter exchange between John the Patrician and Photios, in which John, Baronius claimed, criticized Photios for involving himself in sacred matters, though a eunuch. This view of Photios as eunuch had, in turn, been accepted by the monk Matheus Raderus, in his annotations to his edition of the eighth ecumenical council (1604); by Nicholas Serarius, in his book on the history of Mainz (1604); by the Protestant polemicist Samuel Maresius, in his work on Pope Joan (1658); and by Philippe Labbe, in volume 2 of his work on ecclesiastical writers (1660). Thus, Hanke quietly observed that Baronius's view had spread to both Protestant and Catholic learned communities.

The problem, however, was that Baronius had switched the sender and recipient of the letter, which Hanke demonstrated with a detailed textual analysis: rather than John attacking Photios for being a eunuch, Photios had attacked John. Yet the proof of Baronius's error went further and drew on Hanke's extensive knowledge of the bitter ecclesiastical controversies of the time: "There is this in addition: it is well known that Theognostus the Monk, Nicetas David Paphlago, Metrophanes of Smyrna, Stylianos of Neocaesarea, and others—men who disseminated anything negative that either they themselves could find or find invented by others to destroy Photios's reputation—did not teach in their own writings that Photios was a eunuch"

52 *Sed est, cur ea quae videtur Procopius ut homo paganus scripsisse, mitius interpretemur. Etenemi nonnullis in locis, se non modo Christianum, sed orthodoxum quoque Christianum [nisi forte nimis perversus et protervus Religionis Christianae simulator fuerit].*

(*B* 272). Intimately familiar with the polemical writings of the time and also conscious of the mechanisms of ad hominem attack, Hanke had pointed out the simple fact that although Photios had many critics and enemies who would have delighted in deploying such information as a weapon, not one of them ever accused the patriarch of being a eunuch. It must not, therefore, have been something contemporaries actually said or even lied about. An indication of his argument's success comes in Johannes Fabricius's treatment of this biographical detail in his *Bibliotheca Graeca*. Almost as an antiquarian footnote, he remarked: "This fable about Photius the eunuch which Baronius persuaded many to believe and which was gobbled up in order to declare that [Photios's] ordination was contrary to the canons, Martin Hankius, who has written the life of Photius accurately and carefully, has refuted."[53] Hanke would have been pleased.

While highly polemical and *parti-pris* writers could sometimes serve the Byzantine historian well, they posed essential problems of perspective and bias. Consequently, as he dealt with authors whose careers coincided with major ecclesiastical controversies in Byzantium, Hanke often devoted extensive discussion to the events and theological positions themselves, almost producing at times free-standing histories of these moments. But his aim remained to present his readers with a full understanding of the historical writers' biases and tendencies. Thus, in his accounts of Theophanes Confessor, Nikephoros of Constantinople, and Ignatios the Deacon, the unfolding controversy over images constituted a leitmotif that helped organize and assess the witnesses who were both participants in and narrators of these events (*B* 200–251). In his discussion of the later ninth-century sources, it was the internal conflict between supporters of Ignatios and supporters of Photios, and the conflict with Rome that would come to be known as the Photian Schism, to which he devoted extended, nuanced attention as he drew on Byzantine, papal, and Carolingian sources.[54]

Through careful comparative work with an abundance of sources available in print and manuscript, Hanke highlighted those places where the partisan animus of contemporaries—Latin and Greek—seemed to have gotten the better of their narrative of events and people. At the same time, he pointed out the places where his own contemporaries' partisanship led them to selectively represent or distort the historical record (e.g., *B* 336–37, 355–58, 359–60, 377–78). Of Baronius, for example, he noted, "Just as Baronius serves his love for the Roman pontiff to excess, so he is led excessively by hatred against Photios, the Roman pontiff's opponent"[55] (*B* 337).

53 J. A. Fabricius, *Bibliotheca graeca*, 14 vols. (Hamburg, 1705–28), 9:304.

54 These sources included Theognostos the Monk, Metrophanes of Smyrna, and Photios (*B* 251–395).

55 *Sed Baronius, ut in pontificem Romanum nimis amori servet, sic in Photium, Romani pontificis adversarium, nimis odio ducitur.*

Likewise, when Baronius interpreted Photios's comment in a letter to a deacon Gregory that God saved him through his exile from an earthquake as clear evidence of the patriarch's egotism and impiety, Hanke was more cautious: "Baronius takes this [passage] in a negative way.... But if you look at it more deeply without the zeal of partisanship, you will notice that what Photios says offers no evidence of an impious mind, and what Baronius says no evidence of fair judgment"[56] (*B* 354–55). Indeed, Baronius's own predispositions came through clearly when he asserted, first, that the written *acta* of the Council of Constantinople in 879–80 had been corrupted by Photios and, more seriously, that the patriarch had invented the entire council. Hanke's critique was multifaceted and showed again his ability to enter sympathetically into complex historically processes.

> Their argument is weaker when they contend that [Pope] John [VII]'s altered letter was read in council. Let's pretend, though, that this is truly strong: they nonetheless cannot show that John's letter of guidance to the legates was altered, since they admit that the Greek [version], as it was read out in council, is found in the manuscripts, not the Latin version, as it was written by John. But let us admit that John's letter was recited in council in altered, rather than full, form. They conclude wrongly from this that it was changed by Photios, for another could have changed it without Photios's knowledge or wish.... But does [Photios] alone bear the fault for the John's [supposedly] altered letter of guidance and other letters read out in council? Don't others bear this, too, such as the emperors of Constantinople and especially the legates of the Roman pontiff, unless we think that they were ignorant of Greek and therefore were little suited to be legates?[57] (*B* 377–78)

Having deconstructed these arguments for Photios's corruption of papal documents by applying a more complex understanding of the conciliar process, Hanke turned to

56 *Haec in partem malam Caesar Baronius accipit.... Haec, nullo partium studio, si penitius inspicias, Photiana quidem nihil impii animii, Baroniana vero nihil aequi judicii prodere notabis.*

57 *Horum minus validum argumentum, quo Joannis epistolas mutatas in Concilio recitatas fuisse contendunt. Fingamus esse quam validissimum: eo tamen Joannis epistolam ad Legatos monitoriam, quoniam Graecam quidem, sicut in Concilio legebatur, non autem Latinam, sicut a Joanne scribebatur, in MStis reperiri fatentur, mutatam ostendere non valent. Sed demus, Joannis epistolas mutatas, non integras, in Concilio recitatas: male tamen inde colligunt, a Photio mutatas: quas alius, Photio vel ignorante, vel invito, mutare potuerit.... Numquid autem propter mutatas Joannis literas, tum alias, tum ad Legatos monitorias, in Concilio recitatas, siquam Photius culpam, solus eam sustinet? non eandem sustinentibus aliis, Imperatoribus Constantinopolitanis, maxime Romanis Legatis Pontificiis, nisi Graecarum literarum ignaros, adeoque parum aptos Legatos statuamus?*

the claim that the council of Constantinople never happened and that Photios had made it up for political convenience, a view whose author was Baronius. The ecclesiastical historian had seized on the fact that none of the Greek historians of Basil's reign reported the council, concluding from this "that the whole thing was the work of Photios's pen and tinted with the paintbrush of his lies"[58] (*B* 378).Yet such a view rested on a profoundly problematic assumption that only things reported by *historians* as such could be believed to be true; anything reported by anyone else was either made up or suspect. To be sure, none of the historians for Michael III's reign report it, but was it necessary to dismiss the other sources that do report that the council occurred (including Baronius himself, Hanke noted with characteristic care and probable delight)? Rejecting this view, which was at once radically credulous (of historians) and radically skeptical (of all other sources), Hanke in the end saw no valid reason to doubt that the council had happened. Rather, such suspicions, and the simplistic reasonings of convenience that lay behind them, had been motivated by Baronius's own institutional loyalties and convictions that had blinded his historian's eye.

The final ecclesiastical controversy to which Hanke devoted unusually extended attention was the debate over hesychasm, a conflict that played a significant role in the life of Nikephoros Gregoras: "For the sake of our Nicephorus, we will treat this controversy in a more articulated manner, because he interposed his own person between the disputants" (*B* 588). In order to trace Nikephoros's intervention, Hanke embarked on a narration of the evolving contest between the proud and irascible Barlaam of Calabria and the hesychasts represented by Gregory Palamas and the Byzantine emperors. He was conscious that his impartiality would be challenged by the sources themselves, many of which favored the hesychasts—and, also, the chief protagonist of the opposition, Barlaam the Calabrian, was a deeply unpleasant man: "Although we may have greater faith in Nicephorus Gregoras, Barlaam was condemned on certain charges as mean spirited and too desirous of glory, without being either vanquished or even heard"[59] (*B* 593). Hanke sought therefore to provide such a forum, stating the criticisms of hesychasm as well as the complex factionalized political landscape within which Nikephoros moved and portrayed himself moving. In these sustained moments of attention to Byzantium's own religious conflicts and their effects on the record of historical truth, one cannot help wondering whether Hanke saw, and was trying to teach, lessons for his own world.

58 *Ut ea tota ita fuerit Photii stilo conficta, et eiusdem penicillo mendacii colorata.* Hanke is quoting Baronius's *Annales* a.C. 879, num.lxxiii.

59 *Quod si potius Nicephoro Gregorae fidem habemus, Barlamus quidem certis de causis ne satis quidem auditus, nedum victus, sed tamen, ut malevolentia praeditus et gloriae nimis studiosus, damnatum.*

Hanke as Scholar: Between Guide and Guardian

In its self-conscious construction of a Byzantine literary corpus; its critical interventions in fundamental historical questions of identity, chronology, and reliability; its careful attention to clarity and accessibility through ordered treatments and meticulous bibliographical documentation; its efforts to offer a synoptic view of the accumulating crowd of diverse scholarly testimony; and its extensive quotations from sources and scholarship, Martin Hanke's *De Byzantinarum rerum scriptoribus Graecis liber* reveals a mind actively battling the problem of "too much to know" with the full complement of tools described so evocatively by Ann Blair.[60] At the same time, Hanke bears eloquent witness to the polyhistor's ambition for comprehensiveness and the compelling power of Jean Bodin's valuation of history as a subject profoundly worthy of study but full of obstacles, traps, and challenges of comprehension.[61] In the ever-growing ocean of sources, translations, commentaries, and studies that was the seventeenth-century Republic of Letters, where were the safe harbors, where the shoals and reefs, and where the monsters? Bodin had emphasized the importance of selecting the best sources on which to build one's knowledge,[62] a sentiment with which Hanke concurred. But, in contrast to the general—and often idiosyncratic—approach taken by Bodin, Hanke saw the safe way forward in the construction of a meticulously documented, source-based biobibliography of the most important authors, a criterion he was able to implement because he narrowed his focus.

Similarly, by systematically mobilizing the early modern scholarship on specific historical issues, Hanke offered his readers not blanket or impressionistic opinions but specific guidance regarding which modern scholars they could rely on for what questions and where they needed to seek other counsel. Yet this approach to the editors and commentators also vividly demonstrated how historical error could spread through the uncritical acceptance of undocumented and undemonstrated assertions as well as partisan readings and misreadings. Through rigorous, systematic, and amply documented treatments of each historical author, he sought to stop these epidemics of error before they spread.

Because of these qualities, aims, and methods, Hanke's work offers the modern Byzantinist an exceptionally rich and nuanced portrait of the state of Byzantine studies a generation after the beginning of the Paris Corpus. It challenges significant

60 A. Blair, *Too Much to Know: Managing Scholarly Information before the Modern Age* (New Haven, 2010). Focused primarily on the 16th century, Blair does not discuss Hanke.

61 Jean Bodin, *Method for the Easy Comprehension of History*, trans. B. Reynolds (New York, 1945). On Bodin, see J. Franklin, *Jean Bodin and the Sixteenth-Century Revolution in the Methodology of Law and History* (New York, 1963).

62 Bodin, "The Choice of Historians," chap. 2 of *Method*, 41–84.

elements of the common narratives of Byzantine historiography in its level of interpretive sophistication, its level of critical attention to sources, and the abundance of source materials available in original language editions and translations. Johannes Fabricius, whose *Bibliotheca Graeca* became the standard reference work in the next generation, characterized it as a "noteworthy and careful commentary" and, as was noted above, drew on Hanke's judgments.[63]

Given this reputation and the book's regular presence in eighteenth-century libraries around Europe, it may seem odd that Hanke did not remain more visible. In part, this invisibility may reflect a defect in vision and may change as the history of Byzantine studies in the early modern period becomes less of a terra incognita. In other words, Hanke may be invisible because scholars have not yet read enough and examined archives and libraries with the right questions.

Yet there is also an important question of genre. Like Fabricius and so many other polyhistors, Hanke worked to produce scholarly tools that rationalized and ordered editions and interpretations and established, to the extent possible, a firm foundation of authorial identity, textual authenticity, and accurate chronology upon which his contemporaries could then build more securely. He wrote not *sub specie aeternitatis* but to root out the errors faced by his contemporaries—whether those were caused by ignorance, sloppiness, or bias—and to expose voices in his world that were promoting such views and the faulty methods that permitted them. His project was like a vaccine, whose measure of success lies not in its continued use but in the disappearance of the diseases that it was designed to defeat. If modern scholars no longer find Hanke's lengthy examinations of names, chronology, accusations, and attributions worthy of much attention, it is because Hanke helped to develop scholarly resistance to such infections of uncertainty and error and to identify the scholarly vectors that threatened to spread them. At the same time, many aspects of Hanke's scholarly methods—citing evidence completely and accurately, going back to the primary sources, and providing one's evidence in the course of historical argument in convenient and comprehensible forms—have endured and developed as scholarly ideals.[64]

Having begun with writers on ancient Rome, Hanke engaged Byzantine writers as the next witnesses to that empire's evolution. In this sense, he was a historian of the Roman Empire's *longue durée* and, in that way, a forefather of Edward Gibbon. As Hanke looked forward, he saw his next challenge in producing a similar guide to the historical writers on the empire's existence in the hands of the "Germans," for

63 Fabricius, *Bibliotheca Graeca*, 6:751: *insignem et accuratum Commentarium*.

64 On the history of scholarly documentation, see A. Grafton, *The Footnote: A Curious History* (Cambridge, MA, 1999).

thus readers might finally have complete guidance to that most fundamental and rewarding of histories. It is perhaps with this later project in mind as much as his work on Byzantium that Hanke dedicated the *De Byzantinarum rerum scriptoribus Graecis* to the emperor Leopold I of Austria (1640–1705). As he had with his volume on Byzantine authors, he declared that he already had piles of notes; the question was would he—amid his growing responsibilities at the Elisabeth-gymnasium and Rehdiger Library—ever have the time. For those duties slowed him down and occasionally even sapped his will (*B* Ad Lectorem, d4–d4v.).[65] Yet he was restored when he remembered, "The common good in Human Society, civil as well as literary, is that most beautiful and preeminent goal on which we fix our eyes" (*B* Dedicatio, b4v)—and that good needed a historian it could trust.

65 Hanke's later historical works focused on the history of Silesia: *De Silesiorum nominibus antiquitates* (Leipzig, 1702), and *De Silesiorum rebus ab anno Christi 550 ad 1170 exercitationes* (Leipzig, 1705).

TEN

MONTFAUCON'S BYZANTIUM

SHANE BOBRYCKI

> I cast my scythe into a very ample harvest, more than I had hoped, and more than many had thought.

IN THOSE WORDS BERNARD DE MONTFAUCON (1655–1741) DESCRIBED HIS THREE-year journey (1698–1701) through Italy in search of Greek books.[1] Montfaucon's *Diarium Italicum* (1702) explained that Italian libraries were rich in Greek manuscripts for two reasons. First, learned Greeks had fled with books to Italy when "the

1 Bernard de Montfaucon, *Diarium Italicum, sive monumentorum veterum, bibliothecarum, musæorum, etc. Notitiæ singulares in Itinerario Italico collectæ* (Paris, 1702), 2: *imo exitu meliore quam sperabam, præterque opinionem multorum, in satis amplam messem injecimus falcem.* For Montfaucon's Italian journey, see *Voyage en Italie: Diarium italicum. Un journal en miettes*, ed. A. Galliano (Geneva, 1987); J. L. Lemaître, "Le voyage en Italie et le *Diarium italicum*," in *Dom Bernard de Montfaucon: Actes du Colloque de Carcassonne, Octobre 1996*, ed. D.-O. Hurel and R. Rogé (Carcassonne, 1998), 159–86; A. Momigliano, "Mabillon's Italian Disciples," in his *Essays in Ancient and Modern Historiography*, with a new foreword by A. Grafton (Chicago, 2012), 277–93, at 285–87. Paul Briois (or Brioys) (1666–1700), Montfaucon's fellow Maurist and traveling companion, died at Rome in February 1700. Briois's diary of the trip (now Bibliothèque nationale de France [hereafter BnF], MS fr. 19640, fols. 1–56) was published by H. Omont, "Voyage littéraire de Paris à Rome en 1698: Notes de D. Paul Briois, compagnon de Montfaucon," *Revue des bibliothèques* 40 (1904): 1–45, at 3–41.

Greek state was cut down" (*accisis Græcorum rebus*).[2] Second, the Mezzogiorno and Sicily, like the eastern Adriatic and mainland Greece, remained Greek-speaking.[3]

Montfaucon's two explanations reflect two ways of thinking about postclassical Greek books, people, and things in the eighteenth century: one political and historical, the other editorial and antiquarian. This chapter argues that Montfaucon saw Byzantium through the second framework, but was conversant with the first. The first framework—political and historical—is the focus of this collection: the emergence of a construct of "the Byzantine" organized around the Roman, Christian, and Greek state that began with Constantine and ended in 1453. Montfaucon invokes this fallen state in his hunt for Greek books. Before him, Wolf, Hoeschel, Leunclavius, Crusius, Allacci, and others had treated the Eastern or Constantinopolitan or Greek Empire as a distinct historical entity.[4] Charles du Fresne, sieur Du Cange (1610–1688), had authored the two-volume *Historia Byzantina* (1680) and the mighty

2 Montfaucon, *Diarium Italicum*, 1: *Accisis quippe Græcorum rebus, in primisque post excidium Constantinopolitanum, plerique omnes litterarum cultores Græci cum ampla codicum supellectile in Italiam se proripuerunt.* On the transfer of Greek learning to Italy before 1515, see N. G. Wilson, *From Byzantium to Italy: Greek Studies in the Italian Renaissance*, 2nd ed. (London, 2017); J. J. Yiannias, ed., *The Byzantine Tradition after the Fall of Constantinople* (Charlottesville, VA, 1991); J. Monfasani, *George of Trebizond: A Biography and a Study of His Rhetoric and Logic* (Leiden, 1976).

3 Montfaucon, *Diarium Italicum*, præfatio, n.p. [pp. 4–5 of preface]: *Non Romanas modo, Mediolanenses, Venetianas & Florentinas bibliothecas adire primitus destinaveram, sed etiam Calabrenses & Sicilianas: nam iis in partibus festivam codicum Græcorum superesse copiam, non rumore nuntio, sed narratu complurium fide dignorum accepi. iis enim in locis cum non ita pridem Græcæ linguæ usus obtinuerit; obsoletâ tandem ipsâ, libri multi Græci manuscripti in Cœnobiorum Ecclesiarumque bibliothecis supersunt inobservati, intacti*; 211: *In Calabria enim, & in aliis Neapolitani regni regionibus, atque in Sicilia, ad proxima usque sæcula Græca lingua obtinuit; ut non plebeio solum usu, sed etiam Ecclesiastico, in officiis suis Græca lingua frequentaretur. . . . Hactenus tamen in plerisque Regni partibus populares Græco, sed vitiato, idiomate fabulantur.* Montfaucon was ultimately unable to visit Calabrian and Sicilian monasteries. Political instability and lack of funds prevented him from crossing the Adriatic to the Dalmatian coast and the Peloponnese, where he feared Greek manuscripts were at the mercy of "bookworms and moths," and where Greeks living "in filth and poverty" were known to sell manuscripts for a pittance (præfatio, n.p. [p. 5 of preface]). Montfaucon also drew up "recherches à faire" for an (ideal) trip to Constantinople, published a year after his death in the *Mercure de France* (1742): see C. Duckworth, "Montfaucon's Antiquarian Shopping-List: d'Antraigues's Delayed Deliveries," in *Voltaire and His World: Studies Presented to W. H. Barber*, ed. R. J. Howells, A. Mason, H. T. Mason, and D. Williams (Oxford, 1985), 349–61, at 356–61. See also A. Momigliano, "Ancient History and the Antiquarian," *JWarb* 13.3 (1950): 285–315, at 306–7, for the early modern rediscovery of *Magna Graecia*.

4 For the earlier generation, see A. Pertusi, *Storiografia umanistica e mondo bizantino*, Istituto siciliano di studi bizantini e neoellenici, quaderni 5 (Palermo, 1967). For the later generation, see D. R. Reinsch, "The History of Editing Byzantine Historiographical Texts," in *The Byzantine World*, ed. P. Stephenson (London, 2010), 435–44.

Glossarium ad scriptores mediæ & infimæ Graecitatis (1688) to shed light on its peculiarities.[5] Philippe Labbe's (1607–1667) *Corpus Byzantinae Historiae* had defined its literary corpus: "la Byzantine."[6]

On the other hand, a second, older framework was also available. The Greek manuscripts that Montfaucon found in Italy could be classed under a more generic category: Greek from Homer to Athanasius to Psellos to the present, Greek of the antiquaries, Greek of the editors.[7] When Montfaucon traveled through Italy in search of Greek manuscripts, he went as an editor of Greek fathers. And when he published on palaeography and antiquities, he avoided the grand questions of political periodization that preoccupied other important contributors to early Byzantine studies. Instead, his focus was on dating and locating books by script, and, increasingly over time, on recording curiosities notable for beauty, interest, or rarity.

5 J.-M. Spieser, "Du Cange and Byzantium," in *Through the Looking Glass: Byzantium through British Eyes. Papers from the Twenty-Ninth Spring Symposium of Byzantine Studies, London, March 1995*, ed. R. Cormack and E. Jeffreys, SPBS 7 (Aldershot, 2000), 199–210; see also J. Considine, *Dictionaries in Early Modern Europe: Lexicography and the Making of Heritage* (Cambridge, 2008), 250–87.

6 The *Corpus Byzantinae Historiae* (1645–88), begun by Labbe and patronized by Colbert, goes by many names: the *Byzantine du Louvre*, the Paris Corpus (Corpus Parisiense), or simply *la Byzantine* (as Montfaucon calls it in his letters). See Reinsch, "Byzantine Historiographical Texts," 440–41. Among its most distinguished editors were Leone Allacci (Chronicle of Joel, 1651; George Akropolites, 1656) and Du Cange (Kinnamos in 1670). After a hiatus, Du Cange revived the project with editions of Zonaras (1686–87, 2 vols.) and the *Chronicon Paschale* (1688). See H. Omont, "Du Cange et la Collection Byzantine du Louvre," *REG* 17 (1904): 33–34; Spieser, "Du Cange and Byzantium," 201–2. Thereafter supplements included important editions, such as the Gregoras of Jean Boivin (1702), which superseded that of Wolf, and the Leo Diaconus (1819) of Karl Benedikt Hase, forger of the *Toparcha Gothicus*. For Hase, see I. Ševčenko, "The Date and Author of the So-Called Fragments of Toparcha Gothicus," *DOP* 25 (1971): 117–88.

7 For postclassical conceptions of Greek as a literary and linguistic corpus, see M. Alexiou, *After Antiquity: Greek Language, Myth, and Metaphor* (Ithaca, NY, 2002). For earlier Western engagement with Greek, see W. Berschin, *Greek Letters and the Latin Middle Ages from Jerome to Nicholas of Cusa*, trans. J. C. Frakes, rev. and expanded ed. (Washington, DC, 1988). For the Renaissance rediscovery of Greek, see Wilson, *From Byzantium to Italy*; R. Weiss, *Medieval and Humanist Greek: Collected Essays* (Padua, 1978); H. Lamers, *Greece Reinvented: Transformations of Byzantine Hellenism in Renaissance Italy*, Brill's Studies in Intellectual History 247 (Leiden, 2015); R. Sabbadini, *Le scoperte dei codici latini e greci ne' secoli XIV e XV*, ed. E. Garin, 2 vols. (Florence, 1967); R. R. Bolgar, *The Classical Heritage and Its Beneficiaries* (Cambridge, 1954). For individual authors, consult F. E. Cranz, V. Brown, P. O. Kristeller et al., *Catalogus translationum et commentariorum: Medieval and Renaissance Latin Translations and Commentaries; Annotated Lists and Guides*, 13 vols. (Washington, DC, 1960–). For the history of early printing of Greek authors, see O. Mazal, *Die Überlieferung der antiken Literatur im Buchdruck des 15. Jahrhunderts*, 4 vols. (Stuttgart, 2003); R. Bunker, *A Bibliographical Study of the Greek Works and Translations Published in France during the Renaissance: The Decade 1540–1550* (New York, 1939). For Renaissance teaching techniques of Greek, see F. Ciccolella, *Donati Graeci: Learning Greek in the Renaissance* (Leiden, 2008). For a history of Greek as a language, see G. C. Horrocks, *Greek: A History of the Language and Its Speakers*, 2nd ed. (Malden, MA, 2010).

This means that Montfaucon's Byzantium is not as conceptually distinct as, say, Du Cange's Byzantium. Montfaucon was in dialogue with those who defended the peculiarity of Byzantine history. His career as an editor and translator of Greek began, at the age of thirty, with (what we would call) "Byzantine" texts: the twelfth-century *typikon* of the Constantinopolitan monastery of Mary Kecharitomene founded by Irene Doukaina (and a tribute list for her husband, Alexios I Komnenos).[8] In the preface to the 1688 anthology in which these texts appeared, Montfaucon explained that the *typikon* preserved "useful and serviceable matters pertaining to the history of the imperial family of Constantinople at that time," a recommendation alluding to one of the volumes of Du Cange's 1680 *Historia Byzantina*.[9] Montfaucon read Du Cange all his life. As an old man hunting for dragons said to adorn the robe of Theodosius the Great, he told an audience in Paris in 1737, "I ran through everything Du Cange had had engraved, and others whose appearance did not come to his knowledge, and I found nothing there approaching it."[10]

Yet Montfaucon approached what we would today call Byzantine books, subjects, and artifacts as an editor and antiquary. His first aim was to facilitate editing, by dating manuscripts and explaining particularities of Greek. For much of his adult life, he was engaged upon a vast edition of John Chrysostom. His second aim, however, emerges over time: a desire to popularize the curiosities of postclassical Greek culture, which fascinated him. He was "antiquarian" in the sense of this term popularized by Arnaldo Momigliano and others—a compiler and presenter rather than a synthesizer of historical texts and objects.[11]

8 Monachi Benedictini Congregationis Sancti Mauri, ed., *Analecta Graeca sive Varia opuscula græca hactenus non edita*, 4 vols. (Paris, 1688), 1:136–307 (Montfaucon named on p. 128). Modern edition: P. Gautier, "Le typikon de la Théotokos Kécharitôménè," *REB* 43 (1985): 5–165, at 19–155. Translation: R. Jordan, trans., "*Kecharitomene: Typikon* of Empress Irene Doukaina Komnene for the Convent of the Mother of God *Kecharitomene* in Constantinople," in *Byzantine Monastic Foundation Documents: A Complete Translation of the Surviving Founders' "Typica" and Testaments*, ed. J. Thomas and A. C. Hero (Washington, DC, 1998), 649–724 (no. 27).

9 Montfaucon, *Analecta Graeca*, praefatio, n.p., part 3: *Multa etiam ibidem extant ad Familiæ Imperatoriæ Constantinopolitanæ illius temporis Historiam utilia & opportuna*. Charles du Fresne, sieur Du Cange, *Historia Byzantina duplici commentario illustrata* (Paris, 1680), divided into two volumes: *Familiae Byzantinae* (vol. 1) and *Constantinopolis Christiana, seu descriptio urbis Constantinopolitana, qualis extitit sub imperatoribus Christianis, ex variis scriptoribus contexta & adornata* (vol. 2).

10 Bernard de Montfaucon, "Les modes et les usages du siècle de Théodose le Grand et d'Arcadius son fils, avec quelques réflexions sur le moyen & le bas Age" (delivered 15 February, 1737), *Mémoires de littérature tirez des registres de l'Académie Royale des Inscriptions et Belles Lettres* 13 (1740): 474–79, at 475: "J'ay parcouru tous ceux que M. du Cange a fait graver, & d'autres dont la figure n'estoit pas venue à sa connoissance, & je n'y ay rien trouvé d'approchant."

11 This sense of "antiquary," "antiquarian," and "antiquarianism" was popularized by Momigliano, "Ancient History and the Antiquarian," esp. 286–94; cf. P. N. Miller, *Peiresc's Mediterranean World*

That is not to deny Montfaucon's place in Byzantine studies. Montfaucon laid the groundwork for Byzantine palaeography and codicology.[12] His edition of Chrysostom influenced generations of subsequent editors.[13] Yet in contrast with early modern scholars of Byzantium working with a political or historical orientation, Montfaucon approached what we might today call Byzantine manuscripts, texts, and artifacts as either, in general terms, Greek products or, in specific terms, products of one region, ruler, or century. That was not accidental, I argue here, but central to Montfaucon's editorial and antiquarian commitments. Montfaucon set out to categorize, not to contextualize.

■■■

Bernard de Montfaucon was one of the giants of seventeenth- and eighteenth-century scholarship.[14] Born in 1655 to an illustrious Languedoc family, Montfaucon

---

(Cambridge, MA, 2015), 5–8, and idem, "A Tentative Morphology of European Antiquarianism, 1500–2000," in *World Antiquarianism: Comparative Perspectives*, ed. A. Schnapp (Los Angeles, 2014), 67–87. See also P. N. Miller, ed., *Momigliano and Antiquarianism: Foundations of the Modern Cultural Sciences* (Toronto, 2007).

12 V. Gardthausen, *Griechische Palaeographie*, 2nd ed., 2 vols. (Leipzig, 1911–13), 1:7: "Die *Palaeographia Graeca* (Paris 1708) ist und bleibt eine der hervorragendsten Leistungen, durch die eine neue Disziplin nicht nur begründet, sondern, wie es schien, auch vollendet wurde; sie ist um so hervorragender, als Montfaucon fast gar keine Vorgänger hatte, sondern alles aus Nichts geschaffen hat." Cf. B. Bischoff, *Paläographie des römischen Altertums und des abendländischen Mittelalters*, rev. W. Koch, 4th ed. (Berlin, 2009), 17. For Montfaucon's importance to codicology, see P. Petitmengin, "Montfaucon, dom Le Maître et la *Bibliotheca Bibliothecarum*," in *Du copiste au collectionneur: Mélanges d'histoire des textes et des bibliothèques en l'honneur d'André Vernet*, ed. D. Nebbiai-Dalla Guarda and J.-F. Genest (Turnhout, 1998), 537–84. A measure of Montfaucon's legacy is a collection of essays celebrating the three hundredth anniversary of Montfaucon's *Palaeographia Graeca*, though they do not deal with Montfaucon: A. Bravo García and I. Pérez Martín, ed., *The Legacy of Bernard de Montfaucon: Three Hundred Years of Studies on Greek Handwriting: Proceedings of the Seventh International Colloquium of Greek Palaeography, Madrid-Salamanca, 15–20 September 2008* (Turnhout, 2010).

13 L. Brottier, "L'apport de Bernard de Montfaucon à l'édition de Jean Chrysostome," in *Érudition et commerce épistolaire: Jean Mabillon et la tradition monastique*, ed. D.-O. Hurel (Paris, 2003), 269–83, esp. 282.

14 See E. de Broglie, *Bernard de Montfaucon et les Bernardins, 1715–1750*, 2 vols. (Paris, 1891), with a rich, hagiographic account of Montfaucon (vol. 1) and his followers at Saint-Germain-des-Prés (vol. 2). Excellent shorter studies are J. Irigoin, "Dom Bernard de Montfaucon," in *L'Académie des inscriptions et belles lettres et l'Académie des Beaux-Arts face au message de la Grèce ancienne: Actes* (Paris, 1996), 71–85, and B. Mondrain, "Bernard de Montfaucon et l'étude des manuscrits grecs," *Scriptorium* 66 (2012): 281–316. H. Omont, "Bernard de Montfaucon, sa famille et ses premières années," *Annales du Midi* 4 (1892): 84–90, publishes a letter illuminating Montfaucon's youth. Overviews include J. E. Sandys, *A History of Classical Scholarship*, 3 vols. (Cambridge, 1906–08), 2:385–89; J. W. Thompson, "The Age of Mabillon and Montfaucon," *AHR* 47.2 (1942): 225–44, at 237–40; L. D. Reynolds and N. G. Wilson, *Scribes and Scholars: A Guide to the Transmission of Greek and Latin Literature*, 4th ed. (Oxford, 2013), 191–92; and, with more detail, H. Leclercq,

was, as he himself reports, a voracious reader from youth. As a fourteen- or fifteen-year-old he loved history, and could remember all the Indian cities ending in "-or" that he read about in his father's castle near the wild pine forests of southwestern France.[15] After a brief career (1673–75) as a soldier in Louis XIV's German wars, Montfaucon joined the famous congregation of Saint Maur at Toulouse in 1675.[16] He learned Greek at Sorèze, Grasse, and Bordeaux, where he also began to study Hebrew.[17] "You are just unbearable, my dear brother," his brother told him, "with all your Greek roots.... To the devil with your Greek roots, or Hebrew ones, for I recall that it is Hebrew ones that you desire."[18] In 1687, in recognition of his abilities as a Hellenist, Montfaucon was transferred to Saint-Germain-des-Prés, the capital of Maurist learning.

At Paris, Montfaucon emerged as the Maurists' new Greek talent. As soon as he arrived, he was drafted into the *Analecta Graeca* (1688), where his editorial

---

"Montfaucon (Dom Bernard de)," in *DACL*, vol. 11, part 2, cols. 2608–72, with a list of his publications at 2667–72. See also the essays in Hurel and Rogé, *Dom Bernard de Montfaucon*. For Montfaucon's financing, see H.-J. Martin, "Les Bénédictins, leurs libraires et le pouvoir: Notes sur le financement de la recherche au temps de Mabillon et de Montfaucon," *Revue d'histoire de l'église de France* 43 (1957): 273–87.

15 BnF, MS lat. 11915 (Papiers de Montfaucon), fol. 13r: "Le grand goût pour toute sorte de litterature me prit dès l'age de quatorze ou quinze ans. Après que j'eux fini mes classes a Limoux, mon pere me rappella a notre chateau de Roquetaillade : ou je lus tous les livres, et surtout les historiens, que je pus trouver ; le Plutarque en français, le Jerôme Osorius, aussi en français contenant les navigations et les conquêtes des portugais dans les Indes Orientales. J'avois si bonne memoire que je retenois facilement tout, meme les noms des provinces et des villes de Goa, de Calicut, de Cochin et des autres qui se terminoient Or, Onor, Ravelor, Cananor, Cranganor et Travancore" (printed with modernized spelling in de Broglie, *Bernard de Montfaucon*, 1:3). The "-or" ending is Tamil, Kannada, and Malayalam *ur* for "village, town, city, place." I am grateful to Kalyani Ramnath for explaining South Indian place-names to me.

16 The Maurists dominated 17th- and 18th-century Benedictinism in France: Y. Chaussy, *Les bénédictins de Saint-Maur*, 2 vols. (Paris, 1989–91). For the Maurists' scholarship, see M. D. Knowles, "Great Historical Enterprises, II. The Maurists," *TRHS*, sixth ser., 9 (1959): 169–87.

17 Irigoin, "Dom Bernard de Montfaucon," 75; Sandys, *History of Classical Scholarship*, 2:385. For the young Montfaucon's precocity—producing a translation and commentary of Chrysostom at speed as a challenge in 1686—see B. Gain, "Bernard de Montfaucon, éditeur des Pères grecs," in Hurel and Rogé, *Dom Bernard de Montfaucon*, 121–57, at 124.

18 BNF, MS fr. 17710, fol. 234: "Vous êtes insupportable, mon cher frère, avec vos racines greques, vous êtes toujours occupé à en déterrer quelqu'une, et ne pensés à autre chose, vous creuseriés jusqu'aux abîmes plutôt que d'en perdre une seule.... Au diable vos racines greques ou hébraïques, car je me souviens que c'est aux hébraïques que vous en voulés, la belle passion que la poursuite d'une racine hébraïque" (reprinted with modern orthography and slight changes by de Broglie, *Bernard de Montfaucon*, 1:205–6). "Racines greques" here is likely a reference to the rhyming pedagogical book *Le Jardin des Racines Grecques* (*Le iardin des racines greques, mises en vers françois*) of Claude Lancelot, originally published in 1657 and reprinted, translated, and disseminated continuously thereafter.

contributions included Byzantine and late antique texts. Thereafter he threw himself into questions of chronology pertaining to the book of Judith (1690, 1692), which brought him back to his "Hebrew roots," though he soon returned to Greek.[19] His first stand-alone edition was Athanasius (in three volumes) in 1698.[20] Athanasius and the other Greek fathers brought him to Italy the same year, leading to the *Diarium Italicum* (1702).[21] While in Rome, he published a defense of the Maurist edition of Augustine against the barbs of a Jesuit critic.[22] Returning to Paris, he produced a two-volume edition of Greek fathers in 1706.[23]

In 1708 Montfaucon published his masterpiece, the *Palaeographia Graeca,* on "the rise and development of Greek letters and on the various kinds of Greek writing of all centuries."[24] Montfaucon's book, inspired by Mabillon's *De re diplomatica*

19 Bernard de Montfaucon, *La vérité de l'Histoire de Judith* (Paris, 1690; 2nd ed., 1692). See A. Momigliano, "Persian Historiography, Greek Historiography, and Jewish Historiography," in his *The Classical Foundations of Modern Historiography* (Berkeley, 1990), 5–28, at 11.

20 Bernard de Montfaucon, ed., *Sancti Athanasii archiepiscopi Alexandrini opera omnia Græce et Latine,* 3 vols. (Paris, 1698). See B. Gain, "L'Édition de Saint Athanase par Montfaucon (1698): Genèse, méthodes et résultats," *Sacris Erudiri* 44 (2005): 77–92; Gain, "Bernard de Montfaucon, éditeur des Pères grecs," 126–32. One of Montfaucon's two other original co-editors for Athanasius died; the other abandoned the project before it was finished.

21 Montfaucon, *Diarium Italicum* (n. 1 above), 1. On the *Diarium,* see Galliano's critical edition, *Voyage en Italie* (n. 1 above); Mondrain, "Bernard de Montfaucon et l'étude des manuscrits grecs," 294–98. For Montfaucon's experiences with the Marciana Library of Venice, see B. Cladders, *Französische Venedig-Reisen im 16. und 17. Jahrhundert: Wandlungen des Venedig-Bildes und der Reisebeschreibung* (Geneva, 2002), 42–43, 66, 138–40. See also Irigoin, "Dom Bernard de Montfaucon," 79, for Montfaucon's belated response to his Italian critics (Ficoroni and Maffei).

22 Bernard de Montfaucon, *Vindiciæ editionis S. Augustini a benedictinis adornatæ, adversus epistolam abbatis germani, auctore D. B. de Rivière* (Rome, 1699), soon reprinted in France; on this episode see Leclercq, "Montfaucon," col. 2625.

23 Bernard de Montfaucon, ed., *Collectio nova Patrum et scriptorum Græcorum, Eusebii Cæsariensis, Athanasii, & Cosmæ Ægyptii,* 2 vols. (Paris, 1706). It included Eusebius of Caesarea's commentary on the Psalms (vol. 1) and works by Athanasius, Cosmas Indicopleustes, and Eusebius (vol. 2). These editions relied on Paris manuscripts: R. Devreesse, "L'édition du Commentaire d'Eusèbe de Césarée sur Isaïe: Interpolations et omissions," *RevBibl* 42 (1933): 540–55; M. J. Hollerich, *Eusebius of Caesarea's Commentary on Isaiah: Christian Exegesis in the Age of Constantine* (Oxford, 1999), 15–16.

24 Bernard de Montfaucon, *Palaeographia Graeca sive De ortu et progressu literarum Graecarum et de variis omnium saeculorum scriptionis Graecae generibus: Itemque de abbreviationibus et de notis variarum artium ac disciplinarum, additis figuris et schematibus ad fidem manuscriptorum codicum* (Paris, 1708). See H. Omont, "L'Édition de la 'Palaeographia graeca' de Montfaucon," *REG* 4 (1891): 63–57; B. Mondrain, "La *Palaeographia Graeca* de Bernard de Montfaucon," in *Livret-Annuaire de l'École pratique des Hautes Études, Sciences historiques et philologiques, 141e année (2008–2009)* (2010): 375–78; L. Traube, "Geschichte der Paläographie," in his *Vorlesungen und Abhandlungen,* ed. F. Boll, 3 vols. (Munich, 1909), 1:1–80, at 35–42. Irigoin, "Dom Bernard de Montfaucon," 80, and Mondrain, "Bernard de Montfaucon et l'étude des manuscrits grecs," 298, stress the importance of the *Diarium Italicum* in shaping the *Palaeographia Graeca.*

(1681), surveyed over eleven and a half thousand manuscripts as well as coins, inscriptions, seals, and other archaeological items.[25] But as Traube long ago noted, the *Palaeographia Graeca* was fundamentally different from Mabillon's *De re diplomatica.* It was rooted in book hand and the task of editing, and not in the *discrimen veri ac falsi* of diplomatics.[26] The work was, then and since, a success. The *Palaeographia Graeca* paved the way for all subsequent studies of Greek book hand, even inventing the name *palaeography.*[27]

In 1709 Montfaucon offered the reading public a French translation of Philo of Alexandria's first-century treatise on the contemplative life. In his preface, Montfaucon entered a debate going back to Scaliger over whether Philo's *therapeutai* were early Christians (he thought so).[28] Montfaucon entered several such debates, and he would return to the *therapeutai* in 1712.[29] He edited Origen in 1713 (two volumes) and cataloged the *Bibliotheca Coisliniana* in 1715. In 1718 he produced

25 Montfaucon, *Palaeographia Graeca*, praefatio, i: *Aderant in re pene simili domestica exempla, quæ nos ad id oneris suscipiendum maxime permoverunt: monebat enim laudatum a laudatis viris Mabillonii nostri τοῦ μακαρίτου opus de Re Diplomatica Latina, paria in Græcis literis posse praestari.* In fact, only one chapter of Montfaucon's *Palaeographia Graeca*—chap. 6, titled *De re diplomatica græca* (378–432)—was devoted to diplomatics, and the analysis is patchy (378–90); mostly he publishes and offers brief comments on charters of the Greek monasteries of Italy (391–432).

26 Traube, "Geschichte der Paläographie," 35. Whereas Montfaucon's focus was on the dating of manuscripts by script, Mabillon's work had been motivated by controversies over forged charters. Cf. Mondrain, "Bernard de Montfaucon et l'étude des manuscrits grecs," 283–84; A. Grafton and M. Williams, *Christianity and the Transformation of the Book: Origen, Eusebius, and the Library of Caesarea* (Cambridge, MA, 2006), 242–43. Knowles, "The Maurists," 181–82, treats their difference in character. The literature on Mabillon is much vaster than that on Montfaucon. A convenient starting point is H. Leclercq, "Mabillon," in *DACL*, vol. 10, part 1, cols. 427–724. Idem, *Mabillon*, 2 vols. (Paris, 1953–57), remains useful. For more detail see the first volume of B. Barret-Kriegel, *Les historiens et la monarchie*, 4 vols. (Paris, 1988).

27 Gardthausen, *Griechische Palaeographie*, 1:5–9, for its place in Greek palaeography, though see, e.g., 2:234, for its technical limitations. One missing subject was the palaeography of medieval Greek Italy, which awaited 20th-century studies: R. Devreesse, *Les manuscrits grecs de l'Italie méridionale: Histoire, classement, paléographie* (Modena, 1979); A. Pertusi, *Scritti sulla Calabria greca medievale* (Soveria Mannelli, 1994). Montfaucon had invented the name *palaeography* as early as 29 November 1706, when he signed his book contract: Irigoin, "Dom Bernard de Montfaucon," 71, n. 1.

28 Bernard de Montfaucon, trans., *Le livre de Philon, de la vie contemplative, Traduit sur l'Original Grec* (Paris, 1709), preface [n.p.]. Scaliger, Blondel, Grotius, Étienne Le Moine, Henri Valois, Pagi, and others argued against identifying the *therapeutai* with early Christians. Bellarmine, Baronius, Papebroch, Tillemont, Isaac Vossius, and Thomas Bruno joined Montfaucon in favoring the identification.

29 *Réponse de dom Bernard de Montfaucon aux objections que lui a faites M. contre la dissertation des thérapeutes* (Paris, 1712), which appeared along with "Letters for and against, on the famous question of whether the hermits called *therapeutai*, of which Philo the Jew spoke, were Christians."

the first volume of his mighty Chrysostom (1718–38).[30] This thirteen-volume Chrysostom—"a task so painstaking, so enormous" that the edition, in his words, "constituted a library, not a book"—proved one of Montfaucon's most lasting accomplishments.[31] To finish it, Montfaucon relied on a team of five collators and many assistants and collaborators, including major scholars like Anselmo Banduri (1671/75–1743).[32] Chrysostom occupied decades of Montfaucon's life, and the problems of editing this vast corpus of Greek directly inspired his engagement with palaeographical, linguistic, and antiquarian matters.

Montfaucon always showed interest in Greek as it appeared on coins, inscriptions, and cameos. Later in life, he delved into archaeology. His *Antiquité expliquée,* with more than a thousand copperplate engravings and many more smaller illustrations, appeared volume by volume between 1719 and 1724.[33] It prompted the Académie des Inscriptions et Belles-Lettres to admit him without waiting for a vacancy.[34] Next came the five-volume collection on French antiquities, *Les monumens de la monarchie françoise* (1729–33), a pathbreaking work of medieval archaeology, which popularized a rediscovered Bayeux Tapestry.[35] Finally, a prodigious

30 Origen: *Hexaplorum Origenis quæ supersunt,* 2 vols. (Paris, 1713); catalog: *Bibliotheca Coisliniana, olim Segueriana sive Manuscriptorum omnium græcorum, quæ in ea continentur, accurata descriptio* (Paris, 1715); Chrysostom: Bernard de Montfaucon, ed., *Sancti Patris Nostri Joannis Chrysostomi Arch. Constantinopolitani Opera Omnia,* 13 vols. (Paris, 1718–38).

31 Montfaucon, *Chrysostomi Opera,* vol. 1, præfatio, n.p.: *Diu expetitam S. Joannis Chrysostomi Operum omnium editionem a multis jam annis paramus: neque enim poterat res tam operosa, tam ampla, modico temporis curriculo concinnari. Bibliotheca sunt, non liber, tanti doctoris Opuscula, Commentaria, Epistolæ.* See Brottier, "L'apport de Bernard de Montfaucon" (n. 13 above), for Montfaucon's place in Chrysostom's editorial history. Henry Savile had already established the Greek text in the early 17th century, and Fronton du Duc's Latin translation had made Chrysostom more familiar to the Republic of Letters: as Brottier notes, "Mais c'est Montfaucon qui introduit dans l'édition d'un texte ancien les principes que suivent encore les éditeurs d'aujourd'hui: une présentation de la situation historique, des thèmes et de la problématique de l'œuvre, la confection d'index et d'un lexique" (282).

32 For Banduri, see Leclercq, "Montfaucon," col. 2653. See Irigoin, "Dom Bernard de Montfaucon," 80, for the collators.

33 The first edition was Bernard de Montfaucon, *L'antiquité expliquée et représentée en figures* (Paris, 1719). See E. Vaiani, "*L'Antiquité expliquée* e i *Monumens de la monarchie française* di Bernard de Montfaucon: Modelli per una storia illustrata del Medioevo francese," in *"Conosco un ottimo storico dell'arte": Per Enrico Castelnuovo: Scritti di allievi e amici pisani,* ed. M. M. Donato and M. Ferretti (Pisa, 2012), 337–47; E. Décultot, "Du musée d'images au musée imaginaire: Les recueils d'antiquités et la tradition des musées de papier aux XVIIe et XVIIIe siècles," *Revue de l'Art* 182 (2013): 19–26, esp. 21–22.

34 Irigoin, "Dom Bernard de Montfaucon," 78.

35 Bernard de Montfaucon, *Les monumens de la monarchie françoise, qui comprennent l'histoire de France, avec les figures de chaque règne que l'injure des tems à épargnées,* 5 vols. (Paris, 1729–33). See Décultot, "Du musée d'images au musée imaginaire," 24–25; F. Haskell, *History and Its Images:*

bibliographic project, the *Bibliotheca bibliothecarum* of 1739, made Montfaucon a name famous in book history.[36]

It is a staggering legacy. Yet despite accomplishments in editing, palaeography, archaeology, and bibliography, it seems Montfaucon's curse to be framed as the Vergil to others' Homers. This is especially true of Montfaucon's relation to his fellow Maurist Jean Mabillon (1632–1707). Montfaucon, in one expression of a common sentiment, "did for medieval Greek palaeography what Mabillon had done for medieval Latin palaeography."[37] The comparison tends to lead to lukewarm praise of Montfaucon. Mabillon's *De re diplomatica* (1681) is "immortal"; Montfaucon's *Palaeographia Graeca* (1708) is "valuable."[38] Mabillon has 297 columns in the *Dictionnaire d'archéologie chrétienne et de liturgie* to Montfaucon's 64.[39] The former's street in modern Paris is longer than Montfaucon's, and only Mabillon has a metro stop to his name.[40]

Even Montfaucon's *Diarium Italicum* (1702) is pale fire to Mabillon's earlier *Iter Italicum* (1687). "There is nothing" in it, wrote Arnaldo Momigliano, "of the excitement and of the poetry with which Mabillon discovered Italy for himself."[41] Montfaucon's *Diarium* has its charms, however. Grapevines on an afternoon ascent up Mount Vesuvius "shoot out their branches in all directions, so you would think them one tangled rope."[42] Montfaucon, who nurtured friendships as he journeyed, was a more personable traveler than Mabillon but a less enthralling discoverer of

Art and the Interpretation of the Past (New Haven, 1993), 131–63; A. Rostand, "La documentation iconographique des *Monumens de la Monarchie françoise* de Bernard de Montfaucon," *Bulletin de la société de l'histoire de l'art français* (1932): 104–49; E. C. Pastan, "Montfaucon as Reader of the Bayeux Tapestry," in *Medieval Art and Architecture after the Middle Ages*, ed. J. T. Marquardt and A. A. Jordan (Newcastle, 2009), 89–110. See also E. A. R. Brown and M. Cothren, "The Twelfth-Century Crusading Window of the Abbey of Saint-Denis: *Praeteritorum Enim Recordatio Futurorum Est Exhibitio*," *JWarb* 49 (1986): 1–40, for important medieval stained-glass panels that Montfaucon alone preserved through his description.

36 See Petitmengin, "Montfaucon" (n. 12 above), 538–40, 544–54.

37 Thompson, "The Age of Mabillon and Montfaucon" (n. 14 above), 238. See also R. Stokes, *A Bibliographical Companion* (Metuchen, NJ, 1989), 186; Momigliano, "Ancient History and the Antiquarian" (n. 11 above), 301. Even Montfaucon framed his own palaeographical contribution this way: *Palaeographia Graeca*, praefatio, i.

38 A. A. Vasiliev, *History of the Byzantine Empire, 324–1453*, 2nd ed., 2 vols. (Madison, WI, 1952), 1:5.

39 Leclercq, "Mabillon"; idem, "Montfaucon."

40 Irigoin, "Dom Bernard de Montfaucon," 73.

41 Momigliano, "Mabillon's Italian Disciples" (n. 1 above), 286. Momigliano (286–87, 290–91) also discusses why it was that Montfaucon failed, unlike Mabillon, to gain traction in the Italian Republic of Letters.

42 Montfaucon, *Diarium Italicum*, 307: *In acclivi montis arbores vitibus adrepentibus ornatæ, quæ palmites circumquaque emittunt, alios aliis annexos, continuatum funem diceres.* Montfaucon had been drawn to take the walk both because of the fame of the volcano and in order to see the effects of a recent eruption.

Italy.[43] Partly by design: hoping not to induce "nausea and irritation" by repeating the tropes of Italian travel memoirs, Montfaucon described only "unknown or lesser known things."[44] For that reason, the bulk of the *Diarium* is devoted to the (Greek, especially Christian) contents of libraries.[45]

Montfaucon plays the Vergil to Homers other than Mabillon. He is famous for his contributions to historical archaeology and his use of material evidence—from Greco-Roman tombs to the Bayeux Tapestry—but this work rests on the antiquarianism opened up by Peiresc, whose prints Montfaucon republished, and on the labors of Spon, Fabricius, Spence, and others.[46] And if Montfaucon enjoys a place in the formation of Byzantine studies, he follows Wolf, Hoeschel, Crusius, Labbe, Allacci, and, above all, Du Cange. Du Cange was "the real founder of Byzantine historical studies," wrote George Ostrogorksy at the beginning of his history of the

43 Momigliano, "Mabillon's Italian Disciples," 286.

44 Montfaucon, *Diarium Italicum*, praefatio, n.p. [pp. 1–2 of preface]: *Ad hæc nihil hodie vulgatius, quodque eruditorum studiis ac vigiliis magis frequentetur, quam Italica monumenta, ut non sine nausea atque fastidio toties decantata, de integer recensita quis videat.* Aside from Mabillon's *Iter Italicum* of 1687 (recording his visit of 1685–86), numerous French visitors to Italy wrote up their journeys: Rabelais (1535–36, but published only in 1651), Audebert (1574–78), Montaigne (1580–81), Virey (1592–93), Tarde (1593, 1614–15), Rigaud (1600), Claveson (1608), Bergeron (1603–12), Vinchant (1609–10), Bouchard (1630), Vuillerme (1636–37), Du Val (1641), Gourreau de la Proustière (1654–55), Monconys (1646, 1663–64), le Maistre (1664–65), the marquis de Robias d'Estoublon (1669), Lamayène (1673), Spon (1674–76), Huguetan (1679), Cotte (1689–90), and Bourdin (1695–96). Pierre Duval's *Les Beautez de l'Italie* (1673) and Charles César Baudelot de Dairval's *De l'utilité des voyages* (1686) dealt with Italy's attractions. See A. J. Dumesnil, *Voyageurs français en Italie depuis le seizième siècle jusqu'à nos jours* (Paris, 1865), 105–15; V. C. Minischetti, G. Dotoli, and R. Musnik, *Le voyage français en Italie des origins au XVIIIe siècle: Bibliographie analytique* (Fasano, 2006), 155–56.

45 Cf. Irigoin, "Dom Bernard de Montfaucon," 77: "Éditeur et traducteur d'œuvres grecques, il n'en avait qu'une vision livresque, si j'ose dire, limitée de plus à des auteurs chrétiens ou d'époque byzantine." By contrast, Montfaucon's travel companion, Dom Paul Briois, made laconic references to libraries and their contents (BnF, MS fr. 19640, fols. 1–56; e.g., Omont, "Voyage littéraire" [n. 1 above], 28: "Nous retournâmes à SS. Jean et Paul pour rachever la visite des manuscrits de cette bibliothèque"). Briois preferred medals, curios, treasures, and works of art (Omont, "Voyage littéraire," 28: "Le jeudy, après-midy, nous fûmes voir le médailler de M. Rusini; toutes ses médailles sont en or, en grand nombre, et il s'y en trouve de fort rares. Il a un grand amas de pierres précieuses de toute sorte; il a plusieurs tableaux originaux, entr'autres un *Ecce hommo* [*sic*], la *Visite de la reyne de Saba*, une *Sainte famille*, de Paul Véronèze, etc."). Briois died on 10 February 1700, and was buried at Trinità dei Monti (BnF, MS fr. 16861, p. 32; Omont, "Voyage littéraire," 2). A contemporary ascribed Briois's death to a "pleurisy" contracted from exploring subterranean churches: É. Gigas, ed., *Lettres des Bénédictins de la Congrégation de St-Maur*, 2 vols. (Copenhagen, 1892–93), 2:268–69.

46 Miller, *Peiresc's Mediterranean World* (n. 11 above), 394, 612. Cf. Momigliano, "Ancient History and the Antiquarian," 304. See also E. C. Pastan and S. D. White, with K. Gilbert, *The Bayeux Tapestry and Its Contexts: A Reassessment* (Woodbridge, Suffolk, 2014), 24–35.

Byzantine state. Montfaucon, to whom he devotes a sentence to Du Cange's page and a half, merely "continued" the latter's work.[47]

Montfaucon's ancillary reputation among Byzantinists is also due to the fact that despite inventing Greek palaeography, Montfaucon makes for a negligent founding father of Byzantine studies. By the late seventeenth century, as other contributions to this volume discuss, scholars had found new ways to describe the Greek civilization after Rome: the Eastern Empire, the Empire of the Greeks, the Empire of Constantinople, "Byzantium," or the "more recent" as opposed to the "ancient" Greeks. Montfaucon's friend and collaborator Anselmo Banduri published his *Imperium Orientale* in Paris in 1711 (while the two men were in close contact), a work that spoke of stages of imperial history and referred to the *Byzantina Respublica*.[48] Yet Montfaucon only desultorily used such political categories. He spoke of rulers or coins "of Constantinople."[49] When writing about Greek language, artifacts, or books, he might distinguish *prisci* from *recentes/recentiores*. But what made a codex *recens* he rarely explicitly delineated.[50] In some cases, he borrowed from Du Cange the language of a "Middle and Lower Age" or a "Middle and Lower Greek."[51] In French, he used the phrase "bas Empire," but this might refer to Constantine I or to Constantine VII Porphyrogennetos.[52]

Montfaucon shows little heat or ice in such political periodization. Such equanimity stands in contrast with other "fathers" of Byzantine studies, such as Hieronymus Wolf (1516–1580), who had snarled of the "Byzantines" (*Byzantini*) that "I am

47 G. Ostrogorsky, *History of the Byzantine State*, trans. J. Hussey, rev. ed. (New Brunswick, NJ, 1969), 3–4, quotations at 4.

48 Anselmo Banduri, *Imperium Orientale, sive, Antiquitates Constantinopolitanae in quatuor partes distributatae*, 2 vols. (Paris, 1711), 2:447. On the next page (448), Banduri thanks Montfaucon, *vir inter doctissimos celeberrimus*, for his indispensable assistance.

49 Montfaucon, *Palaeographia Graeca*, 109–10, 176–77.

50 Montfaucon, *Diarium Italicum*, *passim*, lists *codices recentes*, with only occasional dating, at 11 (16th century), 12 (15th century), 16 (15th century), 237 (17th century, implied), 434 (14th century).

51 Montfaucon, *Palaeographia Graeca*, 176: *In nummis Constantinopolitanis medii & infimi ævi . . .*; 266: *vox medio Græcitatis ævo*; 360: *medio et infimo ævo*. The debt to Charles Du Fresne, sieur Du Cange, *Glossarium ad scriptores mediæ & infimæ Græcitatis*, 2 vols. (Lyon, 1688), is clear whenever Montfaucon refers to Du Cange's glossary by name: Montfaucon, *Diarium Italicum*, 78: *Cangius in Glossario mediæ & infimæ Græcitatis*; idem, *Bibliotheca Coisliniana* (n. 30 above), 132: *ut ait Cangius in Glossario mediæ & infimæ Græcitatis*.

52 Montfaucon, *Antiquité expliquée* (n. 33 above), supplément 4, 41: "& personne ne croira que ce soit quelque Empereur du bas Empire où l'on ne portoit point de barbe"; supplément 4, 7: "du bas Empire"; 49: "Je crois que ce trophée est du bas Empire"; 64: "Les Grecs du bas Empire disoient aussi Μινσύριον tire du Latin Missorium, qui revenoit à l'idée de Disque; et l'on trouve dans Constantin Porphyrogenete τὰ ἀργυρᾶ μινσύρια τὰ ἀνάγλυφα, c'étoient des Disques d'argent gravez sous Arcadius, & que l'on conservoit comme des curiositez dans le cabinet de l'Empereur."

surprised, not sorry, that such a dregs and a bilge water of an iniquitous people so long remained unmolested, and were not conquered earlier."[53] His edition of Byzantine historiography had opened with a poetic composition, an *Epilogus Byzantinae Historiae* in dactylic hexameters, which began,

> You who read the histories of the East, and the harsh fortunes
> of Christians, and their weak souls and wicked actions,
> and realms cut apart by discord and tumult...

and persisted in that spirit for four pages.[54] But while Wolf painted Byzantium as a country for old mores, bad Greek, internal conflict, and self-destructive theological caviling, he also depicted a historical coherency, with a beginning and an end (Constantine I and Constantine XI). Wolf's picture was of resilience, the forerunner to the depraved and decadent Byzantiums of Montesquieu, Voltaire, le Beau, and Gibbon.

Affect can define through warmth as well as antipathy, and Montfaucon was more engaged with Byzantium's early admirers. Montfaucon took little notice of Wolf, but he knew Crusius's *Turcograecia*, a more sympathetic, if critical, characterization of the Byzantines.[55] The enthusiastic Banduri was a friend and collaborator. Most important, as we have seen, was Du Cange. Montfaucon often mined Du Cange's *Historia Byzantina* (1680) and his *Glossarium ad scriptores mediæ & infimæ Graecitatis* (1688).[56] Du Cange could be ambivalent toward the Byzantines, but he was committed to the historical and linguistic coherency of a medieval Greek world. It was with passion that he had petitioned Colbert in 1679 to continue patronizing the *Byzantine du Louvre* (that is, Labbe's *Corpus Byzantinae Historiae*).[57] Scholarly

53 Hieronymus Wolf, *Nicephori Gregorae, Romanae, hoc est Byzantinae historiae Libri XI* (Basel, 1562), *praefatio*, n.p. [p. 2 of preface]: *fecem ac sentinam illam nefariorum hominum tam diu fuisse incolumem, nec citius oppressam esse, mirarer potius quàm miserarer.* For "Byzantini" see the previous page, where Wolf notes that the *Byzantini se Romanos... nominarunt.* On Wolf, see D. R. Reinsch, "Hieronymus Wolf as Editor and Translator of Byzantine Texts," in *The Reception of Byzantium in European Culture Since 1500*, ed. P. Marciniak and D. C. Smythe (Burlington, VT, 2016), 43–53; Pertusi, *Storiografia umanistica* (n. 4 above), 51–67.

54 Wolf, *Nicephori Gregorae historiae*, "Epilogus Byzantinae Historiae," n.p.

55 Montfaucon, *Palaeographia Graeca*, 110. For Crusius, see K.-H. Suchland, "Das Byzanzbild des Tübinger Philhellenen Martin Crusius (1526–1607)" (PhD diss., Universität Würzburg, 2001). See also Richard Calis in Chapter 4 of this volume.

56 E.g., Du Cange's *Historia Byzantina*: Montfaucon, *Palaeographia Graeca*, 48, 272, 382; *Bibliotheca Coisliniana*, 42. Du Cange's *Glossarium*: Montfaucon, *Analecta Graeca*, 148, 156, 208, 246, 260, 262, 265, 270, 278, 298; *Diarium Italicum*, 78; *Palaeographia Graeca*, xvii, 18, 22, 46, 59, 172, 302, 344, 374, 385. Cf. *Palaeographia Graeca*, 382–33.

57 Omont, "Du Cange et la Collection Byzantine du Louvre" (n. 6 above), 34.

affect helped solidify Byzantium in space and time for these earlier scholars, and motivated their explanations of what was distinct about Byzantine dynasties, aristocrats, administration, and language.

Part of the difference was generational. There had been good reason to meditate upon Byzantium as a distinct political-historical entity in the sixteenth and seventeenth centuries. Early modern scholars of Byzantium from Wolf to Du Cange wrote with the threat of the Turks in mind.[58] The moral of Byzantine political history was that the empire had succumbed. Writers and their patrons tended to regard Byzantium as either a cautionary tale or a spur to action. Montfaucon's work, on the other hand, postdated the unsuccessful Ottoman siege of Vienna in 1683. In Montfaucon's lifetime, the Turks became less a threat than a subject of exotic fascination for learned Westerners.[59]

As an editor, Montfaucon was interested in historical context predominantly as a groundwork for the work of editing texts. Montfaucon's writing on Byzantine subjects fulfilled antiquarian goals of situating and categorizing artifacts. Location was one part of this work. Montfaucon was unable to establish the same grounding for the localizing of Byzantine *scriptoria* that Mabillon and Maffei had attempted (and Traube would perform) for Latin *scriptoria*.[60] Yet Montfaucon made efforts to localize archaeological objects, both in the *Antiquité expliquée* and *Monumens* and in his palaeographical and codicological works. Montfaucon's real interest, however, lay in dating. There is a pronounced chronological logic to Montfaucon's antiquarianism, which explains his engagement with Du Cange's chronological and dynastic work—the source of many of his working assumptions.[61] Du Cange's lexicology was never far from hand, as we have seen. Montfaucon also used the Byzantine *anno mundi* system to perform chronology.[62] He placed a statue in time by knowing when emperors wore beards.[63] He was aware of which Byzantine rulers, like the empress Eudokia Makrembolitissa, had a bibliophilic reputation, as a means of placing manuscripts in

58 N. Bisaha, *Creating East and West: Renaissance Humanists and the Ottoman Turks* (Philadelphia, 2004), 94–134. This framing of Byzantine history extended to literature. In the 1570s, the Portuguese epic poet Luís Vaz de Camões (*Os Lusíadas*, canto 3, strophe 12) described the subjugation of "Bizâncio" to the Turks as a "boa injúria do grande Constantino" (a mighty insult to the great Constantine), and framed Byzantine defeat as a motivation for Da Gama's rounding of the Cape of Good Hope; Luís de Camões, *Os Lusiadas*, ed. F. Pierce (Oxford, 1973), 52.

59 A. Bevilacqua and H. Pfeifer, "Turquerie: Culture in Motion, 1650–1750," *Past and Present* 221 (2013): 75–118, esp. 77–79.

60 J. Irigoin, "Pour une étude des centres de copie byzantins," *Scriptorium* 12 (1958): 208–27, at 208.

61 E.g., Montfaucon, *Bibliotheca Coisliniana*, 42 (using Du Cange's research on Stefan Dušan).

62 Montfaucon, *Palaeographia Graeca*, 362; Mondrain, "Bernard de Montfaucon et l'étude des manuscrits grecs" (n. 14 above), 310.

63 Montfaucon, *Antiquité expliquée*, Supplément 4, 41.

time.[64] In deploying knowledge about Byzantium, Montfaucon consistently translated factual into chronological insight.[65]

Such categorization was rooted in Montfaucon's lifelong work of editing. Location and date were key considerations in establishing a text from manuscripts. But from early in his career Montfaucon was also drawn to manuscripts that were rare or otherwise exceptional in their own right. Though Montfaucon was mainly interested in datable manuscripts, he often paused to note curious or striking finds. The *Diarium Italicum* is full of examples. On a late August day in Padua, Montfaucon examined one of two "elegant" Greek manuscripts, both clearly datable thanks to colophons, in the otherwise unpromising collection of the Abbey of Santa Giustina:

> Parchment manuscript of the tenth century, beautifully written, of the Homilies of Saint *Basil* on the Psalms, on whose first pages there reads in the first hand: Θευδάτου τοῦ ἐνδοξοτάτου Πατρικίου καὶ στρατηγοῦ τοῦ ὀψικίου. That is: *For Theudatus the most-illustrious Patrician Duke of Obsequium.* On the dignities of *Obsequium*: Du Cange in his Glossary of Middle and Lower Greek at the word ὀψίκιον. On the next page, it reads, Πακουριανοῦ τοῦ ἐνδοξοτάτου Πατρικίου καὶ στρατηγοῦ τῆς Σάμου. *For Pacurianus illustrious Patrician and Duke of the island of Samos.* On the third page, ἐγράφη ἐπὶ Βασιλέων Βασιλείου καὶ Κωνσταντίνου. *The codex was written under the emperors Basil and Constantine.* For under these emperors there was a great verve for copying manuscripts; that is, at the end of the tenth and the beginning of the eleventh century.[66]

Certain features called for explanation. Theudatos's curious title—the "Duke of Service" (*Obsequium*)—might confuse the uninitiated. The reference to Du Cange

64 Montfaucon, *Palaeographia Graeca*, 109–10.

65 E.g., Montfaucon, *Palaeographia Graeca*, x: *nono sæculo*; 96: *XII. sæculo*; 97: *sæculo decimo-quarto*; 102: *XI. sæculo*; 104: *sexto sæculo*; 105: *septimo circiter sæculo*; 107: *sæculo nono*; 260: *cujus character uncials nonum quidem sæculum præfert*; 260: *decimo & undecimo sæculo* (aspects of the same MS); 276: *Qui character uncialis, hoc circiter tempore desiit. A nono enim sæculo nullum vidimus Codicem unciali charactere descriptum, ut supra dictum est, exceptis tamen libris Choralibus*; 510: *nono circiter sæculo*; 510: *X. sæculo*.

66 Montfaucon, *Diarium Italicum*, 78: *Codex membranaceus x. sæculi pulcrè exaratus, Homiliæ S.* Basilii *in Psalmos, in cujus primis foliis hæc leguntur primâ manu.* Θευδάτου τοῦ ἐνδοξοτάτου Πατρικίου καὶ στρατηγοῦ τοῦ ὀψικίου. *Id est:* Theudati præclarissimi Patricii Ducis Obsequii. *De Obsequii dignitatibus Cangius in Glossario mediæ & infimæ Græcitatis ad vocem* ὀψίκιον. *In sequenti pagina legitur,* Πακουριανοῦ τοῦ ἐνδοξοτάτου Πατρικίου καὶ στρατηγοῦ τῆς Σάμου. Pacuriani clarissimi Patricii & Ducis insulæ Samo. *In tertia pagina,* ἐγράφη ἐπὶ Βασιλέων Βασιλείου καὶ Κωνσταντίνου. Scriptus est codex Basilio & Constantino Imperatoribus. *His autem imperantibus magna vis codicum exscripta fuit; in fine scilicet decimi, & initio undecimi sæculi.*

clarifies that *Obsequium* was the Latin name of the Anatolian theme of *Opsikion* (Ὀψίκιον), whose name derived from the "service" of imperial soldiers.[67] The reign of Basil II (r. 976–1025) and Constantine VIII (co-ruler with Basil, sole ruler 1025–1028) is significant mainly for the *magna vis*, the verve, that these Macedonian rulers breathed into book copying. Montfaucon is not here concerned with which of the brothers (Basil) held the real power during their joint reign. What motivates his description is the artifact itself: above all, its dating thanks to the colophon, but also its loveliness (*elegantia*) and the fact it was beautifully executed (*pulcrè exaratus*).[68]

Editorial utility was Montfaucon's guiding star, and this elevated the importance of dating. Montfaucon sought to offer more precise dating criteria, starting with clearly dated manuscripts like the homilies of Basil in Padua, and moving from there to manuscripts that could be dated only by their script. A firm grasp of Byzantine political history was essential in supporting assessments by script. An anecdote circulated by Montfaucon's circle, no doubt embellished, shows the scholar using Byzantine history to corroborate his judgment when a jealous papal librarian attempted to embarrass him:

> While D. B. [Dom Bernard] was in the Vatican Library in good company, Monsieur the under-librarian by the name of Zacagni [Lorenzo Alessandro Zaccagni, 1652–1712] came up to him rather suddenly, opened before him a Greek manuscript around the middle and said to him: "You who know so well the age of manuscripts, how old is this one here?" (he said this to test him, since he did not know anything about it; he held to the false principle that one could not know the age of a manuscript beyond roughly three centuries). D. B., without losing his calm, responded to him: "The age of this manuscript is rather easy to recognize by the script: it is around seven centuries old." "You are mistaken," Monsieur Zacagni told him. "If I am mistaken," D. B. told him in front of the whole company, "I wish to renounce all my knowledge." "It was written under Basil the Macedonian [Basil I, r. 867–886]," insisted the under-librarian. "If it was written under Basil the Macedonian, I repeat to you before the whole company, I wish to renounce all my knowledge. But let us see, evidently this manuscript will have some note." Indeed, it had twelve verses at the opening, of which the first began with βασίλειος. "Did I not tell you," Monsieur Zacagni went on, "that this manuscript was written under Basil the Macedonian." "It is Basil Porphyrogenitos [Basil II, r. 976–1025]," replied D. Bernard: "but let us go

67 Cf. *ODB*, s.v. "Opsikion" (C. Foss).

68 Montfaucon, *Diarium Italicum*, 78.

> to the end of the twelve verses, perhaps we will find ourselves some clarification." Indeed, from the second [verse] there was ἐκ τῆς πορφύρας [from the purple], and everyone was convinced, even Monsieur Zacagni himself, that this could not pertain to anyone other than to Basil Prophyrogenitos and not to the Macedonian, who was a herdsman. Monsieur de Zacagni, having given up, said: "It must be therefore that the Jesuits of Flanders [the Bollandists] were mistaken in saying that this manuscript was written under Basil the Macedonian." "If the Jesuits of Flanders said that," replied D. B., "you see well that they were mistaken, since the thing is obvious." The company had a difficult time restraining themselves and not heavily mocking the under-librarian, who burst with chagrin and desired to have his revenge.[69]

The manuscript in question seems to have been the *Menologion of Basil II*, now Biblioteca Apostolica Vaticana, Vaticanus gr. 1613. This synaxarion (collection of saints' lives) of the tenth-century hagiographer Symeon Metaphrastes, with luscious illuminations, is one of the most famous Byzantine manuscripts—and, as Montfaucon argued, an eleventh-century manuscript.[70]

69 "Notice biographique sur B. de Montfaucon, par un contemporain," in Gigas, *Lettres des Bénédictins de la Congrégation de St-Maur* (n. 45 above), 2:250–53: "D. B. étant dans la Bibliothèque du Vatican en belle compagnie, M^r le sousbibliothécaire, qui s'appelle Zacagni, le vint aborder assez brusquem[en]t, lui ouvrit un Manuscrit Grec vers le milieu et lui dit: 'Vous qui connoissez si bien l'aage des Mss., quel aage a celui ci?' (il disoit cela pour le tenter, car il n'y connoissoit rien: il étoit dans le faux principe qu'on ne pouvoit connoître l'aage d'un M^t à trois cent ans près). D. B., sans s'étonner, lui répondit: 'L'aage de ce M^t est assez aisé a connoître par le charactère: il a environ sept cent ans.' 'Vous vous trompez,' lui dit Mr Zacagni. 'Si je me trompe,' lui dit D. B. devant toute la compagnie, 'je veux renoncer à toutes mes connoissances.' 'Il est écrit sous Basile le Macédonien,' insista le sousbibliothécaire. 'S'il est écrit sous Basile le Macédonien, je vous le répète devant toute la compagnie, je veux renoncer à toutes mes connoissances. Mais voyons, apparamment ce M^s aura quelque note.' En effet, il avoit douze vers au commencem[en]t, dont le premier commençoit par βασιλειος. 'Ne vous avois-je pas bien dit,' poursuivit Mr Zacagni, 'que ce Ms étoit écrit sous Basile le Macédon.' 'C'est Basile Porphyrogenite,' répliqua D. Bernard: 'mais allons jusqu'au bout des 12 vers, peutestre trouverons nous quelque éclaircissement.' En effect, dès le second il y avoit ἐκ τῆς πορφυρας et tous le monde convint, et Mr Zacagni même, que cela ne pouvoit convenir qu'au Porphyrogenite et [n]o[n] pas au Macédonien qui étoit un bouvier. Mr de Zacagni, avant que se rendre, dit: 'Il faut donc que les Jésuites de Flandre se soient trompés en disant que ce Ms avoit été écrit sous Basile le Macédonien.' 'Si les Jésuites de Flandre ont dit cela,' repartit D. B., 'vous voyez bien qu'il se sont trompés, car la chose est claire.' La compagnie avoit peine à se retenir et à ne se pas mocquer hautem[en]t du sousbibioth., qui crevoit de dépit et vouloit avoir sa revanche."

70 F. D'Aiuto and I. Pérez Martín, eds., *El "Menologio de Basilio II": Città del Vaticano, Biblioteca Apostolica Vaticana, Vat. gr. 1613: Libro de estudios con ocasión de la edición facsímil* (Vatican City, 2008). See also *ODB*, s.v. "Menologion of Basil II" (N. P. Ševčenko).

This tale has a revealing coda. Zaccagni tried to discomfit Montfaucon another time. Complaining that French scholars were always "undermining tradition," he lamented that "you French" had done away with Saint Longinus, the soldier who had pierced Jesus's side, because his name was too suspiciously close to λόγχη (spearhead). Yet when Montfaucon examined the book that Zaccagni had thrust before him to prove that Longinus was so called on good authority, Montfaucon said, "Ah ah, I see well that it is on *your* authority, because only you say here that this centurion was called Longinus and that he pierced the side of Our Lord, since neither the Gospel nor Saint Gregory of Nyssa makes this claim." Zaccagni lacked the Greek to check his own work, having merely put his name on the work of another. "I made a mistake," he replied—"dejectedly"—and thereafter Montfaucon's circle gave him the sobriquet "Monsieur Longinus."[71]

Three elements emerge from this eighteenth-century anecdote. First, there was, or was remembered to be, something performative about Montfaucon's antiquarianism. Montfaucon did his work "in good company" (*en belle compagnie*). Montfaucon's bravura adds dramatic tension: "If I am mistaken, I wish to renounce all my knowledge."[72] Second, Montfaucon successfully dated the manuscript by script, before his assessment was corroborated. This was the technique that Montfaucon, unlike Mabillon, became famous for: not differentiating between true and false, but situating a script on the continuum of time—something that Zaccagni felt to be impossible. Third, the anecdote makes Byzantine history the handmaid of antiquarianism. Byzantine imperial history, particularly the meaning of "the purple," is the means of winning a public argument. The anecdote—however embellished (at the very least the story appears to demote Zaccagni, who was not under-librarian but prefect of the Vatican Library)[73]—assumes familiarity with basic facts of Byzantine history. Even Zaccagni knows he is defeated when Montfaucon draws attention to the phrase "in the purple." The "gentlemen" around the table who stifled their laughter all found this proof to be self-evident, as did those who repeated the tale.

The danger of Zaccagni's challenge, aside from its obstructionism, had been its repudiation of Montfaucon's central principle: that manuscripts are datable by script.[74] Zaccagni's logic, if this account can be trusted, was doubly flawed. First, he had mixed up his Basils (even if he had been right, this would have given him only

71 "Notice," ed. Gigas, *Lettres des Bénédictins de la Congrégation de St-Maur*, 252–53.

72 Ibid., 250 ("en belle compagnie"), 251 ("Si je me trompe . . . je veux renoncer à toutes mes connoissances").

73 J. Irigoin, "Bernard de Montfaucon et la *Palaeographia Graeca*," in Hurel and Rogé, *Dom Bernard de Montfaucon* (n. 1 above), 211–23, at 214.

74 Irigoin (ibid., 214–15) notes that Montfaucon's difficulties with librarians owed to fears that he would publish treasures of their collection before they did.

a terminus post quem, since a text of Basil I's time could have been copied later). Second, he had ascribed to the "false principle" that one could not date manuscripts with precision "par le charactère." Montfaucon's refutation, admittedly, does a better job of correcting Zaccagni's first mistake than the second. It depended on his audience's familiarity with facts of (what we would call) Byzantine history—Basil I's humble origins as opposed to his great-great-grandson's lofty birth—but this did not depend upon any grand theory of, or special devotion to, Byzantine history. After all, the savant and the librarian also clashed over Longinus, a character from sacred history.

Montfaucon rarely used terms like *Byzantine* or *Byzantium*. He tended to reserve these for ancient Byzantium, authors like the sixth-century Stephen of Byzantium, or book and series titles like the *Byzantine du Louvre / Corpus Byzantinae Historiae* and Du Cange's *Historia Byzantina*.[75] He deployed other terms of analysis, like *bas Empire*, sporadically, as we have seen. Montfaucon's analysis avoids the political categories of the historian, but Montfaucon was dedicated to the proposition that all books and artifacts should be datable, and that meant sometimes using the insights produced by the historical method. If Montfaucon inhabited the antiquaries' "province" of the Republic of Letters, he sojourned with the historians.[76]

Montfaucon's Byzantium was part of his broader editorial and antiquarian commitment to Greek antiquities. Montfaucon's editorial projects—Athanasius, Origen, Chrysostom, and the other fathers—had convinced him that a broad mastery of ancient culture was necessary for their completion. In the preface to the first volume of his *Antiquité expliquée*, he reported that for thirty-four years he had devoted himself to all aspects of "antiquity" as a necessary precondition for success in editing, but he also hoped his findings would be a subject of interest for the reading public.[77] His travels to study monuments in Italy, for instance, had served "to augment my collections, and to acquire new knowledge about this vast sea of antiquity."[78]

The historian's Byzantium, organized around the chronology of the Byzantine state, is a drop in this ocean. In his writings, Montfaucon usually takes a wider purview. While discussing the historical forms taken by the upsilon (Υ, υ) in book 4 of the *Palaeographia Graeca*, for instance, Montfaucon must trace the development of letter through ancient texts, cameos, inscriptions, and the "very oldest coins

75 E.g., *Diarium Italicum*, 408: *Fragmentum historiæ Byzantinæ anonymi.*

76 A. Grafton, "Jean Hardouin: The Antiquary as Pariah," *JWarb* 62 (1999): 241–67, at 263.

77 Montfaucon, *Antiquité expliquée*, 1:i–ii.

78 Ibid., 1:ii: "La meilleure partie de ce tems fut emploiée à visiter les monumens antiques & les cabinets qui s'y trouvent en grand nombre, à augmenter mes recueils, & à acquerir de nouvelles connoissances sur cette vaste mer de l'antiquité."

of Byzantium" (meaning ancient Byzantium), before reaching what we would call Byzantine (meaning belonging to the medieval Greek East) "manuscripts of the sixth, seventh, eighth, and ninth centuries written in uncial script."[79] The closest Montfaucon comes to political periodization is when he wishes to date artifacts such as coins and monuments produced in given political milieus. Thus, in book 5 of the *Palaeographia Graeca*, Montfaucon describes Greek coins before and during the *Romanum Imperium*, and then "after the Roman Empire was translated to Constantinople."[80] In his *Antiquité expliquée*, he calls the Column of Theodosius "the last work that bears the seal of antiquity."[81]

The breadth of Montfaucon's interests emerges from the lectures he gave to the Académie des Inscriptions et Belles-Lettres. The scholar was so long-lived that two days before his death on 21 December 1741, he could joke at the Académie that in thirteen years he would be a hundred.[82] Montfaucon gave numerous lectures at the Académie. The topics reflected his omnivorous interests: the papyrus plant (read 1720, published 1729), the Alexandrian lighthouse (1729), Roman monuments in Paris (read 1734, published 1740), the aspects of court life in the time of Theodosius and Arcadius (read 1737, published 1740), a passage of Herodotus dealing with Libya (1740), and ancient Egyptian divinities (1743).[83]

In his lecture on Theodosius and Arcadius, Montfaucon paused to offer "some reflections on the Middle and the Lower Age (*le moyen et le bas âge*)."[84] These reflections were interpretations of John Chrysostom, who "preached with so much success under the empire of the great Theodosius and Arcadius his son."[85] Montfaucon had finally completed, two years before, his vast edition of the saint's *opera omnia*. The goal of the lecture was to derive lost antiquities from Chrysostom's prose. True to form, the article ends not with broad reflections on the nature of the age but with information Chrysostom provides about palimpsest tablets, "where after having erased the first writing, one wrote over the same erasure something new, ἐν δέλτῳ ἐξηλειμμένῃ."[86]

79 Montfaucon, *Palaeographia Graeca*, 338.

80 Ibid., 359; see also Montfaucon, *Antiquité expliquée*, supplément 4, 60. Compare Banduri's numismatic periodization of the Roman to Byzantine emperors: A. Banduri, *Numismata imperatorum Romanorum a Trajano Decio ad Palaeologos augustos*, 2 vols. (Paris, 1718).

81 Montfaucon, *Antiquité expliquée*, 2nd ed., vol. 1, preface, 14.

82 Sandys, *History of Classical Scholarship* (n. 14 above), 2:387.

83 Leclercq, "Montfaucon" (n. 14 above), cols. 2671–72.

84 Montfaucon, "Les modes et les usages" (n. 10 above), 474–79.

85 Ibid., 474: "Saint Jean Chrysostome, qui prêchoit avec tant de succès sous l'empire du grand Théodose & d'Arcadius son fils."

86 Ibid., 479 (from ἐξαλείφω).

A grand political category like Byzantium was for Montfaucon's antiquarian purposes both chronologically too broad and geographically too narrow. Geographically, one of Montfaucon's insistent observations had been that the evidence for "Greek" materials was not confined to Greece. Italy was rich in Greek books not only because of the Bessarions of the world but because of the historical Greek of Calabria, Sicily, and Dalmatia.[87] Chronologically, even Banduri's four stages of Byzantine history were too imprecise for Montfaucon's aims.[88] His preference in every case was to date by century. Admittedly, he favored the same emperors and empresses: Theodosius, Arcadius, Basil I, Leo the Wise, Constantine Porphyrogennetos, Basil II, and Eudokia Makrembolitissa.[89] He returned to the same texts. Montfaucon's "Byzantium" was shaped by his antiquarian's reading of Chrysostom, which he knew so well as an editor. The *typikon* of Irene Doukaina that he had edited as a thirty-three-year-old in 1688 was a text to which he would return again and again.[90] Otherwise, Byzantine authors, texts, and objects are sprinkled among his works like isolated stars in a broad sky. They do not constellate.

This is true not only in the treatises, where this pattern might be ascribed to their structure, but also in Montfaucon's correspondence. Take a 1703 letter from Montfaucon to the Florentine scholar and librarian Antonio Magliabechi, describing the latest publications in France.[91] There are new editions of patristics, including one by Montfaucon that uses a new "thirteenth-century manuscript," and there is a new French theology "for ladies without Latin." An ongoing edition of Clement of Alexandria by another scholar is dragging on because Clement is "difficult, and calls for much erudition and phlegm." Boivin's new Gregoras, replacing Wolf's, has appeared. A new edition of Michael Psellos, the famous eleventh-century writer, is deemed newsworthy. Montfaucon wryly notes that while Psellos speaks highly of Patriarch Michael Keroularios in one speech as "[le] plusgrand, [le] plus savant personage de son temps," in another speech "he describes him rather differently." Now Keroularios is guilty of superstition, idolatry, heresy, divining, homicide, sedition, rebellion, and tyranny (et cetera). Neither Psellos nor Keroularios gets category markers here, and Montfaucon does not ascribe Psellos's inconsistency to his Byzantine nature (as Gibbon would condemn Byzantine writers later in the

87 Montfaucon, *Diarium Italicum, præfatio*, n.p. [pp. 4–5 of preface], 211.

88 Banduri, *Imperium Orientale* (n. 48 above), 2:446–47.

89 Cf. Montfaucon, *Palaeographia Graeca*, 109–10.

90 Montfaucon, *Diarium Italicum*, 54; Montfaucon, *Palaeographia Graeca*, 3, 17–18, 30, 46–47, 58, 102, 110, 299–302, 367.

91 Bernard de Montfaucon to Antonio Magliabechi, April 1703, in *Correspondance inédite de Mabillon et de Montfaucon avec l'Italie*, ed. Antoine-Claude Pasquin Valéry, 3 vols. (Paris, 1846), 3:146–54 (no. 374).

century). Montfaucon notes only that the publisher felt Psellos's speeches to be "the loveliest pieces he had yet printed *de la Byzantine*"—that is, the *Byzantine du Louvre*.[92] But the letter to Magliabechi is most preoccupied with two cameos with Greek lettering, one Ptolemaic and one Roman. These occupy by far the greater space of his letter to a fellow member of the Republic of Letters.

■■■

All of this speaks to Montfaucon's scholarly priorities, in an age of cooling confessional tensions and diminishing fears about the Turks. While earlier early modern "inventors" of Byzantium—Wolf and Crusius especially—were interested in the Byzantine Empire with an eye to the Turks or to confessional vendettas, Montfaucon's engagement was more obviously academic. Editing the Fathers brought him to Italy. Editing and dating, not the pointed *veri ac falsi discrimen* of Mabillon's project, were the raison d'être of the *Palaeographia Graeca*. Momigliano sees this when he compares Montfaucon to Mabillon. Monfaucon, he writes, "was not just a second Mabillon. He stood for something of his own."[93]

Regarding Byzantium, that "something" was situational. It meant his developing the tools from which to conduct editorial work. It meant his developing a temporally and geographically situated picture of Greek as a *corpus*: a language, a set of scripts, a family of artifacts, and a body of knowledge. This made Montfaucon different from Du Cange, too. Du Cange had periodized comfortably using political history: witness the essay that opens his lexicographical work. Montfaucon sought more generic divisions. He united under one heading the Greek of Greece, the Greek of the Fathers, the Greek of the Byzantines, and the Greek of medieval Italy. For Montfaucon, taxonomy and categorization came after years of sustained contact with the cultural products of a much broader master category.[94] Political history was important, but as one of many ancillary disciplines that shed light on the work of editing and the presentation of antiquities. In a debate with a hostile librarian, you had to know the difference between Basil the herdsman and Basil the purple-born, but in the same way you had to be able to recognize an allusion to the *Odyssey* to understand the work of Gregory of Nazianzus.[95]

92 Ibid., 3:147 (French theology, Clement of Alexandria), 150 (Gregoras), 150–51 (Psellos).

93 Momigliano, "Mabillon's Italian Disciples" (n. 1 above), 286.

94 See Grafton, "Jean Hardouin" (n. 76 above), 259: "Hardouin seems never to have shared Montfaucon's belief that only continual exposure to the brute material sources could enable a scholar to assess them."

95 Montfaucon, *Antiquité expliquée*, 1:i–ii.

This, then, was Montfaucon's Byzantium. Part of a much wider story, it was an incidental share of a wider editorial and antiquarian vocation particularly situated in the early eighteenth century. By the 1740s, however, Montfaucon had survived into a new age. As he delivered his lectures on usages in Chrysostom, a new vision of Byzantine degeneration was reviving Wolf's negative mind-set. For hostile observers like le Beau and Gibbon, there were new reasons to be interested in the Byzantine state. A new Enlightenment antipathy would soon construct the Byzantines as a deplorable civilization. Antiquarianism too was becoming an object of fun. The satirical *Mémoire de l'Académie des Sciences, Inscriptions, Belles Lettres, Beaux Arts* describes an episode from "the extracts of Constantine Porphyrogenitus" about a Median prince who died of lovesickness for queen "Zarine."[96]

Where does that leave Montfaucon's Byzantium? Montfaucon's technical achievements remain fundamental.[97] Modern scholars still turn to him for otherwise unpublished material.[98] And because the Byzantine state did not stand at the center of Montfaucon's studies, he was pioneering in studying medieval Greek texts produced at the margins of Byzantium. The *Palaeographia Graeca* continues to offer valuable discussion of texts that do not conform to traditional categories of ancient or medieval, Byzantine or Western, like the ninth-century Greek Psalter written out by the Carolingian-Irish scholar Sedulius Scottus, who concluded with the Greek colophon, "I Sedulios Skottos wrote this out."[99]

Montfaucon's antiquarianism may still hold attractions for scholars who hope to take seriously Greek as it lived in the medieval West. Montfaucon's interest in Greek language and artifacts offers a vantage point on cultural products, like those of Italo-Byzantine culture, at the margins of now accepted categories. Montfaucon's method—immerse first, ask questions later—encourages us to constantly rethink our categories. Yet it is strange to think that Montfaucon's main analytical legacy to Byzantine studies may his implicit reminder that Byzantium is a fragile historical category.[100]

This leaves Bernard de Montfaucon in an unusual position among the inventors of Byzantine studies. He inventively and extensively built on scholarship that

96 "Projet d'un Voyage en Espagne," in *Mémoire de l'Académie des Sciences, Inscriptions, Belles Lettres, Beaux Arts, etc. Nouvellement établie à Troyes en Champagne*, 2 vols. in one (Troyes, 1756), 2:21.

97 A. Dain, *Les manuscrits*, 3rd ed. (Paris, 1975), 60.

98 Irigoin, "Dom Bernard de Montfaucon" (n. 14 above), 77, and 77, n. 15.

99 Paris, Bibliothèque de l'Arsenal, MS 8407, fol. 55r: "CHΔΥΛΙΟC CKOTTOC ΕΓΩ ΕΓΡΑΨΑ"; Montfaucon, *Palaeographia Graeca*, 235–50. See now M. W. Herren, "Sedulius Scottus and the Knowledge of Greek," in *Early Medieval Ireland and Europe: Chronology, Contacts, Scholarship*, ed. P. Moran and I. Warntjes (Turnhout, 2015), 515–35, at 524–29.

100 Compare A. Cameron, "Byzantium and the Limits of Orthodoxy," *ProcBrAc* 154 (2008): 129–52, at 152.

took seriously the distinctness of the Byzantine world. With the attention of a man used to reaching out to living colleagues, he assiduously courted the scholarship of the dead. Sometimes the insights he drew on—Crusius's discussion of manuscripts, Banduri's discussion of coins, or Du Cange's lexicographical insights—were steeped in an analysis organized around the lifespan of the Byzantine state. Yet Montfaucon's periodizations were only lightly sketched, and his appeals to political history tended to be in the service of antiquarianism. The translation of the empire to Constantinople, the last statue of Theodosius, the fall of the eastern empire to Mehmed II, even the disappearance of imperial beards: these contextual facts underpinned his categorizing endeavors.

Yet over the course of Montfaucon's career, artifacts also became an end in themselves. It was as an antiquarian—even more than as an editor—that Montfaucon was impelled to study Byzantine materials. This is easy to see from such works as the *Diarium Italicum*, the *Palaeographia Graeca*, and the two bibliographies—texts that are not as bloodless as critics have suggested,[101] since they let us follow Montfaucon into the library. True, Montfaucon "omitted those things which are bandied about on every tongue."[102] But his excitement when he stepped into a new collection is obvious. He took stock of the Arabic, Syriac, and Hebrew manuscripts. He printed lines of old French poetry hidden and unpublished in a manuscript of Dares Phrygius.[103] Greek, though, was always his passion.[104] Greek books, whether they were classics, the Fathers, authors like Procopius, or obscure astronomers and court historians, whether written on parchment, paper, or so-called eastern paper (*charta bombycina*), drew and kept his attention.[105] Noteworthy elements—dragons on a robe, rulers mentioned in passing, the names of themes—might bring him to Du Cange; and if he had omitted some interesting artifact or phenomenon, there might be room for a few lines in a lecture at the Académie. Montfaucon's attention was devoted to information that helped establish or explain texts to be edited—but, increasingly over time, also to the rare, the old, and the beautiful. Montfaucon's Byzantium was only a part of these larger passions.

101 Momigliano, "Mabillon's Italian Disciples," 286: "Montfaucon's prosaic and businesslike nature."

102 Montfaucon, *Diarium Italicum*, praefatio, n.p. [pp. 1–2 of preface].

103 Ibid., 19. For Dares Phrygius's early modern reputation, see F. Clark, "Authenticity, Antiquity, and Authority: Dares Phrygius in Early Modern Europe," *Journal of the History of Ideas* 72 (2011): 183–207.

104 Irigoin, "Dom Bernard de Montfaucon," 77.

105 For Montfaucon's understanding of different writing surfaces, including *charta bombycina*, see Montfaucon, *Palaeographia Graeca*, 13–20 (book 1, chap. 2). For a more recent perspective, see J. Irigoin, "Les premiers manuscrits grecs écrits sur papier et le problème du bombycin," *Scriptorium* 4 (1950): 154–204.

Montfaucon died in 1741. He lived almost three decades longer than the long-lived Sun King for whose armies he had fought as a boy, dying during the reign of Louis XIV's great-grandson. Already the wits of the Enlightenment were mocking the antiquaries of the Académie. In seven years, Montesquieu would cast barbs against the Byzantines. In sixteen, le Beau would publish his history of imperial senescence. In thirty-five, Gibbon would solidify an enduring image of Byzantine degeneracy, which Voltaire's pen would dramatize. These Enlightenment critics disdained a Byzantium that still intrigued them. But for the span of three generations, a scholarly Nestor in the Republic of Letters had welcomed Psellos and Basil and Constantine and Irene and Eudokia, with all their elegant books and artifacts, to the broader court of Greek antiquities.

ELEVEN

HAGIOGRAPHY, ERUDITION, AND THE EMERGENCE OF *BYZANTINISME* (SIXTEENTH–NINETEENTH CENTURIES)

XAVIER LEQUEUX

TRANSLATED BY
NATHANAEL ASCHENBRENNER AND JAKE RANSOHOFF

IN 1607 A JESUIT FROM UTRECHT, HÉRIBERT ROSWEYDE (1569–1629), PUBLISHED a book of only ninety-two pages titled *Fasti Sanctorum quorum Vitae in Belgicis bibliothecis manuscriptae*.[1] Like others, the scholar had discerned the less than satisfactory character of the collections of saints' lives that claimed authority in his time. For instance, in pursuit of the goal of rendering the saints' lives more pleasant to read, the Carthusian scholar Lorenz Sauer (1522–1578) had not hesitated to entirely rewrite certain texts in order to improve their Latinity, nor had he abstained from purging the accounts of certain passages he deemed unsuitable or insufficiently edifying.

The Catholic Church at that time, shaken by the criticisms of Protestants, was in the midst of reassessing its traditions. Scholars undertook grand new editions of scripture and patristic texts. Beside writing his *Annales ecclesiastici*, Cardinal Caesar Baronius (1538–1607) had been the animating force of the new *Martyrologium Romanum* (1584) published under the auspices of Pope Gregory XIII (r. 1572–1585). This work furnished an official calendar for the feasts of saints, martyrs, and confessors. Two years later, a historical commentary, also written by Baronius, appeared as a useful complement to the notices in the *Martyrologium*.[2] It was in this same

1 On Rosweyde's project and its reception, see R. Godding, "L'œuvre hagiographique d'Héribert Rosweyde," in *De Rosweyde aux "Acta Sanctorum": La recherche hagiographique des Bollandistes, à travers quatre siècles*, ed. R. Godding, B. Joassart, X. Lequeux, and F. De Vriendt, SubsHag 88 (Brussels, 2009), 35–62.

2 The bibliography concerning this enterprise is significant; see, among others, G. A. Guazzelli, "Cesare Baronio e il *Martyrologium Romanum*: Problemi interpretativi e linee evolutive di un

context that Rosweyde conceived the idea to produce, for the lives of medieval saints, some editions that would faithfully record the original texts, and to furnish these texts with an explanatory apparatus. His *Fasti* announced the project, which had recently been approved by the Jesuit leadership. Rosweyde intended to collect the lives of saints "of every epoch, gender, and nation."[3] This desire for completeness was coupled with philological considerations: the texts would henceforth be published unredacted and in full, and furnished with a commentary supplying all the explication required for their proper understanding. Rosweyde hoped to obtain numerous copies of lives from manuscripts kept abroad, so he sought the collaboration of scholars across Europe.

The publication as he then conceived it would encompass eighteen volumes. The first three would be dedicated to the feasts of Christ, the Virgin, and the other major ritual celebrations (*solemnitates*) of the liturgical year. The next twelve volumes would follow the months of the year, with each saint listed on the date of his or her commemoration. The next would then treat the martyrologies. The penultimate volume would collect the supplementary material essential for understanding the edited texts: it would explore the authors of the lives, the sufferings of the martyrs, the iconography of different saints, and the liturgical rites encountered in the lives, along with the profane customs and practices, chronology and topography. There the reader would also find a list of uncommon or difficult words. The final volume would present thirteen indexes, and the last fifty pages of the *Fasti* would contain an alphabetical list of some thirteen hundred saints and martyrs. This list encompassed all those for whom Rosweyde knew of an extant life or passion preserved in one of the libraries of the southern Low Countries or northern France, which, taken together, constituted a considerable amount of material.

Leaving aside figures known from Holy Scripture, around 160 entries in this *Index Sanctorum* concern saints who ended their lives in some part of the Christian East.[4] Here we encounter church fathers: the ubiquitous Athanasius of Alexandria, Basil of Caesarea, Gregory of Nazianzus, and John Chrysostom. Among the bishops, Frumentius, the apostle of Ethiopia; Polychronius of Babylon; Symeon Bar Sabba of Ctesiphon; and Jacob of Nisibis bore a touch of the exotic, and illustrate

rapporto diacronico," in *"Nunc alia tempora, alii mores": Storici e storia in età postridentina, Atti del convegno internazionale, Torino, 24–27 sett. 2003*, ed. A. Firpo (Florence, 2005), 47–89; idem, "Baronio attraverso il *Martyrologium Romanum*," in *Cesare Baronio tra santità e scrittura storica*, ed. G. A. Guazzelli, R. Michetti, and F. Scorza Barcellona, Studi e Ricerche 29 (Rome, 2012), 67–110.

3 Héribert Rosweyde, *Fasti Sanctorum quorum Vitae in Belgicis bibliothecis manuscriptae* (Antwerp, 1607), 7: *omnis aetatis, sexus, nationis.*

4 X. Lequeux, "Les saints orientaux dans les *Fasti Sanctorum* de Rosweyde," in Godding et al., *De Rosweyde*, 63–70.

Rosweyde's pursuit of universality. Saints of priestly rank receive less extensive coverage: there we find Ananias of Damascus, martyred in Phoenicia; Hermolaus of Nicomedia; Lucian prebyster *Antiochenus*; and Mocius of Amphipolis. Anthony, Pachomius, Macarius, Onuphrius, Fronto of Nitria, Hilarion of Gaza, and other Serapions lead the procession of monks and anchorites. We should note as well the presence of two practitioners of an ascetic mode that met with little success in the West: the Stylites, Symeon the Elder and Symeon *solitarius*, otherwise known as the Younger. Female saints were present as well: appearing there among others were Apollonia of Alexandria, Barbara and Euphrasia of Nicomedia, Dorothea of Caesarea, Euphemia of Chalcedon, Mary the Egyptian, Melania, Pelagia the Penitent, Thaïs, and the inevitable Thekla.

Rosweyde's list of "eastern" saints was hardly systematic. A significant number of those whose exploits are commemorated in Byzantine synaxaries, or collections of abridged records of saints, are notable by their absence. But this lack is easily explained, for the texts collected by Rosweyde came from his personal visits to the libraries of the southern Low Countries and northern France, institutions poorly furnished on the whole with Greek manuscripts. One might be inclined to think that the credit for introducing these "new" saints to the West goes to Baronius and his *Martyrologium Romanum*. But this was not the case: most of them were already well attested in two collections printed during the second half of the sixteenth century, Luigi Lippomano's *Sanctorum priscorum Patrum Vitae* (1551–60) and Lorenz Sauer's *De probatis Sanctorum historiis* (1570–75).[5] Several of these individuals were already included in medieval historical martyrologies. The notices on Bishop Moses, on the martyrs of Tyre, on John of Nicomedia, and the bishops Thraseas of Eumenia and Dionysius of Alexandria had first been included by Ado of Vienne (d. 875), while that of Meletius—if indeed this is Meletius, the bishop of Pontus—had already been introduced by Usuard (d. 877).[6]

When he had no extant hagiographic account for a saint, Rosweyde was content to simply transcribe the testimony of Greek ecclesiastical historians, which he found in the Latin translation of John Christopherson published in Louvain in 1570. A kind of forerunner of the Bollandists, Christopherson had also made some rare transcriptions of Greek hagiographic texts: from the library of the king of France, he notably recovered the *Acts of St. George* (*BHG* 674); a *Passion of Theodota* (*BHG*

5 On these two publications, see S. Boesch Gajano, "Dalle raccolte di Vite di Santi agli *Acta Sanctorum*: Persistenze e trasformazioni fra Umanesimo e Controriforma," in Godding et al., *De Rosweyde*, 5–34.

6 On Ado of Vienne, see J. Dubois and G. Renaud, *Le martyrologe d'Adon: Ses deux familles, ses trois recensions*, Sources d'histoire médiévale (Paris, 1984), 82, 90, 301–2, 346, 384; on Usuard, see J. Dubois, *Le martyrologe d'Usuard*, SubsHag 40 (Brussels, 1965), 353.

1781), martyred along with her three sons at Nicaea; and Symeon Metaphrastes' *Life of the SS. Xenophon and Maria* (*BHG* 1878).

At the end of his register of saints, Rosweyde had appended a sample text, the complete Latin *Acts of the Martyrs Tarachus, Probus, and Andronicus of Cilicia* (*BHL* 7984), from which Baronius had presented only selections taken from an incomplete manuscript. The new publication of the *Acts* marked a step forward, even though Rosweyde did not specify the provenance of the manuscript he used and claimed (incorrectly) that the text was an authentic transcript of the Roman court that had condemned these martyrs.

The scholarly program he announced was titanic in its scope, and Rosweyde solicited critiques and suggestions. Some remained skeptical, including Cardinal Robert Bellarmine (1542–1621), who had previously traveled through the southern Low Countries between 1569 and 1576. Dismayed at the magnitude of the task and fearing that the original texts would contain many passages likely to provoke derision, the cardinal suggested that Rosweyde content himself with editing those texts which had escaped his predecessors, Lippomano and Sauer, and that he cautiously add the full texts of those lives surreptitiously reworked by the same Sauer. Bellarmine's reservations, informed in part by his desire to defend the church, indirectly revealed the radical novelty of the new initiative.[7]

Unfortunately, Rosweyde was constantly diverted from this research by a series of tasks assigned by his superiors and was never able to complete his project. He nevertheless found the time to publish, alongside a few religious pamphlets, several preparatory works for his program. Having spotted in Cologne a manuscript of the martyrology known as the "Little Roman," which the forger Ado of Vienne claimed to have used during a stay in Ravenna, Rosweyde brought forth the *editio princeps* in 1613.[8] The Jesuit also recognized the importance of another martyrology, the *Hieronymianus*, and in particular its oldest witness, a manuscript from the beginning of the eighth century kept at Echternach Abbey.[9] To facilitate the faithful printing of the text, Rosweyde borrowed the codex from the abbey and entrusted it to Antwerp's famous printer Christophe Plantin, who engraved the folios containing the martyrology (2–32v) on copper plate. Unfortunately, this edition—the first facsimile in the history of printing—took much longer to produce than either Rosweyde or Plantin had expected, and it was only partially printed in nine copies

7 Godding, "L'œuvre hagiographique de Rosweyde," 41–43, with references to the relevant archival documents.

8 R. Godding, "Héribert Rosweyde," in *Bollandistes, saints et légendes: Quatre siècles de recherche*, ed. R. Godding, B. Joassart, X. Lequeux, F. de Vriendt, and J. van der Straeten (Brussels, 2007), 28–29.

9 This manuscript is now Bibliothèque Nationale de France, MS lat. 10837, viewable online at https://gallica.bnf.fr/ark:/12148/btv1b6001113z/f19.image.r=martyrolohium%20hieronymianum.

in 1660, long after Rosweyde's death.[10] His name is associated with yet another major publication: the *Vitae Patrum*, a heavy tome of more than eleven hundred pages printed in Antwerp in 1615. Developed over the course of the Middle Ages, this collection, which gathered together the foundational texts of eastern and western monasticism, was a huge success. It was copied repeatedly and was printed in numerous editions throughout the sixteenth century. After collating twenty-three manuscripts and comparing twenty printed editions, Rosweyde established a text that remained authoritative until the twentieth century. In a series of twenty-six prolegomena, Rosweyde exposed the critical problems encountered over the course of his editorial labors: attribution of authorship, identification of the translators from Greek to Latin, the doctrinal authority and spiritual utility of the included texts, a catalog of the available manuscripts and editions, and the contribution of the new edition. The newly edited texts were furnished both with marginal summaries to facilitate their consultation and with abundant annotation, in which proper names and obscure expressions were explained. A glossary of rare or difficult words (running to thirty-seven pages) and three indexes (themes, *nomina*, and *loci*) completed the collection. The new publication of the *Vitae Patrum* made an impression, for it inspired, a few decades later, the initiator of the *Acta Sanctorum* (*AASS*).

Just as he was preparing the saints' lives of January for printing, Rosweyde died on 4 October 1629 of a contagious disease contracted from tending to a sick patient. He left behind a rich archive—manuscripts, transcriptions, scattered notes, catalogs, printed books—and a voluminous correspondence with the scholars who had aided his research over the years. What was to be done with this legacy? The Jesuit superiors called Father Jean Bolland (1596–1665), then prefect of studies at the Jesuit college in Malines, to examine Rosweyde's papers and to suggest a practical solution. Bolland proposed that he himself pursue Rosweyde's work, on two conditions: he would be free to modify the initial plan as needed, and he would be able to have at his disposal all of Rosweyde's papers. The superiors accepted these conditions and Bolland installed himself in Antwerp to take up his task.

Bolland did not hesitate to expand Rosweyde's project. He aimed henceforth to include *all* saints, not only those for whom a life or passion was available. Enlarging the field of investigation in this way opened the door to saints who were revered in Byzantium but of whom the West knew all too little. Though he did not renounce the philological principles of his predecessor, Bolland was not content to provide only editions of the texts and relegate the commentary to a supplementary volume. Instead, Bolland decided that each text would be framed by an introduction and an explanatory commentary. The young Jesuit Godefroid Henschen (1601–1681), who

10 Godding, "Héribert Rosweyde," 29–31.

had meanwhile joined Bolland, proposed some adaptations to the plan set out by his superior. Tasked with preparing an edition of the *Lives of St. Vaast and St. Amand*, Bolland's new collaborator did not avoid any of the difficulties posed by the text: the list and description of the sources, questions of chronology and topography, identification of historical figures, explanation of rare words, and study of the origins and development of the cult. Impressed by his young charge's labors, Bolland decided to rewrite the first volume for January, which had already been prepared for printing. From that point onward, he would not only edit the texts but also complement them with a historical treatise, as complete as possible, on *each* saint and *all* the sources in which he or she was attested.[11] The concept of the "hagiographic dossier" had been born. Unfortunately, in the eighteenth century, the attention accorded to the quality of these editions and their primacy in the arrangement of the dossier gave ground little by little to the fashion for treatises that ostentatiously displayed stifling erudition.[12] Only with the reform of Charles De Smedt (1833–1911) in the following century would this trend be abandoned.

The first two volumes of the *AASS* were published in 1643. Covering the whole month of January, they totaled more than 2,400 pages and 1,170 saints. The frontispiece of the two books, the work of the painter Abraham van Diepenbeeck (1596–1675), demands attention as well (fig. 11.1).[13] At the center of the engraving, an unfurled sheet conceals the entrance to a cave, in which the authors of the lives and passions of the saints have found refuge; these authors are holding in their hands the writings contained in the volumes.[14] The entrance to the cave is guarded by three young girls, who in beauty and youth yield nothing to the Three Graces. On the right, Truth (*Veritas*) uses a mirror to illuminate the interior of the cave, while the base of her pedestal is inscribed with her motto: *Obscura revelo*, "I reveal the obscured." From this ray of light, a cherub lights a torch to enter the cave and extract the precious testimonies within. Below this scene Time slumps, having placed an hourglass on a pile of volumes. As this old man, Time, greedily devours a book, a cherub wrests a leaf from him, saving the text from total destruction. Emerging from the cave, another cherub presents his spoils, recently extracted from the cave, to Learning (*Eruditio*), who stands to the left; the young woman examines those writings and resolves their difficulties, embodying her motto: *Antiqua reduco*, "I restore

11 R. Godding, "Jean Bolland et les débuts des *Acta Sanctorum*," in Godding et al., *Bollandistes*, 37–38.

12 See F. Dolbeau, "Les sources manuscrites des *Acta Sanctorum* et leur collecte (XVIIe–XVIIIe siècles)," in Godding et al., *De Rosweyde*, 105–47, esp. 115–17.

13 Godding, "Jean Bolland et les débuts des *Acta Sanctorum*," 39.

14 Contrary to what the viewer might conclude at first glance, the individuals in the cave cannot be saints themselves, since they lack the customary halo.

Fig. 11.1. Frontispiece from vol. 1 of January in the *Acta Sanctorum* (Antwerp, 1643). Image courtesy Wikimedia Commons and N. Português.

ancient texts." The manuscripts are then passed by another cherub to a third figure, anonymous, enthroned majestically above the cave. This personification works to transcribe the texts delivered by the cherubs to ensure their dissemination. Celestial rays, representing heavenly inspiration, elucidate this last scene with two biblical quotations: *Dedit illi scientiam sanctorum* (Sap. 10:10), "He gave to him the knowledge of the saints"; *In plenitudine sanctorum detentio mea* (Sir. 24:16), "In the full company of the saints is my abode."[15] The frontispiece, whose plump cherubs seem to have escaped from the studio of the Antwerp painter Peter Paul Rubens (1577–1640), depicts the methodology adopted by Bolland and Henschen. The recuperation of original texts, their analysis, and their publication—these stages demanded all the energy of the Antwerp scholars.

The title, written on the parchment partially concealing the entrance to the cave, informs the reader of the contents of the work:

Acta Sanctorum quotquot toto orbe coluntur, vel a catholicis scriptoribus celebrantur, quae ex latinis et graecis, aliarumque gentium antiquis monumentis collegit, digessit, notis illustravit Ioannes Bollandus Societatis Iesu theologus, servata primigenia Scriptorum phrasi. Operam et studium contulit Godefridus Henschenius[.]

The Acts of the Saints, as far as they are honored throughout the whole world, or as celebrated by Catholic writers, Jean Bolland, theologian of the Society of Jesus, has collected, classified, and annotated from Latin, Greek, and the ancient testimonies of other nations, retaining them in the original style of the authors. Godefroid Henschen also lent his labor and devotion[.]

The title, along with the iconography of the engraving, announced the editors' intentions to recover the life of every saint and exploit all available documentation. In fact, saints honored in Byzantium and in other regions of the Christian East made a triumphant entry into the consciousness of the Catholic Church through the first volume of the collection. Using several synaxaries, often (incorrectly) called *menologia*,[16] enabled Bolland to reveal the existence of countless saints hitherto unknown in the West.

15 This programmatic frontispiece was temporarily replaced, in the volumes of the *AASS* for the month of June (1695–1717), by another engraving inspired by current religious circumstances: see R. Godding, "D'un frontispice à l'autre," in Godding et al., *Bollandistes*, 101–4.

16 On this traditional confusion in nomenclature, see J. Noret, "Ménologes, synaxaires, ménées: Essai de clarification d'une terminologie," *AB* 86 (1968): 21–24.

At the beginning, Bolland and his collaborators never imagined that one day their publications would be read beyond the borders of western Europe, and they were content to print Latin translations of the Greek texts that celebrated the Byzantine saints they had recovered for the *AASS*. Hence, for Basil of Caesarea's *Praise of the Martyr Gordius* (*BHG* 703), Bolland recycled the translation completed by Sauer, adding some corrections to it.[17] For two *Lives of Symeon the Stylite* (*BHG* 1682–83e and 1686–87), he used the earlier translations made by the Jesuit Guillaume de Graet (d. 1629).[18] In the case of the *Life of Theodosius the Cenobiarch* (*BHG* 1778), Bolland borrowed the translation from Sauer (who took it from Lippomano), though Bolland checked it against the recension preserved in a Greek manuscript from the Vatican Library.[19] When no translation was available, the Jesuit scholars would translate the Greek text themselves. For example, the *Life of Alexander the Acemete* (*BHG* 47) and the *Life of Polycarp of Smyrna* by Pionius (*BHG* 1561) were translated "from ancient Greek manuscripts."[20] The *Metaphrastic Life of John the Calybite* (*BHG* 869) was translated by Rosweyde "from a Greek manuscript kept in the Vatican Library."[21]

Greek was by no means absent from the first volumes of the *AASS*.[22] A Greek font was used for brief notations: extracts from synaxaries, variant readings, citations from Byzantine historians, and even lexical explanations. Certain Hellenists, including Cardinal Francesco Barberini (1597–1679), Leone Allacci (1586–1669), and Ottavio Falconieri (1636–1675), regretted that the *AASS* did not give the Greek documents in their original language. The Jesuit Pierre Poussines echoed these grievances in a missive addressed to Bolland on 7 August 1666.[23] In Antwerp, Bolland and his collaborators were then putting the finishing touches on the first volume of March; it was decided to retain the Latin translations within the relevant dossiers and to print the original Greek texts as a supplement at the end, also divided into

17 First volume of *AASS* January, 130–33.

18 Ibid., 264–69, 274–85.

19 Ibid., 685–701.

20 Ibid., 1020–29; the *Life of Polycarp of Smyrna* is in the second volume of *AASS* January, 695–702 (quotation at 695).

21 First volume of *AASS* January, 1031–35, at 1031. The translator is identified in the *Commentarius praevius*, 1029.

22 X. Lequeux, "Les *Acta Sanctorum* et le grec," in Godding et al., *Bollandistes*, 59.

23 Document published by B. Joassart, "Lettres du Jésuite Pierre Poussines à Bolland, Henchen, Papebroch et Janning," *AB* 129 (2011): 123–24. By chance, the first work of this French scholar (1609–1686) was an edition of a hagiographic text: the *Nicetae laudatio SS. Archangelorum Michaelis et Gabrielis* [*BHG* 1291] (Toulouse, 1637).

paragraphs and furnished with identical marginal summaries; this patch helped the scholars avoid rewriting the whole book. Consultation of Greek texts relegated to the end of the volume quickly proved inconvenient. In volume 4 of the *AASS* of May (Antwerp, 1685), dedicated to Cardinal Carlo Barberini (1630–1704), Henschen and Daniel Papebroch (1628–1714), who had joined the Bollandist workshop in 1660,[24] opted for a different presentation of the sources: Greek text and Latin translation were printed side by side in two parallel columns. Such a layout was not new: the two Jesuits may have taken their example from the editions of Greek texts published by the Dominican François Combefis (1605–1679), who had so kindly welcomed them during their stay in Paris, from 11 August to 9 November 1662, on return from a research trip that had taken them to Rome.[25] By henceforth providing the Greek text and its Latin version in parallel, the early Bollandists helped lay the groundwork for what would later become the standard format for the scholarly publication of ancient texts: a substantial introduction, a text based on all available witnesses, a translation into a common language, and commentary notes.[26]

From the start of his work, Bolland understood that Byzantine synaxaries constituted a source of primary importance for the study of the cult of saints in the lands east of Trieste. At the beginning of the seventeenth century, these works were virtually inaccessible in the Catholic Low Countries. For this reason, Bolland contented himself mainly with the brief notices translated into Latin in the *Menologium Graecorum ex bibliotheca et interpretatione Gulielmi Sirleti cardinalis*, printed by Hendrik Kanis in the second volume of his *Antiquae lectionis*.[27] The research trip of his young collaborators Papebroch and Henschen to Italy (22 July 1660–21 December 1662) made it possible to expand the *AASS*'s textual foundations. In the Vatican Library, the two collaborators unearthed a deluxe eleventh-century manuscript (now Vaticanus gr. 1613) containing the months from September to February of the synaxary compiled on

24 B. Joassart, "Papebroch (van Papenbroeck), Daniel," *Lexikon für Theologie und Kirche*, ed. W. Kasper, 3rd ed., vol. 7 (Freiburg, 1998), 1324–25.

25 On the journey of Papebroch and Henschen through Germany, Italy, and France, which inaugurated other scholarly expeditions, see B. Joassart, "Les voyages scientifiques," in Godding et al., *Bollandistes*, 61–73, esp. 61–65. On the relationships and mutual esteem between the hagiographers of Antwerp and Combefis, see B. Joassart, "François Combefis, Jacques Quétif et les Bollandistes," *AB* 118 (2000): 147–79, esp. 149–52. Combefis also sent the Bollandists numerous transcriptions of Greek texts from manuscripts in Paris's rich libraries.

26 In vol. 4 of the November *AASS* (Brussels, 1925), however, Hippolyte Delehaye abandoned the Latin translation, which he probably considered superfluous.

27 See the preface to vol. 1 of the *AASS* of January, LIV–LVI; for Kanis's translation, see *Antiquae lectionis*, vol. 2 (Ingolstadt, 1602), 730–941. On the so-called menologion (in reality a collection of disparate extracts) associated with the name of the illustrious cardinal, see I. Backus and B. Gain, "Le cardinal Sirleto (1514–1585), sa bibliothèque et ses traductions de saint Basile," *MÉFR: Moyen Âge–Temps Modernes* 98 (1986): 889–955, esp. 907–8.

the order of Emperor Basil II (r. 976–1025).[28] They completed the missing months with a manuscript from Grottaferrata Abbey (*Cryptensis* B.γ.III),[29] containing the following six months; the transcription of March to August—in all likelihood produced by Giovanni Francesco Albani (the future Pope Clement XI)[30]—was published month by month, from 1668 to 1733.[31] On their return journey, at the Bibliotheca Ambrosiana in Milan, Bolland's collaborators perused five synaxaries and three *menaia* (liturgical books containing the texts for a month's fixed feasts), with their synaxaries, which enabled them to track down more than 230 new saints.[32] The two travelers then stopped in Dijon, at the home of the Jesuit Pierre-François Chifflet, who allowed them to take, among other things, a Greek synaxary (today Troyes, Bibliothèque municipale, MS 1204).[33] Continuing their journey to Paris,[34] they visited the library at the Collège de Clermont, where they consulted the famous *Synaxarion of Sirmond* (now Berlin, Staatsbibliothek, Phillipps 1622 [219]), which was to serve as the basis for the critical edition of the *Synaxarion of the Great Church of Constantinople* by Hippolyte Delehaye in 1902.[35]

The publication of the second half-year of Basil II's *Menologion* demonstrates that the *AASS* cannot be reduced to a mere collection of hagiographical dossiers,

28 *Synaxarium CP*, XXIII–XXIV (sig. B). The so-called Menologion of Basil II is now available online: https://digi.vatlib.it/view/MSS_Vat.gr.1613. For bibliography, see "Vat.gr.1613," Digivatlib, https://digi.vatlib.it/mss/detail/Vat.gr.1613.

29 The exemplar was identified by A. Luzzi, "Per l'individuazione del codice modello delle prime edizioni a stampa del semestre estivo del 'Menologio' di Basilio II," *Bollettino della Badia Greca di Grottaferrata*, n.s. 52 (1998): 95–115.

30 Ibid., 96.

31 *AASS*, vol. 1 of March (Antwerp, 1668), 864–75; vol. 1 of April (1675), I–XIII; vol. 1 of May (1680), 720–32; vol. 6 of June (1715), I–VII (between p. 274 and the historical index); vol. 1 of July (1719), 687–98; vol. 1 of August (1733), 663–69. This episodic edition completed the Latin version of the winter months published by Ferdinando Ughelli, *Italia sacra*, vol. 6 (Rome, 1659).

32 See X. Lequeux, "L'apport des manuscrits grecs de l'Ambrosienne dans les 'Acta Sanctorum,'" in *Nuove ricerche sui manoscritti greci dell'Ambrosiana: Atti del Convegno, Milano, 5–6 giugno 2003*, ed. C. M. Mazzucchi and C. Pasini, Bibliotheca erudita (Milan, 2005), 179–89, with a list of other hagiographic texts transcribed from the Ambrosian manuscripts.

33 F. Halkin, "Le synaxaire grec de Chifflet retrouvé à Troyes (manuscrit 1204)," *AB* 65 (1947): 61–106. The location of this manuscript was unknown in Delehaye's time.

34 On this stage of their journey, see B. Joassart, "Henschen et Papebroch à Paris en 1662," *AB* 124 (2006): 359–400.

35 *Synaxarium CP*, V–VIII (sig. S). This codex had once belonged to the Jesuit Jacques Sirmond (1559–1651), who very quickly expressed his interest in the Antwerp project, even during Rosweyde's lifetime: B. Joassart, "Jacques Sirmond et les débuts du bollandisme," *AB* 119 (2001): 345–56. See A. Luzzi, "Synaxaria and the Synaxarion of Constantinople," in *The Ashgate Research Companion to Byzantine Hagiography*, ed. S. Efthymiadis, vol. 2, *Genres and Contexts* (Farnham, Surrey, 2014), 197–208.

succeeding one another in the order of commemorations proposed by the liturgical calendar. The early Bollandists did not hesitate to insert into the *AASS* a series of *diatribae*, *tractatus*, and other *exegeses*, dealing with various issues encountered during their research.[36] At the front of the first volume of the May *AASS* (Antwerp, 1680), Papebroch published two illustrated calendars—one Byzantine, the other Slavonic—in his *Ephemerides ecclesiasticus graeco-slavicus*, which constituted the Bollandists' first foray in the Slavic world, foreshadowing the *Annus ecclesiasticus graeco-slavicus* (Brussels, 1863) later compiled by the Jesuit Ivan Martynov.[37] Jean Stilting (1703–1762) wrote a *dissertatio* on the birth date of Gregory of Nazianzus in volume 3 of the September *AASS* (Antwerp, 1750); seven years later, in volume 6 of the same month, he inquired whether James, Joseph, Jude, and Simon—the Lord's brothers—belonged to the twelve apostles.[38] Several contributions list the holders of episcopal seats in the East. One of them deserves the attention of scholars interested in the history of the patriarchate of Constantinople: volume 1 of the August *AASS* (Antwerp, 1733) contains *Tractatus praeliminaris de patriarchis Constantinopolitanis*, which spans its inception to the eighteenth century in over 250 pages; through this initiative, Guillaume Cuypers (1686–1741) intended to help scholars frustrated by the delayed publication of Michel Le Quien's (1661–1733) *Oriens christianus in quatuor patriarchatus digestus*. The Dominican had announced this project in 1722, but it was published only in 1740, after his death.

The Greek texts published in the *AASS* inevitably caught the attention of Charles Du Cange (1610–1688), who initiated Byzantine studies in France.[39] Du Cange, who was then preparing his *Glossarium ad scriptores mediae et infimae Graecitatis*, which was to appear in Lyon in 1688, found in the *AASS* sources of the first order: among the sixty-six *Vitae et martyria edita Sanctorum, auctoribus incertis* mentioned at the end of the second volume of the *Glossarium Graecitatis*,[40] there are forty-six references to editions printed in the *AASS*. Enthralled by the publications of the Bollandist workshop, in 1665 Du Cange sent Bolland a copy of his *Traité historique du chef de S. Jean Baptiste*, newly published in Paris. Since their mentor had recently died, it was Henschen and Papebroch who expressed their gratitude

36 B. Joassart, "Les dissertations spéciales dans les *Acta Sanctorum*," in Godding et al., *Bollandistes*, 47–48.

37 Originally published in a separate volume, the *Annus* was reprinted the following year, at the beginning of vol. 11 of the *AASS* of October (Brussels, 1864).

38 Vol. 3, September *AASS* (Antwerp, 1750), I–XVIII; vol. 6, September *AASS* (Antwerp, 1757), I–XXII.

39 Du Cange similarly paid attention to the Latin texts, when he was preparing his *Glossarium ad Scriptores mediæ & infimæ Latinitatis* (Paris, 1678).

40 *Synaxarium CP*, 65–68.

in a letter dated 23 October 1665. Contact was initiated. There followed an intense correspondence between Amiens, where Du Cange resided, and Antwerp, the epicenter of hagiography.[41] The Frenchman was regularly informed of the progress of the *AASS*, while the Bollandists took advantage of the contacts of their correspondent, who notably sent them, on 19 March 1683, a list of hagiographic texts among the manuscripts of Colbert's library.[42] In exchange for this good turn, Papebroch reported to Du Cange, on 22 June, a series of difficult words taken from the *Life of Saint Andrew the Fool* (*BHG* 116–17), many of which were duly recorded in the *Glossarium Graecitatis*.[43]

To describe the early Bollandists in the same way as Du Cange, as precursors of *Byzantinisme* in the Catholic Low Countries, would be presumptuous. Taking an interest in all the saints of Christendom, they helped gradually familiarize Western readers with the literature inspired by the cult of saints in Byzantium. We can reasonably assume that were it not for the curiosity and the zeal of Bolland's successors, this important part of the Greek literary and religious heritage bequeathed by late antiquity and the Byzantine period would have languished in the gloom of libraries until the last decades of the nineteenth century, when the lives of saints and the passions of the martyrs became an object of study among academic researchers.

■■■

On 21 July 1773, Pope Clement XIV ordered the suppression of the Society of Jesus, and the property of the order was immediately liquidated. Subject to much harassment, and forced to move three times, the *Museum bollandianum*, which in May 1794 had published volume 6 of the October *AASS* in Tongerlo, found itself, the following year, unable to continue its activities. The heterogeneous materials (books, manuscripts, transcripts, correspondence, and various notes) accumulated since Rosweyde were dispersed.[44] But in 1837, at the urging of Monseigneur François-Xavier De Ram, first rector of the Catholic University of Louvain and member of the Commission royale d'Histoire, the superiors of the Belgian Jesuit Province—restored in 1832—agreed to form a new group of hagiographers to continue Bolland's project. The enterprise faced difficulties at the outset, since the secret of the *AASS*'s

41 B. Joassart, *Pierre-François Chifflet, Charles Du Cange et les Bollandistes: Correspondance*, Tabularium hagiographicum 4 (Brussels, 2005), 189–269.

42 Ibid., 207–34 (doc. 51).

43 Ibid., 236–41 (doc. 53). The Greek text the *Life of Saint Andrew the Fool* had been published by Janning in vol. 6 of the May *AASS* (Antwerp, 1688), as a supplement to 28 May and with separate pagination.

44 On these dark years, see B. Joassart, "La fin du Musée bollandien, 1773–1799," in Godding et al., *Bollandistes*, 116–25.

production had been lost. Nevertheless, volume 7 of the October *AASS*, containing the dossiers of saints honored on the 15th and 16th of the month, appeared in Brussels in 1845. The achievement garnered praise, even though the weaknesses of the work—which gave too much importance to learned treatises at the expense of carefully edited texts—were manifest.

In 1876 Charles De Smedt joined the Bollandist workshop to replace the late Victor De Buck.[45] The new recruit, who taught ecclesiastical history at the Jesuit theological college in Louvain, had gained renown for having published a series of contributions that were later brought together in his *Principes de la critique historique* (1883). As Hippolyte Delehaye reports, "During his years of teaching, Father De Smedt had closely followed the progress of historical methods and the extraordinary development of works of scholarship in all fields."[46] Easy access to the riches of libraries through the publication of printed catalogues, as well as the emergence of new disciplines such as modern textual criticism or comparative literature, made it necessary to revisit the traditional working methods of the Bollandists. The first volume of the November *AASS*, which covers the first three days of the month, provides an opportunity to review how their *modus operandi* was updated.[47] At first glance the new volume, published in 1887, does not differ from the previous ones: we find the same general layout, and the content of the entries relating to the saints honored on the day in question conforms to the earlier directives drawn up by Bolland and Henschen.[48] In the preface, however, the editors draw attention to two innovations. Henceforth, the editors would include for each saint all the hagiographical texts, no longer neglecting the interpolated, apocryphal, or purely legendary documents. Entries would set forth the whole of the literature honoring a given saint, while also indicating the relative value of each document. The second novelty concerns the method of editing the texts: the editors would take care to identify all

45 On these two scholars, see B. Joassart, "Victor De Buck (1817–1876), Charles De Smedt (1833–1911), Hippolyte Delehaye (1859–1941): Trois figures de bollandistes contemporains," in *Les intellectuels catholiques en Belgique francophone aux 19ᵉ et 20ᵉ siècles*, ed. G. Zelis, Espaces et temps 10 (Louvain-la-Neuve, 2009), 195–207.

46 H. Delehaye, *L'œuvre des Bollandistes à travers trois siècles, 1615–1915*, 2nd ed., SubsHag 13A2 (Brussels, 1959), 148.

47 On the background to this reform, see B. Joassart, "Deux projets du Père Charles De Smedt: Une réforme des *Acta Sanctorum*, une École des hautes études historiques," *AB* 110 (1992): 353–72, esp. 358–62. The methodological change initiated in 1887 is already reflected four years earlier in a notice of 30 October 1883, devoted to Foilannus, written by Remi De Buck but "probably reviewed by young colleagues": Dolbeau, "Les sources manuscrites des *Acta Sanctorum*" (n. 12 above), 116–17, n. 38.

48 "Caractéristiques de la collection des *AASS*"; see B. Joassart, *Aspects de l'érudition hagiographique aux XVIIᵉ et XVIIIᵉ siècles*, École des hautes études, Sciences historiques et philologiques 5 = Hautes études médiévales et modernes 99 (Geneva, 2011), 20–21.

manuscripts, classify them as far as possible, and note all variant readings. Thus, the dossier on Saints Caesarius and Julian of Terracina in Campania includes five texts[49]—four passions plus the legend of the healing of Galla Placidia—while an introduction clarifies their mutual relationships and respective value. Among these texts, only the *Passio maior* (*BHL* 1511) had already been the subject of an edition by Mombritius.[50] Nonetheless, William Van Hooff did not content himself with reproducing that venerable edition but took pains to establish the text anew: he collated sixty-six manuscripts and added the Greek version (*BHG* 284), drawn from the only known witness, Vaticanus gr. 1608.

This concern for exhaustiveness in the presentation of sources led the Bollandists to visit the main libraries in Europe to draw up inventories of their hagiographic resources. The results obtained during these investigations gave rise to the series of *Catalogi codicum hagiographicorum*; its first installments were published in the *Revue des Analecta Bollandiana*, a journal the Bollandists had recently created to communicate their findings as quickly as possible and to welcome contributions from other researchers.[51] All these inventories follow the same pattern: the manuscripts are examined folio by folio; a brief codicological description is followed by a list of hagiographic texts, referencing the relevant manuscript folios; an edition is referenced when it exists, and if not, the newly edited texts are published in the appendix.

This approach led to many repetitions in each issue. In particular, the *Catalogi* lacked a register containing all the hagiographic texts already published and dispersed throughout separate publications. Such a register could also facilitate the formulation of *status quaestionum*, which requires, as far as possible, a complete inventory of sources. The Bollandists set to work, combing through thousands of volumes. The first fruits of this ambitious project appeared in 1895 in Brussels, under the title *Bibliotheca hagiographica graeca*; the new publication aimed to provide an inventory, in a succinct form, of hagiographic literature written in Greek

49 *AASS*, Nov. 1:84–130.

50 Bonino Mombritius, *Sanctuarium, seu Vitae sanctorum*, novam hanc editionem curaverunt duo monachi Solesmenses, 2 vols. (Paris, 1910), 1:195–97.

51 On the chaotic creation of this periodical, see B. Joassart, "Les origines des *Analecta Bollandiana*," *AB* 112 (1994): 139–58. The first issue, which appeared in 1882, included only articles, all written in Latin. In 1891 the review would admit its first articles in French, as well as offering a "Bulletin of hagiographic publications" in that language (*AB* 10 [1891]: 57–72, 366–84, 471–88). In this new section, the Bollandists pursued a double objective: to present to the readers works and articles relating to the history of the saints and their worship, published the previous year, and, more prosaically, to receive free copies for review in order to minimize the budget necessary to acquire new books.

during Christian antiquity and the Byzantine period.[52] In the second edition of Karl Krumbacher's *Geschichte der byzantinischen Litteratur*, published in 1897, the young Albert Ehrhard described the *BHG* as the "the most highly praiseworthy publication of the Bollandists,"[53] and it would go on to become the standard reference for all those interested in literature relating to the worship of saints in Byzantium.

52 On the genesis of the *BHG*, see X. Lequeux, "La *Bibliotheca hagiographica graeca*: Origine—développements—mise à jour," in *Byzantine Hagiography: Texts, Themes and Projects*, ed. A. Rigo, Studies in Byzantine History and Civilization 13 (Turnhout, 2018), 19–35. On the Latin front, the printing of installments of the *Bibliotheca hagiographica latina* began in 1898 and was completed in 1901, while a *Bibliotheca hagiographica orientalis* was published in Beirut in 1910.

53 K. Krumbacher, *Geschichte der byzantinischen Litteratur von Justinian bis zum Ende des Oströmischen Reiches (524–1453)*, 2nd ed. (Munich, 1897); the section reserved for theology was entrusted to Albert Ehrhard. Hagiography is treated there on pp. 176–205, esp. 183 (about the Bollandists).

PART FOUR

CHRONOLOGIES OF BYZANTIUM FROM THE ENLIGHTENMENT TO MODERNITY

TWELVE

FROM THE RISE OF CONSTANTINE TO THE FALL OF CONSTANTINOPLE

Defining Byzantium and the "Middle Age" in Early Modern Scholarship

FREDERIC CLARK

WHAT DOES BYZANTIUM TELL US ABOUT OUR METHODS OF PERIODIZATION? IN other words, what does our now commonplace division of historical time into separate and distinct ancient, medieval, and modern segments have to do with the invention of Byzantine studies in early modern Europe? This volume explores many ways that the Latin West, broadly speaking, used the Greek East as counterpoint and foil. But how did the former also use the latter to divide and compartmentalize its own past? How did western European scholars use the presence or absence, rise or fall, of a Christian empire centered in Constantinople to mark off periods and units in their own, supposedly *Western* history? The present essay attempts to answer this question, and in so doing it begins at the end, with a historian who (depending on how one wishes to periodize) lived either at the very end of early modernity or else at the dawn of modernity proper—however dubious a label that may be. This was Edward Gibbon, author of the six-volume *History of the Decline and Fall of the Roman Empire*, published between 1776 and 1788.

Perhaps no western European scholar's treatment of Byzantium is more notorious than Gibbon's. Although his name, for better or for worse, was long synonymous with *ancient* history, those who have descended into the less-celebrated final volumes of the *Decline and Fall* also know Gibbon as a medieval and Byzantine historian.[1] He

1 On Gibbon's approaches to historiography, see above all J. G. A. Pocock, *Barbarism and Religion*, 6 vols. (Cambridge, 1999–2015). On his Byzantine scholarship, see especially S. Runciman, "Gibbon and Byzantium," *Daedalus* 105.3 (1976): 103–10, and the chapters dealing with Byzantine

assumed this role despite much hesitation—and proffered distaste—for the subject. This ambivalence was not the isolated quirk of a fatigued historian—even if, by the time he published his Byzantine volumes in 1788, he had already written three volumes and thousands of pages of Roman history. Rather, his indecision was symptomatic of a larger quandary, one with which so many of Gibbon's predecessors had also wrestled: Was Byzantium integral to how the "West" divided up its own past and separated that past from the present? In other words, did the Enlightenment narrative of "how we got here"—that is, from ancient Rome to modern Europe—have to wind its way through medieval Constantinople? This quandary was not just central to our definitions of Byzantium but also raised more macroscopic questions about the scope and limits of historical writing. How was one to write a truly universal—or to use our contemporary categories—global history? Did Byzantium offer a kind of conduit between the "West" (itself something of unstable definition, as much in early modernity as today) and cultures further beyond it? And was this universalizing undertaking desirable?

In his memoirs, Gibbon reflected upon his decision—and the indecision preceding it—to become a Byzantine historian. He described how, having finished the first three volumes of his work, he considered throwing in the towel and calling it concluded. After all, he had just brought his history to what seemed a natural stopping point—namely, the fall of the Western Roman Empire in 476. And there, on the final page of his third volume, he had left things ambiguous. He noted that the "victorious nations of Germany established a new system of manners and government in the western countries of Europe." These "western countries" were no longer Roman, at least in the political or juridical sense. But the situation was far more ambiguous in the East. There "the majesty of Rome was faintly represented by the princes of Constantinople, the feeble and imaginary successors of Augustus." In Gibbon's estimation, these princes were feeble, but they were not so feeble as to have "fallen" like their Western counterparts; as a result, maybe they were still worth writing about. And so Gibbon closed the third volume of the *Decline and Fall* with a cliffhanger of a conclusion, teasing his readers with what would follow if indeed he chose to write more volumes: "Yet they [i.e., those 'princes of Constantinople'] continued to reign over the East... and the history of the *Greek* emperors may still afford a long series of instructive lessons, and interesting revolutions."[2]

---

themes by A. Cameron, J. Howard-Johnston, J. Shepard, and A. Buyer in *Edward Gibbon and Empire*, ed. R. McKitterick and R. Quinault (Cambridge, 1996). Most recently, see *The Cambridge Companion to Edward Gibbon*, ed. K. O'Brien and B. Young (Cambridge, 2018), especially M. Whittow, "Do Byzantine Historians Still Read Gibbon?," 78–92.

2 Edward Gibbon, *History of the Decline and Fall of the Roman Empire*, ed. D. Womersley, 6 vols. in 3 (London, 1994), 2:507.

Perhaps "may" was the key word here. The historian had not yet committed to this project. Would Gibbon bother treating this "faint" imitation of the old Rome, the domain of "feeble" rulers whose links to antiquity proper were imaginary at best? Would he bother writing of those "instructive lessons" that the history of these *Greek* (and hence not Roman) emperors would furnish? In other words, if the organizing principle of Gibbon's historiographical project was the decline and fall of *Rome*, was the thousand-year history of those supposedly feeble Greeks in Constantinople within or rather beyond its purview? Was it enough that his historical subjects would have answered the question in the affirmative, even if their proffered links to the glory days of Augustus seemed deceptive or illusory to Gibbon himself?[3] If their rhetoric alone merited their inclusion, then where was the responsible historian to end? After all, there were still emperors proclaiming themselves "Roman" in Gibbon's own eighteenth century. But Gibbon did not seriously consider including *them* in his *Decline and Fall.*

We will return to Gibbon at the conclusion, but for now it should merely be noted how, in retrospective fashion, he described his decision to proceed from West to East, from the old Rome to Byzantium. As will soon become clearer, whether consciously or otherwise, Gibbon participated in a form of indecision that was several centuries old, reflecting the ambiguities of whether what we now label Byzantium counted as a proper continuation of ancient, Roman history. With the benefit of hindsight, Gibbon described in his memoirs how he ultimately elected to continue his history, and became a Byzantine historian despite his many misgivings:

> So flexible is the title of my History, that the final aera might be fixed at my own choice; and I long hesitated whether I should be content with the three volumes, the fall of the Western empire, which fulfilled my first engagement with the public. In this interval of suspence, nearly a twelvemonth, I returned by a natural impulse to the Greek authors of antiquity.[4]

During this moment of hesitation, Gibbon buried himself in his library, by "natural impulse," with such canonical favorites as Homer, Herodotus, Thucydides, Xenophon, and the Socratic dialogues. But reading them in this desultory fashion could not sustain him:

3 For an analysis of this issue in contemporary Byzantine scholarship, see A. Kaldellis, *Romanland: Ethnicity and Empire in Byzantium* (Cambridge, MA, 2019), with discussion of Gibbon at 13–14 and 22.

4 E. Gibbon, *Memoirs of My Life and Writing*, in *The Miscellaneous Works of Edward Gibbon* (Dublin, 1796), 163.

> Yet in the luxury of freedom I began to wish for the daily task, the active pursuit, which gave a value to every book, and an object to every inquiry: the preface of a new edition announced my design, and I dropped without reluctance from the age of Plato to that of Justinian.[5]

Dropping "from the age of Plato to that of Justinian" was no small task, and it was one that ran counter to many canons of taste and thought in Gibbon's own eighteenth century.[6] However, Gibbon described it as an almost inevitable decision, forced upon him by the unforgiving logic that compels authors not to let go of their work. Whatever Gibbon's specific motivations for continuing beyond 476, we can justly regard his *Decline and Fall* as formalizing a periodization that would have massive consequences for the next two hundred years and more. Not only did Gibbon set the terms for debates about why the ancient world had fallen, but he also defined *when* it had fallen, and how to classify what followed it—including something as nebulous as Byzantium. This is an important story. But just as important is what preceded his contributions. If we reverse our temporal perspective, we can also see Gibbon's indecision about Byzantium as the culmination of a process of negotiation that had been ongoing throughout early modernity. Gibbon was hardly the first to grapple with the question of when antiquity had come to its end. The remainder of this essay considers the decisions of his predecessors, and what they can tell us about the links between Byzantium and periodization.

Constantine and Constantinople among the Early Humanists

The invention of Byzantine studies in early modern Europe depended on another early modern invention, which went by various names: this was the *medium aevum*, the *media aetas*, the *media tempestas*, or, as it came into English, the "Middle Age." Before the invention of the Middle Ages, there were only ancients and moderns, *antiqui* and *moderni*. Although the latter went by many names, the specific use of *modernus* in this temporal sense was the invention of late antiquity: some of its most frequent early usages are found in the *Variae* of the sixth-century Italian scholar Cassiodorus.[7] Even the fourteenth-century Petrarch, long credited with inventing

5 Ibid.

6 On Gibbon's attitudes toward late antique sources, see G. Kelly, "Edward Gibbon and Late Antique Literature," in *A Companion to Late Antique Literature*, ed. S. McGill and E. J. Watts (Malden, MA, 2018), 611–26.

7 See, e.g., Cassiodorus, *Variae* 4.51.2, ed. A. J. Fridh, CCSL 96 (Turnhout, 1973), 177, where the patrician Quintus Aurelius Memmius Symmachus is praised as *antiquorum diligentissimus imitator, modernorum nobilissimus institutor*. Variations upon *modernus* appear throughout the

the "dark ages," still imagined a bipartite system of antiquity and modernity. The clearest evidence for his bipolar conception of temporality comes from an epistle he wrote to his friend Giovanni Colonna, a mendicant friar. In this letter, likely composed in 1337, Petrarch recounted how he and Colonna, antiquarian raconteurs, used to wander the ruins of Rome and regale each other with tales of the Roman past. Between them they utilized a division of labor, which also revealed a system of periodization:

> When we passed through the walls of the shattered city (*menia fracte urbis*) and sat there, the fragments of its ruins (*ruinarum fragmenta*) were before our eyes. What did we say then? We had much discussion about historical works (*historiis*), which we seemed to share out so that you might appear the more expert in new histories (*novis*) and I in ancient histories (*antiquis*)—and let us call "ancient" whatever came before the celebration and worship of Christ's name by the Roman emperors, and "new" from then up to this age (*hanc etatem*).[8]

Petrarch did not offer any more specifics, but his chronology was clear: the border between antiquity and modernity occurred at that point in history when the Roman emperors began to venerate the name of Christ. In other words, Constantine and his embrace of Christianity in the early fourth century marked the division point. And although Petrarch did not allude to it here, we know what other epochal change Constantine accomplished: he founded a new capital in the east—named after himself. When *historia antiqua* gave way to *historia nova,* Rome also ceased to be Rome in an important sense.

Petrarch made no mention of Constantinople; this consequential passage did not even invoke Constantine by name. Neither did he venture any outright value

---

Variae. For discussion of the term *modernus,* see W. Freund, *Modernus und andere Zeitbegriffe des Mittelalters* (Cologne, 1957); J. Moorhead, "The Word 'Modernus,'" *Latomus* 65 (2006): 425–33; and M. S. Bjornlie, *Politics and Tradition between Rome, Ravenna, and Constantinople: A Study of Cassiodorus and the "Variae," 527–554* (Cambridge, 2013), esp. 244–46.

8 Petrarch, *Ad familiares* 6.2.15–16, in Francesco Petrarca, *Selected Letters,* trans. E. Fantham, 2 vols. (Cambridge, MA, 2017), 1:70–71: *Et euntibus per menia fracte urbis et illic sedentibus, ruinarum fragmenta sub oculis erant. Quid ergo? multus de historiis sermo erat, quas ita, partiti videbamur, ut in novis tu, in antiquis ego viderer expertior, et dicantur antique quecunque ante celebratum Rome et veneratum romanis principibus Cristi nomen, nove autem ex illo usque ad hanc etatem.* I have used Fantham's translation with slight modifications. On this passage, and on Petrarch's conception of periodization in general, see T. E. Mommsen, "Petrarch's Conception of the 'Dark Ages,'" *Speculum* 17 (1942): 226–42, esp. 232–33. See also R. Black, "The Donation of Constantine: A New Source for the Concept of the Renaissance," in *Language and Images of Medieval Italy,* ed. A. Brown (Oxford, 1995), 51–85.

judgments about the relative merits of *historia antiqua* and *historia nova*. He did not explicitly declare that the onset of *historia nova* marked the onset of decline, the category that Gibbon would immortalize centuries later. Yet his letter was not devoid of hints on this score. In other words, although silent about the original culprits, he narrated what happened when Rome ceased to be Rome.[9] The tone and contents of his letter as a whole offered a sharp contrast between antiquity's glories and the dismal state of those "new" or "recent" times that followed. Right before he divided antiquity and modernity, he placed himself amid "the walls of the shattered city" (*menia fracte urbis*) and the "fragments of its ruins" (*ruinarum fragmenta*). Petrarch did not explain *what* had shattered Rome, or when exactly in *historia nova* this formerly grand city of *historia antiqua* had been reduced to a fragmentary shell. But he had been (perhaps hyperbolically) clear, in fact just directly before this passage, about the sorry state to which Rome was now reduced. "Today in fact who are more ignorant of Roman history than Rome's citizens? I hate to say this, but nowhere is Rome less known than at Rome itself." Nonetheless, he also hinted that this did not necessarily need to remain the case, and that a bit more knowledge—specifically self-knowledge—could change the city's predicament. "Indeed who can doubt that Rome will rise up again (*surrectura sit*) once she begins to recognize herself?"[10]

Why had Rome fallen into this state of physical ruin and historical ignorance? Again, Petrarch did not fault Christianity per se, even if he made the Christianization of Rome's emperors and its consequent geopolitical consequences coterminous with the start of *historia nova*.[11] In fact, he spoke with reverence of pre-Constantinian Christian Rome, describing legends of Christian martyrs, derived from the medieval *mirabilia* tradition, alongside tales of pagan antiquity from the likes of Livy and Suetonius.[12] Maybe Rome would begin to recognize itself as a political and cultural center once again, and take pride in its history, both pagan and Christian? Petrarch hinted—with his telling phrase *surrectura sit*—at that future epoch of which later generations would name him the founder: in other words, Rome required a rebirth or renaissance. In our now regnant scheme of periodization, this coming of what

9 For hints that Petrarch placed the beginnings of this decline centuries before Constantine, with the first accession of non-Italians to the imperial throne, see Mommsen, "Petrarch's Conception," 234–35, with reference to Petrarch's epic *Africa* 2.274–78.

10 Petrarch, *Ad familiares* 6.2.14, trans. Fantham, 70–71: *Qui enim hodie magis ignari rerum romanarum sunt, quam romani cives? invitus dico: nusquam minus Roma cognoscitur quam Rome. . . . Quis enim dubitare potest quin illico surrectura sit, si ceperit se Roma cognoscere?*

11 Here see Black, "The Donation of Constantine."

12 Petrarch, *Ad familiares* 6.2.5–13, trans. Fantham, 64–69.

we render the capital-R Renaissance marked the end of the Middle Ages.[13] But it remains an open question just how much historical actors like Petrarch adumbrated this scheme. Did Petrarch imagine, or at least desire, a future that would be post-*modern* in the literal sense of the term, a *historia* that would be post-*nova*? Did Petrarch occupy a time both modern and medieval, a present defined by a lost antiquity on the one hand and a still unrealized future on the other? Was he the first to make modernity medieval, at least implicitly?

While it is far beyond the scope of the present essay to answer these questions definitively, it can shed some light on just where Constantine and Constantinople fit into the nascent Renaissance time-scape. There is perhaps an irony at work here insofar as Petrarch mourned another, more recent abandonment of Rome. When he wrote to Colonna of Rome's ruins, the papacy was no longer at Rome but rather at Avignon, and it would stay there throughout the remainder of Petrarch's life. If Rome's emperors abandoned her for Constantinople at the beginning of *historia nova*, her popes had abandoned her for southern France centuries later, when *historia nova* was in full swing. Nor was Petrarch a fan of the notion of *translatio imperii* in general, by which Rome's *imperium* had been transmitted to others. He famously scorned one of the stars of *historia nova*, Charlemagne, and bristled at the use of the appellation "great" to describe the Frankish emperor.[14] He rejected visions of *Romanitas* that did not center on Rome itself.

In the fifteenth century, the humanists who followed in Petrarch's wake began to articulate more fully an ideology of cultural renewal.[15] At the same time, some also assigned a periodizing significance, whether explicit or implicit, to Constantine and Constantinople. The Byzantine émigré scholar Manuel Chrysoloras composed his *Comparison of the New and Ancient Rome*, in which he described Rome to the

13 See the essays collected in *Medieval/Renaissance: After Periodization*, ed. J. Summit and D. Wallace, special issue of *JMEMS* 37.3 (2007).

14 See Mommsen, "Petrarch's Conception," citing Petrarch, *Ad familiares* 1.4. For Petrarch and Charlemagne, see A. J. Romig, "Charlemagne the Sinner: Charles the Great as Avatar of the Modern in Petrarch's *Familiares* 1.4," in *The Charlemagne Legend in Medieval Latin Texts*, ed. W. J. Purkis and M. Gabriele (Cambridge, 2016), 181–201.

15 On humanist historical thought and humanist conceptions of Renaissance, see, e.g., the midcentury work of W. Ferguson, *The Renaissance in Historical Thought: Five Centuries of Interpretation* (Cambridge, MA, 1948), and H. Weisinger, "The Renaissance Theory of the Reaction against the Middle Ages as a Cause of the Renaissance," *Speculum* 20 (1945): 461–67. Recent studies include P. Baker, *Italian Renaissance Humanism in the Mirror* (Cambridge, 2015); J. Hankins, *Virtue Politics: Soulcraft and Statecraft in Renaissance Italy* (Cambridge, MA, 2019); and C. Hirschi, *The Origins of Nationalism: An Alternative History from Ancient Rome to Early Modern Germany* (Cambridge, 2012), esp. 144–52.

emperor Manuel II and compared it to Constantinople.[16] Lorenzo Valla famously singled out the anachronism of the presence of Constantinople in the *Donation of Constantine* as proof that it was a forgery, given that the "Constantine" of the document had yet to thus rename the city.[17] And humanists began to articulate what would become that famous narrative of reverse *translatio*, this time from Constantinople back to Italy. For instance, the mid-fifteenth-century humanist scholar and antiquarian Flavio Biondo theorized in his *Italy Illuminated* that the importation of Greek learning by Chrysoloras and others in the years around 1400 had stimulated a broader renewal of eloquence (*eloquentia*). As Biondo explained, approximately a century after Petrarch had written to Colonna, his age had surpassed Petrarch's own: "We can see that the benefit brought to our countrymen by so many books—the tinder of eloquence itself—resulted in our age (*nostram … aetatem*) having richer and finer resources of expression at its disposal than Petrarch enjoyed. The arrival of Greek letters was no small help in the acquisition of eloquence; and it was actually a stimulus to doing so[.]"[18]

A reader of this passage might wonder whether Biondo considered his own *aetas* to be Petrarch's *historia nova*, or if the revival of Greek and Latin eloquence made it something still newer or more recent. Of course, the arrival of Chrysoloras and company in Italy presaged a process of decline in another part of the world. Biondo, who wrote his *Italy Illuminated* between 1448 and 1453, finished it with the benefit of the hindsight of one who lived through the decline and fall of Constantinople.[19] Biondo and his colleagues were also interested in a parallel and far earlier decline—which brought down the old Rome in the West as opposed to the new Rome in the East. In fact, they even debated whether Constantine deserved some blame for it.

16 Manuel Chrysoloras, "Manuele Crisolora: Confronto tra l'antica e la nuova Roma," ed. C. Billò, *Medioevo Greco: Rivista di storia e filologia bizantina* 0 (2000): 1–26.

17 For Valla on the anachronistic invocation of Constantinople, see Lorenzo Valla, *On the Donation of Constantine*, trans. G. W. Bowersock (Cambridge, MA, 2007), 74–75 (¶45). On approaches to Byzantium along the early humanists, see H. Lamers, *Greece Reinvented: Transformations of Byzantine Hellenism in Renaissance Italy*, Brill's Studies in Intellectual History 247 (Leiden, 2015), and for later contexts, see the essays collected in *Receptions of Hellenism in Early Modern Europe: 15th–17th Centuries*, ed. N. Constantinidou and H. Lamers (Leiden, 2020).

18 Flavio Biondo, *Italia illustrata* 6.30, ed. and trans. J. A. White as *Italy Illuminated*, 2 vols. (Cambridge, MA, 2005–16), 1:306–7: *Quo ex tot librorum, ipsius eloquentiae fomitum, allato nostris hominibus adiumento factum videmus ut maior meliorque ea quam Petrarcha habuit dicendi copia in nostram pervenerit aetatem. Nec parvum fuit cum adiumentum ad discendum eloquentiam tum etiam incitamentum Graecarum accessio litterarum*[.] On the importance of this passage, see Baker, *Italian Renaissance Humanism*, 59.

19 G. Marcellino, "Lo studio delle antichità romane e la propaganda antiturca nella *Roma triumphans* di Biondo Flavio," *Studi classici e orientali* 60 (2014): 163–86.

This should not surprise us. Narratives of renewal by nature necessitated narratives of the decline preceding it. Whereas Petrarch articulated a bipartite scheme that was only implicitly tripartite, both Biondo and his fellow humanist, the Florentine Leonardo Bruni, conjured something like an intervening middle age, even if still mostly *avant la lettre*.[20] Their implicit middle time began with the decline of Rome. However, they did not exactly agree upon where to fix its onset. Bruni, for instance, in his *History of the Florentine People*, did not mince words when it came to Constantine. Although he traced the remote causes of Rome's decline all the way back to the loss of liberty at the end of the Republic (some four centuries before the main drama!), he also condemned Constantine for abandoning the western empire to barbarian invasions:

> The Emperor Constantine, however, enlarged the city of Byzantium and moved the capital to the east. The emperors thereafter began to view Italy and the western part of the empire almost as the abandoned part, to be neglected and left exposed to the invasions of tyrants and barbarians. The latter rushed into the deserted property, as it were, at various times like the waters of a flood and inundated these lands altogether.[21]

Biondo took this project a step further, although intriguingly he resisted speaking so decisively about Constantine (and curiously neither he nor Bruni discussed the pre-Constantinian decentering of Rome by Diocletian's Tetrarchy and the like).[22] One of Biondo's other works was his *Decades of Histories from the Decline (ab*

20 On Bruni on Rome's decline, see Pocock, *Barbarism and Religion* (n. 1 above), vol. 3, *The First Decline and Fall*, 160–78. On Bruni as historian, see G. Ianziti, *Writing History in Renaissance Italy: Leonardo Bruni and the Uses of the Past* (Cambridge, MA, 2012).

21 Leonardo Bruni, *Historiarum Florentini populi libri XII* 1.40, ed. and trans. James Hankins as *History of the Florentine People*, 3 vols. (Cambridge, MA, 2001–07), 1:54–55: *Postquam vero Constantinus, amplificato Bizantio, ad orientem subsedit, Italia et caeterae occidentales imperii partes, quasi pro derelictis habitae, negligi coeperunt, ac tyrannorum barbarorumque invasionibus exponi; qui ceu in vacuam possessionem ruentes, variis temporibus, tanquam diluvia quaedam, has terras inundarunt.*

22 Flavio Biondo, *Historiarum ab inclinatione Romanorum imperii decades* (Venice, 1483). On Biondo's scholarship, see, e.g., R. Cappelletto, *Recuperi Ammianei da Biondo Flavio* (Rome, 1983), and O. Clavuot, *Biondos "Italia illustrata"—Summa oder Neuschöpfung? Über die Arbeitsmethoden eines Humanisten* (Tübingen, 1990). For Biondo on Rome's decline, see D. Hay, "Flavio Biondo and the Middle Ages," *ProcBrAc* 45 (1959): 97–125; I. G. Mastrorosa, "'Inclinatio inchoavit': Decadenza e fine dell'impero romano d'Occidente nelle storiografia umanistica. Leonardo Bruni e Biondo Flavio," *Historika* 4 (2014): 243–75; Pocock, *Barbarism and Religion*, 3:179–202; and F. Delle Donne, "La fasi redazionali e le concezioni della storia nelle *Decadi* di Biondo: Tra storia particolare e generale, tra antica e moderna Roma," in *A New Sense of the Past: The Scholarship of Biondo Flavio (1392–1463)*, ed. A. Mazzocco and M. Laureys, Supplementa Humanistica Lovaniensia 39

inclinatione) of the Empire of the Romans (composed ca. 1439–53), a kind of melancholy inversion of Livy's decades of Roman history "from the founding of the city" (*ab urbe condita*). Biondo's overt theorization of "decline" or *inclinatio* is key to the history of periodization: he chose to date the beginning of this *inclinatio* a full century after Petrarch had inaugurated *historia nova*, and selected as his starting point the Goth Alaric's sack of Rome in 410 (although he curiously misdated it to 412). Biondo refrained from singling out Constantine as the key turning point in the story of decline: while he allowed that Constantine's decision may have constituted a "remote cause of future decline" (*remotam inclinationis future causam*), he refused to speak of it as an immediate turning point à la Bruni, since, as he pointed out, Constantine and his successors had preserved and even occasionally enlarged the empire.[23]

In the half century that followed, others coined names for those distinctions that Biondo and Bruni attempted to express, even though it would take centuries for these terms to become anything close to standard or conventional. The year 1469 produced what appears to be one of the earliest extant uses of a term for "medieval": the humanist Giovanni Andrea Bussi, writing in the preface to his edition of Apuleius, spoke of a *media tempestas* (middle time). Several decades later, in 1496, the Bolognese philologist and commentator Filippo Beroaldo, reviving a term used in a literary sense by the ancient miscellanist Aulus Gellius, deployed the adjective *classicus* (classical).[24] Although the full history of these temporal terms and their relation to notions of antiquity's decline is a story that still needs to be told, it is perhaps no accident that *media tempestas* and *classicus* emerged in the half century following Bruni's and Biondo's articulation of the narratives that their use assumes. Yet as we will see, these terms and narratives sometimes raised more problems than they solved.

(Leuven, 2016), 55–88. For an overview of theories of Roman decline, see A. Demandt, *Der Fall Roms: Die Auflösung des römischen Reiches im Urteil der Nachwelt* (Munich, 1984).

23 Biondo, *Historiarum decades*, sig. a ii v: *Pari ratione translationem sedis imperii: factam a Constantino Bizantium: quemadmodum remotam inclinationis future causam fuisse non abnuerim: ita illius principium non concesserim appellandam, cum et ipse et alii decem in imperio successores: quos ea habuit translata Bizantium sedes: imperii iura partim auxerint partim in maiestate solita conseruauerint.*

24 Apuleius, *Metamorphosis sive de asino aureo*, ed. Giovanni Andrea Bussi (Rome, 1469), fols. 4v, 5r. Bussi's first use of the term occurs in a discussion of Nicholas of Cusa, and the second in an encomium to Plato. For Beroaldo's use of *classicus*, see for instance *Commentarii questionum Tusculanarum editi a Philippo Beroaldo* (Bologna, 1496), fol. 89r. See discussion in S. Rizzo, "Il latino nell'Umanesimo," in *Letteratura italiana V: Le questioni*, ed. A. Asor Rosa (Turin, 1986), 389–90; M. Citroni, "Gellio, 19, 8, 15, et la storia di classicus," *Materiali e discussioni per l'analisi dei testi classici* 58 (2007): 181–205, esp. 201–2 for analysis of Beroaldo; and S. Settis, "Classical," in *The Classical Tradition*, ed. A. Grafton, G. W. Most, and S. Settis (Cambridge, MA, 2010), 205–6.

Petrarch's ambiguities, and Biondo's and Bruni's disagreements, demonstrate just how tricky a business periodization could prove. Although designed as a tool of simplification, it often multiplied complexities.[25] And when it came to the tripartite scheme of ancient–medieval–modern, chief among these complexities was the problematic status of Byzantium. Was Byzantine history coterminous with this newfound notion of a middle time? In the middle decades of the sixteenth century we find the term *Byzantine* used in a manner that might suggest an attempt at periodization, almost a century after *media tempestas* had entered the scholarly lexicon. In 1557 the Augsburg scholar Hieronymus Wolf published the first installment of what would become his *Corpus historiae Byzantinae* (*Corpus of Byzantine History*), a compendium of Byzantine historians including Zonoras, Choniates, Gregoras, and Chalkokondyles. Thanks in part to his use of this term, Wolf was long considered one of the founders of Byzantine studies in early modern Europe. Yet some have also sounded notes of caution. Indeed, Asaph Ben-Tov has recently argued that Wolf himself likely did not come up with his title, pointing out that he did not otherwise use the term or discuss it in his preface.[26]

Whether or not Wolf himself was responsible for this use of the adjective *Byzantina*, the long title of the *Corpus* described that millennium from Constantine to the final fall of Constantinople as a coherent unit of history: it too was a kind of middle, caught somewhere between the ancient and the contemporary. Intriguingly, the title page of the 1568 edition of the *Corpus* also used the language of *inclinatio*, reminiscent of Biondo, while transferring that doleful concept to the collapse of the Byzantine world in 1453. It advertised the last of the volume's historians, Chalkokondyles, as describing "the decline, fall, and ruin of the empire of the Greeks" (*Graecorum imperii inclinationem, casum, atque interitum*).[27] Yet the *Corpus of Byzantine History* was far more than a record of decline and fall: it encompassed "things done not only by the Greek emperors from the time of Constantine the Great, to the last Constantine, and

25 For a selection of reflections on this problem, see *The Challenge of Periodization: Old Paradigms and New Perspectives*, ed. L. Besserman (New York, 1996); K. Davis, *Periodization and Sovereignty: How Ideas of Feudalism and Secularization Govern the Politics of Time* (Philadelphia, 2008); and J. Le Goff, *Must We Divide History into Periods?*, trans. M. B. DeBevoise (New York, 2015).

26 A. Ben-Tov, *Lutheran Humanists and Greek Antiquity: Melanchthonian Scholarship between Universal History and Pedagogy* (Leiden, 2009), esp. 106–8. See also Anthony Kaldellis in Chapter 13 of this volume.

27 *Corpus historiae Byzantinae* (Frankfurt, 1568), title page: *IIII. Laonicus Chalcondyles ab Andronici Iunioris imperio, in quo Gregoras historiam suam finiit, exorsus, Graecorum imperii inclinationem, casum, atque interitum, cum commemoratione originis atque progressus tyrannidis Turcicae libris X exacte miroque ordine exponit.*

the capture of Constantinople by the Turks, but also things done here and there in various parts of the globe, from the beginning of the world (*ab exordio mundi*)."[28] In other words, Byzantine historians were useful not just for what they told about Byzantium but rather for their contributions to something much larger—namely, universal history. According to Wolf, one could find in his sources information stretching all the way back to Creation itself (*ab exordio mundi*), and touching on parts of the world far removed from the environs of Constantinople. Granted, Christian universal history of this sort was rather different from what Gibbon would attempt near the close of the eighteenth century; yet as we will see, both projects treated Byzantium as a crucial link in a more macroscopic enterprise. Byzantium, taken in its broadest sense, could traverse the ancient, medieval, and modern. The connections between Byzantium and this sense of universalism are explored more fully in the pages that follow.

Things here might now seem tidy: use of the term *Byzantine* followed almost inevitably after scholars conjured labels such as *classical* and *medieval*. Perhaps this might strike us as a natural drive for precision, reflecting not only the maturation of humanist philology in the sixteenth century but also an emergent sixteenth-century need, whether for good or for ill, for temporal or even protodisciplinary compartmentalization.[29] After all, one cannot easily imagine Byzantine studies—or medieval or classical studies, for that matter—without at least a rough consensus of the start and end dates of Byzantium, the Middle Ages, and classical antiquity. If scholars wished to specialize in such a fashion, perhaps it was only natural that they, like Petrarch and Colonna, would have to subscribe to some periodization in order to divide up their collective labors. And by the middle decades of the sixteenth century, perhaps the old binary of ancient and modern simply was not good enough anymore.

28 The long title of Wolf's compendium reads as follows: *Corpus historiae Byzantinae in quo non solum res a Graecis imperatoribus a tempore Constantini Magni, ad Constantinum postremum, et Constantinopolim a Turcis occupatam, sed et ab exordio mundi in variis orbis partibus hinc inde gestae, continua serie, erudite ac luculenter exponuntur a quatuor Scriptoribus Graecis . . .*

29 On the circulation of designations for the Middle Ages in the early modern period, and corresponding notions of medievalism, see, e.g., P. Lehmann, "Vom Mittelalter und von der lateinischen Philologie des Mittelalters," in *Quellen und Untersuchungen zur lateinischen Philologie des Mittelalters* (Munich, 1914); G. S. Gordon, "*Medium Aevum* and the Middle Age," *Society for the Propagation of English, Tracts* 19 (1925): 3–28; P. Schaeffer, "The Emergence of the Concept 'Medieval' in Central European Humanism," *Sixteenth Century Journal* 7 (1976): 21–30; M. Fumaroli, "Aux origines de la connaissance historique du Moyen Âge: Humanisme, réforme et gallicanisme au XVIe siècle," *XVIIe siècle* 114–15 (1977): 5–29; and F. C. Robinson, "Medieval, the Middle Ages," *Speculum* 59 (1984): 745–56. This literature is outlined and expanded with additional references in J. Considine, *Dictionaries in Early Modern Europe: Lexicography and the Making of Heritage* (Cambridge, 2008), esp. 259–61. See also discussion of these contributions in E. G. Stanley, "The Early Middle Ages = The Dark Ages = The Heroic Age of England and in English," in *The Middle Ages after the Middle Ages in the English-Speaking World*, ed. M.-F. Alamichel and D. Brewer (Cambridge, 1997), 43–77.

But this is only half the story. It is unquestionably the case that from the sixteenth century onward, many humanist scholars engaged in enterprises that we would term Byzantine studies or medieval studies. But the triad that would seemingly make it all possible—the explicit division of history into ancient–medieval–modern—was not yet widely accepted or commonplace; such acceptance would not happen until the eighteenth century, in that world of Gibbon with which this essay began. Perhaps this is a routine feature of intellectual history: implicit categories required time, even centuries, to be made explicit. *Begriffsgeschichte* must confront a necessary time lag, made all the more problematic in cases when the objects of its analysis are terms for time itself.[30] But this confusion over periodization also reflects the fact that other possibilities were debated and considered, even if some of them—as we will see below—seemed to violate basic rules of chronological order.

Put more specifically, if Byzantine history were an extension of Roman history, and Roman history was ipso facto ancient, where exactly did one put it? Did "Byzantine" belong to antiquity, to the Middle Ages, or to something else in between? This became a question for the many chronologers and universal historians who wrote in the intervening period *between* Wolf and Gibbon. Some of them also began to use variations on "medieval," with different degrees of frequency. The variations on such terms opened up new possibilities, and new confusions. Not a few of them wrestled with where to put Byzantium. Petrarch, Bruni, and Biondo may have ensured that the periodizers who followed in their wake would have to reckon with Constantine and company, but they offered no easy answers.

Space permits discussion of only a few of these periodizations here. For instance, the early seventeenth-century Dutch classical scholar G. J. Vossius showed a broad-minded willingness to read texts and authors whom we would classify as medieval alongside those we would deem ancient. Among his voluminous output were encyclopedic collections of Greek and Latin historians—first a 1624 *De historicis Graecis*, and then a 1627 *De historicis Latinis*. But he did not define these labels in a strictly classical sense; rather, as he explained in his preface to the latter volume, the value of those writers "whom they commonly call barbarians" (*quos vulgo barbaros vocant*) had compelled him to continue his encyclopedic efforts far beyond the terminus point of *historia antiqua* that Petrarch had proposed.[31] And he did so via analogy with Byzantium, even if here he did not use the term. He described his thinking as

30 On the limitations of *Begriffsgeschichte* when applied to temporal categories, see D. Edelstein, *The Enlightenment: A Genealogy* (Chicago, 2010), 15.

31 Gerhard Johannes Vossius, *De historicis Latinis libri tres* (Leiden, 1627), sig. * 2 r: *Sciebam etiam, quos vulgo barbaros vocant, ingenio non caruisse: imo saepe iis, pro aevo, quo vixere, et eruditionem, et facundiam fuisse singularem.*

follows: "Just as I had extended the history of the Greek historians all the way to the capture of Constantinople by Mehmed, so I would bring this history of the Latins all the way to the times of the emperor Charles V."[32] In other words, if it were desirable to extend Greek history to 1453, then it was necessary to extend Latin history in analogous fashion, and in fact still further—all the way up to the Holy Roman emperor Charles V, who lived from 1500 until 1558. Vossius did not explicitly use the term Byzantium, but he made clear that he thought of later Greek historiography much as he thought of medieval Latin historiography. In other words, the domain of "Greek history" stretched until two centuries before Vossius's own; "Latin history" up to less than a century before Vossius's day. If one included Byzantium in one's purview, it only made sense to do the same for the Latin Middle Ages. And both were somehow commensurate with antiquity, or at least merited inclusion in a book alongside more conventional ancients.

Vossius used the expression "medieval" only a few times in his published work; it was not his default term for referring to the approximate millennium that we now identify with the Middle Ages.[33] Yet just a few decades later, in the latter half of the seventeenth century, the designation had grown more popular. The ambiguities raised by this new periodization—and its equally ambiguous implications for Byzantium—were on particular display in the 1666 universal history of the Leiden historian Georg Horn, or Georgius Hornius. This was the aptly titled *Arca Noae, sive historia imperiorum et regnorum a condito orbe ad nostra tempora* (*Ark of Noah, or History of Empires and Kingdoms from the Creation of the World to Our Times*). Not unlike Petrarch some three centuries prior, Horn still officially divided all time into two categories: *historia antiqua* (ancient history) and the appropriately comparative (and appropriately nebulous) *historia recentior* (more recent history).[34] Petrarchan *historia nova*, defined by its presentness, was now "more recent," a strange admixture of present and past.

As a result, Horn divided his book into two sections. In the former, his *historia antiqua*, he stuck to traditional schemes, including that of the Four Monarchies. Rome was the last of these monarchies, and Byzantine history was a continuation

32 Ibid.: *Atque haec impulerunt; ut quemadmodum historiam de historicis Graecis pertexuissem usque ad Constantinopolim a Muhammede captam: ita hanc de Latinis perducerem usque ad tempora imperatoris Karoli V.* On Vossius see C. S. M. Rademaker, *Life and Work of Gerardus Joannes Vossius, (1577–1649)*, trans. H. P. Doezema (Assen, 1981), and N. Wickenden, *G. J. Vossius and the Humanist Concept of History* (Assen, 1993).

33 See, e.g., Gerhard Johannes Vossius, *Ars historica* (Leiden, 1653), 48: *Si medii aevi scriptores quaerimus, quam fabulose Karoli magni vitam scripsit Turpinus, Archiepiscopus Rhemensis, qui ejusce imperatoris et Ludovici filii temporibus vixit?*

34 Georg Horn, *Arca Noae, sive historia imperiorum et regnorum a condito orbe ad nostra tempora* (Leiden, 1666), 183. On Horn's project, see A. Grafton, *New Worlds, Ancient Texts* (Cambridge, MA, 1992), 233–37.

of the Roman monarchy. But this decision created some structural issues. Horn included a terse description of the capture of Constantinople both by the Latins in 1204 and by the Ottomans in 1453 just a few pages before he drew *historia antiqua* to a close and announced his inauguration of *historia recentior*.[35] Yet almost twenty pages later, already deep into his "more recent history," he included an entry for the Franks. It was in this section that Horn discussed Charlemagne's assumption of the Roman imperial crown in the year 800[36]—that act of *translatio* Petrarch had notoriously belittled. Never mind that this "modern" event occurred some six and a half centuries *before* the Ottoman capture of Constantinople—an event that Horn stuck in an appendix to his ancient volume. In other words, not everything in *historia recentior* was literally "more recent" than *historia antiqua*!

So just how did Horn define the *difference* between ancient and modern? *Historia recentior* comprised "the empires and kingdoms of the middle and more recent age (*Imperia et regna medii et recentioris aevi*), and those which survive and endure today."[37] It was far more ample than ancient history, on account both of the extent of its lands and of the multitude of its peoples. Strangely enough, it was here that Horn used the designation *medium aevum*, as he described the Middle Ages as but a component of his non-ancient "more recent" history. And in this "more recent" age, he assigned to those old labels East and West, Orient and Occident, which had a precise meaning in *ancient* history, new and altogether more capacious connotations. Here they marked entire hemispheres. All of "more recent history" was to be divided into three parts: Eastern or *Orientalis*, Western or *Occidentalis*, and Southern or *Australis*. The East now comprised all of Europe, Asia, and Africa; the West constituted the Americas; and the South included the "peoples and lands toward the Antarctic Pole."[38] Ironically, the Greek and Latin worlds were no longer East and West, respectively; rather, both were now East when compared to the Americas. The Latin "West" was no longer western. And the *medium aevum*, including Charlemagne and his Franks, constituted an introduction to this new global world, whereas Byzantium remained in antiquity, on the other side of the gap. Significantly enough, the Turks also appeared in Horn's

35 Horn included this entry on the events of 1204 and 1453 in Constantinople at p. 175 in *Arca Noae*, i.e., still in *historia antiqua*, and then began his *historia recentior* just a few pages later at p. 183.

36 Horn, *Arca Noae*, 211: *KAROLUS Magnus Imperium* Occidentis *instaurat.*

37 Ibid., 183: *Hactenus Historiam* antiquam *exposuimus. Sequitur* Recentior, *quae complectitur Imperia et regna* medii et recentioris *aevi, quae hodieque supersunt et durant.*

38 Ibid.: *Quandoquidem autem Historia recentior spatio terrarum et multitudine populorum longe amplior antiqua est, ac praeter Asiam, Africam et Europam, ipsum quoque novum orbem et australes terras nondum plane cognitas complectitur; hinc dividenda fuit in* Orientalem, *quae Europam, Asiam et Africam:* Occidentalem, *quae Americam, et* Australem, *quae terras populosque versus polum antarcticum continet.*

"more recent history": they were a *modern* people like the Franks, and both were on the other side of the gap from Byzantium.[39]

Horn had used the term "Middle Ages," whereas Vossius, with only a few exceptions, had avoided it. But as the seventeenth century progressed it grew more standard. In 1678 the Parisian Jesuit Jean Garnier released an important work in library classification, the *Systema bibliothecae Collegii Parisiensis Societatis Jesu* (*System of the Library of the Parisian College of the Society of Jesus*). It explicitly employed "medieval" as a recommended subject heading for organizing books. The *Systema* appeared in a busy year for medieval studies in France, for it was also in 1678 that the French scholar Charles Du Cange (discussed elsewhere in this volume) published his dictionary of medieval Latin, which he followed up ten years later with a trailblazing dictionary of Byzantine Greek.[40] Garnier is not as celebrated in the history of Byzantine studies as is Du Cange, but his *Systema* nevertheless illustrates the creative ways in which scholars of the period approached the temporal problems raised by Byzantium. A patristic scholar, Garnier served as librarian at the Parisian Collège de Clermont, later renamed the Collège Louis-le-Grand. In his guide to library science, he described how one should organize books in various subjects according to *ordo temporum* (chronological order),[41] and when doing so he made several uses of the term *media aetas* (middle age).

39 Ibid., 243–69. Horn also discussed the Turks in a related historical work, his *Orbis imperans*, where he took note of the vastness of the Turkish kingdom following the events of 1453. See Georg Horn, *Orbis imperans* (Leipzig, 1668), 274: *Potiti Imperio Orientis: A. 1453. 29. Maii Constantinopolis a* Muhammede *II Imperatore Turcarum expugnata, atque occiso Constantino XV Palaeologo Imperium Graecum penitus eversum et ad Turcas translatum fuit, qui ab eo tempore suam regiam Constantinopoli fixerunt. Incredibile dictu, quantum terrarum sub* Muhammede *II Turcae occuparint, nimirum tria Imperia, 4 Regna, Provincias 20, et 200 Urbes.*

40 See Charles Du Cange, *Glossarium ad scriptores mediæ & infimæ Latinitatis, in quo Latina vocabula novatæ significationis, aut usus rarioris, Barbara & Exotica explicantur, eorum Notiones & Originationes reteguntur: Complures aevi medii Ritus & Mores, Legum, Consuetudinum municipalium, & Iurisprudentiæ recentioris Formulæ, & obsoletæ voces…* (Paris, 1678). Du Cange reused this important formulation in his corresponding Greek dictionary, published a decade later: *Glossarium ad scriptores mediæ & infimæ Græcitatis, in quo Græca vocabula novatæ significationis, aut usus rarioris, Barbara, Exotica, Ecclesiastica, Liturgica, Tactica, Nomica, Jatrica, Botanica, Chymica explicantur, eorum Notiones & Originationes reteguntur: Complures ævi medii Ritus & Mores; Dignitates Ecclesiasticæ, Monasticæ, Palatinæ, Politicæ, et quamplurima alia observatione digna, et ad Historiam Byzantinam praesertim spectantia, recensentur ac enucleantur* (Paris, 1688). On Du Cange's project and the significance of early modern lexicography to the study of the Middle Ages, see D. Bloch, "Charles Du Cange (1610–1688): Exposition organisée à l'occasion du tricentenaire du *Glossarium mediae et infimae Latinitatis* par la Bibliothèque nationale," in *La lexicographie du latin médiéval et ses rapports avec les recherches actuelles sur la civilisation du Moyen-Âge*, ed. Y. Lefèvre (Paris, 1981), 509–47, and Considine, *Dictionaries in Early Modern Europe*, 250–87. See also Teresa Shawcross in Chapters 5 and 6 and Appendixes I and II of this volume.

41 Jean Garnier, *Systema bibliothecae Collegii Parisiensis Societatis Jesu* (Paris, 1678). For biographical details (and an evaluation of the *Systema* from the perspective of 20th-century library science),

Before introducing his variations on the tripartite schema of ancient–medieval–modern, Garnier took an ancient metaphor of the life cycle—deployed by the Roman historian Florus and others,[42] and used more recently by various early moderns—and reapplied it to an avowedly postclassical terrain: the Greek patristic canon. As he explained it, "Four ages of the Greek fathers can be distinguished: adolescence, which precedes the Council of Nicaea and contains the three prior centuries; adulthood or the period of erudition, which contains the next three centuries until the Seventh Council; the elderly phase, which extends from the Seventh Council until the Photian Schism; and the age of senility, from then until our own times."[43] For a Jesuit like Garnier, it was understandable that the history of theology should be periodized in this fashion. The Photian Schism of 863–67 concerned the question of the relationship between the Roman pope and the Constantinopolitan patriarch, and whether the former could intervene in matters concerning the latter. Hence, from his point of view, as the ecclesiastical distance between Rome and Constantinople grew wider, Greek theology degenerated into senility.

But in other instances, Garnier turned from the life cycle to the new periodization. In so doing he deployed intriguing variations on both "medieval" and "Byzantine." His usage shows how the two could diverge quite starkly. He suggested that libraries should divide their Greek history into three classes: the first was "ancient" (*vetus*), the second was "that of the Middle Age" (*mediae aetatis*), and the third was "recent" (*recens*). He then dated these phases: the ancient would extend up to the establishment of the empire at Constantinople, the Middle Age from the founding of Constantinople until its storming by the Turks, and the recent, or new, from the Turks' capture of Constantinople until the present day.[44] Garnier

---

see W. T. Kane, *Jean Garnier: Librarian* (Chicago, 1940). See also the entry for Garnier in Carlos Sommervogel, *Bibliothèque de la Compagnie de Jésus*, 11 vols. (Brussels, 1890–1932), 3:1228–32. For the wider context of French medievalism, see N. Edelman, *Attitudes of Seventeenth-Century France towards the Middle Ages* (New York, 1946), and B. Barret-Kriegel, *Les historiens et la monarchie*, vol. 1, *Jean Mabillon* (Paris, 1988).

42 Florus, *Epitome* 1.1.4, trans. E. S. Forster, *Epitome of Roman History* (Cambridge, MA, 1929), 6–7: *Si quis ergo populum Romanum quasi unum hominem consideret totamque eius aetatem percenseat, ut coeperit utque adoleverit, ut quasi ad quandam iuventae frugem pervenerit, ut postea velut consenuerit, quattuor gradus processusque eius inveniet.*

43 Garnier, *Systema*, 21: *Graecorum Patrum distingui possunt aetates quatuor; Adolescens, quae ante Concilium Nicaenum, quaeque tria priora saecula tenuit; Adulta sive erudita, quae tria consequentia, usque ad septimum Concilium; Provecta, quae a septimo Concilio ad Schisma usque Photianum; Senescens, quae inde ad nostra usque tempora.*

44 Ibid., 64: *Quae vetus dicitur, a primis temporibus ad constitutum Constantinopoli Imperium extenditur: quae mediae aetatis, a condita Constantinopoli ad expugnationem a Turcis: quae recens, ab expugnatione Constantinopolis ad hunc usque diem. Vetus Historia nomen Graecae retinuit; quae mediae aetatis, Byzantina dicitur; recens, Turcica est.*

then named each of the three periods: the first and oldest period was simply to be styled Greek, the middle was to be styled Byzantine, and the final was to be labeled Turkish.

For Garnier, the triad Greek–Byzantine–Turkish lined up with ancient–medieval–modern. However, like Horn's categories, Garnier's antiquities and modernities could be different things in different places. When Garnier got to Roman history, he started off in familiar fashion: "the history of Rome ought to be divided like the Greek, into the ancient, the medieval, and the more recent (*in veterem, mediae aetatis, et recentiorem*)." But *where* he drew the divisions between these categories might surprise us. As Garnier proposed, "The ancient extends from the founding of the city until the emperors; the middle age, from the emperors until the translation of the empire; and the more recent, from the translation of the empire up to our own times."[45] Instead of synchronizing Rome's "middle age" with that of Greece, he fixed the birth of the Roman *media aetas* centuries earlier, with the rise of Augustus and Rome's political transition from republic to empire. And Rome's *historia recentior*, which Garnier explained was to be called *Historia Imperii Occidentalis* (History of the Western Empire), corresponded to the midpoint of his Greek Middle Ages. For Garnier, the "Middle Ages" was not a universal designation, and hence he saw no need to fit multiple histories and contexts into a single periodizing straightjacket. Temporal designations of this sort were labile and elastic; the Roman Middle Ages were not necessarily the Greek Middle Ages, because what was medieval in one place was not necessarily medieval in another. And what was Byzantine was not necessarily always medieval—or ancient, for that matter. Garnier took all the terms floating about in the late seventeenth-century lexicon and combined them together. Indeed, the mere fact that such combination was possible suggests that periodization was not yet a one-size-fits-all category. Nor was Byzantium stable.

From Temporal Indeterminacy to the Consolidation of the New Periodization

But this temporal flexibility would not last for long. Which model would win? Would the tripartite scheme of ancient–medieval–modern be defined by the creation and destruction of Constantinople, or by a more "Western" chronology, marked off by the likes of Augustus, Charlemagne, or Charles V? To answer this question it

45 Ibid., 65: *Historia Romana dividi debet perinde ac Graeca; in veterem, mediae aetatis, et recentiorem. Vetus ab Urbe condita ad Imperatores; mediae aetatis, ab Imperatoribus ad translationem Imperii; recentior, a translatione Imperii ad nostra usque tempora extenditur. Prima, propria est Romanae Reipublicae; secunda, Imperii Romani; tertia, Imperii Occidentalis. Prima retinuit nomen Historiae Romanae, secunda dicitur Augusta, tertia Imperii simpliciter.*

is necessary to examine the figure who did more than anyone else to canonize the new tripartite periodization. This was the German scholar Christopher Cellarius, a professor at Halle and a tireless compiler of textbooks. Not unlike Edward Gibbon a century later, he first composed a circumscribed *Historia antiqua,* first published in 1675 and subsequently revised in 1685. In 1688 there followed *Historia medii aevi a temporibus Constantini Magni ad Constantinopolim a Turcis captam* (*History of the Middle Age from the Times of Constantine the Great to the Capture of Constantinople by the Turks*). In 1696 he wrote up a modern history that covered the sixteenth and seventeenth centuries. In 1702 he went one step further: couching his project in an explicitly universal register, he organized his preceding histories into our now-familiar three-part scheme. His combination volume of these prior works, titled *Historia universalis in antiquam, et medii aevi, ac novam divisa* (*Universal History Divided into Ancient, Medieval, and New Times*) soon became a best-selling textbook across Europe.[46] Over the course of the eighteenth century, Cellarius's three-part history became standard. It enjoyed immense popularity in school instruction, and it survives today in numerous editions.

Much as Gibbon would begin his *Decline and Fall* a century later, Cellarius started off his project as a scholar of antiquity. In the preface to his 1688 *Historia medii aevi,* he described how he wished to continue his "ancient" history, and as a result waded into waters that were no longer ancient. Significantly enough, here he described this next stage of his history, from Constantine to the taking of Constantinople, as "Byzantine."[47] Fourteen years later, in his prologue to his explicitly tripartite *Historia universalis,* Cellarius issued a programmatic defense of periodization. He extolled its practical benefits to the reader: "This universal history is divided into three parts, so that the whole thing may be more ordered and more distinct (*ordinatior distinctiorque*), lest it trouble or confuse the reader by a continuous multitude (*multitudine continua*)."[48] The very title of the *Historia universalis*

46 See the discussion of Cellarius in A. Kamp, *Vom Paläolithikum zur Postmoderne: Die Genese unseres Epochen-Systems,* vol. 1, *Von den Anfängen bis zum Ausgang des 17. Jahrhunderts* (Amsterdam, 2010), esp. 90–91, and also J. H. van der Pot, *Sinndeutung und Periodisierung der Geschichte: Eine systematische Übersicht der Theorien und Auffassungen* (Leiden, 1999), esp. 316–17.

47 Christopher Cellarius, *Historia medii aevi a temporibus Constantini Magni ad Constantinopolim a Turcis captam deducta* (1688; repr., Jena, 1724), "Praefatio editionis primae" (n.p.): *Duodecim anni circumacti sunt, cum Historiae antiquae breuiarium, quod anno superiore vulgaueramus, ita continuauimus, vt in saeculis ante Constantinum latius excurreremus, in ceteris, usque ad Constantinopolim captam, historiam potissimum Byzantinam consectati.*

48 Christopher Cellarius, *Historia universalis breviter ac perspicue exposita, in antiquam, et medii aevi ac nova tempora divisa, cum notis perpetuis* (Jena, 1702), "Prooemium generale," 13: *Vt vero res omnis ordinatior distinctiorque sit, nec multitudine continua lectorem turbet aut impediat; in tres partes uniuersa haec Historia est distributa*[.]

proclaimed that its accompanying contents were *breviter ac perspicue exposita* (briefly and clearly set forth). These three parts, of course, were the ancient, medieval, and modern. Although *antiquity* and *modernity* were long-established categories, *medieval* required a little glossing. And so, Cellarius reprinted the definition of it that he had first offered in his preface of 1685:

> It constitutes a custom of speech of the more learned to call those things that occurred in the barbarous ages (*barbara saecula*), or were not all that far from them, matters of the MIDDLE AGE (*MEDII AEVI*). Therefore we will seem to have composed this history in a rather appropriate fashion if we extend ancient history to Constantine the Great, the history of the middle age (*medii aevi historiam*) to the storming of Constantinople, and then modern (*novam*) history to our times.[49]

He then went on to define some of the salient characteristics of each period. The first, the ancient world, embraced "the whole of paganism" (*universam gentilitatem*). The third, modernity, was defined by political revolution: "the new appearance of the regnant world and the reformation of states." But what was between the two was something unusually specific, insofar as it was the only one of his three periods that he outfitted with a *geographic* label: for it contained "the times of the Constantinopolitan empire of the Christians" (*temporibus imperii Christianorum Constantinopolitani*).

Speaking of this second component in his tripartite scheme, he elsewhere explained how it "shall encompass twelve centuries, setting forth the varying fates of the East and the West for as long as the city of Constantine was under the authority of the Christians, and a little further."[50] This definition included a puzzling qualifier: namely, *et paulo ultra* (and a little beyond).[51] But it was accurate: Cellarius's

49 Christopher Cellarius, *Historia antiqua* (Zeitz, 1685), "Praefatio ad Lectorem," sig.)(6 r–v: *Accedit doctiorum loquendi consuetudo, qui illa MEDII AEVI vocant, quae in barbara saecula inciderunt, aut ab illis abfuerunt propius. Accommodatius ergo facturi videmur, si antiquam ad Constantinum Magnum: medii aevi historiam, ad Constantinopolis expugnationem: nouam denique, ad nostra tempora deducemus, ut ista complectatur uniuersam gentilitatem: illa temporibus imperii Christianorum Constantinopolitani contineatur: haec nouam regnantis orbis faciem rerumque publicarum reformationem recenseat.*

50 Cellarius, *Historia universalis*, "Prooemium generale," 14: *Altera inde res duodecim saeculorum, quamdiu Constantini vrbs in Christianorum ditione fuit, et paullo vltra, comprehendat, Orientis aeque, vt Occidentis fata varia exponens.* For reflections on the role of 1453 in the history of periodization, see D. Lawton, "1453 and the Stream of Time," in Summit and Wallace, *Medieval/Renaissance: After Periodization* (n. 13 above), 469–91.

51 On Cellarius and the phrase *et paulo ultra*, see Kamp, *Vom Paläolithikum zur Postmoderne*, 97.

Historia medii aevi did not end right at 1453 with the fall of Constantinople. This was partially due to structural issues of book organization, similar to those that had jumbled Georg Horn's periodization. Cellarius divided his history both chronologically and thematically: his chapters progressed by centuries (*saecula*), but within them he began with political and ecclesiastical matters and thereafter continued with what we would term literary or cultural history. He started his final chapter, on the fifteenth century, with a lament for the "unhappiness of the century" (*saeculi infelicitas*).[52] And in it he soon delivered a detailed account of the demise of Constantinople and the triumph of the Ottomans.[53]

But this was technically not the end of Cellarius's history, even if that was how it was advertised on the title page. After discussing the fortunes of various western European states, he left high politics behind, and in the final four pages of the *Historia medii aevi* he sped through matters related to literature, culture, and religious piety, including developments both before and after 1453. As a result, he indeed went *paulo ultra*, even as he simultaneously looked backward, to the world of Chrysoloras and others whom Biondo had so praised. "In this age," Cellarius described, "letters fell in the East, and they rose out of long-lasting barbarism (*diuturna barbarie*) in the West, with even the most learned of the Greeks fleeing to Italy to escape the Turks."[54] In this final act of *translatio*, Italy absorbed Greek learning, and at the same time "recalled Latin letters, out of the shadows in which they had been immersed, to their pristine splendor."[55] The inflection point that Biondo had celebrated some two and a half centuries earlier was now firmly canonized.

Adumbrating his "new history" (*historia nova*), Cellarius spent the end of his *historia medii aevi* briefly narrating a lucky chain of events. All of these had become familiar historiographic tropes by the close of the seventeenth century: they included Greek scholars who fled to Italy, the rise of Greek studies and the concomitant revival of Latinity, the *translatio* of such learning across the Alps, Columbus's voyage to the Americas, and that auspicious invention of print in *Germania nostra* (our Germany).[56] He closed by hinting at the coming Reformation, with an invocation of how earlier figures like Jean Gerson and Thomas à Kempis prepared the road for a return to sanctity.[57] This itself was highly significant: to a committed Protestant

52 Cellarius, *Historia medii aevi*, 182.

53 Ibid., 188–93.

54 Ibid., 214: *Hoc saeculo cadebant litterae in Oriente, surgebant ex diuturna barbarie in Occidente, doctissimo quoque Graecorum, ut Turcos euaderet, in Italiam confugiente.*

55 Ibid., 215: *Non segnis erat Italia, quae horum industriam aemularetur, et Latinas simul litteras ex tenebris, quibus immersae fuerant, ad pristinum nitorem reuocaret*[.]

56 Ibid., 215–17.

57 Ibid., 218.

like Cellarius, perhaps the onset of *historia nova* was coeval with the Reformation, and the *medium aevum* was hence an unfortunate middle—defined by Catholicism and papal power—between pure pre-Constantinian Christianity and its Protestant renewal. Perhaps—although addressing the question is beyond the scope of this chapter—Constantine to 1517 would have been a better fit than Constantine to 1453. Did Luther, or Columbus, or Gutenberg—and hence *not* the fall of the capital of the Byzantine world—mark the *actual* end of the Middle Ages? Maybe events in the western half of Europe, and not its eastern Byzantine counterpart, had inaugurated something akin to modernity? Whatever his precise reason, Cellarius tried to have his cake and eat it too, both underscoring and undercutting the epochal status of Byzantine history. In the process, he vacillated *between* criteria for historical change, alternately emphasizing everything from philological and technological to political and theological causation.

But Cellarius's periodization did not necessarily mark the end of formal adherence to the old two-part scheme, and the use of that binary to adjudicate the dueling claims of East and West. To cite but one example, when the Leiden classical scholar Jacob Perizonius lectured on *historia universalis*, he divided it into old and new: *historia vetus* and *historia nova.*[58] As a student's dictation from 1714—today preserved in the library of Thomas Jefferson—reveals, Perizonius preferred a western division: for him, *historia nova* began with Charlemagne, because with his death the world had assumed a political order that was still discernible in Perizonius's own contemporary eighteenth-century moment.[59] Yet in other schools, Perizonius acknowledged, teachers began *historia nova* from Justinian. Even after the triumph of Cellarius and his three-part scheme of history, punctuated by Constantine and the fall of Constantinople, the question of whether to divide time according to a Western or a Byzantine emperor remained open. Indeed, this question was far more of a luxury now than it would have been to someone like Petrarch, for whom Byzantium constituted a real-time counterpart and rival to Rome and the Latin world. Perhaps Byzantium gained in theoretical relevance once it was safely an object of the past, and no longer a political alternative in the present. For whatever reason, its status

58 Washington, DC, Library of Congress, MS Sowerby 45, vol. 1, 1: *Historia systematica, chronologica seu universalis vulgo dividitur in veterem et novam. Historia vetus juxta quosdam se extendit ad Carolum M., vel ut alii volunt ad Iustinianum. Quicquid sit, illa multum confert ad omnem eruditionem, unde nemo vel mediocriter doctus censeri potest, si illius plane rudis reperiatur*[.] On Perizonius and universal history, see F. Clark, "Universal History and the Origin Narrative of European Modernity: The Leiden Lectures of Jacob Perizonius (1651–1715) on *Historia Universalis*," *Erudition and the Republic of Letters* 2 (2017): 359–95.

59 Ibid., 3: *Historia nova incipit a Carolo M., quia eo mortuo terrarum orbis illum statum, in quo nunc cernitur, induit, Europa enim mutata est per divisionem inter Caroli posteros; sic Gallia ante Carolum se extendebat ad Rhenum. Nunc autem Germania adhuc ultra Rhenum porrigitur.*

was still an open question near the close of the eighteenth century, when Gibbon turned to the purported end of the ancient world and the beginning of the modern.

Coda: Edward Gibbon and the Passive Center of Byzantium

In the 1776 preface to his first installment of *The History of the Decline and Fall of the Roman Empire*, Edward Gibbon outlined an ambitious—though rather melancholy—undertaking. He would set out to narrate "the memorable series of revolutions, which, in the course of about thirteen centuries, gradually undermined, and at length destroyed, the solid fabric of Roman greatness[.]"[60] The term *revolution* occurs often in Gibbon: for example, on the very first page of his text proper, he defined the decline and fall of Rome as "a revolution which will ever be remembered, and is still felt by the nations of the earth."[61] Like Garnier, Cellarius, and others before him, he announced in his preface that he would divide these thirteen centuries of destructive revolution into three neat periods: the first would extend from the age of the Antonines to the "subversion of the Western Empire, by the barbarians of Germany and Scythia, the rude ancestors of the most polished nations of modern Europe." The second would range from Justinian, who momentarily revived the East, to Charlemagne, who founded a second empire in the West. The third and final phase would extend from 800 to 1453—that is, from Charlemagne to the capture of Constantinople by the Ottomans.[62]

As J. G. A. Pocock has explored in detail, by choosing this path and keeping his focus on Constantinople, Gibbon made a highly significant decision about the story he would *not* tell: he would not repeat that quintessentially enlightened narrative of the purported triumph of western Europe over "barbarism and religion."[63] He would not focus on how those "rude" barbarians—the peoples of Horn's *historia recentior* and Perizonius's *historia nova,* such as the Franks or others—had become "the most polished nations of modern Europe." It is not that Gibbon necessarily *doubted* that story, and he was not always happy with his alternative. In fact in many places he did subscribe to that narrative—most notably in his "General Observations on the Fall of the Roman Empire in the West," where he maintained that the modern Europe that had emerged out of the Middle Ages was stronger and more stable than its Roman predecessor.[64] But Gibbon could not afford to tarry too long in the West. He was

60 Gibbon, preface of *Decline and Fall* (n. 2 above), 1:1.

61 Gibbon, *Decline and Fall,* 1:31.

62 Gibbon, preface of *Decline and Fall,* 1:1–2.

63 See Pocock, *Barbarism and Religion* (n. 1 above), esp. vol. 2, *Narratives of Civil Government.*

64 See Gibbon, *Decline and Fall,* 2:508–16.

writing a history of Roman decline and he had to follow those who self-identified as Romans, wherever they took him. Yet even if he did not use the Latin term for the genre, *historia universalis*, Gibbon also aimed to write a kind of universal history. What he said next in his preface is highly significant. Although he allowed that "it would require many years of health, of leisure, and of perseverance," he proclaimed that "the execution of this extensive plan" would do nothing less than "connect the ancient and modern history of the World."[65]

Twelve years later, when he described the plan of his final volumes, Gibbon vented, recording some of his notoriously vitriolic statements on Byzantium: writing Byzantine history was an "ungrateful and melancholy task," for it was a "tedious and uniform tale of weakness and misery."[66] According to Gibbon, Byzantium itself could not save Byzantine history, but its connections to antiquity and modernity could: "from these considerations, I should have abandoned without regret the Greek slaves and their servile historians, had I not reflected that the fate of the Byzantine monarchy is *passively* connected with the most splendid and important revolutions which have changed the state of the world."[67] Destructive revolutions were now "splendid." Indeed, Byzantium for Gibbon became the *passive* center of a new world; it gave his narrative coherence as he ranged far from the old Rome and recorded everything from a detailed account of the rise of Islam to the Mongol Empire. It became a vehicle for a global history that was far more than just the story of how western Europe supposedly made itself modern.[68] It was rather a middle time that could connect the ancient to the modern writ large. Gibbon summarized it thus: "As, in his daily prayers, the Musulman of Fez or Delhi still turns his face towards the temple of Mecca, the historian's eye shall be always fixed on the city of Constantinople. The excursive line may embrace the wilds of Arabia and Tartary, but the circle will be ultimately reduced to the decreasing limit of the Roman monarchy."[69]

Whatever they thought of Byzantium itself, Gibbon and his humanist predecessors agreed that it could not be "abandoned without regret," especially if they wished to define their own modernity against an ancient and medieval past. Their ambivalences—and even their regrets—live on in the paradoxes that arise from the

65 Ibid., 1:3.

66 Ibid., 3:23.

67 Ibid., 3:25.

68 On this point see Pocock, *Barbarism and Religion*, vol. 6, *Barbarism: Triumph in the West*, 8: "[T]he second trilogy [i.e., volumes 5 and 6 of the *Decline and Fall*] takes on the dimensions of a world history; but only in name is it a Decline and Fall of the Roman Empire."

69 Gibbon, *Decline and Fall*, 5:25.

nomenclature and categories that we still use when dividing time, and those paradoxes remain productive as we continue to debate the boundaries between historical eras. Periodization is a matter of perspective and is by nature teleological, whether for good or for ill. It is far more than an exercise in chronology. Rather, moments in the past either remain ancient or become modern, according to their perceived distance or closeness to the world of the periodizer. And some moments inevitably fall between the cracks, quite literally into a middle. This is itself one key legacy of the origins of Byzantine studies in early modern Europe, and it remains important today not only to Byzantinists but also to all those engaged in defining the temporal limits and possibilities of their respective fields.

I wish to thank Nathanael Aschenbrenner and Jake Ransohoff for inviting me to participate in the conference "The Invention of Byzantine Studies in Early Modern Europe" at Harvard University in October 2017, and for their stellar work in organizing such a stimulating gathering and bringing the resultant volume to publication. I also workshopped a version of this chapter at a virtual gathering of the Center for Early Modern History at the University of Minnesota, and I thank J. B. Shank for both the invitation and his insightful feedback. I am most grateful to Alexander Bevilacqua, Ann Blair, Anton Matytsin, and Alexander Statman for sharing their erudition on the history of historiography, and I owe a special debt to Richard Calis for his expertise in early modern Byzantine studies. The detailed and incisive comments of an anonymous reader for Dumbarton Oaks immeasurably improved this piece. Finally, my thanks as always to Anthony Grafton for guiding me through the world of early modern scholarship with generosity and wisdom.

THIRTEEN

FROM "EMPIRE OF THE GREEKS" TO "BYZANTIUM"

The Politics of a Modern Paradigm Shift

ANTHONY KALDELLIS

HOW DID THE TERM *BYZANTIUM* COME TO REFER NOT JUST TO THE CAPITAL CITY of the eastern empire but to the empire as a whole and, by extension, to its entire population and civilization? The question is not merely lexicographical but conceptual: the rise of "Byzantium" displaced other notions about what the empire was (e.g., Roman, Greek), detached it from previous narratives, and asserted it as a distinct and separate civilization with its own "essence" that could and should be studied by a discrete scholarly discipline. As we know, the Byzantines themselves—rather, the Greek-speaking Romans of the East whom we now call Byzantines—used this term to refer only to their capital city, as an alternative to its legal names, Constantinople and New Rome, and so its inhabitants could be called "Byzantines." They did not use this name to refer to their empire as a whole. "Byzantios" (Βυζάντιος) was just another word for a Constantinopolitan. For example, the twelfth-century canonist Theodore Balsamon called himself "a Constantinopolitan through-and-through" (Κωνσταντινουπολίτης ἀκραιφνέστατος), while the medical writer Meletios (of the middle Byzantine period) illustrated the concept of individual identity by defining himself as "a Byzantiaios (Βυζαντιαῖος), a doctor, short, snub-nosed, the son of Gregorios," and so on.[1] It is commonly believed that the proper noun *Byzantium* as

1 Balsamon: G. R. Rallis and A. Potlis, eds., *Σύνταγμα τῶν θείων καὶ ἱερῶν κανόνων*, 6 vols. (Athens, 1852–1859), 2:285–86; the translation is from P. Magdalino, "Constantinople and the Outside World," in *Strangers to Themselves: The Byzantine Outsider*, ed. D. C. Smythe (Aldershot, 2000),

a term for the empire as a whole was coined in the sixteenth century by the German scholar Hieronymus Wolf and became conventional thereafter. Thus was "Byzantine studies" founded.

This conventional narrative is inaccurate, however. Some of its elements must be adjusted in a relatively minor way. But one part of this story is glaringly false, and the truth about it changes the big picture considerably: the circumstances under which "Byzantium" became the term of art for our discipline were more politicized, interesting, and recent than the traditional narrative would have it. The transition occurred not in the sixteenth century but in the nineteenth. The history of this paradigm shift requires that we change our understanding of how "Byzantium" came about in the first place, and why. But first, I will present the minor quibbles that relate to earlier periods and work my way forward.

Two eastern Romans do seem to have experimented with using the term *Byzantine* for the empire as a whole, namely the historians Priskos and Malchos, who wrote in Greek in the later fifth century. Priskos, a functionary of the eastern empire who among other duties accompanied official embassies, recounted the history of the mid-fifth century in a detailed narrative that he finished in the mid- or late 470s. He was probably the most important historian of the fifth century, and his work was used by many of his successors. Although his writings did not survive, we have many quotations and fragments preserved in the *Excerpta* commissioned by Constantine VII Porphyrogennetos in the tenth century. Judging from the surviving fragments, Priskos paid more or less equal attention to what he called the "western" and the "eastern" halves of the Roman Empire. For Priskos these two halves were equally Roman, and he refers throughout his narrative either to Romans generally or to "eastern Romans" and "western Romans" specifically. The two groups were distinguished by geography and by having their own emperors and administration, but not by degrees of Romanness; the eastern Romans had no other collective identity.

What is interesting for us, however, is the possible title of Priskos's work. According to the *Suda*, a tenth-century encyclopedia of classical studies, it was titled the *Byzantine History* (*Byzantiakē*, *Βυζαντιακή*). We do not know how reliable this information is. The entry goes on to add that Priskos also wrote *The Events Concerning Attila*, along with various rhetorical works and letters. This list suggests that the *Attila* was separate from the *History*, though the fragments of the history that survive feature Attila extensively. Meanwhile, the tenth-century compilation *Excerpta de legationibus* calls the work the *Gothic History* (there are Goths in the fragments too).

149–61, at 150. Meletios, *A Brief Account of Human Nature*, in *Anecdota Graeca e codd. manuscriptis bibliothecarum Oxoniensium*, ed. J. A. Cramer, vol. 3 (Oxford, 1836), 5–157, at 155.

Priskos's somewhat later contemporary the historian Malchos, about whom we know much less, also called his history the *Byzantiaka* (*Βυζαντιακά*).[2]

These two eastern Romans, then, took the archaic name of the capital of their half of the empire and used it as a rubric for the history of the empire as a whole, or perhaps their intention was to signal that their histories were written from an eastern Roman (or Constantinopolitan) standpoint. We do not know exactly what they meant by it, nor if anyone else used the name in such a broad sense. It was, after all, a unique moment in the history of the Roman Empire. Its institutional division into two halves had become more or less fixed, and perhaps Priskos and Malchos were looking for a name by which to identify their half. But that moment soon passed. The western empire fell, leaving the eastern half as the only Roman Empire in existence. The East did not need to differentiate itself from the West. Under Justinian there was a vigorous assertion of the eastern empire's Romanness.[3] For the duration of the eastern empire's history, its people and rulers were "Romans" (*Romaioi*) in a sense that was both political and ethnic, and they called their state "the polity of the Romans," "the monarchy of the Romans," or just Romanía (Ῥωμανία)—that is, "Romanland."[4]

This bring us to early modern times. It is formulaic to claim that the story of *Byzantium* as a term for the empire as a whole begins with Hieronymus Wolf in the sixteenth century, but this unlikely to be true. The term may have already had that sense in some Western medieval texts. At conferences, colleagues invariably tell me that they remember seeing it in some papal chronicle or medieval romance. Research on this would be most welcome. I expect that most of these texts will turn out to be using Byzantium as a synonym for Constantinople in the phrases "empire of Constantinople" and "emperor of Constantinople." For example, in the medallion made by Costanzo da Ferrara for Sultan Mehmed II in 1481, he is called (among other things) *Byzantii imperator*.[5] This is not (yet) our modern concept of Byzantium but instead the usual medieval metonym (the whole named after the capital). What we would need is a territorial label—for example, if someone on the frontier far from

2 For Priskos see R. C. Blockley, *The Fragmentary Classicising Historians of the Later Roman Empire*, 2 vols. (Liverpool, 1981–83), 1:49, 2:222. Blockley rejects the title *Byzantiakē*, but I do not see why. At any rate, even he has to admit that a later Byzantine reader thought it appropriate, so the name does not go away, it just is pushed to a later time. Also, we have to correct the *Suda*'s *Attalos* to *Attilas*. For Malchos see 1:71, 2:402 (from Photios, *Bibliotheca* cod. 78). For a discussion of the works' titles, see A. Karpozilos, *Βυζαντινοὶ ἱστορικοὶ καὶ χρονογράφοι*, vol. 1 (Athens, 1997), 310–11, 324–25.

3 M. Kruse, *The Politics of Roman Memory from the Fall of the Western Empire to the Age of Justinian* (Philadelphia, 2019).

4 A. Kaldellis, *Romanland: Ethnicity and Empire in Byzantium* (Cambridge, MA, 2019).

5 The reader can view the medal on the website of the Metropolitan Museum of Art in New York, by searching accession no. 1975.1.1269 at https://www.metmuseum.org/art/collection.

the capital is said to "enter Byzantium." Such passages, I suspect, would be rare in Western texts and unsystematic, and they probably are not the source for the modern scholarly use of the term Byzantine.

That tradition likely starts with another historian writing in Greek, Laonikos Chalkokondyles, in the mid-fifteenth century, immediately after the fall of Constantinople to the Ottoman Turks. Laonikos was an Athenian, a student of the radical Platonist philosopher Pletho at Mistra, and, like Pletho, he also advocated a neo-Hellenic identity for the people who had hitherto called themselves Romans. In his preface, he admits that the inhabitants of the empire of Constantinople had called themselves Romans for the past thousand years, but he believed that they were really Greeks and should be called that. To this degree, his neo-Hellenic ideology dovetailed perfectly with the long-standing perspective of western Europeans. They had long denied that the Byzantines were Romans, a label that they reserved exclusively for Western institutions such as the German empire and the Church of Rome. For centuries, Westerners had instead called the Byzantines "Greeks," *Graeci*, a term that also had many negative connotations. This was the origin of the Western denial that Byzantium was "really" Roman, a tradition of denialism that continues to this day and is propagated by many Byzantinists themselves.[6] But Laonikos's Greek interpretation of Byzantium does not appear to stem from a Western, or Latin, bias. He does not side with Latins, Westerners, or Catholics in his history, and it is clear that he had positive nationalistic and possibly religious (neopagan) reasons for claiming the Byzantines as Hellenes: he wanted to get rid of the Roman name as an impediment to his project of national Hellenic reawakening.[7]

Thus, Laonikos calls the Byzantines "the Greeks" and their ruler "the king of the Greeks." He calls their capital "Byzantion," not Constantinople or New Rome, probably because he preferred its ancient Greek name over its Roman names, and so he calls its ruler the "king of Byzantion" and his subjects "the Byzantines." This was, for him, "the kingdom of Byzantion" (*basileus* and *basileia* are ambiguous in Greek between "king" and "emperor"; I believe that Laonikos meant the former in this case). To be sure, in the period that he was discussing (mostly the late fourteenth and the fifteenth century) the empire was limited to Constantinople and a few outlying territories, so the two possible senses of the term "kingdom *of* Byzantion"—that is, the kingdom that simply consisted *of* the city of Byzantion and the kingdom that

6 See Kaldellis, *Romanland*, chap. 1 (3–37), for a survey of this tradition.

7 For the text and translation, see A. Kaldellis, *Laonikos Chalkokondyles: The Histories*, 2 vols. (Cambridge, MA, 2014); for a study, see A. Kaldellis, *A New Herodotos: Laonikos Chalkokondyles on the Ottoman Empire, the Fall of Byzantium, and the Emergence of the West* (Washington, DC, 2014). For his teacher Pletho, see N. Siniossoglou, *Radical Platonism in Byzantium: Illumination and Utopia in Gemistos Plethon* (Cambridge, 2011), and Fabio Pagani in Chapter 1 of this volume.

was governed *from* Byzantion, as belonging to it—basically overlapped. The provinces for him were "the territory of Byzantion,"[8] which could easily just be taken as "Byzantion" *simpliciter*. In this way, we end up with a concept of Byzantion as the empire as a whole, an equation facilitated by the much-diminished state of the empire at that time. The same goes for the empire's population: there was considerable overlap between the inhabitants of the capital ("the Byzantines") and the subjects of the emperor as a whole (the rest of "the Greeks").

Thus, Laonikos detached Byzantine history from its native Roman matrix and reembedded it within a Greek narrative, which he highlights in his opening remarks by mentioning that the history of the Greeks began with Dionysos, Herakles, the Athenians and the Spartans, and Alexander the Great. By contrast, he does not mention Constantine the Great by name when talking about the foundation of Byzantion (the city). In Laonikos, therefore, "Byzantium" was not its own separate category: the question for him was whether it belonged to Greek or to Roman national history.

Manuscripts of Laonikos's *Histories* quickly traveled to the West. Already in the sixteenth century, the work was being paraphrased; "translated" into Latin, French, and Italian; and merged with other histories of the Turks, a process that possibly was already under way in the late fifteenth century.[9] These versions were widely read by sixteenth-century scholars.[10] The Latin translation of Laonikos by Conrad Clauser (1556) renders the key terms as *rex Byzantius, rex Byzantii*, and *regnum Byzantii*, although it follows Laonikos in mostly calling the Byzantines *Graeci*.[11] A reluctant Hieronymus Wolf was meanwhile ordered by the banker Anton Fugger to edit and translate the previous Byzantine historians John Zonaras and Niketas Choniates, editions that were published in 1557 by Oporinus in Basel. In 1562 Clauser's popular Chalkokondyles was added to that edition, along with the history of Nikephoros Gregoras, to form what was only now called a complete "Byzantine" history. That term (*Corpus universae historiae byzantinae*) was probably not Wolf's but the publisher's,[12] and it may have been legitimated by its prior use in both the Greek original and the Latin translation of Laonikos, which had been circulating widely. The original 1557 publication of Wolf's Zonaras and Choniates did not contain the

8 E.g., Laonikos Chalkokondyles, *Histories* 4.5.

9 Kaldellis, *A New Herodotos*, 238–40.

10 A. Pippidi, *Visions of the Ottoman World in Renaissance Europe* (New York, 2013), 45–46, 78–79, 94.

11 Clauser's translation was reprinted in the Bonn Corpus (1843) and PG 159 editions of Laonikos.

12 A. Ben-Tov, *Lutheran Humanists and Greek Antiquity: Melanchthonian Scholarship between Universal History and Pedagogy* (Leiden, 2009), 106–9; for more information and references about the background, see D. R. Reinsch, "The History of Editing Byzantine Historiographical Texts," in *The Byzantine World*, ed. P. Stephenson (London, 2010), 435–44, at 438–39.

word "Byzantine" in the title; this was added in the 1562 edition, which also featured Laonikos. The source of this category, therefore, was likely Laonikos.

What's important about all this is that it was not very important in the long run. The emergence of the adjective *byzantinus* for designating the eastern empire, its history, and its regime did not fundamentally change how western Europeans perceived the people we call the Byzantines. From the later eighth until the later nineteenth century, the dominant interpretive category was that the eastern empire was "the empire of the Greeks," because its rulers and subjects were (allegedly) ethnic Greeks. Occasionally the term "empire of Constantinople" was used too. None of this changed with the introduction of the term Byzantine, which in the early modern period was used almost exclusively in its adjectival form and usually as a synonym for Constantinople; that is, early modern scholars typically used "Byzantine" as a shorter and more archaic way of saying "Constantinopolitan." But the majority of the subjects of the empire in their eyes remained Greek. Western Europeans did not view them as non-ethnic "Orthodox" people, in the way that modern scholarship does. In Western eyes, the heresy or schism of the "Greeks"—that is, their deviation from the Church of Rome—was a function of their bad ethnic traits (faithlessness, fickleness, excessive sophistication, etc.). There was as yet no "Byzantium" as a separate category. There was only the empire of the Greeks, a phase in the long history of the Greek people that began in antiquity.

This statement requires some qualification. The eastern empire was, at various moments in its history, regarded in western Europe as powerful, rich, and sophisticated (because it was); it had direct access to the founding traditions of imperial Christianity; its spectacular capital was the only surviving late Roman imperial city; and Byzantium was a direct continuation of the ancient empire of the East, for all that Western writers insisted that there had been a categorical rupture at some point in its history from "Roman" to "Greek." Thus, Western regimes that sought to look or to sound authentically Roman or to connect themselves to the Roman Empire would sometimes borrow elements such as images, symbols, terms, and forms of dress from contemporary Byzantium, which always called itself "the empire of the Romans." However, they did not always acknowledge this borrowing or explicitly concede that it amounted to a recognition of Byzantium as Roman.[13]

Also, the "Greek" rubric did not establish itself immediately and universally in Latin perceptions of Byzantium. When Westerners wanted a favor from the eastern

13 C. Raffensperber, "The Byzantine Ideal," chap. 1 of his *Reimagining Europe: Kievan Rus' in the Medieval World* (Cambridge, MA, 2012), 10–46, documents many of these implicit borrowings; see also K. N. Ciggaar, *Western Travellers to Constantinople: The West and Byzantium, 962–1204* (Leiden, 1996).

emperors—for example, when Hugh Capet wanted an imperial bride for his son—they referred to them as emperors of the "Romans."[14] Western pilgrims passing through Byzantium before the Crusades sometimes reported that the easterners called themselves Romans, using variant forms such as *Romanites*.[15] Such concessions to emic perceptions continued to be made down to the modern times, when Western travelers to the Ottoman Empire reported that the locals called themselves, and their language, "Roman."[16] But this did not change the dominant view of their essential Greekness in Western eyes. Modern scholars of Byzantium will also routinely concede, based on the evidence of the primary written sources, that the Byzantines "called themselves Romans," but they will also not then call them Romans themselves.

Western medieval writers who wanted to endow their patrons with a Roman genealogy would sometimes include Byzantine emperors in their invented lineages, in some cases emperors as late as Herakleios.[17] Other chapters in this volume show how this tradition continued into early modern times. Yet none of these practices resulted in any explicit theorization of the Byzantines as Romans. These were exceptions of convenience to the otherwise constant background refrain of "Greeks" and "empire of the Greeks." It was locked in by ethnic prejudice (negative depictions of the Byzantines, especially during the era of the Crusades, stressed their "Greek vices"), and also by Catholic religious polemic, which produced many treatises *Contra Errores Graecorum*, thereby further nailing Byzantium, here in the guise of its religion, to its perceived ethnic identity.[18]

After Laonikos and Wolf, the term Byzantium was used, as noted above, primarily as an adjective. European scholars had not yet drawn a clear distinction between ancient Greece and the medieval empire of the Greeks, for they viewed these as successive phases of the same ethnic-national history. But they still needed

14 The sources are collected and discussed by A. G. Panagopoulou, *Οι διπλωματικοί γάμοι στο Βυζάντιο (6ος–12ος αιώνας)* (Athens, 2006), 170–72.

15 E. Joranson, "The Great German Pilgrimage of 1064–1065," in *The Crusades and Other Historical Essays*, ed. L. J. Paetow (New York, 1928), 3–43, at 17–18.

16 R. Chandler, *Travels in Greece* (Oxford, 1776), 136; see more in G. Koubourlis, *Οι ιστοριογραφικές οφειλές των Σπ. Ζαμπέλιου και Κ. Παπαρρηγόπουλου: Η συμβολή Ελλήνων και ξένων λογίων στη διαμόρφωση του τρίσημου σχήματος του ελληνικού ιστορισμού (1782–1846)* (Athens, 2012), 53, n. 12; 161–62.

17 E.g., Godfrey of Viterbo; see A. A. Latowsky, *Emperor of the World: Charlemagne and the Construction of Imperial Authority, 800–1229* (Ithaca, NY, 2013), 202–3.

18 The bibliography on Western perceptions of Byzantium is extensive. I cite here an older and a more recent study: H. Hunger, *Graeculus perfidus, Ἰταλὸς ἰταμός: Il senso dell'alterità nei rapporti Greco-Romani ed Italo-Bizantini* (Rome, 1987); Ch. Messis, "Lectures sexuées d l'altérité: Les Latins et identité romaine menacée les derniers siècles de Byzance," *JÖB* 61 (2011): 151–70.

an adjective to refer to the medieval phase, and "Greek" would not do unless the context was absolutely clear. That is where "Byzantine" was useful—as an adjective for the empire of Constantinople. For example, the seventeenth-century Louvre edition of Byzantine historians was called the *Corpus Byzantinae Historiae* (or *Byzantine du Louvre*), and its Bonn replacement in the nineteenth century was called the *Corpus Scriptorum Historiae Byzantinae*. There was yet no *Historia Byzantii*, a "history of Byzantium," only "Byzantine histories." The editor of the Louvre series, the Jesuit Philippe Labbe, published a *protreptikon* for the study of the corpus of the Byzantine historians in 1648, and in the preface he uses "Byzantine History" and "Constantinopolitan History" interchangeably.[19] Between 1672 and 1685, Louis Cousin published translations of the Byzantine historians in eight volumes under the name *Histoire de Constantinople*. Thus, "Byzantium" had not yet become a proper noun referring to the empire as a whole; it was still too closely linked to Constantinople and was used as an adjective for it, though it pointed through metonymy to the empire as a whole.

In Edward Gibbon's *History of the Decline and Fall of the Roman Empire*, "Byzantium" is the city, never the empire, and its inhabitants are always "the Greeks" (he calls them by their correct Roman name only on the rare occasions that they win a battle).[20] Gibbon uses the adjective *Byzantine* for the court, palace, throne, and patriarch—that is, to mean "of Constantinople"—and occasionally it refers (but only by extension from the capital) to the empire, the monarchy, its history, and its historians. Writers such as Rousseau and Voltaire who wanted to refer to the empire in a random context—that is, where readers would not be expecting a reference to it and where "the Greeks" would be confusing—called it "the empire of Constantinople" (though occasionally "the Greek empire" too).[21] The adjective *Byzantine* could sometimes be used with a nominal force. In one of his letters, for example, Barthold Georg Niebuhr (1776–1831) says that he wanted to write a book about Greek literature "from Homer to the Byzantines (*die Byzantiner*)."[22] We can see why he made this choice: saying "from Homer to the Greeks" would be nonsense. In his *Lectures on the Philosophy of History* (part 3, chap. 3), Hegel (1770–1831) called the

19 Philippe Labbe, *De Byzantinae historiae scriptoribus . . . ad omnes per orbem eruditos προτρεπτικόν* (Paris, 1648), 5–6.

20 G. Fowden, "Gibbon and Islam," *EHR* 131 (2016): 261–92, at 265, n. 10.

21 See, e.g., Rousseau's *Discourse on the Sciences and the Arts*, originally published as *Discours qui a remporté le prix a l'Academie de Dijon en l'année 1750: Sur cette question proposée par la même académie: Si le rétablissement des sciences & des arts a contribué à épurer les mœurs* (Geneva, 1750); for Voltaire, see N. Giakovaki, *Ευρώπη μέσω Ελλάδας: Μια καμπή στην ευρωπαϊκή αυτοσυνείδηση, 17ος–18ος αιώνας* (Athens, 2006), 410, n. 8.

22 *Die briefe Barthold Georg Niebuhrs*, ed. D. Gerhard and W. Norvin, vol. 2 (Berlin, 1929), 306, no. 432.

empire "das Byzantinische Reich" and "das östliche Kaiserreich" but he too clearly thought that it was "of the Greeks" (*der Griechen*).

European writers, intellectuals, and historians continued to rely primarily on the category "empire of the Greeks" for what we call "Byzantium," straight through the Enlightenment and into the nineteenth century—in fact, well into the nineteenth century. It remained the dominant label by far. During the War of Greek Independence (1821–32), Western philhellenes championed the idea of Greek continuity since antiquity, a continuity which included "the empire of the Greeks" that every educated person had heard of, even if no one educated in the traditions of the Enlightenment was enthusiastic about that particular phase of Greek history. All this has challenging implications for the origin of modern Greek national historiography. It is often assumed that the historians of modern Greece in the mid- to later nineteenth century (especially Spyridon Zambelios and Konstantinos Paparrigopoulos) invented the historical paradigm of Greek continuity, but it has now been shown that they found it ready-made in western European historiography (in German, French, and English texts). They took it from there and appropriated it, adapting it to their own national ideology and schematizing it into the tripartite division of ancient, medieval, and modern Hellenism.[23] What is interesting about their use of the schema of Greek continuity is that they picked it up at precisely the moment when the West was abandoning it, a development to which we may now turn.

A dramatic shift occurred in the nineteenth century, especially its second half. It was then that *Byzantium* and *the Byzantines* became the established and dominant terms of art, as we know them today, displacing the "empire of the Greeks" and the "empire of Constantinople." These concepts did not just separate themselves from the Greek rubric: they led to its extinction (except in modern Greek national historiography). The average educated Westerner today would not understand a casual reference to "the empire of the Greeks," at least not without explanation. Why did this happen?

The explanation has a specific political context: the Eastern Question. In brief, the Eastern Question was the concern among the major Christian empires over the failing Ottoman Empire: they all wanted large portions of it for themselves, but they also did not want their rivals to succeed in this, so they generally agreed to keep it in place.[24] This position was consistent with the conservative order that was put in place in Europe after Napoleon's defeat, the Concert of Europe. Soon, however,

23 Koubourlis, *Οι ιστοριογραφικές οφειλές*, passim, esp. 10, 525.

24 The concise survey is A. L. Macfie, *The Eastern Question, 1774–1923* (London, 1996); additional bibliography is cited by D. Vovchenko, *Containing Balkan Nationalism: Imperial Russia and Ottoman Christians, 1856–1914* (New York, 2016), 6, n. 12.

that order was challenged by the Greek Revolution, which carved a new state out of the Ottoman Empire. Greece was recognized by the major powers, especially Russia, England, and France, but reluctantly, because its independence disturbed the established order. Exactly as conservatives feared, Muslims in the European colonies abroad began to ask that if a Christian people (the Greeks) could be allowed to free themselves of their Muslim imperial master (the Turks), why could Muslims not be freed of their Christian colonial overlords?[25]

Greek independence was facilitated in the West by philhellenism, a narrative that recognized the revolutionary Greeks of the 1820s as the heroic descendants of the ancient Greeks who were struggling valiantly to regain their independence after centuries of oppression by the barbaric Turks. However, the ideology of the new Greek state did advance the possibility, indeed the hope, that it would liberate all Greeks elsewhere in the Ottoman Empire; in fact, some leaders of the Greek Revolution from the very start believed that they were doing nothing other than restoring the Christian empire of their ancestors.[26] Some believed that Athens might not or should not be the permanent capital of the new state, for in time Constantinople would be liberated as well.[27] There were no specific plans for making this happen. Even so, none of the Great Powers wanted to see a Greek empire in Constantinople or anywhere else. They had given limited support to the descendants of the ancient Greeks to free themselves from the barbarous Turkish yoke, a limited project of national revival; they had surely *not* endorsed a reconstitution of "the Greek empire." Yet their own romantic love of Greece and historiographical traditions, which were full of references to the "empire of the Greeks," seemed to legitimate that prospect of imperial restoration.

The problem in the West was not just Greek imperial irredentism: it was more specifically Russia. The fear was that Russia would capture Constantinople and revive an Orthodox empire of its own, or that it would use the Greeks, their junior Orthodox clients in the Balkans, to do so as proxies. These fears were not without warrant. There was, for example, the ambitious "Greek Project" hatched and broadcast by Catherine the Great (r. 1762–1796) to lead the Greeks and other Orthodox peoples in a rebellion against the Ottoman Empire and to liberate Constantinople—"the capital of the ancient Greek emperors," as she called it (note how meaningless

25 C. Aydin, *The Idea of the Muslim World: A Global Intellectual History* (Cambridge, MA, 2017), 40, 49–54.

26 E. K. Bogli, *"Έλληνες το γένος": Η ιθαγένεια και η ταυτότητα στο εθνικό κράτος των Ελλήνων (1821–1844)* (Heraklion, 2007), 86, 175, 327, 330; Koubourlis, *Οι ιστοριογραφικές οφειλές*, 57, n. 21.

27 E. Skopetea, *Τό "Πρότυπο βασίλειο" καί ἡ Μεγάλη Ἰδέα: Ὄψεις τοῦ ἐθνικοῦ προβλήματος στήν Ἑλλάδα (1830–1880)* (Athens, 1988), 274, 285, 292–93; cf. V. Kremmydas, *Η Μεγάλη Ιδέα: Μεταμορφώσεις ενός εθνικού ιδεολογήματος* (Athens, 2010), 19.

that phrase would sound in the modern rubric of Byzantine studies). Catherine's plan resulted in an insurgency in the Peloponnese in the 1770s, fifty years before the Greek Revolution. She proposed another such plan to the Austrians in 1782.[28] Down to 1830, Russian statesmen proposed plans for the dismemberment of the Ottoman Empire and the establishment, under Russian protection, of a new Greek or Orthodox empire in Constantinople. Western observers also commented on the close relationship between Greece and Russia that was forged by Orthodoxy (Napoleon called Tsar Alexander I "a shifty Byzantine").[29] At the end of the Greek Revolution, it was Russia that intervened militarily and decisively to force the Porte to accept Greek independence; and the first governor of independent Greece, Ioannis Kapodistrias, had made his career in the Russian foreign service. This connection caused the English and French to suspect that he was an agent of Russian domination in Greece, which he denied.[30] In his analysis of Russian policy between 1821 and 1844, Lucien Frary has argued that the tsar had no actual intention of annexing Constantinople or reviving the Greek empire, but the fear that he might do so was widespread in the West and contributed to mounting Russophobia.[31] In Greece and Russia many hoped for such a restoration, and private societies disseminated propaganda to that end.

The historian and essayist-at-large Jakob Philipp Fallmerayer (1790–1861) had an extreme reaction to these developments. Today he is infamous for having claimed that not a single drop of ancient Greek blood flows in the veins of the so-called modern Greeks of Greece. He believed that in Byzantine times Greece had been overrun entirely by Slavs, who were thinly Hellenized only in their speech (he later came to believe in a heavy admixture of Albanian blood too). Moreover, he shared the Enlightenment's biases against Byzantium, viewing it as the distillation of all human vice and depravity. For him, the barely Hellenized Slavs who called themselves Hellenes in his own day were the worst type of human being, and there are a couple of passages where he fantasizes about killing them all.[32] But this bias was only part of a broader political agenda. Fallmerayer was preoccupied with the rising power of Russia. He saw the Slavs, the medieval and modern Greeks (who were just thinly disguised Slavs), and the Russians as part of the same threat against liberal

28 L. Frary, *Russia and the Making of Modern Greek Identity, 1821–1844* (Oxford, 2015), 24, citing bibliography; also Vovchenko, *Containing Balkan Nationalism*, 40–42 (a summary).

29 A. Roberts, *Napoleon the Great* (London, 2015), 295.

30 Frary, *Russia*, 25–46; fear of Russian influence in Greece: 106, 137, 180, 192.

31 Ibid., 60–61, 202.

32 J. P. Fallmerayer, *Geschichte der Halbinsel Morea während der Mittelalters*, 2 vols. (Stuttgart, 1830–36), 2:168; and a passage from his notebooks quoted by E. Skopetea, *Φαλλμεράϋερ: Τεχνάσματα του ἀντίπαλου δέους* (Athens, 1999), 91, n. 19.

Enlightenment Europe, and he believed that a German hegemony would inaugurate an era of peace for all.[33] For him it was a terrible mistake that the Europeans had allowed a "modern Greece" to happen, because of course Russia had her eye on Constantinople. He viewed the Greeks as in league with the Russians not only because of Orthodoxy but because they were not really Greeks at all, and the same was true of their Byzantine ancestors.

This ideology may have affected how Fallmerayer talked about Byzantium. While he continued to refer to it as the "Greek empire" ruled by the "Greek emperors" (even though he believed that they were really Slavs), he also used the substantives *Byzanz* (Byzantium) and *der Byzantiner* (the Byzantines).[34] This marks a move toward seeing "Byzantium" as a separate entity, not just as a phase of Greek history. Indeed, it had to be a separate entity if you believed that the Byzantines were not really Greeks at all—not Greeks by "blood." (Interestingly, Fallmerayer was ready to concede that the Greeks of the islands and of Asia Minor—i.e., those still subject to the Ottoman Empire—had not been overwhelmed by Slavic blood and still had some ancient nobility about them.)

These threads came together in the Crimean War (1853–56), which, I propose, among its many other consequences marked the turning point in how Europeans talked about Byzantium. Specifically, it heralded the end of "the empire of the Greeks" as the dominant paradigm and the onset of our "Byzantium." The reader will recall that this war, fought mostly in the Crimea, was an intervention by Britain and France to defend the Ottoman Empire against Russia.[35] It was accompanied by a surge in European Russophobia, including the fear of an Orthodox empire established in Constantinople (the term *jingoism* originated in a ditty sung by the British at this very time boasting that they would not let the Russians take Constantinople). Though the tsar apparently had no plan to give the Greeks a new empire, the latter, to their detriment, believed that this was their chance to free more Greeks from the Turkish yoke and gain more territory for the nascent Greek state. These ambitions were labeled the Megali Idea, or "Grand Vision." Although this idea had been articulated previously in vague terms, during the Crimean War it first became a platform for territorial expansion.[36] Greece sided with Russia. Some Greeks joined the Russian army as volunteers, while others incited rebellions—all of which failed—against the

33 Fallmerayer's politics are elucidated by Skopetea, *Φαλλμεράϋερ*.

34 I have skimmed through the volumes of his works and found numerous attestations of these terms.

35 Extensive literature on the war is cited by Vovchenko, *Containing Balkan Nationalism*, 66–67, n. 2. In this period, Britain's policy on the Eastern Question was primarily to contain Russia: G. D. Clayton, *Britain and the Eastern Question: Missolonghi to Gallipoli* (London, 1971).

36 Kremmydas, *Μεγάλη Ιδέα*, 38–39.

Ottoman authorities in Epeiros, Thessaly, and Macedonia. With the blessing of the Greek king, officers of the Greek army resigned their formal commissions to join these revolutionary movements in the guise of private citizens.

It was at this time, I believe, that the concept of "the empire of the Greeks" became politically toxic in the West. A Greek leader of the fighting in Epeiros who sought to free Arta—one Spyridon Karaïskakis, the son of a famous revolutionary fighter whose name every Greek knows today—issued a proclamation that ended with the rousing cry "Greek Empire or Death!" (Ἑλληνικὴ αὐτοκρατορία ἢ θάνατος!). Greeks generally took up this slogan during the war. Another captain, Theodoros Grivas, wrote that "the struggle which we have undertaken is great; it is higher than 1821 [the Greek Revolution], inasmuch as we aim at the restoration of the Greek empire." Another former revolutionary warrior published articles in the newspaper *Aion*, an instrument of the pro-Russian party in Athens, calling for a "Greek Empire" as God's will. Some of these articles in *Aion* were addressed to the English state. The Western response was swift. The British and French armies occupied Athens and confiscated or destroyed the printing presses of *Aion* and other papers. King Otto was not deposed at the end of the war, but his pro-Russian stance during it cost him British support, contributing to his overthrow a few years later.[37]

The Greek stance during the war prompted an outburst of anti-Greek editorials in the Western press targeting Greek "Russianism."[38] One of the greatest journalists of the nineteenth century, Karl Marx, wrote a leader editorial in the *New-York Daily Tribune* on "the Greek insurrection" of 1854. The Greeks, he opined, "may even dream of a Byzantine restoration, although, on the whole, they are too astute a people to believe in such a fancy. But these plans of national aggrandizement and independence on the part of the Greeks [are] proclaimed in consequence of Russian intrigues."[39]

The Crimean War, I believe, was a pivotal moment for Western perceptions of the empire. Just as Greek national historians such as Zambelios and Paparrigopoulos began to invest heavily in the narrative of Greek continuity and to cast "the medieval Greek empire" as a phase of Greek history, picking up the thread from *early* nineteenth-century Western historians, in the latter part of the century we see a

37 L. Divani, *Η εδαφική ολοκλήρωση της Ελλάδας, 1830–1947 (Απόπειρα πατριδογνωσίας)* (Athens, 2001), 23, 147–48, 196.

38 Skopetea, *Tό "Πρότυπο βασίλειο,"* 179, 277–78; for Greece and Greeks during the war, see J. V. Kofas, *International and Domestic Politics in Greece during the Crimean War* (New York, 1980), 69, for Grivas's letter; M. N. Todorova, "The Greek Volunteers in the Crimean War," *BalkSt* 25 (1985): 539–63; S. I. Papadopoulos, "Ο προσανατολισμός των Ελλήνων προς τη Ρωσία κατά τον Κριμαϊκό Πόλεμο (1853–1856)," *Βαλκανικά Σύμμεικτα* 3 (1989): 71–82 (79–80 for the *Aion* articles).

39 K. Marx, "The Greek Insurrection," *New-York Daily Tribune*, 29 March 1854.

falling off of references in the West to "the empire of the Greeks" and a rise in the use of "Byzantium" and "the Byzantines" as proper nouns. These choices, which we currently inhabit, were just as political as the one made in the ninth century to call the eastern empire "the empire of the Greeks" to begin with. Both were attempts to refuse to see it for it was and label it in ways that accommodated Western political ideologies. The change from "empire of the Greeks" to "Byzantium" was gradual but was basically complete by the beginning of the twentieth century. Given that the earlier term and its paradigm had dominated Western perceptions for over a thousand years, the change was actually remarkably swift.

There was only one place where the change did not happen until much later in the twentieth century, and even then incompletely: that place was (as you might guess) Greece. During and after the Crimean War, the idea of "the empire of the Greeks" took off in Greece itself, where professional and amateur historians alike made it the organizing rubric for medieval Greek history.[40] And the idea of restoring some kind of Greek empire that included Constantinople did not die until 1922, with the complete failure of the Asia Minor campaign and the ensuing population exchange. The idea also had supporters among Romantic philhellenic historians in the West, such as Ferdinand Gregorovius, who wrote the history of medieval Athens and fantasized about the cross flying again over Hagia Sophia.[41] For their part, Russian thinkers and planners promoted their own ideas of an Orthodox empire in Constantinople—under Russian protection or direct control, of course—even if this idea did not shape the actual policy of tsars. This cut across Russian political lines. Right before the Crimean War, the socialist and anti-tsarist Alexander Herzen (1812–1870) was in favor of reviving Catherine's Greek project. Months before the Russo-Turkish War of 1877–78, Fyodor Dostoyevsky (1821–1881) "justified Russia's right to take possession of Constantinople 'as the leader, protector, and guardian of Orthodox Christianity'"; so too argued the Pan-Slavist theorists Nikolai Danilevsky (1822–1885) and Konstantin Leontiev (1831–1891), the latter a conservative tsarist.[42] After the Crimean War, Russia largely turned away from Greece, which it increasingly regarded as a Western client, and cultivated Slavic proxies in the Balkans under the rubric of Pan-Slavism. But interest in Constantinople did not just die out. Just as Catherine the Great had issued medallions featuring Hagia Sophia, so during the Crimean War a wealthy Greek of Odessa, Grigorios Maraslis, gave money to the tsar

40 There are many surveys: see D. Christodoulou, "Byzantium in Nineteenth-Century Greek Historiography," in Stephenson, *The Byzantine World* (n. 12 above), 445–61.

41 P. Stephenson, "Pioneers of Popular Byzantine History: Freeman, Gergorovius, Schlumberger," in idem, *The Byzantine World*, 462–80, at 469.

42 See Vovchenko, *Containing Balkan Nationalism*, 68–69, 1, 131–32, 187–88, respectively; for Russian planners (in 1912), 290.

to repair Hagia Sophia when the city fell into Russian hands, and in World War I a Russian officer of Greek descent was assigned the task of placing a cross on Hagia Sophia if the Russians succeeded then.[43]

All this made the idea of "the Greek empire of Constantinople" increasingly more toxic in the West. To be sure, the change was not abrupt, especially among writers educated during the first half of the century. In Lady Hornby's *Constantinople during the Crimean War* (published in London in 1863), the Byzantine Empire is throughout called "the Greek empire" and associated with the Greek race, while the term "Byzantium" is rare (six occurrences in 1,200 pages) and used only for the capital. This is unreconstructed usage: no one would employ that language today. The transition to Byzantium was slow and occurred in the titles of books before their actual contents changed. In the Francophone tradition, for instance, we have Alfred Rambaud's 1870 *L'Empire grec au Xe siècle*. But the historian whom he inspired in the next generation, Gustave Schlumberger (1844–1929), another philhellene, always called the empire *Byzance* and *byzantine* in the titles of his books and other projects, even though inside he freely referred to the Byzantines and their empire as Greek. In the first volume of his "epic history" of Byzantium (*L'épopée byzantine*, 1890), he calls them Greek about twice as often as he calls them Byzantine; but by the third volume (1905), the frequency of the two is about equal. And when he wrote up his memoirs, mostly during World War I and in the 1920s, he referred back to his publications on Byzantium using that word exclusively for the empire, never the term *Greek*—except once, for an emperor of the thirteenth century.[44] Something fundamental had shifted during his career, though he never explained it in print.

43 Russian interest in Hagia Sophia: O. Figes, *The Crimean War: A History* (New York, 2010), 23–27; under Catherine: see above and A. Cutler, "Recovering St. Sophia: Cameron, Catherine II, and the Idea of Constantinople in Late Eighteenth-Century Russia," in *An Architectural Progress in the Renaissance and Baroque*, ed. H. A. Millon and S. S. Munshower, 2 vols. (University Park, PA, 1992), 2:888–909; in World War I: L. Gerd, "Russian Imperial Policy in the Orthodox East and Its Relation to Byzantine Studies," in *Imagining Byzantium: Perceptions, Patterns, Problems*, ed. A. Alshanskaya, A. Gietzen, and C. Hadjiafxenti (Mainz, 2018), 93–100, at 97–98; Maraslis: G. Kordatos, *Ἱστορία τῆς νεώτερης Ἑλλάδος*, vol. 3 (Athens, 1957), 601; Russian officer in World War I: P. Sarris, *Byzantium: A Very Short Introduction* (Oxford, 2015), 127. I am grateful to Jake Ransohoff for helping me track down the last two references. For rival claims to Constantinople and Hagia Sophia during World War I, see P. Mansel, *Constantinople: City of the World's Desire, 1453–1924* (New York, 1995), 373–74, 382–84.

44 G. Schlumberger, *Mes souvenirs, 1844–1928*, 2 vols. (Paris, 1934), 1:174–76, 263–73; 2:91, 96–97 (the exception for John III Vatatzes). At the conference from which this volume originated, Joel Kalvesmaki kindly showed me how to generate graphs via Google that indeed document the steep decline in references to the "empire of the Greeks" and "Greek empire" during the second half of the nineteenth century and the simultaneous steep rise of "Byzantine" and "the Byzantines." I played around with this online system, which showed similar graphs for all the main languages of

A scholarly field was gradually institutionalizing itself around that name (*Byzanz, Byzance*) and shying away from the ethnic Greek label. This was a quiet revolution, tacitly accomplished, but it becomes visible with striking clarity if we compare Western usage before 1851 to what had become the established norm by the early twentieth century. The shift surely had a number of causes. What makes it harder to explain is that nonhagiographic research on the origins of the academic discipline of Byzantine studies in the second half of the nineteenth century remains rudimentary.[45] In part, the increased prominence of the term Byzantium was due to the need to establish clear disciplinary boundaries between scholarship on the ancient Greeks and on the medieval eastern empire. But the imperial politics of the Great Powers of the nineteenth century and their anxieties formed the ideological matrix for these decisions.

At Munich, holding what was effectively the first academic chair in Byzantine studies, Karl Krumbacher (1856–1909) founded *Byzantinische Zeitschrift* in 1892. The foreword to the first volume, where he explains the journal's rationale, is revealing. His goal is to prove that Byzantine studies is (or should be) a coherent, autonomous, and self-standing discipline. Nowhere does he refer to the empire and its inhabitants as Greeks, but always as Byzantium, the Byzantines, and so on. He uses "Greek" only for the language of Byzantine literature and its church. He acknowledges that his subjects called themselves not Byzantines but Romans, yet he justifies the former term by saying that it is conventional in all modern languages and, surprisingly, that there is no alternative (p. 12). This was not true, as there were prominent scholars at that very time, such as J. B. Bury, who thought that the made-up term "Byzantium" was a bad name for what was in fact the Roman Empire.[46] Krumbacher does not explain, moreover, why he excluded the ethnic label "Greek" or the more conventional, indeed traditional, term "empire of the Greeks." He addresses the issue only obliquely, by saying that a deep study of the history of Byzantium is necessary if the modern Greeks are to understand their medieval history (p. 7)—but even that statement is evasive and noncommittal, for he says the same about all of Byzantium's "successors." In fact, on the very first page of the foreword he claims that modern Greece would be a less suitable place for the publication of this journal than is "Europe" (his quotation marks). Indeed,

research. As I am not an expert in the appropriate use of this technology, I leave this methodology to others.

45 See, e.g., H.-G. Beck, "Die byzantinischen Studien in Deutschland vor Karl Krumbacher," in *ΧΑΛΙΚΕΣ: Festgabe für die Teilnehmer am XI. Internationalen Byzantinistenkongress, München 15.–20. September 1958* (Freising, 1958), 67–119.

46 J. B. Bury, *A History of the Later Roman Empire from Arcadius to Irene*, 2 vols. (New York, 1889), 1:v–viii.

> The Orthodox East is a world of its own, a peculiar, half-educated, half-savage state and ethnic tangle situated between civilized Europe and barbarian Asia. This multifarious whirl of cultures, which in the past formed the protective wall of Europe against Asian barbarism, and which seems to be called for the future to serve as a cultural bridge from Europe to Asia, has been little noticed and widely ignored up to the present time.[47] (p. 2)

We need to know more about Krumbacher's politics, especially vis-à-vis Russia and the Eastern Question (for example, German liberals and socialists tended to be more Russophobic). Looking beyond Krumbacher, it would also be nice to find a smoking gun, someone on record as saying that the term "empire of the Greeks" was too politically compromised given the current state of the world, and that the neutral term "Byzantium" would be preferable. But rarely are explicit explanations of these kinds of tectonic shifts left conveniently lying around. One year before issuing the first volume of the *Byzantinische Zeitschrift*, Krumbacher published his pioneering *Geschichte der byzantinischen Litteratur* (*History of Byzantine Literature*). The choice of title is significant, for the one area where one could use the term Greek without problem or ambiguity was for the language and literature of the "Byzantines," as he himself used it in the foreword to the first issue of *Byzantinische Zeitschrift*. Indeed, the chair to which Krumbacher was appointed in 1892 was called a professorship "für mittel- und neugriechische Litteratur." But in Krumbacher's hands, *Byzantine* was edging out *Greek* as a category even for the study of literature.

The transformation had thus come full circle. Whereas in early modern usage *Byzantine* was the adjective that corresponded to the "empire of the Greeks" and *Greek* was the proper noun and "essence" of that civilization, by Krumbacher's time the relationship was entirely inverted: Byzantium had become the proper noun and the "essence" of the civilization, whereas Greek was only the adjective that characterized its language. We have reached the threshold of modern Byzantine studies, the air that we ourselves breathe. By this point, the early twenty-first century, we are so oblivious as to how we got here that we can project the invention of the "Byzantine" paradigm back to the sixteenth century and to Wolf (stealing it, in the process, from the Athenian Laonikos Chalkokondyles).

However, the road that brought us here took some interesting detours along the way, and it is interesting to consider alternative paths that were proposed but not

47 "Der orthodoxe Osten bildet eine Welt für sich, die als ein eigenartiger, halb gebildeter, halb wilder Staaten- und Völkerkomplex zwischen dem civilisierten Europa und dem barbarischen Asien liegt. Dieses vielgestaltige Völkergewirr, das in der Vergangenheit die Schutzmauer Europas gegen die asiatische Barbarei bildete und für die Zukunft berufen scheint als Kulturbrücke von Europa nach Asien zu dienen, ist bis auf die neueste Zeit wenig beachtet und viel verkannt worden."

taken by the field at large. The English historian E. A. Freeman (1823–1892) periodically turned his attention to Byzantine history. In 1879 he published a revised version of his paper on the topic, where he had dismissed the category of the "Greek empire" and advocated the rubric "Byzantine empire." Freeman had strong opinions on the Eastern Question, and by the third page of this essay he was already referring to the negative impact of the Crimean War on perceptions of Byzantium in the West. And yet the politics behind Freeman's choices were not at all what we might expect from just those facts (i.e., Graecophobia stemming from Russophobia). He lobbied for the freedom of the Balkan nations from Ottoman oppression and was knighted by Greece in 1875. He argued against the idea of the "Greek empire" because he saw correctly, based on the sources, that it was really *Roman*. In his mind, *Byzantine* was just a convenient way of saying *eastern Roman*; the empire only really became *Greek* for him after 1204, though even after that it remained Roman in important ways.[48] Freeman honestly believed that the Byzantium paradigm could be a vehicle for rehabilitating its Romanness, though in practice, we now know, it turned out to be only yet another mechanism for denying that Romanness.

Freeman was not making purely verbal concessions, of the kind routinely found in the pages of modern *Byzantinistik*, where scholars (such as Krumbacher) reluctantly admit that the Byzantines called themselves Romans but also make it clear that we will not be calling them that and that no effort will be made to document, explain, or understand why they called themselves that. Unlike subsequent Byzantinists, Freeman did not shirk the historian's duty to explain his labels in substantive terms. Accordingly, he explicated as well as he could why and how he believed the Byzantine Empire to be fundamentally Roman. He did not use "Byzantine" to *evade* this question, as we do.

By the end of the nineteenth century the Byzantine label had largely displaced the Greek one. The West had stripped the eastern empire of its Romanness already during the medieval period, and "Byzantium" now stripped it of any claim to ethnicity as well—even its alleged "Greek" ethnicity. Thus, with Romanness forbidden, and with Hellenism confined to various aspects of language and literary culture, the historians of the twentieth century had to fill the hollow shell of "Byzantium" with the only element left: Orthodoxy.

I hope to have shown how the specific political and intellectual currents of the nineteenth century catalyzed scholarship on Byzantium, and in this case even reshaped the basic categories that enabled the professional discipline of Byzantine

48 E. A. Freeman, *Historical Essays* (London, 1879), 231–78, esp. 232–33, 244–46. For his politics, see Stephenson, "Pioneers of Popular Byzantine History," 463–66.

studies to emerge.[49] The Crimean War had a profound—and unrecognized—impact by forging a new distinction between "Byzantine/Byzantium" and "Greek/Greece," in a context in which the "empire of the Greeks" had become a politically toxic concept to the Great Powers of Europe. In response, European intellectuals increasingly began to lean on the conceptually adjacent and neutral term *Byzantium,* in order to create a semantic bulwark between the acceptable national aspirations of the new Greek state, on the one hand, and its dangerous imperial fantasies and its (perceived) Russian patrons, on the other. This tactic effectively situated the dominant narrative of Byzantine studies at an ever further remove from what we find in the Byzantine sources.

Modern scholars prefer to see Byzantium as an autonomous civilization with its own distinctive culture, institutions, and identity, separate from the ancient Greek and Roman past and the modern Greek present. But this intellectual project, tied to the formation of a professional discipline, has an untold political and ideological history: it is deeply implicated in the specific circumstances of the Great Power politics of the mid- and late nineteenth century. The empire had already been relabeled once in medieval times (from Roman to Greek). What was new about the rebranding of the nineteenth century was that it did not connect Byzantium to any other historical genealogy or preexisting civilizational categories, but rather cordoned its subject off from what came both before and after. This walling off allowed for the rise of Byzantine studies in a wider sense as a separate discipline.

49 My conclusion draws on comments sent to me by the volume's editors, which nicely tied the contribution of the present chapter to the overall themes of the volume.

CONCLUSION

BYZANCE AVANT BYZANCE

Toward a New History of Byzantine Scholarship

NATHANAEL ASCHENBRENNER AND JAKE RANSOHOFF

THIS VOLUME HAS AIMED AT SEVERAL TARGETS. FIRST, IT HAS ATTEMPTED TO diagnose and discard some problematic aspects of current histories of Byzantine scholarship, especially regarding the "invention of Byzantium" from which we drew our title. Some scholars continue to steadfastly maintain that "Byzantium" emerged only with the institutionalization of the discipline in the second half of the nineteenth century; indeed, it is hard to imagine that anyone would deny the profundity of the changes—institutional, administrative, conceptual—that occurred in those generative decades, when titans like Diehl and Krumbacher, Vasil'evskij and Uspenskij held the field. But we need not strain our eyes to see how much these figures (not unlike the fifteenth-century humanists before them) depended on the labors of their predecessors, whether they acknowledged it or not. Texts had been discovered, edited (if often only too poorly), and translated; lexica had been compiled; coins had been collected, monumental architecture described, genealogies excavated. To invert the famous phrase of Nicolae Iorga, there was a *Byzance avant Byzance*—one that still lingers in the shadows.

Against this institutionalizing frame, others take a purely lexical approach and attribute the "invention of Byzantium" to the "first" emergence of the phrase *Byzantinae Historiae* in the title to Hieronymus Wolf's 1562 edition of Gregoras and Chalkokondyles—or attribute it more generally to the sixteenth-century humanists. Asaph Ben-Tov and, in this volume, Anthony Kaldellis have together refuted this spurious origin for the term and, by extension, the discipline. The term appears to have been neither Wolf's nor all that much of an innovation. Latinate writers had been calling Constantinople *Byzantium*—at least in part a conscious archaism—for centuries. And as Kaldellis notes, we should be dubious about what was implied conceptually by this cryptic genitive adjective, *byzantinae*.[1]

Thus we have argued that it is not accurate to say that "Byzantium" was an invention chiefly of the nineteenth century, nor of the sixteenth. Instead, this volume has illustrated how the concept of Byzantium—its temporality, bounds, emphases, coherence—was subject to constant interpretation and negotiation as scholars tried to find suitable frames in which to understand the empire's long and turbulent history. This process began even before the empire's political termination in 1453, as Fabio Pagani demonstrates. Examining a cadre of early fifteenth-century intellectuals around George Gemistos Pletho (ca. 1355–1452), Pagani shows that the visions of the empire's historical and moral significance were even here in tension, as Pletho in particular went to great lengths to lionize the Greek and diminish the Roman origins of late Byzantine society.[2] And as Anthony Kaldellis demonstrates, these reconfigurations of the Byzantine world continued up to the eve of the formation of the scholarly discipline in the nineteenth century, as new semantics for the empire's history took shape in the political jostling of the Great Powers after the end of the Crimean War.[3] Taken together, the volume's thirteen chapters encourage us to approach the story of Byzantium's emergence in a new way: as a continuous process of invention, distortion, reconfiguration, and negotiation over the course of nearly five centuries, as "inventions" of Byzantium that always occurred in close contact with the contemporary political and religious concerns of the day.

We hope, if nothing else, that we have permanently interred the reductive historiographies anatomized in the introduction, in which the snobbish disregard of humanists gave way to the brief flurry of Baroque *byzantinisme* before being subsumed in the torrent of Enlightenment vitriol. As the articles in the volume illustrate, the attitudes associated with each of these periods—disdain, enthusiasm, vituperation—did not succeed one another but were in constant, clamorous conflict. We have aimed not only to disassemble and discard the old armature but also to propose an alternate one in its stead, a provisional new history of Byzantine scholarship that emphasizes three key points: (1) the discipline's deep roots in genres of scholarship as diverse as historiography, classical philology, lexicography, drama, palaeography, and artistic representation; (2) the constant contemporary relevance of scholarly engagement with texts, objects, and ideas we would now classify as "Byzantine"; and (3) the enduring struggle between advocates and critics over the

1 See Chapter 13 in this volume by Anthony Kaldellis, pp. 349–67, esp. 353–56.

2 See Chapter 1 in this volume by Fabio Pagani, pp. 27–45.

3 Kaldellis in Chapter 13, pp. 357–67.

legacy of the Byzantine world. This contest over the significance and import of the Byzantine past—whether it was an annex of Greek, Roman, or Christian history, for instance—did not retard the progress of scholarship; on the contrary, these struggles kept research into the Byzantine Middle Ages receptive to new applications, a key to its enduring vitality. Through this project, we hope to have provided a new narrative (if only to galvanize critique and correction), to have both deepened our understanding of figures like Wolf and Du Cange and expanded the canon of formative early modern "Byzantinists" beyond them, and to have opened new vistas for research in this field.

1400–1550: Preliminary Encounters

Many early humanists brought a classical philologist's disdain to texts from the Byzantine world. Much of this affect no doubt reenacted cultural scripts of the ancient world, in which the Greeks—even preeminent philosophers, poets, and dramatists—were less virile, less upright, less virtuous than the Romans. Dante's encounter with the Greek heroes Odysseus and Diomedes deep within his *Inferno* condemned these warriors for their crimes of perfidy, echoing Vergil's famous suspicion of "Greeks bearing gifts."[4] Not only language but politics and religion refracted the humanist gaze toward the Byzantine East. Flavio Biondo (1392–1463), while arguing for a crusade against the Ottomans, denounced the eastern emperor Alexios I Komnenos (r. 1081–1118) as a "semi-infidel," while others viewed the impending Ottoman conquest of Constantinople as just retribution for centuries of schismatic contumacy or the degradation of the once imposing edifice of Hellenic knowledge and literature.[5] These episodes testify to the early contempt among humanists, but also among intellectuals of all commitments, at the end of the Middle Ages.

But this stark picture becomes more nuanced when situated within its intellectual context. First, the sense that the Byzantine Empire had declined politically and culturally was hardly a view held only by Western elites. Many Byzantine intellectuals shared these sentiments, mourning the diminution of their territory

4 See Dante's encounter with Ulysses and Diomedes in his *Inferno* 26.55–63, in *La Commedia secondo l'antica vulgata*, ed. G. Petrocchi, 4 vols. (Milan, 1966), 2:442–43, and its emphasis on the "craft" or "cunning" for which they wept: "Piangevisi entro l'arte per che, morta, / Deïdamìa ancor si duol d'Achille" (lines 61–62). See also Vergil's infamous condemnation at *Aeneid* 2.49: "Timeo Danaos et dona ferentes."

5 See Flavio Biondo, *Oratio coram serenissimo imperatore Frederico et Alphonso*, in *Scritti inediti e rari di Biondi Flavio*, ed. B. Nogara (Rome, 1927), 112.28; a useful account of other humanist attitudes toward the Ottoman conquest of Constantinople can be found in J. Hankins, "Renaissance Crusaders: Humanist Crusade Literature in the Age of Mehmed II," *DOP* 49 (1995): 111–207, esp. 131–35.

and the decline of literary accomplishment. Yet they also disagreed about what to make of this decline. Some of those clustered around the idiosyncratic philosopher Gemistos Pletho saw the state's decline as a manifestation of the Platonic principle of inexorable corruption.[6] Most others continued to see the empire as the Roman state, whether suffering under the lash of God's fury or being purified for a return to political preeminence. Gennadios Scholarios (ca. 1400–1473), patriarch of Constantinople under Sultan Mehmed II, glumly reckoned the chronology of creation and concluded that the end of the Roman (i.e., Byzantine) Empire would coincide with the end of the world.[7] Meditating on and moralizing the political, cultural, and literary decline of the empire, then, was not an exercise only for those with the privilege to observe the empire's peril from afar.

Nor was contempt the only affect adopted by Western observers. As Anthony Grafton shows, religious reformers like Johann Lange (1487–1548) and Philipp Melanchthon (1497–1560) turned to Byzantine ecclesiastical historians to recover the lost traditions of the early church. Historians like Leonardo Bruni (1370–1444) and Flavio Biondo reconstructed the origins of their own nations using materials on "barbarian" peoples found in Procopius, among others. Humanist historians like Johannes Cuspinian (1473–1529) and Battista Egnazio (1478–1553), who both wrote ecumenical histories of the Roman emperors from Julius Caesar to Maximilian I (albeit with sharp differences in nuance and sophistication), utilized Byzantine historians little known to Latin readers to supplement their accounts of the eastern empire. And all these scholars relied on Byzantine texts for precise, practical information about Western Christendom's great nemesis: the Ottoman Empire.[8]

Moreover, if many humanists approached Byzantine literature and language not as an independent offshoot of later Greek but rather as the downward slope of a long arc that stretched back—unbroken—to Homer and Herodotus, this very lack of "separateness" could prove generative. As an integral part of the Greek tradition, Byzantine texts, in the minds of humanists, both deserved and rewarded close attention. Scholars eagerly studied historians such as Zonaras and Xanthopoulos in hopes of shedding light backward on classical and late antiquity,[9] while, in a process examined by John Considine, lexicographers scoured Greek dictionaries of the postclassical world, from Hesychius to the tenth-century *Suda*, for unfamiliar words to swell

6 Pagani in Chapter 1, pp. 27–45.

7 George Scholarios, *Chronographia* 4:504–12, at 510.3–4, in *Oeuvres complètes de George Scholarios*, ed. L. Petit, X. A. Siderides, and M. Jugie, 8 vols. (Paris, 1928–36).

8 See Anthony Grafton in Chapter 3 of this volume, pp. 71–104.

9 Grafton in Chapter 3, pp. 71–104, esp. 83–89.

their bourgeoning lexica.[10] Such efforts may not, in the fifteenth and early sixteenth centuries, have been directed toward understanding "Byzantium" as a historical entity in its own right. But the meticulous labor of these scholars in resolving old problems and posing new ones informed the work of future generations.

Nor was "Greek" the only frame available to humanists of the fifteenth and sixteenth centuries. True, lexicographers located Byzantium within the Hellenic tradition; but travelers and antiquarians such as Cyriac of Ancona (1391–1452), dazzled by the monuments of Constantinople, were more liable to remember the city's identity as "New Rome."[11] In part, this willingness to recognize Byzantine "Romanness" was a consequence of the profound reconfigurations that followed the Ottoman destruction of the empire. In the wake of 1453, some artists and orators tacitly cast off the medieval conventions that had contemptuously derided the empire as "Greek" in favor of more pregnant associations with the Roman Empire. As Elena Boeck shows, Andrea Mantegna (ca. 1431–1506) drew on antiquarian scholarship to integrate one of Constantinople's most recognizable monuments—Justinian's column—into his tableau of Roman imperial splendor.[12] Meanwhile, in crusade oratory, figures like Enea Silvio Piccolomini (1405–1464) sought new frames for viewing the empire's significance by lamenting it as the *imperium orientale*, the eastern empire of late antiquity.[13] As for so much in the fifteenth and sixteenth centuries, the Ottomans served as a catalyst for reimagining the historical, didactic, and moral role of Byzantium. Of course, not all agreed that the empire, in retrospect, had been Roman. Gemistos Pletho had cast the threatening Ottomans as descendants of Alexander the Great's vanquished enemies, the Parapamisadai, to strengthen his argument for the state's Hellenic essence.[14] But the very plasticity of the Byzantine past in the hands of these scholars shows more ambivalence and uncertainty about the empire's significance than was evident during the Middle Ages.

Early humanist engagement with the Byzantine world, then, was characterized by much more than despair over the perceived decline of postclassical Greek

10 See John Considine in Chapter 8 of this volume, pp. 225–48.

11 See Elena Boeck in Chapter 2 of this volume, pp. 47–68, esp. 48–59.

12 Boeck in Chapter 2, pp. 59–68.

13 See, e.g., Enea Silvio Piccolomini's oration *Quamvis omnibus*, to the assembly at the imperial diet in Regensburg in May 1454, edited most recently in *Deutsche Reichstagsakten: Ältere Reihe*, vol. 19/1, *Deutsche Reichstagsakten unter Kaiser Friedrich III, Fünfte Abteilung: 1453–1454*, ed. H. Weigel and H. Grüneisen (Göttingen, 1969), 1:265–70 (no. 34), esp. at 266. On Piccolomini's concept of *imperium orientale*, see further N. Aschenbrenner, "Reframing Empire: Byzantium and the Transformation of European Identity, c. 1400–1520" (PhD diss., Harvard University, 2019), 176–228, esp. 208–10 for the Regensburg oration.

14 Pagani in Chapter 1, pp. 34–36.

literature. Rather, scholars of law and history, lexicography and philosophy, and even antiquarians and artists, recognized the Byzantine past as a world full of narratives, exemplary characters, and symbols useful for the dilemmas of early modern Europe. Where the Western Middle Ages had largely settled into a comfortable contempt for the Byzantine Empire, early humanist encounters with Byzantium—especially after the fall of Constantinople—show a reevaluation of those paradigms and a willingness to explore alternative inventions of Byzantium.

1550–1700: Canonizing and Synthesizing

The appearance, between 1557 and 1562, of Hieronymus Wolf's editions and Latin translations of Byzantine historians—Zonaras, Choniates, and Gregoras (the last published with a revision of Conrad Clauser's translation of Laonikos Chalkokondyles)—has often been cited as the origin of Byzantine studies. As detailed above, such a view is too reductive in identifying this moment as the discipline's genesis; it also attributes too much agency to Wolf himself, who was a scholar fulfilling a task for his patrons.[15] Yet it remains true that the publications of these volumes marked an inflection point in the study of the Byzantine Middle Ages. Above all, they made the rudiments of Byzantine history and chronology available to a much wider readership: not only to scholars who knew no Greek but also to those who had little or no access to Byzantine sources in manuscript. In the fifteenth and early sixteenth centuries, the relative paucity of printed editions especially privileged scholars residing or working in Italy, whose libraries abounded in postclassical Greek manuscripts. To be sure, Italy's status as treasure-house of Greek manuscripts persisted even after the multiplication of printed editions. In the seventeenth century, the rich harvest of Byzantine synaxaries and menologia reaped from Italian libraries by Godfrey Henschen and Daniel Papebroch during their travels (1660–62) expanded the horizons of the *Acta Sanctorum*.[16] Even at the dawn of the eighteenth century, Bernard de Montfaucon spent three years in Italy (1698–1701) hunting for manuscripts of the Greek fathers.[17] Nonetheless, Wolf's editions and translations placed a "complete and perfect corpus of Byzantine history" within reach of scholars across Europe for the first time, and his labors sparked a new burst of interest in editing and publishing other Byzantine texts.[18]

15 See the Introduction to this volume, pp. 1–23, esp. 4–5, 8–12.

16 See Xavier Lequeux in Chapter 11 of this volume, pp. 305–20, esp. 314–15.

17 See Shane Bobrycki in Chapter 10 of this volume, pp. 279–303, esp. 279–80, 285, 288–89.

18 See, for Wolf's formulation "complete and perfect corpus," Grafton in Chapter 3, p. 79.

The centers of these editorial and scholarly efforts varied over the next several generations. Within the Holy Roman Empire, Wilhelm Xylander (1532–1576) and David Hoeschel (1556–1617) published important editions of George Kedrenos's universal history, Photios's *Bibliotheca*, Constantine VII's *De legationibus*, and Anna Komnene's *Alexiad*. Protestant Leiden soon followed Germany as a second home for enterprising scholars recovering postclassical Greek texts. Here Joseph Scaliger (1540–1609), Bonaventura Vulcanius (1538–1614), Johannes Meursius (1579–1639), and Franciscus Junius (1545–1602), among others, published and revised editions of Byzantine authors from Agathias to Pseudo-Kodinos, and used the fruits of their investigations to compile lexica, revise ancient chronology, and compose literary histories.

Yet Byzantium was hardly the preserve of Protestants alone. Caesar Baronius's (1538–1607) twelve-volume *Annales Ecclesiastici*, the great trumpet blast of Counter-Reformation historiography, made frequent use of printed Byzantine histories, and the wide circulation of his work brought Byzantium to the attention of playwrights like the Jesuit Joseph Simons (1593–1671), who—as Przemysław Marciniak notes—plucked choice stories from Baronius's account for his own entertaining and edifying Byzantine-themed moral plays.[19] Elsewhere, Jesuit imperatives fueled projects that aided not the cultivation of morality but rather the reconstruction of late antique and medieval Christianity. In Antwerp the Jesuit Jean Bolland (1596–1665) adapted Héribert Rosweyde's ambitious plan to publish a new corpus of hagiography to incorporate Byzantine saints as well, as Xavier Lequeux recounts.[20] Meanwhile, scholars like Jakob Gretser (1562–1625) and his colleagues in Ingolstadt steeped themselves in the sources of Orthodox Christianity to defend the validity of Catholic theology and practice. And the Benedictine Congregation of Saint Maur in Paris embarked on editions of patristic authors like Athanasius of Alexandria and John Chrysostom. In the course of these researches, Bernard de Montfaucon brought unparalleled sophistication to the study and dating of Greek script, as Shane Bobrycki illustrates, though Montfaucon resisted the formation of Byzantium as a category in his own work.[21]

As the reforming impulse led to the recovery and publication of Byzantine hagiography, so political ambitions fueled the development of a new corpus of Byzantine historiography. In the heady atmosphere of Bourbon France, the first advances beyond Wolf's attempts at a comprehensive corpus appeared under the auspices of the French royal court. The resulting *Corpus Parisinum* (sometimes known as the *Byzantine du Louvre* or Louvre Corpus) spoke, as Agostino Pertusi showed, to the

19 See Przemysław Marciniak in Chapter 7 of this volume, pp. 205–21, esp. 207–11.

20 Lequeux in Chapter 11, pp. 305–17.

21 Bobrycki in Chapter 10, pp. 279–303.

imperial ambitions of Louis XIV and the glorification of French monarchy.[22] First Charles Annibal Fabrot (1580–1659) and later the Jesuit Philippe Labbe (1607–1667) presided over a flurry of new editions of Byzantine histories under the imprimatur of the Royal Press.[23] Though Labbe may not have directed the enterprise from its inception, he gave it a new vision, a plan of thirty-two volumes to be published collaboratively over more than sixty years. Labbe's project eventually attracted the talents of Byzantium's most brilliant early modern scholar, Charles Du Cange (1610–1688). As Teresa Shawcross details, Du Cange had long been captivated by the Crusades, which—given the continued menace of the Ottomans—remained an urgent concern in the second half of the seventeenth century. But while crusading interests introduced Du Cange to Byzantium, it was the circumstances of patronage that made him a "Byzantinist." Rebuffed in his attempts to elicit royal sponsorship for a series of sources on medieval France, Du Cange instead transitioned to Byzantine texts, and publications on Byzantium occupied his final decades: new editions of Zonaras, John Kinnamos, and the *Chronicon Paschale* for the Louvre Corpus; treatises on genealogy, topography, and numismatics, published under the title *Historia Byzantina*; and his magisterial *Glossarium ad scriptores mediae et infimae Graecitatis*.[24]

French royal patronage extended beyond the editing of Byzantine texts to the collection and study of Byzantine monuments, coins, and inscriptions. Travel to the Ottoman world had always generated results of consequence for Byzantine studies in the West; Wolf's corpus relied in part on manuscripts brought to Augsburg from Constantinople by the adventurer and sometime Fugger agent Hans Dernschwam (1494–1568/69).[25] But just as wider access to Byzantine texts stoked demand for new, specialized lexica and spurred the creation of a more comprehensive collection of literary sources, so wider access to nonliterary evidence—by way of engravings, travel accounts, and numismatic cabinets—fostered new technical resources for the study of Byzantine material culture. Louis XIV's minister Jean-Baptiste Colbert—the impresario of the *Byzantine du Louvre*—also commissioned scholars such as Johann Michael Vansleb (1635–1679), Jacob Spon (1647–1685), and Jean Foy-Vaillant (1632–1706) to travel east, with instructions to acquire antiquities for the Royal Library and to make systematic copies of inscriptions encountered in their

22 A. Pertusi, *Storiografia umanistica e mondo bizantino*, Istituto siciliano di studi bizantini e neoellenici, quaderni 5 (Palermo, 1967), 86–87.

23 See Teresa Shawcross in Chapter 5 of this volume, pp. 156–59.

24 Shawcross in Chapter 5, pp. 143–80.

25 Grafton in Chapter 3, p. 76; further D. R. Reinsch, "Hieronymus Wolf as Editor and Translator of Byzantine Texts," in *The Reception of Byzantium in European Culture since 1500*, ed. P. Marciniak and D. C. Smythe (New York, 2016), 43–53, at 47.

journeys.[26] All three of these travelers visited Constantinople, and the coins, transcriptions, drawings, and testimonies they brought back to France helped propel a new class of studies dedicated to the antiquities of the Byzantine world. Du Cange, for one, mined Spon's *Voyage d'Italie, de Dalmatie, de Grèce et du Levant* (1678) for his extensive treatise on the monuments of Christian Constantinople. Later, Anselmo Banduri (1671/75–1743) leveraged the newly augmented numismatic collection of the Royal Library for his study of "Roman" imperial coinage from the third century to 1453.[27] The seventeenth and early eighteenth centuries thus witnessed the first stirrings of what might be called a kind of "Byzantine" antiquarianism—even if, as was also true of literary evidence, its early practitioners did not always share a common terminology, or agree on the identity and chronological bounds of their subject.

Examining the locus of scholarship in this age reveals one of its distinctive developments. Where previously scholars had worked alone or for individual patrons, from the late sixteenth century onward scholarly encounters with Byzantium increasingly obtained diverse institutional support. In Jesuit colleges, university towns, royal libraries, and learned chapters of religious orders, scholars found financial security and material resources conducive to their Byzantine research. They also found collaborators—Gretser and Pontanus in Ingolstadt, Vulcanius and Meursius in Leiden, Fabrot and Labbe in Paris, Bolland and Papebroch in Antwerp. As a result, these places became something like the first research centers, where like-minded colleagues worked on separate but related aspects of the late ancient and medieval world in a supportive environment.

But this was not only an age in which the production of editions, translations, and antiquarian treatises accelerated. The explosion of available Byzantine materials offered scholars new fields to explore and also new puzzles—lexical, terminological, genealogical—to solve. Grafton reveals how Joseph Scaliger used the ninth-century chronicle of George Synkellos to reconstruct a "proleptic" chronology that antedated the Creation, exploding conventional accounts of man's origins.[28] Through Richard Calis, we encounter Martin Crusius as a dogged researcher using biobibliography, the incessant cross-reading and referencing within his own substantial library, to resolve thorny questions of chronology.[29] Considine illustrates how the new editions

26 See, in general, the documents in H. Omont, *Missions archéologiques françaises en Orient aux XVIIe et XVIIIe siècles*, 2 vols. (Paris, 1902), 1:1–382. For an introduction to this aspect of Colbert's patronage, see N. Dew, *Orientalism in Louis XIV's France* (Oxford, 2009), 16–40.

27 A. Banduri, *Numismata imperatorum Romanorum a Trajano Decio ad Palaeologos augustos*, 2 vols. (Paris, 1718).

28 Grafton in Chapter 3, pp. 97–100.

29 See Richard Calis in Chapter 4 of this volume, pp. 105–42.

of Byzantine sources—alongside manuscripts, of course—enabled ambitious lexicographical projects that sought to cleave *graecobarbarus* from the more classical attestations, resulting in a class of lexica such as Meursius's *Glossarium graecobarbarum* specially devoted to postclassical Greek.[30] Montfaucon utilized Byzantine materials to pioneer methods for dating Greek documents and manuscripts.[31] Even far from learned congregations in Paris and Leiden, the Silesian schoolmaster Martin Hanke (1633–1709) established a new canon of explicitly Byzantine literature with his treatise *De Byzantinarum rerum scriptoribus Graecis* (1677).[32]

Over the course of the seventeenth century, the resources for Byzantine scholarship began to assume a critical mass: constellations of texts and scholars, increasingly specialized *instrumenta*, handbooks on Byzantine coins and monuments, and the support of courts, universities, and religious orders. These developments were sufficient to enable scholars to begin to engage the various strands of Byzantine civilization, tentatively at first, as separate provinces or subdisciplines of their own—as in the case of language with Meursius and Du Cange, or literature with first Vossius and then Hanke. As publications on the history and material culture of the Byzantine world grew too profuse for the empire to remain a vague annex of late ancient or medieval Christendom, we see the first steps toward the disciplinary autonomy that would be celebrated by modern Byzantinists such as Vasiliev and Ostrogorsky. Even so, the difference vis-à-vis earlier paradigms was one of degree rather than kind. Scholars of the seventeenth century still located Byzantine history, language, and culture within sweeping developmental arcs. Meursius's labors, for instance, reflect both a broad interest in "universal" Greek lexicography and a specific attempt to outline a distinctively postclassical idiom.[33] Similarly, Hanke saw his history of Byzantine literature as part of the *longue durée* of Roman literature.[34] Like many transitions, scholarly approaches to Byzantium reveal subtle shifts in emphasis rather than the abrupt abandonment of one paradigm for another.

Such novel developments existed alongside deep continuities. The prime movers for seventeenth-century Byzantine encounters remained much the same as they had been in the fifteenth and sixteenth centuries: the search for historical exemplars of contemporary relevance, the reconstruction of ancient thought and culture, enduring anxiety over Ottoman ascendance, and religious polemics over the authentic modes of Christian belief and practice. As in the age of preliminary encounters, the

30 Considine in Chapter 8, pp. 225–48, esp. 240–47.

31 Bobrycki in Chapter 10, pp. 294–300.

32 See William North in Chapter 9 of this volume, pp. 249–78.

33 Considine in Chapter 8, pp. 243–47.

34 North in Chapter 9, pp. 253–65.

guises of Byzantium in this period were hardly stable or undisputed. Crusius linked Byzantine and post-Byzantine in a continuum of Greek literature and culture that stretched from Homer to Theodosios Zygomalas (1544–1607),[35] similar to the frame Gerhard Johannes Vossius (1577–1649) used for his compendium of Greek historians. But Martin Hanke wrote his history of Byzantine literature explicitly as an extension of the culture of the Roman Empire, while the Bollandists eventually framed Byzantine hagiography as part of an ecumenical history of Christian sanctity.[36] Montfaucon saw in Byzantine monuments and coinage evidence for the end of the ancient world, at the same time that his younger colleague Banduri framed these materials within a continuous history of Roman imperial power that spanned from Augustus to Constantine XI Palaiologos.[37] And in the context of seventeenth-century politics, Byzantium could serve both to exalt and to critique absolutism. In Bourbon France, the rulers of Constantinople appeared in the imperial genealogy fabricated for Louis XIV,[38] while across the Channel in Restoration England, "secret histories" modeled on Procopius offered new ways to criticize authoritarianism, and popular pamphlets and plays used the story of Andronikos I Komnenos (r. 1183–1185) to dramatize the moral hazards of tyranny.[39] These conceptualizations were not only divergent but in productive discord. It was the very ambiguity of the Byzantine past—its indeterminate connections to Greek antiquity, Roman Empire, and medieval Christianity—as well as its status as a kind of historical orphan, belonging solely to no single group, that made it such a charged and protean field for the pursuit of scholarship.

1700–1850: Fabrication of Consensus, Emergence of Autonomy

The end of the seventeenth century marks another transition in the history of Byzantine scholarship. It also, significantly, marks the cessation of serious Ottoman threat to central Europe. It was perhaps only half in jest that John Monfasani, during the conference at which most of these papers were presented, argued that Prince Eugene of Savoy, commander at the decisive victory of the Holy Roman Empire over the Ottomans at Zenta in 1697, should be considered a major figure in the history of Byzantine studies.[40] It seems evident that the diminishing fear of Ottoman expansion

35 Considine in Chapter 8, pp. 234–38; Calis in Chapter 4, pp. 105–42.

36 North in Chapter 9, pp. 259–65.

37 Bobrycki in Chapter 10, pp. 297–98.

38 Shawcross in Chapter 5, pp. 173–79.

39 Grafton in Chapter 3, pp. 101–3; Marciniak in Chapter 7, pp. 215–16.

40 J. Monfasani, "Byzantium and the End of the Middle Ages," *Mediterranea: International Journal for the Transfer of Knowledge* 4 (2019): 245–53, at 250, 252.

vitiated a chief raison d'être for inquiry into the Byzantine past, inquiries that since the sixteenth century had been framed as a kind of defensive ethnography. Teresa Shawcross's detailed investigation of Du Cange's posthumous reputation offers a stark illustration of this change in relevance. Du Cange's contemporaries such as Banduri lauded him as the *pater* of Byzantine scholarship, but two generations later his great-nephew Jean-Charles du Fresne D'Aubigny reconstructed his archive as the *Nachlass* of a historian of France.[41] Once the Ottoman threat had subsided, Du Cange needed to be recast to retain relevance in eighteenth-century France.

The eighteenth century also gave rise to grand, moralizing narratives that positioned Byzantium in accounts of decline from the glories of the ancient world. As Frederic Clark details, Edward Gibbon (1737–1794) sought to justify his historical labors by emphasizing Byzantium as the "passive center of a new world," an account more global in its breadth than those that had come before.[42] Even so, Gibbon—like the seventeenth-century polyhistors who popularized new tripartite periodizations of the postclassical world—remained bound to what Johannes Fabian called "the politics of time": schemes that established hierarchies for societies based on their cultural, rather than chronological, proximity to the modernity of the present.[43] Another perspective on Gibbon and his contemporaries would be that they exemplify a drift away from the generative discord of previous centuries and toward a hegemonic consensus—both in the widespread acceptance of Byzantium as one of the legatees of the postclassical Roman Empire, and in the view that the empire represented the moral nadir of medieval civilization. Such a drift did not completely immobilize the interpretive horizons of the empire; as Anthony Kaldellis points out, even Gibbon engaged in subtle vacillation by calling the empire's inhabitants "Greeks" when they lost battles and "Romans" when they were victorious.[44] And in the late eighteenth century, when Gibbon's lapidary denunciations of the empire were still freshly etched, voices continued to dispute these interpretations of the empire's moral significance. One anonymous treatise from 1798 on the literature of the late Middle Ages tacitly challenged Gibbon's estimations, noting that several emperors had been "what all sovereigns ought to be, munificent patrons, and what so few sovereigns are, distinguished scholars."[45]

41 See Teresa Shawcross in Chapter 6 of this volume, pp. 181–203.

42 See Frederic Clark in Chapter 12 of this volume, pp. 345–47.

43 Clark in Chapter 12, pp. 323–47. On "the politics of time," see Johannes Fabian, *Time and the Other: How Anthropology Makes Its Object* (New York, 1983).

44 Kaldellis in Chapter 13, p. 356.

45 *An Introduction to the Literary History of the Fourteenth and Fifteenth Centuries* (London, 1798), 44.

Kaldellis has recovered a final "invention" of Byzantium in the Great Power politics of the mid-nineteenth century. In this crucible, "Byzantium" became a politically neutral historical space—one that resisted the irredentist imperial projects of the Greeks and Russians that western European nations deemed dangerous. Instead of a "Greek empire," or indeed a "Roman empire," scholars from western Europe enforced terminological and conceptual consensus around "Byzantium" as an autonomous field—not ancient, nor Western medieval, nor strictly Greek.[46] This final transformation gave us the field much as we know it now, converting it from the loosely related but discordant efforts of the previous centuries, which advanced variously under the banners of classical philology, ecclesiastical history, medieval literature, and the study of Greek culture and history, into "Byzantine studies," a truly autonomous and professional discipline.

The final, recognizable emergence of "Byzantine studies" merits two last observations. Kaldellis's piece provides critical background to what we have suggested became the field's hegemonic narrative of triumph, of emerging institutional maturity. The first is that this moment, undeniably critical in the formation of Byzantine studies as a discipline, is better seen as "professionalization" than "institutionalization." As the contributions to this volume have suggested, and this conclusion has highlighted, Byzantine scholarship by the seventeenth century was already occurring under the auspices of several institutions, including colleges, universities, courts, and religious orders. One decisive change was that the university largely displaced other institutions—though certain religious societies, such as the Bollandists and the Assumptionists, remained active—as the home for continued research. The second point is that from the perspective Kaldellis provides, the developments of the chairs, seminars, journals, monographs, conferences, and *Hilfsmittel* devoted specifically to Byzantine civilization appear as not only the signifiers of disciplinary autonomy but also the palisades that fortified this most recent "invention" of Byzantium. That is, they served to defend this neutral Byzantium against the incursions of rival interpretations. The long history of Byzantine scholarship explored in this volume illustrates that we must view this professionalization as another in a continuous series of inventions and reinventions, a process that is likely not yet complete.

■■■

This brief synthesis has attempted to integrate the wide-ranging contributions of the preceding thirteen chapters into a coherent and revisionist account of the development of Byzantine scholarship in early modern Europe. To hazard a synthesis on such a basis may seem presumptuous, even gratuitous, when the present

46 Kaldellis in Chapter 13, pp. 361–67.

volume makes no pretense to exhaustiveness, and when so much of the landscape of Byzantine scholarship remains so imperfectly known.[47] Yet it is worth the risks if our sketch stimulates others to fill its blank spaces, revise or redraw its contours, and continue to explore the history of Byzantine studies in early modern Europe as an unrelentingly political endeavor: a series of encounters attuned as much to contemporary politics, religion, and culture as to the historical conditions of the medieval world. Such work, we believe, will advance us toward the new history of Byzantine scholarship for which this volume is but a prolegomenon, and this conclusion but a beginning.

47 See the Introduction, pp. 12–13, on areas for further work in the history of Byzantine scholarship, and pp. 21–22, for a discussion of specific omissions in the present volume.

APPENDIX I

WORKS BY DU CANGE PUBLISHED DURING HIS LIFETIME OR IN PRESS AT HIS DEATH

TERESA SHAWCROSS

Histoire de l'empire de Constantinople sovs les emperevrs françois, divisée en deux Parties, dont la premiere contient l'Histoire de la conquéte de la ville de Constantinople par les François & les Venitiens, écrite par Geoffroy de Ville-Hardovin Maréchal de Champagne & de Romanie: Reueuë & corrigée en cette Edition sur le Manuscrit de la Bibliotheque du Roy, & illustrée d'Obseruations Historiques, & d'vn glossaire, pour les termes de l'Auteur, à present hors d'vsage. Avec la Suitte de cette Histoire, iusques en l'an MCCXL. tirée de l'Histoire de France MS. de Philippes Movskes Chanoine & depuis Euesque de Tournay. La seconde contient vne Histoire Generale de ce que les François & les Latins ont fait de plus memorable dans l'empire de Constantinople, depuis qu'ils s'en rendirent maistres, iusques à ce que les Turcs s'en sont emparez: Iustifiée par les ecriuains du temps, & par plusieurs Chroniques, Chartes, & autres Pieces non encore publiées. With a dedication to Louis XIV. Paris: Imprimerie royale, 1657.

Traité historiqve dv chef de S. Iean Baptiste, contenant vne discussion exacte de ce que les auteurs anciens & modernes en ont écrit, & particulierement de ses trois Inuentions. Il y est aussi parlé par occasion des autres Reliques du mesme Saint. Et à la fin sont inserez quelques Traitez Grecs, tirez de la Bibliotheque du Roy, & de celle de M. le Cardinal Mazarin, auec leurs versions latines seruans de fondement & de preuue à toute cette dissertation. With a dedication to François Favre, bishop of Amiens. Paris: Sebastien Cramoisy and Sebastian Mabre-Cramoisy, 1665.

Histoire de S. Lovys IX. dv nom Roy de France, ecrite par Iean Sire de Ioinville Senéchal de Champagne: Enrichie de nouuelles observations & Dissertations Historiques. Avec les Établissemens de S. Lovys, le Conseil de Pierre de Fontaines, & plusieurs autres Pieces concernant ce regne, tirées des Manuscrits. With a dedication to Louis XIV. Paris: Sebastian Marbre-Cramoisy, 1668.

Ἰωάννου Κιννάμου βασιλικοῦ γραμματικοῦ ἱστοριῶν λόγοι ς'. Joannis Cinnami imperatorii grammatici historiarum libri sex, sev de rebvs gestis a Joanne et Manuele Comnenis impp. CP. Accedunt Caroli dv Fresne, D. dv Cange, Regi a Consiliis, & Franciæ apud Ambianos Quæstoris, in Nicephori Bryennii cæsaris, Annæ Commenæ cæsarissæ & ejusdem Joannis Cinnami Historiam Comnenicam Notæ Historicæ & Philologicæ. His adivngitvr Pauli Silentiarii descriptio sanctæ Sophiæ, quæ nunc primum prodit Græce & Latine, cum vberiori Commentario. Paris: Imprimerie royale, 1670.

Glossarium ad Scriptores mediæ & infimæ Latinitatis, in quo Latina vocabula novatæ significationis, aut usus rarioris, barbara & exotica explicantur, eorum Notiones & Originationes reteguntur: Complures ævi medii Ritus & Mores, Legum, Consuetudinum municipalium, & Iurisprudentiæ recentioris Formulæ, & obsoletæ voces: Vtriusque Ordinis, Ecclesiastici & Laici, Dignitates & Officia, & quamplurima alia observatione digna recensetur, enucleantur, illustrantur. E libris editis, ineditis, aliisque monumentis cùm publicis, tum privatis. Paris: Gabriel Martini, 1678.

Historia Byzantina duplici commentario illustrata. Prior familias ac stemmata imperatorum Constantinopolitanorum, cum eorundem Augustorum Nomismatibus, & aliquot Iconibus: Prætererea Familias Dalmaticas & Turcicas complectitur: Alter descriptionem urbis Constantinopolitanæ, qualis extitit sub Imperatoribus Christianis. 2 vols. With a dedication to Jean-Baptiste Colbert. Paris: Louis Billaine, 1680.

Ἰωάννου τοῦ ἀσκητοῦ τοῦ Ζωναρᾶ γεγονότος τοῦ μεγάλου δρουγγαρίου τῆς βίγλας καὶ πρωτοασηκρῆτις χρονικόν. Joannis Zonaræ monachi magni antea vigilum præfecti et primi a secretis annales. Carolus du Fresne, Dom. Du Cange, Regi a Consiliis, & Franciae apud Ambianos Quæstor, Wolfianam Editionem cum scriptis Codicibus contulit: Latinam Versionem recensuit, Annales Notis illustravit. 2 vols. Paris: Imprimerie royale, 1686–87.

Glossarium ad scriptores mediæ & infimæ Græcitatis, in quo Græca vocabula novatæ significationis, aut usus rarioris, Barbara, Exotica, Ecclesiastica, Liturgica, Tactica, Nomica, Jatrica, Botanica, Chymica explicantur, eorum Notiones & Originationes reteguntur: Complures ævi medii Ritus & Mores; Dignitates Ecclesiasticæ, Monasticæ, Palatinæ, Politicæ, & quamplurima alia observatione digna, & ad Historiam Byzantinam præsertim spectantia, recensentur ac enucleantur. E libris editis, ineditis, veteribusque monumentis. Accedit Appendix ad Glossarium mediæ & infimæ Latinitatis, unà cùm brevi

Etymologico Linguæ Gallicæ ex utroque Glossario. 2 vols. Lyons: Jean Anisson, Jean Posuel, and Claude Rigaud, 1688.

Πασχάλιον seu Chronicon paschale a mundo condito ad Heraclii Imperatoris annum vicesimum. Opus Hactenus Fastorum Siculorum nomine laudatum, deinde Chronicæ temporum Epitomes, ac denique Chronici Alexandrini lemmate vulgatum: Nunc tandem auctius et emendatius prodit, cum nova Latina versione & Notis Chronicis ac Historicis. With a dedication to Louis XIV. Paris: Imprimerie royale, 1688.

APPENDIX II

THE 1756 INVENTORY OF DU CANGE'S PAPERS

AN EDITION AND TRANSLATION

TERESA SHAWCROSS

A diplomatic edition of the original inventory, faithful to its spelling, punctuation, and layout, is proposed by me below, together with my translation. The compiler of the inventory is not consistent, most probably because he is writing out his entries while referring to and partially transcribing textual material originating with different authors and dating to different periods—and therefore following different conventions.

Identifications of items in the inventory with manuscripts extant today are given by me in the footnotes.

(fol. 369r)

2. May. 1756. **Etat des MSS. de M. Du Cange acquits de M. D'Aubigny.**

Vol^{e}. in fol^{o}. relié en Veau, cotté sur dos: familles d'Outremer MS. familles Normandes MS.
et intitulé: Histoire des principautés et des Royaumes de Hierusalem, de Cypre et d'Ar-menie, et des familles qui les ont possedées.[a]
Dans ce Vol^{e}. on trouve aussi les titres suivants....
...**A**utres Familles Habituées aux Royaumes de Hie-rusalem et de Cypre..........
...**L**es Grands Officiers du Royaume de Hiérusalem.
...**L**es Grands Officiers du Royaume de Cypre.
...**L**a Syrie Sainte: (contenant les Patriarches de jerusalem et ceux d'Antioche et les Archeveques qui dépendent d'eux, ainsi que les Eveques.)...
...**L**es Abbayes de la Terre Sainte.
...**L**es Archeveques et les Evêques Latins de Cypre......
...**L**es Grands Maitres du Temple.

Les familles Normandes.

Genealogie des Rois de Sicile......
...**L**es Comtes d'Averse, et les Princes de Capoue, de la famille des Normans......
...**G**enealogie abregée de la Maison de Grentemesnil en Normandie, alliée à celle des Rois de Sicile...........
...**D**es Seigneurs Normands et François qui ont servi les Empereurs de Constantinople en leurs armées.

On a joint à la Teste dece Vol.^{e} un cahier separé, intitulé: **Ex** Cartulario Ecclesiæ S. Sepul-chri Hierosolymitani, quod fuit Dm̄. Philippi de Maseriis Cancellarii Regni Cypri.......
Plus haute, dans le coin est ecrit: Ex Bibliothecâ. D. Petavii. Ce Cahier est dans une enveloppe <en> papier, cottée: Suite des preuves pour l'hist<oire> de jerusalem.

Ce Vol^{e}. est enfermé dans une boëte, en for<me> de Livre couverte de velin verd et cotteé sur do<s:> Familles d'Outremer. MSS. D. C.

(369v)

2

Histoire de l'Empire de Constantinople sous les Empereurs françois, Divisée en deux parties.[b]
La 1e. contient l'Histoire de la Conquéte de la Ville de Constantinople par les françois et les Venitiens, ecrite par Geoffroy de Ville-

a Bibliothèque nationale de France (hereafter BnF), MS fr. 9493.

b BnF, MS fr. 9473.

(fol. 369r)

2. May. 1756. **Inventory of the Manuscripts of M. Du Cange acquired from M. D'Aubigny**

Folio volume, bound in Calfskin, labeled on the spine: Manuscript Families of the Crusader States. Manuscript Norman Families, and titled: History of the Principalities and Kingdoms of Jerusalem, Cyprus, and Ar- -menia, and the Families That Possessed Them.
In this volume, one also finds the following titles . . .
. . . **O**ther Families Frequenting the Kingdoms of Je -rusalem and Cyprus.
. . . **The** Grand Officers of the Kingdom of Jerusalem.
. . . The Grand Officers of the Kingdom of Cyprus.
. . . **H**oly Syria: (Containing the Patriarchs of Jerusalem and Those of Antioch and the Archbishops and Also Bishops Who Are Subject to Them) . . .
. . . The Abbeys of the Holy Land.
. . . The Latin Archbishops and Bishops of Cyprus . . . . . .
. . . The Grand Masters of the Temple.

The Norman Families.

Genealogy of the Kings of Sicily . . . . . .
. . . The Counts of Aversa, and the Princes of Capua, of Norman Descent. . . . . .
. . . **A**bridged Genealogy of the House of Grandmesnil in Normandy, Joined to That of the Kings of Sicily . . . . . .
. . . **O**f the Norman and French Lords Who Served the Emperors in Constantinople In Their Armies.

Attached to the top of this volume, a separate booklet titled: **From** the Ecclesiastical Cartulary of the Holy Sepul- -cher of Jerusalem, by Lord Philippe de Mézières, Chancellor of the Kingdom of Cyprus. . . . . . . Higher up, in the corner, is written: From the Library of D. Pétau. This booklet is in a paper envelope labeled: Continuation of the Proofs for the History of Jerusalem.

This volume is enclosed in a box, in the shape of a book, covered in green vellum and labeled on the spine: Families of the Crusader States. Manuscripts D. C.

(369v)

2

History of the Empire of Constantinople under the French Emperors, Divided into Two Parts. The first contains the History of the Conquest of the City of Constantinople by the French and Venetians written by Geoffrey of Ville-

-Hardouin &c revue et corrigée &c et illustrée d'observations, ...et d'un Glossaire. Avec la suite de cette Histoire, ~~XXXX~~ jusques en l'an 1240. tirée de l'Histoire de France MS. de Philippe Mouskes, &c. . . . . .
La 2e. est une histoire generale de ce que les francois et les Latins ont fait de plus memorable dans l'Empire de Constantinople, &c. . . . (avec les Pieces justificatives pour les deux parties.) Paris. Imprimerie Royale. 1657. . . . .

Cet Ouvrage de Charles du Fresne Sr. Du Cange est de nouveau enrichi de quantité d'observations, notes historiques, revisions, collations avec MSS, corrections, et enfin de plusieurs Augmentations considerables et importantes, ecrites soit sur les marges, soit sur des papiers separés joints ~~XX~~ ou inserés – en additions aux endroits necessaires; le tout de la propre main de l'Auteur et disposé pour en publier une seconde Edition revûe corrigée, et augmentée. . . . .
En Teste de ce Volume sont plusieurs Cahiers MSS ajoutés sous une Enveloppe cottée: Pour servir à l'Histoire de Constantinople. Et vers la fin du même Volume est ajoutée pareille-ment une Liasse de plusieurs Copies de titres, chartes &c placée avant le recueil des pieces justificatives, à l'augmentation des-quelles elle paroissoit destinée. Le tout de la main du méme Sr. Du Cange.

Ce Vole.* relié en parchemin,[a] et cotté sur dos: Histoire des Empereurs. D. est aussi enfermé dans une pareille boëte, que le précédent; Elle est cottée sur dos: Histoire de Constantinople MSS. D. C.

(370r)

Boëte semblable aux précédentes, cotteé sur dos: Droit des Armes Mss. D.C.[b] renfermant en effet Les minutes en feuilles détacheés ou en Cahiers separés, de Memoires servants à former un ouvrage complet Sur les Armoiries, sous ce titre:

Traité du Droit des Armes, de leur Origine et usage.

Plus: un autre Cahier broché en papier marbré, contenant un autre ouvrage sur la même matiere. Il est intitulé, en françois:

Du Droit et Comportement des Armes.

et en Latin:

a BnF, MS fr. 9474.

b BnF, MS fr. 9466.

-Hardouin etc., reviewed and corrected etc., and illustrated
with observations . . . and a glossary. With the
continuation of this history, ~~XXXX~~ until the year
1240 taken from the History of France in manuscript by
Philippe Mouskés etc. . . . . . .
The second is a general history of the
most memorable deeds of the Franks and
Latins in the Empire of Constantinople,
etc. . . . (With the supporting documents for the
two parts). Paris. Royal Printing Press.
1657. . . . . . .

This work of Charles Du Fresne, Lord
Du Cange is enriched afresh by a quantity
of observations, historical notes, revisions,
collations with manuscripts, corrections, and, finally, with
many considerable and important
augmentations, written either in the margins or
on separate papers attached ~~XX~~ or inserted
as additions in the necessary places;
all in the author's own hand and readied
for the publication from them of a reviewed,
corrected and augmented second edition. . . . . . .
In front of this volume are many manuscript
notebooks added in an envelope labeled: To Be
Used for the History of Constantinople. And toward
the end of the same volume a bundle is similar-
-ly added of many copies of
titles, charters, etc. apparently intended to
supplement the supporting documents be-
-fore which it is placed. All in the hand
of the same L~~x~~ord Du Cange.

This volume* is bound in parchment and labeled on the spine:
History of the Emperors. D. and is also enclosed
in a box similar to the previous one. It
is labeled on the spine: History of Constantinople.
Manuscripts D. C.

(370r)

A similar box to the previous ones, labeled on the spine:
The Right to Armorial Bearings Manuscripts D.C., which indeed contains,
on single sheets of paper or in unbound
booklets, notes of memoranda to be used to make up a
complete work On Coats of Arms, under the
title:

Treatise on the Right of Armorial Bearings, Their Origin
and Use.

Also: another booklet, covered in marbled
paper, containing another work on the
same subject. It is titled, in French:

On Armorial Bearings and Rights.

and, in Latin:

De Insignibus et Armis, sive de Genti-
-litiorum Stemmatum Origine usu et jure.

outre ces 2. Titres on lit sur ce frontispice differents vers Latins, tirés de Martial et d'Ovide, et appliqués ici pour Epigraphes. Et le nom Dufresne: avec la date, 1635.
Le tout, de la main de M. Du Cange, et sur du papier de differentes formes d'in folio.

Trois Boetes, comme les précédentes, cottées sur le dos: **N**obilier de France. Tom I. II. et III.[a]
et remplies de quantite de papiers detachés, de differentes formes et grandeurs: tous MS̄S. de M[r]. Du Cange même, à la reserve d'un seul imprimé, qui est; la Genealogie de Bournon-
-ville. Ce sont des Minutes, et Recherches, ou, com=
=me il les intitule lui même, des ....

Memoires indigestes pour dresser un No-
-biliaire de france tel qu'il l'avoit commen-
-cé &c ... 1676.

Ils sont disposés suivant l'ordre alphabetique des noms dont ils sont intitulés, et qui sont recueillis en une seule Table mise a la Teste du 1er. Tome, ou de la 1ere. Boete, et qui sert pour toutes les trois:

Le Tome 1.

(370v)

Le Tome 1. ou la 1e. Boete comprend depuis la Lettre **A**. jusqu'à la Lettre **D**. inclusivement.

La Lettre **E**. et les suivantes jusqu'à la Lettre **M**. aussi inclusivement, sont contenues dans le Tome II. ou la seconde Boëte.

Et enfin la Troisième, ou le tome III. comprend tout le reste de l'Alphabet à commencer par la Lettre **N**.

Autre Boëte pareille, cottée sur le dos:
Supplément au Nobiliaire. MSS. D. C.
contenant de même differentes Minutes sembla=
--bles, à la teste des quelles est ✗ l'intitulé suivant:

Table des Royaumes, Duchez, Principau-
-tez, Souverainetez. Marquisats, Comtez, –
Vicomtez, Vidamez et autres grandes Seigneu-
-ries Situées dans l'Enceinte des Gaulles, C'est-à dire tant dans le Royaume de France qu'ez autres Provinces assises entre les Mers oceane et Mediterrannée les Alpes, les Pyrenées et le Rhin, dont l'Histoire est icy descrite.

a BnF, MSS fr. 9469–72, organized in alphabetical order in four volumes: A–B (9469), C–I (9470), J–O (9471), and P–Z (9472).

On Insignia and Coats of Arms, or of the
Origin, Use, and Regulation of the Crests of the Nobility.

Apart from these two titles one reads on this frontispiece various verses in Latin taken from Martial and Ovid, and used here as epigraphs. And the name Dufresne: with the date, 1635. All in the hand of M. Du Cange and on paper of different folio formats.

Three boxes, like the previous ones, labeled on the spine: The Peerage of France, Volumes I, II, and III, and filled with a number of detached sheets of paper of different formats and sizes. All manuscripts by M. Du Cange himself, with the exception of a single printed work, which is: The Genealogy of the Bournon-ville. These are notes, research, or as he himself titled them, the ......

Undigested Memoranda for the Creation of a Peer-age of France Such as He Had Be-gun It etc. . . . 1676.[1]

They are organized according to the alphabetical order of the names with which they have been labeled, which are collected together in a single table placed at the beginning of the first volume, or of the first box, which serves for all three:

Volume one.

(370v)

Volume one, or the first box, contains the letter **A** up to and including the letter **D**.

The letter **E** and those that follow up to and also including the letter **M** are contained in volume two, or the second box.

And, lastly, the third, or volume three, consists of all the rest of the alphabet beginning with the letter **N**.

Another similar box, labeled on the spine: Supplement to the Peerage, Manuscripts D. C., likewise containing different notes of a simi-lar type, at the beginning of which is ~~X~~ the following title:

Table of the Kingdoms, Duchies, Principali-ties, Sovereignties, Marquisates, Counties, – Viscounties, Vidames, and Other Great Lord-ships Situated within the Confines of the Gauls – That is To Say, Both the Kingdom of France and the Other Provinces Located between the Atlantic and the Mediterranean Seas, the Alps, the Pyrenees, and the Rhine, Whose History is Described Here.

1 The use of the third-person pronoun suggests that either the title was adapted as it was copied or it in fact was not by Du Cange himself, despite the comment made by the compiler of the list.

Cet Intitulé est precedé d'une feuille de papier d'ecriture differente: elle porte pour Titre: Tables des Articles remis par M. d'Hozier. . Ce sont tous noms de Terre dispo-sés par ordre Alphabetique. Cette Table paroist répondre à l'arrangement des Minu-tes ou l'on a observé en effet l'Ordre Alpha-bétique, aussi.

Autre Boete Semblable, cottée sur le dos: Catalogues Historiques. MSS.D.C.[a]

Elle renferme un Volume in fol°. relié en Velin verd et cotté sur dos, de même, Catalogues Historiques. D. C.

Ce Volume

(371r)

Ce Volume en effet est formé par quantite de Catalogues sur diverses matieres, mais principalement

1°. Des Catalogues de differens Etats de Noblesse qui ont signé comme Te-moins à plusieurs Actes de Paix, d'Accord de Treves &c. passés entre nos Rois et autres Souverains ou Grands Seigneurs: Ou bien de ceux qui ont rendus leurs hommages, et de ceux qui on assisté à ces hommages lors qu'on les a rendus à nos Rois ou aux Autres Grands Sei-gneurs qui avoient droit d'en recevoir par leurs Etats et Seigneuries, comme les Ducs de Normandie, de Bretagne, de Guyenne; Les Comtes de Champagne &c

2°. Plusieurs Listes de montres et Revûes de Gens d'Armes et Autres Milices reglées, sous differentes Denomina-tions. Des Etats et Rôles de payement de ceux qui ont Servi militairement soit pour remplir les Services des fiefs, soit ~~dans~~ dans les differentes Compagnies d'Ordon-nance, d'Archers &c soit autrement.

3°. Enfin differens Catalogues particuliers, ou d'Affaires particulieres et differentes; parmi lesquels les Suivants sont les principaux:

Noms des Chevaliers de l'Ordre du Croissant, ~~XXXXXXXXXX~~ institué par René, Roi de Sicile, le 11. jour d'Aoust l'an 1448. Ainsi qu'ils ont été creéz jour par jour, l'un après l'autre.

Description des Armoiries de quelqu'uns des Chevaliers précédens.

a BnF, MS fr. 9501.

This title is preceded by a sheet
of paper in different handwriting that has as its
title: Table of Articles Returned by M. d'Hozier. . They are all land names orga-
-nized by alphabetical order. This table
seems to conform to the arrangement of the
notes, where one indeed has observed the alpha-
-betical order likewise.

Another similar Box, labeled on the spine:
Historical Lists. MSS.D.C.

This contains a folio volume, bound
in green vellum and labeled on the spine, in the same manner,
Historical Lists D. C.

This volume

(371r)

This volume indeed consists in a
quantity of lists on various matters,
the main being:

First: Lists of different
persons of noble status who signed as wit-
-nesses to many peace agreements,
truces, etc. between our kings and
other sovereigns or great lords,
or of those who rendered their
homage, and of those who were present when
homage was rendered
to our kings or other great
lords who had the right to receive them because of
their status and their lordships, such as the Dukes
of Normandy, Brittany, Guienne;
the Counts of Champagne etc.

Second: Many lists of musters
and roll calls of men at arms and other
regulated militias, under different
names; the inventories and payrolls
of those who served in a military capacity, either
to fulfill the service due for their fiefs or ~~in~~
in the different companies of mili-
-tias, archers etc., or otherwise.

Third: Lastly, lists
both various and specific, or relating to specific
or various matters, of which the following
are the principal ones:

Names of knights of the Order of the
Crescent, ~~XXXXXXXXXX~~ established by
Réné, King of Sicily, on the 11th day of August
in the year 1448. Listed on the days on which they were knighted
day by day, one after the other.

Description of the coats of arms of some of the
aforementioned knights.

Autres Armes de quelques Chevaliers de l'Ordre du Croissant, ainsi que M. Du Cange les a tirées des Memoires de feu M. de Peiresc, sans autre remarque de famille.

Officiers

(371v)

Officiers et Gouverneurs des places du Duchè de Milan, en l'an 1515. Sous le Regne de François 1er.

Les Noms et titres des Ducs et Grands Seigneurs d'Espagne.

Sermens de Feauté à cause des Temporalitez des Eveschez et Abbayes. Ex-traits des Registres des Hommages de la Chambre des Comptes de Paris.

Cette Compilation de Catalogues est de differentes années depuis 1203. Jusqu'en 1626. Mais principalement des 14e. et 15e. Siecles et surtout du 14e.

Volume petit in fol°. relié en parchemin, cotté sur le dos: Oeuvres de M. Du Cange. Tome.1.er .... Recueil de Blazons.[a] Ces deux Titres sont repetés en dedans, sous la couverture. Mais l'Ouvrage est intitulé:

Recueil d'histoires et de Blazons, tiré de divers Livres manuscripts. Dufresne. 1633.

Ce Volume contient en effet des Catalogues, et divers Extraits de Noms de familles, avec la description de leurs Armoiries, le tout selon qu' il est plus amplement détaillé dans la Table du contenu de ce Volume, et qui est placeé à sa Teste: Elle offre de plus divers traits où mor-ceaux d'Histoire, tels que les suivants .....

La Paix de Gand, l'an 1453.

Traité de M. le Dauphin avec le Roy. 1440.

Des Bacheliers et Chevaliers Bannerets.

L'Ordonnance des Tournois et des joustes.

Des Electeurs de l'Empire.

Des Rois Ducs Comtes et Marquis et comme ils se creént.

Enumeration des Ducs et Comtes de france.

L'Obseque du Connestable du Gueselin &c &c &c

Le tout de la main de M. Du Cange.

Autre

a BnF, MS fr. 9477.

Other armorial bearings of some knights of the Order of the Crescent, as M. du Cange extracted them from the memoranda of the late M. de Peiresc, without any further remarks on their family.

Officers

(371v)

Officers and governors of the places of the Duchy of Milan, in the year 1515. During the reign of François I.

Names and titles of the Dukes and Great Lords of Spain.

Oaths of fealty relating to the jurisdictions of Bishoprics and Abbeys. Ex-
-tracts from the registers of homage from the Exchequer in Paris.

This compilation of lists covers various years from 1203 to 1626, but principally the fourteenth and fifteenth centuries, and most especially the fourteenth.

A small folio volume, bound in parchment, labeled on the spine: Works of M. Du Cange, Volume One . . . Collection of Coats of Arms. These two titles are repeated inside the cover. But the work is titled:

Collection of Histories and Coats of Arms, Drawn from Various Books in Manuscript. Du Fresne. 1633.

Indeed, this volume contains lists and various extracts of family names with the description of their armorial bearings, all this being set out in greater detail in the table of contents of this volume, which is placed at its beginning: It offers in addition various sketches or snip-
-pets of history, such as the following . . .

The Peace of Ghent, in the year 1453.
Treaty of the dauphin with the king.
1440.
On knights bachelor and knights banneret.
Decrees concerning Tournaments and jousts.
On the electors of the Empire.
On kings, dukes, counts and marquises and how they are created.
Enumeration of the dukes and counts of France.
The Burial of the Constable Du Guesclin,
etc. etc. etc.

All in the hand of M. Du Cange.

Another

(372r)

Autre Volume de même forme, relié en velin verd, cotté sur le dos: Blason et Genealogies MSS.[a]

Il contient 3. Ouvrages differens MSS. du 16.e Siecle, dont le dernier est d'une très mauvaise ecriture. Ils sont intitulés:

Le 1er. Instruction pour apprendre à bla-sonner les Armoiries. ~~xxxxxxxxxx~~ à la fin de cet ouvrage on lit: fait et achevé le 3e jour du mois de Novembre l'An 1564. en Vallencienne par jacques Le Boucq.

Le 2e. Ce sont les Ceremonies et Ordonnances qui se appartiennent à gaige de Bataille, faict par querelle selon les Constitutions faictes par le bon Roy Philippe de Franche.
Cet Ouvrage paroist estre ecrit par la même main que le précédent, et du même auteur.

Le 3e. **Genealogie** de ceulx de Thrmnes (sans doute: Therouennes.) M. Du Cange à ajouté de sa main cet autre Titre en teste de l'Ouvrage: Recueil d'Alliances. 1636.

Ce 3e. Ouvrage et le 1er. sont avec les blasons enluminés et expliqués.

Dans les Intervals de ces Ouvrages, sur les feuillets de papier blanc inserés entr'eux, M. Du Cange y a copié divers Extraicts, et entr'autres du Songe du Vergier chape. 148.e &c et diverses autres notes.

Lettres ecrites à Mr. Du Cange,[b] par Mrs. D. Luc d'Achery, Benedictin; Allard; Van Aquen, Chanoine Regulier d'Anvers; jos. Ignace de St. An-toine, Carme déchaussé de Tournay; Bastide, Benedictin de St. Germain d'Auxerre; Bigot; Bil-laine; le Blanc, auteur du Traité des Monnoyes de france; Boispiece; Bonnefons, Benedictin; Bou-teroue, auteur de L'Ouvrage sur les Monnoies; jean de Briais, d'Arras; Le Caron, de St. Quentin; La Caroy, jesuite de Clermonten, Auvergne; Charpen-tier; de Chevaues; Colbert, Ambassadeur en
Angleterre

(372v)

8.

Angleterre; Combefis, de l'Ordre des freres prescheurs; Commine, jesuite; Comnene, aumonier général de la Cavallerie de Savoye; Costar; David, Prestre à Dijon. Dorans, Chanoine de Senlis; Duchambourg; faure, Evêq. d'Amiens; feuquiere; Du fourny; Galloys; Goar; Grœvius; Godefroy Hermant; D'Herouval; D'Hozier; junnez; Baron de Lau-

a BnF, MS fr. 9491.

b BnF, MSS fr. 9502–3.

(372r)

Another volume of the same format, bound in green vellum, labeled on the spine: Coats of Arms and Genealogies in Manuscript.

It contains three different manuscript works of the sixteenth century, of which the last is in a very bad hand. They are titled:

The first: Instruction to Learn the Drawing of Coats of Arms. ~~xxxxxxxxx~~ At the end of this work one reads: made and completed the 3rd day of the month of November in the Year 1564 in Valenciennes by Jacques Le Boucq.

The second: These are the Ceremonies and Orders That Relate to the Waging of Battle by Quarrel According to the Constitutions Established by Good King Philip of France.
This work seems to be written by the same hand as the previous one, and by the same author.

The third: **Genealogy** of Those of Thrm̄nes (undoubtedly: Therouannes). M. Du Cange added in his own hand this other title at the beginning of the work: Collection of Alliances, 1636.

The third and first work have illuminated and explicated coats of arms.

In the breaks between these works, on small sheets of white paper inserted between them, M. Du Cange copied various extracts, among them the Dream of the Orchard; chapter forty-eight etc. and various other notes.

Letters written to M. Du Cange by Messrs:
D. Luc d'Achery, Benedictine; Allard; Van Aken, Canon regular of Antwerp; Jos. Ignace de St. An-
-toine, Discalced Carmelite of Tournai; Bastide, Benedictine of St. Germain d'Auxerre; Bigot; Bil-
-laine; Le Blanc, author of the Treatise on the Coinage of France; Boispiece; Bonnetons, Benedictine; Bou-
-teroue, author of The Work on Coinage; Jean de Briais, from Arras; Le Caron, from St. Quentin; La Caroy, Jesuit of Chermont-en-Auvergne; Charpen-
-tier; De Chevaues; Colbert, Ambassador to
England

(372v)

8.
England; Combefis, of the Order of the Friars Preachers; Commine, Jesuit; Comnène, General Almoner of the Savoyard Cavalry; Costar; David, Priest at Dijon. Dorans, Canon of Senlis; Du Chambourg; Fauré, Bishop of Amiens; Feuquières; Du Fourney; Galloys; Goar; Grotius; Godefroy Hermant; D'Hérouval; D'Hozier; Junnez; Baron de Lau-

-nay; Leibnitz; Mabillon et Germain, Bene-
-dictins; Claude Maltraict de Montauban;
Manessier; De la Mare; de Marillac; Nicaise;
d'Ormesson; Daniel Papebroch; Adrian Par-
-villiers, jesuite, Recteur du College de Caen; fr.
Poilly, jes. à Bourges; Pierre Poussines, jes. à
Rome; Rainssant; Sauvalle; Seguyn, Doyen
De St Germain; Spon; Toynard, d'Orleans; –
Toubeau, de Bourges; Du Trousset; De Valois;
et Ildephonse Vrayer, Benedictin.

Ces Lettres comprennent differentes anneés
depuis 1645. jusqu'en 1686.

Elles concernent principalement son Traité
du chef de S^{t}. jean Baptiste, son Glossaire, des
Explications de Medailles, monnoyes, &c et di-
-verses Questions &c

Plus: Autres Lettres ecrites à M. Du Cange
par le S^{r}. Anisson, Libraire à Lyon, depuis
le 18. fevrier 1682. jusqu'au 5. juillet 1688. –
concernant le Cours de l'Impression de son Glos-
-saire. Ces Lettres sont dans un carton séparé.

Un cahier contenant copie des Lettres ecrites
par M. Du Cange à M^{rs}. De la Mare, David et
Nicaise à Lyon en 1669. 1679. 1683. 1684. 1686.

Une autre Lettre ecrite de Treves le 26. Novem
-bre 1655. dont la signature n'est pas Lisible.

Deux Lettres de M. Du Cange, L'une sans
date et sans adresse, sur l'Etablissement de S^{t}.
Cyr: l'Autre du 6. Aoust 1688. à son neveu,
sur la maison de Boufflers.

Enfin une Lettre de M. Pelletier, Controleur
General ^ ^ à Mr. Baluze du 27. Novembre 1688. 2. autres du
Premier Présid^{t}. de Lamoignon, Et une du 19.
novembre 1688 à M^{r}. Baluze par M. franç.
faure, Evêq. d'Amiens, du 19. novembre 1688. Toutes
sur la mort de M^{r} Du Cange.

A la Teste

(373r)

A la Teste de ces Lettres est un cahier in fol^{o}. conten^{t}.
un sommaire general du contenu de ces Lettres, placé
ensuite du nom de ceux qui les ont ecrites, dont on a fait
une Liste Alphabetique.

L'ordre des Lettres differe un peu de celui de cette
Liste, parce que dans l'arrangement de ces Lettres, on y
a suivi plus exactement l'ordre alphabetique, qu'on
n'a fait dans la liste.

Le tout est renfermé dans une Boete, en forme
de Livre in fol^{o}. couverte de Veau, et cottée sur le dos:
Lettres ecrites à M. D. C.

-nay; Leibnitz; Mabillon and Germain, Bene-
-dictines; Claude Maltraist de Montauban;
Manessier; de la Mare; de Marillac; Nicaise;
d'Ormesson; Daniel Papabroch; Adrien Par-
-villiers, Jesuit, Rector of the College of Caen; Fr.
Poilly, Jesuit at Bourges; Pierre Poussines, Jesuit at
Rome; Rainssant; Sauvalle; Seguin, Dean
of St. Germain; Spon; Touesnard, of Orléans; –
Toubeau, of Bourges; Du Trousset; De Valois;
and Ildephonse Vrayer, Benedictine.

These letters date
from 1645 to 1686.

They principally concern his Treatise
On the Head of St. John the Baptist, his Glossary,
explanations about medals, coins etc. and var-
-ious questions etc.

In addition: Other letters written to M. Du Cange
by Sieur Anisson, Bookseller at Lyon, from
18 February 1682 to 5 July 1688. –
concerning the progress of the printing of his Glos-
-sary. These letters are in a separate cardboard box.

A notebook containing copies of the letters written
by M. Du Cange to Messrs de la Mare, David and
Nicaise in Lyon in 1669, 1679, 1683, 1684, and 1686.

Another letter written from Trier on 26 Novem-
-ber 1655 whose signature is not legible.

Two letters by M. Du Cange: One without
date or address, on the establishment of St.
Cyr: the other dated 6 August 1688 to his nephew,
on the House of Boufflers.

Lastly, a letter dated 27 November 1688 from M. Pelletier, General
Comptroller^ ^to M. Baluze. Two others from the
First President of Lamoignon. And one dated 19
November 1688 to M. Baluze from M. François
Fauré, Bishop of Amiens, dated 19 November 1688. All
on the death of M. Du Cange.

In front

(373r)

In front of these letters is a folio notebook containing
a general summary of the content of these letters, placed
after the names of the those who wrote them, of which there is
an alphabetical list.

The order of the letters differs slightly from that of this
list, because in the organization of the letters the
alphabetical order was followed more exactly
than in the list.

Everything is enclosed in a box, in the shape
of a folio book, covered in calfskin, and labeled on the spine:
Letters Written to M. D. C.

Volume in folio, relié en parchemin, cotté sur dos: Oeuvres de Mr. Du Cange. To. II. Gallia.[a]

C'est un Recueil ou Compilation de diverses Citations et indications relatives aux differens Chefs ou titres sous lesquelles elles sont rangées ou rassemblées, et qui renvoyent aux Auteurs mêsme qui devoient lui servir à composer l'ouvrage qu'il meditoit sans ~~xx~~ doute sur les Gaules: ou à éclaircir l'histoire de ce Païs dans ses differens points tels que sa Geographie; sa division; ses Limites; l'Histoire et la Description de cet Etat en General et de Chacun de ses Lieux en particulier; ses fleuves, Rivieres &c; ses Princes; ses moeurs, Coutûmes et usages; sa Milice; les differen-tes parties de son Gouvernement; sa noblesse, ses familles, ses Monnoyes &c &c

À la fin est une Table Alphabetique. des Lieux.

Le tout sous les Noms Latins.

~~**Autre Volume** in fol°. relie en Bazane, cotté sur le dos: Oeuvres de M. Du Cange M. – V. et au dessous. Authores Græci M.D.~~

(373v) 10.

Deux Autres Volumes in fol°. reliés en Bazane: et Cottés sur le Dos: Oeuvres de Mr. Du Cange To.XI. ~~xxxxxxx~~ A.=L. et To. X. M.=V.
Et au dessous de ces Titres, ces 2 autres.......
I. juris Civilis Cognitio et Interpretatio. M. D.
II. Authores Graeci. M. D.[b]

Ces 2. Volumes sont, ainsi que le Précedent, Deux Recueils ou Compilations où l'Auteur avoit rassemblé sous differens titres ou Chefs et noms, soit françois, soit Latins, ~~xx~~ rangés suivant l'Ordre Alphabetique, les diverses indications renvoyant aux Auteurs mêmes ou etoient contenus les passages et Extraits relatifs à ces matieres ou titres, dont l'Objet etoit sans doute d'éclaircir et d'expliquer plu-sieurs points de la jurisprudence Civile.

Quoique le second vole. soit cotté: Authores Graeci, il ne paroist pas renvoyer ~~xxxxxxxx xxxx~~ plus particulierement aux Autheurs Grecs, que le 1er. Les titres contenus dans ces 2. Voles. ne sont en effet qu'un Mélange de noms et de choses tirées ~~des Sciences, des~~ de differens Auteurs Grecs, François, Latins &c sur les sciences, les

a BnF, MS fr. 9492.

b BnF, MSS fr. 9494–95.

Folio volume, bound in parchment, labeled on the spine:
Works of M. Du Cange. Volume Two. Gallia.

This is a collection or compilation of various quotations and citations relating to the different headings or titles under which they are organized or assembled, and that refer to the authors themselves who were to be used by him to compose the work that he ~~xx~~ doubtless intended to write on the Gauls; or to elucidate different aspects of the history of this country, such as its geography; divisions; boundaries; the history and description of this state in general and with regard to each of its particular places; its waterways and rivers etc.; its princes; its manners, customs and habits; its militia; the differ-
-ent parts of its government; its nobility; its families; its coinage etc. etc.

At the end is an alphabetical table.
of places.

All under the Latin names.

~~**Another folio** volume. Bound in sheepskin, labeled on the spine: Works of M. Du Cange M. – V and underneath. Greek Authors M. D.~~

(373v) 10.

Two further folio volumes bound in sheepskin: and labeled on the spine: Works of M. Du Cange Volume XI, ~~xxxxxxx~~ A–L and Volume X, M–V.
And under these titles, these other two . . . . . .
I. Investigation and Interpretation of Civil Law. M. D.
II. Greek Authors. M. D.

These two volumes are, like the previous one, two collections or compilations where the author had collected – under different titles or headings and names, whether French or Latin, ~~xx~~ organized in alphabetical order – the different citations referring to the very authors in which are contained the passages and extracts relative to these matters or titles whose objective was doubtless to elucidate and explain many points of civil jurisprudence.

Although the second volume is labeled: Greek Authors, it does not seem to refer ~~xxxxxxxx Xxx~~ any more particularly to Greek authors than did the first. Indeed, the titles contained within these two volumes are none other than a mixture of names and things taken ~~from the sciences, from~~ from different Greek, French, Latin, etc. authors on the sciences; the

Arts, les Langues, ~~de~~ la Religion, ~~du~~ le Droit, ~~de~~ la Philosophie, ~~de~~ la fable, ~~de~~ la Poësie, ~~de~~ l'Histoire ancienne, moderne, sacrée, profane, civile, politique &c les Antiquités &c &c. Au dessous desquels noms ou choses sont ecrits ces renvois ou indications d'Auteurs indifféremment, et comme ils se sont ~~xxx~~ présentés.

Le Vol^{e}. cotté XI. est sans doute une faute d'~~inaction~~ inatention ; il n'en est pas moins en son rang, avant le X. selon qu'on peut le remarquer par la division ou séparation des Lettres de l'Alphabet qu'ils contiennent: ce n°. XI. commençant par **A.** et finissant par **L.** et le n°. X commençant par **M.** et finissant par **V.**

Il y a en outre un Index abregé du nom des Titres.

(374r)

11.

Volume in folio, fort mince, relié en velin verd, et cotté sur le dos: de Oraculis.

Il est de même intitulé: De Oraculis. en dedans.[a]

C'est pareillement un recueil de passages et de citations, rassemblées sous différens ti- -tres relatifs aux Oracles attribués aux Dieux de l'Antiquité, et de la fable, à leurs Temples, à leur Culte, à leurs prestres &c en un mot à tout ce qui peut concerner leur Histoire.

MS̄. de M. Du Cange.

Autre Volume, petit in folio, relié en velin verd, et cotté sur le dos: **R.** et au dessous. **D. C.**[b]

contenant un Recueil de Dépouillements en forme de Tables des Noms de familles et de Lieux, et du mot des principales matieres contenues dans les plus Sçavants Auteurs Grecs et Latins, Et Surtout les Historiens, et dans quelques uns des Anciens Romans, Poëtes, et Historiens françois

Ces Tables paroissent avoir été formées à mesure que M. Du Cange faisoit ses Lectures, et la pluspart destinées à lui servir de memoires pour travailler sur l'Histoire. Une partie etoit sans doute preparée pour des Glossaires françois ou Latins, n'etant que de simples Listes de mots, telle que celle à la page 337. intitulée, Vieux mots françois tirés du Romant MS. qui commence par Miserere mei Deus. Et une autre ~~qu'on a supprimée~~

a BnF, MS fr. 9490.

b BnF, MS fr. 9489.

arts; languages; ~~from~~ religion; ~~from~~ the law;
~~from~~ philosophy; ~~from~~ myth; ~~from~~ poetry;
~~from~~ ancient, modern, sacred,
profane, civil, political etc. history;
antiquities etc. etc. These names or
things having below them the references
or citations of authors written indiscriminately
as they ~~xxx~~ came up.

The labeling of the volume "XI" is doubtless an error
caused by ~~omission~~ inattention; regardless, it is in its correct
place before X, as one can
see from the division or separation
of the letters of the alphabet that this number "XI" contains,
beginning with **A** and ending
with **L**, while number X begins with **M**
and ends with **V**.

There is, furthermore, a brief index of the names of the titles.

(374r)

11.
A very thin folio volume, bound in green vellum and
labeled on the spine: On Oracles . . .

It is likewise titled On Oracles
inside.

This is similarly a collection of passages
and quotations assembled under different head-
-ings referring to the oracles attributed to the gods
of antiquity and of myth, to their temples,
to their worship, to their priests etc. – in a word
to everything that might concern their history.

Manuscript of M. Du Cange.

Another small folio volume, bound in green vellum
and labeled on the spine R. and underneath D. C.,

containing a collection of analyses
in the form of tables of the names of families and
of places, and the keywords relating to the principal matters
contained in the most learned Greek
and Latin Authors. And especially the historians,
and in some of the Old French romances,
poets, and historians.

These tables seem to have been created
as M. Du Cange carried out his reading,
and the majority were destined to be used by him as
memoranda for working on history.
One section was doubtless prepared for the
French or Latin Glossaries, since it is made up solely of
simple lists of words such as that on
page 337, titled Old French words taken
from a Romance Manuscript that begins with Have
Mercy upon Me, O God. And another ~~that has been removed~~

intitulée, Glossarium Franco Barbarum, qu'on a supprimée de ce volume pour faire Relier séparément.

Il y en a aussi quelqu'unes pour divers autres objets, comme les officiers de la Couronne et de la maison du Roi; les Officiers de la justice ou Gouverneurs. Divers Droits. Les diverses Dénominations des Biens &c.

Chacun des noms ou mots qui composent ces tables, est suivi du chiffre qui renvoye à la page ~~meme~~ du volume ou de l'ouvrage de l'Auteur même ou il se trouve.

La plupart

(374v)

<1>2

La plupart de ces Tables etant raturées ou bâtonnées d'un Trait de plume du haut de la page en bas: Il y a lieu de Croire qu'elles ont été sans doute recrites au net ailleurs.

Elles ne gardent entr'elles aucun ordre chronologique, alphabetique &c ou autre, mais elles ont en teste du Vol^{e}. ou Recueil une Table alphabetique du nom des Auteurs ou des matieres dont elles sont tirées, avec le chiffre de la page ou elles se trouvent dans ce Recueil.

Le chifre continuel des pages de ce Vo-
-lume est interrompu par une Lacune entre les pages 392. et 436. que est formée par une raison deja indiquée ci dessus: C'est à dire par la suppression du Glossarium franco-
-barbarum qu'on a fait relier séparément etant d'une forme de papier trop petite pour aller avec celui de ce Recueil.

Carton, en forme de boëte, couvert de parchemin; petit in folio, cotté dur le dos:

Familles Germaniques. MSS. D. C.[a]

Contenant en effet, sur autant de Cahiers sé-
-parés ou de feuilles detachées, des Catalogues ou Listes chronologiques et des Recherches sur ces Familles ^* Sçavoir: *Et autres.

Autriche; ses marquis et Ducs. Benevent; ses ducs. Boheme; ses Rois. Bosne; ses Rois. Brandebourg; Ses marquis. Bulgarie; ses Rois. Carinthie; Rois des Sclaves, ou de Carinthie. – Chelmo; ses comtes. Croatie; Ses Comtes. Dannemarck; ses Rois. Dragases. Duras; ses Ducs. Egypte; ses Soudans. Frioul; ses Ducs. Geppide; ses Rois. Holsace; ses comtes. Hongrie; ses Rois, parmi lesquels ^ ^sont aussi ceux de la Mai-

a BnF, MS fr. 9509.

titled Vulgar French Glossary
that has been removed from this volume in order to be
bound separately.

There are also some sections on various
other subjects, such as the officers of the crown
or of the king's household; the officers of the
judiciary or governors; various laws;
various designations relating to property etc.

Each of the names or words that make up
these tables is followed by a number that refers
to the ~~same~~ page of the volume or to the work
of the same author where it is found.

Most

(374v)

<1>2.

Most of these tables being scored through
or crossed out with a stroke of the pen from the top
to the bottom of page. There is reason to think that
clean copies of them were doubtlessly made elsewhere.

They do not follow any order among themselves,
whether chronological, alphabetical etc. or any other,
but they have at the beginning of the volume or collection an
alphabetical table of the Authors
or materials that they are taken from, together with
the number of the page where they are found
in this collection.

The continuous numbering of the pages of this vol-
-ume is interrupted by a lacuna between
pages 392. and 436. which was created for the
aforementioned reason: that is to say
by the removal of the Vulgar French
Glossary that was bound separately,
since its format corresponded to a paper size too small
to fit together with that of the collection.

Cardboard, in the shape of a box, covered with parchment,
small folio size, labeled on the spine:

Germanic Families. Manuscripts Du Cange.

Indeed containing, in a corresponding number of un-
-bound notebooks or single sheets, chronological
catalogs or lists and research on
these families^* That is: *And others.

Austria: its Margraves and Dukes. Benevento:
its dukes. Bohemia: its Kings. Bosnia: its Kings.
Brandenburg: Its margraves. Bulgaria: its Kings.
Karinthia: Kings of the Slavs, or of Karinthia. –
Chelmno: its Counts. Croatia: its Counts.
Denmark: its Kings. Dragases. Durazzo:
its Dukes. Egypt: its Sultans. Friuli: its
Dukes. Gepidia: its Kings. Holsatia: its counts.
Hungary: its Kings, among whom ^ ^are also those of the House

-son de France. Istrie; ses marquis. Lombardie; ses Rois. Meckelbourg; ses Ducs, Princes des Obotrites ou Winites. Méranie; ses Ducs. Moldavie; ses Vaïvodes. Moravie; ses Ducs. Naples; ses Ducs. Perse; ses Rois. Pologne; ses Rois.

(375r)

13<>

ses Rois. Rugie; Rois ou Princes de cette Isle. _ St. Saba; ses Ducs. Salerne; ses Princes. Saxe, sur l'Elbe; ses Ducs. Saxe, sur le Weser; ses Ducs. Saxe; ses comptes palatins. Saxe. ses marquis. Saxe, ses Rois. Sclavonie; ses Ducs. Slesvvic, ses Ducs. Spalato; Ducs de Spolete. Styrie; ses Marquis et Ducs. Thuringe; ses Rois; Toscane; ses marquis. ~~xxxxxxxxxxxxxxx~~ Transsylvanie; ses Vaïvodes: Trente; ses Ducs, Comt~~es~~ de Goricie et de Tyrol. Turcs; leurs Empereurs. Walachie; ses Vaïvodes. Vandales; Leurs Rois. Witelspach; Palatins.

Cinq Volumes in fol°. reliés en veau, cottés sur le dos: . . Recherches Sur l'Histoire de France. MSS. D. C.[a]

Ils sont formés de petits papiers, collés sur les feuillets de ces Volumes, et qui contiennent en effet differentes Recherches, qui, etant ainsi rassemblées, donnent principalement des Listes Chronologiques sur diverses par- -ties de l'Histoire de France, qui sont partagées dans ces Volumes de la Ma- niere Suivante, Sçavoir

Le 1er. Volume, Sur les Regents et Regentes, Les Grands Officiers de la Couronne, les Grands Officiers de la Maison du Roi, les grandes Charges ou Commissions dans le Militaire, dans les Finances, &c et sur les Ambassadeurs.

Il y a une Table du contenu à la Teste de ce Volume, et à la fin une autre feuille détachée, et plus détaillée qui sert de supplément en partie à cette Table.

Le 2d. Volume comprend la suite des Officiers de la Couronne et de la Maison du Roi, dans la partie Ecclesiastique. Ceux qui ont été elevés

(375v)

été élevés aux Dignités dans l'Eglise, dans la Robe &c les Papes François; les Cardinaux François; les Premiers Présidents,

a BnF, MSS fr. 9461–65.

of France. Istria: its Marquises. Lombardy: its Kings. Mecklenburg: its Dukes, Princes of the Obotrites and Wends. Merania: its Dukes. Moldavia: its Voivods. Moravia: its Dukes. Naples: its Dukes. Persia: its Kings. Poland: its Kings.

(375r)

13<>

its Kings. Rügen: Kings or Princes of this Island. St. Saba: its Dukes. Salerno: its Princes. Saxony on the Elbe: its Dukes. Saxony on the Weser: its Dukes. Saxony: its Counts Palatine. Saxony: its Marquises. Saxony: its Kings. Sclavonia: its Dukes. Schleswig: its Dukes. Spoleto: Dukes of Spoleto. Styria: its Marquises and Dukes. Thuringia: its Kings. Tuscany: its Marquises. ~~xxxxxxxxxxxxxx~~ Transylvania: its Voivodes. Trent: its Dukes, Counts of Gorizia and Tyrol. Turks: their Emperors. Wallachia: its Voivodes. Vandals: their Kings. Wittelsbach: Paladins.

Five folio volumes bound in calfskin, labeled on the spine: . . Research into the History of France. Manuscripts D.C.

They consist of small bits of paper, glued onto the sheets of these volumes, and indeed contain different pieces of research that, being collected together here, principally supply chronological lists on various parts of the history of France, which are divided in these volumes in the fol- -lowing manner, that is to say:

The first volume, on the male and female regents, the grand officers of the crown, the grand officers of the king's household, the great commands or commissions in the military, in finances etc., and on ambassadors.

At the beginning of the volume there is a table of contents, and at the end another single sheet, and more detailed, which serves to supplement this table in part.

The second volume contains: the continuation of officers of the crown and of the king's household on the ecclesiastical side; Those who had been raised

(375v)

been raised to dignities in the church, the civil service etc.; the French popes; the French cardinals; the first presidents,

Procureurs Generaux, Avocats generaux, des Parlements, Chambres des Comptes, Cour des Aides, Grand Conseil. &c à Paris ou dans les Provinces. Les Officiers des Reines, des Princes du Sang. Les Grands Officiers des Grandes Provinces de France quand elles etoient gouvernées par leur Princes par--ticuliers &c.

Il y a aussi une Table à la Teste de ce Vol^{e}. Sur un papier détaché.

Le 3e. Vol^{e}. renferme les Chastellains heredi--taires. Les Vidames et Avoués des Eglises Cathedrales, les Senechaux et Baillis et enfin les Chastellains et Capitaines, le tout par ordre alphabetique des Lieux où ils exercoient leurs Charges.

Il y a de meme, une Table en Teste de ce Vol^{e}.

Le 4e. Vol^{e}. ne porte point d'indication et n'est précedé ni suivi d'aucune Table, mais à en juger par ce seul mot Outremer qui fait le titre courant au haut de chaque page; il paroist ~~d'autre~~ que l'Objet de ses recherches est sur les famil--les qui sont d'outremer, ou sur les actions de nostre histoire qui se sont passé aussi outremer.

À la page 165. de ce Vol^{e}. commencent d'autres recherches, sans aucune désignation d'Outremer, ni autre: elles regardent aussi diverses familles, rangées par ordre alpha -betique; et il semble que dans cette partie on ait eu plus d'égard à leur blason. Elles sont terminées par quelques personnes et par quelques lieux Ecclésiastiques sépa--rément.

Le 5.e vol^{e}.

(376r)

Le 5e. Vol^{e}. enfin n'est aussi désigné par aucun titre particulier, et n'est précedé ni suivi d'aucune Table, pareillement; cependant par sa disposition, il est aisé de Comprendre qu'il a eu pour objet les Gouverneurs des Provinces du Royaume, rangez par l'ordre alphabetique du nom de ces Provinces.

Le reste de ce Vol^{e}. est rempli par une espece de Liste Alphabétique de Differents Auteurs et Ecrivains, particulierement sur l'histoire; de Divers Plans de Bibliographie; et Enfin de Recherches ou Extraits sur differens Sujets d'Histoire et de Litterature.

procurators general, general counsel;
parlements, exchequers;
court of aids; grand council etc. in Paris
or in the provinces; the queens' officials
and those of princes of the blood; the grand officers
of the major provinces of France when
they were governed by their sep-
-arate princes etc.

There is also a table at the beginning of this volume. On a separate sheet.

The third volume contains: the heredi-
-tary castellans; the vidames and dependent lords of the cathedral
churches; the seneschals and bailiffs; and
finally the castellans and captains, all
in the alphabetical order of the places
where they would exercise their charges.

There is likewise a table at the head of this volume.

The fourth volume bears no indication and is neither
preceded nor followed by any table, but,
to judge from the single word <u>Outremer</u>
that constitutes the running title at the top of
each page, it appears ~~other~~ that
the subject of its research is the fami-
-lies of the Crusader states or the deeds
in our history that likewise took place
in the Crusader states.

On page 165 of this volume other
research begins, without any designation of
Outremer or any other: it also concerns
various families, organized by alpha-
-betical order; and it seems that in this part
more attention was paid to their coat of arms.
It concludes with some ecclesiastical
persons and places given separ-
-ately.

The fifth volume

(376r)

The fifth volume, lastly, is likewise not designated by any
particular title, and similarly is neither preceded nor followed
by any table; nonetheless
from its configuration it is easy to deduce
that it has as its object the governors of the
provinces of the realm, organized in the alphabetical
order of these provinces.

The rest of this volume is filled with a
sort of alphabetical list of different
authors and writers, especially on
history; by various bibliographic plans;
and finally by research or extracts on
different literary and historical subjects.

Petit Vol[e]. in 4°. fort mince, relié en velin verd, cotté sur le dos: Glossarium Francobar=-barum. et Intitulé en Dedans: ......

Glossarium Francobarbarum, desumptum ex Petro Pithœo, fr. hotomano, Hier. Bignonio, et jac. Sirmondo.[a]

Il contient en effet ce petit Glossaire annoncé ci devant pages 11. et 12. dans le Vol[e]. cotté **R. D.C.** et dont il remplit la Lacune annoncée depuis la page 393. jusqu'à la page 435. inclusivement.

Autre Volume, petit in fol°. et très mince aussi: relié pareillement en parchemin verd, cotté sur le dos: Notes et Corrections sur Monstrelet.[b] contenant effectivement des ...

Notes et Corrections sur les chroniques de Monstrelet: de l'Impression de Guillaume Chaudiere, en 1572.

Autre Vol[e].

(376v)

Autre Volume, in fol°. encore fort mince, relié en Velin verd, et cotté sur le Dos: Histor. Fr. Scriptores. et intitulé en dedans: Idœa et Conspectus Operis.[c] parcequ'il contient l'Idée et l'Exposition détaillée, du projet de la collection des Historiens de France, en un Corps d'Impression. à ce Programe écrit en Latin, sont joints 2. autres Memoires en françois, sur le mesme sujet: l'un, sans titre, et de forme in 4°. l'autre intitulé: Propositions à decider. parcequ'il contient XXVI. propositions relatives à cet Ouvrage dont l'Auteur demandoit la Décision.

Autre pareil Volume, cotté sur le Dos: Pays bas.[d]

Il contient des Memoires Historiques et Geographiques pour servir à la Descrip--tion des Differentes Provinces qui composent les Pays bas; comme, Alost; Le Duché de Brabant; le Duché de Lembourg, et Sei--gneurie de Malines; le Duché de Gueldres; le Pays d'Owerissel; le Comté de Frise occidentale; l'Etat et pays de Groeningue; le Comté et le pays de Hollande, la Seigneurie d'Utrecht; le Comté de Zelande; le Comté de Flandres; Cambray, comme libre et Imperiale; Haynault; Luxem-

a BnF, MS fr. 9486.

b BnF, MS fr. 9487.

c BnF, MS fr. 9484.

d BnF, MS fr. 9485.

Small, very thin quarto volume bound in green vellum, labeled on the spine: Vulgar French Glos- -sary. And titled inside: . . . . . .

Vulgar French Glossary, Extracts from Pierre Pitou, François Hotman, Jérôme Bignon, and Jacques Sirmond.

Indeed, it contains the small glossary announced earlier on pages 11 and 12 in the volume labeled **R. D.C.**, filling the announced lacuna from page 393 to page 435, inclusive.

Another volume, also a small folio and very thin and similarly bound in green parchment, labeled on the spine: Notes and Corrections on Monstrelet, which does indeed contain:

Notes and Corrections to the Chronicle of de Monstrelet, as printed by Guillaume Chaudière in 1572.

Another volume.

(376v)

Another volume, folio, also very thin and bound in green vellum, labeled on the spine: Writers of the History of France, and titled inside: Idea and Outline of Work because it contains the idea and detailed exposition of the project of col- -lecting the historians of France in a single printed corpus. To this program written in Latin are attached two other memoranda in French, on the same subject: one without title and in quarto format, the other titled: Proposals to Be Decided, because it contains 26 proposals concerning this work regarding which the author was asking for a decision.

Another similar volume, labeled on the spine: Low Countries.

It contains historical and geographical memoranda to be used for the descrip- -tion of the different provinces that make up the Low Countries, such as: Aalst; the Duchy of Brabant; the Duchy of Limburg and Lord- -ship of Mechelen; the Duchy of Guelders; the Land of Overijssel; the County of West Frisia; the State and Country of Groeningen; the County and Land of Holland; the Lordship of Utrecht; the County of Zeeland; the County of Flanders; Cambrai, both Free and Imperial; Hainault; Luxem-

-bourg; Le Comté de Namur; le Liege;
Et enfin, Aix La Chapelle.

Tous les 4. Volumes ci dessus sont de la main de M. Du Cange.

Carton, en forme de Boete et couvert de parchemin; cotté sur le Dos:
Geographie de la France.......
Dissertations préliminaires.[a]

contenant

(377r)

Contenant des Recherches, Extraits, depouil-lements, observations &c recueillis de dif-ferents Ouvrages et auteurs, et servant de renvois et d'indications pour les rassembler en corps d'ouvrages, ou en former des memoires sur les differents points et Sujets qui peuvent servir d'Introduction et de préliminaires à la Description Historique et Geographi-que de la France; comme: les noms anciens des Gaules, l'Origine des Gaulois, &c les Itine-raires, la Division des Gaules, par jules Cesar et sous Auguste &c celle par Archeveschés, Eveschés &c &c les Gouverneurs des Provin-ces et Villes des Gaules sous les Romains, les Prefets du Pretoire, l'Histoire des Gaules sous les Empereurs Romains, Le Nom de France, l'Origine des François, Les Ducs et Comtes, (Missi) la forme du Gouvernement des Provinces et Villes des Gaules sous les François &c l'Etat de la France sous la 3[e]. race de nos Rois &c &c. &c.

Le tout de la main de M. du C.

Deux autres Cartons, de même forme, cottés sur le Dos....... Gaule Belgique: Part. I. et II.[b]

Contenant de pareilles Recherches sur les Provinces Suivantes: Sçavoir

Partie I.

Hollande, Gueldre, Brabant, Flan-dres, Artois, Hainaut, Namur, Luxem-bourg, Limbourg, Liege, jullierre, Cologne, Treves, ~~xxxxxx~~ Palatinat.

Partie II.

Picardie, Champagne, Barrois, Lorraine, Alsace.

aussi de la main de M. Du Cange.

Deux

a BnF, MS fr. 9504.

b BnF, MS fr. 9507.

-burg; the County of Namur; Liège;
and, finally, Aix-la-Chapelle.
All four of the above volumes are in the hand of M. Du Cange.

Cardboard in the shape of a box covered in parchment; labeled on the spine:
Geography of France......
Preliminary Dissertations,

containing

(377r)

containing research, excerpts, extracts, observations etc. collected from different works and authors and serving as references and indications for the collection of these in a corpus of works, or to form memoranda on the different points and subjects that could be used as the introduction and preliminaries to a historical and geographical description of France, such as: the ancient names of the Gauls; the Origins of the Gauls etc.; the itineraries and division of the Gauls by Julius Caesar and under Augustus etc.; that by archbishops, bishops etc. etc.; the governors of the provinces and cities of the Gauls under the Romans; the prefects of the Praetorium; the history of the Gauls under the Roman Emperors; the name of France; the origins of the French; the dukes and counts; (palatine inspectors) the form of government in the provinces and towns of the Gauls under the French etc.; the state of France under the third race of our kings etc. etc. etc.

All in the hand of M. Du Cange.

Two other boxes of the same shape, labeled on the spine...... Belgian Gaul, Parts I and II.
Containing similar research on the following provinces, namely:

Part I.

Holland, Guelders, Brabant, Flanders, Artois, Hainault, Namur, Luxemburg, Limburg, Liège, La Julienne, Köln, Trier, ~~xxxxxx~~ the Palatinate.

Part II.

Picardy, Champagne, Barrois, Lorraine, Alsace.
Also in the hand of M. Du Cange.

Two

(377v)

Deux autres Cartons de même Forme, cottés sur le Dos: . . . .
. . . Gaule Narbonoise ou Vienoise. Part.I. et II.[a]
Contenant de Pareilles Recherches sur les Provinces suivantes; sçavoir:

Partie I.

Le Comté de Foix, Roussillon, Languedoc.

Partie II.

Dauphiné, Comtat d'Avignon, Princi=
=pauté d'Orenge, Provence, Savoye.

Deux autres Cartons semblables, cottés sur dos:
Gaule Celtique ou Lyonoise. Part.I. et II.[b]
Contenant de pareilles Recherches sur les Provinces suivantes; sçavoir:

Partie I.

L'Isle de France, Brie, Vexin, Normandie, Bretagne, Maine, Perche, Anjou, Loudunois, Touraine, Pays-Chartrain, Orleanois, Gas-
-tinois.

Partie II.

Lyonnois Forest et Beaujolois, Bour-
-gogne, Auxerrois, Bresse, Bugey, Franche-
-Comté; Suisses, alliés des Suisses, Bailliages des Suisses; Genevois, Vallais, Pays des Vaux.

Deux autres Cartons pareils, cottés sur le Dos:
Gaule Aquitanique. Part. I. et II.[c]
Contenant de semblables Recherches sur les Provinces suivantes; sçavoir:

Partie I.

Poitou, Berry, Aulnis, Saintonge, Angou-
-mois, Limosin, La Marche, Bourbonois, Nivernois, Auvergne.

Partie II.

Guienne; Gascogne; Perigord; Bearn; Basques et Labour, Soule et Basse=
Navarre; Bigorre, Commenge, –
Coserant.

(378r)

Cinq Volumes in folio, de differentes formes, reliés en veau, et cottés sur dos:
Recueils A. B.C.D.E. MSS. D.C.[d]
Contenant en général un Mélange d'Extraits de Titres Originaux de differentes Archives, de Chartes, Cartulaires, obituaires et Necro-
-loges, Martyrologes, Inventaires de Titres,

a BnF, MS fr. 9505.

b BnF, MS fr. 9506.

c BnF, MS fr. 9508.

d BnF, MSS fr. 9496–500.

(377v)

Two other boxes of the same shape, labeled on the spine: . . . . . .
. . . Narbonnese or Viennois Gaul, Parts I and II, containing similar research on the following provinces, namely:

Part I.

County of Foix, Roussillon, Languedoc.

Part II.

Dauphiné, County of Avignon, Princi-pality of Orange, Provence, Savoy.

Two other comparable boxes, labeled on the spine: Celtic or Lyonnaise Gaul, Parts I and II, containing analogous research on the following provinces, namely:

Part I.

The Île-de-France, Brie, Vexin, Normandy, Brittany, Maine, Perche, Anjou, Loudunais, Touraine, Pays Chartrain, Orléanais, Gas-tinais.

Part II.

Forest of the Lyonnais and Beaujolais, Bur-gundy, Auxerrois, Bresse, Bugey, Franche-Comté; Swiss Cantons, allies of the Swiss, bailiwicks of the Swiss, Genevois, Vallais, Pays de Vaux.

Two other comparable boxes, labeled on the spine: Aquitaine Gaul, Parts I and II. containing analogous research on the following provinces, namely:

Part I.

Poitou, Berry, Aulnay, Saintonge, Angou-mois, Limousin, La Marche, Bourbonnais, Nivernais, Auvergne.

Part II.

Guyenne, Gascony, Périgord, Béarn, Basque Country and Labour, Soule and Lower Navarre, Bigorre, Commenge, Cosérant.

(378r)

Five folio volumes, of different shapes, bound in calfskin and labeled on the spine:

Collections A. B. C. D. E. Manuscripts D.C. In general containing a mixture of extracts of original titles from different archives, charters, cartularies, obituaries and necro-logies, martyrologies, lists of titles,

Inventaires de productions de pieces dans des
procedures, Titres de Familles, Contracts de
mariages, Testamens, Fondations, &c
Titres des Provinces &c et Enfin de divers
Manuscrits de tous genres, Ecclesiastiques,
Civiles, politiques, et surtout historiques;
Les Registres des Parlements, Chambres des
Comptes &c concernant principalement
Les familles, soit du Royaume, soit étrangeres;
Leurs Genealogies, Armoiries, &c Les Antiqui-
-tés, L'histoire generale et particuliere; celle
du Royaume et des Provinces, parmi lesquel-
-les celle de la Picardie en General, et notam-
-ment celle de la Ville d'Amiens en particulier
tiennent le plus d'étenduë. Le tout ainsi
que l'on peut juger par les détails suivans
propres à chacun de ces Volumes en particu-
-lier. Sçavoir:

Recueil A.

Il contient entr'autres, des Extraits de
Titres concernant les Seigneurs d'Encre; des
Extraits de plusieurs MSS. qui sont des anciens
Romans, et autres Ouvrages de devotion, et
de Sciences, dont quelques uns etoient d'impres-
sion ancienne. Plusieurs Genealogies; des
Extraits concernant l'histoire et les familles
d'Amiens, d'Arras, d'Abbeville &c des ~~xxxx~~
Extraits de l'histoire de France de Philippe
Mouskes; &c &c &c.

Recueil B.

Il concerne principalement l'histoire
d'Amiens, et contient des Extraits de
Cartulaires

(378v)

Cartulaires, Martyrologes &c et autres titres de
ses Eglises de N^{e}. D^{e}., de S^{t}. Firmin, &c leurs fon-
-dations; celle des chapelles &c Des Epitaphes;
Des Inscriptions qui se lisent aux Vitres &c
des Extraits de l'Inventaire du Tresor des
Chartes de France: d'Autres d'une Histoire
des Empereurs, Rois, Princes, Souverains, Ducs
Comtes, &c et Seigneurs particuliers de
l'Europe, et principalement de la France.
Des Extraits de plusieurs Titres et Rouleaux de
La Chambre des Comptes: et surtout relative-
-ment à l'Histoire d'Amiens et de la Picardie.
un Extrait de la Vie de S^{t}. Denis, en Vers, inti-
-tulée le Rosier de S^{t}. Denis. &c &c &c.

Recueil C.

Concernant aussi principalement l'histoire
d'Amiens; et en outre contenant, ainsi que
dans les Volumes précédents, des Extraits
de Titres, Cartulaires, Comptes &c de

lists of documents produced in
lawsuits, family titles, marriage
contracts, wills, foundations etc.,
titles of provinces etc., and finally various
manuscripts of all genres: ecclesiastical,
civil, political, and especially historical;
the registers of parlements and
exchequers etc. principally concerning
families, whether of the kingdom, or foreign;
their genealogies, coats of arms etc.; antiqui-
-ties; general and particular history – that
of the kingdom and the provinces – among which
that of Picardy in general, and nota-
-bly that of the City of Amiens in particular
take up the most space. The whole,
as one may judge from the following details,
is specific to each of these individual vol-
-umes, namely:

Collection A.

This contains, among other things, extracts of
titles concerning the Lords of Encre;
extracts from several manuscripts that are of old
romances and other works of devotion and
science, some of which were from old print-
-ed editions; several genealogies;
extracts concerning the history of families
of Amiens, Arras, Abbeville etc. ~~xxxx~~;
extracts of the History of France by Philippe
Mouskés etc. etc. etc.

Collection B.

This principally concerns the history
of Amiens, and contains: extracts from
cartularies

(378v)
cartularies, martyrologies etc. and other titles of
its Churches of Our Lady, St. Firmin etc.; their foun-
-dations; that of the chapels etc.; epitaphs;
inscriptions that can be read on the stained-glass windows etc.;
extracts from the Inventory of the Treasury of
the Charters of France: and others from a History of
the Emperors, Kings, Princes, Sovereigns, Dukes,
Counts etc. and Individual Lords of
Europe and Principally of France;
extracts of several titles and scrolls of the
Exchequer, and especially concern-
-ing the history of Amiens and Picardy;
an extract of the Life of St. Denis, in verse, ti-
-tled, the Rosebush of St. Denis etc. etc. etc.

Collection C.

This is also principally concerned with the history
of Amiens; and moreover contains, as in the
previous volumes, extracts
from titles, cartularies, accounts, etc.;

Livres de Voyages, d'histoire &c MSS. et
plusieurs Inscriptions trouvées en Syrie, en
Egypte, &c Differens Sceaux, &c &c &c.

Recueil D.

Concernant encore beaucoup l'histoire d'Amiens, et de Picardie; ainsi que celle des Comtes de Champagne, de Boulogne, de Montfort, de Bethune, de Pontieu, &c le Domaine d' Hesdin &c Les Seigneurs du nom de Bour--bon, &c des Extraits de Cartulaires des Abbayes de Long-pré, Corbie, de S[t]. Magloire de Paris, &c &c La Revocation d'un Droit particulier aux Evêques d'Amiens &c des Extraits de Comptes &c &c &c.

Recueil E.

Enfin concernant encore l'histoire d'Amiens, Ses Coustûmes, &c avec des Extraits de quantité de Cartulaires de differentes

Eglises

(379r)

Eglises de toutes les Provinces du Royaume, et aussi de l'Eglise de Paris, et de plusieurs autres deja citées dans les Volumes précédents, Long-pré, Corbie &c Des Remarques parti--culieres entre lesquelles; les Inscriptions et la forme de la Croix de l'Abbaye du Mont Saint Quentin près Peronne: Les Antiquités de Bretheuil, la Liste de ses Seigneurs avec leurs Armes; &c &c &c.

Il y a des Tables très détaillées à la Teste de chacun de ces volumes, qu'on a collationnées très exactement avec le contenu du Volume.

Tous ces Vol.[es] sont, à peu de choses près, de la main de M. Du Cange.

Vol[e]. in folio cotté sur dos: <u>Histoire des Comtes d'A= =miens</u>. MS̄. <u>Histoire des Comtes de Pontieu</u>.[a]
MS̄. contenant en effect l'

Histoire de l'Etat de la Ville d'Amiens et de ses Comtes, avec un Recueil de plu--sieurs Titres concernans l'histoire de cette Ville, qui n'ont pas encore été publiez. par Charles Du Fresne S[r]. Du Cange, Conseiller du Roy Tresorier de France, et general des Finances en la Generalité de Picardie. Plus l'

Histoire des Comtes de Monstreuil et de Pontieu.

Ces deux Histoires ecrites en plusieurs Livres et suivies de differens Titres concer-

a BnF, MS fr. 9478.

travelogues and historical works etc. in manuscript; and
several inscriptions found in Syria, in
Egypt etc.; various seals, etc. etc. etc.

Collection D.

This is also to a large extent concerned with the history of Amiens,
and of Picardy; as well as that of the Counts
of Champagne, Boulogne, Montfort,
Bethune, Ponthieu etc. and of the estate of
Hesdin etc.; the Lords of the name of Bour-
-bon etc.; extracts from cartularies of the
Abbeys of Longpré-les-Corps-Saints, Corbie, Saint-Magloire-
-de-Paris etc. etc.; the revocation of a right
particular to the Bishops of Amiens etc.; the
extracts from accounts etc. etc. etc.

Collection E.

This, lastly, also concerns the history of Amiens,
its customs etc., with extracts of
a number of cartularies of different
churches

(379r)

churches of all the provinces of the realm,
and also of the Church of Paris, and of several
others already cited in the previous volumes:
Longpré, Corbie etc.; among them of special
note being the inscriptions and the
shape of the Cross of the Abbey of Mont-Saint-
-Quentin-près-Peronne; the antiquities of
Bretheuil; the list of its lords with
their armorial bearings etc. etc. etc.

There are very detailed tables at the
beginning of each of these volumes, which have been
most accurately collated with the contents
of the volume.

All of these volumes are, with the exception of just a few items, in
the hand of M. Du Cange.

A folio volume, labeled on the spine: Manuscript History of the Counts of A-
-miens. Manuscript History of the Counts of
Ponthieu; containing indeed the

History of the State of the City of Amiens
and of its Counts, with a Collection of Many
Titles Concerning the History of this
City That Have Not Yet Been Published,
by Charles Du Fresne, Lord Du Cange,
King's Counsel Treasurer of France,
and General of Finance for the Whole
of Picardy. In addition, the

History of the Counts of Montreuil
and of Ponthieu.

These two histories, which are written in many
books and followed by different titles concern-

-nant ~~xxx~~ les ~~Provinces~~ divers lieux de ces Provinces, sont toutes prestes à être impri-mées etant parapheés et avec l'Approba-tion du Censeur, M[r]. Saurin, en date du 7. Fevrier 1713.

Ce Vol[e]. relié en veau est enfermé dans une Boete couverte de Velin Verd, Faite en forme de Livre, et cottée sur le dos: Histoire des Comtes d'Amiens: MSS. D.C.

Entierement de la main de M. Du Cange.

(379v)

Boëte, couverte de velin Verd et faite en forme de Livre, in fol[o]. cotté sur dos: Titres de Picardie M[ss]. D.C. et entierrement remplie de papiers, tous ecrits de la main de M. Du Cange, à la réserve d'un très petit Nombre.[a]

Ce sont toutes Copies de quantité de Titres Originaux, tirés d'Archives, ou d'autres endroits, ou Extraits de Cartulaires; et autres ouvrages MSS. avec differens passages extraits de Poëtes ou autres Auteurs. Le tout pour servir à composer l'histoire de Picardie, et pour former les pieces justificati-ves qui devoient la suivre.

A la Teste de ces Copies ou papiers est un Cahier contenant le Dessein de l'Histoire de la Picardie. avec quelques autres notices qui sem-bloient devoir former les préliminaires de cette Histoire sur sa Topographie, l'origine de son nom &c Et parmi tous ces titres les suivans ont paru mériter d'estre détaillés plus particu-lierement, ainsi que quelques pieces qui s'y trouvent inserées, sçavoir:

Memoire touchant les Droits de l'Eglise d'Amiens sur la Terre de Baugency.

Coutumes Locales de la Ville et Banlieue d'Amiens. MS. en Gothique du 16e. Siecle.

Rhetorique pour le feu de meschief ad-venu au Clocher de l'Eglise N[e]. D[e]. d'Amyens, et pour les Guerres regnans en ce temps qui estoit l'an 1527. et 28. (Cahier contenant 47. Strophes, chacune de 8. vers en 2. Colonnes, Ecriture du Temps.

Erection du Marquisat de Magnelers sous le nom de Halluyn, en titre de Dignité de Duché et Pairie de France en faveur de Charles de Hallewyn. 1588.

Erection de la Baronnie d'Encre et dépen-dances, en Marquisat. 1576.

Contract de Vente dud. Marquisat. 1610.

Foy et Hommage pour ce Marquisat. 1617.

Commutation

a BnF, MS fr. 9468.

-ing ~~xxx~~ the ~~provinces~~ various places of these
provinces, are all ready to be print-
-ed, having been initialed by and received the a-
-pproval of the Censor, M. Saurin, on
7 February 1713.

This volume bound in calfskin is enclosed
in a box covered with green vellum
made in the shape of a book, and labeled on the
spine: History of the Counts of Amiens, manuscript
D.C.

Entirely in the hand of M. Du Cange.

(379v)

Box, covered in green vellum and made in the shape
of a folio book, labeled on the spine: Titles of
Picardy Manuscripts D.C., and entirely filled
with papers, all written in the hand of M. Du
Cange, with the exception of a very small number.

They are all copies of a quantity of original
titles, drawn from archives or from other places,
or excerpted from cartularies and other manuscript works,
with some passages coming from poets or other
authors. All to serve in the writing of the history
of Picardy and to make up the supporting documents
that should follow it.

On top of these copies or papers is a
notebook containing the Plan of the History of
Picardy, with some other notes that seem
to have been intended to form the preliminaries to that
history: on its topography, the origin of its
name etc. and among all these titles, the following
seemed especially to merit a more detailed expla-
-nation, as well as a few documents that happen to be
inserted, namely:

Memorandum concerning the rights of the Church
of Amiens in the land of Beaugency.

Local customs of the city and suburb
of Amiens. Manuscript in Gothic letters of the sixteenth century.

Oration on the arson attack on
the bell tower of the Church of Our Lady of Amiens,
and on the wars reigning at that time, which
was the years 1527–28 (Notebook containing 47
stanzas, each of eight verses in two columns,
script of the period).

The raising of the Marquisate of Maignelais
under the name of Halluin to the dignity
of Duchy and to the Peerage of France. In favor of
Charles de Halluin, 1588.

The elevation of the Baronetcy of Encre and its depen-
-dencies to a Marquisate, 1576.

Contract of sale of the aforesaid Marquisate, 1610.

Faith and homage for this Marquisate, 1617.

Commutation

(380r)

Commutation du Nom d'Encre, en celui d'~~xxxx~~ Albert, en 1620.

Relief dud. Marquisat, en 1626.

Erection du Marquisat de Querrieux. 1652.

Arrest de la Cour du Parlement de Paris, du 9. janvier 1651. concernant la liberté et l'ordre convenable dans l'Election des Echevins d'Amiens. Piece imprimée in 4°.

Ces papiers gardent entr'eux l'Ordre sui-vant: d'abord sont tous ceux qui sont sans date, et sans aucun N°. ni Chiffre de pages; ensuite sont tous ceux qui sont datés, rangès chrono-logiquement depuis l'An 169. jusqu'en 1662. inclusivement. Ces derniers sont en outre nu-mérotés, depuis 1. jusqu'à 236. aussi inclusive-ment.

Volume in Quarto relié en velin verd, et cotté sur dos: Antiquitez d'Amiens.[a] contenant l'Ouvrage suivant.

Antiquitez, histoires et choses plus remarquables de la Ville d'Amiens, poëti-quement traictées. 3e. Edition. par Adrian de la Morliere, chanoine d'Amiens. Paris. Denys Moreau. 1627. Avec des Notes, Citations, corrections, Additions, inser-tions en Grec, en Latin, en françois; ecrites sur les Marges, par M^r^. Du Cange.

Plus: entre les Pages 14. et 15. est une insertion de 7. pages in 4°. imprimées en 1636. Sans nom de Lieu, ni d'imprimeur ou de Libraire, intitulée: Extrait des mesmes antiquitez Manuscrites dudit Sieur de la Morliere. pour estre placé page 15. de son Livre après la preuve de Samarobrine. Cet Extrait contient un Chapitre entier d'Addition, pour prouver: Que la Ville d'Amiens, par excellence, est Le Vray Belgium de Cesar. Contre ce que M. Sanson a dit de semblable de sa Ville d'Ab-beville.

(380v)

Boëte couverte de Velin Verd, en forme de Livre in 4°. cottée sur dos: Evesques d'Amiens. MSS. D. C.[b]

Elle contient les Minutes de l'Histoire de ces Evêques ^ ^ qui sont au Nombre de 54. depuis S^t^. Firmin 1er. Evesque d'Amiens decedé environ l'an 350. jusques et compris jean Rollandi

a BnF, MS fr. 9475.

b BnF, MS fr. 9476.

(380r)

Commutation of the name of Encre, to that
of ~~xxxx~~ Albert, in 1620.

Confiscation of the aforesaid marquisate, in 1626.

Elevation of the Marquisate of Querrieu, 1652.

Decree of 9 January 1651 by the Court of the Parlement of Paris, concerning the appropriate liberty and order to be followed in the election of the Eschevins of Amiens. Item printed in quarto.

These papers are in the following or- -der: first, all those that are without date and without any page number or other numeral; then all those that are dated, organized chrono- -logically from the year 169 to 1662, inclusive. These last are additionally num- -bered from 1 to 236, also inclu- -sive.

Quarto volume bound in green vellum and labeled on the spine: Antiquities of Amiens, containing the following work:

The Most Notable Antiquities, Histories and Things of the City of Amiens, Treated Poeti- -cally, 3rd edition. by Adrien de la Morlière, Canon of Amiens. Paris, Denis Moreau, 1627. With notes, citations, corrections, additions, inser- -tions in Greek, in Latin, and in French; written in the margins by M. Du Cange.

In addition: between pages 14 and 15 are inserted seven quarto pages printed in 1636 without the name of the place or printer or bookseller, titled: Extract of the Same Antiquities Handwritten by the Aforementioned Lord de la Morlière. to be placed on page 15 of his book after the proof of Samarobrinus. This extract contains an entire additional chapter, to prove: That the City of Amiens, More Than Any Other, Is the True Belgium of Caesar against What M. Sanson Said on the Same Subject Regarding his City of Ab- -beville.

(380v)

Box covered in green vellum in the form of a quarto book, labeled on the spine: Bishops of Amiens. Manuscripts D. C.

This contains the drafts of the History of these bishops ^ ^who number 54 from Saint Firmin, first Bishop of Amiens who died around the year 350, up to and including Jean Rolland decedé le 16. Decembre 1388. toutes ecrites de la main de M^r Du Cange sur papiers détachés, de forme in 4.° qui ne sont chiffrés que par parties.

Volume en Velin Verd, de forme in 4°. très petite, cotté sur dos:

Histoire et Familles de Picardie.[a]

Ce n'est qu'un Simple Recueil de noms d'Abbayes et de Lieux rangés par ordre Alphabetique; suivi d'un autre Recueil de Noms de Familles, dans le mesme ordre; au dessous desquels noms sont ecrites de simples citations, pour servir de renvoys aux Ouvrages qui en parlent plus ample-ment. Manuscrit de M. Du Cange.

Il n'y a que très peu d'autres recherches, soit historiques soit généalogiques, meslées parmi ces Citations, de façon que ce volume qui est presque tout en blanc, ne semble qu' un simple repertoire disposé ainsi pour y rassembler ses recherches à mesure qu'il les découvroit.

Autre petit Volume in 4°. très mince et aussi en Velin verd. Sur dos: Pays-bas. En dedans. his-toire des Pays bas.[b] Et en autre titre à la Teste de L'ouvrage, ce qui suit:

Extrait et Abregé de l'Histoire des Pays-bas depuis l'an 1560. jusques en l'an 1602. escritte par jean françois le Petit, Greffier de Bethune et imprimée à S.t Gervais. 1604. in 8°.

Ce sont en effet des Extraits tirés des 8. Livres de cette Histoire, et tous de la main de M. Du Cange.

(381r)

Autre Volume, de même couvert de Velin Verd, de forme petit in fol.° cotté sur dos, et intitulé en dedans: Baillifs et Seneschaux.[c]

Contenant des Minutes de Listes des Baillifs et Seneschaux de toutes les Provinces et Villes du Royaume, où il y a des Bailliages et des Sénéchaussées, rangées indistinctement par ordre Alphabetique.

Ces Listes etoient recueillies et formées à mesure que M. Du Cange faisoit ses Lectures. les Noms qui les composent ne sont ordinairement accompagnés que de simples citations en ren-voys aux differens Ouvrages d'où ils sont tirés, et très rarement de notes ou extraits historiques,

a BnF, MS fr. 9480.

b BnF, MS fr. 9482.

c BnF, MS fr. 9488.

who died on 16 December 1388. All written
in the hand of M. Du Cange on unbound
sheets, of quarto size, and numbered only
in part.

Volume in green vellum, quarto size, very
small, labeled on the spine:
History and Families of Picardy.
This is nothing more than a rudimentary collection of the names
of abbeys and places organized in
alphabetical order; followed by another collection
of family names, in the same order;
under these names are written
basic citations to serve as references
to the works that deal with them in greater
length. Manuscript of M. Du Cange.

There is very little other research,
whether historical or genealogical, among
these citations, with the result that this volume
which is almost all blank, seems to be no more than
a simple list organized so that he could
assemble his research there as he made
his discoveries.

Another small quarto volume, very thin and also in
green vellum. On the spine: Low Countries. Inside: His-
-tory of the Low Countries. And at the beginning of
the work, another title, which follows:

Extract and Summary of the History of the Low Countries
from the Year 1560 to the Year 1602, written
by Jean-François le Petit, Registrar of Bethune
and printed at Saint Gervais, 1604, in octavo.

These are indeed Extracts taken from the eight Books of this History, and
all in the hand of M. Du Cange.

(381r)

Another volume, likewise covered in green vellum, of
small folio format, labeled on the spine, and titled
inside: Bailiffs and Seneschals.

Containing notes on lists of the
bailiffs and seneschals of all the provinces
and cities of the realm, where there are bailiwicks
and seneschalies, organized without distinction
in alphabetical order.

These lists were collected and
composed as M. Du Cange did his reading.
The constituent names are ordinarily
accompanied only by basic citations refer-
-ring to the different works from which they are drawn,
and very rarely historical notes and extracts, and

encore sont ils fort courts. Elles sont presque toutes imparfaites. Plusieurs mesmes n'ont que le Titre. Les seuls Baillys et Prevôts de Paris sont détaillés avec un peu plus d'Etendue, et précedés d'une courte notice historique.

le tout de la main de M. Du Cange.

Portefeuille in 4°. en rouge, cotté sur le dos: MSS. de M. Du Cange. contenant divers Ouvra--ges separés, sçavoir:[a]

1°. Differens papiers de diverses formes, détachés et fixés par une Epingle: ce sont des Notes Genealogiques et Historiques sur plusieurs illustres familles d'Angleterre.

2°. Cahier détaché d'un Livre relié, de forme in fol°. Il est cotté sur le 1er. feuillet **A**. et sur le 4.e, Oeuvres de M. Du Cange Tome 9. Il contient les Armes et Blasons des maisons nobles de Provence, tirées de l'histoire de Provence de Cesar Nostredamus imprimée l'An 1614 ....
Plus une Table Alphabetique des Autheurs Ou Livres esquelz sont blasonnées les Armoiries de plusieurs Nobles familles.

3°. Deux aut.

(381v)

3°. Deux autres Cahiers, détachés, et de plus grande forme in fol°. qui sont un Extrait du Livre de Navarre, Herault du très chres--tien et très puissant Roy de France contenant le blason et devis des armes de tous les Rois Chrestiens Princes et Seigneurs du Sang de France, et autres Barons Bannerets Chevaliers et Escuyers ez pays de France, Normandie, Champaigne, Bourgogne, Bretaigne, le Maine, Anjou, Touraine, Vermandois, Beauvoisin, Ponthieu, Artois, Corbiois, Poictou, Berry, Breban, Flandres, Henault et Angleterre.................
le tout tiré d'un Livre en parchemin trouvé en la Librairie de l'Eglise de N.[e] D.[e] de Bayeux. le d. Livre faisant mention de la Conqueste du Royaume de Hierusalem faite par Godefroy de Bouillon en 1098. &c.

4°. Autres Cahiers détachés, de forme in fol°. plus petite; contenant: Les Armes et Blazons des Ducs en Angleterre, Escosse et Irlande.

Le tout de la Main de M. du Cange.

a BnF, MS fr. 9479.

even then they are very short. They are almost all
incomplete. Many, indeed, have no more
than a heading. Only the bailiffs and prevosts
of Paris are expanded in greater
detail, and preceded by a short historical
notice.

All in the hand of M. Du Cange.

Red quarto folder, labeled on the spine:
Manuscripts of M. Du Cange. containing various discrete
works, namely:

First: Various papers in a variety of formats,
unbound and held together with a pin: these are
historical and genealogical notes on
many illustrious English families.

Second: A booklet taken from a bound book
in folio format. This is labeled on the first page,
A, and on the fourth, Works of Du Cange,
Volume 9. It contains the coats of arms in the form of blazons
of the noble houses of Provence, taken from
The History of Provence by César Nostredamus,
printed in the year 1614 ......
Plus an alphabetical table of the authors
or books in which are emblazoned the
coats of arms of many noble families.

Third: Two oth.

(381v)

Third: Two other booklets, unbound and of
a larger folio format, which are an extract
from the Book of Navarre, Herald of the Most Chris-
-tian and Powerful King of France containing
the blazons and devices of the coats of arms of all the Christian
kings, princes and lords of the royal French
blood, and other barons, knights banneret, knights
and squires of the lands of France, Normandy,
Champagne, Burgundy, Brittany,
Maine, Anjou, Touraine, Vermandois,
Beauvoisin, Ponthieu, Artois, Corbais,
Poitou, Berry, Brabant, Flanders, Hainault,
and England.......
All taken from a parchment book found
in the library of the Church of Our Lady of Bayeux.
The aforesaid book making mention of the conquest of the
Kingdom of Jerusalem by Godfrey
of Bouillon in 1098 etc.

Fourth: Other unbound booklets, of
smaller folio format; containing: The coats of arms
and blazons of the dukes in England, Scotland and
Ireland.

All in the hand of M. Du Cange.

CONTRIBUTORS

NATHANAEL ASCHENBRENNER is a postdoctoral research fellow at Princeton University's Seeger Center for Hellenic Studies. His research and publications explore empire and ideology in the medieval and early modern Mediterranean, as well as Byzantium's imperial legacy after 1453.

SHANE BOBRYCKI is an assistant professor of early medieval history at the University of Vienna.

ELENA N. BOECK is a professor of history of art and architecture at DePaul University. Her publications explore intellectual exchange in the Mediterranean and unconventional, fascinating forms of engagement with Byzantium's legacy. She is the author of *The Bronze Horseman of Justinian in Constantinople: The Cross-Cultural Biography of a Mediterranean Monument* (Cambridge, 2021) and *Imagining the Byzantine Past: The Perception of History in the Illustrated Manuscripts of Skylitzes and Manasses* (Cambridge, 2015). She held appointments as the Excellence Initiative Professor at Radboud University, and director of Byzantine Studies at Dumbarton Oaks.

RICHARD CALIS is a postdoctoral research associate with the Department of History at Princeton University and a Title A Fellow at Trinity College, Cambridge. He specializes in the cultural and intellectual history of the early modern period. His current book project is a study of Martin Crusius and his discovery of the Ottoman Greek world. He obtained his PhD from Princeton University in 2020.

FREDERIC CLARK is an assistant professor of classics at the University of Southern California. He is a cultural and intellectual historian who specializes in the afterlife of classical antiquity in medieval and early modern Europe. He is the author of *The First Pagan Historian: The Fortunes of a Fraud from Antiquity to the Enlightenment* (Oxford, 2020), and co-editor (with Alexander Bevilacqua) of *Thinking in the Past Tense: Eight Conversations* (Chicago, 2019). He is currently completing a book on the history of historical periodization, titled "Dividing Time: The Invention of Historical Periods in Early Modern Europe."

JOHN CONSIDINE teaches English at the University of Alberta, Canada. He is the author of three books on lexicography in early modern Europe, and the editor of *The Cambridge World History of Lexicography*.

ANTHONY GRAFTON teaches European history at Princeton University, where he has worked since 1975. His books include *Joseph Scaliger: A Study in the History of Classical Scholarship* (Oxford, 1983–93); *Defenders of the Text* (Cambridge, MA, 1991); *The Footnote: A Curious History* (Cambridge, MA, 1997); with Brian Curran, Pamela Long, and Benjamin Weiss, *Obelisk* (Cambridge, MA, 2008); with Joanna Weinberg, *"I Have Always Loved the Holy Tongue": Isaac Casaubon, the Jews, and a Forgotten Chapter in Renaissance Scholarship* (Cambridge, MA, 2011); and *Inky Fingers: The Making of Books in Renaissance Europe* (Cambridge, MA, 2020).

ANTHONY KALDELLIS is a professor of classics at The Ohio State University. He has published numerous books and articles on various aspects of Byzantine history, literature, and culture, including the reception of classical antiquity and the Roman identity of the Byzantines, and has also translated many Byzantine texts into English. In 2019 he began a podcast called *Byzantium & Friends*, which showcases recent developments in the field.

XAVIER LEQUEUX is a member of the Bollandist Society (Brussels, Belgium). His main field of research is Byzantine hagiography and literary exchanges between the Orient and Occident. With the support of the Institut de Recherche et d'Histoire des Textes (CNRS, France), he has launched the *Bibliotheca hagiographica graeca manuscripta* (BHGms), an online database of the Greek hagiographic manuscripts kept in libraries all over the world (http://pinakes.irht.cnrs.fr/recherche-generale.html). He is preparing the update of the *Bibliotheca hagiographica graeca*, in collaboration with Brepols and KULeuven (https://clavis.brepols.net/clacla/Default.aspx).

PRZEMYSŁAW MARCINIAK (PhD 2003, University of Silesia) is a professor of Byzantine literature at the University of Silesia, Katowice. His research focuses on drama, performance, and satire in Byzantium, especially in the twelfth century. His work has also focused on the reception of Byzantium: for instance, in the coedited volume *The Reception of Byzantium in European Culture since 1500* (Farnam, Surrey, 2016) and the recent article "Oriental like Byzantium: Some Remarks on Similarities between Byzantinism and Orientalism" (2018). His current research concerns animals in the middle Byzantine period.

WILLIAM NORTH, after receiving his PhD in medieval history from the University of California, Berkeley, and holding a postdoctoral fellowship at Dumbarton Oaks, joined the history faculty at Carleton College in Northfield, MN, where he is now a professor and codirector of medieval and Renaissance studies. He regularly teaches courses on the history of Byzantium, and his research focuses on relations between Byzantium and the West, comparative ecclesiology and reform, and intersections of art and ideology. He also has a strong interest in the history of Byzantine and medieval historiography.

FABIO PAGANI is an assistant professor of Greek and Latin at the Catholic University of America (Washington, DC). He holds a PhD from the Scuola Normale Superiore of Pisa. His research focuses on the reception of Greek philosophy (mainly Plato and Aristotle) during the Latin Middle Ages through the Italian Renaissance, with particular attention to the roles played by Byzantine intellectuals. He has published on Byzantine philosophy, the Italian Renaissance, Petrarch, and documentary papyri. He is a member of the board of the Library of Early Christianity.

JAKE RANSOHOFF is a PhD candidate in Byzantine history at Harvard University.

TERESA SHAWCROSS, associate professor of history and Hellenic studies at Princeton University and Senior Member at Robinson College, Cambridge University, is a historian of the late Middle Ages and early Renaissance working at the interstices between the Byzantine, Latin, and Islamic Mediterranean. She is completing a monograph on the ideas and practices of empire—and its alternatives—from the eleventh to the fifteenth centuries. Publications include *The Chronicle of Morea: Historiography in Crusader Greece* (Oxford, 2008) and *Reading in the Byzantine Empire and Beyond,* coedited with Ida Toth (Cambridge, 2018). Her interest in Charles Du Cange resulted from research on the Latin Empire of Constantinople and benefited from access to the collections of the Bibliothèque nationale de France during a residency in Paris.

INDEX

Page numbers in *italics* indicate illustrations. Titles of works with known authors will be found under the name of the author. Individual manuscripts are listed, by location and library, under "manuscripts."